GREAT ISSUES
IN WESTERN CIVILIZATION

VOLUME I

Edited by BRIAN TIERNEY,

DONALD KAGAN,

and L. PEARCE WILLIAMS

CORNELL UNIVERSITY

CONSULTING EDITOR: *Eugene Rice*

COLUMBIA UNIVERSITY

Random House *New York*

GREAT ISSUES

IN WESTERN

CIVILIZATION

VOLUME I

To Frederick G. Marcham

TEACHER—SCHOLAR—COLLEAGUE—FRIEND

Preface

A major purpose of this two-volume work is to convince students in Western civilization courses that the essential task of a historian is not to collect dead facts but to confront live issues. The issues are alive because they arise out of the tensions that men have to face in every generation—tensions between freedom and authority, between reason and faith, between human free will and all the impersonal circumstances that help to shape our lives.

In order to achieve any sophisticated understanding of such matters, a student needs to read the views of great modern historians as they are set out in their own words. He needs to develop a measure of critical historical insight by comparing these often conflicting views with the source material on which they are based. He needs above all to concern himself with the great issues that have shaped the course of Western civilization and not with historical "problems" that are mere artificially contrived conundrums.

This volume is divided into thirteen sections. Each of them presents both original source material and a variety of modern interpretations; and each deals with a truly great issue in Western history.

We believe that there are three major themes whose development and interplay have shaped the distinctive characteristics that set Western civilization apart from the other great historic cultures. They are the growth of a tradition of rational scientific inquiry, the persistence of a tension between Judaeo-Christian religious ideals and social realities, the emergence of constitutional forms of government. These three themes are introduced in the first sections of Volume I. The reader will find them recurring in new forms and changing contexts throughout the rest of the work. We hope that in studying them he will come to a richer understanding of the heritage of Western civilization—and of the historian's approach to it.

Ithaca, 1967   BRIAN TIERNEY

DONALD KAGAN

L. PEARCE WILLIAMS

Contents

Periclean Athens—

Democracy, Aristocracy, or Monarchy?

CONTENTS

QUESTIONS FOR STUDY

1 How does Pericles' picture of Athenian democracy differ from that of the "Old Oligarch"?

2 Which of the ancient authors believe(s) that Athens was not truly democratic?

3 In what sense does Beloch mean that Athens was aristocratic?

4 Is Van Hook's defense against the charge of aristocracy adequate?

5 How does McGregor try to refute the charge that Athens was a disguised monarchy?

6 If Athens may not be called "democratic," can you think of any state at any time that may?

*A*thens in the time of Pericles is usually regarded as the perfect model of direct democracy. With its popular assembly, its law courts, its magistrates popularly elected or chosen by lot, it might seem, beyond any dispute, the most democratic of states. Yet to a contemporary observer, Thucydides, it was a "democracy in name but the rule of the first citizen in fact." Modern scholars have taken up the debate and added an element to it by arguing that a society that included slaves and despised labor can hardly be called "democratic." This section is an attempt to present a picture of Periclean Athens as it appeared to the ancients and to suggest the kinds of dispute that have engaged modern scholars.

1 The Democratic Monarchy of Pericles

Busolt argues that Periclean Athens was not a truly democratic state and makes clear the nature of the controversy.

FROM *Griechische Geschichte* BY GEORG BUSOLT

THE EXTENSIVE AND GLITTERING outfitting of the Panathenaic festival, the construction of a splendid new temple of Athena, the whole building activity in general were features of the Periclean leadership which it shared with the regime of the Peisistratids, a democratic monarchy to which, according to the judgment of Thucydides, it was really related. Both regimes were concerned with the relief of the lower classes, the attempt to give them employment, to provide a livelihood for them, and also with the acquisition of overseas possessions and the provision of landed property for many citizens. Pericles' colonization of the Chersonnese and his restoration of circuit judges join directly with the tradition of the time of the Peisistratids [who introduced similar popular measures.]

*   *   *

[*Busolt describes the ostracism of Thucydides, son of Melesias (not the historian), the leader of the faction opposed to Pericles—D. K.*]

The oligarchic party lost, with its organizer, its firm coherence and its capacity for robust opposition. Pericles was thus without a rival, and therefore, in the eyes of the people, he became something other than what he had been before. If he had earlier felt himself compelled to be at the people's disposal and to yield to the wishes of the masses, he now began to behave independently and to take the bridle into his hand. By using the weight of his personality he ruled the state—on the one hand by means of the official authority given to him, on the other hand by means of his decisive influence

Georg Busolt, *Griechische Geschichte*, III (1893), Part I, 470, 497–9, translated by Donald Kagan.

on the decisions of the popular assembly. For fifteen years he would be elected to the generalship each year. In difficult times of war he received the supreme command, and at the beginning of the Peloponnesian War he also obtained extraordinarily full powers. Although he did not usually have greater official power than the other generals, he nevertheless held the authoritative position in the college of the generals and thereby collected into his own hand its conduct of the military, maritime, financial, and administrative affairs that were in its competence. The unbroken continuity of office, in fact, released him still further from the principle of accountability and gave him an exceptional position, which would nevertheless be held within bounds by the fact that the people, by means of the *epicheirotonia* that took place each prytany, could suspend him from office and place him before a court. In addition to the most important ordinary annual offices, Pericles quite regularly held the extraordinary office of *Epistates* (supervisor) of a public building. . . .

But, as the official power of Pericles was dependent on popular election and the mood of the people, he could only steer the entire ship of state in the direction he set if he could hold the leadership of the popular assembly in his hand. He succeeded by dint of his firmly based authority, his proven political insight, the integrity of his character, the dignity of his bearing, and the power of his speech. As he did not first need to acquire influence by improper means and was not accustomed to speak in order to please but, on the contrary, by virtue of the esteem in which he was already held, he could, under certain circumstances, even sharply oppose the people. He thus would not be led by the people, but instead he led them. As a result there developed a regime that was a popular government in name but one ruled by the first citizen in fact, a monarchical leadership on a democratic base, which frequently resumed the traditions of the democratic monarchy of the Peisistratids.

2 The Greatness of Athens

In the winter following the first campaigns of the Peloponnesian War, Pericles was chosen to pronounce the customary eulogy over the fallen warriors. He turned it instead into an occasion to praise the Athenian state, its constitution, and its way of life. Thucydides, who was almost surely present, reports the speech in full.

FROM *Pericles' Funeral Oration*

MOST OF MY PREDECESSORS in this place have commended him who made this speech part of the law, telling us that it is well that it should be delivered at the burial of those who fall in battle. For myself, I should have thought that the worth which had displayed itself in deeds, would be sufficiently rewarded by honours also shown by deeds; such as you now see in this funeral prepared at the people's cost. And I could have wished that the reputations of many brave men were not to be imperilled in the mouth of a single individual, to stand or fall according as he spoke well or ill. For it is hard to speak properly upon a subject where it is even difficult to convince your hearers that you are speaking the truth. On the one hand, the friend who is familiar with every fact of the story, may think that some point has not been set forth with that fulness which he wishes and knows it to deserve; on the other, he who is a stranger to the matter may be led by envy to suspect exaggeration if he hears anything above his own nature. For men can endure to hear others praised only so long as they can severally persuade themselves of their own ability to equal the actions recounted: when this point is passed, envy comes in and with it incredulity. However, since our ancestors have stamped this custom with their approval, it becomes my duty to obey the law and to try to satisfy your several wishes and opinions as best I may.

I shall begin with our ancestors: it is both just and proper that they should have the honour of the first mention on an occasion like the present. They dwelt in the country without break in the succession from generation to generation, and handed it down free to the present time by their valour.

Thucydides, *History of the Peloponnesian War* (1876), Book 2, Chapters 35–46, translated by Richard Crawley.

And if our more remote ancestors deserve praise, much more do our own fathers, who added to their inheritance the empire which we now possess, and spared no pains to be able to leave their acquisitions to us of the present generation. Lastly, there are few parts of our dominions that have not been augmented by those of us here, who are still more or less in the vigour of life; while the mother country has been furnished by us with everything that can enable her to depend on her own resources whether for war or for peace. That part of our history which tells of the military achievements which gave us our several possessions, or of the ready valour with which either we or our fathers stemmed the tide of Hellenic or foreign aggression, is a theme too familiar to my hearers for me to dilate on, and I shall therefore pass it by. But what was the road by which we reached our position, what the form of government under which our greatness grew, what the national habits out of which it sprang; these are questions which I may try to solve before I proceed to my panegyric upon these men; since I think this to be a subject upon which on the present occasion a speaker may properly dwell, and to which the whole assemblage, whether citizens or foreigners, may listen with advantage.

Our constitution does not copy the laws of neighbouring states; we are rather a pattern to others than imitators ourselves. Its administration favours the many instead of the few; this is why it is called a democracy. If we look to the laws, they afford equal justice to all in their private differences; if to social standing, advancement in public life falls to reputation for capacity, class considerations not being allowed to interfere with merit; nor again does poverty bar the way, if a man is able to serve the state, he is not hindered by the obscurity of his condition. The freedom which we enjoy in our government extends also to our ordinary life. There, far from exercising a jealous surveillance over each other, we do not feel called upon to be angry with our neighbour for doing what he likes, or even to indulge in those injurious looks which cannot fail to be offensive, although they inflict no positive penalty. But all this ease in our private relations does not make us lawless as citizens. Against this fear is our chief safeguard, teaching us to obey the magistrates and the laws, particularly such as regard the protection of the injured, whether they are actually on the statute book, or belong to that code which, although unwritten, yet cannot be broken without acknowledged disgrace.

Further, we provide plenty of means for the mind to refresh itself from business. We celebrate games and sacrifices all the year round, and the elegance of our private establishments forms a daily source of pleasure and helps to banish the spleen; while the magnitude of our city draws the produce of the world into our harbour, so that to the Athenian the fruits of other countries are as familiar a luxury as those of his own.

If we turn to our military policy, there also we differ from our antagonists. We throw open our city to the world, and never by alien acts exclude foreigners from any opportunity of learning or observing, although the eyes of an enemy may occasionally profit by our liberality; trusting less in system and policy than to the native spirit of our citizens; while in education, where our rivals from their very cradles by a painful discipline seek after manliness, at Athens we live exactly as we please, and yet are just as ready to encounter every legitimate danger. In proof of this it may be noticed that the Lacedaemonians do not invade our country alone, but bring with them all their confederates; while we Athenians advance unsupported into the territory of a neighbour, and fighting upon a foreign soil usually vanquish with ease men who are defending their homes. Our united force was never yet encountered by any enemy, because we have at once to attend to our marine and to despatch our citizens by land upon a hundred different services; so that, wherever they engage with some such fraction of our strength, a success against a detachment is magnified into a victory over the nation, and a defeat into a reverse suffered at the hands of our entire people. And yet if with habits not of labour but of ease, and courage not of art but of nature, we are still willing to encounter danger, we have the double advantage of escaping the experience of hardships in anticipation and of facing them in the hour of need as fearlessly as those who are never free from them.

Nor are these the only points in which our city is worthy of admiration. We cultivate refinement without extravagance and knowledge without effeminacy; wealth we employ more for use than for show, and place the real disgrace of poverty not in owning to the fact but in declining the struggle against it. Our public men have, besides politics, their private affairs to attend to, and our ordinary citizens, though occupied with the pursuits of industry, are still fair judges of public matters; for, unlike any other nation, regarding him who takes no part in these duties not as unambitious but as useless, we Athenians are able to judge at all events if we cannot originate, and instead of looking on discussion as a stumbling-block in the way of action, we think it an indispensable preliminary to any wise action at all. Again, in our enterprises we present the singular spectacle of daring and deliberation, each carried to its highest point, and both united in the same persons; although usually decision is the fruit of ignorance, hesitation of reflexion. But the palm of courage will surely be adjudged most justly to those who best know the difference between hardship and pleasure and yet are never tempted to shrink from danger. In generosity we are equally singular, acquiring our friends by conferring not by receiving favours. Yet, of course, the doer of the favour is the firmer friend of the two, in order by continued kindness to keep the recipient in his debt; while the debtor feels less keenly from the very consciousness that the return he makes will be a payment, not a free gift. And it is only the Athenians who, fearless of consequences, confer their benefits not from calculations of expediency, but in the confidence of liberality.

In short, I say that as a city we are the school of Hellas; while I doubt if the world can produce a man, who where he has only himself to depend upon, is equal to so many emergencies, and graced by so happy a versatility as the Athenian. And that this is no mere boast thrown out for the occasion, but plain matter of fact, the power of the state acquired by these habits proves. For Athens alone of her contemporaries is found when tested to be greater than her reputation, and alone gives no occasion to her assailants to blush at the antagonist by whom they have been worsted, or to her subjects to question her title by merit to rule. Rather, the admiration of the present and succeeding ages will be ours, since we have not left our power without witness, but have shown it by mighty proofs; and far from needing a Homer for our panegyrist, or other of his craft whose verses might charm for the moment only for the impression which they gave to melt at the touch of fact, we have forced every sea and land to be the highway of our daring, and everywhere, whether for evil or for good, have left imperishable monuments behind us. Such is the Athens for which these men, in the assertion of their resolve not to lose her, nobly fought and died; and well may every one of their survivors be ready to suffer in her cause.

Indeed if I have dwelt at some length upon the character of our country, it has been to show that our stake in the struggle is not the same as theirs who have no such blessings to lose, and also that the panegyric of the men over whom I am now speaking might be by definite proofs established. That panegyric is now in a great measure complete; for the Athens that I have celebrated is only what the heroism of these and their like have made her, men whose fame, unlike that of most Hellenes, will be found to be only commensurate with their deserts. And if a test of worth be wanted, it is to be found in their closing scene, and this not only in the cases in which it set the final seal upon their merit, but also in those in which it gave the first intimation of their having any. For there is justice in the claim that steadfastness in his country's battles should be as a cloak to cover a man's other imperfections; since the good action has blotted out the bad, and his merit as a citizen more than outweighed his demerits as an individual. But none of these allowed either wealth with its prospect of future enjoyment to unnerve his spirit, or poverty with its hope of a day of freedom and riches to tempt him to shrink from danger. No, holding that vengeance upon their enemies was more to be desired than any personal blessings, and reckoning this to be the most glorious of hazards, they joyfully determined to accept the risk, to make sure of their vengeance and to let their wishes wait; and while committing to hope the uncertainty of final success, in the business before them they thought fit to act boldly and trust in themselves. Thus choosing to die resisting, rather than to live submitting, they fled only from dishonour, but met danger face to face, and after one brief moment, while at the summit of their fortune, escaped, not from their fear, but from their glory.

So died these men as became Athenians. You, their survivors, must determine to have as unaltering a resolution in the field, though you may pray that it may have a happier issue. And not contented with ideas derived only from words of the advantages which are bound up with the defence of your country, though these would furnish a valuable text to a speaker even before an audience so alive to them as the present, you must yourselves realise the power of Athens, and feed your eyes upon her from day to day, till love of her fills your hearts; and then when all her greatness shall break upon you, you must reflect that it was by courage, sense of duty, and a keen feeling of honour in action that men were enabled to win all this, and that no personal failure in an enterprise could make them consent to deprive their country of their valour, but they laid it at her feet as the most glorious contribution that they could offer. For this offering of their lives made in common by them all they each of them individually received that renown which never grows old, and for a sepulchre, not so much that in which their bones have been deposited, but that noblest of shrines wherein their glory is laid up to be eternally remembered upon every occasion on which deed or story shall fall for its commemoration. For heroes have the whole earth for their tomb; and in lands far from their own, where the column with its epitaph declares it, there is enshrined in every breast a record unwritten with no tablet to preserve it, except that of the heart. These take as your model, and judging happiness to be the fruit of freedom and freedom of valour, never decline the dangers of war. For it is not the miserable that would most justly be unsparing of their lives; these have nothing to hope for: it is rather they to whom continued life may bring reverses as yet unknown, and to whom a fall, if it came, would be most tremendous in its consequences. And surely, to a man of spirit, the degradation of cowardice must be immeasurably more grievous than the unfelt death which strikes him in the midst of his strength and patriotism!

Comfort, therefore, not condolence, is what I have to offer to the parents of the dead who may be here. Numberless are the chances to which, as they know, the life of man is subject; but fortunate indeed are they who draw for their lot a death so glorious as that which has caused your mourning, and to whom life has been so exactly measured as to terminate in the happiness in which it has been passed. Still I know that this is a hard saying, especially when those are in question of whom you will constantly be reminded by seeing in the homes of others blessings of which once you also boasted: for grief is felt not so much for the want of what we have never known, as for the loss of that to which we have been long accustomed. Yet you who are still of an age to beget children must bear up in the hope of having others in their stead; not only will they help you to forget those whom you have lost, but will be to the state at once a reinforcement and a security; for never can a fair or just policy be expected of the citizen who does not, like his fellows, bring to the decision the interests and apprehensions of a father. While those of you who have passed your prime must congratulate yourselves with the thought that the best part of your life was fortunate, and that the brief span that remains will be cheered by the fame of the departed. For it is only the love of honour that never grows old; and honour it is, not gain, as some would have it, that rejoices the heart of age and helplessness.

Turning to the sons or brothers of the dead, I see an arduous struggle before you. When a man is gone, all are wont to praise him, and should your merit be ever so transcendent, you will still find it difficult not merely to overtake, but even to approach their renown. The living have envy to contend with, while those who are no longer in our path are honoured with a goodwill into which rivalry does not enter. On the other hand, if I must say anything on the subject of female excellence to those of you who will now be in widowhood, it will be all comprised in this brief exhortation. Great will be your glory in not falling short of your natural character; and greatest will be hers who is least talked of among the men whether for good or for bad.

My task is now finished. I have performed it to the best of my ability, and in words, at least, the requirements of the law are now satisfied. If deeds be in question, those who are here interred have received part of their honours already, and for the rest, their children will be brought up till manhood at the public expense: the state thus offers a valuable prize, as the garland of victory in this race of valour, for the reward both of those who have fallen and their survivors. And where the rewards for merit are greatest, there are found the best citizens.

And now that you have brought to a close your lamentations for your relatives, you may depart.

3 Ancient Authors on Periclean Democracy

> *Thucydides, the historian of the Peloponnesian War, expe-*
> *rienced Athenian democracy in its glory under Pericles and*
> *at its nadir at the end of the war. His account deserves the*
> *most respectful attention, for he was an eyewitness of acute*
> *and discerning judgment. This selection follows an account*
> *of the response of the Athenians to the hardships of war;*
> *only the persuasiveness of Pericles had prevented them*
> *from seeking terms after a short period of fighting.*

FROM *History of the Peloponnesian War* BY THUCYDIDES

THEY NOT ONLY gave up all idea of sending to Lacedaemon, but applied themselves with increased energy to the war; still as private individuals they could not help smarting under their sufferings, the common people having been deprived of the little that they ever possessed, while the higher orders had lost fine properties with costly establishments and buildings in the country, and, worst of all, had war instead of peace. In fact, the public feeling against him [*Pericles—D. K.*] did not subside until he had been fined. Not long afterwards, however, according to the way of the multitude, they again elected him general and committed all their affairs to his hands, having now become less sensitive to their private and domestic afflictions, and understanding that he was the best man of all for the public necessities. For as long as he was at the head of the state during the peace, he pursued a moderate and conservative policy; and in his time its greatness was at its height. When the war broke out, here also he seems to have rightly gauged the power of his country. He outlived its commencement two years and six months, and the correctness of his previsions respecting it became better known by his death. He told them to wait quietly, to pay attention to their marine, to

Thucydides, *History of the Peloponnesian War* (1876), Book 2, Chapter 65, translated by Richard Crawley.

attempt no new conquests, and to expose the city to no hazards during the war, and doing this, promised them a favourable result. What they did was the very contrary, allowing private ambitions and private interests, in matters apparently quite foreign to the war, to lead them into projects unjust both to themselves and to their allies—projects whose success would only conduce to the honour and advantage of private persons, and whose failure entailed certain disaster on the country in the war. The causes of this are not far to seek. Pericles indeed, by his rank, ability, and known integrity, was enabled to exercise an independent control over the multitude—in short, to lead them instead of being led by them; for as he never sought power by improper means, he was never compelled to flatter them, but, on the contrary, enjoyed so high an estimation that he could afford to anger them by contradiction. Whenever he saw them unseasonably and insolently elated, he would with a word reduce them to alarm; on the other hand, if they fell victims to a panic, he could at once restore them to confidence. In short, what was nominally a democracy became in his hands government *Monarchy* by the first citizen. With his successors it was different. More on a level with one another, and each grasping at supremacy, they ended by committing even the conduct of state affairs to the whims of the multitude. This, as might have been expected in a great and sovereign state, produced a host of blunders, and amongst them the Sicilian expedition; though this failed not so much through a miscalculation of the power of those against whom it was sent, as through a fault in the senders in not taking the best measures afterwards to assist those who had gone out, but choosing rather to occupy themselves with private cabals for the leadership of the commons, by which they not only paralysed operations in the field, but also first introduced civil discord at home. Yet after losing most of their fleet besides other forces in Sicily, and with faction already dominant in the city, they could still for three years make head against their original adversaries, joined not only by the Sicilians, but also by their own allies nearly all in revolt, and at last by the king's son, Cyrus, who furnished the funds for the Peloponnesian navy. Nor did they finally succumb till they fell the victims of their own intestine disorders. So superfluously abundant were the resources from which the genius of Pericles foresaw an easy triumph in the war over the unaided forces of the Peloponnesians.

The following selection is from the Constitution of the Athenians, *probably written by Aristotle, although some scholars attribute it to one of his students. There is no doubt, however, that it was written about a century after*

the death of Pericles and represents the thinking of Aris-
totle and his school.

FROM *Constitution of the Athenians* BY ARISTOTLE

XXVI . . . . AFTER THIS there came about an increased relaxation of the constitution, due to the eagerness of those who were the leaders of the People. For it so happened that during these periods the better classes had no leader at all, but the chief person among them, Cimon son of Miltiades, was a rather young man who had only lately entered public life; and in addition, that the multitude had suffered seriously in war, for in those days the expeditionary force was raised from a muster-roll, and was commanded by generals with no experience of war but promoted on account of their family reputations, so that it was always happening that the troops on an expedition suffered as many as two or three thousand casualties, making a drain on the numbers of the respectable members both of the people and of the wealthy. Thus in general all the administration was conducted without the same attention to the laws as had been given before, although no innovation was made in the election of the Nine Archons, except that five years after the death of Ephialtes they decided to extend to the Teamster class eligibility to the preliminary roll from which the Nine Archons were to be selected by lot; and the first of the Teamster class to hold the archonship was Mnesitheides. All the Archons hitherto had been from the Knights and Five-hundred-measure-men, while the Teamsters held the ordinary offices, unless some provision of the laws was ignored. Four years afterwards, in the archonship of Lysicrates, the thirty judges called the Local Justices were instituted again; and two years after Lysicrates, in the year of Antidotus, owing to the large number of the citizens an enactment was passed on the proposal of Pericles confining citizenship to persons of citizen birth on both sides.

XXVII. After this when Pericles advanced to the leadership of the people, having first distinguished himself when while still a young man he challenged the audits of Cimon who was a general, it came about that the constitution became still more democratic. For he took away some of the functions of the Areopagus, and he urged the state very strongly in the direction of naval power, which resulted in emboldening the multitude, who brought all the government more into their own hands. Forty-eight years after the naval battle of Salamis, in the archonship of Pythodorus, the war

Aristotle, *Constitution of the Athenians* (1891), Sections XXVI–XXVIII, translated by F. G. Kenyon.

against the Peloponnesians broke out, during which the people being locked up in the city, and becoming accustomed to earning pay on their military campaigns, came partly of their own will and partly against their will to the decision to administer the government themselves. Also Pericles first made service in the jury-courts a paid office, as a popular counter-measure against Cimon's wealth. For as Cimon had an estate large enough for a tyrant, in the first place he discharged the general public services in a brilliant manner, and moreover he supplied maintenance to a number of the members of his deme; for anyone of the Laciadae who liked could come to his house every day and have a moderate supply, and also all his farms were unfenced, to enable anyone who liked to avail himself of the harvest. So as Pericles' means were insufficient for this lavishness, he took the advice of Damonides of Oea (who was believed to suggest to Pericles most of his measures, owing to which they afterwards ostracized him), since he was getting the worst of it with his private resources, to give the multitude what was their own, and he instituted payment for the jury-courts; the result of which according to some critics was their deterioration, because ordinary persons always took more care than the respectable to cast lots for the duty. Also it was after this that the organized bribery of juries began, Anytus having first shown the way to it after his command at Pylos; for when he was brought to trial by certain persons for having lost Pylos he bribed the court and got off.

XXVIII. So long, then, as Pericles held the headship of the People, the affairs of the state went better, but when Pericles was dead they became much worse. For the People now for the first time adopted a head who was not in good repute with the respectable classes, whereas in former periods those always continued to lead the People.

The following selections are from a pamphlet on the Athenian constitution that has come down to us among the works of Xenophon. In the long debate concerning its authorship, the only fact generally agreed upon is that it could not have been written by Xenophon. Various authors have been proposed, among them Thucydides, the son of Melesias, a political opponent of Pericles. None of these attributions has won wide acceptance, and the anonymous author is usually called the "Old Oligarch." Internal evidence places the date of the treatise toward the beginning of the Peloponnesian War. The author was thus, like Thucyd-

*ides the historian, a contemporary of Pericles. His views,
though contradictory to those of Thucydides, are not to be
dismissed.*

FROM *Constitution of the Athenians*
BY THE "OLD OLIGARCH"
Surcusm

NOW, AS FOR THE CONSTITUTION of the Athenians, and the type
or manner of constitution which they have chosen, I praise it not, in so far as
the very choice involves the welfare of the baser folk as opposed to that of
the better class. I repeat, I withhold my praise so far; but, given the fact that
this is the type agreed upon, I propose to show that they set about its preservation in the right way; and that those other transactions in connection with it,
which are looked upon as blunders by the rest of the Hellenic world, are the
reverse.

In the first place, I maintain, it is only just that the poorer classes and the
common people of Athens should be better off than the men of birth and
wealth, seeing that it is the people who man the fleet, and have brought the
city her power. The steersman, the boatswain, the lieutenant, the look-out-
man at the prow, the shipwright—these are the people who supply the city
with power far rather than her heavy infantry and men of birth and quality.
This being the case, it seems only just that offices of state should be thrown
open to every one both in the ballot and the show of hands, and that the
right of speech should belong to any one who likes, without restriction. For,
observe, there are many of these offices which, according as they are in good
or in bad hands, are a source of safety or of danger to the People, and in
these the People prudently abstains from sharing; as, for instance, it does not
think it incumbent on itself to share in the functions of the general or of the
commander of cavalry. The commons recognises the fact that in forgoing the
personal exercise of these offices, and leaving them to the control of the more
powerful citizens, it secures the balance of advantage to itself. It is only those
departments of government which bring pay and assist the private estate that
the People cares to keep in its own hands.

In the next place, in regard to what some people are puzzled to explain—
the fact that everywhere greater consideration is shown to the base, to poor
people and to common folk, than to persons of good quality,—so far from
being a matter of surprise, this, as can be shown, is the keystone of the
preservation of the democracy. It is these poor people, this common folk, this
worse element, whose prosperity, combined with the growth of their num-

Pseudo-Xenophon, *Constitution of the Athenians* (1942), Sections 1, 3, translated by H. G.
Dakyns.

bers, enhances the democracy. Whereas, a shifting of fortune to the advantage of the wealthy and the better classes implies the establishment on the part of the commons of a strong power in opposition to itself. In fact, all the world over, the cream of society is in opposition to the democracy. Naturally, since the smallest amount of intemperance and injustice, together with the highest scrupulousness in the pursuit of excellence, is to be found in the ranks of the better class, while within the ranks of the People will be found the greatest amount of ignorance, disorderliness, rascality,—poverty acting as a stronger incentive to base conduct, not to speak of lack of education and ignorance, traceable to the lack of means which afflicts the average of mankind.

The objection may be raised that it was a mistake to allow the universal right of speech and a seat in council. These should have been reserved for the cleverest, the flower of the community. But here, again, it will be found that they are acting with wise deliberation in granting to even the baser sort the right of speech, for supposing only the better people might speak, or sit in council, blessings would fall to the lot of those like themselves, but to the commons the reverse of blessings. Whereas now, any one who likes, any base fellow, may get up and discover something to the advantage of himself and his equals. It may be retorted, "And what sort of advantage either for himself or for the People can such a fellow be expected to hit upon?" The answer to which is, that in their judgment the ignorance and the baseness of this fellow, together with his goodwill, are worth a great deal more to them than your superior person's virtue and wisdom, coupled with animosity. What it comes to, therefore, is that a state founded upon such institutions will not be the best state; but, given a democracy, these are the right means to secure its preservation. The People, it must be borne in mind, does not demand that the city should be well governed and itself a slave. It desires to be free and to be master. As to bad legislation it does not concern itself about that. In fact, what you believe to be bad legislation is the very source of the People's strength and freedom. But if you seek for good legislation, in the first place you will see the cleverest members of the community laying down the laws for the rest. And in the next place, the better class will curb and chastise the lower orders; the better class will deliberate in behalf of the state, and not suffer crack-brained fellows to sit in council, or to speak or vote in the assemblies. No doubt; but under the weight of such blessings the People will in a very short time be reduced to slavery.

Another point is the extraordinary amount of license granted to slaves and resident aliens at Athens, where a blow is illegal, and a slave will not step aside to let you pass him in the street. I will explain the reason of this peculiar custom. Supposing it were legal for a slave to be beaten by a free citizen, or for a resident alien or freedman to be beaten by a citizen, it would frequently happen that an Athenian might be mistaken for a slave or an alien and receive a beating; since the Athenian People is not better clothed than the slave or alien, nor in personal appearance is there any superiority.

Or if the fact itself that slaves in Athens are allowed to indulge in luxury, and indeed in some cases to live magnificently, be found astonishing, this too, it can be shown, is done of set purpose. Where you have a naval power dependent upon wealth we must perforce be slaves to our slaves, in order that we may get in our slave-rents, and let the real slave go free. Where you have wealthy slaves it ceases to be advantageous that my slave should stand in awe of you. In Lacedaemon my slave stands in awe of you. But if your slave is in awe of me there will be a risk of his giving away his own moneys to avoid running a risk in his own person. It is for this reason then that we have established an equality between our slaves and free men; and again between our resident aliens and full citizens, because the city stands in need of her resident aliens to meet the requirements of such a multiplicity of arts and for the purposes of her navy. That is, I repeat, the justification of the equality conferred upon our resident aliens.

The common people put a stop to citizens devoting their time to athletics and to the cultivation of music, disbelieving in the beauty of such training, and recognising the fact that these are things the cultivation of which is beyond its power. On the same principle, in the case of the choregia, the management of athletics, and the command of ships, the fact is recognised that it is the rich man who trains the chorus, and the People for whom the chorus is trained; it is the rich man who is naval commander or superintendent of athletics, and the People that profits by their labours. In fact, what the People looks upon as its right is to pocket the money. To sing and run and dance and man the vessels is well enough, but only in order that the People may be the gainer, while the rich are made poorer. And so in the courts of justice, justice is not more an object of concern to the jurymen than what touches personal advantage.

To speak next of the allies, and in reference to the point that emissaries from Athens come out, and, according to common opinion, calumniate and vent their hatred upon the better sort of people, this is done on the principle that the ruler cannot help being hated by those whom he rules; but that if wealth and respectability are to wield power in the subject cities the empire of the Athenian People has but a short lease of existence. This explains why the better people are punished with infamy, robbed of their money, driven from their homes, and put to death, while the baser sort are promoted to honour. On the other hand, the better Athenians protect the better class in the allied cities. And why? Because they recognise that it is to the interest of their own class at all times to protect the best element in the cities. It may be urged that if it comes to strength and power the real strength of Athens lies in the capacity of her allies to contribute their money quota. But to the democratic mind it appears a higher advantage still for the individual Athenian to get hold of the wealth of the allies, leaving them only enough to live upon and to cultivate their estates, but powerless to harbour treacherous designs.

Again, it is looked upon as a mistaken policy on the part of the

Athenian democracy to compel her allies to voyage to Athens in order to have their cases tried. On the other hand, it is easy to reckon up what a number of advantages the Athenian People derives from the practice impugned. In the first place, there is the steady receipt of salaries throughout the year derived from the court fees. Next, it enables them to manage the affairs of the allied states while seated at home without the expense of naval expeditions. Thirdly, they thus preserve the partisans of the democracy, and ruin her opponents in the law courts. Whereas, supposing the several allied states tried their cases at home, being inspired by hostility to Athens, they would destroy those of their own citizens whose friendship to the Athenian People was most marked. But besides all this the democracy derives the following advantages from hearing the cases of her allies in Athens. In the first place, the one per cent levied in Piraeus is increased to the profit of the state; again, the owner of a lodging-house does better, and so, too, the owner of a pair of beasts, or of slaves to be let out on hire; again, heralds and criers are a class of people who fare better owing to the sojourn of foreigners at Athens. Further still, supposing the allies had not to resort to Athens for the hearing of cases, only the official representative of the imperial state would be held in honour, such as the general, or trierarch, or ambassador. Whereas now every single individual among the allies is forced to pay flattery to the People of Athens because he knows that he must betake himself to Athens and win or lose his case at the bar, not of any stray set of judges, but of the sovereign People itself, such being the law and custom at Athens. He is compelled to behave as a suppliant in the courts of justice, and when some juryman comes into court, to grasp his hand. For this reason, therefore, the allies find themselves more and more in the position of slaves to the People of Athens.

Furthermore, owing to the possession of property beyond the limits of Attica, and the exercise of magistracies which take them into regions beyond the frontier, they and their attendants have insensibly acquired the art of navigation. A man who is perpetually voyaging is forced to handle the oar, he and his domestic alike, and to learn the terms familiar in seamanship. Hence a stock of skilful mariners is produced, bred upon a wide experience of voyaging and practice. They have learned their business, some in piloting a small craft, others a merchant vessel, while others have been drafted off from these for service on a ship-of-war. So that the majority of them are able to row the moment they set foot on board a vessel, having been in a state of preliminary practice all their lives.

*   *   *

I repeat that my position concerning the constitution of the Athenians is this: the type of constitution is not to my taste, but given that a democratic form of government has been agreed upon, they do seem to me to go the right way to preserve the democracy by the adoption of the particular type which I have set forth.

In the Gorgias *dialogue Plato makes his view of Pericles'*
contribution to the Athenian constitution perfectly clear.
Plato was little more than a generation removed from the
time of Pericles and undoubtedly had good second-hand
evidence of its character. It is possible, however, that his
opinion was influenced by his own experience of the Athe-
nian democracy of the fourth century, which he cordially
disliked.

FROM *Gorgias* BY PLATO

soc. And now, my friend, as you are already beginning to be a public character, and are admonishing and reproaching me for not being one, suppose that we ask a few questions of one another. Tell me, then, Callicles, how about making any of the citizens better? Was there ever a man who was once vicious, or unjust, or intemperate, or foolish, and became by the help of Callicles good and noble? Was there ever such a man, whether citizen or stranger, slave or freeman? Tell me, Callicles, if a person were to ask these questions of you, what would you answer? Whom would you say that you had improved by your conversation? There may have been good deeds of this sort which were done by you as a private person, before you came forward in public. Why will you not answer?

cal. You are contentious, Socrates.

soc. Nay, I ask you, not from a love of contention, but because I really want to know in what way you think that affairs should be administered among us—whether, when you come to the administration of them, you have any other aim but the improvement of the citizens? Have we not already admitted many times over that such is the duty of a public man? Nay, we have surely said so; for if you will not answer for yourself I must answer for you. But if this is what the good man ought to effect for the benefit of his own state, allow me to recall to you the names of those whom you were just now mentioning, Pericles, and Cimon, and Miltiades, and Themistocles, and ask whether you still think that they were good citizens.

cal. I do.   .

soc. But if they were good, then clearly each of them must have made the citizens better instead of worse?

cal. Yes.

soc. And, therefore, when Pericles first began to speak in the assembly, the Athenians were not so good as when he spoke last?

Plato, *Gorgias* (1892), pp. 515-7 (Stephanus pagination), translated by Benjamin Jowett.

CAL. Very likely.

SOC. Nay, my friend, "likely" is not the word; for if he was a good citizen, the inference is certain.

CAL. And what difference does that make?

SOC. None; only I should like further to know whether the Athenians are supposed to have been made better by Pericles, or, on the contrary, to have been corrupted by him; for I hear that he was the first who gave the people pay, and made them idle and cowardly, and encouraged them in the love of talk and of money.

CAL. You heard that, Socrates, from the laconising set who bruise their ears.

SOC. But what I am going to tell you now is not mere hearsay, but well known both to you and me: that at first, Pericles was glorious and his character unimpeached by any verdict of the Athenians—this was during the time when they were not so good—yet afterwards, when they had been made good and gentle by him, at the very end of his life they convicted him of theft, and almost put him to death, clearly under the notion that he was a malefactor.

CAL. Well, but how does that prove Pericles' badness?

SOC. Why, surely you would say that he was a bad manager of asses or horses or oxen, who had received them originally neither kicking nor butting nor biting him, and implanted in them all these savage tricks? Would he not be a bad manager of any animals who received them gentle, and made them fiercer than they were when he received them? What do you say?

CAL. I will do you the favour of saying "yes."

SOC. And will you also do me the favour of saying whether man is an animal?

CAL. Certainly he is.

SOC. And was not Pericles a shepherd of men?

CAL. Yes.

SOC. And if he was a good political shepherd, ought not the animals who were his subjects, as we were just now acknowledging, to have become more just, and not more unjust?

CAL. Quite true.

SOC. And are not just men gentle, as Homer says?—or are you of another mind?

CAL. I agree.

SOC. And yet he really did make them more savage than he received them, and their savageness was shown towards himself; which he must have been very far from desiring.

CAL. Do you want me to agree with you?

SOC. Yes, if I seem to you to speak the truth.

CAL. Granted then.

SOC. And if they were more savage, must they not have been more unjust and inferior?

c a l. Granted again.

s o c. Then upon this view, Pericles was not a good statesman?

c a l. That is, upon your view.

s o c. Nay, the view is yours, after what you have admitted. Take the case of
Cimon again. Did not the very persons whom he was serving ostracize him,
in order that they might not hear his voice for ten years? and they did just
the same to Themistocles, adding the penalty of exile; and they voted that
Miltiades, the hero of Marathon, should be thrown into the pit of death, and
he was only saved by the Prytanis. And yet, if they had been really good
men, as you say, these things would never have happened to them. For the
good charioteers are not those who at first keep their place, and then, when
they have broken-in their horses, and themselves become better charioteers,
are thrown out—that is not the way either in charioteering or in any
profession.—What do you think?

c a l. I should think not.

s o c. Well, but if so, the truth is as I have said already, that in the Athenian
State no one has ever shown himself to be a good statesman—you admitted
that this was true of our present statesmen, but not true of former ones, and
you preferred them to the others; yet they have turned out to be no better
than our present ones; and therefore, if they were rhetoricians, they did not
use the true art of rhetoric or of flattery, or they would not have fallen out of
favour.

c a l. But surely, Socrates, no living man ever came near any one of them in
his performances.

s o c. O, my dear friend, I say nothing against them regarded as the serving-
men of the State; and I do think that they were certainly more serviceable
than those who are living now, and better able to gratify the wishes of the
State; but as to transforming those desires and not allowing them to have
their way, and using the powers which they had, whether of persuasion or of
force, in the improvement of their fellow-citizens, which is the prime object
of the truly good citizen, I do not see that in these respects they were a whit
superior to our present statesmen, although I do admit that they were more
clever at providing ships and walls and docks, and all that.

*Plutarch of Chaeronea was a Greek who lived in the second
century of our era. Certainly the best known of his many
works is the collection of biographies of illustrious Greeks
and Romans. He was not an historian but a biographer,
and he lacked the intellectual power of Thucydides, yet his
Lives are peculiarly valuable. He used all the sources available to him almost indiscriminately. Many of these ancient
sources are known to us only through his citation of them,*

*so that his work often throws important light on the events
he describes. His* Life of Pericles *thus uses* Thucydides *but
compares his views with those of other historians who may
have employed reliable information not used by Thucydides. The first selection describes Pericles' rise to power
and his early career.*

FROM *Pericles* BY PLUTARCH

*Institutions were democracy
but was Pericles a democrat.*

SINCE THUCYDIDES describes the rule of Pericles as an aristocratical
government, that went by the name of a democracy, but was, indeed, the
supremacy of a single great man, while many others say, on the contrary,
that by him the common people were first encouraged and led on to such
evils as appropriations of subject territory, allowances for attending theatres,
payments for performing public duties, and by these bad habits were, under
the influence of his public measures, changed from a sober, thrifty people,
that maintained themselves by their own labours, to lovers of expense,
intemperance, and licence, let us examine the cause of this change by the
actual matters of fact.

At the first, as has been said, when he set himself against Cimon's great
authority, he did caress the people. Finding himself come short of his
competitor in wealth and money, by which advantages the other was enabled
to take care of the poor, inviting every day some one or other of the citizens
that was in want to supper, and bestowing clothes on the aged people, and
breaking down the hedges and enclosures of his grounds, that all that would
might freely gather what fruit they pleased, Pericles, thus outdone in popular
arts, by the advice of one Damonides of Oea, as Aristotle states, turned to the
distribution of the public moneys; and in a short time having bought the
people over, what with moneys allowed for shows and for service on juries,
and what with other forms of pay and largess, he made use of them against
the council of Areopagus of which he himself was no member, as having
never been appointed by lot either chief archon, or lawgiver, or king, or
captain. For from of old these offices were conferred on persons by lot, and
they who had acquitted themselves duly in the discharge of them were
advanced to the court of Areopagus. And so Pericles, having secured his
power in interest with the populace, directed the exertions of his party
against this council with such success, that most of these causes and matters
which had been used to be tried there were, by the agency of Ephialtes,
removed from its cognisance; Cimon, also, was banished by ostracism as a

Plutarch, *Pericles* (abridged) (1683–1693), translated by John Dryden.

favourer of the Lacedaemonians and a hater of the people, though in wealth and noble birth he was among the first, and had won several most glorious victories over the barbarians, and had filled the city with money and spoils of war; as is recorded in the history of his life. So vast an authority had Pericles obtained among the people.

Cimon, while he was admiral, ended his days in the Isle of Cyprus. And the aristocratical party, seeing that Pericles was already before this grown to be the greatest and foremost man of all the city, but nevertheless wishing there should be somebody set up against him, to blunt and turn the edge of his power, that it might not altogether prove a monarchy, put forward Thucydides of Alopece [*the son of Melesias, not the historian*—D.K.], a discreet person, and a near kinsman of Cimon's, to conduct the opposition against him; who, indeed, though less skilled in warlike affairs than Cimon was, yet was better versed in speaking and political business and keeping close guard in the city, and, engaging with Pericles on the hustings, in a short time brought the government to an equality of parties. For he would not suffer those who were called the honest and good (persons of worth and distinction) to be scattered up and down and mix themselves and be lost among the populace, as formerly, diminishing and obscuring their superiority amongst the masses; but taking them apart by themselves and uniting them in one body, by their combined weight he was able, as it were upon the balance, to make a counterpoise to the other party.

For, indeed, there was from the beginning a sort of concealed split, or seam, as it might be in a piece of iron, marking the different popular and aristocratical tendencies; but the open rivalry and contention of these two opponents made the gash deep, and severed the city into the two parties of the people and the few. And so Pericles, at that time, more than at any other, let loose the reins to the people, and made his policy subservient to their pleasure, contriving continually to have some great public show or solemnity, some banquet, or some procession or other in the town to please them, coaxing his countrymen like children with such delights and pleasures as were, however, unedifying. Besides that every year he sent out threescore galleys, on board of which there were numbers of the citizens, who were in pay eight months, learning at the same time and practising the art of seamanship.

He sent, moreover, a thousand of them into the Chersonese as planters, to share the land among them by lot, and five hundred more into the isle of Naxos, and half that number to Andros, a thousand into Thrace to dwell among the Bisaltae, and others into Italy, when the city Sybaris, which now was called Thurii, was to be repeopled. And this he did to ease and discharge the city of an idle, and, by reason of their idleness, a busy meddling crowd of people; and at the same time to meet the necessities and restore the fortunes of the poor townsmen, and to intimidate, also, and check their allies from attempting any change, by posting such garrisons, as it were, in the midst of them.

That which gave most pleasure and ornament to the city of Athens, and the greatest admiration and even astonishment to all strangers, and that which now is Greece's only evidence that the power she boasts of and her ancient wealth are no romance or idle story, was his construction of the public and sacred buildings. Yet this was that of all his actions in the government which his enemies most looked askance upon and cavilled at in the popular assemblies, crying out how that the commonwealth of Athens had lost its reputation and was ill-spoken of abroad for removing the common treasure of the Greeks from the isle of Delos into their own custody; and how that their fairest excuse for so doing, namely, that they took it away for fear the barbarians should seize it, and on purpose to secure it in a safe place, this Pericles had made unavailable, and how that "Greece cannot but resent it as an insufferable affront, and consider herself to be tyrannised over openly, when she sees the treasure, which was contributed by her upon a necessity for the war, wantonly lavished out by us upon our city, to gild her all over, and to adorn and set her forth, as it were some vain woman, hung round with precious stones and figures and temples, which cost a world of money."

Pericles, on the other hand, informed the people, that they were in no way obliged to give any account of those moneys to their allies, so long as they maintained their defence, and kept off the barbarians from attacking them; while in the meantime they did not so much as supply one horse or man or ship, but only found money for the service; "which money," said he, "is not theirs that give it, but theirs that receive it, if so be they perform the conditions upon which they receive it." And that it was good reason, that, now the city was sufficiently provided and stored with all things necessary for the war, they should convert the overplus of its wealth to such undertakings as would hereafter, when completed, give them eternal honour, and, for the present, while in process, freely supply all the inhabitants with plenty. With their variety of workmanship and of occasions for service, which summon all arts and trades and require all hands to be employed about them, they do actually put the whole city, in a manner, into state-pay; while at the same time she is both beautiful and maintained by herself. For as those who are of age and strength for war are provided for and maintained in the armaments abroad by their pay out of the public stock, so, it being his desire and design that the undisciplined mechanic multitude that stayed at home should not go without their share of public salaries, and yet should not have them given them for sitting still and doing nothing, to that end he thought fit to bring in among them, with the approbation of the people, these vast projects of buildings and designs of work, that would be of some continuance before they were finished, and would give employment to numerous arts, so that the part of the people that stayed at home might, no less than those that were at sea or in garrisons or on expeditions, have a fair and just occasion of receiving the benefit and having their share of the public moneys.

When the orators, who sided with Thucydides and his party, were at one time crying out, as their custom was, against Pericles, as one who squandered away the public money, and made havoc of the state revenues, he rose in the open assembly and put the question to the people, whether they thought that he had laid out much; and they saying, "Too much, a great deal," "Then," said he, "since it is so, let the cost not go to your account, but to mine; and let the inscription upon the buildings stand in my name." When they heard him say thus, whether it were out of a surprise to see the greatness of his spirit or out of emulation of the glory of the works, they cried aloud, bidding him to spend on, and lay out what he thought fit from the public purse, and to spare no cost, till all were finished.

At length, coming to a final contest with Thucydides which of the two should ostracise the other out of the country, and having gone through this peril, he threw his antagonist out, and broke up the confederacy that had been organised against him. So that now all schism and division being at an end, and the city brought to evenness and unity, he got all Athens and all affairs that pertained to the Athenians into his own hands, their tributes, their armies, and their galleys, the islands, the sea, and their wide-extended power, partly over other Greeks and partly over barbarians, and all that empire, which they possessed, founded and fortified upon subject nations and royal friendships and alliances.

After this he was no longer the same man he had been before, nor as tame and gentle and familiar as formerly with the populace, so as readily to yield to their pleasures and to comply with the desires of the multitude, as a steersman shifts with the winds. Quitting that loose, remiss, and, in some cases, licentious court of the popular will, he turned those soft and flowery modulations to the austerity of aristocratical and regal rule; and employing this uprightly and undeviatingly for the country's best interests, he was able generally to lead the people along, with their own wills and consents, by persuading and showing them what was to be done; and sometimes, too, urging and pressing them forward extremely against their will, he made them, whether they would or no, yield submission to what was for their advantage. In which, to say the truth, he did but like a skilful physician, who, in a complicated and chronic disease, as he sees occasion, at one while allows his patient the moderate use of such things as please him, at another while gives him keen pains and drug to work the cure. For there arising and growing up, as was natural, all manner of distempered feelings among a people which had so vast a command and dominion, he alone, as a great master, knowing how to handle and deal fitly with each one of them, and, in an especial manner, making that use of hopes and fears, as his two chief rudders, with the one to check the career of their confidence at any time, with the other to raise them up and cheer them when under any discouragement, plainly showed by this, that rhetoric, or the art of speaking, is, in Plato's language, the government of the souls of men, and that her chief business is to address the affections and passions, which are as it were the strings and keys to the soul, and require a skilful and careful touch to be played on as they should be. The source of this predominance was not barely his power of language, but, as Thucydides assures us, the reputation of his life, and the confidence felt in his character; his manifest freedom from every kind of corruption, and superiority to all considerations of money. Notwithstanding he had made the city of Athens, which was great of itself, as great and rich as can be imagined, and though he were himself in power and interest more than equal to many kings and absolute rulers, who some of them also bequeathed by will their power to their children, he, for his part, did not make the patrimony his father left him greater than it was by one drachma.

Thucydides, indeed, gives a plain statement of the greatness of his power; and the comic poets, in their spiteful manner, more than hint at it, styling his companions and friends the new Peisistratidae, and calling on him to abjure any intention of usurpation, as one whose eminence was too great to be any longer proportionable to and compatible with a democracy or popular government. And Teleclides says the Athenians had surrendered up to him—

The tribute of the cities, and with them, the cities too, to do with them as he pleases, and undo;
To build up, if he likes, stone walls around a town; and again, if so he likes, to pull them down;
Their treaties and alliances, power, empire, peace, and war, their wealth and their success forever more.

Nor was all this the luck of some happy occasion; nor was it the mere bloom and grace of a policy that flourished for a season; but having for forty years together maintained the first place among statesmen such as Ephialtes and Leocrates and Myronides and Cimon and Tolmides and Thucydides were, after the defeat and banishment of Thucydides, for no less than fifteen years longer, in the exercise of one continuous unintermitted command in the office, to which he was annually re-elected, of General, he preserved his integrity unspotted.

[*During the years just prior to the Peloponnesian War, Pericles' political control was threatened by attacks on his friends and collaborators, among them the sculptor Phidias—D.K.*]

Phidias then was carried away to prison, and there died of a disease; but, as some say, of poison, administered by the enemies of Pericles, to raise a slander, or a suspicion at least, as though he had procured it. The informer Menon, upon Glycon's proposal, the people made free from payment of taxes and customs, and ordered the generals to take care that nobody should do him any hurt. About the same time, Aspasia was indicted of impiety, upon the complaint of Hermippus the comedian, who also laid further to her charge that she received into her house freeborn women for the uses of Pericles. And Diopithes proposed a decree, that public accusations should be laid against persons who neglected religion, or taught new doctrines about things above, directing suspicion, by means of Anaxagoras, against Pericles himself. The people receiving and admitting these accusations and complaints, at length, by this means, they came to enact a decree, at the motion of Dracontides, that Pericles should bring in the accounts of the moneys he had expended, and lodge them with the Prytanes; and that the judges, carrying their suffrage from the altar in the Acropolis, should examine and determine the business in the city. This last clause Hagnon took out of the decree, and moved that the causes should be tried before fifteen hundred jurors, whether they should be styled prosecutions for robbery, or bribery, or any kind of malversation. Aspasia, Pericles begged off, shedding, as Aeschines says, many tears at the trial, and personally entreating the jurors. But fearing how it might go with Anaxagoras, he sent him out of the city. And finding that in Phidias's case he had miscarried with the people, being afraid of impeachment, he kindled the war, which hitherto had lingered and smothered, and blew it up into a flame; hoping, by that means, to disperse and scatter these complaints and charges, and to allay their jealousy; the city usually throwing herself upon him alone, and trusting to his sole conduct, upon the urgency of great affairs and public dangers, by reason of his authority and the sway he bore.

These are given out to have been the reasons which induced Pericles not to suffer the people of Athens to yield to the proposals of the Lacedaemonians; but their truth is uncertain.

The Lacedaemonians, for their part, feeling sure that if they could once remove him, they might be at what terms they pleased with the Athenians, sent them word that they should expel the "Pollution" with which Pericles on the mother's side was tainted, as Thucydides tells us. But the issue proved quite contrary to what those who sent the message expected; instead of bringing Pericles under suspicion and reproach, they raised him into yet greater credit and esteem with the citizens, as a man whom their enemies most hated and feared. In the same way, also, before Archidamus, who was at the head of the Peloponnesians, made his invasion into Attica, he told the Athenians beforehand, that if Archidamus, while he laid waste the rest of the country, should forbear and spare his estate, either on the ground of friendship or right of hospitality that was betwixt them, or on purpose to give his enemies an occasion of traducing him; that then he did freely bestow upon the state all his land and the buildings upon it for the public use. The Lacedaemonians, therefore, and their allies, with a great army, invaded the Athenian territories, under the conduct of King Archidamus, and laying waste the country, marched on as far as Acharnae, and there pitched their camp, presuming that the Athenians would never endure that, but would come out and fight them for their country's and their honour's sake. But Pericles looked upon it as dangerous to engage in battle, to the risk

of the city itself, against sixty thousand men-at-arms of Peloponnesians and
Boeotians; for so many they were in number that made the inroad at first;
and he endeavoured to appease those who were desirous to fight, and were
grieved and discontented to see how things went, and gave them good
words, saying, that "trees, when they are lopped and cut, grow up again in a
short time, but men, being once lost, cannot easily be recovered." He did not
convene the people into an assembly, for fear lest they should force him to
act against his judgment; but, like a skilful steersman or pilot of a ship, who,
when a sudden squall comes on, out at sea, makes all his arrangements, sees
that all is tight and fast, and then follows the dictates of his skill, and minds
the business of the ship, taking no notice of the tears and entreaties of the
sea-sick and fearful passengers, so he, having shut up the city gates, and
placed guards at all posts for security, followed his own reason and judgment, little regarding those that cried out against him and were angry at his
management, although there were a great many of his friends that urged
him with requests, and many of his enemies threatened and accused him for
doing as he did, and many made songs and lampoons upon him, which were
sung about the town to his disgrace, reproaching him with the cowardly
exercise of his office of general, and the tame abandonment of everything to
the enemy's hands.

Cleon, also, already was among his assailants, making use of the feeling
against him as a step to the leadership of the people, as appears in the
anapaestic verses of Hermippus—

> Satyr-king, instead of swords,
> Will you always handle words?
> Very brave indeed we find them,
> But a Teles lurks behind them.
>
> Yet to gnash your teeth you're seen,
> When the little dagger keen,
> Whetted every day anew,
> Of sharp Cleon touches you.

Pericles, however, was not at all moved by any attacks, but took all
patiently, and submitted in silence to the disgrace they threw upon him and
the ill-will they bore him; and, sending out a fleet of a hundred galleys to
Peloponnesus, he did not go along with it in person, but stayed behind, that
he might watch at home and keep the city under his own control, till the
Peloponnesians broke up their camp and were gone. Yet to soothe the
common people, jaded and distressed with the war, he relieved them with
distributions of public moneys, and ordained new divisions of subject land.
For having turned out all the people of Aegina, he parted the island among
the Athenians according to lot. Some comfort, also, and ease in their miser-
ies, they might receive from what their enemies endured. For the fleet,
sailing round the Peloponnese, ravaged a great deal of the country, and
pillaged and plundered the towns and smaller cities; and by land he himself

entered with an army the Megarian country, and made havoc of it all. Whence it is clear that the Peloponnesians, though they did the Athenians much mischief by land, yet suffering as much themselves from them by sea, would not have protracted the war to such a length, but would quickly have given it over, as Pericles at first foretold they would, had not some divine power crossed human purposes.

In the first place, the pestilential disease, or plague, seized upon the city, and ate up all the flower and prime of their youth and strength. Upon occasion of which, the people, distempered and afflicted in their souls, as well as in their bodies, were utterly enraged like madmen against Pericles, and, like patients grown delirious, sought to lay violent hands on their physician, or, as it were, their father. They had been possessed, by his enemies, with the belief that the occasion of the plague was the crowding of the country people together into the town, forced as they were now, in the heat of the summer-weather, to dwell many of them together even as they could, in small tenements and stifling hovels, and to be tied to a lazy course of life within doors, whereas before they lived in a pure, open, and free air. The cause and author of all this, said they, is he who on account of the war has poured a multitude of people in upon us within the walls, and uses all these men that he has here upon no employ or service, but keeps them pent up like cattle, to be overrun with infection from one another, affording them neither shift of quarters nor any refreshment.

With the design to remedy these evils, and do the enemy some inconvenience, Pericles got a hundred and fifty galleys ready, and having embarked many tried soldiers, both foot and horse, was about to sail out, giving great hope to his citizens, and no less alarm to his enemies, upon the sight of so great a force. And now the vessels having their complement of men, and Pericles being gone aboard his own galley, it happened that the sun was eclipsed, and it grew dark on a sudden, to the affright of all, for this was looked upon as extremely ominous. Pericles, therefore, perceiving the steersman seized with fear and at a loss what to do, took his cloak and held it up before the man's face, and screening him with it so that he could not see, asked him whether he imagined there was any great hurt, or the sign of any great hurt in this, and he answering No, "Why," said he, "and what does that differ from this, only that what has caused that darkness there, is something greater than a cloak?" This is a story which philosophers tell their scholars. Pericles, however, after putting out to sea, seems not to have done any other exploit befitting such preparations, and when he had laid siege to the holy city Epidaurus, which gave him some hope of surrender, miscarried in his design by reason of the sickness. For it not only seized upon the Athenians, but upon all others, too, that held any sort of communication with the army. Finding after this the Athenians ill-affected and highly displeased with him, he tried and endeavoured what he could to appease and re-encourage them. But he could not pacify or allay their anger, nor persuade or prevail with them any way, till they freely passed their votes upon him, resumed their power, took away his command from him, and fined him in a sum of money; which by their account that say least, was fifteen talents, while they who reckon most, name fifty. The name prefixed to the accusation was Cleon, as Idomeneus tells us; Simmias, according to Theophrastus; and Heraclides Ponticus gives it as Lacratidas.

*   *   *

The city having made trial of other generals for the conduct of war, and orators for business of state, when they found there was no one who was of weight enough for such a charge, or of authority sufficient to be trusted with so great a command, regretted the loss of him, and invited him again to address and advise them, and to reassume the office of general. He, however, lay at home in dejection and mourning; but was persuaded by Alcibiades and others of his friends to come abroad and show himself to the people; who having, upon his appearance, made their acknowledgments, and apologised for their untowardly treatment of him, he undertook the public affairs once more.

4 Modern Opinions

*In the following essay, Van Hook supports the view that
Periclean Athens was a true democracy.*

Was Athens in the Age of Pericles Aristocratic?
BY LARUE VAN HOOK

THE MAJORITY of the numerous books which deal with Athenian
political and social life in the latter part of the fifth century B.C. convey to
student and to reader the general, but emphatic, impression that the *polis*
Athens, while theoretically a democracy, was, generally speaking, an aristocracy. It is hardly an exaggeration to say that the composite picture of Athens
under Pericles, as represented in the traditional view of the handbooks,
reveals a society brilliant in its achievements, but quite selfishly constituted,
and gravely defective, save from the viewpoint of the favored few. Profound
social distinctions, even among the citizens themselves, are insisted upon.
The conception still is widely prevalent that the *élite* of Athenian society,
few but fit, led a life of glorious but intensely selfish leisure, which was their
lordly prerogative as the result of the ruthless exploitation of all professional
men, artists, producers, traders, artisans, workers, resident aliens, and slaves.
Almost everywhere we find the time-honored assertion that in Athens all
work was despised, labor was contemned, the workers were disdained, and,
in fact, that *any* service for which financial remuneration was received was
in disrepute and branded the doer with a humiliating social stigma. The free
man is supposed to have done little or no work, for surely the aristocratic
citizen must have a completely independent and carefree existence for his
manifold political, social, and religious duties.

Let me now present some typical quotations from some recent books on
Athens which give this false, or exaggerated, as I think, impression of the
nature of Athenian society in the second half of the fifth century B.C., in that
they assert that it was essentially aristocratic. In the ninth edition (1915) of
that very popular, widely influential, and, in many respects, admirable little

LaRue Van Hook, "Was Athens in the Age of Pericles Aristocratic?" *The Classical Journal*, 14
(1918–1919), 472–9.

book, *The Greek View of Life* by Mr. Lowes Dickinson, we read (italics are mine in every case): "In the Greek conception the citizen was an aristocrat. His excellence was thought to consist in public activity; and to the performance of public duties he ought therefore to be able to devote *the greater part of his time and energy*. But the existence of such a privileged class involved the existence of a class of producers to support them; and *the producers, by the nature of their calling,* be they slave *or free, were excluded from the life of the perfect citizen*. They had not the necessary leisure to devote to public business; neither had they the opportunity to acquire the mental and physical qualities which would enable them to transact it worthily. They were therefore regarded by the Greeks as an inferior class. . . . In Athens the most democratic of all the Greek communities, though they were admitted to the citizenship and enjoyed considerable political influence, *they never appear to have lost the stigma of social inferiority*. And the distinction which was more or less definitely drawn in practice *between the citizens proper* and *the productive class* was even more emphatically affirmed in theory" (pp. 74-75). "The obverse of the Greek *citizen,* who realized in the state the highest life, was *an inferior class of producers who realized only the means to subsistence*" (p. 75). "The *inferiority* of the artisan and the trader was further emphasized by the fact that *they were excluded by their calling* from the cultivation of the higher personal qualities; from the training of the body by gymnastics and of the mind by philosophy; *from habitual conversance with public affairs;* from that perfect balance, in a word, of the physical, intellectual, and moral powers, which was only to be attained by a process of *self-culture, incompatible with the pursuance of a trade for bread*" (p. 82). "The existence of the Greek citizen depended upon that of an inferior class who were regarded, not as ends in themselves, but as means to his perfection." "The aim of modern societies is not to separate off a privileged class of citizens, set free by the labour of others to live the perfect life, but rather to distribute impartially to all the burdens and advantages of the state, so that every one shall be at once a labourer for himself and a citizen of the state. But this idea is clearly incompatible with the Greek conception of the citizen" (p. 130). "It is because labour with the hands or at the desk distorts or impairs the body, and the petty cares of a calling pursued for bread pervert the soul, that so *strong a contempt was felt by the Greeks for manual labour and trade."* "If then the artisan . . . in Athens never altogether threw off *the stigma of inferiority attaching to his trade,* the reason was that the life he was compelled to lead was incompatible with the Greek conception of excellence" (p. 134). "The Greeks, on the whole, were quite content to sacrifice the majority to the minority. Their position was fundamentally aristocratic; they exaggerated rather than minimized the distinctions between men, the freeman and the slave, the gentleman and the artisan, regarding them as natural and fundamental, not as the casual product of circumstances. The 'equality' which they sought was proportional, not arithmetical, not of equal rights to all." "In a modern state it is different though class distinctions are clearly enough marked, yet the point of view from which they are regarded is fundamentally different. They are attributed rather to accidents of fortune than to varieties of nature. The artisan, for example, ranks no doubt lower than the professional man; but no one maintains that he is a different kind of being incapable by nature, as Aristotle asserts, of the characteristic excellence of man" (p. 79).

In *Greek Ideals,* by Mr. C. Delisle Burns, a study of Athenian social life of the period under consideration, the Greek aristocratic conception of individual liberty is likewise, I believe, overemphasized. Thus we find the statements: "It seemed essential that liberty and equality should only be the right of *a few* males. . . . . Slaves and *workingmen had no time and no developed capacity for the 'good life'* " (p. 76). "Society was conceived only in terms . . . . of *a small social caste*" (p. 109). "The Athenian citizen might object to doing manual labour" (p. 112).

Similar assertions are common. Thus Mr. Edwards in Whibley's *Companion to Greek Studies:* "The prejudice against trades and handicrafts was most pronounced in Sparta: elsewhere, though the political disabilities might be reduced or removed, the *social stigma was scarcely diminished*—indeed, even the fullest development of democracy at Athens did but stereotype the conventional horror of hard work, and proclaimed leisure, and not labour, to be the citizen's privilege. . . . . The marvel is that, *amid all this depreciation,* mechanical skill and artistic taste should have attained so high a standard" (p. 437).

Gardner and Jevons, *Manual of Greek Antiquities* (p. 379), quote Aristotle and Plato to show the extreme *popular* prejudice against handiwork and the disesteem in which it was *universally* held—"only those too poor to buy slaves had to work themselves."

Gulick, in his excellent *Life of the Ancient Athenians,* says: "The class of artisans comprised callings which among us are regarded as the most dignified professions. Wherever one of these vocations *was in disrepute,* the cause is found in the fact that the person concerned *took money for his services,* and was to that extent not independent of others. Even the great artists, painters, and sculptors fell under *public contempt* simply because they earned money. A few artists, like Phidias, are said to have enjoyed the friendship of eminent men of aristocratic birth; but most of these stories of intimacy are later exaggerations which have not taken into account the conditions of ancient industrial life. Schoolmasters, teachers of music and gymnastics, sophists and even physicians were not highly regarded" (p. 233). "To the *emporos* attached some of *the stigma of personal labor.*" "Ancient communities (e.g., Athens) whose *citizens despised trade and manual labor*" (p. 65). "Art, letters, and politics, claimed the interest of the ordinary citizen far more than they do today, because it was the policy of Pericles *to render the democracy of Athens a leisure class, supported by their slaves and the revenues of the Empire*" (p. 118).

But enough of such representative quotations, they might be multiplied indefinitely. It is the aim of this paper to endeavor to correct, or, at least, to assist in the modification of this all too general conception of an essentially aristocratic Athenian society, a conception which is certainly false in some of its aspects and exaggerated or overemphasized in others.

Before a consideration of the subject proper it may well be asked, why is it that this view of Athenian society as aristocratic, if erroneous, is generally held? The reasons are, I believe, as follows: (1) Athens, like other Greek states, at an early period in its history, in fact, until after Solon and Cleisthenes, was, in large measure, oligarchic and aristocratic both politically and socially. Modern writers mistakenly assume that these early conditions, particularly in social life, continued. (2) Certain Greek states, e.g., Sparta, Thebes, and Crete never suffered democratization. The strictly aristocratic conditions which were permanently characteristic of these states are sometimes thought of as necessarily existing also in Athens. (3) Modern writers have the tendency implicitly to follow Plato and Aristotle as authorities and imagine that actual fifth century Athenian conditions are accurately reflected in the pages of these philosophers even when the latter are discussing theoretical polities and imaginary and ideal societies. Caution must always be observed surely in the case of these "Laconizing" theorizers who, furthermore, were intense aristocrats and distrusted democracy. (4) It is true that Athens was conservative in the granting of full and technically legal citizenship to foreigners and slaves. (5) Slavery was, of course, a recognized institution from time immemorial throughout the ancient world and Athens as well. (6) Physical *drudgery* was not relished by the Athenians. The ground is now cleared for our discussion.

POLITICAL CONDITIONS

Was Athens in the Age of Pericles really a political democracy? We are fortunate in having no less an authority than Pericles himself to testify for us; Pericles, the aristocrat, as reported by Thucydides, the aristocrat. "Our government is *not copied* from those of our neighbors; we are an example to them rather than they to us. Our constitution is named a *democracy,* because it is in the hands not of the few but of *the many.* Our laws secure *equal* justice for *all* in their private disputes, and our *public opinion* welcomes and honors talent in *every branch of achievement,* not for any sectional reason, but on grounds of excellence alone. And as we give free play to *all* in our public life, so we carry the same spirit into our daily relations with one another. We are obedient to whomsoever is set in authority, and to the laws, more especially to those which offer protection to the oppressed and those unwritten ordinances whose transgression brings admitted shame. Wealth to us is not mere material for vainglory but an opportunity for achievement; and *poverty* we think is *no disgrace* to acknowledge but a real degradation to make no effort to overcome. *Our citizens attend both to public and private duties, and do not allow absorption in their own various affairs to interfere with their knowledge of the city's.* We differ from other states in regarding the man who *holds aloof from public life* not as quiet but as useless. In a word I claim that our city as a whole is an education to Greece, and that her members yield to none, man by man, for independence of spirit, many-sidedness of attainment, and complete self-reliance in limbs and brain."

In Athens, then, if not in Sparta and Plato's *Republic,* the state existed for the individual and not the individual for the state. It is unnecessary to do more than briefly to cite the facts which reveal Athens as a political democracy. *All* citizens over eighteen years of age were members of the Assembly; *all* citizens over thirty were eligible to membership in the Council of Five Hundred, the members of which were elected annually *by lot; all* citizens over thirty were eligible to election *by lot* to serve as jurymen in the Heliastic law courts. As Warde Fowler says: "Every citizen had the right to hold all offices, with the doubtful exception in 450, of the archonship; to serve on the Council; to take part in the Assembly; to sit as judge. There was no privileged class, no skilled politicians, no bureaucracy. The whole Athenian people were identified with, actually were the state. All shared equally in the government, education, and pleasures." For this complete political equality we may let Mr. Dickinson himself eloquently testify. Although he tells us (p. 83) that the artisan and the trader were excluded by their calling from habitual conversance with public affairs, later he says (p. 112): "Among the free citizens, who included persons of every rank, no political distinction at all was drawn. All of them from the lowest to the highest had the right to speak and vote in the great assembly of the people which was the ultimate authority; all were eligible to every administrative post; all sat in turn as jurors in the law courts. The disabilities of poverty were minimized by payment for attendance in the assembly and courts. And what is more extraordinary, even distinctions of ability were levelled by the practice of filling all offices, except the highest, by lot. The citizenship was extended to every rank and calling; the poor man jostled the rich, the shopman the aristocrat, in the Assembly; cobblers, carpenters, smiths, farmers, merchants and retail dealers met together with the ancient landed gentry." "Politically the Athenian trader, and the Athenian artisan, was the equal of the aristocrat of purest blood" (p. 115).

We know that the power of the early Athenian aristocracy had been seriously curtailed by the legislation of Solon and Cleisthenes. After the Persian Wars its influence as an organized party became extremely small because of the democratic reforms of Ephialtes and Pericles through the blows dealt to the prestige of the Areopagus, the exile of Cimon, and the complete ascendency of Pericles. There was, then, in Athens in the Age of Pericles complete political equality among the citizens; poverty, wealth, station, family, occupation, and prestige all were of no consequence

SOCIAL CONDITIONS

SOCIAL STATUS OF CITIZENS IN GENERAL

Let us now turn to an examination of the social conditions of Athenian life and scrutinize it for evidences of caste, class, snobbery, inequality, or injustice. In the city the house of the rich man and that of the poor man differed little in appearance. Private unostentation as constrasted with public magnificence was the rule. In fact, it was considered a breach of good taste to build and occupy a house of conspicuous cost or size. In the next place, simplicity in dress was general. Only the young (and, in particular, the Knights) dared to provoke possible derision or to invite popular prejudice by foppery of attire or appearance. Young Mantitheus apologizes to the Senate for his long hair and Strepsiades is disgusted with his son's "dandyism." Wearing the hair long might arouse suspicion of Spartan or aristocratic sympathies. An ancient witness testifies that "the Athenian people are not better clothed than the slave or alien, nor in personal appearance is there any superiority." Of course the nature of the employment might influence the quality and nature of the costume.

In all forms of social activity all the citizens participated on a parity. All could attend the theater; all joined in the public festivals and in religious sacrifices and observances. In fact, if any element in Athens was favored it was the poor and lowly. Listen to the testimony of that unregenerate old Aristocrat (just quoted) who is bitterly opposed to Democracy as an institution but admits that it really exists in Athens. He says that if you *must* have Democracy Athens is a perfect example of it, "I do not praise the Polity of the Athenians, because the very choice involves the welfare of the *baser* folk as opposed to that of the *better* class. The poorer classes and the people of Athens should have the advantage over the men of birth and wealth because it is the people who row the vessels, and put around the city her girdle of power. Everywhere greater consideration is shown to the base, to poor people, and to common folk, than to persons of good quality—this should not surprise us, this is the keystone of the preservation of the democracy. It is these poor people, this common folk, this riff-raff, whose prosperity, combined with the growth of their numbers, enhance the democracy. All the world over the cream of society is in opposition to the democracy. The objection may be raised that it was a mistake to allow the universal right of speech and a seat in council; privileges which should have been reserved for the cleverest, the flower of the community. But if only the better people sat in council blessings would fall only to that class and the baser folk would get nothing. Whereas it is the other way round. The people desire to be free and to be masters and their bad legislation is the very source of the people's strength and freedom." The happy lot of the common people in ancient Athens is further described by this contemporary witness: "The rich man trains the chorus; it is the people for whom the chorus is trained. The rich man is trierarch or gymnasiarch and the people profit by their labors. The whole state sacrifices at public cost a large number of victims; the Attic Democracy keeps holiday. They build at public cost a number of palaestras, dressing-rooms, bathing establishments; the mob gets the benefit of the majority of these luxuries rather than the select few or the well-to-do. In the theater the people do not like to be caricatured in comedy; it is the wealthy or well-born or influential man who is lampooned."

Enough has been said to show that the door of opportunity was open to all in Athens at this time. Worth, ability, character, not accident of birth or position counted. The rich did not grow richer while the poor grew poorer. Surplus wealth was not at the disposal of the few. It was expended for the good of all upon religious observances, the drama, gymnasia, the navy, public buildings and their adornment, and the state support of orphans and those physically incapacitated for earning a living. The wealthier classes were expected, and, in fact, were compelled, to contribute according to their means to the common welfare through the various liturgies and taxes.

THE SOCIAL STATUS OF THE PRODUCER, ARTISAN, ETC.

We come next to a study of the social and economic position of the workers of various kinds. As we have seen, the handbooks in general tell us that all work was regarded as degrading, every activity for which one was paid was condemned, and producers, artisans, and all workers were branded by a humiliating social stigma. No adequate proof of such a condition of affairs is forthcoming; indeed, the actual situation seems to have been otherwise in democratic Athens at the time of Pericles. Why then is there this general mistaken notion? It is largely because of certain pronouncements in Plato and Aristotle. In the *Laws* and the *Republic* Plato insists on the gulf that should separate the citizen from the mechanic or trader. His ideal state rests upon agriculture and all the citizens are landed gentry forbidden to engage in trade. In this ideal *polis* trade and commerce are to be insignificant and the productive class is actually debarred from all political rights. A caste system is presupposed; governors and governed are sharply differentiated and each class is trained for its predestined position in the state. Aristotle, too, in his ideal state divides the population, on the one hand, into a ruling class of soldiers and judges and, on the other, into a subject class consisting of artisans and producers. As a mechanical trade renders the body and soul and intellect of free persons unfit for the exercise and practice of virtue Aristotle denies to the artisan the proper excellence of man on the ground that his occupation and status are unnatural. In an extreme Democracy the mechanic and hired laborer must needs be citizens; this is impossible in an Aristocracy in which virtue and desert constitute the sole claim to the honors of state. Other radical statements of Aristotle are that the producer only differs from a slave in being subject to all instead of to one man and that the sedentary and within-door nature of the crafts unfitted the man who exercised them for war and the chase, the most dignified employments. Physical labor is condemned by him in that it is cheapening to work for another for pay or material profit as this reduces one to the rank of a slave. This would seem to be the chief source for the curious statement everywhere repeated that all Athenians who did anything for pay were condemned. That Aristotle did not represent Athenian opinion is conclusively shown by his condemnation of agriculture as preventing leisure which is at the basis of virtue. But no one doubts that agriculture was generally and highly esteemed by the Athenians.

In Xenophon in a passage which is represented as spoken by Socrates those base mechanic arts are condemned which ruin the bodies of all those engaged in them, as those who are forced to remain in sitting postures and hug the gloom or crouch whole days confronting a furnace. This results in physical enervation and enfeebling of the soul and the victims have no leisure to devote to the claims of friendship and the state. Such will be sorry friends and ill-defenders of the fatherland.

It is absolutely wrong to accept these passages as conclusively proving that the Athenians regarded work as degrading and workers as social outcasts. (1) These writers do not claim to be describing actual Athenian conditions. (2) They are postulating an "ideal" society. (3) They are ever admirers of Spartan, and not their own Athenian polity. (4) They were intense aristocrats in sympathy and mistrusted democracy. (5) They despised the body and its needs. (6) They had particularly in mind soul-destroying drudgery, not reasonable labor and skilled work; corrupt and petty business, not necessary and honest trade and affairs. Frequently they were contrasting the philosopher-statesmen set apart for ruling with the defective yokel. We can, indeed, if we wish, invoke the above-quoted writers in defense of work and the dignity of producing. Plato says in the *Laws:* "Retail trade in a city is not by nature intended to do any harm, but quite the contrary; for is not he a benefactor who reduces the inequalities and incommensurabilities of goods to equality and common measure? And this is what the power of money accomplishes, and the merchant may be said to be appointed for this purpose." Plato goes on to observe that many occupations have suffered ill-repute because of the inordinate love of gain and consequent corrupt practices on the part of the unscrupulous. He concludes: "If . . . . we were to compel the best men everywhere to keep taverns for a time, or carry on retail trade, or do anything of that sort; or if, in consequence of some fate or necessity, the best women were compelled to follow similar callings, then we should know how agreeable and pleasant all these things are; and if all such occupations were managed on incorrupt principles, they would be honored as we honor a mother or nurse." Aristotle in the *Politics* condemns agriculture as we have seen, yet elsewhere he declares: "We honor the generous and brave and just. Such we conceive to be those who do not live upon others; and *such are they who live by labor* . . . . chiefly agriculturalists, and chief among the agriculturalists, the small farmers." Now these small farmers tilled their own fields; in the remote districts of Attica slavery had scarcely penetrated. Xenophon tells the story of Eutherus, an old friend of Socrates, who, in poverty, as his property had been lost in the war, was gaining a livelihood by bodily toil. Socrates warns him that such employment in his case can be only temporary because of lack of necessary physical strength and urges him to secure a position as assistant to a large proprietor as manager of an estate. Eutherus fears the work may be servile. Socrates replies that heads of departments in a state who manage property are regarded not as performing undignified work but as having attained a higher dignity of freedom.

Eutherus still demurs on the ground that he does not like to be accountable to anyone. Socrates replies that it is difficult to find work that is devoid of liability to account. It is difficult to avoid mistakes or unfriendly criticism. "Avoid captious critics," he says, "attach yourself to the considerate. Whatever you can do, do it heart and soul and make it your finest work." Another interesting and significant opinion of Socrates on this subject is reported by Xenophon which was expressed in a conversation between the philosopher and Aristarchus. The time was during the régime of the Thirty when economic and political conditions were very bad. Aristarchus' house was full of his indigent female relatives, fourteen in all. As these ladies are all expert needlewomen, skilled in the making of garments, Socrates advises his friend to put them to work; Ceramon, for example, with a few slaves, is very prosperous. Aristarchus objects to this proposal; the situations are not comparable; the members of his large household are not barbarian slaves but are kinswomen and free-born. Socrates replies: "Then, on the ground that they are free-born and relatives you think they ought to do nothing but eat and sleep? Or is it your opinion that free-born people who live in this way lead happier lives and are more to be congratulated than those who devote themselves to such useful arts of life as they are skilled in? Are work and study of no value? Did your relatives learn what they know merely for useless information or as a future asset? Is the well-tempered life and a juster one attained rather through idleness or the practice of the useful? If they were called upon to do some shameful work, let them choose death rather than that; but it is otherwise. It is suitable work for women. The things which we know are those we can best perform; it is a joy to do them, and the result is fair."

Plenty of evidence is available to show that work was esteemed, not only in the times portrayed by Homer in the *Iliad* and *Odyssey* and Hesiod in his *Works and Days*, but in Athens of the fifth century, B.C. In Athens there was actually a law directed against idleness. That it was long in force is shown by the fact that Lysias wrote a speech in connection with a prosecution for ἀργία [*argia—D.K.*] for which the penalty on conviction was a fine of one hundred drachmas and ἀτιμία [*atimia—D.K.*] if the accused were thrice convicted. Plutarch tells us that a son who had not been taught a trade by his father was thereby released from the obligation to support his parent in old age. We have already quoted Pericles to the effect that not poverty but indolence is degrading.

Now the old-fashioned assumption that the Athenians found abundant leisure and opportunity for the *real life* (i.e., art, literature, politics, and philosophy) only because hirelings, slaves, and women did everything for them and the state treasury liberally supported them in *dolce far niente* is ridiculous. One thing is certain from all we know of the Athenians; they were not indolent; they were energetic in mind and body. Certainly in any state the wealthy are but a minority of the total population and even upon these rests the duty to manage their property and care for investments.

Participation in public life and fulfilment of the demands and duties of good citizenship did not exact from the average Athenian anything like the major part of his waking hours. The Assembly met four times in each prytany (or tenth of a year period), i.e., less than once a week. As the attendance was voluntary only a fraction of all who were entitled to attend were ever present, as convenience or interest dictated. The Council was limited to five hundred citizens and no one might serve more than twice; furthermore, fifty only of the Council . . . (the standing committee) were continuously on duty so that the majority thus were free to attend to their private affairs. The Heliaea, or Courts of Justice, drew their dicasts or judges for jury service from a list of six thousand citizens. These were usually men of advanced years who had volunteered for such service. Universal military service at this time was not obligatory. Festivals and contests were generally attended but they occurred probably not oftener than once a week on the average. It has been estimated that a total of from two to three years of every citizen's life were required for deliberative and administrative duties. Many writers have emphasized the huge number of citizens who were supposedly pensioners luxuriously supported, apparently permanently and completely, by largess from the Periclean treasury. We have seen that public duties were not constant. As for the compensation it must be remembered that the daily living wage for the workman was from one drachma (about 18 cents), to one and a half. Now at the time under consideration Assemblymen received no compensation; jurymen received two obols (about six cents) daily for service; members of the Council of Five Hundred, elected annually by lot, were paid five obols (about fifteen cents). In the light of these facts how can it be claimed that Pericles *corrupted* the citizens generally by gifts of money, making them idle, cowardly, and greedy or to assume that these citizens were all dependent on public pay and could entirely support their households on these meager stipends. Mr. Grundy declares: "A condition of things in which a large proportion of a community is either practically or wholly dependent on the community for subsistence is unhealthy from both a social and political viewpoint." But only a minority of the fifty to sixty thousand adult male citizens received any state pay. The remuneration given was not a living wage; it was merely a contribution to support by which Pericles provided that *all*, and not merely the well-to-do, might participate, in turn, in civic affairs and obtain that benefit and culture from active personal public service to which he eloquently refers in the Funeral Oration. Nor was the remuneration intended as a sop to placate the discontented and starving proletariat. As Ferguson says: "Pericles did not intend to create a class of salaried officials; nor yet to make an advance toward communism. His ideal was political, not economic, equality—to enable all, irrespective of wealth or station, to use the opportunities and face the obligations which democracy brought in its train. Like all the great democratic leaders who preceded him, he was a nobleman by birth and breeding, and, like them, he did not doubt for a moment that the culture that enobled the life of his class would dignify and uplift that of the masses also. His aim was to unite the whole people in a community of high ideas and emotions. It was to make them a nation of noblemen." If this were not the case, Pericles' noble speech, which stands in history by the side of Lincoln's Gettysburg address, is the most hypocritical document preserved to us from the past.

Since the number of wealthy citizens was small how did the ordinary citizen gain his livelihood? It was by means of agriculture, handicrafts, trades, wholesale and retail business, and daily labor. No occupation was more respected and admired than agriculture. Farms were small, tenancy almost unknown. The small farmer tilled his fields with his own hands. In the arts and crafts and in labor no one needed to be idle for the state policies of Pericles and the great building operations not only gave employment to all the residents of Athens, whether free men or slaves, but attracted workers from far and near. Thousands of citizens, perhaps a third of the whole, gained a livelihood by labor. While commerce was largely in the hands of the resident-aliens, and the heaviest drudgery was performed by slaves, the mass of the skilled workers were free citizens. Stone-cutters, masons, and sculptors had their shops or yards where they worked privately with their apprentices, or they might be engaged in public work, as the building operations on the Acropolis, working side by side with other citizens, with metics, and with slaves.

Modest means, even poverty (certainly *paupertas*), was the rule in Athens and was no bar to achievement and distinction. Life and its needs was simple, and money itself as an accumulation was not desired. A uniform wage was paid practically to all skilled workmen alike. Everyone who had skill or art was an artist, a term applied to sculptors, painters, physicians, and cobblers. Our handbooks generally assert that every occupation or profession which brought any financial return was despised and its practitioner was socially held in contempt. Slight reflection should show the absurdity of this thesis; there is no actual evidence to prove it. Plato, to be sure, who was wealthy and an aristocrat, sneers at those sophists and teachers who were compelled to take money for teaching. Of course there were some charlatans in this profession, but we may be certain that such sophists as Gorgias, Protagoras, Isocrates, and Alcidamas (all professors who accepted tuition from countless students who were only too glad to pay it) were held in high esteem in Athens. So were lawyers and speech-writers for pay, such as Antiphon, Lysias, and Isaeus. Literary men who accepted pay, poets who received purses for prizes, and actors who profited financially by their labors stood in the highest social esteem. The prestige of physicians depended on their skill and personality. The ignoramus and the charlatan were contemned; the skilled and public-spirited surgeon might be richly rewarded and given an honorary crown and public thanks. The elementary-school teacher, the music and gymnastic instructor, were not highly regarded, not because they received money for their services, but because most of them were ignorant men and often of inferior breeding. As for the great artists, sculptors, and painters it is simply impossible to believe such a statement as this: "Even the great artists, painters, and sculptors fell under public contempt simply because they earned money." Could this be true of a Phidias, a Polygnotus, an Ictinus, or a Mnesicles? But we know that Phidias was a warm and extremely intimate personal friend of Pericles. In fact, the statesmen admired the sculptor so highly that the latter was entrusted with the greatest powers in superintending the ornamentation of the great temples. As for Polygnotus, a native of Thasos, he was the personal friend of Cimon, and was actually honored by the Athenians with citizenship. Expert potters and vase-painters were very numerous. While some of these were resident aliens (e.g. Amasis and Brygos), very many were citizens. Thus we find such names of prominent vase-makers as Klitias, Ergotimos, Nikosthenes, Epiktetes, Pamphaios, Euphronios, Hieron, and Megakles. A typical vase-making establishment would engage the services of some twelve persons who might be citizens, metics, and slaves all working side by side in equality. Citizen artists and artisans proclaim with pride, and do not conceal in shame, their occupations. Vase-painters and makers signed their wares. A scene (The Workshop of a Greek Vase-Painter) on a vase shows two Victories and Athena herself crowning the workmen, as Pottier says: "a poetic symbol to glorify the fame of Athenian industry." Indeed, artisans regarded themselves as under the special protection of Hephaestus, the smith, and of Athena, mistress of the arts and crafts, and were proud to claim descent from these deities. The potter, Euphronios, when making an offering to Athena calls himself in his dedication κεραμεύς [*kerameus*— D.K.], and the same procedure is followed by the fuller Simon, the tanner Smikros, and the potters, Mnesiades and Nearchus. On a funereal bas-relief a cobbler was represented in a heroic attitude holding the insignia of his trade. In the neighborhood of the Agora shops were especially numerous. These places served as centers of gossip and of news for Athenians generally, as we are told in a graphic passage in an informative speech of Lysias. It was among these craftsmen that Socrates, who had himself started in life as a stonecutter, spent much time in conversation. When he was, on an occasion, in search of a gentleman, he did not hesitate to go the round of various good carpenters, bronzeworkers, painters, and sculptors.

The comedies of Aristophanes are sometimes taken as proof of great social distinctions and inequalities existing among the citizens of Athens. Thus Mr. Dickinson, in an endeavor to maintain his thesis that Athens was politically democratic but socially intensely aristocratic, quotes at length the passage from the comedy of the *Knights* where the sausage-seller is assured that his crass ignorance, boorish vulgarity, and dense stupidity are the strongest possible recommendations and assets for the highest political distinction. We are apparently to infer that Aristophanes was himself a deep-dyed aristocrat who despised the people and their rule and that he was the spokesman for a large aristocratic section of Athenian society who were extremely hostile to democratic government. These views are unwarranted and, indeed, have been wholly discredited. Aristophanes was not a partisan; he was a conservative. He was not an opponent of democracy nor yet an aristocrat. It is true that he was a well-educated man of keen discernment, a friend of the Knights, and was doubtless on good terms with members of the aristocratic element in Athens. But he was friendly to the cause of democracy and sincerely wished to do it a favor by fearlessly revealing those defects to which a democratic form of government is especially liable and to give warning of possible dangers. This he constantly does in his plays with that exaggeration and caricature which are characteristic of the Old Comedy. In the opinion of the poet grave danger to the democracy might arise from unscrupulous demagogy as represented by such knaves as Cleon. In the case of Cleon, who is lampooned in the play of the *Knights,* Aristophanes is actuated by intense animus as a result of previous personal encounters. Thus Cleon is excoriated as a vulgar, coarse, and despicable individual, and the dramatist tries to discredit his influence and popularity. It is a great mistake to take Aristophanes' savage attacks on vulgar demagogues and criticisms of weaknesses in democratic government as proof that Aristophanes was an aristocrat who condemned and arraigned the people as a whole for vulgarity and incompetency. That he did not despair of the democracy and that he sympathized and fraternized with the "lower classes" is shown by those plays in which the chief personages, although of low degree, are "sympathetic characters," e.g., Dicaeopolis, the charcoal-burner of the *Acharnians* and Strepsiades, the rough countryman of the *Clouds.*

In the opinion of Croiset, "the best Athenian society was the most open-hearted, most variously constituted, and most liberal society that has ever existed. The Athens that Plato shows us is a sort of talking place, where everybody is supposed to know everybody else, and where each person has a perfect right to make acquaintance with those he meets." As typical illustrations of this social democracy he refers to two social gatherings of which we have admirable accounts. In Xenophon's *Symposium* we have a description of a banquet held in 421 B.C., in the house of the wealthy Callias, son of Hipponicus, of a great and rich Athenian family. The guests include all sorts of people, rich, poor, philosophers and ignoramuses, and all converse familiarly on terms of equality and intimacy. In the same way, Plato, in his *Symposium,* an account of a dinner held at the house of Agathon in 416 B.C., reveals the same intermixture of classes and professions.

THE STATUS OF THE METICS

We have now completed our discussion of the essentially democratic political and social status of Athenian citizens. It remains to consider briefly the other two classes of the inhabitants of Attica who are commonly regarded, along with the poorer citizens, as the exploited victims of the Athenian aristocracy. These elements are the metics (resident aliens) and the slaves.

The rapid commercial growth and naval expansion of Athens early caused a shortage of workers and helpers of all kinds. The citizen population was numerically inadequate to assume these new duties in addition to the performance of their regular occupations and the prosecution of agriculture. This demand was met by extending a welcome to foreigners and this policy was continued and encouraged by Pericles. Their exact number in the year 431 B.C. is unknown. Meyer's estimate is adult male metics 14,000 to about 55,000 adult male citizens; Clerc estimates them at 24,000, followed by Zimmern; Ferguson gives the number of adult male citizens as 50,000, and a total population of Attica of 300,000 of which one-sixth was foreign and one-third servile. There may have been, then, one adult male metic for every two citizens.

What was the lot of the metics? It has been asserted that their social position was humiliating and that they were disliked and even despised by the ordinary citizen. But contemporary evidence does not indicate this. Pericles says: "We open our city to all and never drive out foreigners." The scene of Plato's dialogue, *The Republic,* is the house of Cephalus, a prominent and influential man, but a metic who had been invited to Attica by Pericles himself. Another contemporary speaks of "the equality between the metics and the full citizens, because the city stands in need of her resident aliens to meet the requirements of such a multiplicity of arts and for the purposes of her navy." Thucydides has Nicias say to metic sailors that they and not any friends or allies outside were the "only free partners with the Athenians in the Empire." The metics participated fully in the social and religious life of the city. Neither in dress nor appearance could they be distinguished from the citizens. They attended the theater, they had a prominent place and dress in the Panathenaïc procession, they were demesmen and worshipped the same deities as the citizens. Like the citizens they defrayed the expenses of the liturgies and served in the army and the navy. When any list of Athenian inhabitants is given the metics are always named as an essential element of the population. They worked in large numbers side by side and for equal pay with the citizens in all kinds of work as, for example, the construction of the Erechtheum. They are found engaged in all the occupations, as workers and artisans of all kinds, as merchants at Peiraeus and at Athens, as bankers and capitalists, as painters, sculptors, and artists, as architects, and as philosophers and orators. Many of the famous pupils of Isocrates were metics, and no less than three of the celebrated Canon of the Ten Orators were resident aliens, namely, Isaeus of Chalcis, Lysias of Syracuse, and Deinarchus of Corinth.

The fee of twelve drachmas (about $2.16) required of metics was a petty matter, a legal formality of registration and license and not an onerous tax burden, as it is often regarded. The liability to taxes beyond those required of citizens was not great. Perhaps the most serious limitation imposed upon aliens was the inability legally to own real property. But metics might be placed on equal terms as to taxation and the owning of property with the citizens thereby becoming ἰσοτελεῖς [*isoteleis*—D.K.], and full citizenship might be conferred by vote of the Assembly. For example, an inscription is preserved which records the grant of full citizenship on those metics who participated in the return of the democrats from Phyle (in 404–3) and helped in the restoration. In the list occur some strangely sounding foreign names, e.g. Βενδιφάνης [*Bendiphanes—D.K.*] and Ψαμμίς [*Psammis—D.K.*], and their occupations as given are decidedly humble, such as cook, gardener, carpenter, fuller, etc.

The Athenians have been harshly criticized for not freely and generally granting citizenship to the metics. At first thought the criticism may seem valid and Athens illiberal. But the citizenship to the Athenian was not merely a political privilege; it was a sacred and usually an *inherited* possession. Loss of citizenship was to be feared more than death itself. Athens was a small and homogeneous community and the Athenians regarded themselves as autochthonous, like their favorite and symbolic cicada, sprung from the very soil of Attica itself. There is danger to a state in a too rapid influx of aliens who are given the powers of citizenship before real political and social assimilation has taken place. Even free America requires a term of years of probation before naturalization, and one of our greatest problems surely is this very one of the assimilation of the large number of our resident aliens. As Aristotle says: "Another cause for revolution is difference of races which do not acquire a common spirit; for the state is not the growth of a day, neither is it a multitude brought together by accident. Hence the reception of strangers in colonies has generally produced revolution." It is true that the metics of Athens were not on full terms of political equality with the citizens but it has been shown that the yawning social and economic gulf postulated by modern writers between citizen and resident foreigner did not really exist.

THE STATUS OF THE SLAVES

The institution of slavery existed throughout the ancient world from the earliest times. The Athenians, with but few exceptions, regarded slavery as natural and justifiable. It is again Aristotle, the fourth-century theorist and philosopher, who is made the starting-point for most modern discussions of slavery among the Greeks and the iniquity of the institution as maintained even by the cultured Athenians of the time of Pericles. In his treatment of this subject Aristotle characterizes in a cold-blooded legal fashion the slave as being merely "a breathing machine or tool, a piece of animated property" . . . and asserts that some men are so inferior that they may be regarded as slaves by nature. It is interesting to note, however, that Aristotle in another passage admits that there were some who protested against such a view. He says: "Others regard slave owning as doing violence to nature on the ground that the distinction of slave and free man is wholly conventional and has no place in nature, and therefore is void of justice, as resting on mere force." Plato, too, regards slavery as natural and justifiable but would forbid the enslavement of Greeks; he admits, however, that "a slave is an embarrassing possession, the distinction between man and slave being a difficult one and slaves should be well-treated and not abused or insulted." Aristotle, also, advises good treatment for the slave.

Recent writers have been very severe in their strictures on the Athenians for tolerating slavery. Professor Mahaffy writes: "Our real superiority lies in our moral ideals, in our philanthropy, our care of the poor and the sick. I do not know whether the existence and justification of slavery as a natural institution are not the main cause of this difference. Xenophon tells us of the callous and brutal attitude to slaves and prisoners. If it was true then it must have been true ten times more in the colder, harsher, and more selfish society of the preceding generation. The milk of human kindness seems to have run dry among them. . . . . The association of the good with the beautiful and the true seems incomplete. The latter two are attained in no ordinary degree. The former, which is to us the most divine of the three, was but poorly represented." Mr. Dickinson goes so far as to say that Athenian slaves had *no political and social rights at all*. It is true that a minority of the slaves in Attica must have had an unenviable existence. These were the men who, in large numbers, slaved in the silver mines at Laurium. But what was the lot of the majority of the slaves in Attica? A contemporary testifies: "An extraordinary amount of license is granted to slaves . . . . where a blow is illegal, and a slave will not step aside to let you pass him on the street. . . . . The Athenian people is not better clothed than the slave or alien, nor in personal appearance is there any superiority. . . . . Slaves in Athens are allowed to indulge in luxury, and indeed in some cases to live magnificently. . . . . We have established an equality between our slaves and free men." Newly acquired slaves were received into the household with showers . . . of confections. They participated as members of the family in religious rites and sacrifices. They might attend the theater. They worked side by side with their masters in the workshop or might even be permitted to work on their own account exercising an independent profession . . . either paying a commission to their masters or actually purchasing their freedom and gaining thereby the status of metics. The law protected a slave from being the victim of ὕβρις [*hybris—D.K.*] and the aggressor was subject to fine. The slave might not be put to death; a free man who had killed a slave was subject to prosecution for manslaughter. Refuge from a cruel master was afforded by flight to a temple as sanctuary, namely, to the Theseum, the Sanctuary of the Erinyes, and the altar of Athena Polias. Freedom might be granted outright by the master, while the state at times enfranchised slaves who had fought for Athens. In case of illness a slave might be affectionately cared for and at death mourned as a relative.

It is certainly a false assertion to claim that Athenian society *rested on slavery* and that slavery was the *dominant* factor in Athenian economic life. The slaves were in the minority in the total population at this period and the prosperity and greatness of the state was due to the industry, the initiative, and the efficiency of citizen and metic. Mr. Grundy says that "the ultimate controlling fact in Greek politics of the fifth and fourth centuries B.C. is the evil economic condition of the lower classes due to the competition of slave labour as competition with slave labour was impossible for the free proletariat." But this was not the case in the fifth century. There was no unemployment in Athens in the Age of Pericles. As we have seen tı e demand for labor was so great that extensive immigration was encouraged and there was a living wage for all. It is undoubtedly true, however, that in the fourth century and later the competition of slave with free labor gave rise to economic distress at a time when the citizens had decreased in number but the slaves had enormously increased. Mr. Grundy further declares that all hand-labor became associated with slavery and hence became incompatible with the dignity of the free man. The absolute falsity of this conception has already been established.

CONCLUSION

As a result of this study the following conclusions may be made:

1. Perhaps the greatest error and most unscientific procedure of many writers is to disregard or underestimate local conditions and, in particular, the chronological factor. Far too often authors indulge in generalizations regarding "the ancient Greek." It is no more possible to make general sweeping statements correctly characterizing the institutions of "the ancient Greek" than it would be accurately to estimate the civilization of "the modern European." Sparta and Athens were as far apart politically and socially in numerous respects as Germany and America, while Athens of the second half of the fifth century b.c. in its political, social, and economic conditions was by no means the Athens of the sixth or fourth centuries.
2. The ideal, aristocratic conceptions of Plato and Aristotle must not and cannot be taken literally to reflect actual Athenian conditions. Certainly Aristotle should not be taken as having "an average Greek mind" in his attitude toward society nor is he, or Plato, representative of fifth-century popular belief.
3. The time-honored tradition that Athenians despised all work and looked down upon all workers is false and our handbooks need revision in their treatment of this topic. It is true that in Athens, as with us, some occupations were thought less desirable and less dignified than others. In no land and at no time is the day laborer esteemed as highly as the statesman. Drudgery and menial employment the Athenians disliked and avoided; so do we. But the citizen who earned his living in some honest way and accepted money for his services was the rule and not the exception, not was he as a result a social outcast but was a member, in good political and social standing, of the commonwealth.
4. The disabilities of the metics are generally exaggerated. Their position in Athenian society was not humiliating. While the resident aliens did not have full participation in political duties and privileges they did share, in a remarkable measure, the life of the citizens.
5. Slavery was, of course, an Athenian institution, and the right of owning slaves was, in general not questioned. It is clear, however, that as a rule

they were treated by their masters with humaneness and consideration, with the exception of the lowest class of public slaves who were employed in the mines.

6. It would be absurd to claim perfection for the Athenian democracy of the Age of Pericles, or to pretend that the Athenians had completely and happily solved the innumerable and complicated social, political, and economic problems which still vex the world and which still await soluion even today. Athens was not, of course, at any time a perfect democracy. But that it was far more democratic and far less aristocratic in the time of Pericles than is generally assumed and asserted is certain.

Beloch's view of Periclean "aristocracy" is quite different from that of Van Hook.

FROM *Griechische Geschichte* BY K. J. BELOCH

THE LEADERSHIP of the [*democratic—D.K.*] party, and in reality the leadership of the state with it, passed over to Pericles, the son of Xanthippus of Cholargus, the victor of Mycale. He was still a comparatively young man, perhaps at the beginning or middle of his thirties, and he had not yet had the opportunity to distinguish himself in war, since, in general, he did not possess an outstanding military talent. We may even doubt whether he was a great statesman. At least he was not able to preserve the Athenian empire at that height to which Themistocles and Cimon had brought it, and at his departure from the political stage he left behind as a legacy that war in which it finally came to ruin. But he was what we would call today a great parliamentarian. Like no other of his contemporaries he possessed the gift of leading the masses by the power of his speech and of drawing them along with him, and he had a very fine sense of what public opinion demanded. The road to power was opened to him by his family connections, and it was they, too, that determined his place in the party struggle. His mother was the niece of the great Cleisthenes, the founder of Athenian popular liberty. Pericles thus grew up in the tradition of the party of the Alcmaeonidae and in opposition to Cimon, which would necessarily have led him to an association with the reform party, even if he had not realized that the future belonged to it.

Karl Julius Beloch, *Griechische Geschichte* (2nd ed.), II, 154–6. Translated by Donald Kagan by permission of Walter de Gruyter & Co., Berlin.

Pericles moved farther along the road Ephialtes had opened. If the democratization of the law courts were not to remain a dead letter, it was necessary to grant to the poorer classes of the citizenry the material capability to take up its share of the sessions of the Heliaea. So, on the proposal of Pericles, the jurors were granted a daily allowance of two obols per session, corresponding approximately to a minimal day's pay, as things stood in Athens in the mid-fifth century. This measure was all the more urgent as it would not otherwise have been possible to collect the required number of jurors, for the more important cases from the states of the empire were not yet being brought before the Athenian courts. This change soon resulted in a large part of the Athenian citizenry abstaining from productive labor and beginning to see its chief source of subsistence in the jury pay.

It was not far from this point to the demand that the state should provide the livelihood of its citizens altogether. Part of the purpose of the great public buildings that were completed under the Periclean regime in Athens was to offer pay to the poorer classes. Grain was also shared among the masses more often. Above all, the dominant position of Athens provided the possibility of assigning to thousands of Athenian citizens landed property outside Attica. If, for some, these so-called "cleruchies" were chiefly for the purpose of securing militarily important places by means of dependable garrisons, for others, nevertheless, the social-political purpose was of prime importance. Such was the case, for instance, with the assignments of land in the territories of Chalcis and Eretria after the conquest of Euboea in 446 or of Lesbos in 427. The recipients of these lots remained quietly living in Athens and allowed the property to be worked by native tenant farmers. Citizens capable of working were paid pensions from the state treasury, even if only in the amount of an obol a day, which just sufficed to pay for the support of the neediest. The children of citizens who had fallen in war were also supported at state expense until their majority.

But they went still further. If the tyrants had accepted it as their task to offer the people the most splendid shows possible, the democracy did not lag far behind this example. The festivals in Athens under the Periclean administration left behind in numbers as in the splendor of their outfitting all that the Greek world had seen up to then, and, if that were not enough, money payments were made to the citizens on such occasions.

We do not know how far other democracies at that time followed the example given by Athens and even less whether the Periclean measures had found their model already in other states. In any case, outside Athens the more restricted sources of financial help drew narrower bounds to the intervention of the state in behalf of the "disinherited" classes. And we must not forget that even in Athens itself it was still only the citizens, that is, at most half the inhabitants of Attica, on whom the care of the state was bestowed, not to mention the fact that the means for all this care was in large part taken from the allies. Thus even this radical democracy really came out of the exploitation of the majority by a minority.

*In the following selection Malcolm McGregor critically
examines and rejects the Thucydidean assertion that
Athens was a democracy in name only during the Periclean
Age. What is more, he goes on to explain why Thucydides
made such a claim. The problem is posed by the fact that,
although Thucydides tells us that the oligarchic government installed by the Four Hundred in 411 was the best
in his time, he also has high praise for the Athens of
Pericles.*

FROM *The Politics of the Historian Thucydides*
BY MALCOLM MCGREGOR

W II A T W E S E E K , ideally, is reconciliation of those comments by Thucydides on government that seem to conflict. Our investigation commences
with Perikles. From the ostracism of Kimon in 461 to his own death in 429
he was not out of office for more than a year or two; for the last fifteen years
consecutively he was elected *strategos,* often, probably, *strategos autokrator.*
Long tenure of office, as we know, becomes in itself a ground for criticism
and Perikles did not escape. The Olympian figure in Aristophanes surely
reflects a phase of contemporary gossip. Today students are often told that
Athens was not really a democracy at all; rather, it was a dictatorship. In
more fashionable circles, we read of the principate of Perikles, a term which
immediately summons Augustus Caesar from the shades. It must be granted
that for this view there is weighty authority, Thucydides himself: "What
was in theory democracy," he writes, "became in fact rule by the first
citizen." The sentence has since been adopted by many as a fundamental
text.

Perhaps the most quoted of Thucydides' opinions, it withstands analysis
least; a cynic might remark that it is seldom subjected to analysis. Throughout Perikles' tenure of office the *ekklesia* met at least forty times a year. Each
spring it elected the generals for the following year. Each year their fellow-
citizens examined the qualifications of the generals before they took office.
Ten times during the year the *ekklesia* heard reports from the generals. As
they left office each year a jury of their fellow-citizens audited their records.
One may employ other terms: during Perikles' political life the constitution
functioned without interruption and Perikles had to retain the confidence of
the sovereign and sensitive *demos* in order to remain in office. Not only was

Malcolm McGregor, "The Politics of the Historian Thucydides," *Phoenix,* 10 (1956), 97–8,
100–2. Published for the Classical Association of Canada by the University of Toronto Press,
Toronto.

it possible for him to fail of re-election, as indeed he did in 444 B.C.; he might be removed from office, as indeed he was in 430 B.C. In the autumn of that year a disgruntled citizenry deposed and fined Perikles; more than that, they actually despatched a peace-mission to Sparta, *while he remained in office,* in direct contravention of his established policy. Now if democracy means and is government by the citizens, if the *ekklesia* decided policy by vote, if free elections persisted at their constitutional intervals, if Perikles was at all times responsible to the sovereign *demos,* and if an unoppressed political opposition survived, as it surely did,—if all this is so, then Athens was as democratic, not only in theory but in day-to-day practice, as government can conceivably be. How such a system can be related to a dictatorship or to a principate is beyond my comprehension. The term principate is particularly unfortunate; for how does Augustus, the prototype, fit the conditions set out in this paragraph, which are not in dispute?

The principle of responsibility was paramount in the Athenian conception of democracy. The mere length of a responsible magistrate's tenure of office should not, by rational judges, be adopted at any time as a criterion of dictatorship. Within our own memories, however, a prolonged term has evoked the same indefensible protest in democratic countries, which should help us to understand, from our own experience, Perikles' position amidst his critics (and admirers) at the beginning of the Peloponnesian War. And nowhere in the modern world is the citizen's control over his representatives more direct and more constant than was the Athenian's. The truth is that Perikles had so won the confidence of his fellow-citizens that they elected him year after year and (wisely, I should say) allowed him, as their elder statesman, to guide them and shape their policies. But that they never surrendered, or diminished, their control of their own destinies is proved no more convincingly by Perikles' failure at the polls in 444 and his deposition in 430 than by his rapid re-election by a repentant *demos* a few months later. Athens remained a full and direct democracy.

*   *   *

We may find it simpler to understand Thucydides if we recognise that the democratic party at Athens itself developed two wings, one radical and one conservative. Perikles ended his life as a member of the latter. He had had his fling with the radical, aggressively imperialistic type of popular leadership and, by 446/5 B.C., had failed. His failure was remarkable in that he confessed it; he at once abandoned the aggressive policy by land and turned to the consolidation of the naval empire. He was thus able to guide Athens—and so most of the Aegean states—through what was probably the longest period of continuous prosperity and peace that Hellenes could remember. His thorough-going reversal I deem the surest evidence of his superior statecraft. This was the man who commanded the allegiance of Thucydides.

With the death of Perikles the restraining voice was gone and the way cleared for the imperialistic radicals, who offered to an avid *demos* a policy that was to prove as disastrous as Perikles had predicted. This transition allows Thucydides to give vent to his natural antipathy to democracy. His indictment of popular government, implied before the death of Perikles, is explicit in his treatment of Kleon, reaches a climax in the shameful words of the Athenian in the Melian Dialogue, and passes inexorably to the final collapse, which Thucydides, who lived to see it, attributes to the folly of the democracy. The state under Perikles, which we, unlike Thucydides, call democracy, Thucydides could endorse with enthusiasm; but Kleon and his kind, in a state in which the machinery and the system had undergone not the slightest change, the oligarchic Thucydides could not stomach. To him Kleon was democracy; we know that Perikles was too. Worse was to come. Alkibiades, that brilliant renegade, borrowed the foreign policies of Kleon; having greater ability and less sense of responsibility, he wrought greater harm.

Yet there were those upon whom the mantle of Perikles fell. Of these Nikias was most prominent. Sometimes considered an oligarch, he was in truth, with his loyalty to Periklean tradition and policy, a conservative, or Periklean, democrat. Of him Thucydides, not surprisingly, writes with a nice appreciation, and in the increasingly grim pages one can detect a real sympathy for Nikias, so honest, so loyal, and, at the last, so ineffective.

The situation after Perikles has been neatly described by John Finley: "Pericles . . . had four characteristics: he could see and expound what was necessary, he was patriotic and above money. Athens' misfortune and the essential cause of her ruin was that none of his successors combined all these traits. Nicias, who was honest but inactive, had the last two; Alcibiades, who was able but utterly self-interested, had the first two . . . ."

This was Athens' tragedy, that she produced no successor who combined all the qualities of Perikles. I have heard it argued that Perikles was culpable for not having left a political heir, that is, that he did not brook rivalry. This, to be sure, is the charge that is commonly levelled at the great man. Apart from the fact that this assumes a principate that never existed and that Nikias *was* his heir, though not his intellectual peer, it is a formidable undertaking to show how one man could suppress others of comparable talent within his own party in a system in which an office-holder was ever subject to discipline and in which a popular assembly provided the ideal arena for the potential statesman to acquire education, training, and reputation. When we bewail the quality of those who received the reins from Perikles, we perhaps fail sufficiently to emphasise the surpassing genius of one who so excelled his contemporaries. "Perikles," Thucydides points out, "influential because of his reputation and intelligence and obvious integrity, was able freely to restrain the people; he led them rather than was led by them . . . . His successors were more evenly matched with one another, striving, each one of them, to be first."

Perikles commanded the respect and the loyalty of men of various political persuasions. Thucydides was one of those to whom the man was more significant than their own partly inherited political convictions. It is a truism that the inspired leader draws support from the state as a whole, irrespective of party-lines. To Thucydides the events that followed the death of Perikles must have come as a bitter, if not entirely unexpected, disappointment; not unexpected, because he had no real faith in democracy and the death of Perikles removed the source of his self-deception. Steadily, as he saw it, the Periklean state was being destroyed. When Theramenes' moderate oligarchy of Five Thousand, with its unrestricted citizenship but restricted privilege, emerged from the revolution of 411/0, Thucydides, reverting easily to his tradition, could follow the dictates of his intellect and pronounce this the best government enjoyed by the Athenians in his time. It is his only categorical judgement on government; it is the key to his political convictions.

One might draw a parallel between Thucydides and the Old Oligarch. The Old Oligarch, it will be recalled, is so named for the nature of his anti-democratic essay written about 425 B.C. He writes, in effect, "I do not approve of democracy, but, if you *must* have it, I admit that the Athenians make a fine job of it." Thucydides, the oligarch born, might have said, "I do not approve of democracy, I see no strength or wisdom in the rabble; but I do admire and will support the Periklean state, which of course is not democracy at all."

We are ready to summarise. Thucydides was reared in the conservative anti-democratic tradition. His orderly and impartial mind was impressed by the genius of Perikles, and so he became a Periklean, though not a democrat; nor could he admit that by so doing he was, in essence, approving of democracy. Later, the oligarchic tradition of his family that had never been abandoned, reasserted itself, as he saw Periklean ideals forgotten, Periklean warnings ignored. He witnessed, with a brutally piercing eye, what seemed to him the evils of a democracy run to seed, its moral fibre weakening. He ended his life as he had begun it, a confirmed oligarch who had never renounced the creed of his fathers.

Ancient Science—
Metaphysical
or Observational?

CONTENTS

QUESTIONS FOR STUDY

1 In what ways does Hippocrates differ from Plato in his approach to knowledge?

2 How does the Epicurean universe differ from the Aristotelian?

3 What is the difference between Aristotle's approach to the physical world and Plato's?

4 What would Plato have thought of Farrington's definition of science?

5 What are the basic elements of ancient science on which Farrington and Edelstein disagree?

6 How can the diametrically opposed interpretations of Plato's influence on the development of science given by Sarton and Shorey be accounted for?

It is a truism that man is a rational creature who desires to know how the world around him works. Every society has evolved some kind of account of the physical world, most often presented in terms of myths, magic, and occult powers. But only Western civilization has developed a mature science, and the scientific quest began in classical Greece. The big question is how does man create scientific knowledge? There are those who insist that science must begin with observation and rise, through progressive generalizations, to general theories; there are others who insist equally firmly that, given the almost infinite number of possible facts to be observed, the poor, limited mind of man must be given some philosophical guide to the facts that count. The debate began in antiquity; it still rages today. What can man know? How does he know it? What use can be made of this knowledge? These questions are as pertinent in the twentieth century as they were when Hippocrates, Plato, and Aristotle gave their answers in the fourth century B.C.

1   The Problem Defined

Benjamin Farrington is a leading exponent of that school of thought that finds the origins of science in ordinary practice and daily life. It is from this point of view that he describes and evaluates the contributions of the various schools of ancient science.

FROM *Greek Science* BY BENJAMIN FARRINGTON

SCIENCE, whatever be its ultimate developments, has its origin in techniques, in arts and crafts, in the various activities by which man keeps soul and body together. Its source is experience, its aims practical, its only test that it works. Science arises in contact with things, it is dependent on the evidence of the senses, and however far it seems to move from them, must always come back to them. It requires logic and the elaboration of theory, but its strictest logic and choicest theory must be proved in practice. Science in the practical sense is the necessary basis for abstract and speculative science.

As thus conceived, science develops in close correspondence with the stages of man's social progress and becomes progressively more self-conscious as man's whole way of life becomes more purposive. A food-gatherer has one kind of knowledge of his environment, a food-producer another. The latter is more active and purposive in his relation to mother earth. Increased mastery of the environment brings increased productivity, which, in its turn, brings social change. The science of gentile or tribal society cannot be the same as the science of political society. The division of labour has an influence on the development of science. The emergence of a leisured class gives opportunity for reflection and elaboration of theory. It also gives opportunity for theorizing without relation to facts. Furthermore, with the development of classes, the need for a new kind of "science" arises which might be defined as "the system of behaviour by which man acquires mastery over man." When the task of mastering men becomes the preoccu-

---

Benjamin Farrington, *Greek Science* (1949), pp. 14–5, 24–5, 66, 67, 68–71, 91–2, 95–6, 98, 102–4. Reprinted by permission of Penguin Books Ltd., Harmondsworth.

pation of the ruling class and the task of mastering nature becomes the forced labour of another class, science takes a new and dangerous turn. Fully to understand the science of any society, we must be acquainted with the degree of its material advancement and with its political structure. There is no such thing as science *in vacuo*. There is only the science of a particular society at a particular place and time. The history of science can only be understood as a function of the total life of society. . . .

These considerations will be found applicable to the whole development of science in antiquity. They are still even to some degree operative to-day. The history of Greek science, which is our main concern, is unintelligible unless they are constantly borne in mind. To borrow the mechanical arts from Egypt or elsewhere was to borrow also the social consequences, at least to some extent. "What are called the mechanical arts," says Xenophon, "carry a social stigma and are rightly dishonoured in our cities. For these arts damage the bodies of those who work at them or who act as overseers, by compelling them to a sedentary life and to an indoor life, and, in some cases, to spend the whole day by the fire. This physical degeneration results also in deterioration of the soul. Furthermore, the workers at these trades simply have not got the time to perform the offices of friendship or citizenship. Consequently they are looked upon as bad friends and bad patriots, and in some cities, especially the warlike ones, it is not legal for a citizen to ply a mechanical trade." (*Oeconomicus,* iv, 203.)

This contempt of the mechanical arts hindered in Greece, as it did in Egypt, the development of the chemical sciences. Greek science represents an enormous advance on Egyptian science, but it shows the same great limitation. Mathematics, surgery, medicine, and astronomy are not only the main divisions of Egyptian science, but of Greek. Physics, chemistry, mechanics were dishonoured and therefore weak. . . .

Medicine, no doubt, like other practices, first became scientific in Ionia. But now, in the fifth century, there were rival medical schools in the West which did not possess the same understanding of medicine as originating in a technique, but sought to deduce the rules of medical practice from *a priori* cosmological opinions.

*   *   *

It was in the school of Empedocles at Agrigentum that cosmology produced its worst effects on the healing art. There man, like everything else, was supposed to consist of the four elements. The doctrine of the elements included a theory as to their characteristic qualities. Earth was said to be Cold and Dry; Air, Hot and Wet; Water, Cold and Wet; Fire, Hot and Dry. The distemperature of man's body, like the distemperature of nature, was ascribed to the excess of defect of one or other of these qualities. Fever was to be interpreted as an excess of the Hot, a chill as an excess of Cold. This being so, what remedies would a physician who was also a philosopher suggest? Would he not recommend a dose of the Hot to cure a chill and of the Cold to cure a fever?

When the new-fangled doctrines of the western philosophical schools began to be spoken of in his beloved Ionia, anger seized the heart of the author of *Ancient Medicine*. In his opening sentence he leaps to the attack. "All who attempt to discuss the art of healing on the basis of a postulate— heat, cold, moisture, dryness, or anything else they fancy—thus narrowing down the causes of disease and death among men to one or two postulates, are not only obviously wrong, but are especially to be blamed because they are wrong in what is an art or technique (*technè*), and one moreover which all men use at the crises of life, highly honouring the practitioners and craftsmen in this art, if they are good."

Into this first sentence our author has managed to pack four separate objections to the new trend in medicine. As they are all of great significance in the history of science, it will be well for us to pick them out and discuss them one by one.

First he objects to the basing of medicine on postulates. The effect of this objection is to separate medicine as a positive science, depending on observation and experiment, from cosmology where experimental control was not possible in antiquity. . . .

Secondly, he protests that the new-fangled doctors are "narrowing down the causes of death and disease." This is most remarkable. It is a protest by a practising technician, conscious of the richness of his positive science, against the barrenness of metaphysics. The historical significance of this is very great. The technician is appalled at the ignorance of the philosophers. Art had not yet been made tongue-tied by authority. For the Hippocratic doctor the qualities of things which affect a man's health were not three or four. They were infinitely various. . . .

Then he proceeds to supplement the handful of Empedoclean concepts with a list of others more relevant to medical science—in foods, such qualities as sweetness, bitterness, acidity, saltness, insipidity, astringency; in human anatomy, the shapes of the organs; in human physiology, the capacity of the organism to react to an external stimulus. Thus does the cook rebuke the cosmologist.

The third reason for his anger is, not that the philosopher should be wrong, but that he should be wrong in a technique or art (*technè*). The reason why ignorance in respect of a *technè* is inexcusable is, that no knowledge was worthy to be called a *technè* unless it gave results. Here the justifiable pride of the craftsman is noticeable; and it admonishes us that the test of early science was, not the laboratory, but practice. We must not overlook this fact when we debate the point, whether Greek science knew experiment or not. A technique was a mode of imitating nature. If it worked, that was proof that the technician understood nature.

The fourth reason for his anger with the doctor who possesses only philosophical postulates but is ignorant of the art is that it is the patient who suffers. This concern for the patient is specially characteristic of the Hippo-cratic doctors. They were severely scientific at their best, but at their best they also maintained that the first duty of the doctor is to heal the sick rather than to study disease. In this there was a certain measure of disagreement between them and the neighbouring school at Cnidus. We might express the differ-ence by saying that the ideal of the men of Cnidus was science, that of the men of Cos science in the service of humanity.

We have now listed the four chief objections of our practising physician to the medical innovations of the philosophers. At this early date, before much positive knowledge had accumulated, and before specialization had in consequence become necessary, it was natural that a philosopher should embrace every branch of knowledge. There is nothing therefore surprising in Empedocles turning his attention to medicine. But his doing so brought sharply into view the fact that there was a kind of speculation that was admissible in cosmology but inadmissible in medicine. Cosmologists tended to start from some observation, or some few observations (change of water into ice or steam; the mathematical relation between the lengths of vibrating strings; the transmutation of food into flesh), and then elaborate on this slender foundation a theory of the universe, satisfied if the system they evolved hung together with reasonable logic. But this could not satisfy the doctor, whose theories were continually tested in practice, proved right or wrong by their effect on the patient. A stricter conception of the scientific method was formed. It can truly be said that the Hippocratic doctors at their best advanced fully to the idea of a positive science. What differentiated their science from ours was less the failure to realize the importance of experiment than the absence of instruments of exact measurement and of any technique of chemical analysis. They were as scientific as the material conditions of their time permitted.

*   *   *

The Platonic writings have long attracted, and still attract, a degree of attention which the earlier philosophers and sophists cannot claim. But the great prestige of his writings constitutes a difficulty for the historian of science. Plato wrote much about those problems of epistemology which lie on the border between philosophy and science. There is no doubt about his eminence as a philosopher. His contribution to science is, however, open to question. Does he deserve the same place in the history of science which by universal accord he holds in philosophy?

Science before Plato had achieved remarkable advances which we may roughly classify under three heads. The first and decisive step, which we associate especially with the Milesians, was the new attitude of attempting to explain the phenomena of nature, including human nature, without super-natural intervention. Secondly, we find that a rudimentary technique of interrogating nature by means of experiments had begun. There was a growing practice of observation and experiments, in Ionia, in Italy, in Sicily, in Athens itself, accompanied, as its philosophical implications became more clearly understood, by a lively debate on the validity of sense-evidence. Thirdly, although the importance of this has been little recognized and the fact has been denied by some, there was the vital connection between natural philosophy and techniques, which determined the character of the early philosophy of nature. In developing his attack on the Ionian philosophers, Plato accords their recognition of this connection an important place in their general world-outlook. The following are the words in which he describes their point of view: "The arts which make the most serious contribution to human life are those which blend their own power with that of nature, like medicine, agriculture, and gymnastics" (*Laws,* X, 889d). This plainly implies a philosophy of the techniques, an attempt to define their essential character and to assign them their very important place in the development of civilized society. . . . Plato was the author, or propagator, of an astral theology in which the stars were cast for the rôle of patterns of divine regularity. He found it incompatible with this requirement that, conspicuous among the hosts of heaven, where

> Round the ancient track marched rank on rank
> The army of unalterable law,

should be a parcel of five disorderly vagabonds (the word planet means vagabond in Greek). The inconvenience was especially great inasmuch as the problem of human vagabondage had reached a crisis at this time in Greece.

Plato's contemporary, Isocrates, had made a special study of the problem of these sturdy beggars. The remedy he proposed was not increased production and better distribution of this world's goods. Faced with an ever-increasing throng of roving outcasts, his idea was to enlist them, drill them, and hurl them against the Persian Empire. If they could not conquer it outright, they could at least tear enough off its territory to provide living-space for themselves. The alternative was revolution at home. "If we cannot check the growing strength of these vagabonds," wrote Isocrates, "by providing them with a satisfactory life, before we know where we are they will be so numerous that they will constitute as great a danger to the Greeks as to the barbarians" (*Philip,* 121). Under these circumstances it is not surprising that, as a contribution to the liquidation of vagabondage on earth, Plato should have determined to liquidate it in heaven. He "set it as a problem to all earnest students to find 'what are the uniform and ordered movements by the assumption of which the apparent movements of the planets can be accounted for.' " Until this problem could be solved, his astral theology, by which he set much store in his proposed reconstruction of society, risked total failure. Why worship the stars if these divine beings could do no better than set a conspicuous example of irregularity and disorder? It is altogether false to regard Plato's challenge to the mathematicians to reduce the planets to order as proof of a disinterested love of science. It was not an attempt to find out the facts, but to conjure away socially inconvenient appearances on the basis of any plausible hypothesis.

*   *   *

This kind of astronomy, in which natural laws were subordinated to divine principles, and in which more regard was paid to the heavenly bodies as objects of worship than subjects of scientific study, was further developed by Aristotle. Systematizing the doctrines of Plato and the Pythagoreans, he taught, not only that the circular motions of the heavenly bodies are proof of their being under the control of divine intelligence, but that the very substance of which they are made—what he called "the fifth element,'" to distinguish it from Earth, Air, Fire, and Water—is different from any that exists below the circle of the moon. The astronomy which he taught in his theological mood (it must be stressed that it is not characteristic of his scientific outlook) is that inherited by the Middle Ages.

Aristotle's account was that the universe consists of fifty-nine concentric spheres, with the earth at the centre. To the earth were allowed four spheres, one for each of the four elements. Outside the four terrestrial spheres were fifty-five celestial spheres, that of the moon being the lowest and that of the fixed stars the highest. The spheres were supposed to revolve round a stationary earth and carry with them, in their revolutions, the heavenly bodies. Only below the moon, in Aristotle's scheme of the universe, was change possible. There the four elements, whose "natural" movements were up and down, might mingle and be transformed into one another. But above the moon, in the etherial spheres, whose "natural" movement was in circles, no change occurred. In this scheme, as the substance of heaven is different from that of earth, so are the laws of motion different. There is a celestial mechanics and a terrestrial mechanics, and the rules of one are not valid for the other. Not till Newton did terrestrial mechanics regain control of heaven.

*   *   *

Plato added nothing to science in the observational and experimental sense. It is extremely doubtful whether he added anything to mathematics. Heath's judgment on his mathematical attainment is that "he does not appear to have been more than up to date" . . . But he did contribute to the philosophy of mathematics. What fascinated him was the meaning of those mathematical truths which seem to be independent of experience. In *Republic* vi, 510, he says of the geometers: "You know that they make use of visible figures and argue about them, but in doing so they are not thinking of these figures but of the things which they represent; thus it is the absolute square and the absolute diameter which is the object of their argument, not the diameter which they draw." In distinguishing this type of knowledge from the knowledge which appears to be wholly dependent on sensuous impressions, Plato made a fundamental contribution to epistemology. It is his concern for this that must excuse, if anything can excuse, a hostility to practical geometry so great that he regarded the mere construction of figures as essentially antagonistic to a true study of the subject.

When we come to the third point, the connection between philosophy and the techniques, which had proved so fruitful in an earlier period, we find that Plato has nothing to contribute. Preoccupied with theological, metaphysical, or political problems, and disbelieving in the possibility of a science of nature, Plato has little appreciation of the connections between Greek thought and Greek practice which were clear to an earlier age. These connections are many. Astronomy was, of course, not studied out of mere curiosity. It was studied in order to solve those very problems concern with which Plato deprecates—the exact relations of the lengths of day and night, of both to the month, and of the month to the year. On the solution of these problems depended the improvement of the calendar. On the improvement of the calendar depended improvements in agriculture, navigation, and the general conduct of public affairs. Neither was geometry studied, outside the Academy, purely for the good of the soul. It was studied in connection with land-surveying, navigation, architecture, and engineering. Mechanical science was applied in the theatre, the field of battle, the docks and dockyards, the quarries, and wherever building was afoot. Medicine was a conspicuous example of applied science. It was a scientific study of man in his environment with a view to promoting his well-being. But the political programme put forward by Plato in the *Republic* and the *Laws* is all but barren of understanding of the rôle of applied science in the improvement of the lot of humanity. In his *Republic* and *Laws* Plato is wholly occupied with the problem of managing men, not at all with the problem of the control of the material environment. Accordingly the works, if full of political ingenuity, are devoid of natural science.

2 The Search for Knowledge in Greek Antiquity

The greatest physician of antiquity was the almost legendary Hippocrates of Cos (c. 460–375 B.C.), whose effect on medicine is still visible in the Hippocratic oath. The treatise "On Ancient Medicine" laid out the basic medical ideas of the Hippocratic school.

FROM *On Ancient Medicine* BY HIPPOCRATES

WHOEVER having undertaken to speak or write on Medicine, have first laid down for themselves some hypothesis to their argument, such as hot, or cold, or moist, or dry, or whatever else they choose, (thus reducing their subject within a narrow compass, and supposing only one or two original causes of diseases or of death among mankind,) are all clearly mistaken in much that they say; and this is the more reprehensible as relating to an art which all men avail themselves of on the most important occasions, and the good operators and practitioners in which they hold in especial honour. . . . Wherefore I have not thought that it stood in need of an empty hypothesis, like those subjects which are occult and dubious, in attempting to handle which it is necessary to use some hypothesis; as, for example, with regard to things above us and things below the earth; if any one should treat of these and undertake to declare how they are constituted, the reader or hearer could not find out, whether what is delivered be true or false; for there is nothing which can be referred to in order to discover the truth.

But all these requisites belong of old to Medicine, and an origin and way have been found out, by which many and elegant discoveries have been made, during a length of time, and others will yet be found out, if a person possessed of the proper ability, and knowing those discoveries which have been made, should proceed from them to prosecute his investigations. But whoever, rejecting and despising all these, attempts to pursue another course

The Genuine Works of Hippocrates, I (1849), 161–2, 168–73, 174–6, translated by Francis Adams.

and form of inquiry, and says he has discovered anything, is deceived himself and deceives others, for the thing is impossible. And for what reasons it is impossible, I will now endeavour to explain, by stating and showing what the art really is.

*　　*　　*

But I wish the discourse to revert to the new method of those who prosecute their inquiries in the Art by hypothesis. For if hot, or cold, or moist, or dry, be that which proves injurious to man, and if the person who would treat him properly must apply cold to the hot, hot to the cold, moist to the dry, and dry to the moist—let me be presented with a man, not indeed one of a strong constitution, but one of the weaker, and let him eat wheat, such as it is supplied from the thrashing-floor, raw and unprepared, with raw meat, and let him drink water. By using such a diet I know that he will suffer much and severely, for he will experience pains, his body will become weak, and his bowels deranged, and he will not subsist long. What remedy, then, is to be provided for one so situated? Hot? or cold? or moist? or dry? For it is clear that it must be one or other of these. For, according to this principle, if it is one of these which is injuring the patient, it is to be removed by its contrary. But the surest and most obvious remedy is to change the diet which the person used, and instead of wheat to give bread, and instead of raw flesh, boiled, and to drink wine in addition to these: for by making these changes it is impossible but that he must get better, unless completely disorganised by time and diet. What, then, shall we say? whether that, as he suffered from cold, these hot things being applied were of use to him, or the contrary? I should think this question must prove a puzzler to whomsoever it is put. For whether did he who prepared bread out of wheat remove the hot, the cold, the moist, or the dry principle in it?—for the bread is consigned both to fire and to water, and is wrought with many things, each of which has its peculiar property and nature, some of which it loses, and with others it is diluted and mixed.

And this I know, moreover, that to the human body it makes a great difference whether the bread be fine or coarse; of wheat with or without the hull, whether mixed with much or little water, strongly wrought or scarcely at all, baked or raw—and a multitude of similar differences; and so, in like manner, with the cake (maza); the powers of each, too, are great, and the one nowise like the other. Whoever pays no attention to these things, or, paying attention, does not comprehend them, how can he understand the diseases which befall a man? For, by every one of these things, a man is affected and changed this way or that, and the whole of his life is subjected to them, whether in health, convalescence, or disease. Nothing else, then, can be more important or more necessary to know than these things. So that the first inventors, pursuing their investigations properly, and by a suitable train of reasoning, according to the nature of man, made their discoveries, and thought the Art worthy of being ascribed to a god, as is the established belief. For they did not suppose that the dry or the moist, the hot or cold, or any of these, are either injurious to man, or that man stands in need of them; but whatever in each was strong, and more than a match for a man's constitution, whatever he could not manage, that they held to be hurtful, and sought to remove. Now, of the sweet, the strongest is that which is intensely sweet; of the bitter, that which is intensely bitter; of the acid, that which is intensely acid; and of all things that which is extreme, for these things they saw both existing in man, and proving injurious to him. For there is in man the bitter and the salt, the sweet and the acid, the sour and the insipid, and a multitude of other things having all sorts of powers, both as regards quantity and strength. These, when all mixed and mingled up with one another, are not apparent, neither do they hurt a man; but when any of them is separate, and stands by itself, then it becomes perceptible, and hurts a man. And thus, of articles of food, those which are unsuitable and hurtful to man when administered, every one is either bitter, or intensely so, or saltish or acid, or something else intense and strong, and therefore we are disordered by them in like manner as we are by the secretions in the body. But all those things of which a man eats and drinks are devoid of any such intense and well-marked quality, such as bread, cake, and many other things of a similar nature which man is accustomed to use for food, with the exception of condiments and confectionaries, which are made to gratify the palate and for luxury. And from those things, when received into the body abundantly, there is no disorder nor dissolution of the powers belonging to the body; but strength, growth, and nourishment result from them, and this for no other reason than because they are well mixed, have nothing in them of an immoderate character, nor anything strong, but the whole forms one simple and not strong substance.

I cannot think in what manner they who advance this doctrine, and transfer the Art from the cause I have described to hypothesis, will cure men according to the principle which they have laid down. For, as far as I know, neither the hot nor the cold, nor the dry, nor the moist, has ever been found unmixed with any other quality; but I suppose they use the same articles of meat and drink as all we other men do. But to this substance they give the attribute of being hot, to that cold, to that dry, and to that moist. Since it would be absurd to advise the patient to take something hot, for he would straightway ask what it is? so that he must either play the fool, or have recourse to some one of the well-known substances: and if this hot thing happen to be sour, and that hot thing insipid, and this hot thing has the power of raising a disturbance in the body (and there are many other kinds of heat, possessing many opposite powers), he will be obliged to administer some one of them, either the hot and the sour, or the hot and the insipid, or that which, at the same time, is cold and sour (for there is such a substance), or the cold and the insipid. For, as I think, the very opposite effects will result from either of these, not only in man, but also in a bladder, a vessel of wood, and in many other things possessed of far less sensibility than man; for it is not the heat which is possessed of great efficacy, but the sour and the insipid, and other qualities as described by me, both in man and out of man, and that whether eaten or drunk, rubbed in externally, and otherwise applied.

But I think that of all the qualities heat and cold exercise the least operation in the body, for these reasons: as long time as hot and cold are mixed up with one another they do not give trouble, for the cold is attempered and rendered more moderate by the hot, and the hot by the cold; but when the one is wholly separate from the other, then it gives pain; and at that season when cold is applied it creates some pain to a man, but quickly, for that very reason, heat spontaneously arises in him without requiring any aid or preparation. And these things operate thus both upon men in health and in disease. For example, if a person in health wishes to cool his body during winter, and bathes either in cold water or in any other way, the more he does this, unless his body be fairly congealed, when he resumes his clothes and comes into a place of shelter, his body becomes more heated than before. And thus, too, if a person wish to be warmed thoroughly either by means of a hot bath or strong fire, and straightway having the same clothing on, takes up his abode again in the place he was in when he became congealed, he will appear much colder, and more disposed to chills than before. And if a person fan himself on account of a suffocating heat, and having procured refrigeration for himself in this manner, cease doing so, the heat and suffocation will be ten times greater in his case than in that of a person who does nothing of the kind. And, to give a more striking example, persons travelling in the snow, or otherwise in rigorous weather, and contracting great cold in their feet, their hands, or their head, what do they not suffer from inflammation and tingling when they put on warm clothing and get into a hot place? In some instances, blisters arise as if from burning with fire, and they do not suffer from any of those unpleasant symptoms until they become heated. So readily does either of these pass into the other; and I could mention many other examples. And with regard to the sick, is it not in those who experience a rigor that the most acute fever is apt to break out? And yet not so strongly neither, but that it ceases in a short time, and, for the most part, without having occasioned much mischief; and while it remains, it is hot, and passing over the whole body, ends for the most part in the feet, where the chills and cold were most intense and lasted longest; and, when sweat supervenes, and the fever passes off, the patient is much colder than if he had not taken the fever at all. Why then should that which so quickly passes into the opposite extreme, and loses its own powers spontaneously, be reckoned a mighty and serious affair? And what necessity is there for any great remedy for it?

One might here say—but persons in ardent fevers, pneumonia, and other formidable diseases, do not quickly get rid of the heat, nor experience these rapid alterations of heat and cold. And I reckon this very circumstance the strongest proof that it is not from heat simply that men get into the febrile state, neither is it the sole cause of the mischief, but that this species of heat is bitter, and that acid, and the other saltish, and many other varieties; and again there is cold combined with other qualities. These are what proves injurious; heat, it is true, is present also, possessed of strength, as being that which conducts, is exacerbated and increased along with the other, but has no power greater than what is peculiar to itself.

Certain sophists and physicians say that it is not possible for any one to know medicine who does not know what man is [and how he was made and how constructed], and that whoever would cure men properly, must learn this in the first place. But this saying rather appertains to philosophy, as Empedocles and certain others have described what man in his origin is, and how he first was made and constructed. But I think whatever such has been said or written by sophist or physician concerning nature has less connexion with the art of medicine than with the art of painting. And I think that one cannot know anything certain respecting nature from any other quarter than from medicine; and that this knowledge is to be attained when one comprehends the whole subject of medicine properly, but not until then; and I say that this history shows what man is, by what causes he was made, and other things accurately. Wherefore it appears to me necessary to every physician to be skilled in nature, and strive to know, if he would wish to perform his duties, what man is in relation to the articles of food and drink, and to his other occupations, and what are the effects of each of them to every one. And it is not enough to know simply that cheese is a bad article of food, as disagreeing with whoever eats of it to satiety, but what sort of disturbance it creates, and wherefore, and with what principle in man it disagrees; for there are many other articles of food and drink naturally bad which affect man in a different manner. Thus, to illustrate my meaning by an example, undiluted wine drunk in large quantity renders a man feeble; and everybody seeing this knows that such is the power of wine, and the cause thereof; and we know, moreover, on what parts of a man's body it principally exerts its action; and I wish the same certainty to appear in other cases. For cheese (since we used it as an example) does not prove equally injurious to all men, for there are some who can take it to satiety without being hurt by it in the least, but, on the contrary, it is wonderful what strength it imparts to those it agrees with; but there are some who do not bear it well, their constitutions are different, and they differ in this respect, that what in their body is incompatible with cheese, is roused and put in commotion by such a thing; and those in whose bodies such a humour happens to prevail in greater quantity and intensity, are likely to suffer the more from it. But if the thing had been pernicious to the whole nature of man, it would have hurt all. Whoever knows these things will not suffer from it.

Plato (429–347 B.C.) was one of the greatest philosophers of all time. In The Republic, *Plato was intent upon examining*

*the requirements of the perfect political state. Science en-
tered in as part of the training of those who were to guide
the state.*

FROM *The Republic* BY PLATO

AND NOW, I said, let me show in a figure how far our nature is enlightened or unenlightened:—Behold! human beings living in an underground
den, which has a mouth open towards the light and reaching all along the
den; here they have been from their childhood, and have their legs and necks
chained so that they cannot move, and can only see before them, being
prevented by the chains from turning round their heads. Above and behind
them a fire is blazing at a distance, and between the fire and the prisoners
there is a raised way; and you will see, if you look, a low wall built along the
way, like the screen which marionette players have in front of them, over
which they show the puppets.

I see.

And do you see, I said, men passing along the wall carrying all sorts of
vessels, and statues and figures of animals made of wood and stone and
various materials, which appear over the wall? Some of them are talking,
others silent.

You have shown me a strange image, and they are strange prisoners.

Like ourselves, I replied; and they see only their own shadows, or the
shadows of one another, which the fire throws on the opposite wall of the
cave?

True, he said; how could they see anything but the shadows if they were
never allowed to move their heads?

And of the objects which are being carried in like manner they would
only see the shadows?

Yes, he said.

And if they were able to converse with one another, would they not
suppose that they were naming what was actually before them?

Very true.

And suppose further that the prison had an echo which came from the
other side, would they not be sure to fancy when one of the passers-by spoke
that the voice which they heard came from the passing shadow?

No question, he replied.

To them, I said, the truth would be literally nothing but the shadows of
the images.

The Dialogues of Plato, I (1937), 773–6, 780, 781–4, 786–90, translated by Benjamin Jowett.

That is certain.

And now look again, and see what will naturally follow if the prisoners are released and disabused of their error. At first, when any of them is liberated and compelled suddenly to stand up and turn his neck round and walk and look towards the light, he will suffer sharp pains; the glare will distress him, and he will be unable to see the realities of which in his former state he had seen the shadows; and then conceive some one saying to him, that what he saw before was an illusion, but that now, when he is approaching nearer to being and his eye is turned towards more real existence, he has a clearer vision,—what will be his reply? And you may further imagine that his instructor is pointing to the objects as they pass and requiring him to name them,—will he not be perplexed? Will he not fancy that the shadows which he formerly saw are truer than the objects which are now shown to him?

Far truer.

And if he is compelled to look straight at the light, will he not have a pain in his eyes which will make him turn away to take refuge in the objects of vision which he can see, and which he will conceive to be in reality clearer than the things which are now being shown to him?

True, he said.

And suppose once more, that he is reluctantly dragged up a steep and rugged ascent, and held fast until he is forced into the presence of the sun himself, is he not likely to be pained and irritated? When he approaches the light his eyes will be dazzled, and he will not be able to see anything at all of what are now called realities.

Not all in a moment, he said.

He will require to grow accustomed to the sight of the upper world. And first he will see the shadows best, next the reflections of men and other objects in the water, and then the objects themselves; then he will gaze upon the light of the moon and the stars and the spangled heaven; and he will see the sky and the stars by night better than the sun or the light of the sun by day?

Certainly.

Last of all he will be able to see the sun, and not mere reflections of him in the water, but he will see him in his own proper place, and not in another; and he will contemplate him as he is.

Certainly.

He will then proceed to argue that this is he who gives the season and the years, and is the guardian of all that is in the visible world, and in a certain way the cause of all things which he and his fellows have been accustomed to behold?

Clearly, he said, he would first see the sun and then reason about him.

And when he remembered his old habitation, and the wisdom of the den and his fellow-prisoners, do you not suppose that he would felicitate himself on the change, and pity them?

Certainly, he would.

And if they were in the habit of conferring honours among themselves on those who were quickest to observe the passing shadows and to remark which of them went before, and which followed after, and which were together; and who were therefore best able to draw conclusions as to the future, do you think that he would care for such honours and glories, or envy the possessors of them? Would he not say with Homer,

> Better to be the poor servant of a poor master,

and to endure anything, rather than think as they do and live after their manner?

Yes, he said, I think that he would rather suffer anything than entertain these false notions and live in this miserable manner.

Imagine once more, I said, such an one coming suddenly out of the sun to be replaced in his old situation; would he not be certain to have his eyes full of darkness?

To be sure, he said.

And if there were a contest, and he had to compete in measuring the shadows with the prisoners who had never moved out of the den, while his sight was still weak, and before his eyes had become steady (and the time which would be needed to acquire this new habit of sight might be very considerable), would he not be ridiculous? Men would say of him that up he went and down he came without his eyes; and that it was better not even to think of ascending; and if any one tried to loose another and lead him up to the light, let them only catch the offender, and they would put him to death.

No question, he said.

This entire allegory, I said, you may now append, dear Glaucon, to the previous argument; the prison-house is the world of sight, the light of the fire is the sun, and you will not misapprehend me if you interpret the journey upwards to be the ascent of the soul into the intellectual world according to my poor belief, which, at your desire, I have expressed—whether rightly or wrongly God knows. But, whether true or false, my opinion is that in the world of knowledge the idea of good appears last of all, and is seen only with an effort; and, when seen, is also inferred to be the universal author of all things beautiful and right, parent of light and of the lord of light in this visible world, and the immediate source of reason and truth in the intellectual; and that this is the power upon which he who would act rationally either in public or private life must have his eye fixed.

*   *   *

Who then are those whom we shall compel to be guardians? Surely they will be the men who are wisest about affairs of State, and by whom the State is best administered, and who at the same time have other honours and another and a better life than that of politics?

They are the men, and I will choose them, he replied.

And now shall we consider in what way such guardians will be produced, and how they are to be brought from darkness to light,—as some are said to have ascended from the world below to the gods?

By all means, he replied.

*　　*　　*

Well, I said, there may be nothing left of our special subjects; and then we shall have to take something which is not special, but of universal application.

What may that be?

A something which all arts and sciences and intelligences use in common, and which every one first has to learn among the elements of education.

What is that?

The little matter of distinguishing one, two, and three—in a word, number and calculation:—do not all arts and sciences necessarily partake of them?

Yes.

Then the art of war partakes of them?

To be sure.

Then Palamedes, whenever he appears in tragedy, proves Agamemnon ridiculously unfit to be a general. Did you never remark how he declares that he had invented number, and had numbered the ships and set in array the ranks of the army at Troy; which implies that they had never been numbered before, and Agamemnon must be supposed literally to have been incapable of counting his own feet—how could he if he was ignorant of number? And if that is true, what sort of general must he have been?

I should say a very strange one, if this was as you say.

*　　*　　*

I should like to know whether you have the same notion which I have of this study?

What is your notion?

It appears to me to be a study of the kind which we are seeking, and which leads naturally to reflection, but never to have been rightly used; for the true use of it is simply to draw the soul towards being.

Will you explain your meaning? he said.

*　　*　　*

I mean to say that objects of sense are of two kinds; some of them do not invite thought because the sense is an adequate judge of them; while in the case of other objects sense is so untrustworthy that further enquiry is imperatively demanded.

You are clearly referring, he said, to the manner in which the senses are imposed upon by distance, and by painting in light and shade.

No, I said, that is not at all my meaning.

Then what is your meaning?

When speaking of uninviting objects, I mean those which do not pass from one sensation to the opposite; inviting objects are those which do; in this latter case the sense coming upon the object, whether at a distance or near, gives no more vivid idea of anything in particular than of its opposite. An illustration will make my meaning clear:—here are three fingers—a little finger, a second finger, and a middle finger.

Very good.

You may suppose that they are seen quite close: And here comes the point.

What is it?

Each of them equally appears a finger, whether seen in the middle or at the extremity, whether white or black, or thick or thin—it makes no difference; a finger is a finger all the same. In these cases a man is not compelled to ask of thought the question what is a finger? for the sight never intimates to the mind that a finger is other than a finger.

True.

And therefore, I said, as we might expect, there is nothing here which invites or excites intelligence.

There is not, he said.

But is this equally true of the greatness and smallness of the fingers? Can sight adequately perceive them? and is no difference made by the circumstance that one of the fingers is in the middle and another at the extremity? And in like manner does the touch adequately perceive the qualities of thickness or thinness, of softness or hardness? And so of the other senses; do they give perfect intimations of such matters? Is not their mode of operation on this wise—the sense which is concerned with the quality of hardness is necessarily concerned also with the quality of softness, and only intimates to the soul that the same thing is felt to be both hard and soft?

You are quite right, he said.

And must not the soul be perplexed at this intimation which the sense gives of a hard which is also soft? What, again, is the meaning of light and heavy, if that which is light is also heavy, and that which is heavy, light?

Yes, he said, these intimations which the soul receives are very curious and require to be explained.

Yes, I said, and in these perplexities the soul naturally summons to her aid calculation and intelligence, that she may see whether the several objects announced to her are one or two.

True.

And if they turn out to be two, is not each of them one and different?

Certainly.

And if each is one, and both are two, she will conceive the two as in a state of division, for if they were undivided they could only be conceived of as one?

True.

The eye certainly did see both small and great, but only in a confused manner; they were not distinguished.

Yes.

Whereas the thinking mind, intending to light up the chaos, was compelled to reverse the process, and look at small and great as separate and not confused.

Very true.

Was not this the beginning of the enquiry "What is great?" and "What is small?"

Exactly so.

And thus arose the distinction of the visible and the intelligible.

Most true.

This was what I meant when I spoke of impressions which invited the intellect, or the reverse—those which are simultaneous with opposite impressions, invite thought; those which are not simultaneous do not.

I understand, he said, and agree with you.

And to which class do unity and number belong?

I do not know, he replied.

Think a little and you will see that what has preceded will supply the answer; for if simple unity could be adequately perceived by the sight or by any other sense, then, as we were saying in the case of the finger, there would be nothing to attract towards being; but when there is some contradiction always present, and one is the reverse of one and involves the conception of plurality, then thought begins to be aroused within us, and the soul perplexed and wanting to arrive at a decision asks "What is absolute unity?" This is the way in which the study of the one has a power of drawing and converting the mind to the contemplation of true being.

And surely, he said, this occurs notably in the case of one; for we see the same thing to be both one and infinite in multitude?

Yes, I said; and this being true of one must be equally true of all number?

Certainly.

And all arithmetic and calculation have to do with number?

Yes.

And they appear to lead the mind towards truth?

Yes, in a very remarkable manner.

Then this is knowledge of the kind for which we are seeking, having a double use, military and philosophical; for the man of war must learn the art of number or he will not know how to array his troops, and the philosopher also, because he has to rise out of the sea of change and lay hold of true being, and therefore he must be an arithmetician.

*   *   *

And, for all these reasons, arithmetic is a kind of knowledge in which the best natures should be trained, and which must not be given up.

I agree.

Let this then be made one of our subjects of education. And next, shall we enquire whether the kindred science also concerns us?

You mean geometry?

Exactly so.

Clearly, he said, we are concerned with that part of geometry which relates to war; for in pitching a camp, or taking up a position, or closing or extending the lines of an army, or any other military manoeuvre, whether in actual battle or on a march, it will make all the difference whether a general is or is not a geometrician.

Yes, I said, but for that purpose a very little of either geometry or calculation will be enough; the question relates rather to the greater and more advanced part of geometry—whether that tends in any degree to make more easy the vision of the idea of good; and thither, as I was saying, all things tend which compel the soul to turn her gaze towards that place, where is the full perfection of being, which she ought, by all means, to behold.

True, he said.

Then if geometry compels us to view being, it concerns us; if becoming only, it does not concern us?

Yes, that is what we assert.

Yet anybody who has the least acquaintance with geometry will not deny that such a conception of the science is in flat contradiction to the ordinary language of geometricians.

How so?

They have in view practice only, and are always speaking, in a narrow and ridiculous manner, of squaring and extending and applying and the like —they confuse the necessities of geometry with those of daily life; whereas knowledge is the real object of the whole science.

Certainly, he said.

Then must not a further admission be made?

What admission?

That the knowledge at which geometry aims is knowledge of the eternal, and not of aught perishing and transient.

That, he replied, may be readily allowed, and is true.

Then, my noble friend, geometry will draw the soul towards truth, and create the spirit of philosophy, and raise up that which is now unhappily allowed to fall down.

*   *   *

And suppose we make astronomy the third—what do you say?

I am strongly inclined to it, he said; the observation of the seasons and of months and years is as essential to the general as it is to the farmer or sailor.

I am amused, I said, at your fear of the world, which makes you guard against the appearance of insisting upon useless studies; and I quite admit the difficulty of believing that in every man there is an eye of the soul which, when by other pursuits lost and dimmed, is by these purified and re-illumined; and is more precious far than ten thousand bodily eyes, for by it alone is truth seen. Now there are two classes of persons: one class of those who will agree with you and will take your words as a revelation; another class to whom they will be utterly unmeaning, and who will naturally deem them to be idle tales, for they see no sort of profit which is to be obtained from them. And therefore you had better decide at once with which of the two you are proposing to argue. You will very likely say with neither, and that your chief aim in carrying on the argument is your own improvement; at the same time you do not grudge to others any benefit which they may receive.

I think that I should prefer to carry on the argument mainly on my own behalf.

Then take a step backward, for we have gone wrong in the order of the sciences.

What was the mistake? he said.

After plane geometry, I said, we proceeded at once to solids in revolution [*astronomy—L. P. W.*], instead of taking solids in themselves; whereas after the second dimension the third, which is concerned with cubes and dimensions of depth, ought to have followed.

That is true, Socrates; but so little seems to be known as yet about these subjects.

Why, yes, I said, and for two reasons:—in the first place, no government patronises them; this leads to a want of energy in the pursuit of them, and they are difficult; in the second place, students cannot learn them unless they have a director. But then a director can hardly be found, and even if he could, as matters now stand, the students, who are very conceited, would not attend to him. That, however, would be otherwise if the whole State became the director of these studies and gave honour to them; then disciples would want to come, and there would be continuous and earnest search, and discoveries would be made; since even now, disregarded as they are by the world, and maimed of their fair proportions, and although none of their votaries can tell the use of them, still these studies force their way by their natural charm, and very likely, if they had the help of the State, they would some day emerge into light.

Yes, he said, there is a remarkable charm in them. But I do not clearly understand the change in the order. First you began with a geometry of plane surfaces?

Yes, I said.

And you placed astronomy next, and then you made a step backward?

Yes, and I have delayed you by my hurry; the ludicrous state of solid geometry, which, in natural order, should have followed, made me pass over this branch and go on to astronomy, or motion of solids.

True, he said.

Then assuming that the science now omitted would come into existence if encouraged by the State, let us go on to astronomy, which will be fourth.

The right order, he replied. And now, Socrates, as you rebuked the vulgar manner in which I praised astronomy before, my praise shall be given in your own spirit. For every one, as I think, must see that astronomy compels the soul to look upwards and leads us from this world to another.

Every one but myself, I said; to every one else this may be clear, but not to me.

And what then would you say?

I should rather say that those who elevate astronomy into philosophy appear to me to make us look downwards and not upwards.

What do you mean? he asked.

You, I replied, have in your mind a truly sublime conception of our knowledge of the things above. And I dare say that if a person were to throw his head back and study the fretted ceiling, you would still think that his mind was the percipient, and not his eyes. And you are very likely right, and I may be a simpleton: but, in my opinion, that knowledge only which is of being and of the unseen can make the soul look upwards, and whether a man gapes at the heavens or blinks on the ground, seeking to learn some particular of sense, I would deny that he can learn, for nothing of that sort is matter of science; his soul is looking downwards, not upwards, whether his way to knowledge is by water or by land, whether he floats, or only lies on his back.

I acknowledge, he said, the justice of your rebuke. Still, I should like to ascertain how astronomy can be learned in any manner more conducive to that knowledge of which we are speaking?

I will tell you, I said: The starry heaven which we behold is wrought upon a visible ground, and therefore, although the fairest and most perfect of visible things, must necessarily be deemed inferior far to the true motions of absolute swiftness and absolute slowness, which are relative to each other, and carry with them that which is contained in them, in the true number and in every true figure. Now, these are to be apprehended by reason and intelligence, but not by sight.

True, he replied.

The spangled heavens should be used as a pattern and with a view to that higher knowledge; their beauty is like the beauty of figures or pictures excellently wrought by the hand of Daedalus, or some other great artist, which we may chance to behold; any geometrician who saw them would appreciate the exquisiteness of their workmanship, but he would never dream of thinking that in them he could find the true equal or the true double, or the truth of any other proportion.

No he replied, such an idea would be ridiculous.

And will not a true astronomer have the same feeling when he looks at the movements of the stars? Will he not think that heaven and the things in heaven are framed by the Creator of them in the most perfect manner? But he will never imagine that the proportions of night and day, or of both to the month, or of the month to the year, or of the stars to these and to one another, and any other things that are material and visible can also be eternal and subject to no deviation—that would be absurd; and it is equally absurd to take so much pains in investigating their exact truth.

I quite agree, though I never thought of this before.

Then, I said, in astronomy, as in geometry, we should employ problems, and let the heavens alone if we would approach the subject in the right way and so make the natural gifts of reason to be of any real use.

That, he said, is a work infinitely beyond our present astronomers.

Plato's greatest pupil was Aristotle (384–322 B.C.). After some twenty years of close association with Plato, he broke with Platonism and created his own system. Like his master, he felt it essential to ask what knowledge was and how it could be attained. In The Physics *he analyzed the concept of causation.*

FROM *The Physics* BY ARISTOTLE

NOW THAT WE HAVE ESTABLISHED these distinctions, we must proceed to consider causes, their character and number. Knowledge is the object of our inquiry, and men do not think they know a thing till they have grasped the "why" of it (which is to grasp its primary cause). So clearly we too must do this as regards both coming to be and passing away and every kind of physical change, in order that, knowing their principles, we may try to refer to these principles each of our problems.

In one sense, then, (1) that out of which a thing comes to be and which persists, is called "cause," e.g. the bronze of the statue, the silver of the bowl, and the genera of which the bronze and the silver are species.

In another sense (2) the form or the archetype, i.e. the statement of the essence, and its genera, are called "causes" (e.g. of the octave the relation of 2:1, and generally number), and the parts in the definition.

W. D. Ross, ed., *The Works of Aristotle*, II (1930), 194b–195a, translated by R. P. Hardie and R. K. Gaye. Reprinted by permission of The Clarendon Press, Oxford.

Again (3) the primary source of the change or coming to rest; e.g. the man who gave advice is a cause, the father is cause of the child, and generally what makes of what is made and what causes change of what is changed.

Again (4) in the sense of end or "that for the sake of which" a thing is done, e.g. health is the cause of walking about. ("Why is he walking about?" we say. "To be healthy," and, having said that, we think we have assigned the cause.) The same is true also of all the intermediate steps which are brought about through the action of something else as means towards the end, e.g. reduction of flesh, purging, drugs, or surgical instruments are means towards health. All these things are "for the sake of" the end, though they differ from one another in that some are activities, others instruments.

This then perhaps exhausts the number of ways in which the term "cause" is used.

As the word has several senses, it follows that there are several causes of the same thing (not merely in virtue of a concomitant attribute), e.g. both the art of the sculptor and the bronze are causes of the statue. These are causes of the statue *qua* statue, not in virtue of anything else that it may be— only not in the same way, the one being the material cause, the other the cause whence the motion comes. Some things cause each other reciprocally, e.g. hard work causes fitness and *vice versa,* but again not in the same way, but the one as end, the other as the origin of change. Further the same thing is the cause of contrary results. For that which by its presence brings about one result is sometimes blamed for bringing about the contrary by its absence. Thus we ascribe the wreck of a ship to the absence of the pilot whose presence was the cause of its safety.

In The Metaphysics, *Aristotle examined the basic nature of science and applied his principles to the motion of the heavenly bodies. There is one difficulty that deserves some editorial comment. According to Plato, the planets, as divine heavenly bodies* must *move with the only kind of motion that is perfect and unchangeable, that is, uniform circular motion. But observation clearly reveals that the planets do* not *revolve in circles; rather, their motion as observed from the earth is:*

The great problem, then, was to resolve this motion into the motion of circles. The solution that Aristotle gave in The Metaphysics *was that proposed by the great mathematician*

Eudoxos and is known as "the doctrine of homocentric spheres." Each sphere rotates on its axis; the combination of these rotations produces the observed motion of the planet. This system is the one described in Dante's Divine Comedy, *some 1,600 years later.*

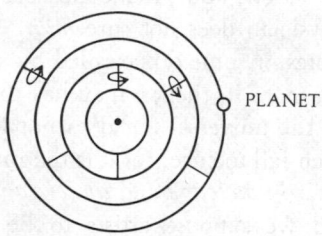

FROM *The Metaphysics* BY ARISTOTLE

ALL MEN by nature desire to know. An indication of this is the delight we take in our senses; for even apart from their usefulness they are loved for themselves; and above all others the sense of sight. For not only with a view to action, but even when we are not going to do anything, we prefer seeing (one might say) to everything else. The reason is that this, most of all the senses, makes us know and brings to light many differences between things.

By nature animals are born with the faculty of sensation, and from sensation memory is produced in some of them, though not in others. And therefore the former are more intelligent and apt at learning than those which cannot remember; those which are incapable of hearing sounds are intelligent though they cannot be taught, e.g. the bee, and any other race of animals that may be like it; and those which besides memory have this sense of hearing can be taught.

The animals other than man live by appearances and memories, and have but little of connected experience; but the human race lives also by art and reasonings. Now from memory experience is produced in men; for the several memories of the same thing produce finally the capacity for a single experience. And experience seems pretty much like science and art, but really science and art come to men *through* experience; for "experience made art," as Polus says, "but inexperience luck." Now art arises when from many notions gained by experience one universal judgement about a class of objects is produced. For to have a judgement that when Callias was ill of this disease this did him good, and similarly in the case of Socrates and in many individual cases, is a matter of experience; but to judge that it has done good to all persons of a certain constitution, marked off in one class, when they

W. D. Ross, ed., *The Works of Aristotle*, VIII (1928), 980a–981b, 982b, 1073a–1074a, translated by W. D. Ross. Reprinted by permission of The Clarendon Press, Oxford.

were ill of this disease, e.g. to phlegmatic or bilious people when burning with fever,—this is a matter of art.

With a view to action experience seems in no respect inferior to art, and men of experience succeed even better than those who have theory without experience. (The reason is that experience is knowledge of individuals, art of universals, and actions and productions are all concerned with the individual; for the physician does not cure *man,* except in an incidental way, but Callias or Socrates or some other called by some such individual name, who happens to be a man. If, then, a man has the theory without the experience, and recognizes the universal but does not know the individual included in this, he will often fail to cure; for it is the individual that is to be cured.) But yet we think that *knowledge* and *understanding* belong to art rather than to experience, and we suppose artists to be wiser than men of experience (which implies that Wisdom depends in all cases rather on knowledge); and this because the former know the cause, but the latter do not. For men of experience know that the thing is so, but do not know why, while the others know the "why" and the cause. Hence we think also that the master-workers in each craft are more honourable and know in a truer sense and are wiser than the manual workers, because they know the causes of the things that are done (we think the manual workers are like certain lifeless things which act indeed, but act without knowing what they do, as fire burns,—but while the lifeless things perform each of their functions by a natural tendency, the labourers perform them through habit); thus we view them as being wiser not in virtue of being able to act, but of having the theory for themselves and knowing the causes. And in general it is a sign of the man who knows and of the man who does not know, that the former can teach, and therefore we think art more truly knowledge than experience is; for artists can teach, and men of mere experience cannot. . . .

And the science which knows to what end each thing must be done is the most authoritative of the sciences, and more authoritative than any ancillary science; and this end is the good of that thing, and in general the supreme good in the whole of nature. Judged by all the tests we have mentioned, then, the name in question falls to the same science; this must be a science that investigates the first principles and causes; for the good, i.e. the end, is one of the causes.

That it is not a science of production is clear even from the history of the earliest philosophers. For it is owing to their wonder that men both now begin and at first began to philosophize; they wondered originally at the obvious difficulties, then advanced little by little and stated difficulties about the greater matters, e.g. about the phenomena of the moon and those of the sun and of the stars, and about the genesis of the universe. And a man who is puzzled and wonders thinks himself ignorant (whence even the lover of myth is in a sense a lover of Wisdom, for the myth is composed of wonders); therefore since they philosophized in order to escape from ignorance, evidently they were pursuing science in order to know, and not for any utilitarian end. And this is confirmed by the facts; for it was when almost all the necessities of life and the things that make for comfort and recreation had been secured, that such knowledge began to be sought. Evidently then we do not seek it for the sake of any other advantage; but as the man is free, we say, who exists for his own sake and not for another's, so we pursue this as the only free science, for it alone exists for its own sake. . . .

Evidently there *is* a first principle, and the causes of things are neither an infinite series nor infinitely various in kind. For (1) neither can one thing proceed from another, as from matter, *ad infinitum* (e.g. flesh from earth, earth from air, air from fire, and so on without stopping), nor can the sources of movement form an endless series (man for instance being acted on by air, air by the sun, the sun by Strife, and so on without limit). Similarly the final causes cannot go on *ad infinitum,*—walking being for the sake of health, this for the sake of happiness, happiness for the sake of something else, and so one thing always for the sake of another. And the case of the essence is similar. For in the case of intermediates, which have a last term and a term prior to them, the prior must be the cause of the later terms. For if we had to say which of the three is the cause, we should say the first; surely not the last, for the final term is the cause of none; nor even the intermediate, for it is the cause only of one. (It makes no difference whether there is one intermediate or more, nor whether they are infinite or finite in number.) But of series which are infinite in this way, and of the infinite in general, all the parts down to that now present are alike intermediates; so that if there is no first there is no cause at all.

*   *   *

It is clear, then, why these things are as they are. But we must not ignore the question whether we have to suppose one such substance or more than one, and if the latter, how many; we must also mention, regarding the opinions expressed by others, that they have said nothing about the number of the substances that can even be clearly stated. For the theory of Ideas has no special discussion of the subject; for those who speak of Ideas say the Ideas are numbers, and they speak of numbers now as unlimited, now as limited by the number 10; but as for the reason why there should be just so many numbers, nothing is said with any demonstrative exactness. We however must discuss the subject, starting from the presuppositions and distinctions we have mentioned. The first principle or primary being is not movable either in itself or accidentally, but produces the primary eternal and single movement. But since that which is moved must be moved by something, and the first mover must be in itself unmovable, and eternal movement must be produced by something eternal and a single movement by a single thing, and since we see that besides the simple spatial movement of the universe, which we say the first and unmovable substance produces, there are other spatial movements—those of the planets—which are eternal (for a body which moves in a circle is eternal and unresting; we have proved these points in the physical treatises), each of *these* movements also must be caused by a substance both unmovable in itself and eternal. For the nature of the stars is eternal just because it is a certain kind of substance, and the mover is eternal and prior to the moved and that which is prior to a substance must be a substance. Evidently, then, there must be substances which are of the same number as the movements of the stars, and in their nature eternal, and in themselves unmovable, and without magnitude, for the reason before mentioned.

That the movers are substances, then, and that one of these is first and another second according to the same order as the movements of the stars, is evident. But in the number of the movements we reach a problem which must be treated from the standpoint of that one of the mathematical sciences which is most akin to philosophy—viz. of astronomy; for this science speculates about substance which is perceptible but eternal, but the other mathematical sciences, i.e. arithmetic and geometry, treat of no substance. That the movements are more numerous than the bodies that are moved is evident to those who have given even moderate attention to the matter; for each of the planets has more than one movement. But as to the actual number of these movements, we now—to give some notion of the subject—quote what some of the mathematicians say, that our thought may have some definite number to grasp; but, for the rest, we must partly investigate for ourselves, partly learn from other investigators, and if those who study this subject form an opinion contrary to what we have now stated, we must esteem both parties indeed, but follow the more accurate.

Eudoxus supposed that the motion of the sun or of the moon involves, in either case, three spheres, of which the first is the sphere of the fixed stars, and the second moves in the circle which runs along the middle of the zodiac, and the third in the circle which is inclined across the breadth of the zodiac; but the circle in which the moon moves is inclined at a greater angle than that in which the sun moves. And the motion of the planets involves, in each case, four spheres, and of these also the first and second are the same as the first two mentioned above (for the sphere of the fixed stars is that which moves all the other spheres, and that which is placed beneath this and has its movement in the circle which bisects the zodiac is common to all), but the *poles* of the third sphere of each planet are in the circle which bisects the zodiac, and the motion of the fourth sphere is in the circle which is inclined at an angle to the equator of the third sphere; and the poles of the third sphere are different for each of the other planets, but those of Venus and Mercury are the same.

Callippus made the position of the spheres the same as Eudoxus did, but while he assigned the same number as Eudoxus did to Jupiter and to Saturn, he thought two more spheres should be added to the sun and two to the moon, if one is to explain the observed facts; and one more to each of the other planets.

But it is necessary, if all the spheres combined are to explain the observed facts, that for each of the planets there should be other spheres (one fewer than those hitherto assigned) which counteract those already mentioned and bring back to the same position the outermost sphere of the star which in each case is situated below the star in question; for only thus can all the forces at work produce the observed motion of the planets. Since, then, the spheres involved in the movement of the planets themselves are—eight for Saturn and Jupiter and twenty-five for the others, and of these only those involved in the movement of the lowest-situated planet need not be counteracted, the spheres which counteract those of the outermost two planets will be six in number, and the spheres which counteract those of the next four planets will be sixteen; therefore the number of all the spheres—both those which move the planets and those which counteract these—will be fifty-five. And if one were not to add to the moon and to the sun the movements we mentioned, the whole set of spheres will be forty-seven in number.

Let this, then, be taken as the number of the spheres, so that the unmovable substances and principles also may probably be taken as just so many; the assertion of *necessity* must be left to more powerful thinkers. But if there can be no spatial movement which does not conduce to the moving of a star, and if further every being and every substance which is immune from change and in virtue of itself has attained to the best must be considered an end, there can be no other being apart from these we have named, but this must be the number of the substances. For if there are others, they will cause change as being a final cause of movement; but there cannot *be* other movements besides those mentioned. And it is reasonable to infer this from a consideration of the bodies that are moved; for if everything that moves is for the sake of that which is moved, and every movement belongs to something that is moved, no movement can be for the sake of itself or of another movement, but all the movements must be for the sake of the stars. For if there is to be a movement for the sake of a movement, this latter also will have to be for the sake of something else; so that since there cannot be an infinite regress, the end of every movement will be one of the divine bodies which move through the heaven.

There were other ways in antiquity to account for the physical world than through recourse to Platonic Ideas or Aristotelian Forms. Might not reality consist of atoms, themselves not capable of being perceived but constituting the bodies around us? The atomic theory was to have a most successful future, but in antiquity it was regarded as atheistic and subversive of public order. One of the philosophical problems the atomic theory had to confront was how, if atoms were imperceptible, we could know anything of them. And could we know enough to use them to explain things? These were the questions that Epicurus (341–270 B.C.) set out to answer in his letter to Herodotus.

Epicurus' Letter to Herodotus

HAVING MADE THESE POINTS CLEAR, we must now consider things imperceptible to the senses. First of all, that nothing is created out of that which does not exist: for if it were, everything would be created out of everything with no need of seeds. And again, if that which disappears were destroyed into that which did not exist, all things would have perished, since that into which they were dissolved would not exist. Furthermore, the universe always was such as it is now, and always will be the same. For there is nothing into which it changes: for outside the universe there is nothing which could come into it and bring about the change.

Moreover, the universe is (bodies and space): for that bodies exist, sense itself witnesses in the experience of all men, and in accordance with the evidence of sense we must of necessity judge of the imperceptible by reasoning, as I have already said. And if there were not that which we term void and place and intangible existence, bodies would have nowhere to exist and nothing through which to move, as they are seen to move. And besides these two nothing can even be thought of either by conception or on the analogy of things conceivable such as could be grasped as whole existences and not spoken of as the accidents or properties of such existences. Furthermore, among bodies some are compounds, and others those of which compounds are formed. And these latter are indivisible and unalterable (if, that is, all things are not to be destroyed into the non-existent, but something permanent is to remain behind at the dissolution of compounds): they are completely solid in nature, and can by no means be dissolved in any part. So it must needs be that the first-beginnings are indivisible corporeal existences.

Moreover, the universe is boundless. For that which is bounded has an extreme point: and the extreme point is seen against something else. So that as it has no extreme point, it has no limit; and as it has no limit, it must be boundless and not bounded. Furthermore, the infinite is boundless both in the number of the bodies and in the extent of the void. For if on the one hand the void were boundless, and the bodies limited in number, the bodies could not stay anywhere, but would be carried about and scattered through the infinite void, not having other bodies to support them and keep them in

C. Bailey, *Epicurus: The Extant Remains* (1926), pp. 21, 23, 25, 27, 29, 31, 33, 49, 51, 53. Reprinted by permission of The Clarendon Press, Oxford.

place by means of collisions. But if, on the other hand, the void were limited, the infinite bodies would not have room wherein to take their place.

Besides this the indivisible and solid bodies, out of which too the compounds are created and into which they are dissolved, have an incomprehensible number of varieties in shape: for it is not possible that such great varieties of things should arise from the same (atomic) shapes, if they are limited in number. And so in each shape the atoms are quite infinite in number, but their differences of shape are not quite infinite, but only incomprehensible in number.

And the atoms move continuously for all time, some of them falling straight down, others swerving, and others recoiling from their collisions. And of the latter, some are borne on separating to a long distance from one another, while others again recoil and recoil, whenever they chance to be checked by the interlacing with others, or else shut in by atoms interlaced around them. For on the one hand the nature of the void which separates each atom by itself brings this about, as it is not able to afford resistance, and on the other hand the hardness which belongs to the atoms makes them recoil after collision to as great a distance as the interlacing permits separation after the collision. And these motions have no beginning, since the atoms and the void are the cause.

These brief sayings, if all these points are borne in mind, afford a sufficient outline for our understanding of the nature of existing things.

Furthermore, there are infinite worlds both like and unlike this world of ours. For the atoms being infinite in number, as was proved already, are borne on far out into space. For those atoms, which are of such nature that a world could be created out of them or made by them, have not been used up either on one world or on a limited number of worlds, nor again on all the worlds which are alike, or on those which are different from these. So that there nowhere exists an obstacle to the infinite number of the worlds.

*   *   *

Now we must suppose too that it is when something enters us from external objects that we not only see but think of their shapes. For external objects could not make on us an impression of the nature of their own colour and shape by means of the air which lies between us and them, nor again by means of the rays or effluences of any sort which pass from us to them— nearly so well as if models, similar in colour and shape, leave the objects and enter according to their respective size either into our sight or into our mind; moving along swiftly, and so by this means reproducing the image of a single continuous thing and preserving the corresponding sequence of qualities and movements from the original object as the result of their uniform contact with us, kept up by the vibration of the atoms deep in the interior of the concrete body.

*   *   *

Moreover, we must suppose that the atoms do not possess any of the qualities belonging to perceptible things, except shape, weight, and size, and all that necessarily goes with shape. For every quality changes; but the atoms do not change at all, since there must needs be something which remains solid and indissoluble at the dissolution of compounds, which can cause changes; not changes into the non-existent or from the non-existent, but changes effected by the shifting of position of some particles, and by the addition or departure of others. For this reason it is essential that the bodies which shift their position should be imperishable and should not possess the nature of what changes, but parts and configuration of their own. For thus much must needs remain constant. For even in things perceptible to us which change their shape by the withdrawal of matter it is seen that shape remains to them, whereas the qualities do not remain in the changing object, in the way in which shape is left behind, but are lost from the entire body. Now these particles which are left behind are sufficient to cause the differences in compound bodies, since it is essential that some things should be left behind and not be destroyed into the non-existent.

*   *   *

Furthermore, the motions of the heavenly bodies and their turnings and eclipses and risings and settings, and kindred phenomena to these, must not be thought to be due to any being who controls and ordains or has ordained them and at the same time enjoys perfect bliss together with immortality (for trouble and care and anger and kindness are not consistent with a life of blessedness, but these things come to pass where there is weakness and fear and dependence on neighbours). Nor again must we believe that they, which are but fire agglomerated in a mass, possess blessedness, and voluntarily take upon themselves these movements. But we must preserve their full majestic significance in all expressions which we apply to such conceptions, in order that there may not arise out of them opinions contrary to this notion of majesty. Otherwise this very contradiction will cause the greatest disturbance in men's souls. Therefore we must believe that it is due to the original inclusion of matter in such agglomerations during the birth-process of the world that this law of regular succession is also brought about.

Furthermore, we must believe that to discover accurately the cause of the most essential facts is the function of the science of nature, and that blessedness for us in the knowledge of celestial phenomena lies in this and in the understanding of the nature of the existences seen in these celestial phenomena, and of all else that is akin to the exact knowledge requisite for our happiness: in knowing too that what occurs in several ways or is capable of being otherwise has no place here, but that nothing which suggests doubt or alarm can be included at all in that which is naturally immortal and blessed. Now this we can ascertain by our mind is absolutely the case. But what falls within the investigation of risings and settings and turnings and eclipses, and all that is akin to this, is no longer of any value for the happiness which knowledge brings, but persons who have perceived all this, but yet do not know what are the natures of these things and what are the essential causes, are still in fear, just as if they did not know these things at all: indeed, their fear may be even greater, since the wonder which arises out of the observation of these things cannot discover any solution or realize the regulation of the essentials. And for this very reason, even if we discover several causes for turnings and settings and risings and eclipses and the like, as has been the case already in our investigation of detail, we must not suppose that our inquiry into these things has not reached sufficient accuracy to contribute to our peace of mind and happiness. So we must carefully consider in how many ways a similar phenomenon is produced on earth, when we reason about the causes of celestial phenomena and all that is imperceptible to the senses; and we must despise those persons who do not recognize either what exists or comes into being in one way only, or that which may occur in several ways in the case of things which can only be seen by us from a distance, and further are not aware under what conditions it is impossible to have peace of mind. If, therefore, we think that a phenomenon probably occurs in some such particular way, and that in circumstances under which it is equally possible for us to be at peace, when we realize that it may occur in several ways, we shall be just as little disturbed as if we know that it occurs in some such particular way.

And besides all these matters in general we must grasp this point, that the principal disturbance in the minds of men arises because they think that these celestial bodies are blessed and immortal, and yet have wills and actions and motives inconsistent with these attributes; and because they are always expecting or imagining some everlasting misery, such as is depicted in legends, or even fear the loss of feeling in death as though it would concern them themselves; and, again, because they are brought to this pass not by reasoned opinion, but rather by some irrational presentiment, and therefore, as they do not know the limits of pain, they suffer a disturbance equally great or even more extensive than if they had reached this belief by opinion. But peace of mind is being delivered from all this, and having a constant memory of the general and most essential principles.

Wherefore we must pay attention to internal feelings and to external sensations in general and in particular, according as the subject is general or particular, and to every immediate intuition in accordance with each of the standards of judgement. For if we pay attention to these, we shall rightly trace the causes whence arose our mental disturbance and fear, and, by learning the true causes of celestial phenomena and all other occurrences that come to pass from time to time, we shall free ourselves from all which produces the utmost fear in other men.

3   What Is Ancient Science?

*George Sarton's life work was promoting the history of
science as an essential bridge between the "two cultures" of
science and the humanities. For Sarton, science was "positive" knowledge, which related to the real world in a very
direct way. Hence his evaluation of the relative merits of
Plato and Aristotle in the selection that follows.*

FROM *A History of Science* BY GEORGE SARTON

WE HAVE NO INTENTION of describing the details of Plato's philosophy, but we must discuss the theory of Ideas, which is the core of it and
dominates Plato's thought on every subject.

The objects that we see with our own eyes are only appearances, like the
shadows in the cave. If there is any truth, there must be things that really
exist. These things are the "Ideas" or "Forms." To each kind of being or
object there corresponds an Idea, which is as it were its womb and its cause.
For example, we see "horses" all of which are different and imperfect;
however good they may seem to be, they are bound to weaken and sooner or
later to pass away. The Idea of the horse, however, or let us call it the "ideal
horse," is perfect and eternal. The ideal horse cannot be seen or touched, but
while the horses of sense are as ephemeral and nonexistent as shadows, it
truly exists; it is the archetype of all possible horses, born or unborn.

This theory enables one to classify all the objects in their reality, instead
of having to consider only their evanescent appearances. It helps us to
understand the law of change and decay, which seems to be universal, and it
gives us new principles of thought and conduct. The sensible world is
submitted to corruption and death, but the Ideas, being immaterial, are
incorruptible and ageless; the world of Ideas is real and permanent. The Idea
is not only the essential reality of a thing, it is also its definition and its
name; hence, we are given at one and the same time the tools of knowledge
and its valid elements. The Ideas are not fancies, but beings, living and

Reprinted by permission of the publishers from George Sarton, *A History of Science*, pp. 402–
4, 496–7. Cambridge, Mass.: Harvard University Press, Copyright, 1952, by the President and
Fellows of Harvard College.

eternal; they are Forms, patterns, wombs, standards; at the same time they are like magical names.

The Ideas lend themselves easily to classification and hierarchy. The supreme Idea is the Idea of Good, which comes very close to God.

We may have opinions concerning the material objects, but real knowledge can be built only upon the basis of the immaterial Ideas. The aim of science is thus to investigate, understand, and know those Ideas. The real philosopher is the man whose soul can grasp them beyond the fleeting and deceiving appearances, and he derives his greatest reward from the contemplation of the purest and highest Ideas.

* * *

The Platonic point of view allured poets and metaphysicians, who fancied that it made divine knowledge possible; unfortunately, it made the more earthbound scientific knowledge impossible. The Platonic method of leading from the general to the particular, from the abstract to the concrete, is intuitive, swift, and sterile. It is sterile because it is unworkable, or, to use our modern terminology, it is not "operational": abstract good is no good and one cannot ride an ideal horse. The opposite method . . . leading from known particulars to abstract notions of increasing generality, is slow but fruitful; it prepared very gradually the way for modern science. In spite of the incredible fertility and power of science, Platonism is not dead and will never die, for there will always be impatient metaphysicians wanting universal and immediate answers to their queries, and there will always be (let us hope) poets electing dreams instead of realities.

* * *

Aristotle's scientific views and achievements will be discussed in the following pages, but we must try to show him at once in his wholeness. Perhaps the simplest way of doing that is to compare him with his old master, Plato. The latter's scientific training had been restricted to mathematics and astronomy; Aristotle's was primarily medical. His father, Nicomachos, was an Asclepiad, and the Asclepiadean tradition was handed down directly from father to son. The young Aristotle may have visited patients with his father or assisted him in his treatment of them in the surgery; at any rate, he could not help, wide-awake as he was, learning much from his father's lips and above all absorbing the empirical point of view. A mathematician, especially one like Plato, inspired by Pythagorean arithmology, would satisfy himself with a priori conceptions of the universe; a physician soon realized that one should assume and foretell as little as possible, but observe, take notes, induce and deduce prudently. Plato was imaginative and tender-minded; Aristotle, experimental and tough-minded; yet, one should remember that Aristotle had begun his intellectual life as a Platonist and never shook off completely some of his Platonic fantasies. To my mind, this illustrates his greatness; he never was as dogmatic as his master had been and was so keenly aware of the mysteries of life that he remained somewhat Platonic in his growing resistance to Plato.

Aristotle had some experience of the occult practices of Greek religion and like Plato he compared intuitive knowledge with the initiation into the mysteries, yet he evaded mystical exaggerations. . . . His residual mysticism was very much like that of the great scientists of every age who are humble and prudent and never unmindful of the infinite complexity of the universe.

One of his fundamental ideas, expressed by the word teleology, may be called mystical, for its validity cannot be completely proved. The idea is very typical of the Plato–Aristotle relation, for it was derived from the Platonic conceptions of Idea or Form as prior to the existing object, as their metaphysical womb, as it were; for Aristotle the Idea is an unattainable goal. Plato tended to assimilate change with corruption; Aristotle, on the contrary, conceives change as a motion toward an ideal. Plato rejected the possibility of progress, while Aristotle accepted it. Things change because of the potentialities inherent in them; they change in order to attain or to approach their perfection. The Idea or Form is *in* the thing (like the adult in the embryo), not outside. The destiny of a thing is foretold by its hidden unrealized essence. Evolution proceeds as it does, not because of material causes producing natural consequences, pushing them on . . . but by final causes pulling them ahead. . . . All the things that exist are directed toward an end (which is potentially inside of them); their development is shaped by a purpose. The world is gradually realized because of a transcendental Design, or call it Divine Providence.

Aristotle realized that mechanism and purpose are complementary and inseparable aspects; in the study of nature one must seek for a mechanical explanation or for the leading reason; sometimes the mechanism is clearer, sometimes the reason. In his time practically no mechanism (for example, a physiologic mechanism) was conceivable; hence, there remained only the teleologic explanation.

To a hard-boiled man of science of today such an explanation is mere verbiage. It is futile to ask the "why" of things, he would say; it suffices to answer as carefully as possible the question "how?" Aristotle was trying prematurely to answer the question "why?" and was giving that question first place. Was he all wrong? The question might be premature, but it was not futile; it had in a first approximation a guiding value. To his credit we should bear in mind also: (1) that his conception of terminal ideas (teleology) was an enormous improvement upon Plato's conception of germinal ideas; (2) that the teleologic explanations, even if insufficient, are yet very useful; every man of science uses them wittingly or unwittingly; the purpose of an organ helps us to understand and to remember its anatomy and physiology; (3) that the vitalists use teleologic language, and there are still many of them among us; it is impossible to suppress the vitalist point of view; it dodges every blow and reappears under a new form; (4) finally, if one accepts Divine Providence one cannot reject teleology.

The teleologic appearances of nature are obvious enough; do they correspond to an inner reality or are they simply illusions? The question can be put this way: Is the argument of design valid or is it a paradox? Aristotle was the first to use that argument and to attach considerable importance to it. Who will be the last? Aristotelian teleology is one of the proofs of his genius.

The teleologic point of view implied the concept of evolution, evolution toward an ideal, progress. To understand things we must penetrate their purpose, their genesis and growth. Aristotle applied these ideas to natural history, rather than to human history; otherwise he would have been one of the ancestors of the historians of science.

Aristotle was primarily an encyclopedist and with the partial exception of Democritos he was the first one. Earlier philosophers had tried to explain the universe, but Aristotle, who shared their ambition, was the first to realize that such an explanation should be preceded by as complete an inventory and description of it as possible. He did not simply understand that need but, what is more remarkable, he satisfied it. The totality of his work represents an encyclopedia of the available knowledge, much of which was obtained by himself or because of his leadership. It is easy to find holes or errors in that encyclopedia, but the amazing thing is that it was as good, as comprehensive and durable, as it was.

The encyclopedic purpose implies the belief that there is some unity and order in the universe and the conviction that the same unity and order should be transparent in our knowledge of it. The unity is proved by one's study of first principles (philosophy, theology), the order by proper classification and description.

As to first principles, there is a soul in every living thing and there is in each soul something divine, something connected with pure reason. God exists, for it is the necessary principle and end of everything, the first motor. All motion and all life symbolize an immense and universal impulse to perfection, to God; that impulse is obscure in the lower forms of existence, but it becomes clearer and clearer in men according to their degree of intelligence. Much of this could and did eventually lead to scholasticism and to mysticism, but in Aristotle's mind these sublime thoughts were restrained by his matter-of-factness and moderation. Aristotle's classification made a first distinction between the various branches of science, theoretical, productive, and practical. The theoretical ones have no aim but the apprehension and contemplation of truth; they are mathematics, physics, metaphysics (first philosophy, theology). The productive branches concern the arts. Practical philosophy seeks to regulate human actions; its two chief branches are ethics and politics. In spite of its insufficiency, Aristotle's classification exerted a very strong influence upon the whole development of philosophy and science down to our own day.

His encyclopedic ambition was a very elementary one as compared with ours. He could not help believing that it could be achieved by an accumulation of definitions (that is why I used the word "inventory" above), and his definitions were verbal, not truly explicative. To the modern mind this is very insufficient indeed, but one had to begin with such inventories and fill them in gradually with more and deeper meaning.

Scientific knowledge of a thing is possible when we know its causes, and the main cause is the essence. We should know the varieties of each kind of thing, and this means enumeration and description. Ideas of increasing generality are not established a priori but are derived from the observation of increasing numbers of things. Aristotle, his colleagues, and his disciples accumulated a large number of observations; they provided good analyses and descriptions, and intelligent interpretations. Their terminology was often artificial, but much of it was apposite and has survived in modern languages. Unfortunately, the search for the essence of things opened the door to metaphysics; explanations were often wordy, and the enumerations incomplete. Aristotle did not realize their incompleteness and often concluded an enumeration with the words *cai para tauta uden* (and beyond that nothing else); he believed himself nearer to the goal than he was, or than he could possibly be. That was natural enough. His school had done so much that its illusions were pardonable; illusions of complete knowledge are far less pardonable today.

That philosophy was satisfying, because it is full of common sense and is moderate. Aristotle's love of order, of clearness and tidiness, of the *via media,* appealed to the Greek mind. After the days of paganism, when religious fervor increased, all that was necessary to preserve the popularity of his philosophy was to harmonize it with the dogmatic theology of other nations, and this was done by various doctors, for example, Ibn Rushd for the Muslims, Maimonides for the Jews, St. Thomas Aquinas for the Christians.

It has sometimes been said that Aristotelianism as compared with mystical deviations lacked humanity, tenderness, and even ideals. This was very misleading. Its main ideal was the scientific ideal, the discovery of the truth, an ideal that is always far ahead of men, yet a guide in the darkness. Aristotle's conception of science was very insufficient as compared with ours, but that was unavoidable. Because of his willingness to compromise he has been accused of mediocrity; that is another way of saying that he lacked ideals. That seems very unfair to me. He was trying hard to reach the truth; he could not realize as clearly and strongly as we do that truth (scientific truth) is not attainable, though we may approach it indefinitely.

Not everyone would agree with Sarton that Plato's approach to nature was "poetic and metaphysical." It was also mathematical, and it is this aspect that Shorey stressed in his defense of Platonism in science.

FROM *Platonism and the History of Science* BY P. SHOREY

THE CHIEF VALUES of humanism are cultural rather than scientific. And so far as they are scientific, I would stress rather the training of the judgment than the investigation and discovery of fresh truth. Critical judgment of the meaning of books, documents, the written word, is one of the latest, rarest, and most easily lost of human attainments. Lawyers cultivate it with great precision in a narrow field; experts, including men of science, must have something of it in their own specialty. But the majority of educated men, including lawyers and men of science, do not even know that they lack it in the broader domain of literature and general criticism of life. They do not know that they cannot trust themselves to understand what they read (especially in the literature of the past) or to translate, quote, interpret, or apply it correctly and rationally.

Classical studies will not of themselves impart this discipline to recalcitrant minds. But rightly taught, there is no better educational instrument for training this kind of judgment than the classics, and no field in which it is more needed than in the interpretation of the two great literatures separated from us by the chasm of the Middle Ages and composed in languages we call dead. Misunderstandings of the classics naturally multiply in an age which has so many more pressing things to think about. Trivial errors, which amuse the scholar and delight the gloating pedant, are of no concern. But in the light of the new interest in the evolution of human thought and the history of science, the perpetuation and broadcasting of error about Greek philosophy is a more serious matter. I am not now speaking of doubtful points of metaphysics or the philosophy of history but of the quite definite and demonstrable misapprehensions—"howlers" in fact—which the index of almost any book of recent philosophy, science, or the history of science that mentions Plato, Aristotle and the pre-Socratics at all, will reveal. Writers who expect us to accept on faith their would-be scientific and critical interpretation of special and general relativity, symbolic and mathematical logic, the quantum theory, the constitution of the cell, the structure of the atom, the evidence for the inheritance of acquired qualities, will gravely refer us to a page of Plato or Aristotle for an idea that isn't there, and that intelligent and attentive reading of any good translation even, would have shown them is not there. The limits of my time and the courtesies of the occasion forbid me to mention names. But I have them, and there are astonishingly few exceptions to what may be thought a petulant generali-

P. Shorey, "Platonism and the History of Science," *Proceedings of the American Philosophical Society*, 66 (1927), 159–61, 176–7, 180.

zation. The fact surely indicates some defect in our education, or else the failure of the cautious scientific temper to function in this field. But this is not a paper on education, and in place of further generalization I will confine myself to one widespread and frequently reiterated error about Plato.

Though there are honorable exceptions, it is currently taught that Platonism is the antithesis of the scientific spirit and that Plato is a reactionary in relation to the evolutionary and mechanistic philosophies of the pre-Socratics, and a dreamer, spinning the world out of his inner consciousness, as contrasted with the fact-loving Aristotle.

*   *   *

In . . . defending Plato against the charge that, because he emphatically demanded mathematics, he would have rejected observation and experiment, I might invoke the dangerous alliance of modern mathematical mysticism, which is only too ready to exalt Plato and Pythagoras before him for anticipating the proposed reduction of all philosophy and all science to mathematics. I need not quote illustrations of a view which you meet everywhere in philosophical literature to-day. When it is not bluff, mysticism, or the mathematician's magnifying of his office, it can only be a prophecy of the final triumph of materialism. Philosophy and science can be swallowed up in mathematics only in so far as all qualities can be definitely correlated with measurable quantities. We may leave that consummation to the unknown future. There is no prediction of it in Plato; and the passages in which he praises mathematics and opposes measurement to guessing do not justify attributing it to him.

As for Pythagoras, of whom we know nothing, the wise reader turns the page when he sees that name, as Tyndall (or was it Huxley?) did when he saw the word "polarity."

But in these passages Plato has some notable anticipations of recent dicta of leaders of modern science on this subject, which are worth quoting. In "Republic" 602D, he says that measuring, counting and weighing are most gracious aids against the illusions of sense and the subjectivities of opinion; in "Philebus" 55E he says still more notably that if one divorces arithmetic, measurement and weighing, from the arts and sciences, that which remains is of little value—there is left only conjecture and guess-work and the exercise of the senses by empiricism and habit.

These utterances surely differ little from Lord Kelvin's statements that he understood a thing only when he could construct a working model of it, and that if you can measure a thing and express it by number, you have some knowledge of it, otherwise not; from Kant's declaration that the only part of any theory of nature that is scientific in the strict sense of the word is the quantity of mathematics which it contains; from Clerk Maxwell's statement that progress is symbolized in the clock, the balance and the foot-rule.

*   *   *

Plato not only advocated education in science, but practiced it. Various steps in the progress of mathematics and astronomy are attributed to Plato as head of the Academy and director of research. He himself uses language that implies this conception of his function. One legend assigns to him the solution of the Delian Problem of the duplication of the cube. His friend Theaetetus, whose name is attached to one of the profoundest dialogues, apparently discovered and constructed some or all of the five regular solids. The astronomer Eudoxus, whose theory of the celestial spheres prepares that of Aristotle and the Middle Ages, was a friend of Plato and attended his lectures. . . .

Once more, from the point of view of working science and material progress, and flying the Atlantic in a night, all this is of no significance. All depends on whether we are as much interested in the ascertainable history of the civilized human mind, as we seem to be in that of the hypothetic psychology of the cave-man. If we are, it is worth while to get it right.

Educated ancients, men like Cicero and Plutarch, understood the facts which I have related and knew that the real scientific men of antiquity were Platonists and Aristotelians, not Epicureans. The mere dogmatic assertion of atomic materialism, and the denunciation of every form of the idea of design could not in their eyes make a true scientific thinker out of a poet who supposed the moon and sun to be about their apparent size and who denied the possibility of the antipodes. Many also of the great scientific men of the Renaissance and the following centuries understood the matter and spoke respectfully of Plato's scientific attainments and conceptions. It is enough to mention Galileo and Leibniz.

> *Addressing himself to the same ultimate questions as Far-*
> *rington, the late Professor Edelstein of Johns Hopkins Uni-*
> *versity brings the argument full circle. It might be well for*
> *the student, after finishing this selection, to go back and*
> *reread Farrington before addressing himself to the problem*
> *of ancient science.*

FROM *Motives and Incentives for Science in Antiquity*
BY LUDWIG EDELSTEIN

SO FAR I HAVE CONSIDERED science merely as theoretical understanding and have left out of consideration its usefulness for practical ends. Of the

Ludwig Edelstein, "Motives and Incentives for Science in Antiquity," A. C. Crombie, ed., *Scientific Change*, pp. 22–7, 28–32. Reprinted by permission of Heinemann Educational Books Ltd., London; published by Basic Books, Inc., New York, 1963.

applicability of their findings the scientists were of course quite conscious, as the testimony shows. Archytas's studies in the theory of mechanics led him to construct instruments and machines, and even a rattle, "a good invention," Aristotle says, "which people give to children in order that while occupied with this they may not break any furniture, for young things cannot keep still." Archimedes, the "geometrical Briareus" as the Roman aggressors called him, invented weapons for the defence of his native city. Astronomers and geographers applied their knowledge to drawing maps that could be used by sailors and travellers. It is true, scientists did not undertake their research with practical purposes in mind; they did not feel that their labours were more valuable or justifiable on account of the practical fruits they bore. The latter rather were by-products, so to say. Yet science did not shy away from technology, as is often assumed.

On the other hand, one cannot deny that applied science, as all ancient technology, did not advance as far as it could conceivably have done. During the thousand years of scientific studies in which the intellect on its "flight through the universe" revolutionized man's understanding of nature and achieved ever greater triumphs, the forms of daily existence changed relatively little, less perhaps than during the later Middle Ages, surely much less than in some of the decades since the middle of the nineteenth century. That the usefulness of science in Graeco-Roman times was comparatively unexploited, that it was, strictly speaking, no motive for developing scientific knowledge, is due I think mainly to three factors.

First, the "empirical" scientists, who considered speculation and theory of less importance, if of importance at all, and who on account of their prevalent concern with reality might have taken a special interest in applying their knowledge, were the ones to curtail research and thereby to curtail also the chances of mastering the phenomena. For in the Hellenistic theory of empiricism, the possibility of comprehending nature is severely narrowed down. Everything inaccessible to the senses is regarded as hidden from exploration and thus closed to scientific study. It was the empirical physician who denied that anatomy and physiology could become sciences and rendered useful for medical treatment. Also, reading of books—the treasured-up experience of the past—for him took precedence over making new experiments and accumulating more data. Extension of knowledge, the opening-up of new opportunities for applied science, was therefore left almost exclusively to the "theoretical" scientists—the "dogmatists" as they were derisively called by their opponents, and yet in fact the only ones to venture beyond the already known. But with them, of course, knowledge for the sake of knowledge was the prime motive and the prime concern.

Second, one must not forget that ancient sciences have by their very nature so to say a slant towards the theoretical rather than the practical. Some, physics and psychology for instance, were really "philosophical" sciences. For they remained in the domain of the philosopher and were studied by him as part of his analysis of the physical world and of human nature.

When the original unity of philosophy and all the sciences, obtaining in the pre-Socratic period, dissolved, and independent, particular sciences were established—sciences pursued by specialists—they still kept in close touch with philosophy. Their first principles, their methodology rested on philosophical grounds. The issue between mechanism and teleology, the controversy about the respective values of empirical observation and theoretical reasoning were fought not with scientific but with philosophical arguments, and these discussions occupied a much larger part of scientific writing than they would in later science. Not that the scientist slavishly followed the dictates of a philosophic law-giver. Rather he took an active interest in philosophy, he became himself a philosopher. The title of Galen's essay "That the best physician is also a philosopher" epitomizes the prevailing attitude. On the other hand, there was a feeling that men of experience, as Aristotle says, are better in practical matters, better equipped to handle particulars, than is the scientist who knows the universals. Thus the improvement of the technical apparatus remained largely in the hands of artisans and craftsmen, who changed things slowly and cautiously in their traditional conservative manner.

Last though not least, the relative neglect of the practical must I think be viewed against the background of the ancients' general attitude towards life, of which it seems characteristic that they acknowledged and respected boundaries set to their actions. They would, to be sure, aim at perfection in rational insight and in right conduct; they would fashion their cities or states in accordance with political ideals; they would above all civilize human existence so that it became truly human. They did not feel that it was their business to take the world over altogether. Men no more claimed than did their gods to be creators out of nothing, to act with a free will that imposes its law on things that have no nature of their own. Rather did they feel called upon to shape matter that was given and, here below at any rate, refractory to reason. The gods but mould, or to use a Platonic phrase, persuade the physcal universe to accommodate itself to their wishes as far as possible. It does not stand otherwise with that universe which men build. Having accomplished what appeared possible and essential, the pagans were satisfied to use knowledge mostly for taking care of their daily wants which were modest, for defending their country when there was need, for adorning temple services and festivals, for increasing pleasure through play and amusement.

It is mainly for such reasons, I think, that ancient science remained relatively useless, that changes which in principle were within reach were actually not made. But to a certain extent the ineffectiveness of science in altering conditions depended also on social factors, as should become clear from the discussion of the incentives for science, to which I shall now turn.

The new venture of science which started in the pre-Socratic centuries was a venture undertaken by individuals; it lacked the support of society. In the opinion of the citizens of the Greek communities, the scientist's "activity" was "idleness"—indeed withdrawal from the realities of life. They neither cared to be like him nor had they any use for him. Why then should they have given support to science? Far from supporting it, they did not even pay homage to it, as they did honour and reward poets or athletes. One who wished to engage in scientific studies had to be a man of independent means, free to indulge his fancies. At most he might maintain himself by teaching converts to the new cause. He certainly had no other hope of making a living. There were no schools with which one could be associated, no careers that one could follow as a scientist. The few who favoured the scientific movement advocated redress of the situation, for they were well aware of the fact that what society does not pay for or prize does not flourish. No one listened to their remonstrances. Throughout the classical age science remained beyond the pale of society.

Why did science fail to secure more recognition and encouragement? The responsibility certainly does not lie with distrust of science, with political schemes of any class of society designed to prevent science from becoming a weapon in the fight for freedom and enlightenment. If fear was felt regarding the relationship of society and science, it was the scientists who were suspicious. For they were well aware of the fact that royal support or support from any outside quarters was potentially a danger to the objectivity of their research, because favours might be expected in return, favours that could necessitate distortions of the truth or actions irreconcilable with their ideals. The true explanation for the reaction of society is I think to be found first of all in the scientific situation as it had taken shape by the time of Hellenism.

It was a situation not dissimilar to that of modern philosophy. Rival systems of science were competing with one another, rival systems which were in fact rival sciences. For there was nothing one could call science in the modern sense of the term, a body of knowledge valid everywhere, a system of principles, of rules of procedure and of theories, well defined and generally accepted. With the exception perhaps of mathematics, there were but "sciences," the adherence to which was optional. A science of mathematical astronomy faced a science of empirical astronomy. Empirical medicine, discarding anatomy and physiology, opposed dogmatic medicine based on anatomy and physiology. Descriptive geography rejecting quantitative analysis stood against a highly mathematized geography. Each of these sciences of course in the opinion of its proponents was true, but their claim to this effect clashed with counter-claims. This "dissension" as the ancients called it—a dissension not concerning particular results but concerning the basic presuppositions and aims of the scientific enterprise as such—made it almost impossible for anyone not a partisan to say what science was and what it was about, let alone to decide which of the existing systems of science should be encouraged and rewarded.

That science in general or science as the Greeks knew it begins one day, and that, after the liberating word has been spoken, everyone knows the right course to follow, seems an ineradicable historical prejudice. In fact, the history of Greek science, in addition to being the story of the discovery of true and false data—true and false from the modern point of view—is also the story of the gradual discovery of the meaning of science. The concept of science itself has a history. It took almost eight hundred years to work out the implications of the enterprise on which the ancients had ventured and to create general agreement on it. . . . The last step was only taken in the second century A.D., when largely through the work of Galen and of Ptolemy —theoreticians of science no less than scientists—a *scientia aeterna* began to be built up, science as it was to be understood from then on.

Yet, one may object, if men had been wiser, if they had recognized the value of science, if they had encouraged it as so many of the ancients themselves desired, the "dissension" of which I spoke could have been resolved earlier, and science would then have become integrated into civilization in Antiquity as it was later on. In such an objection there is I think a kernel of truth. The neglect of science on the part of society was undoubtedly due also to the predominance of other intellectual and emotional concerns.

Even those friendly to science often did not accept it altogether. The pre-Socratics and most of the classical philosophers to be sure were its fervent devotees. But among the minor Socratics emphasis on ethics began to grow, not to mention the fact that with Cynicism a conscious revolt of the civilized against civilization set in, which, though never spectacularly successful, left its mark on subsequent thought. Primitivism, the dream of a Golden Age of the past or future, a Rousseauesque admiration for the "noble savage" who has not eaten from the tree of knowledge, was the shadow of ancient rationalism and progressionism. Hellenistic philosophies, Stoicism as well as Epicureanism, were interested in science; in their last phases they even showed a strong appreciation of the significance of science. But they were given to the study of moral values at least as much as to the study of brute facts; if to them God was visible in nature, he was even more manifest in man and his actions. Rhetorical training, whose hold was probably greater than that of philosophical education, never included more than the rudiments of science, for everything beyond them was considered useless. The so-called liberal arts led to the threshold of science but no farther. And education in general, being a matter of the individual's free choice, continued to consist mainly in the study of poetry and music. Centuries after the eclipse of the sun had been proved to be a natural, recurrent phenomenon, such an event was still taken even by men in prominent positions as a divine omen, without their incurring the least censure except from the *avant garde* of intellectuals. For not everybody was willing to resign himself to the disenchantment of the world which followed from the attempt to comprehend nature in rational terms. Without the pressure of a general school system through which the results of science would be filtered down to the people, they did not feel obliged to believe in the results of science and preferred to cling to the mythos, to live in it, to think in its categories. Science never succeeded in breaking the power of mythology. No less an achievement than art and poetry, it was in contrast to them but a thin layer over ancient civilization and not at all as important to the Greeks and Romans as it was destined to become to the future.

It goes without saying that the lack of institutionalization of ancient science accounts for many of its shortcomings. Without adequate prestige and recognition, without promise of financial security, it did not attract many people, not as many at any rate as could profitably have worked on securing the terrain which had been laid out. On the other hand, what was accomplished seems even more impressive because it was done with so little outside assistance. Considering why "men originally instituted a prize for competitions of the body, but none for wisdom," a pupil of Aristotle considers it a satisfactory answer to the puzzle that "the prize must be more desirable than the competition"; and he adds that though in the case of athletic contests such a prize can be found, "what prize could be better than wisdom?" It would be carrying flattery to extremes if one believed that ancient society failed to pay scientists because kings and citizens admiringly realized that wisdom is its own reward. But one may fairly say, I think, that in a world in which science was not a career, the overwhelming majority of those who studied science must have done so for the sake of science. This is perhaps not the least of the reasons for the strength and the survival of the ideal of the theoretical life in all periods of ancient history. For motives rather than incentives, desire for the truth rather than outward allurement, had to persuade men to enter the service of science.

Christianity in the Roman Empire—Why Did It Succeed?

CONTENTS

QUESTIONS FOR STUDY

1 How does Gibbon make use of the evidence of the Bible in his explanation of the Christian victory?

2 What does the correspondence of Pliny and Trajan show us about the Roman attitude toward Christianity?

3 On what grounds did Trajan permit the persecution of Christians?

Christianity, which conquered the Roman Empire, was to provide the religious basis of Western civilization. This religion, originating among poor fishermen in an insignificant oriental province of the empire, competed, not only against the official pagan cults of Rome, but also against such popular mystery cults as those of Isis and Osiris, Mithra, and many others. It came into a world educated by the philosophies of Plato, Aristotle, the Stoa, and Epicurus. Without armies it resisted the force and oppression of emperors. In spite of all, it won out, first gaining tolerance, then absolute control. The problem of its astonishing success is the subject of this chapter.

4   *How did the organization of the early Christian church help it to survive?*

5   *What does Latourette add to the reasons offered by Gibbon for the Christian success?*

6   *In what ways did Christianity differ from Judaism?*

7   *Are these differences significant in explaining the success of Christianity?*

1 Gibbon on the Victory of Christianity

FROM *The History of the Decline and Fall of the Roman Empire* BY EDWARD GIBBON

THE PROGRESS OF THE CHRISTIAN RELIGION, AND THE SENTIMENTS, MANNERS, NUMBERS, AND CONDITION, OF THE PRIMITIVE CHRISTIANS

A CANDID BUT RATIONAL INQUIRY into the progress and establishment of Christianity may be considered as a very essential part of the history of the Roman empire. While that great body was invaded by open violence, or undermined by slow decay, a pure and humble religion gently insinuated itself into the minds of men, grew up in silence and obscurity, derived new vigour from opposition, and finally erected the triumphant banner of the cross on the ruins of the Capitol. Nor was the influence of Christianity confined to the period or to the limits of the Roman empire. After a revolution of thirteen or fourteen centuries, that religion is still professed by the nations of Europe, the most distinguished portion of human kind in arts and learning as well as in arms. By the industry and zeal of the Europeans it has been widely diffused to the most distant shores of Asia and Africa; and by the means of their colonies has been firmly established from Canada to Chile, in a world unknown to the ancients.

But this inquiry, however useful or entertaining, is attended with two peculiar difficulties. The scanty and suspicious materials of ecclesiastical history seldom enable us to dispel the dark cloud that hangs over the first age of the church. The great law of impartiality too often obliges us to reveal the

Edward Gibbon, *The History of the Decline and Fall of the Roman Empire*, J. B. Bury, ed., II (1896), 1–2, 54–70.

imperfections of the uninspired teachers and believers of the gospel; and, to a careless observer, *their* faults may seem to cast a shade on the faith which they professed. But the scandal of the pious Christian, and the fallacious triumph of the Infidel, should cease as soon as they recollect not only *by whom,* but likewise *to whom,* the Divine Revelation was given. The theologian may indulge the pleasing task of describing Religion as she descended from Heaven, arrayed in her native purity. A more melancholy duty is imposed on the historian. He must discover the inevitable mixture of error and corruption which she contracted in a long residence upon earth, among a weak and degenerate race of beings.

Our curiosity is naturally prompted to inquire by what means the Christian faith obtained so remarkable a victory over the established religions of the earth. To this inquiry, an obvious but satisfactory answer may be returned; that it was owing to the convincing evidence of the doctrine itself, and to the ruling providence of its great Author. But, as truth and reason seldom find so favourable a reception in the world, and as the wisdom of Providence frequently condescends to use the passions of the human heart, and the general circumstances of mankind, as instruments to execute its purpose; we may still be permitted, though with becoming submission, to ask not indeed what were the first, but what were the secondary causes of the rapid growth of the Christian church. It will, perhaps, appear that it was most effectually favoured and assisted by the five following causes: I. The inflexible, and, if we may use the expression, the intolerant zeal of the Christians, derived, it is true, from the Jewish religion, but purified from the narrow and unsocial spirit which, instead of inviting, had deterred the Gentiles from embracing the law of Moses. II. The doctrine of a future life, improved by every additional circumstance which could give weight and efficacy to that important truth. III. The miraculous powers ascribed to the primitive church. IV. The pure and austere morals of the Christians. V. The union and discipline of the Christian republic, which gradually formed an independent and increasing state in the heart of the Roman empire.

*   *   *

In the course of this important, though perhaps tedious, inquiry, I have attempted to display the secondary causes which so efficaciously assisted the truth of the Christian religion. If among these causes we have discovered any artificial ornaments, any accidental circumstances, or any mixture of error and passion, it cannot appear surprising that mankind should be the most sensibly affected by such motives as were suited to their imperfect nature. It was by the aid of these causes, exclusive zeal, the immediate expectation of another world, the claim of miracles, the practice of rigid virtue, and the constitution of the primitive church, that Christianity spread itself with so much success in the Roman empire. To the first of these the Christians were indebted for their invincible valour, which disdained to capitulate with the enemy whom they were resolved to vanquish. The three succeeding causes supplied their valour with the most formidable arms. The last of these causes united their courage, directed their arms, and gave their efforts that irresistible weight which even a small band of well-trained and intrepid volunteers has so often possessed over an undisciplined multitude, ignorant of the subject, and careless of the event of the war. In the various religions of Polytheism, some wandering fanatics of Egypt and Syria, who addressed themselves to the credulous superstition of the populace, were perhaps the only order of priests that derived their whole support and credit from their sacerdotal profession, and were very deeply affected by a personal concern for the safety or prosperity of their tutelar deities. The ministers of Polytheism, both in Rome and in the provinces, were, for the most part, men of a noble birth, and of an affluent fortune, who received, as an honourable distinction, the care of a celebrated temple, or of a public sacrifice, exhibited, very frequently at their own expense, the sacred games, and with cold indifference performed the ancient rites, according to the laws and fashion of their country. As they were engaged in the ordinary occupations of life, their zeal and devotion were seldom animated by a sense of interest, or by the habits of an ecclesiastical character. Confined to their respective temples and cities, they remained without any connexion of discipline or government; and, whilst they acknowledged the supreme jurisdiction of the senate, of the college of pontiffs, and of the emperor, those civil magistrates contented themselves with the easy task of maintaining, in peace and dignity, the general worship of mankind. We have already seen how various, how loose, and how uncertain were the religious sentiments of Polytheists. They were abandoned, almost without control, to the natural workings of a superstitious fancy. The accidental circumstances of their life and situation determined the object, as well as the degree, of their devotion; and, as long as their adoration was successively prostituted to a thousand deities, it was scarcely possible that their hearts could be susceptible of a very sincere or lively passion for any of them.

When Christianity appeared in the world, even these faint and imperfect impressions had lost much of their original power. Human reason, which, by its unassisted strength, is incapable of perceiving the mysteries of faith, had already obtained an easy triumph over the folly of Paganism; and, when Tertullian or Lactantius employ their labours in exposing its falsehood and extravagance, they are obliged to transcribe the eloquence of Cicero or the wit of Lucian. The contagion of these sceptical writings had been diffused far beyond the number of their readers. The fashion of incredulity was communicated from the philosopher to the man of pleasure or business, from the noble to the plebeian, and from the master to the menial slave who waited at his table, and who eagerly listened to the freedom of his conversation. On public occasions the philosophic part of mankind affected to treat with respect and decency the religious institutions of their country; but their secret contempt penetrated through the thin and awkward disguise; and even the people, when they discovered that their deities were rejected and derided by those whose rank or understanding they were accustomed to reverence, were filled with doubts and apprehensions concerning the truth of those doctrines to which they had yielded the most implicit belief. The decline of ancient prejudice exposed a very numerous portion of human kind to the danger of a painful and comfortless situation. A state of scepticism and suspense may amuse a few inquisitive minds. But the practice of superstition is so congenial to the multitude that, if they are forcibly awakened, they still regret the loss of their pleasing vision. Their love of the marvellous and supernatural, their curiosity with regard to future events, and their strong propensity to extend their hopes and fears beyond the limits of the visible world, were the principal causes which favoured the establishment of Polytheism. So urgent on the vulgar is the necessity of believing that the fall of any system of mythology will most probably be succeeded by the introduction of some other mode of superstition. Some deities of a more recent and fashionable cast might soon have occupied the deserted temples of Jupiter and Apollo, if, in the decisive moment, the wisdom of Providence had not interposed a genuine revelation, fitted to inspire the most rational esteem and conviction, whilst, at the same time, it was adorned with all that could attract the curiosity, the wonder, and the veneration of the people. In their actual disposition, as many were almost disengaged from their artificial prejudices, but equally susceptible and desirous of a devout attachment; an object much less deserving would have been sufficient to fill the vacant place in their hearts, and to gratify the uncertain eagerness of their passions. Those who are inclined to pursue this reflection, instead of viewing with astonishment the rapid progress of Christianity, will perhaps be surprised that its success was not still more rapid and still more universal.

It has been observed, with truth as well as propriety, that the conquests of Rome prepared and facilitated those of Christianity. In the second chapter of this work we have attempted to explain in what manner the most civilized provinces of Europe, Asia, and Africa were united under the dominion of one sovereign, and gradually connected by the most intimate ties of laws, of manners, and of language. The Jews of Palestine, who had fondly expected a temporal deliverer, gave so cold a reception to the miracles of the divine prophet that it was found unnecessary to publish, or at least to preserve, any Hebrew gospel. The authentic histories of the actions of Christ were composed in the Greek language, at a considerable distance from Jerusalem, and after the Gentile converts were grown extremely numerous. As soon as those histories were translated into the Latin tongue, they were perfectly intelligible to all the subjects of Rome, excepting only to the peasants of Syria and Egypt, for whose benefit particular versions were afterwards made. The public highways, which had been constructed for the use of the legions, opened an easy passage for the Christian missionaries from Damascus to Corinth, and from Italy to the extremity of Spain or Britain; nor did those spiritual conquerors encounter any of the obstacles which usually retard or prevent the introduction of a foreign religion into a distant country. There is the strongest reason to believe that before the reigns of Diocletian and Constantine, the faith of Christ had been preached in every province, and in all the great cities of the empire; but the foundation of the several congregations, the numbers of the faithful who composed them, and their proportion to the unbelieving multitude, are now buried in obscurity, or disguised by fiction and declamation. Such imperfect circumstances, however, as have reached our knowledge concerning the increase of the Christian name in Asia and Greece, in Egypt, in Italy, and in the West, we shall now proceed to relate, without neglecting the real or imaginary acquisitions which lay beyond the frontiers of the Roman empire.

The rich provinces that extend from the Euphrates to the Ionian sea were the principal theatre on which the apostle of the Gentiles displayed his zeal and piety. The seeds of the gospel, which he had scattered in a fertile soil, were diligently cultivated by his disciples; and it should seem that, during the two first centuries, the most considerable body of Christians was contained within those limits. Among the societies which were instituted in Syria, none were more ancient or more illustrious than those of Damascus, of Beroea or Aleppo, and of Antioch. The prophetic introduction of the Apocalypse has described and immortalized the seven churches of Asia: Ephesus, Smyrna, Pergamus, Thyatira, Sardes, Laodicea, and Philadelphia; and their colonies were soon diffused over that populous country. In a very early period, the islands of Cyprus and Crete, the provinces of Thrace and Macedonia, gave a favourable reception to the new religion; and Christian republics were soon founded in the cities of Corinth, of Sparta, and of Athens. The antiquity of the Greek and Asiatic churches allowed a sufficient space of time for their increase and multiplication, and even the swarms of Gnostics and other heretics serve to display the flourishing condition of the orthodox church, since the appellation of heretics has always been applied to the less numerous party. To these domestic testimonies we may add the confession, the complaints, and the apprehensions of the Gentiles themselves. From the writings of Lucian, a philosopher who had studied mankind, and who describes their manners in the most lively colours, we may learn that, under the reign of Commodus, his native country of Pontus was filled with Epicureans and *Christians*. Within fourscore years after the death of Christ, the humane Pliny laments the magnitude of the evil which he vainly attempted to eradicate. In his very curious epistle to the emperor Trajan, he affirms that the temples were almost deserted, that the sacred victims scarcely found any purchasers, and that the superstition had not only infected the cities, but had even spread itself into the villages and the open country of Pontus and Bithynia.

Without descending into a minute scrutiny of the expressions, or of the motives of those writers who either celebrate or lament the progress of Christianity in the East, it may in general be observed that none of them have left us any grounds from whence a just estimate might be formed of the real numbers of the faithful in those provinces. One circumstance, however, has been fortunately preserved, which seems to cast a more distinct light on this obscure but interesting subject. Under the reign of Theodosius, after Christianity had enjoyed, during more than sixty years, the sunshine of Imperial favour, the ancient and illustrious church of Antioch consisted of one hundred thousand persons, three thousand of whom were supported out of the public oblations. The splendour and dignity of the queen of the East, the acknowledged populousness of Caesarea, Seleucia, and Alexandria, and the destruction of two hundred and fifty thousand souls in the earthquake which afflicted Antioch under the elder Justin, are so many convincing proofs that the whole number of its inhabitants was not less than half a million, and that the Christians, however multiplied by zeal and power, did not exceed a fifth part of that great city. How different a proportion must we adopt when we compare the persecuted with the triumphant church, the West with the East, remote villages with populous towns, and countries recently converted to the faith with the place where the believers first received the appellation of Christians! It must not, however, be dissembled that, in another passage, Chrysostom, to whom we are indebted for this useful information, computes the multitude of the faithful as even superior to that of the Jews and Pagans. But the solution of this apparent difficulty is easy and obvious. The eloquent preacher draws a parallel between the civil and the ecclesiastical constitution of Antioch; between the list of Christians who had acquired Heaven by baptism and the list of citizens who had a right to share the public liberality. Slaves, strangers, and infants were comprised in the former; they were excluded from the latter.

The extensive commerce of Alexandria, and its proximity to Palestine, gave an easy entrance to the new religion. It was at first embraced by great numbers of the Therapeutae, or Essenians of the lake Mareotis, a Jewish sect which had abated much of its reverence for the Mosaic ceremonies. The austere life of the Essenians, their fasts and excommunications, the community of goods, the love of celibacy, their zeal for martyrdom, and the warmth though not the purity of their faith, already offered a very lively image of the primitive discipline. It was in the school of Alexandria that the Christian theology appears to have assumed a regular and scientifical form; and, when Hadrian visited Egypt, he found a church, composed of Jews and of Greeks, sufficiently important to attract the notice of that inquisitive prince. But the progress of Christianity was for a long time confined within the limits of a single city, which was itself a foreign colony, and, till the close of the second century, the predecessors of Demetrius were the only prelates of the Egyptian church. Three bishops were consecrated by the hands of Demetrius, and the number was increased to twenty by his successor Heraclas. The body of the natives, a people distinguished by a sullen inflexibility of temper, entertained the new doctrine with coldness and reluctance; and even in the time of Origen it was rare to meet with an Egyptian who had surmounted his early prejudices in favour of the sacred animals of his country. As soon, indeed, as Christianity ascended the throne, the zeal of those barbarians obeyed the prevailing impulsion; the cities of Egypt were filled with bishops, and the deserts of Thebais swarmed with hermits.

A perpetual stream of strangers and provincials flowed into the capacious bosom of Rome. Whatever was strange or odious, whoever was guilty or suspected, might hope, in the obscurity of that immense capital, to elude the vigilance of the law. In such a various conflux of nations, every teacher, either of truth or of falsehood, every founder, whether of a virtuous or a criminal association, might easily multiply his disciples or accomplices. The Christians of Rome, at the time of the accidental persecution of Nero, are represented by Tacitus as already amounting to a very great multitude, and the language of that great historian is almost similar to the style employed by Livy, when he relates the introduction and the suppression of the rites of Bacchus. After the Bacchanals had awakened the severity of the senate, it was likewise apprehended that a very great multitude, as it were *another people,* had been initiated into those abhorred mysteries. A more careful inquiry soon demonstrated that the offenders did not exceed seven thousand; a number, indeed, sufficiently alarming, when considered as the object of public justice. It is with the same candid allowance that we should interpret the vague expressions of Tacitus, and in a former instance of Pliny, when they exaggerated the crowds of deluded fanatics who had forsaken the established worship of the gods. The church of Rome was undoubtedly the first and most populous of the empire; and we are possessed of an authentic record which attests the state of religion in that city, about the middle of the third century, and after a peace of thirty-eight years. The clergy, at that time, consisted of a bishop, forty-six presbyters, seven deacons, as many sub-deacons, forty-two acolytes, and fifty readers, exorcists, and porters. The number of widows, of the infirm, and of the poor, who were maintained by the oblations of the faithful, amounted to fifteen hundred. From reason, as well as from the analogy of Antioch, we may venture to estimate the Christians of Rome at about fifty thousand. The populousness of that great capital cannot, perhaps, be exactly ascertained; but the most modest calculation will not surely reduce it lower than a million of inhabitants, of whom the Christians might constitute at the most a twentieth part.

The western provincials appeared to have derived the knowledge of Christianity from the same source which had diffused among them the language, the sentiments, and the manners of Rome. In this more important circumstance, Africa, as well as Gaul, was gradually fashioned to the imitation of the capital. Yet, notwithstanding the many favourable occasions which might invite the Roman missionaries to visit their Latin provinces, it was late before they passed either the sea or the Alps; nor can we discover in those great countries any assured traces either of faith or of persecution that ascend higher than the reign of the Antonines. The slow progress of the gospel in the cold climate of Gaul was extremely different from the eagerness with which it seems to have been received on the burning sands of Africa.

The African Christians soon formed one of the principal members of the primitive church. The practice introduced into that province of appointing bishops to the most inconsiderable towns, and very frequently to the most obscure villages, contributed to multiply the splendour and importance of their religious societies, which during the course of the third century were animated by the zeal of Tertullian, directed by the abilities of Cyprian, and adorned by the eloquence of Lactantius. But if, on the contrary, we turn our eyes towards Gaul, we must content ourselves with discovering, in the time of Marcus Antoninus, the feeble and united congregations of Lyons and Vienna; and, even as late as the reign of Decius, we are assured that in a few cities only, Arles, Narbonne, Toulouse, Limoges, Clermont, Tours, and Paris, some scattered churches were supported by the devotion of a small number of Christians. Silence is indeed very consistent with devotion, but, as it is seldom compatible with zeal, we may perceive and lament the languid state of Christianity in those provinces which had exchanged the Celtic for the Latin tongue; since they did not, during the three first centuries, give birth to a single ecclesiastical writer. From Gaul, which claimed a just preeminence of learning and authority over all the countries on this side of the Alps, the light of the gospel was more faintly reflected on the remote provinces of Spain and Britain; and, if we may credit the vehement assertions of Tertullian, they had already received the first rays of the faith when he addressed his apology to the magistrates of the emperor Severus. But the obscure and imperfect origin of the western churches of Europe has been so negligently recorded that, if we would relate the time and manner of their foundation, we must supply the silence of antiquity by those legends which avarice or superstition long afterwards dictated to the monks in the lazy gloom of their convents. Of these holy romances, that of the apostle St. James can alone, by its single extravagance, deserve to be mentioned. From a peaceful fisherman of the lake of Gennesareth, he was transformed into a valorous knight, who charged at the head of the Spanish chivalry in their battles against the Moors. The gravest historians have celebrated his exploits; the miraculous shrine of Compostella displayed his power; and the sword of a military order, assisted by the terrors of the Inquisition, was sufficient to remove every objection of profane criticism.

The progress of Christianity was not confined to the Roman empire; and, according to the primitive fathers, who interpret facts by prophecy, the new religion within a century after the death of its divine author, had already visited every part of the globe. "There exists not," says Justin Martyr, "a people, whether Greek or barbarian, or any other race of men, by whatsoever appellation or manners they may be distinguished, however ignorant of arts or agriculture, whether they dwell under tents, or wander about in covered waggons, among whom prayers are not offered up in the name of a crucified Jesus to the Father and Creator of all things." But this splendid exaggeration, which even at present it would be extremely difficult to reconcile with the real state of mankind, can be considered only as the rash sally of a devout but careless writer, the measure of whose belief was regulated by that of his wishes. But neither the belief nor the wishes of the fathers can alter the truth of history. It will still remain an undoubted fact, that the barbarians of Scythia and Germany who afterwards subverted the Roman monarchy were involved in the darkness of paganism; and that even the conversion of Iberia, of Armenia, or of Aethiopia, was not attempted with any degree of success till the sceptre was in the hands of an orthodox emperor. Before that time the various accidents of war and commerce might indeed diffuse an imperfect knowledge of the gospel among the tribes of Caledonia, and among the borderers of the Rhine, the Danube, and the Euphrates. Beyond the last-mentioned river, Edessa was distinguished by a firm and early adherence to the faith. From Edessa the principles of Christianity were easily introduced into the Greek and Syrian cities which obeyed the successors of Artaxerxes; but they do not appear to have made any deep impression on the minds of the Persians, whose religious system, by the labours of a well-disciplined order of priests, had been constructed with much more art and solidity than the uncertain mythology of Greece and Rome.

From this impartial, though imperfect, survey of the progress of Christianity, it may, perhaps, seem probable that the number of its proselytes has been excessively magnified by fear on the one side and by devotion on the other. According to the irreproachable testimony of Origen, the proportion of the faithful was very inconsiderable when compared with the multitude of an unbelieving world; but, as we are left without any distinct information, it is impossible to determine, and it is difficult even to conjecture, the real numbers of the primitive Christians. The most favourable calculation, however, that can be deduced from the examples of Antioch and of Rome will not permit us to imagine that more than a twentieth part of the subjects of the empire had enlisted themselves under the banner of the cross before the important conversion of Constantine. But their habits of faith, of zeal, and of union seemed to multiply their numbers; and the same causes which contributed to their future increase served to render their actual strength more apparent and more formidable.

Such is the constitution of civil society that, whilst a few persons are distinguished by riches, by honours, and by knowledge, the body of the people is condemned to obscurity, ignorance, and poverty. The Christian religion, which addressed itself to the whole human race, must consequently collect a far greater number of proselytes from the lower than from the superior ranks of life. This innocent and natural circumstance has been improved into a very odious imputation, which seems to be less strenuously denied by the apologists than it is urged by the adversaries of the faith; that the new sect of Christians was almost entirely composed of the dregs of the populace, of peasants and mechanics, of boys and women, of beggars and slaves; the last of whom might sometimes introduce the missionaries into the rich and noble families to which they belonged. These obscure teachers (such was the charge of malice and infidelity) are as mute in public as they are loquacious and dogmatical in private. Whilst they cautiously avoid the dangerous encounter of philosophers, they mingle with the rude and illiterate crowd, and insinuate themselves into those minds, whom their age, their sex, or their education has the best disposed to receive the impression of superstitious terrors.

This unfavourable picture, though not devoid of a faint resemblance, betrays, by its dark colouring and distorted features, the pencil of an enemy. As the humble faith of Christ diffused itself through the world, it was embraced by several persons who derived some consequence from the advantages of nature or fortune. Aristides, who presented an eloquent apology to the emperor Hadrian, was an Athenian philosopher. Justin Martyr had sought divine knowledge in the schools of Zeno, of Aristotle, of Pythagoras, and of Plato, before he fortunately was accosted by the old man, or rather the angel, who turned his attention to the study of the Jewish prophets. Clemens of Alexandria had acquired much various reading in the Greek, and Tertullian in the Latin, language. Julius Africanus and Origen possessed a very considerable share of the learning of their times; and, although the style of Cyprian is very different from that of Lactantius, we might almost discover that both those writers had been public teachers of rhetoric. Even the study of philosophy was at length introduced among the Christians, but it was not always productive of the most salutary effects; knowledge was as often the parent of heresy as of devotion, and the description which was designed for the followers of Artemon may, with equal propriety, be applied to the various sects that resisted the successors of the apostles. "They presume to alter the holy scriptures, to abandon the ancient rule of faith, and to form their opinions according to the subtile precepts of logic. The science of the church is neglected for the study of geometry, and they lose sight of Heaven while they are employed in measuring the earth. Euclid is perpetually in their hands. Aristotle and Theophrastus are the objects of their admiration; and they express an uncommon reverence for the works of Galen. Their errors are derived from the abuse of the arts and sciences of the infidels, and they corrupt the simplicity of the Gospel by the refinements of human reason."

Nor can it be affirmed with truth that the advantages of birth and fortune were always separated from the profession of Christianity. Several Roman citizens were brought before the tribunal of Pliny, and he soon discovered that a great number of persons of *every order* of men in Bithynia had deserted the religion of their ancestors. His unsuspected testimony may, in this instance, obtain more credit than the bold challenge of Tertullian, when he addresses himself to the fears as well as to the humanity of the proconsul of Africa, by assuring him that, if he persists in his cruel intentions, he must decimate Carthage, and that he will find among the guilty many persons of his own rank, senators and matrons of noblest extraction, and the friends or relations of his most intimate friends. It appears, however, that about forty years afterwards the emperor Valerian was persuaded of the truth of this assertion, since in one of his rescripts he evidently supposes that senators, Roman knights, and ladies of quality were engaged in the Christian sect. The church still continued to increase its outward splendour as it lost its internal purity; and in the reign of Diocletian the palace, the courts of justice, and even the army concealed a multitude of Christians who endeavoured to reconcile the interests of the present with those of a future life.

And yet these exceptions are either too few in number, or too recent in time, entirely to remove the imputation of ignorance and obscurity which has been so arrogantly cast on the first proselytes of Christianity. Instead of employing in our defence the fictions of later ages, it will be more prudent to convert the occasion of scandal into a subject of edification. Our serious thoughts will suggest to us that the apostles themselves were chosen by providence among the fishermen of Galilee, and that, the lower we depress the temporal condition of the first Christians, the more reason we shall find to admire their merit and success. It is incumbent on us diligently to remember that the kingdom of heaven was promised to the poor in spirit, and that minds afflicted by calamity and the contempt of mankind cheerfully listen to the divine promise of future happiness; while, on the contrary, the fortunate are satisfied with the possession of this world; and the wise abuse in doubt and dispute their vain superiority of reason and knowledge.

We stand in need of such reflections to comfort us for the loss of some illustrious characters, which in our eyes might have seemed the most worthy of the heavenly present. The names of Seneca, of the elder and the younger Pliny, of Tacitus, of Plutarch, of Galen, of the slave Epictetus, and of the emperor Marcus Antoninus, adorn the age in which they flourished, and exalt the dignity of human nature. They filled with glory their respective stations, either in active or contemplative life; their excellent understandings were improved by study; Philosophy had purified their minds from the prejudices of the popular superstition; and their days were spent in the pursuit of truth and the practice of virtue. Yet all these sages (it is no less an object of surprise than of concern) overlooked or rejected the perfection of the Christian system. Their language or their silence equally discover their contempt for the growing sect, which in their time had diffused itself over the Roman empire. Those among them who condescend to mention the Christians consider them only as obstinate and perverse enthusiasts, who exacted an implicit submission to their mysterious doctrines, without being able to produce a single argument that could engage the attention of men of sense and learning.

It is at least doubtful whether any of these philosophers perused the apologies which the primitive Christians repeatedly published in behalf of themselves and of their religion; but it is much to be lamented that such a cause was not defended by abler advocates. They expose with superfluous wit and eloquence the extravagance of Polytheism. They interest our compassion by displaying the innocence and sufferings of their injured brethren. But, when they would demonstrate the divine origin of Christianity, they insist much more strongly on the predictions which announced, than on the miracles which accompanied, the appearance of the Messiah. Their favourite argument might serve to edify a Christian or to convert a Jew, since both the one and the other acknowledge the authority of those prophecies, and both are obliged, with devout reverence, to search for their sense and their accomplishment. But this mode of persuasion loses much of its weight and influence, when it is addressed to those who neither understand nor respect the Mosaic dispensation and the prophetic style. In the unskilful hands of Justin and of the succeeding apologists, the sublime meaning of the Hebrew oracles evaporates in distant types, affected conceits, and cold allegories; and even their authenticity was rendered suspicious to an unenlightened Gentile by the mixture of pious forgeries, which, under the names of Orpheus, Hermes, and the Sibyls, were obtruded on him as of equal value with the genuine inspirations of Heaven. The adoption of fraud and sophistry in the defence of revelation too often reminds us of the injudicious conduct of those poets who load their *invulnerable* heroes with a useless weight of cumbersome and brittle armour.

But how shall we excuse the supine inattention of the Pagan and philosophic world to those evidences which were presented by the hand of Omnipotence, not to their reason, but to their senses? During the age of Christ, of his apostles, and of their first disciples, the doctrine which they preached was confirmed by innumerable prodigies. The lame walked, the blind saw, the sick were healed, the dead were raised, daemons were expelled, and the laws of Nature were frequently suspended for the benefit of the church. But the sages of Greece and Rome turned aside from the awful spectacle, and, pursuing the ordinary occupations of life and study, appeared unconscious of any alterations in the moral or physical government of the world. Under the reign of Tiberius, the whole earth, or at least a celebrated province of the Roman empire, was involved in a praeternatural darkness of three hours. Even this miraculous event, which ought to have excited the wonder, the curiosity, and the devotion of mankind, passed without notice in an age of science and history. It happened during the lifetime of Seneca and the elder Pliny, who must have experienced the immediate effects, or received the earliest intelligence, of the prodigy. Each of these philosophers, in a laborious work, has recorded all the great phenomena of Nature, earthquakes, meteors, comets, and eclipses, which his indefatigable curiosity could collect. Both the one and the other have omitted to mention the greatest phenomenon to which the mortal eye has been witness since the creation of the globe. A distinct chapter of Pliny is designed for eclipses of an extraordinary nature and unusual duration; but he contents himself with describing the singular defect of light which followed the murder of Caesar, when, during the greatest part of the year, the orb of the sun appeared pale and without splendour. This season of obscurity, which cannot surely be compared with the praeternatural darkness of the Passion, had been already celebrated by most of the poets and historians of that memorable age.

2 The Evidence of the Bible

One of the most attractive features of Christianity has always been the high standard of morality preached by its founder. Much of the moral message of Christianity is contained in the Sermon on the Mount.

FROM *The Gospel According to Matthew*

5 ¹SEEING THE CROWDS, he went up on the mountain, and when he sat down his disciples came to him. ² And he opened his mouth and taught them, saying:

³ "Blessed are the poor in spirit, for theirs is the kingdom of heaven.

⁴ "Blessed are those who mourn, for they shall be comforted.

⁵ "Blessed are the meek, for they shall inherit the earth.

⁶ "Blessed are those who hunger and thirst for righteousness, for they shall be satisfied.

⁷ "Blessed are the merciful, for they shall obtain mercy.

⁸ "Blessed are the pure in heart, for they shall see God.

⁹ "Blessed are the peacemakers, for they shall be called sons of God.

¹⁰ "Blessed are those who are persecuted for righteousness' sake, for theirs is the kingdom of heaven.

¹¹ "Blessed are you when men revile you and persecute you and utter all kinds of evil against you falsely on my account. ¹² Rejoice and be glad, for your reward is great in heaven, for so men persecuted the prophets who were before you.

¹³ "You are the salt of the earth; but if salt has lost its taste, how shall its saltness be restored? It is no longer good for anything except to be thrown out and trodden under foot by men.

¹⁴ "You are the light of the world. A city set on a hill cannot be hid. ¹⁵ Nor do men light a lamp and put it under a bushel, but on a stand, and it gives light to all in the house. ¹⁶ Let your light so shine before men, that they may see your good works and give glory to your Father who is in heaven.

¹⁷ "Think not that I have come to abolish the law and the prophets; I

have come not to abolish them but to fulfil them. ¹⁸ For truly, I say to you, till heaven and earth pass away, not an iota, not a dot, will pass from the law until all is accomplished. ¹⁹ Whoever then relaxes one of the least of these commandments and teaches men so, shall be called least in the kingdom of heaven; but he who does them and teaches them shall be called great in the kingdom of heaven. ²⁰ For I tell you, unless your righteousness exceeds that of the scribes and Pharisees, you will never enter the kingdom of heaven.

²¹ "You have heard that it was said to the men of old, 'You shall not kill; and whoever kills shall be liable to judgment.' ²² But I say to you that every one who is angry with his brother shall be liable to judgment; whoever insults his brother shall be liable to the council, and whoever says, 'You fool!' shall be liable to the hell of fire.²³ So if you are offering your gift at the altar, and there remember that your brother has something against you, ²⁴ leave your gift there before the altar and go; first be reconciled to your brother, and then come and offer your gift. ²⁵ Make friends quickly with your accuser, while you are going with him to court, lest your accuser hand you over to the judge, and the judge to the guard, and you be put in prison; ²⁶ truly, I say to you, you will never get out till you have paid the last penny.

²⁷ "You have heard that it was said, 'You shall not commit adultery.' ²⁸ But I say to you that every one who looks at a woman lustfully has already committed adultery with her in his heart. ²⁹ If your right eye causes you to sin, pluck it out and throw it away; it is better that you lose one of your members than that your whole body be thrown into hell. ³⁰ And if your right hand causes you to sin, cut it off and throw it away; it is better that you lose one of your members than that your whole body go into hell.

³¹ "It was also said, 'Whoever divorces his wife, let him give her a certificate of divorce.' ³² But I say to you that every one who divorces his wife, except on the ground of unchastity, makes her an adultress; and whoever marries a divorced woman commits adultery.

³³ "Again you have heard that it was said to the men of old, 'You shall not swear falsely, but shall perform to the Lord what you have sworn.' ³⁴ But I say to you, Do not swear at all, either by heaven, for it is the throne of God, ³⁵ or by the earth for it is his footstool, or by Jerusalem, for it is the city of the great King. ³⁶ And do not swear by your head, for you cannot make one hair white or black. ³⁷ Let what you say be simply 'Yes' or 'No'; anything more than this comes from evil.

³⁸ "You have heard that it was said, 'An eye for an eye and a tooth for a tooth.' ³⁹ But I say to you, Do not resist one who is evil. But if any one strikes you on the right cheek, turn to him the other also; ⁴⁰ and if any one would sue you and take your coat, let him have your cloak as well; ⁴¹ and if any one forces you to go one mile, go with him two miles. ⁴² Give to him who begs from you, and do not refuse him who would borrow from you.

⁴³ "You have heard that it was said, You shall love your neighbor and hate your enemy.' ⁴⁴ But I say to you, Love your enemies and pray for those

who persecute you, ⁴⁵ so that you may be sons of your Father who is in heaven; for he makes his sun rise on the evil and on the good, and sends rain on the just and on the unjust. ⁴⁶ For if you love those who love you, what reward have you? Do not even the tax collectors do the same? ⁴⁷ And if you salute only your brethren, what more are you doing than others? Do not even the Gentiles do the same? ⁴⁸ You, therefore, must be perfect, as your heavenly Father is perfect.

6 ¹ "Beware of practicing your piety before men in order to be seen by them; for then you will have no reward from your Father who is in heaven.

² "Thus, when you give alms, sound no trumpet before you, as the hypocrites do in the synagogues and in the streets, that they may be praised by men. Truly, I say to you, they have their reward. ³ But when you give alms, do not let your left hand know what your right hand is doing, ⁴ so that your alms may be in secret; and your Father who sees in secret will reward you.

⁵ "And when you pray, you must not be like the hypocrites; for they love to stand and pray in the synagogues and at the street corners, that they may be seen by men. Truly, I say to you, they have their reward. ⁶ But when you pray, go into your room and shut the door and pray to your Father who is in secret; and your Father who sees in secret will reward you.

⁷ "And in praying do not heap up empty phrases as the Gentiles do; for they think that they will be heard for their many words. ⁸ Do not be like them, for your Father knows what you need before you ask him. ⁹ Pray then like this:

> Our Father who art in heaven,
> Hallowed be thy name.
> ¹⁰ Thy kingdom come,
> Thy will be done,
> On earth as it is in heaven.
> ¹¹ Give us this day our daily bread;
> ¹² And forgive us our debts,
> As we also have forgiven our debtors;
> ¹³ And lead us not into temptation,
> But deliver us from evil.

¹⁴ For if you forgive men their trespasses, your heavenly Father also will forgive you; ¹⁵ but if you do not forgive men their trespasses, neither will your Father forgive your trespasses.

¹⁶ "And when you fast, do not look dismal, like the hypocrites, for they disfigure their faces that their fasting may be seen by men. Truly, I say to you, they have their reward. ¹⁷ But when you fast, anoint your head and wash your face, ¹⁸ that your fasting may not be seen by men but by your Father who is in secret; and your Father who sees in secret will reward you.

¹⁹ "Do not lay up for yourselves treasures on earth, where moth and rust

consume and where thieves break in and steal, [20] but lay up for yourselves treasures in heaven, where neither moth nor rust consumes and where thieves do not break in and steal. [21] For where your treasure is, there will your heart be also.

[22] "The eye is the lamp of the body. So, if your eye is sound, your whole body will be full of light; [23] but if your eye is not sound, your whole body will be full of darkness. If then the light in you is darkness, how great is the darkness!

[24] "No one can serve two masters; for either he will hate the one and love the other, or he will be devoted to the one and despise the other. You cannot serve God and mammon.

[25] "Therefore I tell you, do not be anxious about your life, what you shall eat or what you shall drink, nor about your body, what you shall put on. Is not life more than food, and the body more than clothing? [26] Look at the birds of the air; they neither sow nor reap nor gather into barns, and yet your heavenly Father feeds them. Are you not of more value than they? [27] And which of you by being anxious can add one cubit to his span of life? [28] And why are you anxious about clothing? Consider the lilies of the field, how they grow; they neither toil nor spin; [29] yet I tell you, even Solomon in all his glory was not arrayed like one of these. [30] But if God so clothes the grass of the field, which today is alive and tomorrow is thrown into the oven, will he not much more clothe you, O men of little faith? [31] Therefore do not be anxious, saying, 'What shall we eat?' or 'What shall we drink?' or 'What shall we wear?' [32] For the Gentiles seek all these things; and your heavenly Father knows that you need them all. [33] But seek first his kingdom and his righteousness, and all these things shall be yours as well.

[34] "Therefore do not be anxious about tomorrow, for tomorrow will be anxious for itself. Let the day's own trouble be sufficient for the day.

7 [1] "Judge not, that you be not judged. [2] For with the judgment you pronounce you will be judged, and the measure you give will be the measure you get. [3] Why do you see the speck that is in your brother's eye, but do not notice the log that is in your own eye? [4] Or how can you say to your brother, 'Let me take the speck out of your eye,' when there is the log in your own eye? [5] You hypocrite, first take the log out of your own eye, and then you will see clearly to take the speck out of your brother's eye.

[6] "Do not give dogs what is holy; and do not throw your pearls before swine; lest they trample them underfoot and turn to attack you.

[7] "Ask, and it will be given you; seek, and you will find; knock, and it will be opened to you. [8] For every one who asks receives, and he who seeks finds, and to him who knocks it will be opened. [9] Or what man of you, if his son asks him for a loaf, will give him a stone? [10] Or if he asks for a fish, will give him a serpent? [11] If you then, who are evil, know how to give good gifts to your children, how much more will your Father who is in heaven give good things to those who ask him? [12] So whatever you wish that men would do to you, do so to them; for this is the law and the prophets.

[13] "Enter by the narrow gate; for the gate is wide and the way is easy, that leads to destruction, and those who enter by it are many. [14] For the gate is narrow and the way is hard, that leads to life, and those who find it are few.

[15] "Beware of false prophets, who come to you in sheep's clothing but inwardly are ravenous wolves. [16] You will know them by their fruits. Are grapes gathered from thorns, or figs from thistles? [17] So, every sound tree bears good fruit, but the bad tree bears evil fruit. [18] A sound tree cannot bear evil fruit, nor can a bad tree bear good fruit. [19] Every tree that does not bear good fruit is cut down and thrown into the fire. [20] Thus you will know them by their fruits.

[21] "Not every one who says to me, 'Lord, Lord,' shall enter the kingdom of heaven, but he who does the will of my Father who is in heaven. [22] On that day many will say to me, 'Lord, Lord, did we not prophesy in your name, and cast out demons in your name, and do many mighty works in your name?' [23] and then will I declare to them, 'I never knew you; depart from me, you evildoers.'

[24] "Every one then who hears these words of mine and does them will be like a wise man who built his house upon the rock; [25] and the rain fell, and the floods came, and the winds blew and beat upon that house, but it did not fall, because it had been founded on the rock. [26] And every one who hears these words of mine and does not do them will be like a foolish man who built his house upon the sand; [27] and the rain fell, and the floods came, and the winds blew and beat against that house, and it fell; and great was the fall of it."

[28] And when Jesus finished these sayings, the crowds were astonished at his teaching, [29] for he taught them as one who had authority, and not as their scribes.

The tradition of miracles performed by Jesus and his disciples played a powerful part in attracting heathens to the Christian faith. The story of Lazarus is a striking example of the miraculous tradition.

FROM *The Gospel According to John*

11 [1] NOW A CERTAIN MAN was ill, Laz'arus of Bethany, the village of Mary and her sister Martha. [2] It was Mary who anointed the Lord with ointment and wiped his feet with her hair, whose brother Laz'arus was

---

John 11: 1–44, Revised Standard Version Bible, copyright 1946, 1952.

ill. [3] So the sisters sent to him, saying, "Lord, he whom you love is ill." [4] But when Jesus heard it he said, "This illness is not unto death; it is for the glory of God, so that the Son of God may be glorified by means of it."

[5] Now Jesus loved Martha and her sister and Laz'arus. [6] So when he heard that he was ill, he stayed two days longer in the place where he was. [7] Then after this he said to the disciples, "Let us go into Judea again." [8] The disciples said to him, "Rabbi, the Jews were but now seeking to stone you, and are you going there again?" [9] Jesus answered, "Are there not twelve hours in the day? If any one walks in the day, he does not stumble, because he sees the light of this world. [10] But if any one walks in the night, he stumbles, because the light is not in him." [11] Thus he spoke, and then he said to them, "Our friend Laz'arus has fallen asleep, but I go to awake him out of sleep." [12] The disciples said to him, "Lord, if he has fallen asleep, he will recover." [13] Now Jesus had spoken of his death, but they thought that he meant taking rest in sleep. [14] Then Jesus told them plainly, "Laz'arus is dead; [15] and for your sake I am glad that I was not there, so that you may believe. But let us go to him." [16] Thomas, called the Twin, said to his fellow disciples, "Let us also go, that we may die with him."

[17] Now when Jesus came, he found that Laz'arus had already been in the tomb four days. [18] Bethany was near Jerusalem, about two miles off, [19] and many of the Jews had come to Martha and Mary to console them concerning their brother. [20] When Martha heard that Jesus was coming, she went and met him, while Mary sat in the house. [21] Martha said to Jesus, "Lord, if you had been here, my brother would not have died. [22] And even now I know that whatever you ask from God, God will give you." [23] Jesus said to her, "Your brother will rise again." [24] Martha said to him, "I know that he will rise again in the resurrection at the last day." [25] Jesus said to her, "I am the resurrection and the life; he who believes in me, though he die, yet shall he live, [26] and whoever lives and believes in me shall never die. Do you believe this?" [27] She said to him, "Yes, Lord; I believe that you are the Christ, the Son of God, he who is coming into the world."

[28] When she had said this, she went and called her sister Mary, saying quietly, "The Teacher is here and is calling for you." [29] And when she heard it, she rose quickly and went to him. [30] Now Jesus had not yet come to the village, but was still in the place where Martha had met him. [31] When the Jews who were with her in the house, consoling her, saw Mary rise quickly and go out, they followed her, supposing that she was going to the tomb to weep there. [32] Then Mary, when she came where Jesus was and saw him, fell at his feet, saying to him, "Lord, if you had been here, my brother would not have died." [33] When Jesus saw her weeping, and the Jews who came with her also weeping, he was deeply moved in spirit and troubled; [34] and he said, "Where have you laid him?" They said to him, "Lord, come and see." [35] Jesus wept. [36] So the Jews said, "See how he loved him!" [37] But some of them said, "Could not he who opened the eyes of the blind man have kept this man from dying?"

 ³⁸ Then Jesus, deeply moved again, came to the tomb; it was a cave, and a stone lay upon it. ³⁹ Jesus said, "Take away the stone." Martha, the sister of the dead man, said to him, "Lord, by this time there will be an odor, for he has been dead four days." ⁴⁰ Jesus said to her, "Did I not tell you that if you would believe you would see the glory of God?" ⁴¹ So they took away the stone. And Jesus lifted up his eyes and said, "Father, I thank thee that thou hast heard me. ⁴² I knew that thou hearest me always, but I have said this on account of the people standing by, that they may believe that thou didst send me." ⁴³ When he had said this, he cried with a loud voice, "Laz'arus, come out." ⁴⁴ The dead man came out, his hands and feet bound with bandages, and his face wrapped with a cloth. Jesus said to them, "Unbind him, and let him go."

> *At the center of Christianity is the Resurrection of Jesus. The story of the crucifixion and resurrection is movingly told in the Book of John.*

FROM *The Gospel According to John*

²⁸ THEN THEY LED JESUS from the house of Ca'iaphas to the praetorium. It was early. They themselves did not enter the praetorium, so that they might not be defiled, but might eat the passover. ²⁹ So Pilate went out to them and said, "What accusation do you bring against this man?" ³⁰ They answered him, "If this man were not an evildoer, we would not have handed him over." ³¹ Pilate said to them, "Take him yourselves and judge him by your own law." The Jews said to him, "It is not lawful for us to put any man to death." ³² This was to fulfill the word which Jesus had spoken to show by what death he was to die.

 ³³ Pilate entered the praetorium again and called Jesus, and said to him, "Are you the King of the Jews?" ³⁴ Jesus answered, "Do you say this of your own accord, or did others say it to you about me?" ³⁵ Pilate answered, "Am I a Jew? Your own nation and the chief priests have handed you over to me; what have you done?" ³⁶ Jesus answered, "My kingship is not of this world; if my kingship were of this world, my servants would fight, that I might not be handed over to the Jews; but my kingship is not from the world." ³⁷ Pilate said to him, "So you are a king?" Jesus answered, "You say that I am a king. For this I was born, and for this I have come into the world, to bear witness to the truth. Every one who is of the truth hears my voice." ³⁸ Pilate said to him, "What is truth?"

John 18:28–21:25, Revised Standard Version Bible, copyright 1946, 1952.

After he had said this, he went out to the Jews again, and told them, "I find no crime in him. [39] But you have a custom that I should release one man for you at the Passover; will you have me release for you the King of the Jews?" [40] They cried out again, "Not this man, but Barab'bas!" Now Barab'bas was a robber.

19 [1] Then Pilate took Jesus and scourged him. [2] And the soldiers plaited a crown of thorns, and put it on his head, and arrayed him in a purple robe; [3] they came up to him, saying, "Hail, King of the Jews!" and struck him with their hands. [4] Pilate went out again, and said to them, "Behold, I am bringing him out to you, that you may know that I find no crime in him." [5] So Jesus came out, wearing the crown of thorns and the purple robe. Pilate said to them, "Here is the man!" [6] When the chief priests and the officers saw him, they cried out, "Crucify him, crucify him!" Pilate said to them, "Take him yourselves and crucify him, for I find no crime in him." [7] The Jews answered him, "We have a law, and by that law he ought to die, because he has made himself the Son of God." [8] When Pilate heard these words, he was the more afraid; [9] he entered the practorium again and said to Jesus, "Where are you from?" But Jesus gave no answer. [10] Pilate therefore said to him, "You will not speak to me? Do you not know that I have power to release you, and power to crucify you?" [11] Jesus answered him, "You would have no power over me unless it had been given you from above; therefore he who delivered me to you has the greater sin." [12] Upon this Pilate sought to release him, but the Jews cried out, "If you release this man, you are not Caesar's friend; every one who makes himself a king sets himself against Caesar." [13] When Pilate heard these words, he brought Jesus out and sat down on the judgment seat at a place called The Pavement, and in Hebrew, Gab'batha. [14] Now it was the day of Preparation for the Passover; it was about the sixth hour. He said to the Jews, "Here is your King!" [15] They cried out, "Away with him, away with him, crucify him!" Pilate said to them, "Shall I crucify your King?" The chief priests answered, "We have no king but Caesar." [16] Then he handed him over to them to be crucified.

[17] So they took Jesus, and he went out, bearing his own cross, to the place called the place of a skull, which is called in Hebrew Gol'gotha. [18] There they crucified him, and with him two others, one on either side, and Jesus between them. [19] Pilate also wrote a title and put it on the cross; it read, "Jesus of Nazareth, the King of the Jews." [20] Many of the Jews read this title, for the place where Jesus was crucified was near the city; and it was written in Hebrew, in Latin, and in Greek. [21] The chief priests of the Jews then said to Pilate, do not write, 'The King of the Jews,' but, 'This man said, I am King of the Jews.'" [22] Pilate answered, "What I have written I have written."

[23] When the soldiers had crucified Jesus they took his garments and made four parts, one for each soldier. But his tunic was without seam, woven

from top to bottom; [24] so they said to one another, "Let us not tear it, but cast lots for it to see whose it shall be." This was to fulfil the scripture.

> They parted my garments among them,
> and for my clothing they cast lots.

[25] So the soldiers did this; but standing by the cross of Jesus were his mother, and his mother's sister, Mary the wife of Clopas, and Mary Mag'dalene. [26] When Jesus saw his mother, and the disciple whom he loved standing near, he said to his mother, "Woman, behold your son!" [27] Then he said to the disciple, "Behold your mother!" And from that hour the disciple took her to his own home.

[28] After this Jesus, knowing that all was now finished, said (to fulfil the scripture), "I thirst." [29] A bowl full of vinegar stood there; so they put a sponge full of the vinegar on hyssop and held it to his mouth. [30] When Jesus had received the vinegar, he said, "It is finished"; and he bowed his head and gave up his spirit.

[31] Since it was the day of Preparation, in order to prevent the bodies from remaining on the cross on the sabbath (for that sabbath was a high day), the Jews asked Pilate that their legs might be broken, and that they might be taken away. [32] So the soldiers came and broke the legs of the first, and of the other who had been crucified with him; [33] but when they came to Jesus and saw that he was already dead, they did not break his legs. [34] But one of the soldiers pierced his side with a spear, and at once there came out blood and water. [35] He who saw it has borne witness—his testimony is true, and he knows that he tells the truth—that you also may believe. [36] For these things took place that the scripture might be fulfilled, "Not a bone of him shall be broken." [37] And again another scripture says, "They shall look on him whom they have pierced."

[38] After this Joseph of Arimathe'a, who was a disciple of Jesus, but secretly, for fear of the Jews, asked Pilate that he might take away the body of Jesus, and Pilate gave him leave. So he came and took away his body. [39] Nicode'mus also, who had at first come to him by night, came bringing a mixture of myrrh and aloes, about a hundred pounds' weight. [40] They took the body of Jesus, and bound it in linen cloths with the spices, as is the burial custom of the Jews. [41] Now in the place where he was crucified there was a garden, and in the garden a new tomb where no one had ever been laid. [42] So because of the Jewish day of Preparation, as the tomb was close at hand, they laid Jesus there.

20 [1] Now on the first day of the week Mary Mag'dalene came to the tomb early, while it was still dark, and saw that the stone had been taken away from the tomb. [2] So she ran, and went to Simon Peter and the other disciple, the one whom Jesus loved, and said to them, "They have taken the Lord out of the tomb, and we do not know where they have laid him." [3] Peter then came out with the other disciple, and they went toward the tomb. [4] They both

ran, but the other disciple outran Peter and reached the tomb first; [5] and stooping to look in, he saw the linen cloths lying there, but he did not go in. [6] Then Simon Peter came, following him, and he went into the tomb; he saw the linen cloths lying, [7] and the napkin, which had been on his head, not lying with the linen cloths but rolled up in a place by itself. [8] Then the other disciple, who reached the tomb first, also went in, and he saw and believed; [9] for as yet they did not know the scripture, that he must rise from the dead. [10] Then the disciples went back to their homes.

[11] But Mary stood weeping outside the tomb, and as she wept she stooped to look into the tomb; [12] and she saw two angels in white, sitting where the body of Jesus had lain, one at the head and one at the feet. [13] They said to her, "Woman, why are you weeping?" She said to them, "Because they have taken away my Lord, and I do not know where they have laid him." [14] Saying this, she turned round and saw Jesus standing, but she did not know that it was Jesus. [15] Jesus said to her, "Woman, why are you weeping? Whom do you seek?" Supposing him to be the gardener, she said to him, "Sir, if you have carried him away, tell me where you have laid him, and I will take him away." [16] Jesus said to her, "Mary." She turned and said to him in Hebrew, "Rab-bo'ni!" (which means Teacher). [17] Jesus said to her, "Do not hold me, for I have not yet ascended to the Father; but go to my brethren and say to them, I am ascending to my Father and your Father, to my God and your God." [18] Mary Mag'dalene went and said to the disciples, "I have seen the Lord"; and she told them that he had said these things to her.

[19] On the evening of that day, the first day of the week, the doors being shut where the disciples were, for fear of the Jews, Jesus came and stood among them and said to them, "Peace be with you." [20] When he had said this, he showed them his hands and his side. Then the disciples were glad when they saw the Lord. [21] Jesus said to them again, "Peace be with you. As the Father has sent me, even so I send you." [22] And when he had said this, he breathed on them, and said to them, "Receive the Holy Spirit. [23] If you forgive the sins of any, they are forgiven; if you retain the sins of any, they are retained."

[24] Now Thomas, one of the twelve, called the Twin, was not with them when Jesus came. [25] So the other disciples told him, "We have seen the Lord." But he said to them, "Unless I see in his hands the print of the nails, and place my finger in the mark of the nails, and place my hand in his side, I will not believe."

[26] Eight days later, his disciples were again in the house, and Thomas was with them. The doors were shut, but Jesus came and stood among them, and said, "Peace be with you." [27] Then he said to Thomas, "Put your finger here, and see my hands; and put out your hand, and place it in my side; do not be faithless, but believing." [28] Thomas answered him, "My Lord and my God!" [29] Jesus said to him "Have you believed because you have seen me? Blessed are those who have not seen and yet believe."

[30] Now Jesus did many other signs in the presence of the disciples, which are not written in this book; [31] but these are written that you may believe that Jesus is the Christ, the Son of God, and that believing you may have life in his name.

21 [1] After this Jesus revealed himself again to the disciples by the Sea of Tibe'ri-as; and he revealed himself in this way. [2] Simon Peter, Thomas called the Twin, Nathan'a-el of Cana in Galilee, the sons of Zeb'edee, and two others of his disciples were together. [3] Simon Peter said to them, "I am going fishing." They said to him, "We will go with you." They went out and got into the boat; but that night they caught nothing.

[4] Just as day was breaking, Jesus stood on the beach; yet the disciples did not know that it was Jesus. [5] Jesus said to them, "Children, have you any fish?" They answered him, "No." [6] He said to them, "Cast the net on the right side of the boat, and you will find some." So they cast it, and now they were not able to haul it in, for the quantity of fish. [7] That disciple whom Jesus loved said to Peter, "It is the Lord!" When Simon Peter heard that it was the Lord, he put on his clothes, for he was stripped for work, and sprang into the sea. [8] But the other disciples came in the boat, dragging the net full of fish, for they were not far from the land, but about a hundred yards off.

[9] When they got out on land, they saw a charcoal fire there, with fish lying on it, and bread. [10] Jesus said to them, "Bring some of the fish that you have just caught." [11] So Simon Peter went aboard and hauled the net ashore, full of large fish, a hundred and fifty-three of them; and although there were so many, the net was not torn. [12] Jesus said to them, "Come and have breakfast." Now none of the disciples dared to ask him, "Who are you?" They knew it was the Lord. [13] Jesus came and took the bread and gave it to them, and so with the fish. [14] This was now the third time that Jesus was revealed to the disciples after he was raised from the dead.

[15] When they had finished breakfast, Jesus said to Simon Peter, "Simon, son of John, do you love me more than these?" He said to him, "Yes, Lord; you know that I love you." He said to him, "Feed my lambs." [16] A second time he said to him, "Simon, son of John, do you love me?" He said to him, "Yes, Lord; you know that I love you." He said to him, "Tend my sheep." [17] He said to him the third time, "Simon, son of John, do you love me?" Peter was grieved because he said to him the third time, "Do you love me?" And he said to him, "Lord, you know everything; you know that I love you." Jesus said to him, "Feed my sheep. [18] Truly, truly, I say to you, when you were young, you girded yourself and walked where you would; but when you are old, you will stretch out your hands, and another will gird you and carry you where you do not wish to go." [19] (This he said to show by what death he was to glorify God.) And after this he said to him, "Follow me."

[20] Peter turned and saw following them the disciple whom Jesus loved, who had lain close to his breast at the supper and had said, "Lord, who is it

that is going to betray you?" [21] When Peter saw him, he said to Jesus, "Lord, what about this man?" [22] Jesus said to him, "If it is my will that he remain until I come, what is that to you? Follow me!" [23] The saying spread abroad among the brethren that this disciple was not to die; yet Jesus did not say to him that he was not to die, but, "If it is my will that he remain until I come, what is that to you?"

[24] This is the disciple who is bearing witness to these things, and who has written these things; and we know that his testimony is true.

[25] But there are also many other things which Jesus did; were every one of them to be written, I suppose that the world itself could not contain the books that would be written.

3　The Spread of Christianity
and the Roman Response

*In the first century after Christ the religion of the cross
spread rapidly throughout the Roman Empire, especially in
the eastern provinces. Pliny the Younger was an intimate
of the Emperor Trajan (A.D. 98–117) and governor of the
province of Bithynia in Asia Minor. His letter to the
emperor and Trajan's answer give us evidence of the attitude of Rome toward the new religion at the end of the
first century.*

FROM *Pliny's Letters*

EP.96. It is my custom, my lord, to refer to you all questions about which
I have doubts. Who, indeed, can better direct me in hesitation, or enlighten
me in ignorance? In the examination of Christians I have never taken part;
therefore I do not know what crime is usually punished or investigated or to
what extent. So I have no little uncertainty whether there is any distinction
of age, or whether the weaker offenders fare in no respect otherwise than the
stronger; whether pardon is granted on repentance, or whether when one
has been a Christian there is no gain to him in that he has ceased to be such;
whether the mere name, if it is without crimes, or crimes connected with the
name are punished. Meanwhile I have taken this course with those who were
accused before me as Christians: I have asked them whether they were
Christians. Those who confessed I asked a second and a third time, threatening punishment. Those who persisted I ordered led away to execution. For I
did not doubt that, whatever it was they admitted, obstinacy and unbending
perversity certainly deserve to be punished. There were others of the like
insanity, but because they were Roman citizens I noted them down to be sent
to Rome. Soon after this, as it often happens, because the matter was taken

Reprinted with the permission of Charles Scribner's Sons from *A Source Book for Ancient
Church History*, pp. 20–2, by Joseph Cullen Ayer. Copyright 1913 Charles Scribner's Sons;
renewal copyright 1941 Joseph Cullen Ayer, Jr.

notice of, the crime became wide-spread and many cases arose. An unsigned paper was presented containing the names of many. But these denied that they were or had been Christians, and I thought it right to let them go, since at my dictation they prayed to the gods and made supplication with incense and wine to your statue, which I had ordered to be brought into the court for the purpose, together with the images of the gods, and in addition to this they cursed Christ, none of which things, it is said, those who are really Christians can be made to do. Others who were named by an informer said that they were Christians, and soon afterward denied it, saying, indeed, that they had been, but had ceased to be Christians, some three years ago, some many years, and one even twenty years ago. All these also not only worshipped your statue and the images of the gods, but also cursed Christ. They asserted, however, that the amount of their fault or error was this: that they had been accustomed to assemble on a fixed day before daylight and sing by turns [i. e., antiphonally] a hymn to Christ as a god; and that they bound themselves with an oath, not for any crime, but to commit neither theft, nor robbery, nor adultery, not to break their word and not to deny a deposit when demanded; after these things were done, it was their custom to depart and meet together again to take food, but ordinary and harmless food; and they said that even this had ceased after my edict was issued, by which, according to your commands, I had forbidden the existence of clubs. On this account I believed it the more necessary to find out from two maid-servants, who were called deaconesses [ministrae], and that by torture, what was the truth. I found nothing else than a perverse and excessive superstition. I therefore adjourned the examination and hastened to consult you. The matter seemed to me to be worth deliberation, especially on account of the number of those in danger. For many of every age, every rank, and even of both sexes, are brought into danger; and will be in the future. The contagion of that superstition has penetrated not only the cities but also the villages and country places; and yet it seems possible to stop it and set it right. At any rate, it is certain enough that the temples, deserted until quite recently, begin to be frequented, that the ceremonies of religion, long disused, are restored, and that fodder for the victims comes to market, whereas buyers of it were until now very few. From this it may easily be supposed what a multitude of men can be reclaimed if there be a place of repentance.

EP. 97 (*Trajan to Pliny*). You have followed, my dear Secundus, the proper course of procedure in examining the cases of those who were accused to you as Christians. For, indeed, nothing can be laid down as a general law which contains anything like a definite rule of action. They are not to be sought out. If they are accused and convicted, they are to be punished, yet on this condition, that he who denies that he is a Christian and makes the fact evident by an act, that is, by worshipping our gods, shall obtain pardon on his repentance, however much suspected as to the past. Papers, however, which are presented anonymously ought not to be admitted in any accusation. For they are a very bad example and unworthy of our times.

Not all the emperors were as humane as Trajan, and there were several persecutions of various degrees of severity. It is not too much to say that the persecutions were ultimately helpful to the Christian cause, for they were too sporadic and inefficient to destroy the sect yet enabled the Christians to win sympathy for their faith and courage.

FROM *Acts of the Scillitan Martyrs*

WHEN PRAESENS, for the second time, and Claudianus were the consuls, on the seventeenth day of July, at Carthage, there were set in the judgment-hall Speratus, Nartzalus, Cittinus, Donata, Secunda and Vestia.

Saturninus the proconsul said: Ye can win the indulgence of our lord the Emperor, if ye return to a sound mind.

Speratus said: We have never done ill, we have not lent ourselves to wrong, we have never spoken ill, but when ill-treated we have given thanks; because we pay heed to OUR EMPEROR.

Saturninus the proconsul said: We too are religious, and our religion is simple, and we swear by the genius of our lord the Emperor, and pray for his welfare, as ye also ought to do.

Speratus said: If thou wilt peaceably lend me thine ears, I can tell thee the mystery of simplicity.

Saturninus said: I will not lend mine ears to thee, when thou beginnest to speak evil things of our sacred rites; but rather swear thou by the genius of our lord the Emperor

Speratus said: The empire of this world I know not; but rather I serve that God, *whom no man hath seen, nor* with these eyes *can see.* I have committed no theft; but if I have bought anything I pay the tax; because I know my Lord, the King of kings and Emperor of all nations.

Saturninus the proconsul said to the rest: Cease to be of this persuasion.

Speratus said: It is an ill persuasion to do murder, to speak false witness.

Saturninus the proconsul said: Be not partakers of this folly.

Cittinus said: We have none other to fear, save only our Lord God, who is in heaven.

Donata said: Honour to Caesar as Caesar: but fear to God.

Vestia said: I am a Christian.

Secunda said: What I am, that I wish to be.

"Acts of the Scillitan Martyrs" in *Selections from Early Writers Illustrative of Church History to the Time of Constantine* (1961), pp. 79–83, translated by H. M. Gwatkin. Reprinted by permission of James Clarke & Co. Ltd., London.

Saturninus the proconsul said to Speratus: Dost thou persist in being a Christian?

Speratus said: I am a Christian. And with him they all agreed.

Saturninus the proconsul said: Will ye have a space to consider?

Speratus said: In a matter so straightforward there is no considering.

Saturninus the proconsul said: What are the things in your chest?

Speratus said: Books and epistles of Paul, a just man.

Saturninus the proconsul said: Have a delay of thirty days and bethink yourselves.

Speratus said a second time: I am a Christian. And with him they all agreed.

Saturninus the proconsul read out the decree from the tablet: Speratus, Nartzalus, Cittinus, Donata, Vestia, Secunda and the rest having confessed that they live according to the Christian rite, since after opportunity offered them of returning to the custom of the Romans they have obstinately persisted, it is determined that they be put to the sword.

Speratus said: We give thanks to God.

Nartzalus said: To-day we are martyrs in heaven; thanks be to God.

Saturninus the proconsul ordered it to be declared by the herald: Speratus, Nartzalus, Cittinus, Veturius, Felix, Aquilinus, Lactantius, Januaria, Generosa, Vestia, Donata and Secunda, I have ordered to be executed.

They all said: Thanks be to God.

And so they all together were crowned with martyrdom; and they reign with the Father and the Son and the Holy Ghost, for ever and ever. Amen.

In 313 Constantine and Licinius, joint emperors, granted toleration to the Christians. The following document is not the actual edict, but a letter to a prefect referring to the edict.

FROM *De Mortibus Persecutorum* BY LACTANTIUS

WHEN I, CONSTANTINE AUGUSTUS, and I, Licinius Augustus, had happily met together at Milan, and were having under consideration all things which concern the advantage and security of the State, we thought that, among other things which seemed likely to profit men generally, we ought, in the very first place, to set in order the conditions of the reverence paid to the Divinity by giving to the Christians and all others full permission to follow whatever worship any man had chosen; whereby whatever divinity there is in heaven may be benevolent and propitious to us, and to all placed under our authority. Therefore we thought we ought, with sound counsel and very right reason, to lay down this law, that we should in no way refuse to any man any legal right who had given up his mind either to the observance of Christianity or to that worship which he personally feels best suited to himself; to the end that the Supreme Divinity, whose worship we freely follow, may continue in all things to grant us his accustomed favor and good-will. Wherefore your devotion should know that it is our pleasure that all provisions whatsoever which have appeared in documents hitherto directed to your office regarding Christians and which appeared utterly improper and opposed to our clemency should be abolished, and that every one of those men who have the same wish to observe Christian worship may now freely and unconditionally endeavor to observe the same without any annoyance or molestation. These things we thought it well to signify in the fullest manner to your carefulness, that you might know that we have given free and absolute permission to the said Christians to practise their worship. And when you perceive that we have granted this to the said Christians, your devotion understands that to others also a similarly full and free permission for their own worship and observance is granted, for the quiet of our times, so that every man may have freedom in the practice of whatever worship he has chosen. And these things were done by us that nothing be taken away from any honor or form of worship. Moreover, in regard to the Christians, we have thought fit to ordain this also, that if any appear to have bought, either from our exchequer or from others, the places in which they were accustomed formerly to assemble, and concerning which definite orders have been given before now, and that by letters sent to your office, the same be restored to the Christians, setting aside all delay and dispute, without payment or demand of price. Those also who have obtained them by gift shall restore them in like manner without delay to the said Christians; and those, moreover, who have bought them, as well as those who have obtained them by gift, if they request anything of our benevolence, they shall apply to the deputy that order may be taken for them too by our clemency. All these must be delivered over at once and without delay by your intervention to the corporation of the Christians. And since the same Christians are known to have possessed not only the places where they are accustomed to assemble, but also others belonging to their corporation, namely, to the churches and not to individuals, all these by the law which we have described above you will order to be restored without any doubtfulness or dispute to the said Christians—that is, to their said corporations and assemblies; provided always, as aforesaid, that those who restore them without price, as we said, shall expect a compensation from our benevolence. In all these things you must give the aforesaid Christians your most effective intervention, that our command may be fulfilled as soon as may be, and that in this matter also order may be taken by our clemency for the public quiet. And may it be, as already said, that the divine favor which we have already experienced in so many affairs, shall continue for all time to give us prosperity and successes, together with happiness for the State. But that it may be possible for the nature of this decree and of our benevolence to come to the knowledge of all men, it will be your duty by a proclamation of your own to publish everywhere and bring to the notice of all men this present document when it reaches you, that the decree of this our benevolence may not be hidden.

Whatever weight one gives the several reasons for the success of Christianity, there is no denying the important role of the church and its organization. The following selections illustrate the nature of the organization and the place it had in early Christian thought.

FROM *A Source Book for Ancient Church History*
BY J. C. AYER

No subject in Church history has been more hotly discussed than the organization of the primitive Christian Church. Each of several Christian confessions have attempted to justify a polity which it regarded as *de fide* by appeal to the organization of the Church of the primitive ages. Since it has been seen that the admission of the principle of development does not invalidate claims for divine warrant for a polity, the acrimonious debate has been somewhat stilled. There seems to have been in the Church several forms of organization, and to some extent the various contentions of conflicting creeds and polities have been therein justified. The ultimately universal form, episcopacy, may in some parts of the Church be traced to the end of the apostolic age, but it seems not to have been universally diffused at that time. Since Christian communities sprang up without official propaganda, at least in many instances, and were due to the work of independent Christian believers moving about in the Empire, this variety of organization was what might have been expected, especially as the significance of the organization was first felt chiefly in connection with the danger from heresy. That various external influences affected the development is also highly probable.

CLEMENT OF ROME,

EP. AD CORINTHIOS, I, 42, 44.

CH. 42. The Apostles have preached the Gospel to us from the Lord Jesus Christ; Jesus Christ was sent forth from God. Christ, therefore, was from God, and the Apostles from Christ. Both these appointments, then, came about in an orderly way, by the will of God. Having, therefore, received their orders, and being fully assured by the resurrection of our Lord Jesus Christ, and established in the word of God, with full assurance of the Holy Ghost, they went forth proclaiming that the kingdom of God was at hand. And thus preaching through countries and cities, they appointed their first-fruits, having proved them by the Spirit, to be bishops and deacons of those who should afterward believe. Nor was this a new thing; for, indeed, many ages before it was written concerning bishops and deacons. For thus saith the Scripture in a certain place: "I will appoint their bishops in righteousness, and their deacons in faith."

CH. 44. Our Apostles also knew, through our Lord Jesus Christ, that there would be strife on account of the office of the episcopate. For this cause, therefore, inasmuch as they had obtained a perfect foreknowledge of this, they appointed those already mentioned, and afterward gave instructions that when these should fall asleep other approved men should succeed them in their ministry. We are of the opinion, therefore, that those appointed by them, or afterward by other eminent men, with the consent of the whole Church, and who have blamelessly served the flock of Christ in lowliness of mind, peaceably, and with all modesty, and for a long time have borne a good report with all—these men we consider to be unjustly thrust out of their ministrations. For it will be no light sin for us, if we thrust out those who have offered the gifts of the bishop's office blamelessly and holily. Blessed are those presbyters who have gone before seeing their departure was fruitful and ripe; for they have no fear lest any one should remove them from their appointed place. For we see that ye have displaced certain persons, though they were living honorably, from the ministration which had been honored by them blamelessly.

DIDACHE, 7–15.

The *Didache* is a very early manual of the instruction for Christian converts. It consists of two quite distinct parts, viz., a brief account of the moral law (chapters 1–6), which appears to be based upon a Jewish original to which the name of *The Two Ways* has been given, and a somewhat longer account of the various rites of the Church and the regulations governing its organization. Its date is in the first half of the second century and belongs more probably to the first quarter than to the second. It is a document of first-class importance, especially in the part bearing on the organization of the Church, which is here given. The extensive literature on the subject may be found in Krüger, *op. cit.,* § 21.

CH. 7. But concerning baptism, thus shall ye baptize. Having first recited all these things, baptize in the name of the Father and of the Son and of the Holy Spirit in living [i. e., running] water. But if thou hast not living water, then baptize in any other water; and if thou art not able in cold, in warm. But if thou hast neither, pour water upon the head thrice in the name of the Father and of the Son and of the Holy Spirit. But before baptism let him that baptizeth and him that is baptized fast, and any others also who are able; and thou shalt order him that is baptized to fast a day or two before. CH. 8. And let not your fastings be with the hypocrites. For they fast on the second and the fifth days of the week; but do ye keep your fast on the fourth and on the preparation [i. e., the sixth day]. Neither pray ye as the hypocrites, but as the Lord commanded in His Gospel, thus pray ye: Our Father who art in heaven, hallowed be Thy name; Thy kingdom come; Thy will be done, as in heaven, so also on earth; give us this day our daily bread; and forgive us our debt, as we also forgive our debtors; and lead us not into temptation, but deliver us from the Evil One; for Thine is the power and the glory forever. Three times in the day pray ye so. CH. 9. But as regards the eucharist [thanksgiving], give ye thanks thus. First, as regards the cup: We give Thee thanks, O our Father, for the holy vine of David, Thy Son, which Thou madest known unto us through Jesus, Thy Son; Thine is the glory forever. Then as regards the breaking [i. e., of the bread]: We give thanks to Thee, O our Father, for the life and knowledge which thou madest known unto us through Jesus, Thy Son; Thine is the glory forever. As this broken bread was scattered upon the mountains and being gathered together became one, so may Thy Church be gathered together from the ends of the earth into Thy kingdom; for Thine is the glory and the power through Jesus Christ for ever and ever. But let no one eat or drink of this eucharist [thanksgiving] but they that have been baptized into the name of the Lord; for concerning this also the Lord hath said: Give not that which is holy unto the dogs. CH. 10. After ye are satisfied give thanks thus: We give Thee thanks, Holy Father, for Thy holy name, which Thou hast made to tabernacle in our hearts, and for the knowledge and faith and immortality, which Thou hast made known unto us through Thy Son Jesus; Thine is the glory forever. Thou, Almighty Master, created all things for Thy name's sake, and gave food and drink unto men for enjoyment, that they might render thanks to Thee; but bestowed upon us spiritual food and drink and eternal life through Thy Son. Before all things we give Thee thanks that Thou art powerful; Thine is the glory forever. Remember, Lord, Thy Church to deliver us from all evil and to perfect it in Thy love; and gather it together from the four winds—even the Church which has been sanctified—into Thy kingdom which Thou hast prepared for it; for Thine is the power and the glory forever. May grace come and may this world pass away. Hosanna to the God of David. If any one is holy, let him come; if any one is not, let him repent. Maran Atha. Amen. But permit the prophets to offer thanksgiving as much as they will.

CH. 11. Whosoever, therefore, shall come and teach you all these things that have been said receive him; but if the teacher himself be perverted and teach a different doctrine to the destruction thereof, hear him not; but if to the increase of righteousness and knowledge of the Lord, receive him as the Lord.

But concerning the apostles and prophets, so do ye according to the ordinance of the Gospel: Let every apostle coming to you be received as the Lord; but he shall not abide more than a single day, or if there be need, a second likewise; but if he abide three days, he is a false prophet. And when he departs, let not the apostle receive anything save bread until he find shelter; but it he ask money, he is a false prophet. And any prophet speaking in the Spirit ye shall not try, neither discern; for every sin shall be forgiven, but this sin shall not be forgiven. Yet not every one that speaketh in the Spirit is a prophet, but only if he have the ways of the Lord. From his ways, therefore, the false prophet and the [true] prophet shall be recognized. And no prophet when he ordereth a table in the Spirit shall eat of it; otherwise he is a false prophet. And every prophet teaching the truth, if he doeth not what he teacheth, is a false prophet. And every prophet approved and found true, working unto a worldly mystery of the Church, and yet teacheth not to do what he himself doeth, shall not be judged before you; he hath his judgment in the presence of God; for in like manner also did the ancient prophets. And whosoever shall say in the Spirit, Give me silver or anything else, do not listen to him; but if he say to give on behalf of others who are in want, let no one judge him.

CH. 12. But let every one coming in the name of the Lord be received; and when ye have tested him ye shall know him, for ye shall have understanding on the right hand and on the left. If the comer is a traveller, assist him as ye are able; but let him not stay with you but for two or three days, if it be necessary. But if he wishes to settle with you, being a craftsman, let him work and eat. But if he has no craft, according to your wisdom provide how without idleness he shall live as a Christian among you. If he will not do this, he is trafficking upon Christ. Beware of such men.

CH. 13. But every true prophet desiring to settle among you is worthy of his food. In like manner, a true teacher is also worthy, like the workman, of his food. Every first-fruit, then, of the produce of the wine-vat and of the threshing-floor, of thy oxen and of thy sheep, thou shalt take and give as the first-fruit to the prophets; for they are your chief priests. But if ye have not a prophet, give them to the poor. If thou makest bread, take the first-fruit and give according to the commandment. In like manner, when thou openest a jar of wine or oil, take the first-fruit and give to the prophets; yea, and of money and raiment and every possession take the first-fruit, as shall seem good to thee, and give according to the commandment.

c h . 1 4 . And on the Lord's day gather yourselves together and break bread and give thanks, first confessing your transgressions, that your sacrifice may be pure. And let no man having a dispute with his fellow join your assembly until they have been reconciled, that your sacrifice may not be defiled; for this is the sacrifice spoken of by the Lord: In very place and at every time offer me a pure sacrifice; for I am a great king, saith the Lord, and my name is wonderful among the nations. [Mal. 1:11, 14.]

c h . 1 5 . Appoint [i.e., lay hands on], therefore, for yourselves bishops and deacons worthy of the Lord, men meek, not lovers of money, truthful, and approved; for they also render you the service of prophets and teachers Despise them not, therefore, for they are your honored ones together with the prophets and teachers.

IGNATIUS, *EP. AD TRALLIANOS*, 2, 3.

c h . 2 . For since ye are subject to the bishop as Jesus Christ, ye appear to me to live not after the manner of men, but according to Jesus Christ, who died for us, in order that by believing in His death ye may escape death. It is therefore necessary that just as ye indeed do, so without the bishop ye should do nothing, but should also be subject to the presbytery, as to the Apostles of Jesus Christ, our Hope, living in whom we shall be found [i. e., at the last]. It is right, also, that the deacons, being [ministers] of the mysteries of Jesus Christ, should in every respect be well-pleasing to all. For they are not the ministers of meats and drinks, but servants of the Church of God. It is necessary, therefore, that they guard themselves from all grounds of accusation as they would from fire.

c h . 3 . In like manner, let all reverence the deacons as Jesus Christ, as also the bishop, who is a type of the Father, and the presbyters as the sanhedrim of God and the assembly of the Apostles. Apart from these there is no Church.

IGNATIUS, *EP. AD SMYRNAEOS*, 8.

See that ye follow the bishop as Jesus Christ does the Father, and the presbyters as ye would the Apostles; and reverence the deacons as a commandment of God. Without the bishop let no one do any of those things connected with the Church. Let that be deemed a proper eucharist which is administered either by the bishop or by him to whom he has intrusted it. Wherever the bishop shall appear there let also the multitude be, even as wherever Jesus Christ is there is the Catholic Church. It is not lawful without the bishop either to baptize or to make an agape. But whatsoever he shall approve that is also pleasing to God, so that everything that is done may be secure and valid.

4 The Victory of Christianity— Modern Views

K. S. Latourette places great importance on the uniqueness of Jesus' message in contributing to the success of Christianity.

FROM *A History of the Expansion of Christianity*
BY K. S. LATOURETTE

WHY IS IT that Christianity won? Why, among all the many cults and philosophics which competed in the Graeco-Roman world and in spite of more severe opposition than was encountered by any other, did this faith outstrip them all? What reasons account for the fact that, in the course of three centuries, a religion which began as an obscure Jewish sect with no influential backing in high places, developed an organization second only in extent to that of the Empire, forced the state to come to terms with it, and within another two centuries became the one official religion, held the nominal allegiance of the vast majority of the population of the Mediterranean basin, and then outlived the Empire which had sought to uproot it? The question has often been asked and many answers have been given. Closely allied with it are three other problems. Why, of the several Jewish sects, was Christianity the only one which proved successful in achieving a permanent place outside the parent stock? Why did that parent stock, of all the religious groups in the Roman Empire, prove the most resistant to the new faith and why was it never absorbed by it? Why did Christianity make headway first in the cities and in the elements touched by Hellenistic Judaism and Hellenism?

To these questions no single reply will suffice. A number of factors contributed to the result. One, as we shall suggest, was determinative. Without it the others would have been insufficient. Yet it may be that without the others that main factor would have proved unequal to bringing

Kenneth Scott Latourette, *A History of the Expansion of Christianity*, I, 162–9. Copyright 1937 by Harper & Brothers. Reprinted by permission of Harper & Row, Publishers.

about the eventual triumph of Christianity. The answer is not simple, but complex.

One factor has been suggested—the endorsement of Constantine. Had that Emperor been less able or had his reign been brief, his support might not have led to such consequences. It was no minor cause of the part that Christianity was later to play in the world that the Church obtained the active endorsement of the head of the most powerful state of the time and that the particular monarch who initiated the policy stood out as among the ablest of the imperial succession and enjoyed a sufficiently long tenure of office to place the Church firmly in its new position. Had he been a weaker man or had he died soon after he granted toleration, the inevitable reaction might have embarrassed the Church much more than it did. As we have suggested, however, the Church was growing so rapidly before Constantine and the persecutions had so clearly failed of their purpose that he seems merely to have hastened an already probable consummation. To account for this victory of Christianity one must go back of Constantine and seek for the causes of growth before his day and of the attraction of the faith for him.

Another factor, and one which we have mentioned more than once, appears to have been the disintegration of society. From at least the time of Alexander the Mediterranean world had been in a state of flux. The passing of the old was hastened by the wars which culminated in the founding of the Roman Empire and was further accelerated by the Empire itself. The construction of a universal state could not but dissolve the barriers which divided people from people. In the consequent intermingling of individuals and ideas old cultures, with their religions, were weakened. In the great cities especially were thousands of deracinated individuals, some of them slaves, some freedmen, and some merchants, who had been separated by force or voluntarily from their hereditary milieu. Often insecure, subject to oppression from the powerful, presumably many of them welcomed the fellowship afforded by the strong Christian organization and the security which the faith promised for the life to come. It is notable that Christianity had its first strongholds in the large cities, where these conditions were particularly prominent. The disintegration of existing cultures had become especially marked in the hundred and thirty years between Marcus Aurelius and Constantine. The disasters of these decades had weakened the established order, had made it less able to resist the inroads of a new faith, and had started many men on a quest for the sort of security which an authoritative religion seemed to offer. Had Christianity been born in a vigorous young culture whose adherents were confident of its virtues, it might have met a different fate. Then, too, at first the government was relatively indifferent and did not exert itself to support the state religion against this rival. Later, when it became alarmed and took drastic measures, it proved too weak to crush the Church. In Persia, as we shall see in later chapters, Christianity confronted a state religion actively sustained by the crown and never became the faith of more than a minority. Yet it must be remembered that Christianity was only one of many competing cults in the decaying Roman Empire. Some of these, notably Neoplatonism, had the endorsement of a much larger proportion of the upper classes than did the eventual victor. Why was it that of all these rivals Christianity gained the day?

A third cause of Christianity's victory was the organization which it developed. No one of its rivals possessed so powerful and coherent a structure as did the Church. No other gave to adherents quite the same feeling of coming into a closely knit community. To be sure, that organization was far from perfect. Never, unless possibly in the first generation after Jesus, and probably not even then, had all who called themselves Christians been embraced within a single visible fellowship. Long before Constantine, sectarian differences developed and leaders of rival Christian bodies engaged in reciprocal recrimination. Yet for a combination of inclusiveness, strength against attack, and flexibility, the Christian Churches were without parallel among the religious bodies in the Graeco-Roman world. In this respect the nearest approach to them was Judaism. It was probably in part to this fact that the parent faith owed its survival. However, it did not equal its victorious scion. The Church proved able to instil in its members a loyalty and a feeling of solidarity which proved inestimable assets in the struggle for existence. Yet what was the source of this organization and of its strength?

A fourth reason for Christianity's success is to be found in its inclusiveness. More than any of its competitors it attracted all races and classes. Even in the days of its most active proselyting activities Judaism never quite escaped from its racial bonds, and after the second century infrequently overpassed them. It usually remained an encysted minority. Christianity, however, gloried in its appeal to Jew and Gentile, Greek and barbarian. The philosophies never really won the allegiance of the masses. In spite of attempts at popularization they appealed primarily to the educated. It was one of the charges against Christianity, however, that it drew the lowly and unlettered multitude. The essence of its teachings was so simple that all could understand, and in its story of the life, death, and resurrection of Jesus it could be comprehended by even the ignorant. Yet Christianity also developed a philosophy which commanded the respect of many of the learned. In this respect it was more successful than the mystery cults, although some of the latter were fortified by elaborate intellectual systems. To the educated Christianity could offer what the rival philosophies could not. Thus Augustine said that in Neoplatonism he found philosophical concepts which he also discovered in Christianity, but that in that last great rival of the conquering faith he missed the incarnation and the humility of Christ. Christianity, too, was for both sexes, whereas at least two of its main rivals were primarily for men. The Church welcomed both rich and poor. In contrast with it, the mysteries were usually for people of means: initiation into them was expensive. No other cult, therefore, took in so many groups and strata of society. Here, too, the query must be raised of why this comprehensiveness came to be. It was not in Judaism. Why did it appear in Christianity?

A fifth source of strength was in the fact that Christianity was both intransigent and flexible. In its refusal to compromise with the current paganism and with many of the social customs and moral practices of the times it developed a coherence and an organization which set it over against society. The very break required to join it gave to its adherents a conviction which constituted a source of strength against persecution and of zeal in winning converts. Here it was not unlike its parent faith, Judaism. Yet Christianity proved able to adjust itself to many current intellectual beliefs and to popular practices as Judaism did not—or at least as the Rabbinic Judaism which ultimately became the dominant form of the older faith failed to do. It must also be recalled that Christianity, while adaptable, was not primarily a syncretic product. On what it deemed its essential and central doctrines the main body of the Church refused to compromise. Again one must seek to go behind the superficial reason and to ask the cause. Why this combination of intolerance and adaptability?

A sixth factor of which much is made is that Christianity supplied what the Graeco-Roman world was asking of religion and philosophy, and did it better than any of its competitors. As we have seen, the ancient world, and especially those portions of it in which Hellenistic influence was strong, believed in the distinction between matter and spirit. The former it regarded as evil and the latter as good. For it salvation meant the emancipation of the soul from the thraldom of matter and immortality through union with God. This was the object of the mysteries, of gnosticism, and of Neoplatonism. That salvation Christianity supplied. It had in the cross and the resurrection a dramatization of redemption which resembled the myths around which the mysteries were built. The Christians were convinced that they were heirs of a joyous immortality and in this assurance lay no small part of their appeal. Christianity had, too, the advantage of a connexion with Judaism and in the Jewish Scriptures could trace for itself what the time craved—the authority of a long tradition and the support of ancient sacred books. For the many who despaired of reason as a road to salvation it could offer a divine revelation in these Scriptures and in Jesus. For those who still wished the undergirding of reason, it provided a theology which claimed to have all that the best philosophies possessed. Some of the teachers led their pupils to Christianity by the way of philosophy. Among the apologists were those who claimed that the Greek philosophers derived many of their ideas from the Hebrew Scriptures. It will be recalled that it was in the Hellenistic world that Christianity achieved its first major successes. Again, however, it must be asked: How did it happen that Christianity could offer a way of salvation which made so powerful an appeal?

As has been suggested, its Jewish origin assisted Christianity in its growth. The Hebrew Scriptures supplied the sanctity of a long development and the authority of antiquity. Then, too, in Hellenistic Judaism Christianity found communities prepared for its message. Hellenistic Judaism, as we have seen, was an adaptation of the ancient Hebrew belief to the Greek intellectual and spiritual environment. It had translated the Hebrew Scriptures into Greek. The synagogues of the Dispersion had attracted many Gentiles. Through these synagogues and their constituencies Christianity made most of its first adventures into the Gentile world. It drew to itself some of the Jewish and many of the Gentile adherents of Hellenistic Judaism. The Jews whom it did not win reacted from the direction in which Gentile Christianity was moving. Retiring within Rabbinic Judaism, they no longer reached out into the Hellenistic world. Christianity, therefore, was left the sole heir of Hellenistic Judaism. Again the question recurs, Why? What gave Christianity the qualities which enabled it to win those to whom Hellenistic Judaism had appealed?

Still another reason for the triumph of the faith was the miracles attributed to it. Christianity was by no means the only cult which could claim the endorsement of the miraculous, but people looked to it to do for them what they expected of other religions and were not disappointed. To the Graeco-Roman world the existence of demons was almost as axiomatic as molecules, atoms, electrons, and germs have been to those reared in the science of the twentieth century. Christians claimed the power to expel evil spirits and could cite many instances of their success. The physical cures wrought by Christianity were among its claims for consideration. As we have seen, it was apparently because Constantine believed that the Christian God had aided him in achieving the mastery of the Empire and so had demonstrated his ability to do what was required by pagans of their divinities but to do it better, that he gave him his allegiance. Again the question arises as to whence came the confidence and the energy which gave rise to achievements which were regarded as manifestations of superhuman power.

In its moral qualities lay another of the reasons for Christianity's success. It was not merely that high ethical standards were held up before an age in which many were seeking moral improvement. Numbers of Christians found as well the power to forsake evil and to approximate to those standards. The experience of thoroughgoing moral and spiritual renewal was probably shared by only a minority of Christians. Enough of them had it, however to give a tone to the Christian community. Part of the morality of Christians showed itself in the care for the unfortunate members of the community. The poor, the widows, the orphans, and the sick were the charge of the Church. As time passed thousands of underprivileged persons were supported by their fellow believers. It is important, too, to remind ourselves again that the Church did not seek retaliation against its persecutors. In the Christian writings of the period is little or nothing of bitterness or of desire for revenge against those who were hounding the faithful. In the fate of some of the persecutors Christian writers believed they saw divine retribution, but so far as we are aware no imprecatory prayers were offered against them. Once more the source of this moral and spiritual dynamic must be sought if the reason for the triumph of Christianity is to be discovered.

The more one examines into the various factors which seem to account for the extraordinary victory of Christianity the more one is driven to search for a cause which underlies them. It is clear that at the very beginning of Christianity there must have occurred a vast release of energy, unequalled in the history of the race. Without it the future course of the faith is inexplicable. That burst of energy was ascribed by the early disciples to the founder of their faith. Something happened to the men who associated with Jesus. In his contact with them, in his crucifixion and in their assurance of his resurrection and of the continued living presence with his disciples of his spirit, is to be found the major cause of the success of Christianity. That experience and that assurance were transmitted to succeeding generations. Why this occurred may lie outside the realms in which historians are supposed to move. One reason is probably to be found in the continued study of the earliest written records of Christianity and in the effort to preserve intact the belief and the experience of the circle of apostles who had been the intimates of Jesus. Whatever the cause, that the stream flowed on is clear. It is the uniqueness of Jesus which seems the one tenable explanation of the fact that Christianity is the only one of the many Jewish sects to break off from the parent stem and outstrip it in size and influence. In the impulse which came from Jesus is the primary reason for that growth and that strength which attracted Constantine, for that vitality which enabled Christianity, in the keen competition among religions, to emerge the victor, and for the vision of a fellowship of disciples which led to its organization. Here, too, is the main source of Christianity's inclusiveness. Members of both sexes and of all races, the learned and the ignorant, so Christians held, might share in the salvation made possible by Christ. This new life might express itself in many different cultural forms: hence the flexibility of Christianity. On certain matters of morals and of worship and belief, however, Christians were convinced they must not compromise: hence the intransigence of the Church. For those accustomed to the mysteries Christianity could offer in Jesus the sufferings and triumph of a Saviour-God. One appeal to those influenced by Hellenistic Judaism was the claim that the prophecies of the Jewish Scriptures pointed to Christ and had their fulfilment in him. The use of the name of Christ and faith in him were held to account for the miracles. With those touched by Christ began, too, that moral strength, that enthusiasm, and that overflowing charity which had so much to do with the success of the faith. In Jesus, therefore, and in his death and the conviction of his resurrection and of moral and spiritual rebirth and immortality through him, is to be found the chief reason for the triumph of Christianity. Without Jesus Christianity would not have sprung into existence, and from him and beliefs about him came its main dynamic.

With the question of the possible cosmic significance of Jesus we are not here concerned. Inevitably to the thoughtful mind that question obtrudes itself. It is apart from our purpose, however, to enter upon the discussion—which, it may be noted, began during his lifetime and has been in progress ever since. Simply as a plain matter of history, however, the vitality of the movement which we call Christianity, when traced back to its source, has its origin primarily in the impulse which came from Jesus.

It must be immediately added that Jesus and the beliefs about him, central though they are among the causes for the remarkable growth of Christianity in the Roman Empire, are not alone sufficient to account for it. In the course of our story we shall see the faith planted again and again by representatives as convinced and as zealous as were those who spread it in the Graeco-Roman world. Yet repeatedly they have met with failure or with meagre success. Christianity has been continuously in China for a longer time than elapsed between the crucifixion and Constantine, propagated by devoted missionaries. Yet as against the probable tenth of the population of the Roman Empire who called themselves Christian at the accession of Constantine, scarcely one out of a hundred Chinese would now so denominate himself. In India, where a Christian community has been present for at least fourteen or fifteen centuries and in which missionaries from the Occident have been active for over four centuries, scarcely two out of a hundred confess to being Christian. In vast sections of Asia and Africa, Christianity, once vigorous, has died out. It requires more than the dynamic which came from Jesus, powerful though that has been, and embodied though it may be in earnest and devoted missionaries, to win and hold any large proportion of a people to Christianity. More even is demanded than the organization, the combination of compromise and unyielding adherence to principle, the active charity, and the moral and spiritual qualities which played so large a part in the triumph of the Church in the Mediterranean world. It was to the entire combination of factors which we have attempted to enumerate that the phenomenal outcome must be ascribed. We must conclude as we began by saying that the causes of the victory of Christianity were many, but that of one it can be said that without it the others would either not have existed or would have availed nothing.

> *Dawson emphasizes the importance of the organization of the Christian Church.*

FROM *The Making of Europe* BY CHRISTOPHER DAWSON

THE INFLUENCE OF CHRISTIANITY on the formation of the European unity is a striking example of the way in which the course of historical

From *The Making of Europe* by Christopher Dawson, pp. 42–9, published by Sheed & Ward Inc., New York. Reprinted by permission of The Society of Authors, London.

development is modified and determined by the intervention of new spiritual influences. History is not to be explained as a closed order in which each stage is the inevitable and logical result of that which has gone before. There is in it always a mysterious and inexplicable element, due not only to the influence of chance or the initiative of the individual genius, but also to the creative power of spiritual forces.

Thus in the case of the ancient world we can see that the artificial material civilisation of the Roman Empire stood in need of some religious inspiration of a more profound kind than was contained in the official cults of the city-state; and we might have guessed that this spiritual deficiency would lead to an infiltration of oriental religious influences, such as actually occurred during the imperial age. But no one could have foretold the actual appearance of Christianity and the way in which it would transform the life and thought of ancient civilisation.

The religion which was destined to conquer the Roman Empire and to become permanently identified with the life of the West was indeed of purely oriental origin and had no roots in the European past or in the traditions of classical civilisation. But its orientalism was not that of the cosmopolitan world of religious syncretism in which Greek philosophy mingled with the cults and traditions of the ancient East, but that of a unique and highly individual national tradition which held itself jealously aloof from the religious influences of its oriental environment, no less than from all contact with the dominant Western culture.

The Jews were the one people of the Empire who had remained obstinately faithful to their national traditions in spite of the attractions of the Hellenistic culture, which the other peoples of the Levant accepted even more eagerly than their descendants have received the civilisation of modern Europe. Although Christianity by its very nature broke with the exclusive nationalism of Judaism and assumed a universal mission, it also claimed the succession of Israel and based its appeal not on the common principles of Hellenistic thought, but on the purely Hebraic tradition represented by the Law and the Prophets. The primitive Church regarded itself as the second Israel, the heir of the Kingdom which was promised to the People of God; and consequently it preserved the ideal of spiritual segregation and the spirit of irreconcilable opposition to the Gentile world that had inspired the whole Jewish tradition.

It was this sense of historic continuity and social solidarity which distinguished the Christian Church from the mystery religions and the other oriental cults of the period, and made it from the first the only real rival and alternative to the official religious unity of the Empire. It is true that it did not attempt to combat or to replace the Roman Empire as a political organism. It was a supernatural society, the polity of the world to come, and it recognised the rights and claims of the state in the present order. But, on the other hand, it could not accept the ideals of the Hellenistic culture or cooperate in the social life of the Empire. The idea of citizenship, which was the fundamental idea of the classical culture, was transferred by Christianity to the spiritual order. In the existing social order Christians were *peregrini*— strangers and foreigners—their true citizenship was in the Kingdom of God, and even in the present world their most vital social relationship was found in their membership of the Church, not in that of the city or the Empire.

Thus the Church was, if not a state within the state, at least an ultimate and autonomous society. It had its own organisation and hierarchy, its system of government and law, and its rules of membership and initiation. It appealed to all those who failed to find satisfaction in the existing order, the poor and the oppressed, the unprivileged classes, above all those who revolted against the spiritual emptiness and corruption of the dominant material culture, and who felt the need of a new spiritual order and a religious view of life. And so it became the focus of the forces of disaffection and opposition to the dominant culture in a far more fundamental sense than any movement of political or economic discontent. It was a protest not against material injustice but against the spiritual ideals of the ancient world and its whole social ethos.

This opposition finds an inspired expression in the book of the Apocalypse, which was composed in the province of Asia at a time when the Church was threatened with persecution owing to the public enforcement of the imperial cult of Rome and the Emperor in the time of Domitian. The state priesthood that was organised in the cities of the province is described as the False Prophet that causes men to worship the Beast (the Roman Empire) and its image, and to receive its seal, without which no man might buy or sell. Rome herself, whom Virgil described as "like the Phrygian Mother of the Gods, crowned with towers, rejoicing in her divine offspring," now appears as the Woman sitting upon the Beast, the mother of harlots and abominations, drunken with the blood of the saints and the blood of the martyrs of Jesus. And all the heavenly hosts and the souls of the martyrs are shown waiting for the coming of the day of vengeance when the power of the Beast shall be destroyed and Rome shall be cast down for ever, like a mill-stone into the sea.

This is an impressive witness to the gathering forces of spiritual hostility and condemnation that were sapping the moral foundations of the Roman power. The Empire had alienated the strongest and most living forces in the life of the age, and it was this internal contradiction, far more than war or external invasion, that caused the downfall of ancient civilisation. Before ever the barbarians had broken into the Empire and before the economic breakdown had taken place, the life had passed out of the city-state and the spirit of classical civilisation was dying. The cities were still being built with their temples and statues and theatres as in the Hellenistic age, but it was a sham façade that hid the decay within. The future lay with the infant Church.

Nevertheless, Christianity won the victory only after a long and bitter struggle. The Church grew under the shadow of the executioner's rods and axes, and every Christian lived in peril of physical torture and death. The thought of martyrdom coloured the whole outlook of early Christianity. It was not only a fear, it was also an ideal and a hope. For the martyr was the complete Christian. He was the champion and hero of the new society in its conflict with the old, and even the Christians who had failed in the moment of trial—the *lapsi*—looked on the martyrs as their saviours and protectors. We have only to read the epistles of St. Cyprian or the *Testimonia* which he compiled as a manual for the "milites Christi," or the treatise *de Laude Martyrum* which goes under his name, to realise the passionate exaltation which the ideal of martyrdom produced in the Christian mind. It attains almost lyrical expression in the following passage of St. Cyprian's epistle to Nemesianus, which is deservedly famous: "O feet blessedly bound, which are loosed not by the smith but by the Lord! O feet blessedly bound, which are guided to paradise in the way of salvation! O feet bound for the present time in the world that they may be always free with the Lord! O feet lingering for a while among the fetters and crossbars but to run quickly to Christ on a glorious road! Let cruelty, envious or malignant, hold you here in its bonds and chains as long as it will, from this earth and from these sufferings you shall speedily come to the Kingdom of Heaven. The body is not cherished in the mines with couch and cushions, but it is cherished with the refreshment and solace of Christ. The frame wearied with labours lies prostrate on the ground, but it is no penalty to lie down with Christ. Your limbs unbathed are foul and disfigured with filth; but within they are spiritually cleansed, though the flesh is defiled. There the bread is scarce, but man liveth not by bread alone but by the Word of God. Shivering, you want clothing; but he who puts on Christ is abundantly clothed and adorned." This is not the pious rhetoric of a fashionable preacher; it is the message of a confessor, who was himself soon to suffer death for the faith, to his fellow bishops and clergy and "the rest of the brethren in the mines, martyrs of God."

In an age when the individual was becoming the passive instrument of an omnipotent and universal state it is difficult to exaggerate the importance of such an ideal, which was the ultimate stronghold of spiritual freedom. More than any other factor it secured the ultimate triumph of the Church, for it rendered plain to all the fact that Christianity was the one remaining power in the world which could not be absorbed in the gigantic mechanism of the new servile state.

And while the Church was involved in this life-and-death struggle with the imperial state and its Hellenistic culture, it also had to carry on a difficult and obscure warfare with the growing forces of oriental religion. Under the veneer of cosmopolitan Hellenistic civilisation, the religious traditions of the ancient East were still alive and were gradually permeating the thought of the age. The mystery religions of Asia Minor spread westwards in the same way as Christianity itself, and the religion of Mithras accompanied the Roman armies to the Danube and the Rhine and the British frontier. The Egyptian worship of Isis and the Syrian cults of Adonis and Atargatis,

Hadad of Baalbek, and the Sun-God of Emesa, followed the rising tide of Syrian trade and migration to the West, while in the oriental underworld new religions, like Manichaeanism, were coming into existence, and the immemorial traditions of Babylonian astral theology were appearing in new forms.

But the most characteristic product of this movement of oriental syncretism was the Gnostic theosophy, which was an ever-present danger to the Christian Church during the second and third centuries. It was based on the fundamental dualism of spirit and matter and the association of the material world with the evil principle, a dualism which derived more, perhaps, from Greek and Anatolian influences than from Persia, since we find it already fully developed in the Orphic mythology and in the philosophy of Empedocles. But this central idea was enveloped in a dense growth of magic and theosophical speculation which was undoubtedly derived from Babylonian and oriental sources.

This strange oriental mysticism possessed an extraordinary attraction for the mind of a society which, no less than that of India six centuries before, was inspired with a profound sense of disillusionment and the thirst for deliverance. Consequently, it was not merely an exterior danger to Christianity; it threatened to absorb it altogether, by transforming the historical figure of Jesus into a member of the hierarchy of divine Aeons, and by substituting the ideal of the deliverance of the soul from the contamination of the material world for the Christian ideals of the redemption of the body and the realisation of the Kingdom of God as a social and historical reality. And its influence was felt not only directly in the great Christian-Gnostic systems of Valentinus and Basilides, but also indirectly through a multitude of minor oriental heresies that form an unbroken series from Simon Magus in the apostolic age down to the Paulicians of the Byzantine period. In the second century this movement had grown so strong that it captured three of the most distinguished representatives of oriental Christianity, Marcion in Asia Minor, and Tatian and Bardesanes, who were the founders of the new Aramaic literature, in Syria.

If Christianity had been merely one among the oriental sects and mystery religions of the Roman Empire it must inevitably have been drawn into this oriental syncretism. It survived because it possessed a system of ecclesiastical organisation and a principle of social authority that distinguished it from all the other religious bodies of the age. From the first, as we have seen, the Church regarded itself as the New Israel, "an elect race, a royal priesthood, a holy nation, a people set apart." This holy society was a theocracy inspired and governed by the Holy Spirit, and its rulers, the apostles, were the representatives not of the community but of the Christ, who had chosen them and transmitted to them His divine authority. This conception of a divine apostolic authority remained as the foundation of ecclesiastical order in the post-apostolic period. The "overseers" and elders, who were the rulers of the local churches, were regarded as the successors of the apostles, and the churches that were of direct apostolic origin enjoyed a peculiar prestige and authority among the rest.

This was the case above all with the Roman Church, for, as Peter had possessed a unique position among the Twelve, so the Roman Church, which traced its origins to St. Peter, possessed an exceptional position among the churches. Even in the first century, almost before the close of the apostolic age, we see an instance of this in the authoritative intervention of Rome in the affairs of the Church of Corinth. The First Epistle of Clement to the Corinthians (*c.*A.D. 96) gives the clearest possible expression to the ideal of hierarchic order which was the principle of the new society. The author argues that order is the law of the universe. And as it is the principle of external nature so, too, is it the principle of the Christian society. The faithful must preserve the same discipline and subordination of rank that marked the Roman army. As Christ is from God, so the apostles are from Christ, and the apostles, in turn, "appointed their first converts, testing them by the spirit, to be the bishops and deacons of the future believers. And, knowing there would be strife for the title of bishop, they afterwards added the codicil that if they should fall asleep other approved men should succeed to their ministry." Therefore it is essential that the Church of Corinth should put aside strife and envy and submit to the lawfully appointed presbyters, who represent the apostolic principle of divine authority.

The doctrine of St. Clement is characteristically Roman in its insistence on social order and moral discipline, but it has much in common with the teaching of the Pastoral Epistles, and there can be no doubt that it represents the traditional spirit of the primitive Church. It was this spirit that saved Christianity from sinking in the morass of oriental syncretism.

In his polemic against the Gnostics in the following century St. Irenaeus appeals again and again to the social authority of the apostolic tradition against the wild speculations of Eastern theosophy. "The true Gnosis is the teaching of the apostles and the primitive constitution of the Church throughout the world." And with him also it is the Roman Church that is the centre of unity and the guarantee of orthodox belief.

In this way the primitive Church survived both the perils of heresy and schism and the persecution of the imperial power and organised itself as a universal hierarchical society over against the pagan world-state. Thence it was but a step to the conquest of the Empire itself, and to its establishment as the official religion of the reorganised Constantinian state. Whether Constantine himself was moved by considerations of policy in his attitude to Christianity is a debatable question. No doubt he was sincere in the conviction he expresses in his letter to the provincials: that he had been raised up by the Divinity from the far west of Britain to destroy the enemies of Christianity, who would otherwise have ruined the Republic; and this belief may well have been reinforced by a conviction that the order and universality of the Christian Church predestined it to be the spiritual ally and complement of the universal Empire. In any case, this was the light in which the official Christian panegyrist of Constantine, Eusebius of Caesarea, interpreted the course of events. "One God," he writes, "was proclaimed to all mankind; and at the same time one universal power, the Roman Empire, arose and flourished. The enduring and implacable hatred of nation for nation was now removed; and as the knowledge of one God and one way of religion and salvation, even the doctrine of Christ, was made known to all mankind; so at the selfsame period, the entire dominion of the Roman Empire being vested in a single sovereign, profound peace reigned throughout the world. And thus, by the express appointment of the same God, two roots of blessing, the Roman Empire and the doctrine of Christian piety, sprang up together for the benefit of mankind."

The Roman Empire—
Why Did It Fall?

CONTENTS

QUESTIONS FOR STUDY

1 Does the evidence fully support Gibbon's estimate of Rome in the second century? What light does Pliny shed on that estimate?

2 What is the relationship among the evidence of Justinian, Herodian, and Salvian?

The problem of the causes of the decline and fall of the classical world as represented by the Roman Empire in the West is at least as old as the Renaissance and was posed in a definitive form by Edward Gibbon in the eighteenth century. It has not yet lost its fascination, for in the twentieth century historians and philosophers of history have continued to use it as the focal point for speculations on the nature of historical change. The Roman Empire is admirably suited to be a subject for such speculations, for it represents a completed cycle of civilization. At the same time it is of special interest to students of Western civilization, for the classical heritage is a vital component of that civilization.

The difficulties presented by the problem of the decline and fall are enormous. The passage of time and the vagaries of fortune have destroyed much of the evidence we should like to have and have preselected the rest; but beyond the problem of sources is the difficult methodological problem of distinguishing cause from effect and assigning the proper weight to each contributing factor. In the light of these difficulties it is not surprising that there seem to be as many interpretations as there are scholars and that each age has seen the problem from a different perspective.

---

3 *Both Walbank and Rostovtzeff emphasize economic and social elements. How do their interpretations differ?*

4 *How does the interpretation of Piganiol compare with that of Gibbon?*

5 *Was the fall of Rome inevitable?*

1 Gibbon on the Decline and Fall

Edward Gibbon framed the question we are considering in the eighteenth century. His formulation remains the basis for modern discussion.

FROM *The History of the Decline and Fall of the Roman Empire* BY EDWARD GIBBON

THE GREEKS, after their country had been reduced into a province, imputed the triumphs of Rome, not to the merit, but to the FORTUNE of the republic. The inconstant goddess, who so blindly distributes and resumes her favours, had *now* consented (such was the language of envious flattery) to resign her wings, to descend from her globe, and to fix her firm and immutable throne on the banks of the Tiber. A wiser Greek, who has composed, with a philosophic spirit, the memorable history of his own times, deprived his countrymen of this vain and delusive comfort by opening to their view the deep foundations of the greatness of Rome. The fidelity of the citizens to each other, and to the state, was confirmed by the habits of education and the prejudices of religion. Honour, as well as virtue, was the principle of the republic; the ambitious citizens laboured to deserve the solemn glories of a triumph; and the ardour of the Roman youth was kindled into active emulation, as often as they beheld the domestic images of their ancestors. The temperate struggles of the patricians and plebeians had finally established the firm and equal balance of the constitution; which united the freedom of popular assemblies with the authority and wisdom of a senate and the executive powers of a regal magistrate. When the consul displayed the standard of the republic, each citizen bound himself, by the obligation of an oath, to draw his sword in the cause of his country, till he had discharged the sacred duty by a military service of ten years. This wise institution continually poured into the field the rising generations of free-men and soldiers; and their numbers were reinforced by the warlike and populous states of Italy, who, after a brave resistance, had yielded to the

Edward Gibbon, *The History of the Decline and Fall of the Roman Empire,* J. B. Bury, ed., IV (1901), 160–3.

valour, and embraced the alliance, of the Romans. The sage historian, who excited the virtue of the younger Scipio and beheld the ruin of Carthage, has accurately described their military system; their levies, arms, exercises, subordination, marches, encampments; and the invincible legion, superior in active strength to the Macedonian phalanx of Philip and Alexander. From these institutions of peace and war, Polybius has deduced the spirit and success of a people incapable of fear and impatient of repose. The ambitious design of conquest, which might have been defeated by the seasonable conspiracy of mankind, was attempted and achieved; and the perpetual violation of justice was maintained by the political virtues of prudence and courage. The arms of the republic, sometimes vanquished in battle, always victorious in war, advanced with rapid steps to the Euphrates, the Danube, the Rhine, and the Ocean; and the images of gold, or silver, or brass, that might serve to represent the nations and their kings, were successively broken by the *iron* monarchy of Rome.

The rise of a city, which swelled into an empire, may deserve, as a singular prodigy, the reflection of a philosophic mind. But the decline of Rome was the natural and inevitable effect of immoderate greatness. Prosperity ripened the principle of decay; the causes of destruction multiplied with the extent of conquest; and, as soon as time or accident had removed the artificial supports, the stupendous fabric yielded to the pressure of its own weight. The story of its ruin is simple and obvious; and, instead of inquiring why the Roman empire was destroyed, we should rather be surprised that it had subsisted so long. The victorious legions, who, in distant wars, acquired the vices of strangers and mercenaries, first oppressed the freedom of the republic, and afterwards violated the majesty of the purple. The emperors, anxious for their personal safety and the public peace, were reduced to the base expedient of corrupting the discipline which rendered them alike formidable to their sovereign and to the enemy; the vigour of the military government was relaxed, and finally dissolved, by the partial institutions of Constantine; and the Roman world was overwhelmed by a deluge of Barbarians.

The decay of Rome has been frequently ascribed to the translation of the seat of empire; but this history has already shewn that the powers of government were *divided* rather than *removed*. The throne of Constantinople was erected in the East; while the West was still possessed by a series of emperors who held their residence in Italy and claimed their equal inheritance of the legions and provinces. This dangerous novelty impaired the strength, and fomented the vices, of a double reign; the instruments of an oppressive and arbitrary system were multiplied; and a vain emulation of luxury, not of merit, was introduced and supported between the degenerate successors of Theodosius. Extreme distress, which unites the virtue of a free people, embitters the factions of a declining monarchy. The hostile favourites of Arcadius and Honorius betrayed the republic to its common enemies; and the Byzantine court beheld with indifference, perhaps with pleasure, the disgrace of Rome, the misfortunes of Italy, and the loss of the West. Under the succeeding reigns, the alliance of the two empires was restored; but the aid of the Oriental Romans was tardy, doubtful, and ineffectual; and the national schism of the Greeks and Latins was enlarged by the perpetual difference of language and manners, of interest, and even of religion. Yet the salutary event approved in some measure the judgment of Constantine. During a long period of decay, his impregnable city repelled the victorious armies of Barbarians, protected the wealth of Asia, and commanded, both in peace and war, the important straits which connect the Euxine and Mediterranean seas. The foundation of Constantinople more essentially contributed to the preservation of the East than to the ruin of the West.

As the happiness of a *future* life is the great object of religion, we may hear, without surprise or scandal, that the introduction, or at least the abuse, of Christianity had some influence on the decline and fall of the Roman empire. The clergy successfully preached the doctrines of patience and pusillanimity; the active virtues of society were discouraged; and the last remains of the military spirit were buried in the cloister; a large portion of public and private wealth was consecrated to the specious demands of charity and devotion; and the soldiers' pay was lavished on the useless multitudes of both sexes, who could only plead the merits of abstinence and chastity. Faith, zeal, curiosity, and the more earthly passions of malice and ambition kindled the flame of theological discord; the church, and even the state, were distracted by religious factions, whose conflicts were sometimes bloody, and always implacable; the attention of the emperors was diverted from camps to synods; the Roman world was oppressed by a new species of tyranny; and the persecuted sects became the secret enemies of their country. Yet party-spirit, however pernicious or absurd, is a principle of union as well as of dissension. The bishops, from eighteen hundred pulpits, inculcated the duty of passive obedience to a lawful and orthodox sovereign; their frequent assemblies, and perpetual correspondence, maintained the communion of distant churches: and the benevolent temper of the gospel was strengthened, though confined, by the spiritual alliance of the Catholics. The sacred indolence of the monks was devoutly embraced by a servile and effeminate age; but, if superstition had not afforded a decent retreat, the same vices would have tempted the unworthy Romans to desert, from baser motives, the standard of the republic. Religious precepts are easily obeyed, which indulge and sanctify the natural inclinations of their votaries; but the pure and genuine influence of Christianity may be traced in its beneficial, though imperfect, effects on the Barbarian proselytes of the North. If the decline of the Roman empire was hastened by the conversion of Constantine, his victorious religion broke the violence of the fall, and mollified the ferocious temper of the conquerors.

2   *The Empire at Its Height*

For Gibbon the empire reached its peak in the Age of the Antonines.

FROM *The History of the Decline and Fall of the Roman Empire* BY EDWARD GIBBON

IN THE SECOND CENTURY of the Christian era, the empire of Rome comprehended the fairest part of the earth, and the most civilized portion of mankind. The frontiers of that extensive monarchy were guarded by ancient renown and disciplined valour. The gentle, but powerful, influence of laws and manners had gradually cemented the union of the provinces. Their peaceful inhabitants enjoyed and abused the advantages of wealth and luxury. The image of a free constitution was preserved with decent reverence. The Roman senate appeared to possess the sovereign authority, and devolved on the emperors all the executive powers of government. During a happy period of more than fourscore years, the public administration was conducted by the virtue and abilities of Nerva, Trajan, Hadrian, and the two Antonines. It is the design of this and of the two succeeding chapters, to describe the prosperous condition of their empire; and afterwards, from the death of Marcus Antoninus, to deduce the most important circumstances of its decline and fall: a revolution which will ever be remembered, and is still felt by the nations of the earth.

*   *   *

    Notwithstanding the propensity of mankind to exalt the past, and to depreciate the present, the tranquil and prosperous state of the empire was warmly felt, and honestly confessed, by the provincials as well as Romans. "They acknowledged that the true principles of social life, laws, agriculture, and science, which had been first invented by the wisdom of Athens, were now firmly established by the power of Rome, under whose auspicious

Edward Gibbon, *The History of the Decline and Fall of the Roman Empire,* J. B. Bury, ed., I (1897), 1, 56, 78.

influence the fiercest barbarians were united by an equal government and common language. They affirm that, with the improvement of arts, the human species was visibly multiplied. They celebrate the increasing splendour of the cities, the beautiful face of the country, cultivated and adorned like an immense garden; and the long festival of peace, which was enjoyed by so many nations, forgetful of their ancient animosities, and delivered from the apprehension of future danger." Whatever suspicions may be suggested by the air of rhetoric and declamation which seems to prevail in these passages, the substance of them is perfectly agreeable to historic truth.

*　　　*　　　*

If a man were called to fix the period in the history of the world during which the condition of the human race was most happy and prosperous, he would, without hesitation, name that which elapsed from the death of Domitian to the accession of Commodus. The vast extent of the Roman empire was governed by absolute power, under the guidance of virtue and wisdom. The armies were restrained by the firm but gentle hand of four successive emperors, whose characters and authority commanded involuntary respect. The forms of the civil administration were carefully preserved by Nerva, Trajan, Hadrian, and the Antonines, who delighted in the image of liberty, and were pleased with considering themselves as the accountable ministers of the laws. Such princes deserved the honour of restoring the republic, had the Romans of their days been capable of enjoying a rational freedom.

3 The Evidence of Decline

Dio Cassius, a historian of the third century, considered the death of Marcus Aurelius and the accession of his son Commodus as the beginning of troubles for Rome. "Our history," he says, "now descends from a kingdom of gold to one of iron and rust." Although Gibbon and others have accepted this date as a starting point, there is good evidence that many of the problems which were to trouble Rome later were already present in the "golden age" of the second century.

The greatness of classical antiquity was based on urban life. Wherever Roman power reached, municipalities sprang up to provide a prosperous and educated class of citizens, soldiers, and administrators. In the first century, participation in municipal duties was lively and desirable, as the following document shows.

Pompeii was destroyed by volcanic eruption in A.D. 79. These notices were painted on the walls of buildings in the city.

Election Posters in Pompeii

THE FRUIT DEALERS together with Helvius Vestalis unanimously urge the election of Marcus Holconius Priscus as duovir with judicial power.

II

The goldsmiths unanimously urge the election of Gaius Cuspius Pansa as aedile.

III

I ask you to elect Gaius Julius Polybius aedile. He gets good bread.

Roman Civilization, I (1955), 326–7, translated by Naphtali Lewis and Meyer Reinhold. Reprinted by permission of Columbia University Press, New York.

IV

The muleteers urge the election of Gaius Julius Polybius as duovir.

V

The worshippers of Isis unanimously urge the election of Gnaeus Helvius Sabinus as aedile.

VI

Proculus, make Sabinus aedile and he will do as much for you.

VII

His neighbors urge you to elect Lucius Statius Receptus duovir with judicial power; he is worthy. Aemilius Celer, a neighbor, wrote this. May you take sick if you maliciously erase this!

VIII

Satia and Petronia support and ask you to elect Marcus Casellius and Lucius Albucius aediles. May we always have such citizens in our colony!

IX

I ask you to elect Epidius Sabinus duovir with judicial power. He is worthy, a defender of the colony, and in the opinion of the respected judge Suedius Clemens and by agreement of the council, because of his services and uprightness, worthy of the municipality. Elect him!

X

If upright living is considered any recommendation, Lucretius Fronto is well worthy of the office.

XI

Genialis urges the election of Bruttius Balbus as duovir. He will protect the treasury.

XII

I ask you to elect Marcus Cerrinius Vatia to the aedileship. All the late drinkers support him. Florus and Fructus wrote this.

XIII

The petty thieves support Vatia for the aedileship.

XIV

I ask you to elect Aulus Vettius Firmus aedile. He is worthy of the municipality. I ask you to elect him, ballplayers. Elect him!

XV

I wonder, O wall, that you have not fallen in ruins from supporting the stupidities of so many scribblers.

> *The Emperor Trajan (A.D. 98–117) found it necessary to send special agents to deal with problems in the provinces. One of them was Pliny the Younger, who was sent to the province of Bithynia in Asia Minor. The following exchange of letters shows how burdensome public service could become, even in the "golden age."*

FROM *Pliny's Letters*

LETTER CXIII. To the Emperor Trajan

THE POMPEIAN LAW, Sir, which is observed in Pontus and Bithynia, does not direct that any money should be given by those who are elected into the public council by the Censors. It has however been usual for such members as have been admitted into those assemblies, in pursuance of the privilege which you were pleased to grant to some particular cities, of receiving above their legal number, to pay one or two thousand denarii. Subsequent to this, the Proconsul Anicius Maximus ordained (tho' indeed his edict extended to some few cities only) that those who were elected by the Censors should also pay into the treasury a certain sum, which varied in different places. It remains therefore for your consideration, whether it would not be proper to settle a certain fixed sum for each member, who is elected into the council, to pay upon his entrance; for it well becomes you, whose every word and action deserves immortality, to give laws that shall for ever be permanent.

LETTER CXIV. Trajan to Pliny

I can give no general directions applicable to all the cities of Bithynia, whether those who are made members of their respective councils shall pay an honorary fee upon their admittance, or not. It seems best therefore, in this case (what indeed upon all occasions is the safest way), to leave each city to its respective laws. But I think, however, that the Censors ought to set the

---

Pliny's Letters (1789), translated by William Melmoth.

sum lower to those who are chosen into the senate contrary to their inclinations, than to the rest.

> *By the third and fourth centuries the troubles of the empire were such that necessary public services could be guaranteed only by the regular use of compulsion. The upper classes who had vied for positions as municipal councillors (decuriones or curiales) in the first century now became a hereditary caste and were compelled to serve. Their chief and sometimes their only function was the collection of taxes, ever more burdensome. The emperors made the cu-riales personally liable for the taxes due. Little wonder that they made every effort to escape service, but gradually the imperial jurists closed all avenues of evasion.*

FROM *Justinian's Digest*

THE GOVERNOR OF THE PROVINCE shall see to it that decurions who are proved to have left the area of the municipality to which they belong and to have moved to other places are recalled to their native soil and perform the appropriate public services. . . .

Persons over fifty-five are forbidden by imperial enactments to be called to the position of decurion against their will, but if they do consent to this they ought to perform the duties, although if they are over seventy they are not compelled to assume compulsory municipal services. . . .

Municipal duties of a personal character are: representation of a municipality, that is, becoming a public advocate; assignment to taking the census or registering property; secretaryships; camel transport; commissioner of food supply and the like, of public lands, of grain procurement, of water supply; horse races in the circus; paving of public streets; grain storehouse; heating of public baths; distribution of food supply; and other duties similar to these. From the above-mentioned, other duties can be deduced in accordance with the laws and long-established custom of each municipality. . . .

The governor of the province shall see to it that the compulsory public services and offices in the municipalities are imposed fairly and in rotation according to age and rank, in accordance with the gradation of public services and offices long ago established, so that the men and resources of municipalities are not inconsiderately ruined by frequent oppression of the

Justinian's Digest in *Roman Civilization*, II (1955), 446–7, translated by Naphtali Lewis and Meyer Reinhold. Reprinted by permission of Columbia University Press, New York.

same persons. If two sons are under parental power, the father is not compelled to support their public services at the same time. . . .

The care of constructing or rebuilding a public work in a municipality is a compulsory public service from which a father of five living children is excused; and if this service is forcibly imposed, this fact does not deprive him of the exemption that he has from other public services. The excusing of those with insufficient resources who are nominated to public services or offices is not permanent but temporary. For if a hoped-for increase comes to one's property by honorable means, when his turn comes an evaluation is to be made to determine whether he is suitable for the services for which he was chosen. . . . A person who is responsible for public services to his municipality and submits his name for military service for the purpose of avoiding the municipal burden cannot make the condition of his community worse.

> *In the third century the Roman Empire's capacity to maintain order and security broke down. The army made and unmade emperors; the upper classes were terrorized and plundered by rapacious armies of peasant-soldiers, increasingly led by peasant-generals. Private and public property were fair game, farm land was ravaged, and cities were destroyed. A good example of this chaotic period is provided by the reign of Gaius Julius Maximinus (235–238). A Thracian peasant, a barbarian of Gothic and Alan stock, he was the first emperor to rise from the ranks. He waged a war against the propertied classes and the prosperous cities of Italy. Previous emperors had attacked elements of the nobility, but Maximinus instituted a systematic terror against the entire bourgeoisie. In 238 he marched against the city of Aquileia.*

FROM *History of the Roman Empire* BY HERODIAN

BEFORE THESE EVENTS OCCURRED, Aquileia was already a huge city, with a large permanent population. Situated on the sea and with all the provinces of Illyricum behind it, Aquileia served as a port of entry for Italy.

Herodian, *History of the Roman Empire* (1961), pp. 199–207, translated by Edward C. Echols. Reprinted by permission of University of California Press.

The city thus made it possible for goods transported from the interior by land or by the rivers to be traded to the merchant mariners and also for the necessities brought by sea to the mainland, goods not produced there because of the cold climate, to be sent to the upland areas. Since the inland people farm a region that produces much wine, they export this in quantity to those who do not cultivate grapes. A huge number of people lived permanently in Aquileia, not only the native residents but also foreigners and merchants. At this time the city was even more crowded than usual; all the people from the surrounding area had left the small towns and villages and sought refuge there. They put their hope of safety in the city's great size and its defensive wall; this ancient wall, however, had for the most part collapsed. Under Roman rule the cities of Italy no longer had need of walls or arms; they had substituted permanent peace for war and had also gained a participating share in the Roman government. Now, however, necessity forced the Aquileians to repair the wall, rebuild the fallen sections, and erect towers and battlements. After fortifying the city with a rampart as quickly as possible, they closed the gates and remained together on the wall day and night, beating off their assailants. Two senators named Crispinus and Meniphilus, former consuls, were appointed generals. These two had seen to everything with careful attention. With great foresight they had brought into the city supplies of every kind in quantities sufficient to enable it to withstand a long siege. An ample supply of water was available from the many wells in the city, and, a river flowing at the foot of the city wall provided both a defensive moat and an abundance of water.

These are the preparations which had been made in the city. When it was reported to Maximinus that Aquileia was well defended and tightly shut, he thought it wise to send envoys to discuss the situation with the townspeople from the foot of the wall and try to persuade them to open the gates. There was in the besieging army a tribune who was a native of Aquileia, and whose wife, children, and relatives were inside the city. Maximinus sent this man to the wall accompanied by several centurions, expecting their fellow citizen to win them over easily. The envoys told the Aquileians that Maximinus, their mutual emperor, ordered them to lay down their arms in peace, to receive him as a friend, not as an enemy, and to turn from killing to libations and sacrifices. Their emperor directed them not to overlook the fact that their native city was in danger of being razed to its very foundations, whereas it was in their power to save themselves and to preserve their city when their merciful emperor pardoned them for their offenses. Others, not they, were the guilty ones. The envoys shouted their message from the foot of the wall so that those above might understand it. Most of the city's population was on the walls and in the towers; only those standing guard at other posts were absent. They all listened quietly to what the envoys were saying. Fearing that the people, convinced by these lying promises, might choose peace instead of war and throw open the gates, Crispinus ran along the parapet, pleading with the Aquileians to hold out bravely and offer stout resistance; he begged them not to break faith with the senate and the Roman people, but to win a place in history as the saviors and defenders of all Italy.

*   *   *

When the envoys returned unsuccessful, Maximinus, in a towering rage, pressed on toward the city with increased speed. But when he came to a large river sixteen miles from Aquileia, he found it flowing very wide and very deep. The warmth at that season of the year had melted the mountain snow that had been frozen all winter, and a vast, snow-swollen flood had resulted. It was impossible for Maximinus' army to cross this river because the Aquileians had destroyed the bridge, a huge structure of imposing proportions built, by earlier emperors, of squared stones and supported on tapering piers. Since neither bridges nor boats were available, the army halted in confusion. Some of the Germans, unfamiliar with the swift, violent rivers of Italy and thinking that these flowed down to the plains as lazily as their own streams (it is the slow current of the German rivers which causes them to freeze over), entered the river with their horses, which are trained to swim, and were carried away and drowned.

After a ditch had been dug around the camp to prevent attacks, Maximinus halted for two or three days beside the river, considering how it might be bridged. Timber was scarce, and there were no boats which could be fastened together to span the river. Some of his engineers, however, called attention to the many empty wooden kegs scattered about the deserted fields, the barrels which the natives use to ship wine safely to those forced to import it. The kegs are hollow, like boats; when fastened together and anchored to the shore by cables, they float like pontoons, and the current cannot carry them off. Planks are laid on top of these pontoons, and with great skill and speed a bank of earth is piled up evenly on the platform thus fashioned. After the bridge had been completed, the army crossed over and marched to Aquileia, where they found the buildings on the outskirts deserted. The soldiers cut down all the trees and grapevines and burned them, and destroyed the crops which had already begun to appear in those regions. Since the trees were planted in even rows and the interwoven vines linked them together everywhere, the countryside had a festive air; one might even say that it wore a garland of green. All these trees and vines Maximinus' soldiers cut down to the very roots before they hurried up to the walls of Aquileia. The army was exhausted, however, and it seemed wiser not to launch an immediate attack. The soldiers therefore remained out of range of the arrows and took up stations around the entire circuit of the wall by cohorts and legions, each unit investing the section it was ordered to hold. After a single day's rest, the soldiers kept the city under continuous siege for the remaining time.

They brought up every type of siege machinery and attacked the wall with all the power they could muster, leaving untried nothing of the art of siege warfare. They launched numerous assaults virtually every day, and the entire army held the city encircled as if in a net, but the Aquileians fought back determinedly, showing real enthusiasm for war. They had closed their houses and temples and were fighting in a body, together with the women and children, from their advantageous position on the parapet and in the towers. In this way they held off their attackers, and no one was too young or too old to take part in the battle to preserve his native city. All the buildings in the suburbs and outside the city gates were demolished by Maximinus' men, and the wood from the houses was used to build the siege engines. The soldiers made every effort to destroy a part of the wall, so that the army might break in, seize everything, and, after leveling the city, leave the area a deserted pasture land. The journey to Rome would not be fittingly glorious if Maximinus failed to capture the first city in Italy to oppose him. By pleading and promising gifts, Maximinus and his son, whom he had appointed his Caesar, spurred the army to action; they rode about on horseback, encouraging the soldiers to fight with resolution. The Aquileians hurled down stones on the besiegers; combining pitch and olive oil with asphalt and brimstone, they ignited this mixture and poured it over their attackers from hollow vessels fitted with long handles. Bringing the flaming liquid to the walls, they scattered it over the soldiers like a heavy downpour of rain. Carried along with the other ingredients, the pitch oozed onto the unprotected parts of the soldiers' bodies and spread everywhere. Then the soldiers ripped off their blazing corselets and the rest of their armor too, for the iron grew red hot, and the leather and wooden parts caught fire and burned. As a result, soldiers were seen everywhere stripping themselves, and the discarded armor appeared like the spoils of war, but these were taken by cunning and treachery, not by courage on the field of battle. In this tragedy, most of the soldiers suffered scarred and disfigured faces and lost eyes and hands, while every unprotected part of the body was severely injured. The Aquileians hurled down torches on the siege engines which had been dragged up to the walls. These torches, sharpened at the end like a javelin, were soaked in pitch and resin and then ignited; the firebrands, still blazing, stuck fast in the machines, which easily caught fire and were consumed by the flames.

During the opening days, then, the fortunes of war were almost equal. As time passed, however, the army of Maximinus grew depressed and, cheated in its expectations, fell into despair when the soldiers found that those whom they had not expected to hold out against a single assault were not only offering stout resistance but were even beating them back. The Aquileians, on the other hand, were greatly encouraged and highly enthusiastic, and, as the battle continued, their skill and daring increased. Contemptuous of the soldiers now, they hurled taunts at them. As Maximinus rode about, they shouted insults and indecent blasphemies at him and his son. The emperor became increasingly angry because he was powerless to retaliate. Unable to vent his wrath upon the enemy, he was enraged at most of his troop commanders because they were pressing the siege in cowardly and half-hearted fashion. Consequently, the hatred of his supporters increased, and his enemies grew more contemptuous of him each day.

As it happened, the Aquileians had everything they needed in abundant quantities. With great foresight they had stored in the city all the food and drink required for men and animals. The soldiers of the emperor, by contrast, lacked every necessity, since they had cut down the fruit trees and devastated the countryside. Some of the soldiers had built temporary huts, but the majority were living in the open air, exposed to sun and rain. And now many died of starvation; no food was brought in from the outside, as the Romans had blocked all the roads of Italy by erecting walls provided with narrow gates. The senate dispatched former consuls and picked men from all Italy to guard the beaches and harbors and prevent anyone from sailing. Their intent was to keep Maximinus in ignorance of what was happening at Rome; thus the main roads and all the bypaths were closely watched to prevent anyone's passing. The result was that the army which appeared to be maintaining the siege was itself under siege, for it was unable to capture Aquileia or leave the city and proceed to Rome; all the boats and wagons had been hidden, and no vehicles of any kind were available to the soldiers. Exaggerated rumors were circulated, based only on suspicion, to the effect that the entire Roman people were under arms; that all Italy was united; that the provinces of Illyricum and the barbarian nations in the East and South had gathered an army; and that everywhere men were solidly united in hatred of Maximinus. The emperor's soldiers were in despair and in need of everything. There was scarcely even sufficient water for them. The only source of water was the nearby river, which was fouled by blood and bodies. Lacking any means of burying those who died in the city, the Aquileians threw the bodies into the river; both those who fell in the fighting and those who died of disease were dropped into the stream, as the city had no facilities for burial.

And so the completely confused army was in the depths of despair. Then one day, during a lull in the fighting, when most of the soldiers had gone to their quarters or their stations, Maximinus was resting in his tent. Without warning, the soldiers whose camp was near Rome at the foot of Mount Alba, where they had left their wives and children, decided that the best solution was to kill Maximinus and end the interminable siege. They resolved no longer to ravage Italy for an emperor they now knew to be a despicable tyrant. Taking courage, therefore, the conspirators went to Maximinus' tent about noon. The imperial bodyguard, which was involved in the plot, ripped Maximinus' pictures from the standards; when he came out of his tent with his son to talk to them, they refused to listen and killed them both [A.D. 238]. They killed the army's commanding general also, and the emperor's close friends. Their bodies·were handed over to those who wished to trample and mutilate them, after which the corpses were exposed to the birds and dogs. The heads of Maximinus and his son were sent to Rome. Such was the fate suffered by Maximinus and his son, who paid the penalty for their savage rule.

> *The obvious and immediate cause of Rome's fall was the invasion of the barbarians. The following selection illustrates the Romans' attitude toward the tribes who pressed on their frontiers.*

FROM *Res Gestae* BY AMMIANUS MARCELLINUS

THE PEOPLE CALLED HUNS, barely mentioned in ancient records, live beyond the sea of Azof, on the border of the Frozen Ocean, and are a race savage beyond all parallel. At the very moment of birth the cheeks of their infant children are deeply marked by an iron, in order that the hair, instead of growing at the proper season on their faces, may be hindered by the scars; accordingly the Huns grow up without beards, and without any beauty. They all have closely knit and strong limbs and plump necks; they are of great size, and low legged, so that you might fancy them two-legged beasts, or the stout figures which are hewn out in a rude manner with an ax on the posts at the end of bridges.

They are certainly in the shape of men, however uncouth, and are so hardy that they neither require fire nor well flavored food, but live on the roots of such herbs as they get in the fields, or on the half-raw flesh of any animal, which they merely warm rapidly by placing it between their own thighs and the backs of their horses.

They never shelter themselves under roofed houses, but avoid them, as people ordinarily avoid sepulchers as things not fit for common use. Nor is there even to be found among them a cabin thatched with reeds; but they wander about, roaming over the mountains and the woods, and accustom themselves to bear frost and hunger and thirst from their very cradles. . . .

There is not a person in the whole nation who cannot remain on his horse day and night. On horseback they buy and sell, they take their meat and drink, and there they recline on the narrow neck of their steed, and yield to sleep so deep as to indulge in every variety of dream.

And when any deliberation is to take place on any weighty matter, they

Ammianus Marcellinus, *Res Gestae* (1862), 3–1, 2–4, 13, translated by C. D. Yonge.

all hold their common council on horseback. They are not under kingly authority, but are contented with the irregular government of their chiefs, and under their lead they force their way through all obstacles. . . .

None of them plow, or even touch a plow handle, for they have no settled abode, but are homeless and lawless, perpetually wandering with their wagons, which they make their homes; in fact, they seem to be people always in flight. . . .

This active and indomitable race, being excited by an unrestrained desire of plundering the possessions of others, went on ravaging and slaughtering all the nations in their neighborhood till they reached the Alani. . . .

[After having harassed the territory of the Alani and having slain many of them and acquired much plunder, the Huns made a treaty of friendship and alliance with those who survived. The allies then attacked the German people to the west.] In the meantime a report spread far and wide through the nations of the Goths, that a race of men, hitherto unknown, had suddenly descended like a whirlwind from the lofty mountains, as if they had risen from some secret recess of the earth, and were ravaging and destroying everything which came in their way.

And then the greater part of the population resolved to flee and to seek a home remote from all knowledge of the new barbarians; and after long deliberation as to where to fix their abode, they resolved that a retreat into Thrace was the most suitable for these two reasons: first of all, because it is a district most fertile in grass; and secondly, because, owing to the great breadth of the Danube, it is wholly separated from the districts exposed to the impending attacks of the invaders.

Accordingly, under the command of their leader Alavivus, they occupied the banks of the Danube, and sent ambassadors to the emperor Valens, humbly entreating to be received by him as his subjects. They promised to live quietly, and to furnish a body of auxiliary troops if necessary.

While these events were taking place abroad, the terrifying rumor reached us that the tribes of the north were planning new and unprecedented attacks upon us; and that over the whole region which extends from the country of the Marcomanni and Quadi to Pontus, hosts of barbarians composed of various nations, which had suddenly been driven by force from their own countries, were now, with all their families, wandering about in different directions on the banks of the river Danube.

At first this intelligence was lightly treated by our people, because they were not in the habit of hearing of any wars in those remote districts till they were terminated either by victory or by treaty.

But presently the belief in these occurrences grew stronger and was confirmed by the arrival of ambassadors, who, with prayers and earnest entreaties, begged that their people, thus driven from their homes and now encamped on the other side of the river, might be kindly received by us.

The affair now seemed a cause of joy rather than of fear, according to the skillful flatterers who were always extolling and exaggerating the good fortune of the emperor. They congratulated him that an embassy had come from the farthest corners of the earth, unexpectedly offering him a large body of recruits; and that, by combining the strength of his own people with these foreign forces, he would have an army absolutely invincible. They observed further that the payment for military reënforcements, which came in every year from the provinces, might now be saved and accumulated in his coffers and form a vast treasure of gold.

Full of this hope, he sent forth several officers to bring this ferocious people and their carts into our territory. And such great pains were taken to gratify this nation which was destined to overthrow the Empire of Rome, that not one was left behind, not even of those who were stricken with mortal disease. Moreover, so soon as they had obtained permission of the emperor to cross the Danube and to cultivate some districts in Thrace, they poured across the stream day and night, without ceasing, embarking in troops on board ships and rafts and on canoes made of the hollow trunks of trees. . . .

In this way, through the turbulent zeal of violent people, the ruin of the Roman Empire was brought about. This, at all events, is neither obscure nor uncertain, that the unhappy officers who were intrusted with the charge of conducting the multitude of the barbarians across the river, though they repeatedly endeavored to calculate their numbers, at last abandoned the attempt as hopeless. The man who would wish to ascertain the number might as well (as the most illustrious of poets says) attempt to count the waves in the African sea, or the grains of sand tossed about by the zephyrs. . . .

> Salvian the Presbyter wrote in the middle of the fifth century A.D. His book, On the Governance of God, contrasted the excellence of the barbarians with the decadence and corruption of the Roman Empire. In the following selection he indicates how serious was the effect of taxation.

FROM *On the Governance of God* BY SALVIAN

BUT WHAT ELSE can these wretched people wish for, they who suffer the incessant and even continuous destruction of public tax levies. To them there is always imminent a heavy and relentless proscription. They desert their

The Writings of Salvian, the Presbyter (1947), pp. 138–41, translated by J. F. O'Sullivan. Reprinted by permission of The Catholic University of America Press.

homes, lest they be tortured in their very homes. They seek exile, lest they suffer torture. The enemy is more lenient to them than the tax collectors. This is proved by this very fact, that they flee to the enemy in order to avoid the full force of the heavy tax levy. This very tax levying, although hard and inhuman, would nevertheless be less heavy and harsh if all would bear it equally and in common. Taxation is made more shameful and burdensome because all do not bear the burden of all. They extort tribute from the poor man for the taxes of the rich, and the weaker carry the load for the stronger. There is no other reason that they cannot bear all the taxation except that the burden imposed on the wretched is greater than their resources.

They suffer from envy and want, which are misfortunes most diverse and unlike. Envy is bound up with payment of the tax; need, with the ability to pay. If you look at what they pay, you will think them abundant in riches, but if you look at what they actually possess, you will find them poverty stricken. Who can judge an affair of this wretchedness? They bear the payment of the rich and endure the poverty of beggars. Much more serious is the following: the rich themselves occasionally make tributary levies which the poor pay.

But, you say, when the assessment due from the rich is very heavy and the taxes due from them are very heavy, how does it happen that they wish to increase their own debt? I do not say that they increase the taxes for themselves. They increase them because they do not increase them for themselves. I will tell you how this is done. Commonly, new envoys, new bearers of letters, come from the imperial offices and those men are recommended to a few well-known men for the mischief of many. For them new gifts are decreed, new taxes are decreed. The powerful levy what the poor are to pay, the courtesy of the rich decrees what the multitude of the wretched are to lose. They themselves in no way feel what they levy.

You say they who were sent by our superiors cannot be honored and generously entertained otherwise. Therefore, you rich men, you who are the first to levy, be the first to give. Be the first in generosity of goods, you who are the first in profusion of words. You who give of mine, give of thine. Most justly, whoever you are, you who alone wish to receive favor, you alone should bear the expense. But to your will, O rich men, we the poor accede. What you, the few, order, we all pay. What is so just, so humane? Your decrees burden us with new debts; at least make your debt common to us all. What is more wicked and more unworthy than that you alone are free from debt, you who make us all debtors?

Indeed, the most wretched poor thus pay all that I have mentioned, but for what cause or for what reason they pay, they are completely ignorant. For, to whom is it lawful to discuss why they pay; to whom is permitted to find out what is owed? Then it is given out most publicly when the rich get angry with each other, when some of them get indignant because some levies are made without their advice and handling.

Then you may hear it said by some of them, "What an unworthy crime!

Two or three decree what kills many; what is paid by many wretched men is decreed by a few powerful men." Each rich man maintains his honor by being unwilling that anything is decreed in his absence, yet he does not maintain justice by being unwilling that evil things be done when he is present. Lastly, what these very men consider base in others they themselves later legalize, either in punishment of a past contempt or in proof of their power. Therefore, the most unfortunate poor are, as it were, in the midst of the sea, between conflicting, violent winds. They are swamped by the waves rolling now from one side, now from the other.

But, surely, those who are wicked in one way are found moderate and just in another, and compensate for their baseness in one thing by goodness in another. For, just as they weigh down the poor with the burden of new tax levies, so they sustain them by the assistance of new tax reliefs; just as the lower classes are oppressed by new taxes, so they are equally relieved by tax mitigations. Indeed, the injustice is equal in taxes and reliefs, for, as the poor are the first to be burdened, so they are the last to be relieved.

For when, as has happened lately, the highest powers thought it would be advisable that taxation should be lessened somewhat for the cities which were in arrears in their payments, the rich alone instantly divided among themselves the remedy given for all. Who, then, remembers the poor? Who calls the poor and needy to share in the common benefit? Who permits him who is first in bearing the burden even to stand in the last place for receiving redress? What more is there to say? In no way are the poor regarded as taxpayers, unless when the mass of taxes is imposed upon them; they are not reckoned among the number of taxpayers when the tax-reliefs are portioned.

Do we think we are unworthy of the punishment of divine severity when we thus constantly punish the poor? Do we think, when we are constantly wicked, that God should not exercise His justice against all of us? Where or in whom are evils so great, except among the Romans? Whose injustice so great except our own? The Franks are ignorant of this crime of injustice. The Huns are immune to these crimes. There are no wrongs among the Vandals and none among the Goths. So far are the barbarians from tolerating these injustices among the Goths, that not even the Romans who live among them suffer them.

Therefore, in the districts taken over by the barbarians, there is one desire among all the Romans, that they should never again find it necessary to pass under Roman jurisdiction. In those regions, it is the one and general prayer of the Roman people that they be allowed to carry on the life they lead with the barbarians. And we wonder why the Goths are not conquered by our portion of the population, when the Romans prefer to live among them rather than with us. Our brothers, therefore, are not only altogether unwilling to flee to us from them, but they even cast us aside in order to flee to them.

4   The Social Problem

F. W. Walbank takes the view that the rigidity of Roman society was a major cause of Rome's fall.

FROM *The Decline of the Roman Empire in the West* BY F. W. WALBANK

THE CAUSE OF THE DECLINE of the Roman Empire is not to be sought in any one feature—in the climate, the soil, the health of the population, or indeed in any of those social and political factors which played so important a part in the actual process of decay—but rather in the whole structure of ancient society. The date at which the contradictions, which were ultimately to prove fatal, first began to appear is not A.D. 200 nor yet the setting-up of the Principate by Augustus Caesar in 27 B.C., but rather the fifth century B.C. when Athens revealed her inability to keep and broaden the middle-class democracy she had created. The failure of Athens epitomised the failure of the City-State. Built on a foundation of slave labour, or on the exploitation of similar groups, including the peasantry, the City-State yielded a brilliant minority civilisation. But from the start it was top-heavy. Through no fault of its citizens, but as a result of the time and place when it arose, it was supported by a woefully low level of technique. To say this is to repeat a truism. The paradoxical contrast between the spiritual achievements of Athens and her scanty material goods has long been held up to the admiration of generations who had found that a rich material inheritance did not automatically ensure richness of cultural life. But it was precisely this low level of technique, relative to the tasks Greek and Roman society set itself, that made it impossible even to consider dispensing with slavery and led to its extension from the harmless sphere of domestic labour to the mines and workshops, where it grew stronger as the contradictions of society became more apparent.

As so often, we find ourselves discussing as cause and effect factors which were constantly interacting, so that in reality the distinction between

F. W. Walbank, *The Decline of the Roman Empire in the West* (1953), pp. 3-7. Reprinted by permission of Lawrence and Wishart Ltd., London.

the effective agent and the result it brought about is often quite arbitrary. But roughly speaking, the City-State, precisely because it was a minority culture, tended to be aggressive and predatory, its claim to autonomy sliding over insensibly, at every opportunity, into a claim to dominate others. This led to wars, which in turn took their place among the many sources of fresh slaves. Slavery grew, and as it invaded the various branches of production it led inevitably to the damping down of scientific interest, to the cleavage, already mentioned, between the classes that used their hands and the superior class that used—and later ceased using—its mind. This ideological cleavage thus reflects a genuine separation of the community into classes; and henceforward it becomes the supreme task of even the wisest sons of the City-State—a Plato and an Aristotle—to maintain this class society, whatsoever the cost.

That cost was indeed heavy. It says much for Plato's singlemindedness that he was willing to meet it. In the *Laws,* his last attempt to plan the just city, he produces a blue-print for implanting beliefs and attitudes convenient to authority through the medium of suggestion, by a strict and ruthless censorship, the substitution of myths and emotional ceremonies for factual knowledge, the isolation of the citizen from the outside world, the creation of types with standardised reactions, and, as a final guarantee, by the sanctions of the police-state, to be invoked against all who cannot or will not conform.

Such was the intellectual and spiritual fruit of this tree, whose roots had split upon the hard rock of technical inadequacy. Materially, the result of increasing slavery was the certainty that new productive forces would not be released on any scale sufficient for a radical transformation of society. Extremes of wealth and poverty became more marked, the internal market flagged, and ancient society suffered a decline of trade and population and, finally, the wastage of class warfare. Into this sequence the rise of the Roman Empire brought the new factor of a parasitical capital; and it spread the Hellenistic system to Italy, where agrarian pauperism went side by side with imperial expansion and domination on an unparalleled scale. From all this arose the typical developments of the social life of the Empire—industrial dispersion and a reversion to agrarian self-sufficiency— and the final attempt to retrieve the crisis, or at least to salvage whatever could be salvaged from the ruins, by the unflinching use of oppression and the machinery of the bureaucratic State. These tendencies we have already analysed, and need not repeat them here. The important point is that they fall together into a sequence with its own logic, and that they follow—not of course in the specific details, which were determined by a thousand personal or fortuitous factors, but in their general outlines—from the premises upon which classical civilisation arose, namely an absolutely low technique and, to compensate for this, the institution of slavery. Herein lie the real causes of the decline and fall of the Roman Empire.

5   The Rostovtzeff Thesis

Like Walbank, M. I. Rostovtzeff sees the chief problem to
be the organization of Roman society, but his analysis is
different from Walbank's, as are his conclusions.

FROM *Social and Economic History of*
the Roman Empire BY M. I. ROSTOVTZEFF

INCOMPLETE AS IT IS, the picture which we have drawn shows very
clearly the chaos and misery that reigned throughout the Roman Empire in
the third century and especially in the second half of it. We have endeavoured to show how the Empire gradually reached this pitiful state. It was
due to a combination of constant civil war and fierce attacks by external foes.
The situation was aggravated by the policy of terror and compulsion which
the government adopted towards the population, using the army as its
instrument. The key to the situation lies, therefore, in the civil strife which
provoked and made possible the onslaughts of neighbouring enemies, weakened the Empire's powers of resistance, and forced the emperors, in dealing
with the population, to have constant recourse to methods of terror and
compulsion, which gradually developed into a more or less logically organized system of administration. In the policy of the emperors we failed to
discover any systematic plan. It was a gradual yielding to the aspirations of
the army and to the necessity of maintaining the existence of the Empire and
preserving its unity. Most of the emperors of this troubled period were not
ambitious men who were ready to sacrifice the interests of the community to
their personal aspirations: they did not seek power for the sake of power.
The best of them were forced to assume power, and they did it partly from a
natural sense of self-preservation, partly as a conscious sacrifice of their own
lives to the noble task of maintaining and safeguarding the Empire. If the
state was transformed by the emperors on the lines described above, on the
lines of a general levelling, by destroying the part played in the life of the
Empire by the privileged and educated classes, by subjecting the people to a

Michael I. Rostovtzeff, *Social and Economic History of the Roman Empire,* 2nd ed., I (1957),
491–501. Reprinted by permission of The Clarendon Press, Oxford.

cruel and foolish system of administration based on terror and compulsion, and by creating a new aristocracy which sprang up from the rank and file of the army, and if this policy gradually produced a slave state with a small ruling minority headed by an autocratic monarch, who was commander of an army of mercenaries and of a militia compulsorily levied, it was not because such was the ideal of the emperors but because it was the easiest way of keeping the state going and preventing a final breakdown. But this goal could be achieved only if the army provided the necessary support: and the emperors clearly believed they could get its help by the policy they pursued.

If it was not the ambition of the emperors that drew the state ever deeper into the gulf of ruin, and threatened to destroy the very foundations of the Empire, what was the immanent cause which induced the army constantly to change the emperors, to slay those whom they had just proclaimed, and to fight their brothers with a fury that hardly finds a parallel in the history of mankind? Was it a "mass psychosis" that seized the soldiers and drove them forward on the path of destruction? Would it not be strange that such a mental disease should last for at least half a century? The usual explanation given by modern scholars suggests that the violent convulsions of the third century were the accompaniment of the natural and necessary transformation of the Roman state into an absolute monarchy. The crisis (it is said) was a political one; it was created by the endeavour of the emperors to eliminate the senate politically and to transform the Augustan diarchy into a pure monarchy; in striving towards this goal the emperors leaned on the army, corrupted it, and provoked the state of anarchy, which formed a transitional phase that led to the establishment of the Oriental despotism of the fourth century. We have endeavoured to show that such an explanation does not stand the test of facts. The senate, as such, had no political importance whatsoever in the time of the enlightened monarchy. Its social prestige was high, for it represented the educated and propertied classes of the Empire, but its direct political participation in state affairs was very small. In order to establish the autocratic system of government there was not the slightest necessity to pass through a period of destruction and anarchy. Monarchy was established in actual fact by the Antonines without shedding a drop of blood. The real fight was not between the emperor and the senate.

The theory that a bloody struggle developed in the third century between the emperors and the senate must therefore be rejected as not fitting the facts. Certainly, the transformation of the principate into a military monarchy did not agree with the wishes of the senate, but that body had no political force to oppose to the emperors. Recognizing this fact, some leading modern scholars have attempted to explain the crisis in another way, but still in terms of political causes; on the assumption that the crisis of the third century arose not so much from the active opposition of the senate as from the relations between the emperors and the army. The new army of the second part of the third century was no longer the army of Roman citizens recruited from Italy and the romanized provinces; the elements of which it was composed were provinces of little or no romanization and warlike tribes recruited beyond its frontiers. No sooner had this army recognized its own power at the end of the Antonine age, than it was corrupted by the emperors with gifts and flattery, and familiarized with bribery; it felt itself master of the state and gave orders to the emperors. The conditions imposed by it were partly of a material, and partly, up to a certain point, of a political, nature: for example, that the privileges enjoyed by the ruling classes should be extended to the army. As the emperors had not succeeded in giving their power a juridical or religious basis which was sufficiently clear to convince the masses and the army without delay, it became increasingly clear that they governed only by the grace of the soldiers; each body of troops chose its own emperor and regarded him as the instrument for the satisfaction of its wishes.

This theory, which I hope I have summarized exactly, is undoubtedly nearer the truth and coincides in the main with the views set forth in this book. I have shown how the Roman emperors tried hard to find a legal basis for their power. Emperors like Vespasian and, even more, Domitian saw clearly that the dynastic principle of hereditary succession, founded upon the Oriental conception of the divine nature of imperial power, and therefore upon the apotheosis of the living emperor, was much more intelligible to the masses than the subtle and complex theory of the principate as formulated by Augustus and applied by the majority of his successors, particularly the Antonines. Yet the simplification proposed by Domitian could not be accepted by the leading classes of the Roman Empire, since it implied the complete negation of the idea of liberty, which they cherished so dearly. These classes fought against the transformation of the principate into an unconcealed monarchy, and in their tenacious struggle they had, if not as an ally, at least not as an enemy, the army composed of citizens who held to a great extent the same opinions as themselves. The result was a compromise between the imperial power on one side, and the educated classes and the senate which represented them, on the other. This compromise was effected by the Antonines. When, at the end of the second century A.D., the barbarization of the army was complete, that body was no longer able to understand the delicate theory of the principate. It was instead prepared to accept the hereditary monarchy established by Septimius Severus, and the emperor, with the army's help, was able to suppress without difficulty the opposition aroused by his action. So far I am in the fullest agreement with the theory described above.

But at this point difficulties begin. Why did the dynasty of the Severi not last, after it had been established, and accepted willingly by the army and unwillingly by the educated classes? How are we to explain the fact that the soldiers murdered Severus Alexander, and later even killed and betrayed the emperors they had themselves elected, thereby creating that political chaos which exposed the Empire to the greatest dangers? The continuous upheavals must have had a deeper cause than the struggle for the hereditary monarchy of divine right. This goal had been reached from the first moment; why did the struggle continue for another fifty years?

Perhaps the wisest course would be to be satisfied with this partial explanation, in the company of the majority of scholars. Our evidence is scanty, and the most comfortable way is always that of *non liquet* and *ignoramus*. In the first edition of this work I dared to offer a theory which is to some extent supported by our inadequate evidence, and which, if it proved acceptable, would enable us to understand the nature of the crisis of the Roman Empire. The five pages devoted to this explanation attracted the attention of the majority of my critics, and much has been written against my "theory," though without a single fact being adduced against it. The chief argument invoked against my "theory" is that the trend of my thoughts was influenced by events in modern Russia. Without entering upon an argument on this topic, I see no reason to abandon my previous explanation simply because I may, or may not, have been led to it by the study of similar events in later history. It still satisfies me and agrees with the facts in so far as I know them.

In my opinion, when the political struggle which has been fought around the hereditary monarchy between the emperors, supported by the army, and the upper classes, came to an end, the same struggle was repeated in a different form. Now, no political aim was at stake: the issue between the army and the educated classes was the leadership of the state. The emperors were not always on the side of the army; many of them tried to preserve the system of government which the enlightened monarchy had based upon the upper classes. These efforts were, however, fruitless, since all concessions made by the emperors, any act which might mean a return to the conditions of the Antonine age, met the half-unconscious resistance of the army. In addition, the *bourgeoisie* was no longer able to give the emperors effective aid.

Such was the real meaning of the civil war of the third century. The army fought the privileged classes, and did not cease fighting until these classes had lost all their social prestige and lay powerless and prostrate under the feet of the half-barbarian soldiery. Can we, however, say that the soldiery fought out this fight for its own sake, with the definite plan of creating a sort of tyranny or dictatorship of the army over the rest of the population? There is not the slightest evidence in support of such a view. An elemental upheaval was taking place and developing. Its final goal may be comprehensible to us, but was not understood even by contemporaries and still less by the actors in the terrible tragedy. The driving forces were envy and hatred, and those who sought to destroy the rule of the bourgeois class had no positive programme. The constructive work was gradually done by the emperors, who built on the ruins of a destroyed social order as well, or as badly, as it could be done and not in the least in the spirit of destroyers. The old privileged class was replaced by another, and the masses, far from being better off than they had been before, became much poorer and much more miserable. The only difference was that the ranks of the sufferers were swelled, and that the ancient civilized condition of the Empire had vanished for ever.

If the army acted as the destroyer of the existing social order, it was not because as an army it hated that order. The position of the army was not bad even from the social point of view, since it was the natural source of recruits for the municipal *bourgeoisie*. It acted as a powerful destructive and levelling agent because it represented, at the end of the second century and during the third, those large masses of the population that had little share in the brilliant civilized life of the Empire. We have shown that the army of M. Aurelius and of Commodus was almost wholly an army of peasants, a class excluded from the advantages of urban civilization, and that this rural class formed the majority of the population of the Empire. Some of these peasants were small landowners, some were tenants or serfs of the great landlords or of the state; as a mass they were the subjects, while the members of the city aristocracy were the rulers; they formed the class of *humiliores* as contrasted with the *honestiores* of the towns, the class of *dediticii* as compared with the burgesses of the cities. In short, they were a special caste separated by a deep gulf from the privileged classes, a caste whose duty it was to support the high civilization of the cities by their toil and work, by their taxes and rents. The endeavours of the enlightened monarchy and of the Severi to raise this class, to elevate it into a village *bourgeoisie,* to assimilate as large a portion of it as possible to the privileged classes, and to treat the rest as well as possible, awakened in the minds of the *humiliores* the consciousness of their humble position and strengthened their allegiance to the emperors, but they failed to achieve their main aim. In truth, the power of the enlightened monarchy was based on the city *bourgeoisie,* and it was not the aim of the *bourgeoisie* to enlarge their ranks indefinitely and to share their privileges with large numbers of newcomers.

The result was that the dull submissiveness which had for centuries been the typical mood of the *humiliores* was gradually transformed into a sharp feeling of hatred and envy towards the privileged classes. These feelings were naturally reflected in the rank and file of the army, which now consisted exclusively of peasants. When, after the usurpation of Septimius, the army became gradually aware of its power and influence with the emperors, and when the emperors of his dynasty repeatedly emphasized their allegiance to it and their sympathy with the peasants, and treated the city *bourgeoisie* harshly, it gradually yielded to its feelings and began to exert a half-conscious pressure on the emperors, reacting violently against the concessions made by some of them to the hated class. The *bourgeoisie* attempted to assert its influence and to save its privileges, and the result was open war from time to time and a ruthless extermination of the privileged class. Violent outbreaks took place after the reign of Alexander, whose ideals were those of the enlightened monarchy, and more especially after the short period of restoration which followed the reaction of Maximinus. It was this restoration that was ultimately responsible for the dreadful experiences of the reign of Gallienus; and the policy consequently adopted by that emperor and most of his successors finally set aside the plan of restoring the rule of the cities, and met the wishes of the peasant army. This policy, although it was a policy of despair, at least saved the fabric of the Empire. The victory of the peasants over the city *bourgeoisie* was thus complete, and the period of the domination of city over country seemed to have ended. A new state based on a new foundation was built up by the successors of Gallienus, with only occasional reversions to the ideals of the enlightened monarchy.

It is, of course, not easy to prove our thesis that the antagonism between the city and the country was the main driving force of the social revolution of the third century. But the reader will recollect the picture we have drawn of Maximinus' policy, of his extermination of the city *bourgeoisie,* of the support given him by the African army of peasants against the city land-owners; and he will bear in mind the violent outbreaks of military anarchy after the reign of Pupienus and Balbinus, of Gordian III, and of Philip. Many other facts testify to the same antagonism between country and city. It is remarkable how easily the soldiers could be induced to pillage and murder in the cities of the Roman Empire. We have already spoken of the destruction of Lyons by the soldiery after the victory of Septimius over Albinus, of the Alexandrian massacre of Caracalla, of the demand of the soldiers of Elagabal to loot the city of Antioch. We have alluded to the repeated outbreaks of civil war between the population of Rome and the soldiers. The fate of Byzantium, pillaged by its own garrison in the time of Gallienus, is typical. Still more characteristic of the mood both of the peasants and of the soldiers is the destruction of Augustodunum (Autun) in the time of Tetri-cus and Claudius in A.D. 269. When the city recognized Claudius, Tetricus sent a detachment of his army against the "rebels." It was joined by gangs of robbers and peasants. They cut off the water supply and finally took the flourishing city and destroyed it so utterly that it never revived. The two greatest creations of the period of urbanization in Gaul—Lyons and Autun— were thus laid in ruins by enraged soldiers and peasants. One of the richest cities of Asia Minor, Tyana, was in danger of suffering the same fate in the time of Aurelian. It was saved by the emperor, and the words he used to persuade the soldiers not to destroy it are interesting: "We are carrying on war to free these cities; if we are to pillage them, they will trust us no more. Let us seek the spoil of the barbarians and spare these men as our own people." It was evidently not easy to convince the soldiers that the cities of the Empire were not their chief enemies. The attitude of the soldiers towards them was like that of the plundering Goths, as described by Petrus Patricius. His words certainly expressed the feelings of many Roman soldiers. "The Scythians jeered at those who were shut up in the cities, saying, They live a life not of men but of birds sitting in their nests aloft; they leave the earth which nourishes them and choose barren cities; they put their trust in lifeless things rather than in themselves."

We have frequently noted also the close relations existing between the peasants and the soldiers. It was through soldiers that the peasants forwarded their petitions to the emperor in the time of Commodus and Septimius as well as in that of Philip and Gordian. In fact, most of the soldiers had no knowledge or understanding of the cities, but they kept up their relations with their native villages, and the villagers regarded their soldiers as their natural patrons and protectors, and looked on the emperor as their emperor and not as the emperor of the cities. In the sixth and seventh chapters we described the important part played during the third century by soldiers and ex-soldiers in the life of the villages of the Balkan peninsula and Syria, the lands of free peasant *possessores,* as contrasted with the lands of tenants or *coloni,* and we pointed out that they formed the real aristocracy of the villages and served as intermediaries between the village and the administrative authorities. We showed how large was the infiltration of former soldiers into the country parts of Africa in the same century; and in describing the conditions of Egypt during that period we repeatedly drew attention to the large part played in the economic life of the land by active and retired soldiers. All this serves to show that the ties between the villages and the army were never broken, and that it was natural that the army should share the aspirations of the villages and regard the dwellers in the cities as aliens and enemies.

Despite the changed conditions at the end of the fourth century, the relations between the army and the villages remained exactly as they had been in the third. The cities still existed, and the municipal aristocracy was still used by the government to collect the taxes and exact compulsory work from the inhabitants of the villages. It was no wonder that, even after the cities almost completely lost their political and social influence, the feelings of the peasants towards them did not change. For the villages the cities were still the oppressors and exploiters. Occasionally such feelings are expressed by writers of the fourth century, both Western (chiefly African) and Eastern, especially the latter. Our information is unusually good for Syria, and particularly for the neighbourhood of Antioch, thanks to Libanius and John Chrysostom. One of the leading themes which we find in both writers is the antagonism between city and country. In this constant strife the government had no definite policy, but the soldiers sided with the peasants against the great men from the cities. The sympathies of the soldiers are sufficiently shown by the famous passage in Libanius' speech *De patrociniis,* where he describes the support which they gave to certain large villages inhabited by free peasants, the excesses in which the villagers indulged, and the miserable situation of the city aristocracy, which was unable to collect any taxes from the peasants and was maltreated both by them and by the soldiers. Libanius, being himself a civilian and a large landowner, experienced all the discomfort of this *entente cordiale* between soldiery and peasants. The tenants on one of his own estates, perhaps in Judaea, who for four generations had not shown any sign of insubordination, became restless and tried, with the help of a higher officer, who was their patron, to dictate their own conditions of work to the landowner. Naturally Libanius is full of resentment and bitterness towards the soldiers and the officers. On the other hand, the support given by the troops to the villagers cannot be explained merely by greed. The soldiers in the provinces were still themselves peasants, and their officers were of the same origin. They were therefore in real sympathy with the peasants and were ready to help them against the despised inhabitants of the cities.

Some scattered evidence on the sharp antagonism between the peasants and the landowners of the cities may be found also in Egypt. In a typical document of the year A.D. 320 a magnate of the city of Hermupolis, a gymnasiarch and a member of the municipal council, Aurelius Adelphius, makes a complaint to the strategus of the nome. He was a hereditary lessee . . . of γῆ οὐσιακή [gê ousiakê—D.K.], a man who had inherited his estate from his father and had cultivated it all his life long. He had invested money in the land and improved its cultivation. When harvest-time arrived, the peasants of the village to the territory of which the estate belonged, "with the usual insolence of villagers" . . . tried to prevent him from gathering in the crop. The expression quoted shows how deep was the antagonism between city and country. It is not improbable that the "insolence" of the peasants is to be explained by their hopes of some support from outside. They may have been justified: the proprietor may have been a land-grabber who had deprived them of plots of land which they used to cultivate; but the point is the deep-rooted mutual hostility between the peasants and the landowners which the story reveals.

I feel no doubt, therefore, that the crisis of the third century was not political but definitely social in character. The city *bourgeoisie* had gradually replaced the aristocracy of Roman citizens, and the senatorial and the equestrian class was mostly recruited from its ranks. It was now attacked in turn by the masses of the peasants. In both cases the process was carried out by the army under the leadership of the emperors. The first act ended with the short but bloody revolution of A.D. 69-70, but it did not affect the foundations of the prosperity of the Empire, since the change was not a radical one. The second act, which had a much wider bearing, started the prolonged and calamitous crisis of the third century. Did this crisis end in a complete victory of the peasants over the city *bourgeoisie* and in the creation of a brand-new state? There is no question that the city *bourgeoisie,* as such, was crushed and lost the indirect influence on state affairs which it had exerted through the senate in the second century. Yet it did not disappear. The new ruling bureacracy very soon established close social relations with the surviving remnant of this class, and the strongest and richest section of it still formed an important element of the imperial aristocracy. The class which was disappearing was the middle class, the active and thrifty citizens of the thousands of cities in the Empire, who formed the link between the lower and the upper classes. Of this class we hear very little after the catastrophe of the third century, save for the part which it played, as *curiales* of the cities, in the collection of taxes by the imperial government. It became more and more oppressed and steadily reduced in numbers.

While the *bourgeoisie* underwent the change we have described, can it be said that the situation of the peasants improved in consequence of their temporary victory? There is no shadow of doubt that in the end there were no victors in the terrible class war of this century. If the *bourgeoisie* suffered heavily, the peasants gained nothing. Any one who reads the complaints of the peasants of Asia Minor and Thrace which have been quoted above, or the speeches of Libanius and the sermons of John Chrysostom and Salvian, or even the "constitutions" of the Codices of Theodosius and Justinian, will realize that in the fourth century the peasants were much worse off than they had been in the second. A movement which was started by envy and hatred, and carried on by murder and destruction, ended in such depression of spirit that any stable conditions seemed to the people preferable to unending anarchy. They therefore willingly accepted the stabilization brought about by Diocletian, regardless of the fact that it meant no improvement in the condition of the mass of the population of the Roman Empire.

6 The Barbarians and the Ruin of the Roman Empire

The interpretation of Piganiol is the simplest and most direct of any recent attempt at an explanation.

FROM *L'Empire Chrétien* BY ANDRÉ PIGANIOL

THE LATE EMPIRE is usually considered as the very model of an epoch of decadence. A useful and happy decadence from the point of view of Augustine and his modern emulators because it liberated new forces, since the fall of Rome permitted the shaking off of the oppression of the past.

Nevertheless, this notion of decadence is quite confused. If one wishes to say that Roman civilization went through a critical period, no one will deny it. The problem is to know if it could not renew itself, transform itself, without going through the catastrophe which was followed, not at all by a miraculous rise, but by the dark age of the beginning of the Middle Ages.

To explain the decadence, the ancient Greek philosophers taught that it was tied to a certain periodicity of the course of the stars. Moderns have not altogether renounced these cosmological explanations.

According to Ellsworth Huntington, periods of decadence coincide with world periods of drought. There would have been a constant decrease in rainfall from 200 to 400, whence the pressure of the barbarians, themselves pressed by others who were dying of hunger. "Thus Rome perished, and its fall was followed by that period of unfavorable climate which is called the dark age of the Middle Ages."

Unfortunately, we possess no statistics of rainfall during Mediterranean antiquity, and we doubt that they can be supplied by determining the periods of growth of old trees in California.

Oliganthropy, Malthusianism, ruined Greece according to Polybius. The apogee of the population of the Roman Empire seems to be placed toward

André Piganiol, *L'Empire Chrétien* (1947), pp. 411–22. Translated by Donald Kagan by permission of Presses Universitaires de France, Paris. Reprinted from Donald Kagan, ed., *Decline and Fall of the Roman Empire* (1962), by permission of D. C. Heath and Company.

the time of Caracalla and a decline, doubtless very sharp, followed in the course of the catastrophes of the third century. The evil was aggravated in the 4th century when one sees cultivated lands return to wasteland, as well in Italy as in North Africa or in Egypt and the cities shrank to very small enclaves. In addition, Christianity aggravated Malthusianism; if Eusebius does not attest to it expressly, the Life of St. Melanie would prove it.

Not only did the population decline, but its very composition was changed. According to the pseudo-biological theory of Seeck, the Romans practiced a reverse selection (*Ausrottung der Besten*): the emperors on the one hand, the popular revolts on the other, worked toward the destruction of men of character, the elite. For the imperial period as a whole must be defined as a period of terror. One would also like to pose the problem of knowing to what degree the mixing of peoples favored cross-breeding, the diffusion of Germanic or Semitic elements; but, without statistics this inquiry will come to naught. Besides, it is useless, since in order to condemn the theory of Seeck it is enough to observe that the fourth century produced some very fine human types and that in this respect the century of the Antonines is far from being able to rival it. When all has been reckoned, moreover, the diminution of the population did not return its number, to what it was at the beginning of the Christian era, and was, in fact, far from it.

G. Ferrero informs us that the fall of Rome had as its cause a crisis of authority. The principal cause of this crisis was the equivocal and badly defined character of the imperial power. What was its source, the people or the senatorial aristocracy? Did the army have the title to speak in the name of the people? Did the imperial power, born of an acclamation, have the right to perpetuate itself in a dynasty? From these uncertainties resulted revolutions, massacres of the elite and anarchy.

But did not the system of Diocletian remedy these evils? It does not appear that the absolutist regime of the late empire was seriously contested. At most one may say that, in the circle of Roman nobles, the dynastic principle was discussed. The theory of the divine character of the prince was susceptible to interpretations which made it acceptable even to the Christians.

G. Ferrero adds that in the late empire the destruction of the elite handed over power to a new oligarchy of the newly wealthy and of high officials who came from barbarous elements of the population. He thus agrees with M. Rostovtzeff, according to whom the revolution of the third century, the victory of the masses, the physical destruction of the cultivated class, had as a consequence a fatal "bolshevization" of civilization.

But when we read Marcus Aurelius we find in his *Meditations* harsher judgments on the incomprehension and incapacity of the ruling class; to save the empire an appeal had to be made to new men. It is not at all proved that the governmental personnel of the late empire could not bear comparison with that of the second century. What debased spirits and broke their *élan* was the deprivation of liberty. Not only had the masses taken no part in government since the republic, but the municipal aristocracy itself was put into tutelage under the empire. It would, however, be rash to assert that the Roman Empire died because liberty died, for it had been dead for centuries.

At the heart of the Roman Empire the conquered nationalities had in no way lost consciousness of their origin and many were the means of resistance to the unifying will of Rome. In the fourth century there was a rebirth of indigenous languages. In the artistic realm one sees very old popular traditions revive. In Africa under cover of the donatist schism, it was the Berbers who rose up against Rome. Egypt had always been like a foreign body in the empire. What is especially new and serious is the growth of a feeling of opposition in Gaul; it is certain that the emperors of the fourth century were preoccupied with it and it is doubtless to overcome it that Valentinian had to consent to take up his home at Trèves. It is not easy to know what elements made up the feeling of opposition of the Gauls. Did they blame Rome for not defending the Rhine attentively enough? Or rather, on the other hand, were the Germanic elements which had infiltrated Gaul during the third century plotting treason? It is quite probable that both parties existed in Gaul and that neither was satisfied with Rome.

But this resistance of nationalities would have been serious only if it was opposed to a Roman nationalism which would try to maintain them in a state of inferiority or slavery. There was none of that, all the people of the empire were equal; the rebirth and multiplication of local diets allowed them to express their wishes.

The nationalities which awoke, moreover, were conscious of the profound tie which united them to one another. A little later than the terms *Francia, Alamannia, Gothia* appeared *Romania*. The wisdom of the imperial policy permitted all nationalities to live fraternally in the bosom of this great family which had only barbarians for enemies.

The Roman state went bankrupt in the third century. It was incapable of continuing to pay its officials and its armies without recourse to confiscations, monetary falsifications, requisition in kind, and unpaid services (*munera*).

Diocletian tried to put order into these improvisations; nevertheless the fiscal system of the fourth century is full of survivals which recall the great crisis of the third. In the time of great distress men supposed that burdens would no longer be placed on individuals but on interdependent groups. In the fourth century they did not succeed in freeing themselves from this convenient and perilous method. It was this fiscal system which led to the transformation of the class of municipal councillors into an army of tax collectors unpaid by the state and the class of free peasants into serfs of the great lords. It is above all because of its financial policies that the Roman state provoked the hatred of the masses. In vain did a pamphleteer in the time of Valentinian demand "fiscal relaxation."

But why did the state have to face these crushing expenses? Because of the squandering of the court, because of the increase of the bureaucracy, but above all, because of the needs of the army. It is easy to discern a series of important events which overturned the ancient economic order:

1. The decline of slavery. "The possessor of slaves," wrote M. Weber, "became the support of ancient culture." But the slave system is a consumer of men as the blast furnace is of coal; it is necessary constantly to supply a complement of slaves. Under the empire this supply dried up, and what happened is what would happen to our industrial civilization if there were no coal.

But may one not object to Weber that this crisis could be the instigator of a renewal? The homage rendered by the Fathers to the labor of the worker is a pleasing thing and so too is the great progress of the construction of the individual house of the peasant succeeding the barracks of the slaves.

2. The decline of the cities and the progress of the autarchy of the estate. The great estate was self-sufficient and allowed the city to die of starvation. Now, says Weber, the estate is the cell of the feudal regime, while the city was the birth-place of liberty.

3. The destruction of capital and the progress of a natural economy. Endemic war since the time of Marcus Aurelius was the cause of this destruction of wealth. The restoration of devastated regions had to absorb a great part of the public revenue; still it was never accomplished; Gaul in the fourth century was strewn with ruins. The state, overwhelmed by expenses, became a counterfeiter.

Is it correct to say, however, that in the fourth century there was a return to a natural economy? It seems to us that in reality two systems of exchange and two price systems had coexisted since the third century. On the one hand, there was the public market, where prices were controlled by the state, where provisions were, in part, on a quota basis; they were furnished by requisitions, the state undertaking their collection. They were bought with those dreadful pieces of debased coinage whose perpetual devaluations the numismatists have disentangled with such difficulty. But there was, on the other hand, a market for the rich. There, gold circulated, not secretly, but under the control of the state, which took a large percentage for itself. For the price of gold one could obtain objects of the greatest luxury. When Ausonius retired he returned to live on his lands and sent his men into the country, provisioning himself, as we say, "on the black market." It was this coexistence of a public market, anemic and badly supplied, and a clandestine and abundant market which was probably the most disquieting feature of the late empire.

4. The removal of the routes of commerce to central Europe. A great continental route connecting the valleys of the Rhine and the Danube tended to compete with Mediterranean commerce at the time of Trajan's death. We pick out the string of new imperial capitals, Trèves, Milan, Sirmium, Serdica, Constantinople. The emperors no longer had any occasion to pass through Rome. It was on both sides of this Rhine-Danube axis that the Celtic

empire was based and on it would one day be founded the new Europe.

Nevertheless, we do not have the right to speak of a decline of Mediterranean commerce. Maritime relations remained active from Narbonne to Alexandria, from Carthage to Constantinople. If the Roman peace had lasted, we might have seen a civilization of central Europe prosper in the radiance of the Mediterranean civilization.

5. The abuse of interventionism. State socialism, says H. M. R. Leopold, made the empire a workshop of forced labor; thus the state committed suicide; it provoked the discontent of the lower classes and ruined economic prosperity.

To this view is opposed that of F. Heichelheim, who believes, on the contrary, that the state had the duty of intervening to save the economy threatened by the crisis and that its intervention was effective. The state, according to him, struggled heroically to save civilization, to arrest tendencies toward feudalism, to maintain circulation.

From all these observations it follows that a new economic system was being born, characterized by associations of free workers, control exercised by the state on the circulation and allotment of provisions, more scientific exploitation of the great estates. But progress was hindered by monetary instability, insecurity, excessive taxation, and all these evils had a single cause, war.

The extraordinary luxury of the mighty was brutally opposed to the wretchedness of the poor who were at the point of abject mendicity. Gaius Gracchus had already asked why should the poor, living in holes, take up arms for the defense of their country. It is not in doubt that the poor of the late Empire sometimes appealed to the barbarians in order to avenge themselves on the rich. It was in the wake of the invasions of the third century that the countryside was depopulated and that the nobles extended their properties without limit: at the source of their scandalous fortunes were all the abuses which made the state of war possible. English scholars, studying the dispossession of the peasants in the fourth century, conclude that in Britain none of the conditions leading to a social revolution were absent.

Rome had been saved formerly, says Ammianus, by its austerity, by the solidarity between rich and poor, by the disregard of death; it was now lost because of its luxury and cupidity. Innumerable are the evidences of the Church Fathers, who stigmatized the immorality of both rich and poor. Salvienus confirms Ammianus in affirming that the cupidity (*avaritia*) was a vice common to almost all Romans.

But this is the common language of moralists which Sallust used in his beautiful gardens; to these black pictures the history of the fourth century would oppose how many examples of heroism, candor and charity! The social transformation since the time of the Severi favored the progress of a morality which was brutal, simplistic, and fraternal.

The conflicts between pagans and Christians were a serious cause of disintegration; we have said that they often served to mask ethnic conflicts.

Christianity did not declare war on Roman society, but it condemned it. It impatiently awaited the fall of the new Babylon which would be the first episode of the end of the world. That is why, before the accession of Constantine, the Christian went on strike, fled the burdens of the state, refused to fight for Rome. The heroic remedy of Constantine, to call in the Christians to govern, is comparable to the one a statesman would apply who gave power to revolutionaries, in the hope that the experience would moderate them. The Catholics in power were enriched and occupied the highest positions; they undertook the defense of property and allowed the hope that the fall of Rome would not take place tomorrow. But when Rome came to the supreme crisis the Christians, seeing it lost, treated it as the city of the devil, and betrayed it once more. The Roman nation had much to complain of these bad citizens.

Nevertheless, if Rome could have overcome this ordeal, is it not evident that Christianity by imposing the unity of faith on the whole empire would have contributed to a political solidification of this great body? Is it not under the form of the unity of Christianity that the empire perpetuated itself after its collapse? One may not say, therefore, that Christianity was responsible for the dissolution of the empire, since it was capable, on the contrary, had there been time, to confirm its moral unity.

M. Rostovtzeff believes that the decadence of Rome is explained by "the gradual absorption of the educated classes by the masses, and in consequence, the simplification of all the functions of political, social, economic and intellectual life which we call the barbarization of the ancient world." Has one really the right to speak of barbarization in the fourth century?

In the same way as, in economic life, gold was reserved for the wealthy while a dreadful bronze coinage was sufficient for the poor, so too did the Romanic languages, sprung from the vulgar language, begin to undermine the beautiful artistic language which was that of the late Latin writers and of polite society. The diversity of these languages will soon correspond to those of the nationalities, and this evolution was doubtless inevitable.

But it is not true that the intellectual was in regression. Certainly the rulers were afraid of books and one cannot think without horror of the *autos da fé* ordered by Constantine on Valens. Certainly the Christians regarded scientific culture with suspicion and St. Augustine held to a theory of obscurantism. It does not alter the fact that the plan of education which he himself traced derives from Hellenistic programs. What is important is the fact that the modern book at last made its appearance in the form of the *codex,* which took the place of the *volumen* and which became a marvelous instrument of culture. What is important is that the Roman nobles by editing the ancient texts showed the way to Byzantium which was the librarian of the world. What is important is that slavery, which for so long was an obstacle to technological progress, declined, for at once it seems that a period of scientific invention was going to open up. The new art was quite clumsy and did not respect the classical formulas and certain works provoke horror: but what is important is that to the old rhetorical and narrative style there succeeded a moving and impressionistic style, that the architects invested new models with disconcerting prodigality, that the miniature was born.

The philosophy and theology of these times discourage us. But let us remember those men whom a text of Filastrius lets us get a glimpse of, who meditated on the innumerable centuries of human prehistory and on the infinity of worlds. The truth seems to be that an admirable blossoming was in preparation if a catastrophe had not occurred. The catastrophe arrived in the form of the barbarian invasions.

The Germans lived in a dreadful land whose sterile soil they were too lazy to clear. They preferred war to ordered work and invaded neighboring states *fame urgente.* Neither the influence of Greece nor of Rome had succeeded in civilizing them after so many centuries. They had a primitive economy, they were ignorant of coinage, they had a rudimentary alphabet. But they were born soldiers. Their social organization was a form of their army; the tribe was divided into hundreds, and the centurion was at the same time leader for agriculture and war. The chief was surrounded by faithful men who wanted to die bravely for him. "The struggle was between the Roman Empire and the rule of the warrior band." These cruel people, according to a contemporary German historian, experienced a kind of ecstasy. Now the pressure of nomads from Asia drove them toward the West.

Against so evident and grave a danger the Romans needed a strong army. Yet the Roman emperors from fear of liberty, since the time of Augustus, had systematically disarmed the citizens and trusted the defense of the empire to mercenaries. They resorted first to the populations of the barbarous regions of the empire, then to foreign barbarians. In the fourth century Rome dared to confide the defense of the frontiers to barbarian tribes which it received into its bosom: it installed the Franks in Toxandria, charging them with the defense of the Rhine. In Pannonia they placed the Vandals and Ostrogoths, in Moesia the Visigoths, charging them with the defense of the Danube. In the reserve army itself the most highly regarded bodies were the barbarian *auxilia,* and barbarian officers occupied the highest ranks up to that of master of the militia. Synesius, addressing Arcadius a short time after the death of Theodosius, denounced the evil in these terms: "We are protected by armies composed of men who are of the same race as our slaves," and he recommends the remedy: obligatory military service. It is chiefly because Rome relinquished compulsory military service for citizens that she perished.

It is false to say that Rome was in decay. Pillaged, disfigured by the barbarian invaders of the third century, it restored its ruins. At the same time, at the price of a serious crisis, a work of internal metamorphosis was accomplished: a new concept of imperial power was formed which is that of Byzantium, a new concept of truth and beauty which is that of the Middle Ages, a new concept of collective and mutually responsible labor in the service of the social interest. And all the evils from which the empire suffered, crushing taxation, overthrow of fortunes and social classes, had as their origin not at all this fecund work of metamorphosis, but the perpetual war carried on by unorganized bands of those Germans who had succeeded in living on the frontiers of the empire for centuries without being civilized.

It is too convenient to assert that at the arrival of the barbarians into the empire "all was dead, it was a worn out body, a corpse stretched out in its own blood," or, again, that the Roman Empire in the West was not destroyed by a brutal shock, but that it had "fallen asleep."

Roman civilization did not die a natural death.

It was murdered.

Charlemagne—

The Maker of Europe?

CONTENTS

Many historians have seen in the age of Charlemagne the first beginnings of a distinctively Western civilization. The Roman Empire had been essentially a Mediterranean state with its greatest centers of population and wealth in the East. And even after the breakdown of the empire it seemed for centuries likely that Italy would continue to be dominated by Byzantium. Italy might well have remained a satellite of Greek culture and northern Europe merely barbarian. There would then have been no western European civilization such as later ages would know.

In the middle of the eighth century, however, a new alliance was formed between the Roman church and the northern kingdom of the Franks. The popes needed a strong ally to protect Rome against marauding Lom-

---

QUESTIONS FOR STUDY

1 What impressions of Charlemagne's ideals of government do you get from reading Dawson? Burns? General Capitulary of 802?

2 What is the major difference between Einhard's account of the coronation and those of other contemporary writers? How can the discrepancy be explained?

3 What evidence can you find in the sources that Charlemagne felt either attraction toward or aversion from the imperial title?

4 Who do you think took the initiative in planning the imperial coronation?

5 What were the motives of the principal participants in the coronation ceremony?

6 Why are the politics of Byzantium relevant to an understanding of the events at Rome?

bards. The Frankish leader, Pepin, who had seized the throne of the Franks in 750, wanted papal approval to legitimize his action. Accordingly, in 754, Pope Stephen II crossed the Alps and crowned Pepin as king. In return, Pepin invaded Italy, defeated the Lombards, and conferred on the Roman church the lands he had seized from the Lombards in central Italy.

Pepin's son, Charlemagne, a great conqueror, made himself ruler of France, western Germany, and northern Italy. His coronation as emperor of the Romans on Christmas Day, 800, symbolized a new ordering of the Western world. Charlemagne's empire did not survive as a political unit, but it retained a certain cultural coherence. Thenceforth there would be a distinctively European civilization, different in character from the Byzantine culture to the East and the Moslem culture to the South.

1 Charlemagne and Christian Culture

Christopher Dawson treated the imperial coronation as an important stage in the emergence of "Western Christendom."

FROM *The Making of Europe* BY CHRISTOPHER DAWSON

THE HISTORICAL IMPORTANCE of the Carolingian age far transcends its material achievement. The unwieldy Empire of Charles the Great did not long survive the death of its founder, and it never really attained the economic and social organisation of a civilised state. But, for all that, it marks the first emergence of the European culture from the twilight of pre-natal existence into the consciousness of active life. Hitherto the barbarians had lived passively on the capital which they had inherited from the civilisation which they had plundered; now they began to co-operate with it in a creative social activity. The centre of mediaeval civilisation was not to be on the shores of the Mediterranean, but in the northern lands between the Loire and the Weser which were the heart of the Frankish dominions. This was the formative centre of the new culture, and it was there that the new conditions which were to govern the history of mediaeval culture find their origin. The ideal of the mediaeval Empire, the political position of the Papacy, the German hegemony in Italy and the expansion of Germany towards the East, the fundamental institutions of mediaeval society both in Church and State, and the incorporation of the classical tradition in mediaeval culture—all have their basis in the history of the Carolingian period.

The essential feature of the new culture was its religious character. While the Merovingian state had been predominantly secular, the Carolingian Empire was a theocratic power—the political expression of a religious unity. This change in the character of the monarchy is shown by the actual circumstances of the installation of the new dynasty; for Pepin obtained

From *The Making of Europe* by Christopher Dawson, pp. 169–71, 175–6, 226–7, published by Sheed & Ward Inc., New York. Reprinted by permission of The Society of Authors, London.

Papal authority for the setting aside of the old royal house and was anointed king in the year 752 by St. Boniface according to the religious coronation rite which had grown up under ecclesiastical influence in Anglo-Saxon England and Visigothic Spain, but which had hitherto been unknown among the Franks. Thus the legitimation of the rule of the Carolingian house sealed the alliance between the Frankish monarchy and the Papacy which St. Boniface had done so much to bring about, and henceforward the Frankish monarchy was the recognised champion and protector of the Holy See. The Papacy had already been alienated from the Byzantine Empire by the Iconoclastic policy of the Isaurian emperors, and the extinction of the last survival of the Byzantine power at Ravenna by the Lombards in 751 forced the Pope to look for support elsewhere. In 754 Stephen II visited Pepin in his own dominions, and obtained from him a treaty which secured to the Papacy the Exarchate of Ravenna and the former Byzantine possessions in Italy, together with the duchies of Spoleto and Benevento. In return the Pope reconsecrated Pepin as King of the Franks, and also conferred on him the dignity of Patrician of the Romans. This was an epoch-making event, for it marked not only the foundation of the Papal State which was to endure until 1870, but also the protectorate of the Carolingians in Italy, and the beginning of their imperial mission as the leaders and organisers of Western Christendom.

The Carolingians were naturally fitted to undertake this mission since they were themselves the representatives of both sides of the European tradition. They traced their descent from Gallo-Roman bishops and saints as well as from Frankish warriors, and they combined the warlike prowess of a Charles Martel with a vein of religious idealism, which shows itself in Carloman's renunciation of his kingdom in order to enter the cloister, and Pepin's sincere devotion to the cause of the Church. But it is in Pepin's successor, Charles the Great, that both these elements find simultaneous expression. He was above all a soldier with a talent for war and military enterprise which made him the greatest conqueror of his time. But in spite of his ruthlessness and unscrupulous ambition he was no mere barbaric warrior; his policy was inspired by ideals and universal aims. His conquests were not only the fulfillment of the traditional Frankish policy of military expansion; they were also crusades for the protection and unity of Christendom. By his destruction of the Lombard Kingdom he freed the Papacy from the menace which had threatened its independence for two hundred years and brought Italy into the Frankish Empire. The long drawn out struggle with the Saxons was due to his determination to put an end to the last remains of Germanic heathenism as well as of Saxon independence. His conquest of the Avars in 793–794 destroyed the Asiatic robber state which had terrorised the whole of Eastern Europe, and at the same time restored Christianity in the Danube provinces, while his war with the Saracens and his establishment of the Spanish March were the beginning of the Christian reaction to the victorious expansion of Islam. In the course of thirty years of incessant warfare he had extended the frontiers of the Frankish monarchy as far as the

Elbe, the Mediterranean and the Lower Danube, and had united Western Christendom in a great imperial state.

The coronation of Charles as Roman Emperor and the restoration of the Western Empire in the year 800 marked the final stage in the reorganisation of Western Christendom and completed the union between the Frankish monarchy and the Roman Church which had been begun by the work of Boniface and Pepin.

*   *   *

As King, Charles had stood outside the Roman tradition; as Emperor, he entered into a definite juridical relationship with the head of the Church. His power was still as formidable as ever, but it was no longer indefinite and incalculable. Moreover, the idea of the Roman Empire was still indispensable to the Church. It was synonymous with Christian civilisation, while the rule of the barbarians was so identified with heathenism and war that the Liturgy couples together, "the enemies of the Roman name and the foes of the Catholic Faith." Consequently, it is by no means improbable that the Papacy as the representation of Roman universalism should have taken the initiative in the restoration of the Empire in 800, as it did once more seventy-five years later in the case of Charles the Bald.

However this may be, it is certain that the restoration of the Roman Empire, or rather the foundation of the new mediaeval Empire, had a religious and symbolic value which far outweighed its immediate importance from a political point of view. Charles used it, no doubt, as a diplomatic counter in his negotiations with the Eastern Empire, but his coronation made no difference in his life or government. He never attempted to ape the ways of a Roman or Byzantine Caesar, as did Otto III and other mediaeval emperors, but remained a thorough Frank, in dress and manners as well as in his political ideals. He even imperilled his whole work of imperial unification by dividing his dominions among his heirs in 806 according to the old Frankish custom, instead of following the Roman principle of indivisible political sovereignty; and the same tradition reasserted itself among his successors and proved fatal to the unity and continuity of the Carolingian Empire.

It was the churchmen and the men of letters, rather than the princes and statesmen, who cherished the ideal of the Holy Roman Empire. To them it meant the end of the centuries of barbarism and a return to civilised order. To Einhard, Charles is a new Augustus, and he views his achievement in the light of the Augustan ideal; while Modoin, the Bishop of Auxerre, writes of his age as the Renaissance of classical antiquity:

> rursus in antiquos mutataque saecula mores;
> aurea Roma iterum renovata renascitur orbe.
>
> [*The changing ages turn to ancient ways;*
> *golden Rome is born again, the world renewed*—B. T.]

In fact, though the learning of the Carolingian age may seem a poor thing to set by the side of that of the great Italian humanists, it was none the less a genuine Renaissance which had no less importance for the development of European culture than the more brilliant movement of the fifteenth century. The gathering together of the scattered elements of the classical and patristic traditions and their reorganisation as the basis of a new culture was the greatest of all the achievements of the Carolingian age.

*   *   *

Thus the culture that we regard as characteristically Western and European was confined in the main within the limits of the former Carolingian Empire, and found its centre in the old Frankish territories of Northern France and Western Germany. In the tenth century it was, as we have seen, hard pressed on every side and even tended to contract its frontiers. But the eleventh century saw the turn of the tide and the rapid expansion of this central continental culture in all directions. In the West the Norman Conquest took England out of the sphere of the Nordic culture that had threatened for two centuries to absorb it, and incorporated it into the continental society; in the North and East it gradually dominated the Western Slavs and penetrated Scandinavia by its cultural influence; while in the South it embarked with crusading energy on the great task of the reconquest of the Mediterranean from the power of Islam.

In this way the peoples of the Frankish Empire imposed their social hegemony and their ideals of culture on all the surrounding peoples, so that the Carolingian unity may be regarded without exaggeration as the foundation and starting-point of the whole development of mediaeval Western civilisation. It is true that the Carolingian Empire had long lost its unity, and France and Germany were becoming more and more conscious of their national differences. Nevertheless they both looked back to the same Carolingian tradition, and their culture was compounded of the same elements, though the proportions were different. They were still in essence the Western and East Frankish realms, though, like brothers who take after different sides of their family, they were often more conscious of their difference than of their resemblance. In both cases, however, the cultural leadership lay with the intermediate regions—the territories of the Empire that were most Latinised, and those in France where the Germanic element was strongest: Northern France, Lorraine and Burgundy, Flanders and the Rhineland. Above all, it was Normandy, where the Nordic and Latin elements stood in sharpest contrast and most immediate contact, that was the leader of the movement of expansion.

It was this middle territory, reaching from the Loire to the Rhine, that was the true homeland of mediaeval culture and the source of its creative and characteristic achievements. It was the cradle of Gothic architecture, of the great mediaeval schools, of the movement of monastic and ecclesiastical reform and of the crusading ideal. It was the centre of the typical development of the feudal state, of the North European communal movement and of the institution of knighthood. It was here that a complete synthesis was finally achieved between the Germanic North and the spiritual order of the Church and the traditions of the Latin culture.

2 Charlemagne as Seen by His Contemporaries

This biography of Charlemagne was written by a member of the imperial court circle about ten years after the emperor's death.

FROM *Life of Charlemagne* BY EINHARD

CHARLES WAS LARGE AND STRONG, and of lofty stature, though not disproportionately tall (his height is well known to have been seven times the length of his foot); the upper part of his head was round, his eyes very large and animated, nose a little long, hair fair, and face laughing and merry. Thus his appearance was always stately and dignified, whether he was standing or sitting; although his neck was thick and somewhat short, and his belly rather prominent; but the symmetry of the rest of his body concealed these defects. His gait was firm, his whole carriage manly, and his voice clear, but not so strong as his size led one to expect. His health was excellent, except during the four years preceding his death, when he was subject to frequent fevers; at the last he even limped a little with one foot. Even in those years he consulted rather his own inclinations than the advice of physicians, who were almost hateful to him, because they wanted him to give up roasts, to which he was accustomed, and to eat boiled meat instead. In accordance with the national custom, he took frequent exercise on horseback and in the chase, accomplishments in which scarcely any people in the world can equal the Franks. He enjoyed the exhalations from natural warm springs, and often practiced swimming, in which he was such an adept that none could surpass him; and hence it was that he built his palace at Aix-la-Chapelle, and lived there constantly during his latter years until his death. He used not only to invite his sons to his bath, but his nobles and friends, and now and then a troop of his retinue or bodyguard, so that a hundred or more persons sometimes bathed with him.

He used to wear the national, that is to say, the Frank, dress—next his

Einhard, *Life of Charlemagne* (1880), pp. 56–65, translated by Samuel Epes Turner.

skin a linen shirt and linen breeches, and above these a tunic fringed with silk; while hose fastened by bands covered his lower limbs, and shoes his feet, and he protected his shoulders and chest in winter by a close-fitting coat of otter or marten skins. Over all he flung a blue cloak, and he always had a sword girt about him, usually one with a gold or silver hilt and belt; he sometimes carried a jeweled sword, but only on great feastdays or at the reception of ambassadors from foreign nations. He despised foreign costumes, however handsome, and never allowed himself to be robed in them, except twice in Rome, when he donned the Roman tunic, chlamys, and shoes; the first time at the request of Pope Hadrian, the second to gratify Leo, Hadrian's successor. On great feastdays he made use of embroidered clothes and shoes bedecked with precious stones, his cloak was fastened by a golden buckle, and he appeared crowned with a diadem of gold and gems, but on other days his dress varied little from the common dress of the people.

Charles was temperate in eating, and particularly so in drinking, for he abominated drunkenness in anybody, much more in himself and those of his household; but he could not easily abstain from food, and often complained that fasts injured his health. He very rarely gave entertainments, only on great feastdays, and then to large numbers of people. His meals ordinarily consisted of four courses, not counting the roast, which his huntsmen used to bring in on the spit; he was more fond of this than of any other dish. While at table, he listened to reading or music. The subjects of the readings were the stories and deeds of olden time: he was fond, too, of St. Augustine's books, and especially of the one entitled "The City of God." He was so moderate in the use of wine and all sorts of drink that he rarely allowed himself more than three cups in the course of a meal. In summer, after the midday meal, he would eat some fruit, drain a single cup, put off his clothes and shoes, just as he did for the night, and rest for two or three hours. He was in the habit of awaking and rising from bed four or five times during the night. While he was dressing and putting on his shoes, he not only gave audience to his friends, but if the Count of the Palace told him of any suit in which his judgment was necessary, he had the parties brought before him forthwith, took cognizance of the case, and gave his decision, just as if he were sitting on the judgment seat. This was not the only business that he transacted at this time, but he performed any duty of the day whatever, whether he had to attend to the matter himself, or to give commands concerning it to his officers.

Charles had the gift of ready and fluent speech, and could express whatever he had to say with the utmost clearness. He was not satisfied with command of his native language merely, but gave attention to the study of foreign ones, and in particular was such a master of Latin that he could speak it as well as his native tongue; but he could understand Greek better than he could speak it. He was so eloquent, indeed, that he might have passed for a teacher of eloquence. He most zealously cultivated the liberal arts, held those who taught them in great esteem, and conferred great honors upon them. He took lessons in grammar of the deacon Peter of Pisa, at that time an aged man. Another deacon, Albin of Britain, surnamed Alcuin, a man of Saxon extraction, who was the greatest scholar of the day, was his teacher in other branches of learning. The King spent much time and labor with him studying rhetoric, dialectics, and especially astronomy; he learned to reckon, and used to investigate the motions of the heavenly bodies most curiously, with an intelligent scrutiny. He also tried to write, and used to keep tablets and blanks in bed under his pillow, that at leisure hours he might accustom his hand to form the letters; however, as he did not begin his efforts in due season, but late in life, they met with ill success.

He cherished with the greatest fervor and devotion the principles of the Christian religion, which had been instilled into him from infancy. Hence it was that he built the beautiful basilica at Aix-la-Chapelle, which he adorned with gold and silver and lamps, and with rails and doors of solid brass. He had the columns and marbles for this structure brought from Rome and Ravenna, for he could not find such as were suitable elsewhere. He was a constant worshipper at this church as long as his health permitted, going morning and evening, even after nightfall, besides attending mass; and he took care that all the services there conducted should be administered with the utmost possible propriety, very often warning the sextons not to let any improper or unclean thing be brought into the building or remain in it. He provided it with a great number of sacred vessels of gold and silver and with such a quantity of clerical robes that not even the doorkeepers who fill the humblest office in the church were obliged to wear their everyday clothes when in the exercise of their duties. He was at great pains to improve the church reading and psalmody, for he was well skilled in both, although he neither read in public nor sang, except in a low tone and with others.

He was very forward in succoring the poor, and in that gratuitous generosity which the Greeks call alms, so much so that he not only made a point of giving in his own country and his own kingdom, but when he discovered that there were Christians living in poverty in Syria, Egypt, and Africa, at Jerusalem, Alexandria, and Carthage, he had compassion on their wants, and used to send money over the seas to them. The reason that he zealously strove to make friends with the kings beyond seas was that he might get help and relief to the Christians living under their rule. He cherished the Church of St. Peter the Apostle at Rome above all other holy and sacred places, and heaped its treasury with a vast wealth of gold, silver, and precious stones. He sent great and countless gifts to the popes, and throughout his whole reign the wish that he had nearest at heart was to re-establish the ancient authority of the city of Rome under his care and by his influence, and to defend and protect the Church of St. Peter, and to beautify and enrich it out of his own store above all other churches. Although he held it in such veneration, he only repaired to Rome to pay his vows and make his supplications four times during the whole forty-seven years that he reigned.

The writer of the following letters, Alcuin, was a leading member of the group of learned churchmen that Charlemagne brought together at his court. The letters were written in 799.

FROM *Alcuin's Letters*

FLACCUS ALBINUS sends greetings to the peaceful lord, King David [*Charlemagne—B. T.*].

. . . If I were present I should have used many words to persuade your venerable dignity, had you the opportunity to listen, or I the eloquence to speak. For the pen is often wont to stimulate the secrets of the love of my heart to write of your excellence, of the stability of the kingdom given to you by God, and of the progress of the holy Church of Christ. She is disturbed greatly by the manifold wickedness of evil men, and tainted by the audacious crimes of the worst of men, not only among low-born persons, but even among the greatest and highest. All this is greatly to be feared.

For three persons have hitherto been the highest in the world: that is, the apostolic sublimity, which is accustomed to rule the throne of St. Peter, the prince of the Apostles, as its vicar. Your venerable goodness has informed me of what should be done in the case of him, who was the ruler of the aforesaid seat. Another is the imperial dignity and secular power of the second Rome, whose governor was impiously deposed, not by foreigners, but by his own relatives and fellow-citizens, as the story was everywhere spread by rumor. The third is the royal dignity, in which the dispensation of our Lord Jesus Christ placed you, as ruler of the Christian people, more excellent in power than the others mentioned above, more renowned for your wisdom, more sublime in the dignity of your realm. Behold, on you alone rests the entire safety of the churches of Christ. You are the avenger of crimes, you are the guide of the erring, you are the consoler of the grieving, you are the exaltation of good men. . . .

Nothing can be concealed from your wisdom: for we know that you are exceedingly well-learned both in the holy Scriptures and in secular histories. In all these things you have been given full knowledge by God, so that through you the holy Church of God might be ruled, exalted, and preserved for the Christian people. Who can describe the magnitude of the reward which God will give you for your greatest devotion? For eye has not seen, nor ear heard, nor the heart of man conceived what God has prepared for those who love Him. . . .

Flaccus, the faithful orator, sends wishes for eternal blessedness in Christ to his most beloved lord of lords, King David.

. . . O most sweet [Charles], glory of the Christian people, O defense of the churches of Christ, consolation of this present life. Because of these virtues, it is necessary that all men should exalt your blessedness in their prayers and aid you by their intercessions, since it is through your prosperity that the Christian Empire may be protected, that the Catholic faith may be defended, and that the rule of justice may become known to all. . . .

And would that you, whenever divine grace grants you enough freedom from the wicked Saxon people, might travel on the roads, govern your realms, do justice, repair churches, discipline the people, decree laws for individual persons and classes, to defend the oppressed, to ordain laws, to comfort pilgrims, and to show the way of righteousness and heavenly life to everyone everywhere. Thus the arrival of your piety would be a consolation to all; and blessings would come to the most famous sons of your nobility through your copious blessings, just as it is read that through the sanctity of your namesake David alone, a king most pleasing to God, the power of the royal throne was preserved for all his descendants. In such exercises of this religion the exaltation of your sons, the felicity of your realm, the well-being of your people, the abundance of harvests, the delight of all good men, and the blessings which the heavenly kingdom holds in store for you shall increase and be augmented through all eternity, with the help of Christ the God, O most sweet David. . . .

3   *The Imperial Coronation*

In 799 there was an attempted rebellion against Pope Leo III in Rome. This trouble was the immediate cause of Charlemagne's visit to the city in 800. Of the following five accounts the first three are by Frankish writers, the fourth by a member of the papal court, and the fifth by a Byzantine chronicler.

FROM *Frankish Royal Annals*

799

THE ROMANS SEIZED POPE LEO during a solemn procession and blinded him and cut out his tongue. [*It is evident from the following account that the chronicler exaggerated the pope's injuries—B. T.*] He was placed in custody but escaped over the wall and came to the legates of the lord king who were at St. Peter's basilica, namely abbot Wirindus and duke Winigis of Spoleto. He was then escorted to Spoleto. The lord king had set out for Saxony and, having crossed the Rhine near Lippeham set up his camp at Paderborn . . . and there received Pope Leo honorably while he was waiting for the return of his son, Charles. The pope was sent away as honorably as he had been received and at once set out for Rome [with a Frankish escort] while the lord king returned to his palace at Aachen.

800

At the beginning of the month of August, when Charles came to Mainz, he announced a journey into Italy. Having arrived at Ravenna with his army he set on foot a campaign against the Beneventans. He commanded his son, Pippin, to ravage their lands with the army while Charles, after seven days' delay, set out for Rome. As he drew near, Pope Leo, accompanied by Romans, went out to meet him at Nomentum which is twelve miles from the city and there received him with great humility and great honor. The pope dined with the king at this place and then at once returned to Rome.

Annales Laurissenses, G. H. Pertz, ed., *Monumenta Germaniae Historiae, Scriptores,* I (1826), 184–9, translated by Brian Tierney.

On the next day the pope stationed himself on the steps of the basilica of the blessed apostle Peter, with the standards of the city of Rome displayed and great crowds of pilgrims and citizens assembled there suitably grouped to shout the praises of him who was coming. Leo, with the clergy and bishops, welcomed the king when he dismounted from his horse and ascended the steps and then, having offered up a prayer, led him into the basilica of the blessed apostle Peter while all around chanted psalms. This happened on November 24.

Seven days later the king summoned a council and explained to all why he had come to Rome, and thenceforth he was daily occupied with the matters he had come to settle. He began with the most important of these, the investigation of the crimes of which the pontiff had been accused. Since no one would undertake to prove the crimes, Leo mounted into the pulpit of the basilica of the blessed apostle Peter before all the people with the Gospel in his hand and, invoking the name of the Holy Trinity, purged himself by oath of the crimes that had been imputed to him.

8 0 1

On the most holy day [*The chronicler reckons December 25 as the first day of the new year—B. T.*] of the nativity of the Lord, as the king rose from praying at Mass before the tomb of the blessed apostle Peter, pope Leo placed a crown on his head and all the Roman people cried out, "To Charles Augustus, crowned by God, great and peace-giving emperor of the Romans, life and victory." And after the laudation he was adored by the pope in the manner of the ancient princes and, the title of patrician being set aside, he was called emperor and Augustus. A few days later he commanded the men who had deposed the pope the year before to be brought before him. They were examined according to Roman law on a charge of treason and condemned to death. However, the pope interceded for them with the emperor and they were spared in life and limb. Subsequently they were sent into exile for so great a crime.

FROM *Annals of Lorsch*

8 0 0

IN THE SUMMER Charles gathered together his lords and faithful men in the city of Mainz. When he saw that there was peace throughout his dominions he called to mind the injuries that the Romans had inflicted on Pope Leo and, setting his face toward Rome, he journeyed there. After his arrival he

---

Annales Laureshamenses, G. H. Pertz, ed., *Monumenta Germaniae Historiae, Scriptores*, I (1826), 38, translated by Brian Tierney.

summoned a great council of bishops and abbots, together with priests, deacons, counts and other Christian people. Those who wished to condemn the apostle Leo came before this assembly. When the king realised that they did not want to condemn the pope for the sake of justice but maliciously, it became clear to the most pious prince Charles and to all the bishops and holy fathers present that, if the pope wished it and requested it, he ought to clear himself, not by judgment of the council, but spontaneously, by his own will; and this was done. When the pope had taken the oath, the holy bishops, together with the clergy and prince Charles and the devoted Christian people, began the hymn, *Te Deum laudamus, te Dominum confitemur.* When this was finished the king and all the faithful people with him gave thanks to God who had preserved the apostle Leo sound in body and mind. And he passed the Winter in Rome.

Now since the title of emperor had become extinct among the Greeks and a woman claimed the imperial authority it seemed to the apostle Leo and to all the holy fathers who were present at the council and to the rest of the Christian people that Charles, king of the Franks, ought to be named emperor, for he held Rome itself where the Caesars were always wont to reside and also other cities in Italy, Gaul, and Germany. Since almighty God had put all these places in his power it seemed to them that, with the help of God, and in accordance with the request of all the Christian people, he should hold this title. King Charles did not wish to refuse their petition, and, humbly submitting himself to God and to the petition of all the Christian priests and people, he accepted the title of emperor on the day of the nativity of our Lord Jesus Christ and was consecrated by the lord Pope Leo.

FROM *Life of Charlemagne* BY EINHARD

THE ROMANS HAD INFLICTED many injuries upon the Pontiff Leo, tearing out his eyes and cutting out his tongue, so that he had been compelled
Nov. 24, 800   to call upon the King for help. Charles accordingly went to Rome, to set in order the affairs of the Church, which were in great confusion, and passed the whole winter there.
Dec. 25, 800   It was then that he received the titles of Emperor and Augustus, to which he at first had such an aversion that he declared that he would not have set foot in the Church the day that they were conferred, although it was a great feast-day, if he could have foreseen the design of the Pope. He bore very patiently with the jealousy which the Roman emperors showed upon his assuming these titles, for they took this step very ill; and by dint of frequent embassies and letters, in which he addressed them as brothers,

Einhard, *Life of Charlemagne* (1880), pp. 65–6, translated by Samuel Epes Turner.

he made their haughtiness yield to his magnanimity, a quality in which he was unquestionably much their superior.

It was after he had received the imperial name that, finding the laws of his people very defective (the Franks have two sets of laws, very different in many particulars), he determined to add what was wanting, to reconcile the discrepancies, and to correct what was vicious and wrongly cited in them. However, he went no further in this matter than to supplement the laws by a few capitularies, and those imperfect ones; but he caused the unwritten laws of all the tribes that came under his rule to be compiled and reduced to writing. He also had the old rude songs that celebrate the deeds and wars of the ancient kings written out for transmission to posterity.

FROM *Life of Leo III*

THE FAITHFUL ENVOYS OF CHARLEMAGNE who had returned with the pope to Rome . . . spent more than a week examining those most evil malefactors to discover what crimes they could impute to the pope. Neither Pascal nor Campulus nor their followers found anything to say against him; so the aforementioned envoys seized them and sent them to France.

After a time the great king joined them in the basilica of the blessed apostle Peter and was received with great honor. He called together a council of archbishops, bishops, abbots and of all the Frankish and Roman nobility. The great king and likewise the most blessed pontiff took their seats and made the most holy archbishops and abbots seat themselves while all the other priests and the Frankish and Roman nobles remained standing. This council was to investigate all the charges that had been made against the holy pontiff. When all the archbishops, bishops and abbots heard this they declared unanimously, "We do not dare to judge the apostolic see which is the head of all the churches of God, for we are all judged by it and its vicar, but it may be judged by no one according to ancient custom. Whatever the supreme pontiff decrees we will obey canonically." The venerable pontiff said, "I follow the footsteps of the pontiffs who were my predecessors. I am ready to clear myself of the false charges that have been basely made against me."

On a later day, in the same church of the blessed apostle Peter, when all were present, namely the archbishops, bishops, abbots, all the Franks who were in the service of the great king and all the Romans, the venerable pontiff mounted to the altar holding the four Gospels of Christ and in a clear

Vita Leonis III, L. Duchesne, ed., *Le Liber Pontificalis*, II (1892), 6–8. Translated by Brian Tierney by permission of Editions E. de Boccard, Paris.

voice declared under oath, "I have no knowledge of these false crimes which the Romans who have persecuted me have basely charged me with, nor any knowledge of having done such things." When this was done all the archbishops, bishops, abbots and all the clergy chanted litanies and gave praise to God and to our lady the ever-virgin Mary, Mother of God, and to the blessed apostle Peter, prince of the apostles and of all the saints of God.

After this, on the day of the nativity of our Lord Jesus Christ, all were again gathered together in the basilica of the blessed apostle Peter. And then the venerable holy pontiff with his own hands crowned Charles with a most precious crown. Then all the faithful Romans, seeing how he loved the holy Roman church and its vicar and how he defended them, cried out with one voice by the will of God and of St. Peter, the key-bearer of the kingdom of Heaven, "To Charles, most pious Augustus, crowned by God, great and peace-giving emperor, life and victory." This was proclaimed three times before the tomb of blessed Peter the apostle, with the invocation of many saints, and he was instituted by all as the emperor of the Romans. Then on that same day of the nativity of our Lord Jesus Christ the most holy bishop and pontiff anointed Charlemagne's most excellent son, Charles, as king, with holy oil.

After the celebration of Mass, the most serene lord emperor presented a silver table weighing . . . pounds with its legs. Likewise, at the tomb of the apostle of God, the emperor and his kingly sons and his daughters presented various vases of pure gold . . .

Afterward those iniquitous malefactors, namely Pascal and Campulus, and their followers were brought into the presence of the most pious lord emperor, with all the noble Franks and Romans standing around, and everyone agreed about the evil words and deeds of those men. Campulus then rebuked Pascal and said, "It was an evil hour for me when I saw your face, for you have put me in this present danger." And so, each condemning the other they made manifest their own guilt. When the most pious emperor realized how cruel and wicked they were he sent them into exile in France.

FROM *Annals of Theophanis*

IN THE SAME YEAR [801] partisans of the Roman pope, Hadrian, of blessed memory, started a riot against Pope Leo and injured his eyesight. The men who were selected to put out his eyes were moved by pity and spared him, so that he was not completely blinded. Leo immediately fled to Charles, king of the Franks. The king took vengeance on the enemies of the

F. Duncalf and A. C. Krey, *Parallel Source Problems in Medieval History* (Harper & Brothers, 1912), pp. 18–9. Reprinted by permission of Harper & Row, Publishers.

pope and restored him to his seat. Thus at this time Rome fell into the hands of the Franks and continued thus. Leo repaid Charles by anointing him from head to foot with oil in the church of the blessed apostle, and, having saluted him with the title of *Imperator,* he crowned him. He also clothed him with the imperial robes and insignia. This happened on the 25th day of the month of December, in the ninth indiction.

> *Charlemagne's behavior after the coronation provides important evidence about his attitude toward the new dignity. The following formulas of greeting from his charters show how he chose to designate himself at different times during his reign.*

Charlemagne's Royal and Imperial Titles

April 1, 772   Charles, by the grace of God king of the Franks . . .

June 5, 774   Charles, by the grace of God king of the Franks and of the Lombards . . .

July 16, 774   Charles, by the grace of God king of the Franks and of the Lombards and patrician of the Romans . . . (This last title was regularly used until after the imperial coronation on December 25, 800.)

March 4, 801   Charles, by the grace of God king of the Franks and of the Lombards and patrician of the Romans . . .

May 29, 801   Charles, most serene Augustus, crowned by God, great and pacific emperor governing the Roman empire who also, through the mercy of God, is king of the Franks and of the Lombards . . .

813   Charles, by divine grace emperor and Augustus and king of the Franks and of the Lombards . . .

E. Mühlbacher, *Diplomatum Karolinorum I, Monumenta Germaniae Historiae* (1906), pp. 95, 116, 264, 265; and E. Dümmler, *Epistolae Variorum I, Monumenta Germaniae Historiae* (1895), p. 556; both translated by Brian Tierney.

4　Some Modern Accounts of the Coronation

C. Delisle Burns presented the imperial coronation as the climax of a political policy deliberately pursued by Charlemagne and his predecessors.

FROM *The First Europe* BY C. DELISLE BURNS

ON CHRISTMAS DAY, A.D. 800, Charles the Great, the king of the Franks, was crowned as Emperor and Augustus in the basilica of St. Peter in the Vatican by Pope Leo III. Each of the chief actors in this episode was playing a part. And in view of the later history of the Holy Roman Empire, which was supposed by some historians to have then come into existence, the parts make the play almost a comedy. But that is from the point of view of a much later age. At the time and throughout the Middle Ages, the majority of men who thought at all on such subjects, no doubt, seriously believed that Charles was a successor of the Emperor Augustus, and that the successor of St. Peter had the power to make him so.

*　　*　　*

THE POLICY OF THE CAROLINGIANS

The steps taken by those in control of social power, which led eventually to the crowning of Charles the Great, may be shortly described as follows. They are all connected with the three names—Charles Martel, Pippin his son, and Charles the Great his grandson. It is the story of the conquest of supreme power by a Frankish family, of its entanglement in Italian rivalries and of the final acceptance of a theocratic authority, as a method of preserving and extending military conquests. Conscious policy was that of barbarian warriors who could extend their power by armed force but found, as all

C. Delisle Burns, *The First Europe*, pp. 569, 580–1, 587–8, 599–603, 609–11. Reprinted by permission of George Allen & Unwin Ltd., London.

barbarians are surprised to find, that they could not hold their conquests except by acquiring some moral authority.

Charles Martel, the illegitimate son of Pippin of Herstal, made his first bid for power at the age of twenty-five, on the death of his father (A.D. 714). His father had secured, at the end of interminable and confused struggles and treacheries, the power to control, as chief of the Palace, the king of the Franks. Charles Martel had to fight battles and employ the traditional treachery, in order to secure his power. But, with the assistance of the Frankish warriors who held land in Austrasia, and of those from Neustria who were discontented with the recent efforts to restore power to the king's Court (*palatium*), he contrived eventually to secure the greatest military power in the kingdom for himself. His control of Neustria or northern France compelled him to take account of the advance of the Saracens northwards from Spain; and in A.D. 732 he defeated the Saracen raiders in a great battle near Poitiers. This battle has been given by some historians an exaggerated importance. It is even said to have saved western Europe from becoming Mohammedan. But it seems likely, in fact, that the Saracen raiders defeated by Charles Martel were only seeking for loot and not for permanent conquest; and besides, the Saracen leaders were already divided among themselves before meeting the Frankish forces. Their dissensions may have largely contributed to their defeat.

For the future policy of the Frankish leaders, however, what was generally believed was more important than what actually occurred. It was believed that Charles Martel had defended the whole of western Christendom and defeated its chief enemies. Thus he became the instrument of God's will and the protector of the Faith against "infidels."

*   *   *

THE FRANKS IN ITALY

The next step in the formation of the imperial idea was taken by Pippin, the son of Charles Martel. The expedition against the Lombards in Italy, which Gregory III had asked Charles to undertake, was eventually led into Italy by Pippin in A.D. 754; but not before the Pope, Stephen II, had travelled North to make intercession himself with Pippin. By this time Pippin had been already crowned and anointed by St. Boniface as king of the Franks; and the Pope himself again anointed Pippin and his two sons at the monastery of St. Denis on January 6, 754. In the early summer after an assembly of the Franks, at which the policy was opposed by Frankish nobles, Pippin advanced into Italy and laid siege to Pavia, the Lombard capital. The Pope returned to Rome in October of that year; and from this time the king of the Franks was addressed in papal letters as *Patricius Romanorum*.

*   *   *

THE ROMAN EMPIRE

In the year following the Council of Frankfurt, Pope Hadrian died and was succeeded by Leo III (A.D. 795–816). The new Pope at once sent an embassy to Charles the Great to announce his election and to present to him the keys of the "Confesson" of St. Peter and the banner of the city of Rome. Leo evidently intended to carry on the policy of Hadrian. But events in Constantinople drastically altered the situation, at any rate in the minds of Charles and his advisers. In A.D. 797 the Emperor, Constantine VI, was blinded by order of his mother, who thrust him from the imperial throne and assumed supreme authority herself. Irene favoured the worship of images and was supported by the monks and most of the clergy in the East. She might, therefore, have expected support for her policy in the West. But evidently the violent deposition of an Emperor by his own mother and the assumption by a woman, for the first time in history, of supreme authority in the Roman Empire, caused consternation among those who followed public policy.

Two years later a still greater shock to sentiment in the North affected the situation. Pope Leo III, going in procession at the Greater Litanies, April 25, 799, was set upon by officials of the Roman Church, relatives of the late Pope, who beat him to the ground and attempted to tear out his eyes and tongue. They left him for dead. But his own friends rescued him; and he fled as a suppliant to Charles the Great at Paderborn. Charles received him with honour; and an elaborate poem by Angilbert, abbot of St. Riquier, describes the procession of Charles and his beautiful daughters and the splendid feast prepared for the Pope. The impression made by these events, in so far as it affected policy, is well expressed in a letter from Alcuin to Charles the Great, containing the following passage.

"There have been until now three persons who were highest in the world. That is, the Apostolic Sublimity which rules as Vicar the seat of St. Peter, Prince of the Apostles. And what has happened to him who was the holder of that seat, your respected kindness has informed me. Another is the Imperial Dignity, the secular power of the second Rome (Constantinople). How impiously the governor of that Empire has been deposed, not by foreigners but by those of his own household and city, is everywhere increasingly narrated. The third is the Kingly Dignity in which the dispensation of Our Lord Jesus Christ has placed you as ruler of the Christian people—a ruler superior in power to the other above-mentioned dignities, more noble in wisdom and higher in the dignity of rule. Lo, now on you alone rests the whole safety of the Churches of Christ—you are the avenger of crime; you are the ruler of the sinful; you are the comforter of those who weep and the exaltation of the virtuous."

It will be noticed that Alcuin does not suggest any change in the status or function of the king of the Franks. Indeed, he definitely makes a distinction between the imperial and the regal power, and treats the second as the instrument for the assistance of the Church and the Christian people. The use of the word *imperium* in an earlier letter of Alcuin to Charles indicates only the same sort of indefinite, superior authority as was intended by Bede when he wrote that the king of Kent had an *imperium* over eastern England. For Alcuin, Charles is always "King David" and not the Emperor Augustus. Thus, in a letter of A.D. 789 to Charles the Great, Alcuin writes: "May God grant eternal salvation and the glory of empire (*decus imperii*) to you, beloved David." Clearly "imperium," in this use, has no definite reference to the Roman Empire.

The same vague use of titles drawn from the ancient tradition before the actual coronation of Charles by Pope Leo, is to be found in the poem of Angilbert, referred to above, which describes the meeting of Charles the Great and the fugitive Pope Leo. In that poem Charles is referred to as "king, ruler, revered chief, augustus"; and some lines farther down as "head of the world, chief of Europe, hero and augustus." When, in the poet's imagination, the Pope appears to Charles in a dream, the phrase from Lucan's *Pharsalia* is used—"cold fear held the limbs of the Augustus." Clearly "augustus" was not intended to imply in any exact sense the traditional imperial authority. It was to Charles, as the great *king,* that his followers turned.

A Pope suppliant at the Court of a Frankish king, asking to be restored to his authority over his rebellious subjects, created a new situation, of which Charles was evidently not unwilling to take advantage. He sent the Pope back to Rome under the protection of Frankish armed forces and himself followed with his Court and retainers, reaching Rome on November 24, 800. For some weeks consultations or discussions of policy were carried on in Rome. The opponents of the Pope had charged him with perjury, adultery and other crimes; and had excused their violence as a legitimate rebellion against tyranny. The king of the Franks, who had restored the Pope and was now in control of the city of Rome, evidently could not altogether disregard the charges brought against Leo. But there was no attempt to set up any public court or council for a decision of the case; and on December 23, 800, in St. Peter's, in the presence of Charles and his warriors, the Pope swore a solemn oath rebutting all the charges against him. The Greek historian, Theophanes, was in no doubt about the political situation thus established. He writes that then "for the first time the city of Rome came under the power of the Franks." And according to Einhard, on the same day on which the Pope's oath was sworn, Charles received an embassy from the patriarch of Jerusalem which brought to him the keys of the Sepulchre, as well as the keys and the banner of the city itself, then in control of the Mohammedans.

THE CORONATION

The play at this point reaches the scene in St. Peter's when Charles was crowned by the Pope; but so many different interpretations have been placed upon what occurred, that it may be well to state explicitly what explanation will be given below. In the view here maintained the coronation was arranged beforehand between the Pope and Charles, and was probably the outcome of the policy, not of the Pope but of Charles himself. Secondly, the ceremony was intended by Charles to indicate the assumption of a *title,* and not the establishment of an *institution*—still less the claim to control an ancient institution already in existence, the Roman Empire. Thirdly, the title was intended to add prestige to the king of the Franks in all his territories indeed but primarily to express his new position in relation to the Pope. It implied the recognition of a higher status than that of Patrician; and from the Pope's point of view, it expressed the assumption that the king of the Franks was the official protector of the papal territories.

What actually occurred in St. Peter's on Christmas Day A.D. 800 is described in four different documents, of which two at least contain accounts amended in view of the political effects of the coronation in later years. These two accounts are in the *Annales Laureshamenses* of about A.D. 803 and in the *Life of Charles* by Einhard, composed about twenty-five years after the event. But even the two more reliable accounts, one in the *Liber Pontificalis,* the other in the *Annals of the Kingdom of the Franks (Annales Laurissenses),* are affected by two different points of view—the former that of the Roman clergy, the latter that of the Frankish Court. Allowance must, therefore, be made for the elements of what would now be called "propaganda" in all the documents now available. Each writer of these documents was affected by the policy current in his circle and by the atmosphere of his time. It is childish to treat any record, however contemporary, as a colourless scientific formula.

The record in the *Liber Pontificalis,* which was probably written at the death of Leo III in A.D. 816, runs as follows: "After this [that is, after the ceremony of Leo's oath] on Christmas Day in the same basilica of St. Peter all were again gathered. And then the venerable and kindly bishop with his own hands crowned him with a precious crown. Then all the Roman faithful, seeing the great protection and love which he had for the Holy Roman Church and its Vicar, unanimously with a loud voice, at a sign from God and St. Peter the key-bearer of the Kingdom of Heaven, cried out—'To Charles, the devout, Augustus, crowned by God, great and pacific Emperor, life and victory!' Before the holy Confession of St. Peter, the Apostle, invoking many saints, it was three times said; and by all he was constituted Emperor of the Romans."

The account in the Frankish *Annals* runs as follows: "On the holy day of Christmas when the king, at Mass before the Confession of St. Peter, rose from prayer, Pope Leo placed a crown on his head and the cry was raised by the whole Roman people—'To Charles, Augustus, crowned by God, great and pacific Emperor of the Romans, life and victory!' And after acclamations, he was adored by the Pope in the manner of the ancient princes; and, dropping the title Patrician, he was called Emperor and Augustus."

It seems clear from these straightforward accounts, first, that Charles was quite well aware of what the Pope was going to do; secondly, that the crowd in the basilica, euphemistically called "the whole Roman people," knew beforehand what to call out; and thirdly, that the ceremony indicated the adoption of a title, not the assertion of new powers. It is extremely doubtful whether anyone in St. Peter's on that day was thinking of the Roman Empire which had its capital at Constantinople; and indeed the Greek historian, Theophanes, mentions the event in the short phrase—"In this year Charles, the king of the Franks, was crowned by Pope Leo"—as if crowning were a habit in the West, of not much importance.

*   *   *

If anything more were needed to show that Charles the Great did not establish an Empire, and was not in anything but name an Emperor, a brief review of the actual situation in which he left Europe would be conclusive. There was no capital or permanent centre of administration and law. The old barbarian custom continued of moving the king's officials and retinue from villa to villa. It made no difference in practice that a villa or country residence of a king might be called a "palace" (*palatium*). Indeed, this use of the word is merely another sign of make-believe by which the central offices of ancient Rome on the Palatine Hill gave their name to any of the scattered houses of a barbarian chieftain. Again there was no central administration. The king's agents (*missi dominici*) were quite unable to control the counts or other local landowners who had established themselves in almost independent power over different districts. Worse still, there was no permanent armed force, either for internal order or for defence against foreign enemies. Charles the Great followed the old practice of summoning for an expedition as many armed men as he could collect in the early summer, and of allowing them to return to their scattered homes in the autumn. He did, indeed, attempt to establish small permanent outposts on his north-eastern frontier, manned by counts and their armed retainers; but that there was no single defensive system is proved by the number of expeditions the king had to make, to help these outposts. Finally, in the system established or rather continued under Charles the Great, there was none of that "providence" (*providentia*) with which the Emperor was credited under the old Roman system. He made no roads. His system of government did not require them. He conceived a plan of a canal between the Main and Danube; but when the work was begun, it was abandoned because the sides fell in, owing to the lack of competent workers. He repaired the old Roman harbour at Boulogne, but seems never to have grasped the need for new harbours, as a protection against the raids of the Northmen. He did, indeed, give money and land for the building and maintenance of churches and monasteries— which may be taken to correspond to the building of temples and public baths by the Roman Emperors; but the administration of what would now be called "social services" was in the hands of the clergy and not of the king or his counts.

In short, Charles the Great, stripped of the romances which adorned "Charlemagne," was simply a barbarian warrior of great energy, limited intelligence, no education and great simplicity of mind. Like Clovis, three hundred years before him, he believed that he could promote Christianity in the form familiar to him by killing some of those who had never heard of it and compelling the others to be baptized. He was intelligent enough to appreciate the services of scholars and to support their efforts for the promotion of learning and music among the clergy. His ambitions and ideals were those of a barbarian chieftain; and his leisure was spent in hunting and swimming. He was frugal in food and drink and clothing, but somewhat expansive in his affections. The number of his concubines and illegitimate children is not known; and he enjoyed having about him all his daughters. But in an age in which savage cruelty and reckless treachery were not uncommon, even at the Court of the Roman Emperor, which claimed to be the centre of civilized life, Charles the Great was exceptional in attracting faithful supporters and in exciting admiration for the power of his personality.

He was a sincere Christian, in one of the many different meanings of that word. His correspondence shows that he was interested in the peculiar habits of the moon, in the status of the Holy Ghost, in the restriction of the use of religious pictures and in the correct method of administering Baptism. He was not interested in the more subtle moral issues which perhaps would have seemed important to Paulinus of Nola or to St. Boniface. He is said by Einhard to have listened with attention to the reading of St. Augustine's *City of God* and to have kept a writing tablet under his pillow at night, in order to practise writing the alphabet, which he never succeeded in doing. He spoke usually his own Germanic dialect but could speak Latin also fluently; and he understood Greek, although he could not speak it. He extended the dominions which Frankish warriors and churchmen controlled; but he left them so badly organized that soon after his death they were continually troubled by civil war and so badly defended that they were raided year after year by the Northmen and by the Saracens.

Karl Heldmann emphasized the role of Pope Leo III.

FROM *The Empire of Charles the Great*
BY KARL HELDMANN

LEO'S OATH OF DECEMBER 23, 800, had formally vindicated the pope —that meant that his opponents were placed formally in the wrong by virtue

Karl Heldmann, *Das Kaisertum Karls des Grossen: Theorien und Wirklichkeit* (1928), translated by R. E. Sullivan in *The Coronation of Charlemagne* (1959), pp. 67–9. Reprinted by permission of D. C. Heath and Company and Hermann Böhlaus Nachfolger, Weimar.

of his action. For every true son of the Church, and for Charles too, their guilt was thereby made clear in a legal sense. The tables were now turned: legal proceedings now not only could but indeed had to be directed against them. With these one could proceed properly only according to the precedents of the Roman law. Only now for the first time did the pope find himself in a position to raise a formal accusation against his opponents. This charge cited them as traitors.

In the writings concerning the problem the statement is often made that the sentencing of the opponents of Leo III followed immediately after the purification oath. But this is not correct. Between the two events lay the imperial coronation. And that is decisive. There can be no doubt about it. Since the imperial coronation cannot be explained in any other way, as my earlier investigations hoped to demonstrate, then it belongs organizationally to the sphere of this trial and is to be understood in the context of this trial.

The purification oath of Leo, in itself, had cleared the way for a criminal procedure against the conspirators. Any independent intervention of the pope or the king-*patricius* into such a procedure would—as things stood before December 25, 800—have signified not only a complete break with the legal traditions and order of Rome, would not only have upset the entire legal system of Rome, but also would have openly sharpened the political opposition and hatred against Leo to the extreme, and furthermore would have extended that feeling to Charles. Could either of them have allowed such a state of affairs to exist? According to the Roman law observed in Rome the urban prefect alone was able to conduct a legal criminal action. Of him, however, there is no mention in any source. Why not? This question has been answered in different ways . . . [and] none of these conjectures can be opposed or confirmed with certainty. But that is clearly not the point. For the essential consideration is something entirely different. . . .

A suitable pronouncement of judgment by the urban prefect—supposing the office was occupied at the time—would not necessarily have ended the struggle. For from his sentence the way was open for an appeal by the defeated party to the emperor: only the emperor's sentence was absolutely final. Furthermore: if the prefect refused [to judge the case in favor of the pope], if he himself perhaps belonged to the conspirators—which we do not know for certain—then only the direct judicial power of the emperor could intervene and the urban prefect himself could not be brought to account except by the emperor and his council of state, as was the case with all holders of the highest imperial offices. Thirdly, however, just at that time the legal organization not only of Rome but also of the empire in general was tottering, threatened most seriously at an unprecedented place in its basic structure, the emperorship, because after the overthrow and death of the Emperor Constantine VI (797), for the first time since the empire had arisen, a woman wielded the scepter of the Caesars with full sovereignty. It is of little consequence how Irene herself had laid her plans to cover up this political anomaly or to what extent the Eastern Empire under the pressure of force endured her overlordship as legitimate. But how did the West and especially Rome come to terms with the new situation? This is decisive for our question. . . . That the imperial urban prefect and the whole administration of justice in Rome could do without an emperor who was recognized on a sound basis, indeed, that anyone can doubt that an urban prefect was authorized to exercise his office at all without the authorization of the emperor needs no further argument after all the previous discussion.

As a result Leo III was in a difficult position. His purification oath had legally cleared him personally, but his position in Rome was still in no way "secure." From a juridical standpoint the possibility of a proper and final conclusion of the treason trial in his favor was completely uncertain as long as the question of the imperial throne, made acute by the *coup d'état* of Irene, appeared not to have been resolved beyond any doubt. From a political standpoint it was absolutely hazardous for the pope to appeal the decision of his dispute, from which the king-*patricius* Charles had to stand apart, to the imperial court in Constantinople which alone was competent to handle it, if on top of everything else, his enemies were in some way associated with the imperial party.

Out of this dilemma arose the new imperial project, built upon the *patricius* Charles. Who it was that brought the project up first we do not know. In any case its agent was none other than Leo III personally, and of him we shall speak as the father of the plan. It was the guarantee through which he could secure a proper and final settlement of the treason trial, favorable to his wishes; it was the political move by means of which he, after his own purification oath of December 23, intended to prepare an absolutely certain method in the form of a criminal procedure to bring about a quick and full defeat of his opponents in Rome, without first having to make juridically and politically precarious evasions with respect to Constantinople. The *patricius* Charles once established as emperor offered a way for the pope not merely to replace a sometimes lacking supreme judge, i.e., the imperial urban prefect, but also to place once again beyond a doubt and on a legitimate basis the whole legal system of Rome and imperial Italy, at least over against the doubtful right of Irene to rule.

This was the real motive which led to the coronation act of December 25, to the elevation of Charles, the king of the Franks and the Lombards and the *patricius* of the Romans to the rank of emperor of the Romans. It was not the wish to sanction formally an outwardly already far developed separation of Rome from the Roman Empire and to establish in place of that Empire a legal supremacy of the Frankish king over Rome that supplied Leo with the imperial concept; rather it was the compelling need to bring into existence, at all costs as quickly and with as little risk as possible, a lord established on the basis of the Roman Empire and its legal organization who would have supreme authority over his opponents in Rome. Not the romantic spell of universal empire, nor thankful respect for the truest son of the Roman Church created the emperorship of Charles the Great, but a sober political consideration of a purely local, yes, even purely personal kind.

Also the fact that such an intent fits in with actual historical events can be proved clearly. After the Mass Charles dedicated to St. Peter a silver table and along with his sons and daughters some golden vases, but this was not his first action in his official capacity as emperor: as simply *patricius*-king he would have brought his offerings there to the church too, especially after the (previously prepared for) coronation of his son Charles as king. The first official action of the new emperor and sovereign of Rome was not "an act of grace" but rather [his assumption of authority in seeing to] the continuation and the conclusion of the undecided quarrel between the pope and his opponents in the form of a criminal procedure against the latter. Whatever might have been the situation in that day with regard to the urban prefect, with an emperor at hand his powers no longer had any bearing on the question. The absolute and highest ranking court was now at hand. "A few days" after Christmas the new emperor took up the proceedings against Leo's opponents. They were subjected to "a severe questioning according to the Roman law" and "sentenced to death as traitors," but that sentence, on the request of the pope, was changed to exile into Francia. . . . Only after the death of their enemy Leo (May 25, 816) and the trip of his successor, Stephen IV (June 22, 816; died, Jan. 24, 817), to the imperial camp of Louis the Pious were they relieved from exile and their return to their homeland made possible.

> *Francis Ganshof maintained that the Frankish court, not Charlemagne himself, planned the coronation.*

FROM *The Imperial Coronation of Charlemagne*
BY FRANCIS GANSHOF

IT SEEMS TO ME that in order to understand Charlemagne's accession to the imperial dignity, we must go back to Alcuin's chief concern. The famous abbot of Saint-Martin de Tours, whose intimacy of thought with his royal protector is well known, was between 796 and 799 full of anxiety concerning the Church. The storm caused by the conflict about the worshipping of the sacred images had only just calmed down; abuses dishonoured the clergy; in Saxony resistance to Christianity was still active; hesitations and misunderstandings threatened to imperil the evangelisation of the Danubian countries and above all the adoptionist heresy preached by Elipand of Toledo and

Francis Ganshof, *The Imperial Coronation of Charlemagne* (1949), pp. 13–28. Reprinted by permission of Jackson Son and Co. (Booksellers) Ltd., Glasgow.

Felix of Urgel was gravely menacing the purity of faith in the West.

In May 799 arrived the news of the criminal attempt against pope Leo III: to Alcuin, deeply devoted to the Holy See, it was the scandal of scandals.

As has been noticed, it is in the midst of these anxious days that, about the year 798, the expression *Imperium Christianum*—"the Christian empire" —appears in Alcuin's correspondence; it was frequently used by him up to 801/802. He used it when writing to Charlemagne and to his friend Arn, archbishop of Salzburg.

That "Christian empire" is the whole of the territories submitted to Charlemagne's authority and inhabited by the *populus christianus,* which is the community of Christians spiritually dependent on Rome. Charles's task is to govern, defend and enlarge it and closely linked with these obligations is his duty to protect Faith and Church. It is in the letters where he most insistently implores Charlemagne to take measures against the adoptionist heresy or to re-establish the pope in his authority, that Alcuin uses these expressions.

It seems to me quite unquestionable that we are here in the presence of an obvious indication.

Charles is master of almost the whole Western Christendom and Rome itself is subject to his protectorate. He is more than a king; his states form a whole which may well deserve to be qualified "empire": the underlying idea is that Charlemagne must be emperor.

When Alcuin begs him to interfere in favour of Leo III he shows him the Holy See humiliated, the imperial throne in Byzantium vacant and he proclaims that on Charles, the king of the Franks, chief of the "christian folk," rests the safeguarding of the Church's highest interests.

That character of guardian of the faith, protector of the church, was precisely the one which ecclesiastical tradition attributed—indeed quite arbitarily—to the Roman emperor; Gregory the Great, in whose writings Alcuin had been steeped, is categorical in this respect. In the eyes of Alcuin it appeared a necessity for the sake of the Church that there should be an emperor, successor of the Christian Roman emperors, who would end the scandals and above all prevent new ones.

If Alcuin has expressed these ideas with particular force, he certainly was not the only one to think as he did. It would be strange if Arn, one of his most faithful correspondents, had had no notion of the kind. We have reason to believe that another of his correspondents, Angilbert, abbot of Saint-Riquier and familiar of Charlemagne as well as declared lover of one of his daughters, shared the same ideas.

We must also remember the insertion in certain liturgical prayers of the name of the king of the Franks next to that of the emperor, and of the *Regnum Francorum* next to the *Imperium Romanum,* and their association in the defence of the Christian world against pagans and in the maintenance of peace. In *Francia* towards the end of the VIIIth century these prayers must have familiarized many a cleric with the idea that the actual power of their king and the way in which he used it, fitted in rather well with the tasks appointed to the imperial institution.

Did Alcuin and the other "imperialists" succeed in convincing Charlemagne of their views? It certainly was a hard task. In the first place because other duties may have appeared to him more urgent than to go to Rome in order to settle the affairs of the papacy. It was difficult also because Charlemagne seems to have been prejudiced against the imperial title; he might even have felt some aversion from it. Finally because Charlemagne, in spite of his appetite for learning, lacked intellectual culture and most likely did not thoroughly grasp what Alcuin and his people meant by the imperial dignity—a notion which required some slight knowledge of history and theology, even if unsophisticated, and some capacity of abstraction.

And yet Charlemagne decided to go the way that, according to me, had been pointed to him.

At the end of the year 799, when Arn had imparted to Alcuin the charges levied against the pope and the anxiety then prevailing in Rome, the necessity for a personal intervention by Charles and for a restoration in Western Europe of the imperial power proved itself even more urgent than ever.

It is most likely during the stay of Charlemagne in Tours, in the spring of the year 800 and during his own stay at the palace of Aachen in June on the occasion of the council that compelled the heresiarch Felix to abjure adoptionism, that Alcuin managed to convince the king. Perhaps he succeeded by using the "hegemoniac" notion of the empire, the very vast kingdom which was not contained by rigorous frontiers: these notions were familiar to the Anglo-Saxon Alcuin and they might have been accessible to the realistic mind of Charlemagne, mostly impressed by reasons of power.

Charlemagne started for Italy some time after the assembly of Mainz, which took place in August. I think that I have shown elsewhere that at the end of summer or at the beginning of autumn, Alcuin knew that this expedition must lead to the restoration of the imperial dignity in favour of his master.

How did things happen in Rome?

The pope whom Charlemagne had re-established on his throne was surrounded by enemies and soon was compelled to clear himself publicly of the accusations brought forward against him. He was but a toy in the hands of the Frankish king and of his counsellors. He would certainly not have been in a position to oppose the realisation of a scheme which Charlemagne had adopted. His interests moreover were quite different: he might well believe that an emperor would efficiently protect him, and besides, he had always been compliant towards Charles. He might also have found pleasure in removing any suggestion of subordination to Byzantium. One must admit that Leo III showed himself quite willing to take his share in the events.

The leading part belongs, according to me, to a few Frankish clerics of the royal circle, namely, I take it, to Arn and to Alcuin's confidential agents, whom he had sent to Rome: Whitto-Candidus, Fridugisus-Nathanael and other monks of Saint-Martin-de-Tours. Thanks to their interference, the ideals of Alcuin and of the other "imperialist clerics" won the day.

They sat together in the council with other ecclesiastics; Frankish, Lombard and Roman. There were very strenuous debates, which resulted in the oath by which on December 23rd, the pope justified himself. After this on the same day, the council and "the whole christian folk"—that is to say the Franks and the Lombards as well as the Romans—decided that Charlemagne must be made emperor. Was not the imperial throne occupied by a criminal woman, vacant? Were not Rome—capital of the Caesars—Italy, Gaul and Germany in his possession? Charlemagne accepted.

The imperial dignity for Western Europe had been restored in his favour on that very day.

There only remained the ceremony at which this was to be celebrated.

On December 25th at St. Peter's, according to the rules that were known in Rome, but which the king and the Franks ignored and did not care about, Charles was regularly elected by the "Roman people" expressing their will by the way of ritual acclamations. But before these had sounded, the pope had himself crowned the new emperor. Like many weak characters, Leo III had played a crooked game. Through his gesture which could be understood as a symbolic livery—as a *traditio*—he had given the impression that it was he who had invested Charlemagne with the imperial dignity.

There lies, in my opinion, the reason of the great displeasure shown by Charlemagne, the reason for which he hesitated during several months to adorn himself with the imperial title in his diplomas and for which he refused to adopt the one which had appeared in the acclamations: *imperator Romanorum*.

He did not wish to seem as if he held his empire from the pope and especially not from a pope who owed him so much and had taken him now by a kind of treachery. When in the palace church of Aachen, on September 11th, 813, he himself crowned his son Louis, emperor—or perhaps ordered him to take the crown from the altar and to put it on his head—without any interference of either pope or clergy, he showed how to his liking things should have taken place on December 25th, 800.

There is no doubt to me that Charlemagne has been considered, and has considered himself, as a Roman emperor, the successor of the Christian Roman emperors, of Constantine the Great and his heirs. His authority however, extended over territories of which some, like the greater part of his possessions beyond the Rhine, had not been part of the *Imperium Romanum*. Because it was for all the territories over which his power extended that he had become emperor, it is all his subjects that in the year 802 had to take an oath of allegiance to him in his capacity of emperor. This did not prevent him from keeping his titles of king of the Franks and of the Lombards; these titles alone were significant of a real political power.

Did he, in the year 800, also become emperor of the countries submitted to the Basileus of Byzantium? One might have admitted it all the more so as one of the reasons put forward in favour of his elevation to his new dignity was the vacancy in the imperial throne. Perhaps for a while in the East, such an attempt by him seemed possible. But he himself does not appear to have contemplated such a thing.

His empire was a Western Christian and Roman empire and on the day on which he could, in the year 812, constrain the emperor of Byzantium to recognise his new imperial dignity, the notion of empire ceased to be one of unique and universal authority.

> *Through most of the eighth century a theological dispute over "iconoclasm" divided the Greek and Roman churches. The iconoclasts at Constantinople rejected the practice of venerating images; the Roman church approved it. Charlemagne, in spite of his regard for the papacy, sympathised with the iconoclastic position. In 787 the queen-regent at Constantinople, Irene, declared in favor of the Roman doctrine and, in 797, she deposed her son and illegitimately assumed sole power.*
>
> *Emphasizing these circumstances, Werner Ohnsorge presented the coronation in Rome as an attempt by the papacy to free itself once and for all from East Roman authority by making Charlemagne—against his own will—a "universal" Roman emperor.*

FROM *The Problem of Two Emperors in the Early Middle Ages* BY WERNER OHNSORGE

THEN THE FACT that Charles' wife died in the summer of 800 gave to the papacy the impulse to try an audacious secret plan to proclaim Charles as universal emperor of the Romans against his will and to establish through a marriage between Charles and Irene a new western emperorship in place of the existing eastern one. What strengthened the curia in its belief in its ability to carry through its project were certain tendencies in the Frankish court circle, which, because it was influenced by older Saxon and Anglo-

Werner Ohnsorge, *Das Zweikaiserproblem im früheren Mittelalter* (1947), translated by R. E. Sullivan in *The Coronation of Charlemagne* (1959), pp. 84–9. Reprinted by permission of D. C. Heath and Company and August Lax, Hildesheim.

Saxon concepts of sovereignty, was inclined to designate Charles in a rather perfunctory way [without bothering about legal formalities] as (Roman) world emperor. Furthermore, as already mentioned, there was the old religious tradition in the West of equating the "Imperium Romanum," the Roman Empire, with the "Imperium Christianum," the Christian world empire; by virtue of the Christian belief of Charles and his veneration for St. Peter this concept was of compelling importance. The papal curia could also understand from the fact that . . . Charles had adopted a gold seal modeled on the Byzantine style for his royal documents [to be used] along with the usual wax seal and that he had taken over the dating method of the so-called Greek indiction for Frankish royal documents, that—in spite of the Franks' aversion in principle to the imperial concept—the Graeco-Roman court always stood as an object of comparison, an example, and a spur behind Charles' concept of kingship.

The papacy prepared its action in all secrecy. For the settlement of a conflict in the city of Rome, in which the pope was involved, Charles had in December, 800, come to Rome. . . . On Christmas day the son of Charles was to be anointed king according to previously arranged plans. Then before this anointment took place Leo III surprised Charles by placing on his head a crown and acclaiming him emperor. The world had a new Roman emperor who through the acclamation of the people, the Senate, and the warriors had been installed in a proper fashion in Irene's place, whose right to hold the imperial power was denied.

The coronation of Charles as emperor, i.e., the replacement of the Roman emperorship of the East with a new Roman emperorship in the West, was the consequence of a development dating back to the original empire. The political world up to this time had known merely one empire, the Roman Empire, whether it was officially designated as this or not. . . . Charles himself was on December 25, 800, called to be emperor and by virtue of that he was Roman emperor. There was no concept of emperor apart from Rome before 800 nor even before 812. . . .

It was completely clear to Charles that there were only two alternatives. The Roman emperorship could exist only as entity either if it were kept in Byzantium as at that time or if it were once again transferred from the East to the West, as it had at another time been transferred by Constantine the Great from the West to the East. But the papacy had taken this transferral into its own hands, from which it might be concluded that just as the transferral met the needs of the West, in view of the world political situation, so also had the curia at the same time made certain of its superiority over the new imperial regime which it had shaped. The coronation of Charles must appear as an organizational formalization of the . . . developing process of union between the Carolingians and the papacy, which had begun in 752 with papal approval of the transfer of the Frankish crown to Pepin.

The research of the last decades . . . has denied the universal character of the imperial coronation and has sought to explain it merely as the by-product of a particular historical moment in connection with the conflicts of the papacy in Roman politics. Certainly, reservations have rightly had to be raised against this modern position: it runs contrary to the line of development of papal policy, especially in the second half of the eighth century. In addition [*the argument raised against—B. T.*] the universalist position rests on a narrow interpretation almost always used in the last few years, yet a completely one-sided one, of the chief source concerning the coronation of the emperor, the *Vita Karoli* of Einhard. . . . an interpretation which says that although Charles actually denied the form in which Leo III had carried through the coronation on December 25, 800, he still did not stand unconditionally opposed to the imperial idea itself. It still is stated . . . clearly and unequivocally by Einhard, Charles' trusted biographer, that Charles so strongly disliked the "word," that is, the imperial title, that he would not have sought out the court of Peter, in spite of the great feast day, had he known beforehand that the pope planned his coronation as emperor. It accordingly remains certain, and this is reinforced by the surviving legal documents, chiefly the protocol of the diplomas of the winter of 800–801, that Charles did not want to be emperor on Christmas day 800; between the Charles of the *Libri karolini* and the Charles of December 25, 800, there was no difference; and in addition it is still certain that it was not just the form of the coronation as such that was extraordinarily painful and unacceptable to the great Frank.

Charles saw at once that the pope had played him against Irene and that this signified the end of the peaceful relations with Byzantium that had been established during the last years of the eighth century and could lead to unforeseen political developments. It signified further that the papal curia had forced him into the acceptance of a dignity which Charles in his whole inner course of development had proudly and consciously denied. He was the king of the Franks, filled with a sense of the greatness of his people, for whom he would provide a world position comparable to that possessed by the emperor in the East, who for all that was only a king as Charles himself was. Now this Roman imperial dignity had been imposed on him in a sanctified place which excluded any immediate resistance, by an act of the pope performed publicly and in a solemn fashion and not to be undone by subsequent protest; all of which he detested. Einhard knew why he designated his master only as king until his death, and it is not accidental that the chief wax seal of Charles, which bore only the inscription: "Christe, protege Carolum regem Francorum [Christ, protect Charles, king of the Franks], was used from 772 to 813, even during the imperial period and was not replaced by a special imperial seal. Charles felt himself to be king of the Franks and wished only for the greatness of his Frankish people; all things Roman were indifferent to him, if not hated.

Step by step in the course of the winter of 800–801 the papal curia through tedious negotiations had subsequently won Charles over to its project. We can follow the steps. A few days passed [after the coronation] before Charles decided to make use of [his new power under] the Roman law in settling the difficulties in the city of Rome. With that step the papacy had already won a victory in principle: Charles had recognized on practical political grounds the necessity for assuming the Roman tradition. But still he thought it might be possible to champion Roman concepts without bearing the imperial title. For some months he had resisted the acceptance of the imperial title in his official documents; for a while in March 801 he believed that he had reached the same end [of exercising legal authority in Rome] when he consented to the honor of being named consul. For the first time in May 801 he finally acknowledged his acceptance of the imperial title through the suitable change of the protocol of his documents.

Very significant as a reflection of Charles' inner opposition is how this title [of May 801] was formed. In the first place he took over the words "Augustus . . . Imperator." So far this was the title of the Roman emperor, but Charles depreciated that title at the same moment to a certain extent by adding to it in a completely unusual way the words: "Romanum gubernans Imperium" [governing the Roman Empire]. The expression "Romanum gubernans Imperium" has, as has long been known, a double meaning. It can signify the Roman Empire as well as the territory of the city of Rome. Research has decided chiefly in favor of the last-named interpretation. But this is clearly not possible, since the words "Romanum gubernans Imperium" are absent in the last expression of Charles' title in the year 813. Charles had not at that time given up his authority over Rome, but rather, as will be shown, [had given up] the Roman emperorship. . . . The words "Romanum gubernans Imperium" thus mean "he who rules the Roman Empire." If this qualifying addition to the words: "Augustus . . . Imperator" in the imperial title, is not a senseless tautology, then at that time [May 801] Charles by this means instinctively distinguished an absolute emperorship from a Roman emperorship; on the basis of the latter he possessed the former. Then he added to the foregoing the title "King of the Franks and Lombards," so that the new title in its full expression with all additions read: "Karolus serenissimus augustus a Deo coronatus magnus pacificus imperator, Romanum gubernans imperium, qui et per misericordiam Dei rex Francorum et Langobardorum" [Charles, the most serene Augustus crowned by God the great pacific emperor, governing the Roman Empire, who through the mercy of God is king of the Franks and Lombards]. This imperial title of Charles was the product of intensive thought, built up, as can be proved, out of older title forms originating in the Frankish realm. It represented an attempt to de-romanize as far as possible the Roman imperial title, which Charles had had to accept under the pressure of the situation, and it already aimed toward shaping an imperial concept which would be independent of Rome without, however, actually being able to realize such a Roman-free imperial concept at this time. What we know about the political reforms made by Charles during the rest of his life is only further proof of the correctness of the explanation of the form of his title of 801 as we have expounded it. Also in the years during which Charles had to acknowledge the Roman emperorship against his will, he never denied his basically purely Frankish position.

Evidently the papal curia was able to convince Charles that at that time [in 801] the struggle for world prestige would be decided on the basis of the Roman imperial concept. The experiment of the *Libri karolini* had been an attempt [to raise the Franks to a supreme position] by unsuitable means. [The curia must have argued] that only by making the decision to continue the Roman tradition would Charles be able to obtain for his Franks the portion of universal power which they deserved.

Along with the political motive there was another one which up to now has not been recognized: a Christian-religious motive. . . . There was no reason why the curia should now hold back with the already noted marriage project . . . ; if in a sense the curia intended to replace the eastern emperorship with a new western one, in that case the change could have been brought to completion through a marriage of Charles with Irene. If from the following events the surprising fact emerges that this project found strong acceptance with Charles, still the motive of the Frank was quite different from that of the curia. A marriage was forbidden from Charles' viewpoint as long as Irene held fast to the worship of the idols. But was it not perhaps possible for Irene to return to her original iconoclastic position? Charles could consider himself a good servant of Christ if through his person he united the East and the West around a dogmatic position sanctioned by the Franks and accepted by them as the only correct one. That this concept did not coincide with papal ideas was for the curia provoking, but for the moment the papacy was willing on the whole to take it into the bargain considering what was at stake. The repeatedly disputed fact . . . that Charles after 801 embraced the universal imperial title merely to please the curia but against his own will, without in any way denying by that act his purely Frankish position, this fact is proved by Charles' position in the marriage affair.

When Charles departed in the spring of 801 from Rome, the pope could feel sure that he who had been newly crowned by the pope would not lay aside his crown. But Charles had declined to take any kind of initiative against the Eastern Romans. It was still in no way clear whether developments could really follow the direction wished by the papacy, and that a western emperorship could be established effectively in place of the eastern. There was the possibility that the East would simply overlook the development in the West; whereupon the imperial problem would become a problem of two emperors, especially inasmuch as Charles would not decide to proceed against Byzantium. First it had to be seen what attitude would be taken by the East. It has been maintained rightly that Charles after his return to Germany had given serious thought to the whole complex question: contrary to custom he remained in his imperial palace at Aachen and undertook no military expeditions. He demanded a new oath of loyalty from his subjects to him as emperor. He issued a new coin, stamped uniformly for his whole empire with a picture of his head. He introduced finally . . . a new form of imperial document, in which in place of the use of the actual signature of the ruler to complete the document there was employed the eastern Roman form of imperial document in which the chancellor's signature, done in red ink, replaced the ruler's signature.

In 802 Irene's legates finally appeared at the Frankish court at Aachen, since Byzantium was interested in finding out how things stood with the new imperial usurper in the West, who now continued the line of earlier Roman emperors raised to power in the West, but who surprisingly made no threat to come to Constantinople and make good his rights with the sword. As a result of the wide reverberations of the political relationship of Charles with the caliph Harun-al-Rachid the political position of Charles had to be considered in the East at least as a cause for anxiety and especially was it to be feared that Charles would attack Sicily. The negotiations [of 802] must have been conducted in a friendly sense. The result was that an embassy of Charles, accompanied by papal legates, went to Constantinople and there set before Irene the marriage project. We know that this was synonymous with a demand for a change in the East from the veneration of the idols to iconoclasm. Also Charles would never have yielded to Eastern Roman custom in order to take up residence in Constantinople. . . . The movement of Irene to the West had to be accepted as the second condition for the marriage. It is very remarkable that in spite of these decisive stipulations . . . Irene reacted positively to the offer of the West. It seemed as if the papacy had comprehended the world political situation correctly, and that in the Roman emperorship it was as if its removal from the East could be brought about through the West.

It was, as far as we can establish, these two stipulations of Charles which brought about the fall of Irene. To the circle on which Irene had depended for protection after her return to the veneration of images, the thought of a reaction was intolerable. The western policy of Irene contained the seeds of her fall.

The Greek legates of her successor, the emperor Nicephorus, who appeared in 803 at Salz in Thuringia at the court of Charles in the company of the returning German negotiators, presented to the West a wholly new situation. Byzantium now had no intention of bowing before the West in any way. The new emperor in the East had been legally enthroned; he repudiated his western rival simply as a usurper. It has been pointed out correctly that the discussions at Salz as well as the letters which the Greeks brought with them must have been not very friendly. A completely changed position had developed: papal theories had been false, and the problem of two emperors had now arisen.

The question was now whether Charles would in the future force the course of events to follow the line desired by the curia, or whether this would be for him the occasion to take a course opposed to what the pope expected and so to seek now an independent political policy.

In the place of a universalist solution to the question of prominence [for the Franks in the] world Charles established a solution of equality, which basically corresponded to what he had stood for in the *Libri karolini* and had already striven for through the marriage of Rotrude. The path to a world emperorship [to be established] in the place of Eastern Rome, along which the papal curia had led him basically against his own will, had proved an impossible course. With a greater energy he now set himself to gain acceptance for his Franks as a power equal to Byzantium.

*   *   *

The first offer for a peaceful co-existence of the western and eastern emperors, which Charles had directed from Salz to Nicephorus, Byzantium passed over with disrespect. Years of war with Byzantium followed, fought in Italy by Charles' son Pepin. Political conditions in the East finally made it appear desirable for Constantinople to bring to an end the conflict in the West. A legate was sent to Pepin, who was no longer living, but the legate was sent on by the Franks to the court at Aachen. Charles himself was in no way inclined to war with Byzantium, but concerned himself only with striving for equality of rights in the realm of world politics. The leader of this Greek legation, Arsaphios, whose fitness was expressly attested by Charles, was a man of the greatest political capabilities. He recognized that Charles' emperorship had no universal, imperialistic tendencies, that Charles was in his way the king of the Franks and really wanted nothing more. . . . Charles' emperorship was only an "exalted kingship," an emperorship in title: that is what at that time became clear to the Greek negotiator. He reported in this sense to Byzantium. The result was that Constantinople decided in 812 to make a virtue of necessity, and through an official act the Byzantine legate in Aachen recognized Charles as the spiritual "brother" of the Byzantines and of the emperor-basileus instead of the previously used "son"—he is the "emperor of the Franks," as [the Byzantine historian] Theophanes says. Political practice rendered necessary the introduction in Byzantium of a new imperial concept for Charles, which was in effect to consider him simply an exalted king. . . . While the eastern ruler up until 812 was designated sometimes simply as "emperor," and sometimes as "Roman emperor," henceforth "Roman emperor" always appeared on the coins and in all of the diplomatic designations, as a conscious expression of the claims of the East for its world emperorship—over against the new Frankish "emperor." Thus Byzantium had in no way departed from its ideology; it had merely introduced into the order of its designations for crowned rulers under the world emperor in Constantinople a special designation for the Frankish king.

Very much stronger was the ideological influence which Byzantium exercised on Charles in a reverse sense. We do not know what the decisive influential event had been for Charles . . . [but] in any case at the end of his life Charles recognized in the Byzantine emperorship a power which was in his eyes basically nothing more than an exalted kingship, whose rulers took the (Roman) imperial title only as a name, and which therefore could serve as a prototype and model for the creation of a native Frankish emperorship which in its internal characteristics had very little more to do with Roman concepts than it did with the Greek.—

5 Imperial Government After the Coronation

The General Capitulary of 802 was a decree regulating the government of Charlemagne's realm.

FROM General Capitulary of 802

1. CONCERNING THE EMBASSY sent out by the lord emperor. Therefore, the most serene and most Christian lord emperor Charles has chosen from his nobles the wisest and most prudent men, both archbishops and some of the other bishops also, and venerable abbots and pious laymen, and has sent them throughout his whole kingdom, and through them by all the following chapters has allowed men to live in accordance with the correct law. Moreover, where anything which is not right and just has been enacted in the law, he has ordered them to inquire into this most diligently and to inform him of it; he desires, God granting, to reform it. And let no one, through his cleverness or astuteness, dare to oppose or thwart the written law, as many are wont to do, or the judicial sentence passed upon him, or to do injury to the churches of God or the poor or the widows or the wards or any Christian. But all shall live entirely in accordance with God's precept, justly and under a just rule, and each one shall be admonished to live in harmony with his fellows in his business or profession; the canonical clergy ought to observe in every respect a canonical life without heeding base gain, nuns ought to keep diligent watch over their lives, laymen and the secular clergy ought rightly to observe their laws without malicious fraud, and all ought to live in mutual charity and perfect peace. And let the *missi* [*traveling agents of the king—B. T.*] themselves make a diligent investigation whenever any man claims that an injustice has been done to him by any one, just as they desire to deserve the grace of omnipotent God and to keep their fidelity promised to Him, so that entirely in all cases everywhere, in accordance with the will and fear of God, they shall administer the law fully

University of Pennsylvannia Translations and Reprints, VI, No. 5 (1900), 16–27, translated by D. C. Munro.

and justly in the case of the holy churches of God and of the poor, of wards and widows and of the whole people. And if there shall be anything of such a nature that they, together with the provincial counts, are not able of themselves to correct it and to do justice concerning it, they shall, without any ambiguity, refer this, together with their reports, to the judgment of the emperor; and the straight path of justice shall not be impeded by any one on account of flattery or gifts from any one, or on account of any relationship, or from fear of the powerful.

2. Concerning the fidelity to be promised to the lord emperor. And he commanded that every man in his whole kingdom, whether ecclesiastic or layman, and each one according to his vow and occupation, should now promise to him as emperor the fidelity which he had previously promised to him as king; and all of those who had not yet made that promise should do likewise, down to those who were twelve years old. And that it shall be announced to all in public, so that each one might know, how great and how many things are comprehended in that oath; not merely, as many have thought hitherto, fidelity to the lord emperor as regards his life, and not introducing any enemy into his kingdom out of enmity, and not consenting to or concealing another's faithlessness to him; but that all may know that this oath contains in itself this meaning:

3. First, that each one voluntarily shall strive, in accordance with his knowledge and ability, to live wholly in the holy service of God in accordance with the precept of God and in accordance with his own promise, because the lord emperor is unable to give to all individually the necessary care and discipline.

4. Secondly, that no man, either through perjury or any other wile or fraud, on account of the flattery or gift of any one, shall refuse to give back or dare to abstract or conceal a serf of the lord emperor or a district or land or anything that belongs to him; and that no one shall presume, through perjury or other wile, to conceal or abstract his fugitive fiscaline serfs who unjustly and fraudulently say that they are free.

5. That no one shall presume to rob or do any injury fraudulently to the churches of God or widows or orphans or pilgrims; for the lord emperor himself, after God and His saints, has constituted himself their protector and defender.

6. That no one shall dare to lay waste a benefice of the lord emperor, or to make it his own property.

7. That no one shall presume to neglect a summons to war from the lord emperor; and that no one of the counts shall be so presumptuous as to dare to dismiss thence any one of those who owe military service, either on account of relationship or flattery or gifts from any one.

8. That no one shall presume to impede at all in any way a ban or command of the lord emperor, or to dally with his work or to impede or to lessen or in any way to act contrary to his will or commands. And that no one shall dare to neglect to pay his dues or tax.

9. That no one, for any reason, shall make a practice in court of defending another unjustly, either from any desire of gain when the cause is weak, or by impeding a just judgment by his skill in reasoning, or by a desire of oppressing when the cause is weak. But each one shall answer for his own cause or tax or debt unless any one is infirm or ignorant of pleading; for these the *missi* or the chiefs who are in the court or the judge who knows the case in question shall plead before the court; or if it is necessary, such a person may be allowed as is acceptable to all and knows the case well; but this shall be done wholly according to the convenience of the chiefs or *missi* who are present. But in every case it shall be done in accordance with justice and the law; and that no one shall have the power to impede justice by a gift, reward, or any kind of evil flattery or from any hindrance of relationship. And that no one shall unjustly consent to another in anything, but that with all zeal and goodwill all shall be prepared to carry out justice.

For all the above mentioned ought to be observed by the imperial oath.

10. That bishops and priests shall live according to the canons and shall teach others to do the same.

11. That bishops, abbots, abbesses, who are in charge of others, with the greatest veneration shall strive to surpass their subjects in this diligence and shall not oppress their subjects with a harsh rule or tyranny, but with sincere love shall carefully guard the flock committed to them with mercy and charity or by the examples of good works.

[*Clauses 12–24 deal with points of ecclesiastical discipline—B. T.*]

*   *   *

25. That counts and *centenarii* [*subordinate officials—B. T.*] shall compel all to do justice in every respect, and shall have such assistants in their ministries as they can securely confide in, who will observe law and justice faithfully, who will oppress the poor in no manner, who will not dare under any pretext, on account of flattery or reward, to conceal thieves, robbers, murderers, adulterers, magicians, wizards or witches, and all sacrilegious men, but instead will give them up that they may be punished and chastised in accordance with the law, so that, God granting it, all of these evils may be removed from the Christian people.

26. That judges shall judge justly in accordance with the written law, and not according to their own will.

27. And we command that no one in our whole kingdom shall dare to deny hospitality to rich or poor or pilgrims, that is, no shall deny shelter and fire and water to pilgrims traversing our country in God's name, or to anyone travelling for the love of God or for the safety of his own soul. If, moreover, any one shall wish to serve them farther, let him expect the best reward from God, who Himself said: "And whoso shall receive one such little child in my name, receiveth me;" and elsewhere: "I was a stranger and ye took me in."

28. Concerning embassies coming from the lord emperor. That the counts and *centenarii* shall provide most carefully, as they desire the grace of the lord emperor, for the *missi* who are sent out, so that they may go through their departments without any delay; and he commands to all everywhere that they ought to see to it that no delay is encountered anywhere, but they shall cause them to go on their way in all haste and shall provide for them in such a manner as our *missi* may direct.

29. Concerning the poor to whom in his mercy the lord emperor has granted the ban which they ought to pay, that the judges, counts or our *missi* shall not, for their own advantage, have the power to compel them to pay the fine which has been granted to them.

30. Concerning those whom the lord emperor wishes, Christ being propitious, to enjoy peace and protection in his kingdom, namely, those who are hastening to his clemency, either Christians or pagans, because they desire to announce some news, or seeking his aid on account of their poverty or hunger, that no one shall dare to constrain them to serve him, or to seize them, or alienate or sell them; but wherever they may wish to remain voluntarily, there under the defence of the lord emperor they shall be aided in his mercy. If any one shall have presumed to act contrary to this, let him who has so presumptuously despised the commands of the lord emperor, know that he shall suffer the loss of his life for it.

31. And against those who announce the justice of the lord emperor, let no one presume to plot any injury or damage, or to stir up any enmity. But if any one shall have presumed, let him pay the imperial ban or, if he deserves a heavier punishment, it is commanded that he shall be brought to the emperor's presence.

32. Murders, by which a multitude of the Christian people perishes, we command in every way to be shunned and to be forbidden; God Himself forbade to His followers hatred and enmity, much more murder. For in what manner does any one trust to placate God, who has killed his son nearest to him? In what manner truly does he, who has killed his brother, think that the Lord Christ will be propitious to him? It is a great and terrible danger also with God the Father and Christ, Lord of heaven and earth, to stir up enmities among men: it is possible to escape for some time by remaining concealed, but nevertheless by accident at some time he falls into the hands of his enemies; moreover, where is it possible to flee from God, to whom all secrets are manifest? By what rashness does any one think to escape His anger? Wherefore, lest the people committed to us to be ruled over should perish from this evil, we have taken care to shun this by every means of discipline; because he who shall not have dreaded the wrath of God, shall find us in no way propitious or to be placated; but we wish to inflict the most severe punishment upon any one who shall have dared to murder a man. Nevertheless, lest sin should also increase, in order that the greatest enmities may not arise among Christians, when by the persuasions of the devil murders happen, the criminal shall immediately hasten to make amends and with all celerity shall pay the fitting composition for the evil

done to the relatives of the murdered man. And we forbid firmly, that the relatives of the murdered man shall dare in any way to continue their enmities on account of the evil done, or shall refuse to grant peace to him who asks it, but having given their pledges they shall receive the fitting composition and shall make a perpetual peace; moreover, the guilty one shall not delay to pay the composition. When, moreover, it shall have happened on account of sins that any one shall have killed his brethren or his neighbor, he shall immediately submit to the penance imposed upon him, and just as his bishop arranges for him, without any ambiguity; but by God's aid he shall desire to accomplish his atonement and he shall compound for the dead man in accordance with the law, and shall make peace in every way with his relatives; and the pledge being given, let no one dare thereafter to stir up enmity against him. But if any one shall have scorned to make the fitting composition, he shall be deprived of his property until we shall render our decision.

33. We prohibit in every way the crime of incest. But if any one shall have been contaminated by sinful fornication, he shall by no means be released without severe punishment, but for this he shall be corrected in such a manner that others shall fear to do likewise and that uncleanness shall be wholly removed from the Christian people, and that the guilty man shall fully atone for this by penance, just as his bishop shall arrange for him; and the woman shall be placed in the hands of her parents until we render our judgment. But if he shall have been unwilling to consent to the judgment of the bishops concerning his amendment, then he shall be brought to our presence, mindful of the example which was made concerning the incest which Fricco perpetrated with the nun of God.

34. That all shall be fully and well prepared, whenever our order or proclamation shall come. But if any one shall then say that he was unprepared and shall have neglected our command, he shall be brought to the palace; and not only he, but also all who dare to transgress our ban or command.

*   *   *

40. Lastly, therefore, we desire all our decrees to be known in our whole kingdom through our *missi* now sent out, either among the men of the church, bishops, abbots, priests, deacons, canons, all monks or nuns, so that each one in his ministry or profession may keep our ban or decree, or where it may be fitting to thank the citizens for their good will, or to furnish aid, or where there may be need still of correcting anything. Likewise also to the laymen and in all places everywhere, whether they concern the guardianship of the holy churches or of widows and orphans and the weaker; or the robbing of them; or the arrangements for the assembling of the army; or any other matters; how they are to be obedient to our precept and will, or how they observe our ban, or how each one strives in all things to keep himself in the holy service of God; so that all these good things may be well done to the

praise of omnipotent God, and we may return thanks where it is fitting. But where we believe there is anything unpunished, we shall so strive to correct it with all our zeal and will that with God's aid we may bring it to correction, both for our own eternal glory and that of all our faithful. Likewise we desire all the above to be fruitfully known by our counts or *centenarii,* our ministerials.

> *In 806 Charlemagne promulgated the following decree providing for an eventual division of his territories among his three sons.*

Charlemagne's Division of the Kingdoms

[handwritten annotation: Could a man committed to being an emperor give / divide his empire?]

IN THE NAME of the Father and Son and Holy Ghost. Charles most serene Augustus, great and pacific Emperor crowned by God, governing the Roman Empire, and also by the mercy of God King of the Franks and Lombards, to all the faithful of the holy church of God and to our subjects present and future.

As we believe it is known to all of you and hidden from none of you how the divine clemency, by whose will earthly tendencies to decay are checked through successive generations, has of His great mercy and kindness richly endowed us by giving to us three sons, because through them in accordance with our vows and our hopes He has strengthened the kingdom and has made the chance of oblivion in the future less; accordingly we wish to make this known to you, namely, that we desire to have these our sons by the grace of God as associates in the kingdom granted to us by God as long as we live, and after our departure from this life we desire to have them as heirs of the empire preserved and protected by God and of our kingdom, if this is the will of the divine majesty. In order that we may not leave it to them in confusion and disorder or provoke strife and litigation by giving them the whole kingdom without division, we have caused to be described and designated the portion which each one of them ought to enjoy and rule; in this manner forsooth so that each one, content with his own portion in accordance with our ordination, may strive with the aid of God to defend the frontiers of his kingdom and preserve peace and charity with his brothers.

It has pleased us to divide the empire, preserved and protected by God, and our kingdom so that to our beloved son Louis we have assigned the whole of Aquitaine and Gascony, except the province of Tours, and whatever is beyond to the west and towards Spain and from the city Nevers, which is situated on the river Loire, with the province of Nevers, the province of Avallon and Auxois, Châlon, Mâcon, Lyons, Savoy, Maurienne, Tarantaise, Mont Cenis, the valley of Susa to the *Clusoe* and thence from the Italian mountains to the sea, these provinces with their cities and whatever is beyond these on the south and west as far as the sea or Spain, that is that portion of Burgundy and Provence and Septimania or Gothia.

To our beloved son Pippin, Italy, which is also called Lombardy and Bavaria, just as Tassilo held it, with the exception of the two villas of Ingolstadt and Lauterhofen which we formerly gave to Tassilo as a benefice and which belong to the district which is called the Northgau, and from Alemannia the part which is on the south bank of the river Danube, and from the source of the Danube in a direct line as far as the river Rhine on the boundary of the districts of Klettgau and Hegau at the place which is called Enge, and thence up the river Rhine to the Alps; whatever is within these limits and extending to the south or east together with the duchy of Chur and the canton of Thurgau.

To our beloved son Charles moreover we have granted all of our kingdom that is outside of these limits, that is France and Burgundy, except that part which we have given to Louis, and Alemannia, except the portion which we have assigned to Pippin, Austria and Neustria, Thüringen, Saxony, Friesland, and the part of Bavaria which is called the Northgau; so that Charles and Louis may be able to go into Italy to bear aid to their brother, if such a necessity should arise, Charles by the valley of the Aosta which is in his kingdom and Louis by the valley of the Susa; Pippin also has the means of ingress and exit by the Norican Alps and Chur.

In 813 Charles succeeded in obtaining recognition of his imperial title from the authorities in Constantinople. The first of the following extracts is from the Annals of Lorsch, the second from a letter of Charlemagne to the Byzantine emperor Michael.

FROM *Annals of Lorsch*

THE EMPEROR, NICEPHORUS, after winning many notable victories in Moesia, fell in battle against the Bulgarians, and his son-in-law Michael

A Source Book for Mediaeval History (1905), pp. 58–9, translated by O. J. Thatcher and E. H. McNeal.

was made emperor. He received the ambassadors in Constantinople whom Karl had sent to Nicephorus and dismissed them, sending back to Karl with them his own ambassadors, Michael, a bishop, and Arsaphius and Theognostus, commanders of the imperial body-guard, to confirm the treaty which had been proposed in the time of Nicephorus. They came to the emperor at Aachen and received a copy of the treaty from him in the church of Aachen. In their address to him on this occasion, which they delivered in Greek, they called him emperor and *basileus*. They then proceeded to Rome on their way back, and received a copy of the treaty from the pope in the church of St. Peter, the apostle.

FROM *Charlemagne's Letter to Emperor Michael*

IN THE NAME of the Father, Son, and Holy Spirit. Karl, by the grace of God emperor and Augustus, king of the Franks and the Lombards, to his dear and honorable brother, Michael, glorious emperor and Augustus, eternal greeting in our Lord Jesus Christ. We bless and praise our Lord Jesus Christ with all our heart and strength for the ineffable gift of his kindness, with which he has enriched us. For he has deigned in our day to establish that peace between the east and the west, which we have long sought for and have always desired, and, in answer to the daily prayers which we have offered to him, has unified the holy immaculate catholic church throughout the whole world and given it peace. We speak of this peace as if it had been already brought about, for we have done our part, and we are sure you are willing to do yours. We put our trust in God who has ordained that this matter, the making of peace between us, should be carried out; for he is faithful and true, giving his aid to all who are engaged in good works, and he will bring to perfection this work which we have begun. Desiring now to bring about this consummation, we have sent you our legates, Amalhar, venerable bishop of Trier, and Peter, abbot of the monastery of Nonantula, to receive from the holy altar by your hands a copy of the treaty of peace, bearing the signatures of your priests, patriarchs, and nobles, just as your legates, Michael, venerable metropolitan, and Arsaphius and Theognostus, commanders of the royal body-guard, received the copy from us, with our signature and the signatures of our priests and nobles.

A Source Book for Mediaeval History (1905), pp. 58–9, translated by O. J. Thatcher and E. H. McNeal.

After the agreement with Byzantium, Charles crowned his surviving son, Louis, emperor. The event is described by Einhard.

FROM *Life of Charlemagne* BY EINHARD

TOWARD THE CLOSE OF HIS LIFE, when he was broken by ill-health and old age, he summoned Louis, King of Aquitania, his only surviving son by Hildegard, and gathered together all the chief men of the whole kingdom of the Franks in a solemn assembly. He appointed Louis, with their unanimous consent, to rule with himself over the whole kingdom, and constituted him heir to the imperial name; then, placing the diadem upon his son's head, he bade him be proclaimed Emperor and Augustus. This step was hailed by all present with great favor, for it really seemed as if God had prompted him to it for the kingdom's good; it increased the King's dignity, and struck no little terror into foreign nations.

Einhard, *Life of Charlemagne* (1880), pp. 58-9, translated by Samuel Epes Turner.

Feudalism—Cause or Cure of Anarchy?

CONTENTS

*C*harlemagne's empire was short-lived. It was soon torn apart by civil wars and by incursions of pagan peoples from beyond its borders. During the ninth and tenth centuries a new pattern of social and political life emerged, which modern historians have called "the feudal system." Feudalism was really anything but systematic. There were all kinds of national and local variations. But most typically a feudal society displayed three main characteristics: *First, the major cohesive force was a relationship of mutual loyalty between individual lords and their vassals—not a common loyalty of all citizens to the state. Second, a vassal held from his lord an estate of land called a "fief" (or "benefice") and* rendered military service in exchange for it. Third, feudal tenure of land carried rights of government over it. Some historians regard such a system as by its very nature anarchic. Others see it as a constructive response to the difficult circumstances of the times.

QUESTIONS FOR STUDY

1 Explain the meaning of the terms "escheat," "relief," "aid," "counsel," "homage," "wardship."

2 Judging from the descriptions of Louis VI of France and William I of England, what qualities were most necessary in an effective feudal king?

3 What elements in feudalism—if any—were conducive to anarchy?

4 Magna Carta has been called a "reactionary feudal document." Which of the clauses given in this section do you consider "feudal"? Can you suggest any reasons why they might be called reactionary?

5 How does the scheme of government described in the Assizes of Romania resemble and differ from that defined in Magna Carta?

6 Compare the views of Calmette, Southern, and Strayer on feudalism as a system of government.

1   Feudal Institutions—
A Modern Description

*The following account describes the institutions and prac-
tices that were characteristic of medieval feudalism.*

FROM *Mediaeval Feudalism* BY CARL STEPHENSON

BY EXAMINING various customs of the Carolingian period we have necessarily concerned ourselves with the development of the institutions called
feudal. Before we proceed further, it might be well to summarize the problem of that development through a series of questions and suggested answers.

What was the origin of vassalage? Since under the Carolingians, as in
the later period, vassalage was an honorable relationship between members
of the warrior class, to derive it from the Romans seems quite impossible. In
spite of all the Latin words that came to be adopted by the Franks in Gaul,
mediaeval vassalage remained essentially a barbarian custom, strikingly akin
to that described by Tacitus as the *comitatus*. Originally this custom was
shared by various Germanic peoples, notably the Anglo-Saxons. The peculiarity of Frankish vassalage resulted, in the main, from the governmental
policy of the Carolingian kings.

What was the Carolingian policy with regard to vassalage? The Merovingian kingdom had been at most a pseudo-Roman sham. By the end of the
seventh century it had utterly disintegrated. The Carolingian kingdom was a
new unit created by the military genius of Charles Martel, Pepin, and
Charlemagne. To preserve and strengthen their authority, these rulers depended less on their theoretical sovereignty than on the fidelity of their
personal retainers, now styled vassals. So the key positions in the army, as
well as the more important offices in church and state, came to be held by
royal vassals. Eventually the rule was adopted that every great official, if not
already a royal vassal, had to become one. The Carolingian policy, as will be

seen in the following pages, utterly failed; yet it established legal precedents that were observed for many centuries.

What was the origin of the fief? In Frankish times, as later, *beneficium* remained a vague term. Various kinds of persons were said to hold benefices, and in return for various kinds of service or rent. Since the benefice of a vassal was held on condition of military service, we may call it a military benefice. At first there was no technical Latin word for such a benefice, though in the Romance vernacular it became known as a *feos* or *fief*. This name, Latinized as *feodum* or *feudum,* ultimately came into official use and so provided the root for our adjective "feudal" (French *féodal*). Whether or not the military benefice existed before the eighth century is still disputed. In any case, it was the Carolingians who made that form of tenure into a common Frankish institution, and the best explanation of their policy is the one presented by Heinrich Brunner. According to his famous thesis, the old Frankish army had been largely made up of infantry—of ordinary freemen who provided their own weapons and served without pay. In the eighth century, as the experience of warfare proved the insufficiency of the traditional system, the Carolingians anxiously sought to enlarge their force of expert cavalry. And to do so they developed what we know as feudal tenure by associating vassalage with benefice-holding.

What was the nature of the fief? In its essence, we may say, a military benefice or fief was the special remuneration paid to a vassal for the rendering of special service. If the rulers had been able to hire mounted troops for cash, recourse to feudal tenure would have been unnecessary; for the Carolingian fief was primarily a unit of agrarian income. To call a fief a piece of land is inaccurate. What value would bare acres have for a professional warrior who considered the work of agriculture degrading? Being the possession of a gentleman, the fief included organized manors, worked by the native peasantry according to a customary routine of labor. Nor was this all. To hold a fief was also to enjoy the important privilege that the Carolingians knew as immunity. Within his own territory the royal vassal, like the clerical immunists of an earlier time, administered justice, collected fines and local taxes, raised military forces, and exacted services for the upkeep of roads, bridges, and fortifications. To some extent, therefore, he was a public official, a member of the hierarchy whose upper ranks included dukes, marquises, counts, and the greater ecclesiastics. As all these magnates came to be royal vassals, their offices, together with the attached estates, naturally appeared to be their fiefs. And as royal vassals passed on bits of their own privilege to subvassals, feudal tenure became inseparable from the exercise of political authority.

What, then, was the original feudalism? In this connection we can do no better than quote a shrewd observation by Ferdinand Lot: "It has become accepted usage to speak of 'feudalism,' rather than of 'vassalage,' from that point in history when, with rare exceptions, there were actually no vassals without fiefs." By "feudalism," in other words, we properly refer to the peculiar association of vassalage with fief-holding that was developed in the Carolingian Empire and thence spread to other parts of Europe.

*   *   *

In actual practice we know that, even before the close of the ninth century, it was customary for fiefs to pass from father to son; and that, within another hundred years or so, a fief was regularly described as hereditary. For reasons stated above, however, such inheritance is found to have been merely the renewal of a feudal contract, to which each of the parties, the lord and the vassal, had to give personal assent. When a vassal died, his fief reverted to the lord and really ceased to be a fief at all until another vassal had been invested with it. In case the vassal had no heir, the reversion was called escheat, and the lord was free to keep the dead man's estate or to regrant it to whomsoever he pleased. In case the vassal had an heir, the lord was legally obliged to accept him as the new holder. Yet even then a regrant was necessary through formal investiture; and in recognition of this fact the heir very commonly paid the lord a sum of money called relief.

Another striking peculiarity of feudal tenure was primogeniture, the rule that a fief should pass intact to the eldest son. No such form of inheritance was known either to Roman or to Germanic law, and allodial property continued to be shared by the children of a deceased owner. The fact that a fief was legally indivisible seems to prove that it was considered a public office rather than a piece of land. This was obviously true in the case of a duchy or county. But it was no less true, at least originally, in the case of an ordinary fief, where the income from agrarian estates combined with a territorial immunity provided remuneration for the service, military and political, of a vassal. It was greatly to the interest of a princely donor that responsibility for the needed service should be concentrated. To allow a fief to be indefinitely partitioned would nullify its value—would, in fact, contravene the very purpose of its establishment. On the other hand, the recipient of a fief might well be permitted to assign parts of it to his own vassals, for their default would remain his liability. Primogeniture thus came to be adopted as a very practical regulation for the continuance of feudal tenure, and with the latter spread widely throughout mediaeval Europe. The only significant modification of the rule for the benefit of younger children was the custom called parage. Under it a fief could be divided among a number of co-heirs if one of them rendered homage for all of it and so in a way guaranteed its integrity.

To introduce the subject of feudal inheritance it has been necessary to re-emphasize the fact that vassalage was always personal. A related fact also had important consequences—that vassalage was properly restricted to fighting-men. When a vassal died leaving an infant son as heir, the lord commonly enjoyed the right of wardship. That is to say, he took the fief into his own hands and, enjoying its revenue, supported the heir until such time as the latter attained majority. Then the youth, having been knighted and declared of age, performed homage to the lord and from him received investiture. This procedure logically solved the problem of a minority. But suppose the holder of a fief had only a daughter. If a girl could not be a vassal, how could she be recognized as an heiress? The answer, of course, was provided by the institution of marriage: a husband could render the necessary homage and acquire legal possession of the fief. Such a marriage required the lord's consent even during the lifetime of the girl's father. When he was dead, the lord as guardian took complete charge of the matter and, very generally, awarded the lady's hand to the noble suitor who bid the highest. True, the relatives of a young heir or heiress often objected to the lord's pretensions, and he was sometimes compelled to recognize one of them as guardian—on condition, however, that the latter became the lord's vassal for the duration of the minority.

Thus, by a series of legal devices, it was arranged that a fief should pass from one mature man to another; for the holder was normally required to perform military service. Although detailed records of the service actually rendered date only from the later Middle Ages, we may be sure that the principles then set forth were much older. Since at least the ninth century vassalage had implied a personal obligation to fight for the lord as a heavy-armed cavalryman, or knight. But, in addition, a royal vassal who had received a valuable fief was expected to bring with him a mounted troop of his own vassals, and the same requirement would apply to most men who held of a duke, a count, or some other magnate. It was in this way that the army of every feudal prince was regularly made up. At first, apparently, the size of each vassal's contingent and the length of his service were not precisely determined in advance. By the twelfth century, however, such determination had become usual in the better-organized states, especially those controlled by the Normans. According to the perfected scheme, the vassal took with him into the field enough knights to complete whatever quota was charged against his fief, but he was obliged to furnish the service at his own cost for no more than forty days once in the year.

* * *

That heavy expense was entailed by military service of this kind is apparent from the fact that it involved the finding, not only of trained men, but also of very superior horses, costly equipment, numerous servants, and enough food to supply the whole troop throughout the campaign. And the vassal's responsibility was by no means restricted to military service. On certain occasions he was required to pay his lord a contribution called aid. The northern French custom, taken by the Normans to England, specified three such occasions: the knighting of the lord's eldest son, the marriage of the lord's eldest daughter, and ransom of the lord when captured. In many regions, however, an aid could be exacted for the knighting of any son or the marriage of any daughter, and sometimes, as well, for a crusade, a journey to the royal court, or some other extraordinary undertaking. The vassal, furthermore, owed his lord hospitality. That is to say, whenever the lord came for a visit, the vassal was expected to provide free entertainment. And since every great lord was constantly moving about with a small army of mounted attendants, one could not afford to be too generous a host. As a consequence, the vassal's obligation in this respect often came to be strictly defined and was sometimes commuted into a money payment.

Every vassal, finally, was responsible for the important service called suit to court. When summoned to attend his lord, the vassal had to go in person and at his own expense. The reasons for the service were as varied as the meanings of the word "court." The occasion might be largely ceremonial, as in the case of a festival or the celebration of a wedding. Perhaps the lord wished to consult his men with regard to a war or a treaty. Very frequently they were asked to approve some act of government or to take part in a trial. For example, if the lord needed military service or financial aid beyond what was specifically owed by his vassals, his only recourse was to ask them for a voluntary grant. He had no right to tax or assess them arbitrarily, for his authority in such matters was determined by feudal contract. Nor did he have a discretionary power of legislation. Law was the unwritten custom of the country. To change or even to define it was the function, not of the lord, but of his court. It was the vassals themselves who declared the law under which they lived; and when one of them was accused of a misdeed, he was entitled to the judgment of his peers, i.e., his fellow vassals.

2 Origins of Feudalism

Feudalism grew up in a society ravaged by incessant inter-
nal warfare and by frequent invasions from beyond the
borders of Christendom. These conditions are illustrated in
the following extracts from ninth-century sources.

FROM *Annals of Fulda*

[handwritten annotations: Civil wars, Oppression of christians, Famine]

841

THE THREE BROTHERS [*Lothaire, Louis, and Charles, grandsons of Charlemagne—B. T.*] met in Auxerre, near Fontenay. They could not agree to divide the Empire because Lothaire, who wished to be sole monarch, was opposed to it. So they agreed that the case should be decided by the power of the sword and so proved by the judgment of God. On the twenty-fifth of June a great battle was fought between them, and the blood shed on both sides was so great that the present age remembers no such carnage among the Frankish people before. On the same day Lothaire began a retreat to his city of Aix-la-Chapelle. Louis and Charles seized his camp and collected and buried the bodies of their slain. They then parted; Charles remained in the West and Louis went in the month of August to the royal town Salz.

Lothaire again collected his forces from all sides. He went to Mayence and ordered the Saxons, with his little son Lothaire, to meet him at Speyer. He himself crossed the Rhine, intending to pursue his brother Louis to the confines of the outlying nations. He returned to Worms, unsuccessful. He celebrated there the marriage of his daughter, and then marched toward Gaul to subdue Charles. He spent the whole winter in fruitless effort and strife and then returned to Aix. On the twenty-fifth of December a comet appeared in the sign of Aquarius.

Annals of Fulda, 841 in *Readings in European History*, I (1904), 156–7, translated by J. H. Robinson.

FROM *Annals of Xanten*

[handwritten: Chronicle of a monastery constant fighting 845 famine pestilence]

TWICE IN THE CANTON OF WORMS there was an earthquake; the first in the night following Palm Sunday, the second in the holy night of Christ's Resurrection. In the same year the heathen broke in upon the Christians at many points, but more than twelve thousand of them were killed by the Frisians. Another party of invaders devastated Gaul; of these more than six hundred men perished. Yet owing to his indolence Charles agreed to give them many thousand pounds of gold and silver if they would leave Gaul, and this they did. Nevertheless the cloisters of most of the saints were destroyed and many of the Christians were led away captive.

*   *   *

846

According to their custom the Northmen plundered Eastern and Western Frisia and burned the town of Dordrecht, with two other villages, before the eyes of Lothaire, who was then in the castle of Nimwegen, but could not punish the crime. The Northmen, with their boats filled with immense booty, including both men and goods, returned to their own country.

In the same year Louis sent an expedition from Saxony against the Wends across the Elbe. He personally, however, went with his army against the Bohemians, whom we called Beu-winitha, but with great risk. . . . Charles advanced against the Britons, but accomplished nothing.

At this same time, as no one can mention or hear without great sadness, the mother of all churches, the basilica of the apostle Peter, was taken and plundered by the Moors, or Saracens, who had already occupied the region of Beneventum. The Saracens, moreover, slaughtered all the Christians whom they found outside the walls of Rome, either within or without this church. They also carried men and women away prisoners. They tore down, among many others, the altar of the blessed Peter, and their crimes from day to day bring sorrow to Christians. Pope Sergius departed life this year.

847

After the death of Sergius no mention of the apostolic see has come in any way to our ears. Rabanus [Maurus], master and abbot of Fulda, was solemnly chosen archbishop as the successor of Bishop Otger, who had died.

Annals of Xanten, 845–854 in *Readings in European History*, I (1904), 158–62, translated by J. H. Robinson.

Moreover the Northmen here and there plundered the Christians and engaged in a battle with the counts Sigir and Liuthar. They continued up the Rhine as far as Dordrecht, and nine miles farther to Meginhard, when they turned back, having taken their booty.

*   *   *

849

While King Louis was ill his army of Bavaria took its way against the Bohemians. Many of these were killed and the remainder withdrew, much humiliated, into their own country. The heathen from the North wrought havoc in Christendom as usual and grew greater in strength; but it is revolting to say more of this matter.

850

On January 1st of that season, in the octave of the Lord, towards evening, a great deal of thunder was heard and a mighty flash of lightning seen; and an overflow of water afflicted the human race during this winter. In the following summer an all too great heat of the sun burned the earth. Leo, pope of the apostolic see, an extraordinary man, built a fortification round the church of St. Peter the apostle. The Moors, however, devastated here and there the coast towns in Italy. The Norman Rorik, brother of the abovementioned younger Heriold, who earlier had fled dishonored from Lothaire, again took Dordrecht and did much evil treacherously to the Christians. In the same year so great a peace existed between the two brothers—Emperor Lothaire and King Louis—that they spent many days together in Osning [Westphalia] and there hunted, so that many were astonished thereat; and they went each his way in peace.

851

The bodies of certain saints were sent from Rome to Saxony,—that of Alexander, one of seven brethren, and those of Romanus and Emerentiana. In the same year the very noble empress, Irmingard by name, wife of the emperor Lothaire, departed this world. The Normans inflicted much harm in Frisia and about the Rhine. A mighty army of them collected by the river Elbe against the Saxons, and some of the Saxon towns were besieged, others burned, and most terribly did they oppress the Christians. A meeting of our kings took place on the Maas.

852

The steel of the heathen glistened; excessive heat; a famine followed. There was not fodder enough for the animals. The pasturage for the swine was more than sufficient.

853

A great famine in Saxony so that many were forced to live on horse meat.

854

The Normans, in addition to the very many evils which they were everywhere inflicting upon the Christians, burned the church of St. Martin, bishop
of Tours, where his body rests.

*The various elements that were combined in feudalism—
personal loyalty, vassalage, fief-holding—all existed separately before the ninth century. As early as the first century
A.D. Tacitus described the loyalty of Teutonic warriors to
their chiefs.*

FROM *Germania* BY TACITUS

THEY UNDERTAKE no business whatever either of a public or a private
character save they be armed. But it is not customary for any one to assume
arms until the tribe has recognized his competence to use them. Then in a
full assembly some one of the chiefs or the father or relatives of the youth
invest him with the shield and spear. This has the same meaning as the
assumption of the toga by Roman boys; it is their first honor. Before this he
was only a member of a household, hereafter he is a member of the tribe.
Distinguished rank or the great services of their parents secure even for mere
striplings the claim to be ranked as chiefs. They attach themselves to certain
more experienced chiefs of approved merit; nor are they ashamed to be
looked upon as belonging to their followings. There are grades even within
the train of followers assigned by the judgment of its leader. There is great
rivalry among these companions as to who shall rank first with the chief, and
among the chiefs as to who shall have the most and the bravest followers. It
is an honor and a source of strength always to be surrounded by a great band
of chosen youths, for they are an ornament in peace, a defence in war. It
brings reputation and glory to a leader not only in his own tribe but also
among the neighboring peoples if his following is superior in numbers and
courage; for he is courted by embassies and honored by gifts, and often his
very fame decides the issue of wars.

Tacitus, *Germania* (American Philological Association Monograph No. 5, 1935), pp. 289–
91, translated by R. P. Robinson. Reprinted by permission of the American Philological
Association.

When they go into battle it is a disgrace for the chief to be outdone in deeds of valor and for the following not to match the courage of their chief; furthermore for any of the followers to have survived his chief and come unharmed out of a battle is life-long infamy and reproach. It is in accordance with their most sacred oath of allegiance to defend and protect him and to ascribe their bravest deeds to his renown. The chief fights for victory; the men of his following, for their chief. If the tribe to which they belong sinks into the lethargy of long peace and quiet, many of the noble youths voluntarily seek other tribes that are still carrying on war, because a quiet life is irksome to the Germans, and they gain renown more readily in the midst of perils, while a large following is not to be provided for except by violence and war. For they look to the liberality of their chief for their war-horse and their deadly and victorious spear; the feasts and entertainments, however, furnished them on a homely but liberal scale, fall to their lot as mere pay. The means for this bounty are acquired through war and plunder. Nor could you persuade them to till the soil and await the yearly produce so easily as you could induce them to stir up an enemy and earn glorious wounds. Nay even they think it tame and stupid to acquire by their sweat what they can purchase by their blood.

From the seventh century onward we have written formulas that show how a man commended himself to a lord. The following examples are from England and France respectively.

Feudal Oaths

[handwritten annotation: Documents show feudal forms had advanced from shapeless form in Tacitus' time to more stringent requirements]

THUS SHALL ONE TAKE the oath of fidelity:

By the Lord before whom this sanctuary is holy, I will to N. be true and faithful, and love all which he loves and shun all which he shuns, according to the laws of God and the order of the world. Nor will I ever with will or action, through word or deed, do anything which is unpleasing to him, on condition that he will hold to me as I shall deserve it, and that he will perform everything as it was in our agreement when I submitted myself to him and chose his will.

*   *   *

University of Pennsylvania Translations and Reprints, IV, No. 3 (1897), 3–4, translated by E. P. Cheyney.

It is right that those who offer to us unbroken fidelity should be protected by our aid. And since *such and such* a faithful one of ours, by the favor of God, coming here in our palace with his arms, has seen fit to swear trust and fidelity to us in our hand, therefore we decree and command by the present precept that for the future *such and such* above mentioned be counted with the number of the antrustions. And if anyone perchance should presume to kill him, let him know that he will be judged guilty of his wergild of 600 shillings.

> *The first recorded example of the great noble accepting a status of "vassalage" dates from 757.*

FROM *Frankish Royal Annals*

KING PEPIN held his court at Compiègne with the Franks. Tassilo, Duke of the Bavarians, came there and commended himself in vassalage by hand. He swore many, indeed innumerable oaths, laying his hand on relics of saints and promising to be faithful to King Pepin and his sons, the aforementioned lords Charles and Carloman, as by law a vassal should be toward his lords, sincerely and with devotion.

> *From about the same period we have documents granting lands as* precaria *or* beneficia, *forms of land-holding that anticipated the later feudal tenure. The following document of 743, issued in France, required a church to lend out part of its lands for the support of royal warriors.*

Capitulary of Lestinnes, 743

BECAUSE OF THE THREATS OF WAR and the attacks of certain tribes on our borders, we have determined, with the consent of God and by

---

F. Kurze, ed., *Annales Regni Francorum* (1895), p. 14, translated by Brian Tierney.

A Source Book for Mediaeval History (1905), p. 357, translated by O. J. Thatcher and E. H. McNeal.

the advice of our clergy and people, to appropriate for a time part of the ecclesiastical property for the support of our army. The lands are to be held as *precaria* for a fixed rent; one solidus, or twelve denarii, shall be paid annually to the church or monastery for each *casata* [farm]. When the holder dies the whole possession shall return to the church. If, however, the exigency of the time makes it necessary, the prince may require the *precarium* to be renewed and given out again. Care shall be taken, however, that the churches and monasteries do not incur suffering or poverty through the granting of *precaria*. If the poverty of the church makes it necessary, the whole possession shall be restored to the church.

> *Sometimes royal grants conferred immunity from the jurisdiction of the king's local officers as in the following example.*

Grant of Immunity

THOSE WHO FROM THEIR EARLY YOUTH have served us or our parents faithfully are justly rewarded by the gifts of our munificence. Know therefore that we have granted to that illustrious man (name), with greatest good will, the villa called (name), situated in the county of (name), with all its possessions and extent, in full as it was formerly held by him *or* by our treasury. Therefore by the present charter which we command to be observed forever, we decree that the said (name) shall possess the villa of (name), as has been said, in its entirety, with lands, houses, buildings, inhabitants, slaves, woods, pastures, meadows, streams, mills, and all its appurtenances and belongings, and with all the subjects of the royal treasury who dwell on the lands, and he shall hold it forever with full immunity from the entrance of any public official for the purpose of exacting the royal portion of the fines from cases arising there; to the extent finally that he shall have, hold, and possess it in full ownership, no one having the right to expect its transfer, and with the right of leaving it to his successors or to anyone whom he desires, and to do with it whatever else he wishes.

A Source Book for Mediaeval History (1905), pp. 352–3, translated by O. J. Thatcher and E. H. McNeal.

3   Lords and Vassals

*Vassals acquired fiefs in various ways. The manner in
which the Duchy of Normandy was established in 911
illustrates the endemic violence of the period. The following account was written about a century after the events it
describes.*

[handwritten annotation: shows that the French people were committed to Feudalism but that the Vikings weren't willing to accept their overlordship]

FROM *The Customs and Acts of the First Dukes
of Normandy*

THE FRANKS, not having the strength to resist the pagans and seeing all
France brought to nothing, came to the king and said unanimously, "Why
do you not aid the kingdom which you are bound by your scepter to care for
and rule? Why is peace not made by negotiation since we cannot achieve it
either by giving battle or by defensive fortifications? Royal honor and power
is cast down; the insolence of the pagans is raised up. The land of France is
almost a desert for its people are dying by famine or by the sword or are
taken captive. Care for the kingdom, if not by arms then by taking counsel". . .

Immediately Charles, having consulted with them, sent Franco, Archbishop of Rouen, to Rollo, Duke of the Pagans. Coming to him he began to
speak with mild words. "Most exalted and distinguished of dukes, will you
quarrel with the Franks as long as you live? Will you always wage war on
them? What will become of you when you are seized by death? Whose
creature are you? Do you think you are God? Are you not a man formed
from filth? Are you not dust and ashes and food for worms? Remember
what you are and will be and by whose judgment you will be condemned.
You will experience Hell I think, and no longer injure anyone by your wars.
If you are willing to become a Christian you will be able to enjoy peace in
the present and the future and to dwell in this world with great riches.
Charles, a long-suffering king, persuaded by the counsel of his men, is

*De Moribus et Actis Primorum Normanniae Ducum, Mémoires de la Société des Antiquaires de
Normandie*, 3e Série, III (1858), 165–9, translated by Brian Tierney.

willing to give you this coastal province that you and Halstigno have grievously ravaged. He will also give you his daughter, Gisela, for a wife in order that peace and concord and a firm, stable and continuous friendship may endure for all time between you and him . . ."

At the agreed time Charles and Rollo came together at the place that had been decided on. . . . Looking on Rollo, the invader of France, the Franks said to one another, "This duke who has fought such battles against the warriors of this realm is a man of great power and great courage and prowess and good counsel and of great energy too." Then, persuaded by the words of the Franks, Rollo put his hands between the hands of the king, a thing which his father and grandfather and great-grandfather had never done; and so the king gave his daughter Gisela in marriage to the duke and conferred on him the agreed lands from the River Epte to the sea as his property in hereditary right, together with all Brittany from which he could live.

Rollo was not willing to kiss the foot of the king. The bishops said, "Anyone who receives such a gift ought to be eager to kiss the king's foot." He replied, "I have never bent my knees at anyone's knees, nor will I kiss anyone's foot." But, urged by the entreaties of the Franks, he commanded one of his warriors to kiss the foot of the king. The warrior promptly seized the king's foot, carried it to his mouth and kissed it standing up while the king was thrown flat on his back. At that there was a great outburst of laughter and great excitement among the people. Nevertheless King Charles, Duke Robert, the counts and nobles, the bishops and abbots swore by the Catholic faith and by their lives, limbs and the honor of the whole kingdom to the noble Rollo that he should hold and possess the land described above and pass it on to his heirs.

A more conventional ceremony, which took place in Flanders in 1127, is described in the next document.

FROM *Chronicle of the Death of Charles the Good*
BY GALBERT OF BRUGES

THROUGH THE WHOLE REMAINING PART of the day those who had been previously enfeoffed by the most pious count Charles, did homage

University of Pennsylvania Translations and Reprints, IV, No. 3 (1897), 18, translated by E. P. Cheyney.

to the count, taking up now again their fiefs and offices and whatever they had before rightfully and legitimately obtained. On Thursday the seventh of April, homages were again made to the count being completed in the following order of faith and security.

First they did their homage thus, the count asked if he was willing to become completely his man, and the other replied, "I am willing"; and with clasped hands, surrounded by the hands of the count, they were bound together by a kiss. Secondly, he who had done homage gave his fealty to the representative of the count in these words, "I promise on my faith that I will in future be faithful to count William, and will observe my homage to him completely against all persons in good faith and without deceit," and thirdly, he took his oath to this upon the relics of the saints. Afterward, with a little rod which the count held in his hand, he gave investitures to all who by this agreement had given their security and homage and accompanying oath.

The following record of the grant of a fief in France (1200) illustrates some of the complexities that could arise when a vassal held land from several lords.

Grant of Fief, 1200

[handwritten: Indefinite as to what a fief consists of.]

I, THIEBAULT, count palatine of Troyes, make known to those present and to come that I have given in fee to Jocelyn d'Avalon and his heirs the manor which is called Gillencourt, which is of the castellanerie of La Ferte sur Aube; and whatever the same Jocelyn shall be able to acquire in the same manor I have granted to him and his heirs in augmentation of that fief. I have granted, moreover, to him that in no free manor of mine will I retain men who are of this gift. The same Jocelyn, moreover, on account of this has become my liege man, saving however, his allegiance to Gerard d'Arcy, and to the lord duke of Burgundy, and to Peter, count of Auxerre. Done at Chouaude, by my own witness, in the year of the Incarnation of our Lord 1200 in the month of January. Given by the hand of Walter, my chancellor; note of Milo.

University of Pennsylvania Translations and Reprints, IV, No. 3 (1897), 15, translated by E. P. Cheyney.

The next group of documents explain in more detail the obligations of a vassal to his lord. The first extract refers to financial "aids."

FROM *Le Grand Coutumier de Normandie*

NEXT IT IS PROPER to see the chief aids of Normandy, which are called chief because they should be paid to the chief lords.

In Normandy there are three chief aids. One is to make the oldest son of his lord a knight; the second, to marry his oldest daughter; the third to ransom the body of his lord from prison when he is taken in the Duke's war.

In 1270 King Louis IX of France defined the military service due from his vassals.

Definition of Knight Service BY LOUIS IX

THE BARON AND ALL VASSALS of the king are bound to appear before him when he shall summon them, and to serve him at their own expense for forty days and forty nights, with as many knights as each one owes; and he is able to exact from them these services when he wishes and when he has need of them. And if the king wishes to keep them more than forty days at their own expense, they are not bound to remain if they do not wish it. And if the king wishes to keep them at his expense for the defence of the realm, they are bound to remain. And if the king wishes to lead them outside of the kingdom, they need not go unless they wish to, for they have already served their forty days and forty nights.

University of Pennsylvania Translations and Reprints, IV, No. 3 (1897), 28, translated by E. P. Cheyney.

University of Pennsylvania Translations and Reprints, IV, No. 3 (1897), 30, translated by E. P. Cheyney.

The followings extracts from the Exchequer Rolls of the medieval English government refer to feudal "reliefs."

FROM *English Exchequer Rolls*

[handwritten: Someone is always paying relief]

WALTER HAIT renders an account of 5 marks of silver for the relief of the land of his father.

Walter Brito renders an account of £66, 13s. and 4d. for the relief of his land.

Richard of Estre renders an account of £15 for his relief for 3 knights' fees which he holds from the honor of Mortain.

Walter Fitz Thomas, of Newington, owes 28s. 4d. for having the fourth part of one knight's fee which had been seized into the hand of the king for default of relief.

John of Venetia renders an account of 300 marks for the fine of his land and for the relief of the land which was his father's and he does homage to the king against all mortals.

Ralph, son and heir of Ralph of Sullega renders an account of £100 for his relief for the lands which were Ralph his father's which he held from the king *in capite*.

John de Balliol owes £150 for the relief of 30 knights' fees which Hugh de Balliol his father held from the king *in capite*, that is 100s. for each fee.

Peter de Bruce renders an account of £100 for his relief for the barony which was of Peter his father.

[handwritten: money is used to get one's way in order to marry or wardship]

The Exchequer Rolls also illustrate how the rights of wardship and marriage were exercised in a feudal society.

ROHEISA DE DOURA renders account of £450 to have half of all the lands which belonged to Richard de Lucy, her grandfather, and which the brother of the same Roheisa had afterward as well in England as in Normandy, and for license to marry where she wishes so long as she does not marry herself to any of the enemies of the king.

Alice, countess of Warwick, renders account of £1000 and 10 palfreys to be allowed to remain a widow as long as she pleases, and not to be forced to marry by the king. And if perchance she should wish to marry, she shall not marry except with the assent and on the grant of the king, where the king shall be satisfied; and to have the custody of her sons whom she has from the earl of Warwick her late husband.

Hawisa, who was wife of William Fitz Robert renders account of 130 marks and 4 palfreys that she may have peace from Peter of Borough to whom the king has given permission to marry her; and that she may not be compelled to marry.

Geoffrey de Mandeville owes 20,000 marks to have as his wife Isabella, countess of Gloucester, with all the lands and tenements and fiefs which fall to her.

Thomas de Colville renders an account of 100 marks for having the custody of the sons of Roger Torpel and their land until they come of age.

William, bishop of Ely, owes 220 marks for having the custody of Stephen de Beauchamp with his inheritance and for marrying him where he wishes.

William of St. Mary's church, renders an account of 500 marks for having the custody of the heir of Robert Young, son of Robert Fitzharding, with all his inheritance and all its appurtenances and franchises; that is to say with the services of knights and gifts of churches and marriages of women, and to be allowed to marry him to whatever one of his relatives he wishes; and that all his land is to revert to him freely when he comes of age.

Bartholomew de Muleton renders an account of 100 marks for having the custody of the land and the heiress of Lambert of Ibtoft, and for marrying the wife of the same Lambert to whomsoever he wishes where she shall not be disparaged and that he may be able to confer her (the heiress) upon whom he wishes.

The forfeiture of a fief for failure to render military service is described in the following extract.

FROM *English Hundred Rolls*

IT IS PRESENTED by the jurors above named that the manor of Chinnore along with the hamlet of Sydenham was held of old, from the time of the Conquest, from the lord king of England, by a certain man who was named Walter de Vernon, as one knight's fee; and because the said Walter de Vernon refused to perform his due service from the said manor to the lord

University of Pennsylvania Translations and Reprints, IV, No. 3 (1897), 36, translated by E. P. Cheyney.

king John in the time of the war which sprang up between the lord king John and the king of France, the lord king John with the advice of his council seized that same manor with its appurtenances and removed the said Walter de Vernon, on account of his ingratitude from the possession of the aforesaid manor forever. And the lord king John granted that same manor with its appurtenances for the services that to the same lord king was due from it to Saer de Quincy formerly earl of Winchester, to hold to himself and his heirs *in capite* from the lord king as one knight's fee; and the heirs of the said Saer held the aforesaid manor in succession, and still hold it, except the hamlet of Sydenham, which the abbot of Thame holds as a gift from Roger de Quincy.

4 Feudal Kingship Versus Feudal Chaos

> It is generally agreed that feudal government worked differently in different countries and at different times. The following documents illustrate some of the problems and potentialities of feudal kingship. The first one describes the pacification of the royal demesne in France by King Louis VI (1108–1135).

FROM *Life of Louis VI* BY SUGER

Vengeance, Distribution capturing

GUY TROUSSEL, son of that violent man and troubler of the kingdom, Milo of Montlhéry, came back home from an expedition to the Holy Sepulcher, weakened by the hardships of the long journey and by many trials. He had been moved by exceeding great fear of Corbaran, and had descended from the wall of Antioch and left the army of God beleaguered within, and so he was forsaken by all. Fearing that his only daughter might in consequence be deprived of her heritage, he yielded to the desire and persuasions of Philip, the king, and of Louis, his son, who ardently longed for his castle, and gave his daughter in marriage to Philip, the king's younger son. . . .

When the castle of Montlhéry fell in this wise into their hands, the king and his son rejoiced as if they had plucked a straw from their eyes or had torn down bars by which they had been confined. And, indeed, we have heard the father say to his son Louis, "Go, son Louis, keep that tower with all vigilance, whose ravages have well-nigh made us grow old, and whose wiles and criminal frauds have never let me rest in good peace and quiet."

Indeed, its unfaithfulness made the faithful faithless, the faithless most faithless. It brought together the treacherous from far and near, and no ill was done in the whole kingdom without its support. And since the territory

Suger, *Life of Louis VI* in *Readings in European History*, I (1904), 201–4, translated by J. H. Robinson.

of Paris was commanded on the river Seine by Corbeil, midway by Montlhéry, on the right by Châteaufort, there resulted such confusion and chaos in the communications between the men of Paris and of Orleans that neither could go to visit the others without the consent of these faithless men, unless they traveled with a strong guard. But the marriage of which we have spoken tore down the barrier and made travel easy between the two cities. . . .

A king, when he takes the royal power, vows to put down with his strong right arm insolent tyrants whensoever he sees them vex the state with endless wars, rejoice in rapine, oppress the poor, destroy the churches, give themselves over to lawlessness which, and it be not checked, would flame out into ever greater madness; for the evil spirits who instigate them are wont cruelly to strike down those whom they fear to lose, but give free rein to those whom they hope to hold, while they add fuel to the flames which are to devour their victims to all eternity.

Such an utterly abandoned man was Thomas of Marle. While King Louis was busied with many wars, he laid waste the territories of Laon, Rheims, and Amiens, devouring like a raging wolf. He spared not the clergy —fearing not the vengeance of the Church—nor the people for humanity's sake. And the devil aided him, for the success of the foolish does ever lead them to perdition. Slaying all men, spoiling all things, he seized two manors, exceeding rich, from the abbey of the nuns of St. John of Laon. He fortified the two exceeding strong castles, Crécy and Nogent, with a marvelous wall and very high towers, as if they had been his own; and made them like to a den of dragons and a cave of robbers, whence he did waste almost the whole country with fire and pillage; and he had no pity.

The Church of France could no longer bear this great evil; wherefore the clergy, who had met together in a general synod at Beauvais, proceeded to pass sentence of condemnation upon the enemy of the Church's true spouse, Jesus Christ. The venerable Cono, bishop of Praeneste and legate of the holy Roman Church, troubled past endurance by the plaints of churches, of the orphans, of the poor, did smite this ruthless tyrant with the sword of the blessed Peter, which is general anathema. He did also ungird the knightly sword belt from him, though he was absent, and by the judgment of all declared him infamous, a scoundrel, unworthy the name of Christian.

And the king was moved by the plaints of this great council and led an army against him right quickly. He had the clergy, to whom he was ever humbly devoted, in his company, and marched straight against the castle of Crécy. Well fortified was it; yet he took it unprepared because his soldiers smote with an exceeding strong hand; or rather, because the hand of the Lord fought for him. He stormed the strongest tower as if it were the hut of a peasant, and put to confusion the wicked men and piously destroyed the impious. Because they had no pity upon other men, he cut them down without mercy. None could behold the castle tower flaming like the fires of hell and not exclaim, "The whole universe will fight for him against these madmen."

After he had won this victory, the king, who was ever swift to follow up his advantage, pushed forward toward the other castle, called Nogent. There came to him a man who said: "Oh, my lord king, it should be known to thy Serenity that in that wicked castle dwell exceeding wicked men who are worthy to lie in hell, and there only. Those are they who, when thou didst issue commands to destroy the commune of Laon, did burn with fire not only the city of Laon, but the noble church of the Mother of God, and many others beside. And well-nigh all the noble men of the city suffered martyrdom because they were true to their faith and defended their lord the bishop. And these evil men feared not to raise their hands against thy venerable Bishop Gaudin, the anointed of the Lord, defender of the church, but did him most cruelly to death, and exposed his naked body on the open road for beasts and birds of prey to feed upon; but first they cut off his finger with the pontifical ring. And they have agreed together, persuaded by the wicked Thomas, to attack and hold your tower."

The king was doubly animated by these words, and he attacked the wicked castle, broke open the abominable places of confinement, like prisons of hell, and set free the innocent; the guilty he punished with very heavy punishment. He alone avenged the injuries of many. Athirst for justice, he ordained that whatsoever murderous wretches he came upon should be fastened to a gibbet, and left as common food for the greed of kites, crows, and vultures. And this they deserved who had not feared to raise their hand against the Lord's anointed.

When he had taken these two adulterine castles and given back to the monastery of St. John the domains that had been seized, he returned to the city of Amiens and laid siege to a tower of that city which was held by a certain Adam, a cruel tyrant who was laying waste the churches and all the regions round about. He held the place besieged for hard upon two years, and at last forced those who defended it to give themselves up. When he had taken it he destroyed it utterly, and thus brought peace to the realm. He fulfilled most worthily the duty of a king who beareth not the sword in vain, and he deprived the wicked Thomas and his heirs forever of the lordship over that city.

Not every king was able to consolidate his power

a king can use his power to become the chief one

leas that every one down th scale doesn't insurrect

Western Crusaders spread feudal practices to the eastern Mediterranean. These extracts from the Assizes of Romania *deal with the operation of feudal jurisdiction in Greece in the thirteenth century.*

FROM *Feudal Institutions as Revealed in the Assizes of Romania* BY P. W. TOPPING

[handwritten annotations: much more advanced stage; Not every quarrel is settled by warfare but by Courts also]

HOW THE PRINCE CANNOT PUNISH ANY BARON OR VASSAL OF HIS WITHOUT THE CONSENT OF HIS LIEGEMEN

THE PRINCE CANNOT PUNISH any baron or vassal of his, either in civil or criminal action, nor injure him, nor place a penalty on him, without the counsel and consent of his liegemen or of the major part of them; nor render a decision concerning someone's fief or commission others to decide his actions at law; but he must render a decision through his liegemen. And the said lord or his officials cannot have any jurisdiction; but, in petty actions, like the matter of the vineyard of a fief or [the disposition] of a serf, the lord can entrust the judgment to his liegemen if the parties agree. And the lord cannot by force place any liegeman in any office against his will, nor punish him, nor retain his fief, unless it is with the judgment of his other liegemen.

HOW NO LIEGEMAN CAN BE HELD BY HIS LORD EXCEPT FOR TWO CAUSES

It has been ordered in the said Usages that no liegeman of the Principality can be detained in person by his lord for any reason except these two, to wit: for the causes of homicide and treason. And it is thus because his fief provides his security.

WHAT SHOULD BE DONE IF A LIEGEMAN COMMITS HOMICIDE OR TREASON?

If it should happen that a liegeman has committed homicide or treason, what should be done? To this the answer is, that according to the customs and usages aforesaid the lord cannot punish or detain him unless the homicide or

---

P. W. Topping, *Feudal Institutions as Revealed in the Assizes of Romania* (1949), pp. 25–31, 56. Reprinted by permission of University of Pennsylvania Press.

treason has first been proved and unless the judgment has been made in the case of the said liegeman by the other liegemen of the Principality. The lord can neither detain nor seize nor take his goods except by the judgment of the liegemen of the Principality.

AND IF IT HAPPENS THAT THE LORD HAS ONE OF HIS VASSALS, THAT IS, A FIEF OF ONE OF THEM, UNJUSTLY SEIZED, WHAT SHOULD BE DONE?

It is further asked, if the lord has the fief of one of his vassals seized unjustly, and this vassal of his has thrice asked for it in one year in the presence of his liegemen (if he can have such), demanding of him that he should return his fief and requesting the judgment of his court, and if the lord does not have the fief returned in full seizin when a year has passed, the homage for this fief passes to the nearest superior lord. And the vassal should first make a request for his fief within forty days, otherwise he shall lose the produce and revenues of that year. This same decision applies to others who have vassals subject to them if these vassals are liegemen. The man of simple homage has no court and can hold none. The liegeman or the man of simple homage shall be able to lodge a complaint before the overlord of his lord for the feudal goods which might have been taken from him unjustly by his lord; and he does this through a procurator appointed to this task.

When a criminal, civil, or feudal action arises between the Prince or another lord and one of his vassals, the Prince or the lord involved in the dispute must delegate one of his liegemen, or one not a liege, in his place. And the lord is required to rise, to give the delegate his baton and to leave the council, in accordance with the custom. And the delegate is to give the counsel of the liegemen of his court as much to the lord as to the party, retaining with him those liegemen who should appear to him most necessary in order to decide the question. And this is understood if the litigant is a liegeman.

*   *   *

By the Usage and Custom of the Empire of Romania, the Prince cannot place upon his vassals or freemen, or even on their serfs, any tallages or collections on any condition or under any name whatever, or anything, for the utility of the country, without the counsel and consent as well of the liegemen and vassals as of the other freemen. And in this case, those who consent are under obligation, and those who do not consent are under none. But in truth, if he wishes to marry his daughter or ransom himself from his enemies when he has been taken by them, in this case he can levy a collection only on the men of simple homage. Moreover, the lord should take care that no vassal, baron, or soldier allows straw, poultry, or any other thing to be taken by force from the serfs of his subjects.

*   *   *

If a liegeman has been injured in his fief or a part thereof by the Prince or by another lord, the said liegeman is bound to request his lord thrice in a year before some of his liegemen that he restore to him that in which he aggrieved him or reinstate him in his fief, demanding the judgment of his court. Moreover, he is not obliged to render service until he has been reinstated in his fief. And, if the lord is not willing to do him full justice, in this case he [the vassal] must summon his peers and together with them summon his lord also. And if the lord is negligent in doing what justice requires, in this case the other lieges who are with him are not bound to serve their lord until the fief in question is reinstated.

> *The next three readings deal with medieval England. The first one, an extract from the* Anglo-Saxon Chronicle, *describes a highly successful feudal king, William the Conqueror (1066–1087).*

FROM *Anglo-Saxon Chronicle*

IF ANYONE WISHES TO KNOW what sort of a man he was, or what dignity he had or of how many lands he was lord—then we will write of him even as we, who have looked upon him, and once lived at his court, have perceived him to be.

This King William of whom we speak was a very wise man, and very powerful and more worshipful and stronger than any predecessor of his had been. He was gentle to the good men who loved God, and stern beyond all measure to those people who resisted his will. In the same place where God permitted him to conquer England, he set up a famous monastery and appointed monks for it, and endowed it well. In his days the famous church at Canterbury was built, and also many another over all England. Also, this country was very full of monks and they lived their life under the rule of St. Benedict, and Christianity was such in his day that each man who wished

D. C. Douglas and G. Greenaway, *English Historical Documents 1042–1189* (1953), pp. 163–4. Reprinted by permission of Oxford University Press, Inc., and Eyre & Spottiswoode Ltd., London.

followed out whatever concerned his order. Also, he was very dignified:
three times every year he wore his crown, as often as he was in England. At
Easter he wore it at Winchester, at Whitsuntide at Westminster, and at
Christmas at Gloucester, and then there were with him all the powerful men
over all England, archbishops and bishops, abbots and earls, thegns and
knights. Also, he was a very stern and violent man, so that no one dared do
anything contrary to his will. He had earls in his fetters, who acted against
his will. He expelled bishops from their sees, and abbots from their abbacies,
and put thegns in prison, and finally he did not spare his own brother, who
was called Odo; he was a very powerful bishop in Normandy (his cathedral
church was at Bayeux)—and was the foremost man next the king, and had
an earldom in England. And when the king was in Normandy, then he was
master in this country: and he [the king] put *him* in prison. Amongst other
things the good security he made in this country is not to be forgotten—so
that any honest man could travel over his kingdom without injury with his
bosom full of gold: and no one dared strike another, however much wrong
he had done him. And if any man had intercourse with a woman against her
will, he was forthwith castrated.

He ruled over England, and by his cunning it was so investigated that
there was not one hide of land in England that he did not know who owned
it, and what it was worth, and then set it down in his record. Wales was in
his power, and he built castles there, and he entirely controlled that race. In
the same way, he also subdued Scotland to himself, because of his great
strength. The land of Normandy was his by natural inheritance, and he
ruled over the county called Maine: and if he could have lived two years
more, he would have conquered Ireland by his prudence and without any
weapons. Certainly in his time people had much oppression and very many
injuries:

> He had castles built
> And poor men hard oppressed.
> The king was so very stark
> And deprived his underlings of many a mark
> Of gold and more hundreds of pounds of silver,
> That he took by weight and with great injustice
> From his people with little need for such a deed.
> Into avarice did he fall
> And loved greediness above all,
> He made great protection for the game
> And imposed laws for the same.
> That who so slew hart or hind
> Should be made blind.
>
> He preserved the harts and boars
> And loved the stags as much

As if he were their father.
Moreover, for the hare did he decree that they should go free.
Powerful men complained of it and poor men lamented it
But so fierce was he that he cared not for the rancour of them all
But they had to follow out the king's will entirely
If they wished to live or hold their land,
Property or estate, or his favour great,
Alas! woe, that any man so proud should go,
And exalt himself and reckon himself above all men.
May Almighty God show mercy to his soul
And grant unto him forgiveness for his sins.

The Chronicle *also provides a picture of an unsuccessful feudal ruler, King Stephen (1135–1154).*

WHEN THE TRAITORS UNDERSTOOD that he was a mild man, and gentle and good, and did not exact the full penalties of the law, they perpetrated every enormity. They had done him homage, and sworn oaths, but they kept no pledge; all of them were perjured and their pledges nullified, for every powerful man built his castles and held them against him and they filled the country full of castles. They oppressed the wretched people of the country severely with castle-building. When the castles were built, they filled them with devils and wicked men. Then, both by night and day they took those people that they thought had any goods—men and women—and put them in prison and tortured them with indescribable torture to extort gold and silver—for no martyrs were ever so tortured as they were. They were hung by the thumbs or by the head, and corselets were hung on their feet. Knotted ropes were put round their heads and twisted till they penetrated to the brains. They put them in prisons where there were adders and snakes and toads, and killed them like that. Some they put in a "torture-chamber"—that is in a chest that was short, narrow and shallow, and they put sharp stones in it and pressed the man in it so that he had all his limbs broken. In many of the castles was a "noose-and-trap"—consisting of chains of such a kind that two or three men had enough to do to carry one. It was so made that it was fastened to a beam, and they used to put a sharp iron around the man's throat and his neck, so that he could not in any direction either sit or lie or sleep, but had to carry all that iron. Many thousands they killed by starvation.

I have neither the ability nor the power to tell all the horrors nor all the torments they inflicted upon wretched people in this country: and that lasted the nineteen years while Stephen was king, and it was always going from bad to worse. They levied taxes on the villages every so often, and called it "protection money." When the wretched people had no more to give, they robbed and burned all the villages, so that you could easily go a whole day's journey and never find anyone ocupying a village, nor land tilled. Then corn was dear, and meat and butter and cheese, because there was none in the country. Wretched people died of starvation; some lived by begging for alms, who had once been rich men; some fled the country.

There had never been till then greater misery in the country, nor had heathens ever done worse than then they did. For contrary to custom, they respected neither church nor churchyard, but took all the property that was inside, and then burnt the church and everything together. Neither did they respect bishops' land nor abbots' nor priests', but robbed monks and clerics, and everyone robbed somebody else if he had the greater power. If two or three men came riding to a village, all the villagers fled, because they expected they would be robbers. The bishops and learned men were always excommunicating them, but they thought nothing of it, because they were all utterly accursed and perjured and doomed to perdition.

Wherever cultivation was done, the ground produced no corn, because the land was all ruined by such doings, and they said openly that Christ and his saints were asleep. Such things, too much for us to describe, we suffered nineteen years for our sins.

The most famous constitutional document that survives from medieval England is Magna Carta—*a "treaty of peace" between a feudal king and his barons (1215).*

FROM *Magna Carta*

JOHN, BY THE GRACE OF GOD, king of England, lord of Ireland, duke of Normandy and Aquitaine, count of Anjou; to the archbishops, bishops, abbots, earls, barons, justiciars, foresters, sheriffs, reeves, servants, and all bailiffs and his faithful people greeting. . . .

1. In the first place we have granted to God, and by this our present charter confirmed, for us and our heirs forever, that the English church shall be free, and shall hold its rights entire and its liberties uninjured; and we will that it thus be observed; which is shown by this, that the freedom of elections, which is considered to be most important and especially necessary to the English church, we, of our pure and spontaneous will, granted, and by our charter confirmed, before the contest between us and our barons had

University of Pennsylvania Translations and Reprints, I, No. 6 (1897), 6–17, translated by E. P. Cheyney.

arisen; and obtained a confirmation of it by the lord Pope Innocent III; which we will observe and which we will shall be observed in good faith by our heirs forever.

We have granted moreover to all free men of our kingdom for us and our heirs forever all the liberties written below, to be had and holden by themselves and their heirs from us and our heirs.

2. If any of our earls or barons, or others holding from us in chief by military service shall have died, and when he has died his heir shall be of full age and owe relief, he shall have his inheritance by the ancient relief; that is to say, the heir or heirs of an earl for the whole barony of an earl a hundred pounds; the heir or heirs of a baron for a whole barony a hundred pounds; the heir or heirs of a knight, for a whole knight's fee, a hundred shillings at most; and who owes less let him give less according to the ancient custom of fiefs.

3. If moreover the heir of any one of such shall be under age, and shall be in wardship, when he comes of age he shall have his inheritance without relief and without a fine.

4. The custodian of the land of such a minor heir shall not take from the land of the heir any except reasonable products, reasonable customary payments, and reasonable services, and this without destruction or waste of men or of property; and if we shall have committed the custody of the land of any such a one to the sheriff or to any other who is to be responsible to us for its proceeds, and that man shall have caused destruction or waste from his custody we will recover damages from him, and the land shall be committed to two legal and discreet men of that fief, who shall be responsible for its proceeds to us or to him to whom we have assigned them; and if we shall have given or sold to any one the custody of any such land, and he has caused destruction or waste there, he shall lose that custody, and it shall be handed over to two legal and discreet men of that fief who shall be in like manner responsible to us as is said above.

5. The custodian moreover, so long as he shall have the custody of the land, must keep up the houses, parks, warrens, fish ponds, mills, and other things pertaining to the land, from the proceeds of the land itself; and he must return to the heir, when he has come to full age, all his land, furnished with ploughs and implements of husbandry according as the time of wainage requires and as the proceeds of the land are able reasonably to sustain.

6. Heirs shall be married without disparity, so nevertheless that before the marriage is contracted, it shall be announced to the relatives by blood of the heir himself.

7. A widow, after the death of her husband, shall have her marriage portion and her inheritance immediately and without obstruction, nor shall she give anything for her dowry or for her marriage portion, or for her inheritance which inheritance her husband and she held on the day of the death of her husband; and she may remain in the house of her husband for forty days after his death, within which time her dowry shall be assigned to her.

8. No widow shall be compelled to marry so long as she prefers to live without a husband, provided she gives security that she will not marry without our consent, if she holds from us, or without the consent of her lord from whom she holds, if she holds from another.

9. Neither we nor our bailiffs will seize any land or rent, for any debt, so long as the chattels of the debtor are sufficient for the payment of the debt; nor shall the pledges of a debtor be distrained so long as the principal debtor himself has enough for the payment of the debt; and if the principal debtor fails in the payment of the debt, not having the wherewithal to pay it, the pledges shall be responsible for the debt; and if they wish, they shall have the lands and the rents of the debtor until they shall have been satisfied for the debt which they have before paid for him, unless the principal debtor shall have shown himself to be quit in that respect towards those pledges.

10. If any one has taken anything from the Jews, by way of a loan, more or less, and dies before that debt is paid, the debt shall not draw interest so long as the heir is under age, from whomsoever he holds; and if that debt falls into our hands, we will take nothing except the chattel contained in the agreement.

11. And if any one dies leaving a debt owing to the Jews, his wife shall have her dowry, and shall pay nothing of that debt; and if there remain minor children of the dead man, necessaries shall be provided for them corresponding to the holding of the dead man; and from the remainder shall be paid the debt, the service of the lords being retained. In the same way debts are to be treated which are owed to others than the Jews.

12. No scutage or aid shall be imposed in our kingdom except by the common council of our kingdom, except for the ransoming of our body, for the making of our oldest son a knight, and for once marrying our oldest daughter, and for these purposes it shall be only a reasonable aid; in the same way it shall be done concerning the aids of the city of London.

13. And the city of London shall have all its ancient liberties and free customs, as well by land as by water. Moreover, we will and grant that all other cities and boroughs and villages and ports shall have all their liberties and free customs.

14. And for holding a common council of the kingdom concerning the assessment of an aid otherwise than in the three cases mentioned above, or concerning the assessment of a scutage we shall cause to be summoned the archbishops, bishops, abbots, earls, and greater barons by our letters under seal; and besides we shall cause to be summoned generally, by our sheriffs and bailiffs all those who hold from us in chief, for a certain day, that is at the end of forty days at least, and for a certain place; and in all the letters of that summons, we will express the cause of the summons, and when the summons has thus been given the business shall proceed on the appointed day, on the advice of those who shall be present, even if not all of those who were summoned have come.

15. We will not grant to any one, moreover, that he shall take an aid from his free men, except for ransoming his body, for making his oldest son

a knight, and for once marrying his oldest daughter; and for these purposes only a reasonable aid shall be taken.

16. No one shall be compelled to perform any greater service for a knight's fee, or for any other free tenement than is owed from it.

17. The common pleas shall not follow our court, but shall be held in some certain place.

*   *   *

20. A free man shall not be fined for a small offence, except in proportion to the measure of the offence; and for a great offence he shall be fined in proportion to the magnitude of the offence, saving his freehold; and a merchant in the same way, saving his merchandise; and the villain shall be fined in the same way, saving his wainage, if he shall be at our mercy; and none of the above fines shall be imposed except by the oaths of honest men of the neighborhood.

21. Earls and barons shall only be fined by their peers, and only in proportion to their offence.

*   *   *

28. No constable or other bailiff of ours shall take anyone's grain or other chattels, without immediately paying for them in money, unless he is able to obtain a postponement at the good-will of the seller.

29. No constable shall require any knight to give money in place of his ward of a castle if he is willing to furnish that ward in his own person or through another honest man, if he himself is not able to do it for a reasonable cause; and if we shall lead or send him into the army he shall be free from ward in proportion to the amount of time by which he has been in the army through us.

30. No sheriff or bailiff of ours or any one else shall take horses or wagons of any free man for carrying purposes except on the permission of that free man.

31. Neither we nor our bailiffs will take the wood of another man for castles, or for anything else which we are doing, except by the permission of him to whom the wood belongs.

32. We will not hold the lands of those convicted of a felony for more than a year and a day, after which the lands shall be returned to the lords of the fiefs.

*   *   *

39. No free man shall be taken or imprisoned or dispossessed, or outlawed, or banished, or in any way destroyed, nor will we go upon him, nor

send upon him, except by the legal judgment of his peers or by the law of the land.

40. To no one will we sell, to no one will we deny, or delay right or justice.

41. All merchants shall be safe and secure in going out from England and coming into England and in remaining and going through England, as well by land as by water, for buying and selling, free from all evil tolls, by the ancient and rightful customs, except in time of war, and if they are of a land at war with us; and if such are found in our land at the beginning of war, they shall be attached without injury to their bodies or goods, until it shall be known from us or from our principal justiciar in what way the merchants of our land are treated who shall be then found in the country which is at war with us; and if ours are safe there, the others shall be safe in our land.

42. It is allowed henceforth to anyone to go out from our kingdom, and to return, safely and securely, by land and by water, saving their fidelity to us, except in time of war for some short time, for the common good of the kingdom; excepting persons imprisoned and outlawed according to the law of the realm, and people of a land at war with us, and merchants, of whom it shall be done as is before said.

43. If anyone holds from any escheat, as from the honor of Wallingford, or Nottingham, or Boulogne, or Lancaster, or from other escheats which are in our hands and are baronies, and he dies, his heir shall not give any other relief, nor do to us any other service than he would do to the baron, if that barony was in the hands of the baron; and we will hold it in the same way as the baron held it.

*   *   *

54. No one shall be seized nor imprisoned on the appeal of a woman concerning the death of anyone except her husband.

55. All fines which have been imposed unjustly and against the law of the land, and all penalties imposed unjustly and against the law of the land are altogether excused, or will be on the judgment of the twenty-five barons of whom mention is made below in connection with the security of the peace, or on the judgment of the majority of them, along with the aforesaid Stephen, archbishop of Canterbury, if he is able to be present, and others whom he may wish to call for this purpose along with him. And if he should not be able to be present, nevertheless the business shall go on without him, provided that if any one or more of the aforesaid twenty-five barons are in a similar suit they should be removed as far as this particular judgment goes, and others who shall be chosen and put upon oath, by the remainder of the twenty-five shall be substituted for them for this purpose.

*   *   *

60. Moreover, all those customs and franchises mentioned above which we have conceded in our kingdom, and which are to be fulfilled, as far as pertains to us, in respect to our men; all men of our kingdom as well clergy as laymen, shall observe as far as pertains to them, in respect to their men.

61. Since, moreover, for the sake of God, and for the improvement of our kingdom, and for the better quieting of the hostility sprung up lately between us and our barons, we have made all these concessions; wishing them to enjoy these in a complete and firm stability forever, we make and concede to them the security described below; that is to say, that they shall elect twenty-five barons of the kingdom, whom they will, who ought with all their power to observe, hold, and cause to be observed, the peace and liberties which we have conceded to them, and by this our present charter confirmed to them; in this manner, that if we or our justiciar, or our bailiffs, or any one of our servants shall have done wrong in any way toward any one, or shall have transgressed any of the articles of peace or security; and the wrong shall have been shown to four barons of the aforesaid twenty-five barons, let those four barons come to us or to our justiciar, if we are out of the kingdom, laying before us the transgression, and let them ask that we cause that transgression to be corrected without delay. And if we shall not have corrected the transgression or, if we shall be out of the kingdom, if our justiciar shall not have corrected it within a period of forty days, counting from the time in which it has been shown to us or to our justiciar, if we are out of the kingdom; the aforesaid four barons shall refer the matter to the remainder of the twenty-five barons, and let these twenty-five barons with the whole community of the country distress and injure us in every way they can; that is to say by the seizure of our castles, lands, possessions, and in such other ways as they can until it shall have been corrected according to their judgment, saving our person and that of our queen, and those of our children; and when the correction has been made, let them devote themselves to us as they did before. And let whoever in the country wishes take an oath that in all the above-mentioned measures he will obey the orders of the aforesaid twenty-five barons, and that he will injure us as far as he is able with them, and we give permission to swear publicly and freely to each one who wishes to swear, and no one will we ever forbid to swear. All those, moreover, in the country who of themselves and their own will are unwilling to take an oath to the twenty-five barons as to distressing and injuring us along with them, we will compel to take the oath by our mandate, as before said. And if any one of the twenty-five barons shall have died or departed from the land or shall in any other way be prevented from taking the above-mentioned action, let the remainder of the aforesaid twenty-five barons choose another in his place, according to their judgment, who shall take an oath in the same way as the others. In all those things, moreover, which are committed to those five and twenty barons to carry out, if perhaps the twenty-five are present, and some disagreement arises among them about something, or if any of them when they have been summoned are not

willing or are not able to be present, let that be considered valid and firm which the greater part of those who are present arrange or command, just as if the whole twenty-five had agreed in this; and let the aforesaid twenty-five swear that they will observe faithfully all the things which are said above, and with all their ability cause them to be observed. And we will obtain nothing from anyone, either by ourselves or by another by which any of these concessions and liberties shall be revoked or diminished; and if any such thing shall have been obtained, let it be invalid and void, and we will never use it by ourselves or by another.

5 Feudalism as a System of Government

The following readings present the views of three modern scholars on feudalism as a political system. J. Calmette saw feudalism as essentially a disintegrative force.

FROM *The Feudal World* BY J. CALMETTE

THE FEUDAL PRINCIPLE

TWO FUNDAMENTAL IDEAS served as the bases of ancient society—the State and property. The feudal principle attacked these two ideas and so to speak disintegrated them. Properly speaking there was neither State nor property in feudalism. How could these two ideas which seem fundamental and solid have been dissolved? To explain it is to explain the emergence of feudalism.

DISSOLUTION OF PROPERTY

Property was undermined first. At the outset the early Middle Ages knew hardly any form of wealth except land, and land belonged chiefly to the great proprietors. These latter could not cultivate it themselves. Moreover, agricultural work could not be carried out, either by slave labor as in former times—slavery being condemned by the morals of the age—nor by paid workers as nowadays—the circulation of currency being insufficient to maintain a class of wage earners. Hence the problem was resolved by making grants of land by means of contracts. The land to be cultivated was partitioned into lots among tenants of divers conditions who, whatever their name or quality, were charged with labor services and rents while, for their part, they enjoyed a right to the use of the land. Words like *precarium, emphyteusis,* etc., refer merely to contractual variants of this system of grants. In the final reckoning,

J. Calmette, *Le Monde Féodal* (1937), pp. 165–75. Translated by Brian Tierney by permission of Presses Universitaires de France, Paris.

their common characteristic was that they were permanent and heredi-tary. . . . When possession was dissociated definitively from ownership the latter diminished to no more than an external right, purely and simply a capacity to exact certain services. Briefly, the right of property, being con-verted into a kind of eminent domain, had practically ceased to exist.

DISSOLUTION OF THE STATE

The State was eclipsed in the same way. On the morrow of the invasions it was personified in a barbarian king who fused together prerogatives of state and his own personal rights. A man governed, not an impersonal entity. This man bound other men to himself by personal oaths. The idea of personal loyalty dissolved the substance of the State just as the permanent and hereditary right of tenure dissolved property. The bond of dependence of man on man—that ancient custom that gave rise to the "clientage" of ancient law—acquired unprecedented importance from the fact of the invasions. Around the barbarian chief are his "companions," bound by oath and paid by booty, a band that forms an instrument of war and conquest. Now it is from his intimate circle derived from this band that the Frankish king usually draws his counts. Soon these, like the king, attach to themselves by oath men whom they intend to make use of or wish to dominate. It is "vassalage" which is taking root. If the word does not appear until the eighth century its rapid success manifests the force of the concept which it ex-presses.

LORDSHIP

Vassalage becomes combined with the granting of land. For, like the worker, the administrator cannot be paid in money in a society where currency is scarce and does not circulate. Hence the administrator, like the worker, is paid by a form of usufruct. In other words the king, who is the greatest of landlords, pays his agents in the same way that the landlord pays his peasants; he gives them the use of part of his domain. This right of use is at the same time payment for and conditional on the performing of formerly public service. This grant in exchange for service, above all military service on horseback, is called a "benefice" or "honor." Vassalage and benefice combined engender the fief. The fief, properly speaking, is a benefice that a vassal holds of his lord.

The lord or seigneur [senior—the oldest, the most exalted in dignity] receives the oath of the vassal and gives him the property whose revenues provide remuneration for the services implied by the oath. Thus, there is created between lord and vassal a contract. This is the feudal contract. But the services owed by virtue of this contract include those which formerly the subject was bound to render to the state from the very fact of his birth. A private right is thus substituted for a public right. Evidently the generalization of such a system impoverishes the State, which is no more than an idea or transcendental concept, deprived of concrete reality—just what has happened to property itself.

APPROPRIATION OF PUBLIC FUNCTIONS

However serious this transformation became the Carolingian regime would have continued as a semblance of a State if its functionaries had continued to obey it. But, on the contrary, they ceased little by little to be under the king's control and adopted the habit of exercising their powers, no longer on behalf of the State, but in their own name. The public function was absorbed into the lordship. The decline did not take place all at once but came about through insensible transitions. The kings did not react against it because they saw lordship as a means of administering. Moreover the struggles of prince against prince put loyalty on the auction block. The counts sell their support to the king. This support is paid for in benefices and the kingship is so thoroughly stripped of its lands that the descendants of Charlemagne will leave to their successors, the Capetians, a domain reduced almost to nothing. Each count, each holder of an immunity, in a word each lord, lives independently and this is the time when, to quote Quicherat, France—one might say all the West—"bristled with castles.". . .

FEUDAL PROTECTION

The success of this system would have been incomprehensible if it had not answered to a need. The need was for protection. Feudalism established itself because at a critical time it offered protection. We have already seen that insecurity worked in its favor. It was above all the Viking invasions—and to a lesser degree the Saracen and Magyar invasions—which brought about the victory of feudal principles in the ninth century. Faced with the peril of invasions in various localities, the central government proved incapable of finding any effective remedy. The royal failure betrayed the people, and local resistance was organized around the lord. The fortified castle was the center of resistance. Life was concentrated in the circle of the lord because the seigneury was a living cell, one in which the individual found relative security. . . .

PRIVATE WAR

The feudal nobility appears most of all as a military caste. The lord remains above all a soldier. Not all conflicts of law or fact are ended by means of a judgment of a feudal court. In case of discord there is war between lord and lord. Not only a clash of interests or personalities, but often sheer love of battle provokes these quarrels, which custom regulates, and which, once the gauntlet has been thrown down and accepted, unleash between two seigneuries all the horrors of steel, fire and blood. The Church, as a civilizing force, tried in vain to limit the evil. The Truce of God, the Peace of God, were palliatives of perceptible effect but insufficient and precarious in application. One might say that private war, the scourge of the feudal centuries, replaced the invasions against which men had sought to protect themselves by placing themselves under the protection of lords.

R. W. Southern saw the feudal principality as a constructive achievement.

FROM *The Making of the Middle Ages*
BY R. W. SOUTHERN

POLITICALLY, THE GREAT QUESTION in the tenth century, outside Germany, was how far the disintegration of authority would go. The immediate cause of the disintegration was lack of loyalty, and with lack of loyalty to persons went a decay and confusion of the ideas for which the persons stood. It was a time when claims of allegiance and duty, however well founded in law or in history, counted for nothing when they went beyond the bounds of effective personal power. It was easy for the Count of Anjou to throw off his obligations to the King of France. Would it prove equally possible for the lord of Loches or of any of the castles of the Loire to throw off the authority of the Count of Anjou? How far would the process go? The answer depended partly on the range of those small bodies of armoured, mounted soldiers who were growing up round the strong points of government. Partly it depended on the extent of the sacrifices people would be prepared to make for peace and security. It was no accident that after the confusion of the tenth century the strongest governmental units appeared where there was least in the way of marsh, mountain or forest to separate one community from another—in the open plains where the competition for power was most intense, and where the need for organization was consequently most keenly felt. But even in the most favourable geographical conditions, man's technical equipment was so primitive that this helplessness before Nature—which added to his misery in one way—saved him from the misery of organized tyranny. There was a mercifully large gap between the will to rule and the power to do so, and it may be that bad

R. W. Southern, *The Making of the Middle Ages* (1953), pp. 80–90. Reprinted by permission of Yale University Press and Hutchinson Publishing Group Ltd., London.

roads and an intractable soil contributed more to the fashioning of familiar liberties than any other factor at this time.

Perhaps more simply than anywhere else in Europe, the shaping of a new political order may be seen in the valley of the river Loire. There was here so clean a sweep of ancient institutions, title deeds and boundaries, that the emergence of new forms of loyalty and authority was facilitated. Elsewhere the same processes are to be observed, men have the same objects in view, but they work towards them less directly and less swiftly. We shall observe the ambitions, and the restraints imposed on the wills, of some of the most powerful personalities of their time, in studying the emergence of one of the strongest new political units of the eleventh century in the Loire valley.

THE COUNTY OF ANJOU[1]

The history of this county from the late tenth to the mid-twelfth century provides a rich portrait gallery of the makers of a medieval "state." Like other families, the counts took a great interest in their past; they were proud of it, and in the course of years they left a large collection of documents, which illuminate their history. Towards the end of the eleventh century, there was a historically minded Count, Fulk Rechin, who set himself to record the traditions of the family and his own recollections of his predecessors. Looking back from the eminence which the family had attained in his time, he could dimly perceive the origins of their good fortune in the career of an ancestor two hundred years earlier. Nothing was clearly reported about this ancestor except that his name was Ingelgarius, nor was much known about his descendants for nearly another hundred years; but the later panegyrists of the family were able to fill this gap by proclaiming that Ingelgarius was descended from an ancient Romano-British family of high rank. No amount of research or invention could discover how the family had lived in the intervening period since the fall of Rome, but it was concluded that "the matter is unimportant for we often read that senators have lived on the land and emperors have been snatched from the plough." This classical background was a twelfth-century addition to the history of the family—it reveals the romantic prejudices of that period—but in essentials the historians of the family were right. They saw that the effective origins of the family were to be sought in the later years of the ninth century—a time when, as one of them remarked, "the men in established positions relied on the merits of their ancestors and not on their own," and allowed themselves to be elbowed out of the way by new men pushing their way to the front by superior energy and military effectiveness.

[1] For what follows, see L. Halphen, *Le Comté d'Anjou au XI Siècle* (Paris, 1906), J. Chartrou, *L'Anjou de 1109–1151* (Paris, 1928), and J. Boussard, *Le Comté d'Anjou sous Henri Plantegenêt et ses fils (1151–1204)* (Bibliothèque de l'école des Hautes Études, CLXXI, Paris, 1938). The chronicle sources are published in *Chroniques des Comtes d'Anjou et des seigneurs d'Amboise,* ed. L. Halphen and R. Poupardin (Collection des Textes pour servir à l'étude d'histoire, 1913).

The family of Ingelgarius were among these new men. War made them conspicuous, grants of land established their position, marriage consolidated it, and the acquisition of ancient titles of honour cloaked their usurpations. Ingelgarius gained the first foothold in the valley of the Loire, but it was his son Fulk the Red—with a name and physical characteristic which kept reappearing in his descendants—who made the family a power to be reckoned with in the neighbourhood: marriage added to his possessions, force held them together, and the comital rights (for what they were worth), which had previously been shared, were now acquired outright. Two more generations, covering the period from 941 to 987, gave the family a place in legend and in general repute, establishing them in a subtle way in men's minds as well as in their physical experience. The time of Fulk the Good (941 to c. 960) was looked back to as a period of growth, though it was not a time of territorial expansion: it was now that the unnatural fertility of the soil—the fruit of long years of depopulation—was discovered, and prodigious crops rewarded the labours of new settlers. The prize of the Loire valley, the capital city of Tours, still lay outside the range of the count's authority, but the family had great claims to the gratitude of the church in that city. It was said that Ingelgarius had restored to it by force of arms the relics of its patron saint, thus starting the family tradition of goodwill towards the church of Tours. Fulk's reputation in this respect was of a more scholarly kind. It was reported that he delighted to take part in the choir services with the canons and that he was the author of a famous rebuke to a king who ridiculed his clerical tastes. The story is exceedingly improbable, but it illustrates the way in which the family was adding to itself fame of a more than military kind. Fulk's son, Geoffrey Greymantle, who was Count from about 960 to 987, added to this legendary reputation: he was one of the select band of tenth-century heroes whose names were handed down to form part of the stock-in-trade of twelfth-century poetic memory. He was pictured as the standard bearer of Charlemagne in the *Song of Roland,* and in his own right he was the hero of various stories, in which his prowess and counsel saved the kingdom from its enemies.[2]

By 987 the family was ready to emerge from its legendary and epic age on to the stage of history. At this moment there appeared one of those powerful figures, who combined all the qualities and ferocity of his race and consolidated the achievements of the last four generations: Fulk Nerra, the Black, Count of Anjou from 987 to 1040. We cannot do better than look at him through the eyes of his grandson, Count Fulk Rechin. This is what he records of Fulk Nerra:

1 He built thirteen castles, which he can name, and many more besides.
2 He won two pitched battles, against his neighbours to East and West.
3 He built two abbeys, one at Angers and the other near Loches, the great outpost of his power in the South East.

[2] For the place of Geoffrey Greymantle in epic tradition, see F. Lot, *Geoffroi Grisegonelle dans l'Épopée* in Romania, 1890, XIX, 377–93, and *Traditions sur Geoffroi Grisegonelle et sur Helgaud de Montreuil* in Romania, 1920, XLVI, 376–81.

4 He went twice to Jerusalem (this is an understatement: it is almost certain that he went three times); and he died on his way home during his last journey.

Each one of these items, properly considered, stamps him as a man of note: taken together they convey a vivid impression of a pioneer in the art of feudal government. In the first place, the castles: they were the guarantee of the stability of the régime. Fulk was a pioneer in the building of stone keeps, and one formidable example of his handiwork still survives at Langeais. The inexpugnable fortresses solved at once the problem of defence and of government—they made loyalty easy. The battles were more speculative—brilliant gambles based on the solid capital of defensive positions. It was a time when he who committed himself to open battle, committed his fortune to the winds. But the reward of successful enterprise was great, as befitted the uncertainty of the outcome; and the battle of Conquereuil in 992 against the Count of Britanny was one of the foundations of Angevin greatness.

We pass to the expressions of Fulk Nerra's religious zeal. He and his contemporary Duke of Normandy were the greatest of the pilgrims who set on foot the movement to Jerusalem. In them the alternation of headlong violence with abrupt acts of remorse and atonement, which characterises the early feudal age, has its full play. Perhaps more than in anything else, the nature of the man is revealed in the documents which recount his religious benefactions. They breathe a vigorous and autocratic spirit, unencumbered by any feeling after intangible things, yet accessible to a sense of guilt and stirred by a sense of littleness before the miraculous disturbances of nature. These documents deal with stark facts:

> I give them (says Fulk's charter to Beaulieu) the blood, the thieves and all evil deeds, of whatsoever kind they are (that is to say, jurisdiction over, and the profits arising from the punishment of, murderers, thieves and other criminals), between the rivulet de Concere and the oak of St. Hilary, and between the vegetable garden and the elm on which men are hanged. And wheresoever, on my land, the abbot does battle for anything, if his champion is beaten, he shall go free and pay no fine to my reeve or any official.[3]

So far as Fulk speaks to us at all, he speaks to us in words like these. Yet, when all is said, we are very far from understanding a man like Fulk Nerra. It is only occasionally that we are allowed to see behind the façade of ruthlessness and activity to the not overconfident humanity which guided arm and hand. It takes some extraordinary event to reveal these men in their more domestic moods. They must often have sat with their wives at the upper windows of their newly built castles, but it is not until a meteor falls into the garden below that we have a picture of Fulk's formidable son Geoffrey Martel and his wife Agnes (the mother of the Empress) racing

[3] L. Halphen, Le Comté d'Anjou au XI Siècle, pp. 351-2.

down to the spot where it fell and vowing to found an abbey dedicated to the Holy Trinity, in memory of the three glowing fragments which had flashed before their awestruck eyes. It was in the face of the miraculous that they became most human. When the Duke of Aquitaine heard that a rain of blood had fallen in his duchy, he did not reflect that he was hostile to the royal pretensions—he humbly wrote and asked the king if he had any learned men who could explain the event. And their answers were such as to make any man pause in a career of wrong-doing.[4] But, on the whole, the secular leaders of the early eleventh century must be judged by what they did, and not by what they thought or intended. Judged by this standard Fulk Nerra is the founder of the greatness of the County of Anjou.

His life-time brings us to an age of serious, expansive wars waged by well-organized and strongly fortified territorial lords. The confused warfare, haphazard battles and obscure acts of force of the first hundred years of the family's history had turned scattered and precarious rights into a complex, but geographically compact and militarily impregnable association, dependent on the Count. The process was directed by an instinctive feeling for strategic advantage, which perhaps lends to the history of these years an appearance of consistency greater than in fact it possessed. The methods were not refined, but they were practised with a consistency of purpose which inspires a certain respect. The swallowing of an important strong point might be preceded by many years of steady encroachment. It was necessary, first, to get established at some point within the territory to be threatened—an operation carried out by a careful marriage, a purchase which the documents represent as a gift, or an act of force or fraud. Then a castle was built as a base of operations. After that, watchfulness: a minority, the chance offered by the enemy's engagement elsewhere, or a lucky battle, might complete the circle. The town of Tours, for instance, was not swallowed until 1044, but in a sense the whole history of the family was a preparation for this event: the good relations with the church of the city seem to go back to the founder of the dynasty; the encircling of the town by a ring of castles at Langeais, Montbazon, Montrichard and Montboyau had been begun by Fulk Nerra fifty years before the final victory. How much was design and how much a kind of inspired opportunism it would be useless to enquire. Once started, the process went on as relentlessly as the operations of the Stock Exchange.

But by the middle of the eleventh century, easy progress by these familiar methods was no longer possible. The weak had been made dependent, the strongholds of intruding neighbours had been taken and, by the same token, distant claims of the Counts outside their own territory had been abandoned. To the west stood Brittany, to the east Blois, to the north—across the still debatable land of Maine—Normandy, to the south Poitou. They

---

[4] These letters were preserved among the correspondence of Fulbert of Chartres and they are printed in P. L. vol. 141, 239–40 and 935–8.

faced each other as equals. Although the armed peace was often broken, the chief interest of the next hundred and fifty years lies in the emergence of stable political institutions and the elaboration of a new system of law. The swashbuckling days were over, and the régimes which had emerged began to clothe themselves in habits of respectability. Up to this point, St. Augustine's dictum that secular governments are nothing but large-scale robbery seemed to be abundantly justified by the facts: but slowly something more complex, more sensitive to the positive merits of organized society, seemed to be required. Government became something more than a system of exactions from a conquered countryside, and there developed a routine for the peaceful exploitation of resources and for the administering of justice. For this, an expert and literate staff was needed, in addition to the menials and military leaders who had satisfied the requirements of a more primitive age. Government by means of the written word returned after a long silence. Until the time of Fulk Rechin, the Count seems not to have felt the need for having someone at hand who could write his letters. All the known comital documents were written by an outsider. It was quite natural that this should be so. The most frequent occasion for writing a document was to make a record of some act of generosity, by which the Count had endowed a religious house: it was the beneficiary who was interested in making the record, and to him fell the labour of making it. If on the other hand, as might sometimes happen, the Count wished to correspond with the Pope or the King of France, he called in some notable scholar for the occasion to write his letters for him. But slowly his needs outgrew this primitive expedient. The necessity for transmitting orders and preserving information became more pressing, and by the end of the eleventh century the Count was not only sealing or witnessing documents which had been written for him by those with whom he was in casual contact; he had men about him who could conduct his correspondence and were eager to manage his affairs. It is an important moment in history, not peculiar to Anjou but common to the governments of northwestern Europe. The continuity of government was re-established. The work required trained men, and the presence of trained men—by a process with which we are familiar—made more work for more trained men.

The rise of the great schools of Northern France and Norman England coincided with and forwarded this movement in government. Slowly the ruling households of Europe, at all levels from the Papal Court to the household of a minor baron, were penetrated by men calling themselves "Masters," men who had studied in the Schools—or as we should say university men. The flow of university men into the Civil Service and into technical positions from the 1870's to our own day is not more significant of the new part played by government in daily affairs, than the similar flow of "Masters" into official positions which began in the early twelfth century and, by the end of our period, had transformed the operations and outlook of secular government. The revolutions in thought which transformed the mainly monastic learning of the eleventh century on the one hand, and the mainly clerical education of the early nineteenth century on the other, had, both of them, wide repercussions in the sphere of government. The "Masters" of the twelfth century brought to government a training, a method and a breadth of vision which had been unknown in the previous century: they were only the instruments of government, but they were finer instruments than had been known before.

> *J. R. Strayer considered that feudalism provided a workable basis of government for the newly emerging European states.*

FROM *Feudalism in Western Europe*
BY J. R. STRAYER

WE COULD HARDLY EXPECT these early feudal governments to be well organized and efficient—they were improvised to meet a desperate situation and they bore all the signs of hasty construction. But they did have two great advantages which made them capable of further development. In the first place, feudalism forced men who had privileges to assume responsibility. In the late Roman Empire, the Frankish kingdom, and the Carolingian monarchy wealthy landlords had assisted the central government as little as possible while using their position and influence to gain special advantages for themselves. Now they had to carry the whole load; if they shirked they lost everything. In the second place, feudalism simplified the structure of government to a point where it corresponded to existing social and economic conditions. For centuries rulers had been striving to preserve something of the Roman political system, at the very least to maintain their authority over relatively large areas through a hierarchy of appointed officials. These efforts had met little response from the great majority of people; large-scale government had given them few benefits and had forced them to carry heavy burdens. Always there had been a dangerous discrepancy between the wide interests of the rulers and the narrow, local interests of the ruled. Feudalism relieved this strain; it worked at a level which was comprehensible to the ordinary man and it made only minimum demands on him. It is probably true that early feudal governments did less than they should,

J. R. Strayer, "Feudalism in Western Europe" in R. Coulborn, ed., *Feudalism in History*, pp. 22–5. Reprinted by permission of Princeton University Press, copyright, © 1956, by Princeton University Press.

but this was better than doing more than was wanted. When the abler feudal lords began to improve their governments they had the support of their people who realized that new institutions were needed. The active demand for more and better government in the twelfth century offers a sharp contrast to the apathy with which the people of Western Europe watched the disintegration of the Roman and the Carolingian Empires.

Feudalism, in short, made a fairly clean sweep of obsolete institutions and replaced them with a rudimentary government which could be used as a basis for a fresh start. Early feudal government was informal and flexible. Contrary to common opinion, it was at first little bound by tradition. It is true that it followed local custom, but there were few written records, and oral tradition was neither very accurate nor very stable. Custom changed rapidly when circumstances changed; innovations were quickly accepted if they seemed to promise greater security. Important decisions were made by the lord and his vassals, meeting in informal councils which followed no strict rules of procedure. It was easy for an energetic lord to make experiments in government; for example, there was constant tinkering with the procedure of feudal courts in the eleventh and twelfth centuries in order to find better methods of proof. Temporary committees could be set up to do specific jobs; if they did their work well they might become permanent and form the nucleus of a department of government. It is true that many useful ideas came from the clergy, rather than from lay vassals, but if feudal governments had not been adaptable they could not have profited from the learning and skill of the clergy.

Feudalism produced its best results only in regions where it became the dominant form of government. France, for example, developed her first adequate governments in the feudal principalities of the north, Flanders, Normandy, Anjou and the king's own lordship of the Ile de France. The first great increase in the power of the French king came from enforcing his rights as feudal superior against his vassals. Many institutions of the French monarchy of the thirteenth century had already been tested in the feudal states of the late twelfth century; others grew out of the king's feudal court. By allowing newly annexed provinces to keep the laws and institutions developed in the feudal period, the king of France was able to unite the country with a minimum of ill-will. France later paid a high price for this provincial particularism, but the existence of local governments which could operate with little supervision immensely simplified the first stages of unification.

England in many ways was more like a single French province than the congeries of provinces which made up the kingdom of France. In fact, the first kings after the Conquest sometimes spoke of the kingdom as their "honor" or fief, just as a feudal lord might speak of his holding. As this example shows, England was thoroughly feudalized after the Conquest. While Anglo-Saxon law remained officially in force it became archaic and inapplicable; the law which grew into the common law of England was the law applied in the king's feudal court. The chief departments of the English government likewise grew out of this court. And when the combination of able kings and efficient institutions made the monarchy too strong, it was checked by the barons in the name of the feudal principles expressed in Magna Carta. Thus feudalism helped England to strike a happy balance between government which was too weak and government which was too strong.

The story was quite different in countries in which older political institutions prevented feudalism from reaching full development. Feudalism grew only slowly in Germany; it never included all fighting men or all lands. The German kings did not use feudalism as the chief support of their government; instead they relied on institutions inherited from the Carolingian period. This meant that the ruler acted as if local lords were still his officials and as if local courts were still under his control. In case of opposition, he turned to bishops and abbots for financial and military aid, instead of calling on his vassals. There was just enough vitality in this system to enable the king to interfere sporadically in political decisions all over Germany, and to prevent the growth of strong, feudal principalities. But while the German kings of the eleventh and twelfth centuries showed remarkable skill in using the old precedents, they failed to develop new institutions and ideas. Royal government became weaker, and Germany more disunited in every succeeding century. The most important provincial rulers, the dukes, were also unable to create effective governments. The kings were jealous of their power, and succeeded in destroying, or weakening, all the great duchies. The kings, however, were unable to profit from their success, because of their own lack of adequate institutions. Power eventually passed to rulers of the smaller principalities, not always by feudal arrangements, and only after the monarchy had been further weakened by a long conflict with the papacy. Thus the German kings of the later Middle Ages were unable to imitate the king of France, who had united his country through the use of his position as feudal superior. Germany remained disunited, and, on the whole, badly governed, throughout the rest of the Middle Ages and the early modern period.

Italy also suffered from competition among different types of government. The German emperor was traditionally king of (north) Italy. He could not govern this region effectively but he did intervene often enough to prevent the growth of large, native principalities. The Italian towns had never become depopulated, like those of the North, and the great economic revival of the late eleventh century made them wealthy and powerful. They were too strong to be fully controlled by any outside ruler, whether king or feudal lord, and too weak (at least in the early Middle Ages) to annex the rural districts outside their walls. The situation was further complicated by the existence of the papacy at Rome. The popes were usually on bad terms with the German emperors and wanted to rule directly a large part of central Italy. In defending themselves and their policies they encouraged the towns' claims to independence and opposed all efforts to unite the peninsula. Thus, while there was feudalism in Italy, it never had a clear field and was unable to develop as it did in France or England. Italy became more and more disunited; by the end of the Middle Ages the city-state, ruled by a "tyrant," was the dominant form of government in the peninsula. There was no justification for this type of government in medieval political theory, and this may be one reason why the Italians turned with such eagerness to the writings of the classical period. In any case, the Italian political system was a failure, and Italy was controlled by foreign states from the middle of the sixteenth to the middle of the nineteenth century.

There are certainly other factors, besides feudalism, which enabled France and England to set the pattern for political organization in Europe, and other weaknesses, besides the absence of fully developed feudalism, which condemned Germany and Italy to political sterility. At the same time, the basic institutions of France and England in the thirteenth century, which grew out of feudal customs, proved adaptable to changed conditions, while the basic institutions of Italy and Germany, which were largely non-feudal, had less vitality. Western feudalism was far from being an efficient form of government, but its very imperfections encouraged the experiments which kept it from being a stagnant form of government. It was far from being a just form of government, but the emphasis on personal relationships made it a source of persistent loyalties. And it was the flexibility of their institutions and the loyalty of their subjects which enabled the kings of the West to create the first modern states.

Gregory VII—
Church Reformer
or World Monarch?

CONTENTS

Gregory VII (1073–1085) led the papacy into the first great conflict of church and state in Western history. The dispute is often called the "Investiture Contest" because the immediate cause of its outbreak was the pope's condemnation of an existing practice whereby kings appointed bishops and "invested" them with the symbols of spiritual office, the episcopal ring and staff. Some historians regard Gregory as a zealous reformer of ecclesiastical morals who was forced reluctantly into a political dispute because a worldly minded monarch resisted his reforming policy. Others see him as a revolutionary figure, determined to create a new world order in which all power over spiritual and temporal affairs would belong to the pope.

QUESTIONS FOR STUDY

1   Why was the right to appoint bishops so important to eleventh-century kings? How could this right be defended in theory?

2   What were the major objectives of the papal reform movement? And why did the reformers concentrate on these particular issues?

3   Was Canossa a victory for Gregory or for Henry?

4   How would you argue for and against the proposition that Gregory was a "revolutionary" in the sphere of politics and in the sphere of religion?

5   Would Gregory VII have approved of the Concordat of Worms?

1   The Church Before the Reform Movement

The problem of church and state has deep roots in Western history. In the year 494 Pope Gelasius I wrote a letter to the Eastern emperor at Byzantium that contained a famous definition of the right relationship between priesthood and kingship. It was quoted by both sides during the Investiture Contest.

Supremacy
of Church

FROM *Gelasius I's Letter to Emperor Anastasius*

TWO THERE ARE, august emperor, by which this world is chiefly ruled, the sacred authority [auctoritas] of the priesthood and the royal power [potestas]. Of these the responsibility of the priests is more weighty in so far as they will answer for the kings of men themselves at the divine judgment. You know, most clement son, that, although you take precedence over all mankind in dignity, nevertheless you piously bow the neck to those who have charge of divine affairs and seek from them the means of your salvation, and hence you realize that, in the order of religion, in matters concerning the reception and right administration of the heavenly sacraments, you ought to submit yourself rather than rule, and that in these matters you should depend on their judgment rather than seek to bend them to your will. For if the bishops themselves, recognizing that the imperial office was conferred on you by divine disposition, obey your laws so far as the sphere of public order is concerned lest they seem to obstruct your decrees in mundane matters, with what zeal, I ask you, ought you to obey those who have been charged with administering the sacred mysteries? Moreover, just as no light risk attends pontiffs who keep silent in matters concerning the service of God, so too no little danger threatens those who show scorn—which God forbid—when they ought to obey. And if the hearts of the faithful should be submitted to all priests in general who rightly administer

Brian Tierney, *The Crisis of Church and State,* © 1964, pp. 13–4. Reprinted by permission of Prentice-Hall, Inc., Englewood Cliffs, N. J.

divine things, how much more should assent be given to the bishop of that see which the Most High wished to be pre-eminent over all priests, and which the devotion of the whole church has honored ever since. As Your Piety is certainly well aware, no one can ever raise himself by purely human means to the privilege and place of him whom the voice of Christ has set before all, whom the church has always venerated and held in devotion as its primate. The things which are established by divine judgment can be assailed by human presumption; they cannot be overthrown by anyone's power.

> *Pope Gelasius I was writing just after the line of Roman emperors in the West had become extinct. The establishment of barbarian kingdoms in the Western world and the subsequent growth of feudalism created new problems for the church. T. M. Parker discusses the impact of feudalism in the next reading.*

FROM *Christianity and the State in the Light of History* BY T. M. PARKER

ALWAYS IN THE MEDIEVAL WEST there is implicit the idea of rights as derived not solely from the state, but from the status of the individuals which make up the political community.

It is not difficult to see how in such an atmosphere the idea of the Church as an institution separate from the State and possessed of its own authority—an idea ultimately derived from the Biblical notion of the Kingdom of God—could develop into that of the Church as an *imperium in imperio.* So long as the classical idea of sovereignty persisted such an evolution was inconceivable or barely possible. But, given feudal conditions, the way was open. For the Church had a history infinitely longer and more impressive than that of the feudal fief. It could claim independence with far better title than any feudal landlord.

Yet this was far from being the immediate outcome of the Church's finding itself living in the new type of society which developed, as the result of a long evolution, towards the end of the first millennium A.D. On the contrary, in the breakdown of centralised power, the Church suffered a loss of independence and not without reason is the volume of the great Fliche et Martin, *Histoire de l'Église,* covering the period 888 to 1057, given the title

T. M. Parker, *Christianity and the State in the Light of History* (1955), pp. 104–8. Reprinted by permission of A. & C. Black Ltd., London.

L'Église au pouvoir des laïques. To understand the reasons we need to turn to a phenomenon in Church history for the elucidation of which we are indebted to comparatively recent historical scholarship—a phenomenon of which the existence was barely recognised before the nineteenth century. I refer to the notion of the "private church," the *Eigenkirche* as it is technically known. It was in October 1894 that Ulrich Stutz delivered his now classical inaugural lecture in the University of Basel entitled *Die Eigenkirche als Element des mittel-alterlich-germanischen Kirchenrechtes* (Berlin, 1895), and thereby set in motion a series of studies and controversies which have to a great extent transformed our notions of ecclesiastical development in the early Middle Ages. It is not my purpose to discuss the disputes which have arisen about the origin of the institution then described by Stutz—disputes which have been so strangely complicated and embittered by nationalistic feeling, as German and French historians have contended on behalf of Teutonic and Latin claims to the doubtful honour of inventing the private church. (These contests remind one of the rivalry between Ipswich and Sudbury to be regarded as the original of Dickens's Eatanswill, for only an idealist could regard the private church as a blessing to mankind or to the Church.) It would probably now be agreed that Stutz's attempt to identify the institution he discovered with a peculiarity of Germanic paganism carried on into early German Arian Christianity and thence into medieval Catholic polity has failed, and that the proprietary church is but one example of the phenomena produced by the general decay of centralism in the decline and fall of the Roman Empire in the West. Let us content ourselves with considering its importance in the history of Church-State relations.

What was an *Eigenkirche?* It was a church built by a landlord on his estate for the spiritual benefit of himself and his dependents. In accordance with the spirit of the times the Dark Ages landlord regarded his foundation as his own property and both Church and State perforce admitted his claim to possess it. Not only was the church and its income his, but he retained also the right to nominate its priest—a right which has survived in this country and in some other parts of Europe in the form of lay parochial patronage, even though other vestiges of the private church system have vanished. In its heyday the landlord claimed not only to appoint but to control his priest. Furthermore, he conceived himself to possess the right to dispose of his church by gift, sale or testamentary disposition, to third parties, if he did not leave it to devolve upon his heir. Short of secularising the building (which would have been sacrilege) he could do almost anything with it, whilst over its incumbent his powers were often greater than those of the diocesan bishop.

The obvious friction between lay and ecclesiastical authority occasioned by this claim of the laity to the ownership of what were to become the parish churches of medieval Europe needs no stressing. What is of even greater significance is the extension, by a natural transition of thought, of a parallel claim to lay control of the larger units of ecclesiastical jurisdiction and property, bishoprics and monasteries. Kings and lesser magnates, accustomed to the idea of owning and controlling churches upon their domains, thought it natural to claim similar rights over the sees and religious houses they had in many cases founded or endowed and of which in any case they were the protectors. In regard to bishoprics there was the earlier precedent of imperial and royal control of episcopal elections to aid their claim: monarchs had long been accustomed to think of the bishops of their realms as *their* bishops. With the decline of royal power in favour of that of local lords, it was equally natural for these latter to regard the greater churches within their sphere of influence as subject to them. So one finds a curious rivalry between kings and nobles for the control of episcopal elections. For example, of 77 sees in eleventh-century France, the king had the control of about 25: the rest were in the hands of dukes, counts or viscounts. That control was exercised chiefly in determining the occupant of the see. The temporal lord might either concede the election to the clergy and people, subject to his own confirmation, or himself appoint a candidate direct. But it did not limit itself to this. The idea of the private church, as we have seen, involved more than the mere right of appointment to it: the church was the lord's property. This notion, too, is applied to bishoprics. The see, with its lands and property, comes to be regarded as an "honour"; the same word is used as that increasingly current to describe a lay fief. As such it is in the overlord's gift. He expects from its tenant homage, fealty and military service: he claims the right to invest him with the honour and when it is vacant take it "into his own hand" until the time comes to grant it again to its newly chosen incumbent.

Here we come face to face with another aspect of the influence of feudal ideas upon ecclesiastical affairs. When political power is localised to the extent required by a feudal organisation of society, and is bound up with the holding of land, it is inevitable that the Church should become, to a greater degree than ever before, a sharer in that power. For, before the development of money investments and finance, endowment of the Church can only be in land. And when land is the measure of power, the greater ecclesiastical landlords, bishops, abbots, cathedral churches and other prelates or corporations, must of necessity be important units in the State, responsible for military service, local jurisdiction, and supervision of agricultural economy. And if they are such, the State cannot be indifferent to their identity. Even in their spiritual capacity, as men wielding great powers of spiritual persuasion and coercion, bishops and other prelates are formidable and we have already seen that the State, from the moment it became Christian, interested itself profoundly in ecclesiastical appointments. But when to spiritual power was added, under feudal conditions, temporal authority over wide areas of territory, bishops and abbots became personages about whose loyalty the State could not take chances. In England the prince-bishop in the full sense, as found in, for example, Germany, was a rare, indeed a unique phenomenon. Yet who can look at Durham Castle and reflect upon the key position of the

Palatinate of Durham in the defence of the Scottish border without realising that no King of England could remain indifferent to the outcome of an election to that see?

The temporal importance of prelates was the ultimate and legitimate reason upon the State's side for its retention of at least some degree of control over ecclesiastical personages and property, a control which came to be regarded by zealous churchmen as out of harmony with any adequate notion of the Church's freedom.

Catherine E. Boyd describes the abuses that arose in the churches of Italy. Similar conditions existed in other parts of Europe.

FROM *Tithes and Parishes in Medieval Italy*

BY CATHERINE E. BOYD

Selling of church for rent in return

THE CONDITONS which had originated in the Italian parishes in the tenth century continued unchanged into the eleventh century, when their disastrous effects upon religious life became clearly visible. The monk Donizo, in his versified life of Matilda of Tuscany, tells how the Tuscan bishops sold parish churches to both laymen and priests, to the demoralization of the people. The history of some of these churches can be traced through the century. In 1009 the parish church of Creti in Arezzo was bestowed by the bishop as a prebend upon the archdeacon of his cathedral, with the right of unrestricted alienation; the archdeacon might assign or bequeath the church to another priest or give it as a benefice to a layman, provided the stipulated rent was paid to the bishop. Two generations later the church had become the benefice of a group of nine *milites*. Now practically in ruins, it was retroceded to the bishopric by the knights, who promised to refrain in the future from violence within the church precincts. Of the tithes of the parish, they restored only a fourth, presumably retaining the rest in their possession.

Numerous other examples illustrate the way in which parish churches and their tithes had come to be regarded as objects of proprietary right, to be exploited by clergy and laymen alike. In Lucca, where the concessions in *livello* were in this period being transformed into fiefs, the charges imposed by the bishops upon the parish priests also assumed a more feudal character. One parish was let by Bishop Grimizzo to a priest in return for a money rent and a horse if needed for service in the imperial host. Bishop Anselm I, though he favored ecclesiastical reform, confirmed the grants of parishes to laymen which had been made by his predecessors. In the regions farther north the same practices obtained. Bishops helped themselves to the tithes of their parish churches or shared them with their vassals for political purposes. Marquis Boniface of Tuscany at one time held thirteen parish churches from the bishop of Reggio, who shared the revenues of fourteen others with the local knights. In the Piedmontese bishoprics numerous churches and tithes were held by laymen, although here, to a greater extent than elsewhere in Italy, the tithe was annexed to manorial churches without parochial rights. Ulric-Manfred, count of Turin, and his daughter Adelaide had in their possession many churches and their revenues. When a reformer in the eleventh century used the term "simony," he had before his eyes this whole complex of mercenary transactions which resulted from the growth of the proprietary system of churches and the extension of the proprietary idea to the parishes. It will be noted that the clergy as well as the laity exercised proprietary rights over the lower churches, treating them as if they were their private property and disposing of their revenues as if they were private income.

Abuses of a moral order were undoubtedly fostered by these practices. Clerical marriage was of course widespread in Italy, as well as less legitimate relations. Rathier of Verona, late in the tenth century, stated that if he tried to enforce clerical celibacy in his diocese, he would be left without a clergy. In Milan the clergy married according to the forms of civil law and claimed that marriage was a custom permitted to the church of St. Ambrose. Clerical marriage became doubly dangerous to ecclesiastical order when combined with the leasing of churches to the clergy under tenurial forms which gave them complete control of church property; there was a real possibility that church offices and property might become hereditary.

> *Clerical immorality and the buying and selling of churches were evident abuses. But the appointment of bishops by kings could be given a theological justification. The following extract (written by an anonymous cleric of the Anglo-Norman kingdom, c. 1100) presents a theory of theocratic kingship that was widely accepted in the eleventh century.*

FROM *York Tractates*

BY DIVINE AUTHORITY and by institution of the holy fathers kings are ordained in the church of God and are consecrated at the altar with sacred

Brian Tierney, *The Crisis of Church and State,* © 1964, pp. 76–7. Reprinted by permission of Prentice-Hall, Inc., Englewood Cliffs, N. J.

unction and benediction, that they may have the power of ruling the people of the Lord, the Christian people, which is the holy church of God—a chosen race, a holy race, a purchased people (cf. 1 Peter 2:9). What else indeed is the church but the congregation of faithful Christians living together in the house of Christ in charity and in the one faith? Therefore kings receive in their consecration the power to rule this church, that they may rule it and strengthen it in judgment and justice and administer it in accordance with the discipline of the Christian law; for they reign in the church, which is the kingdom of God, and reign together with Christ, in order that they may rule, protect and defend it. To reign is to rule the subjects well and to serve God with fear. The episcopal order too is instituted and consecrated with sacred unction and benediction, that it also may rule the holy church according to the form of doctrine given to it by God. Accordingly the blessed pope Gelasius speaks thus, "Two there are by which this world is chiefly ruled, the priestly authority and the royal power." By "this world" he means the holy church, which is a sojourner in this world. In this world, then, the priestly authority and the royal power hold the principate of sacred government. Some seek to divide the principate in this fashion, saying that the priesthood has the principate of ruling souls, the king that of ruling bodies; as if souls could be ruled without bodies and bodies without souls, which cannot be done by any means. For if bodies are well ruled it is necessary that souls are well ruled too and vice versa, since both are ruled for this purpose, that at the resurrection they may both be saved together.

Christ, God and man, is the true and highest king and priest. But he is king from the eternity of his divinity, not made, not created, not below or separate from the Father, but equal to and one with the Father. He is priest from his assumption of humanity, made and created according to the order of Melchisedech and so less than the Father. As king he created all things and rules and preserves all things, governing both men and angels. As priest he only redeemed men that they might reign with him. This is the sole reason why he was made priest, to offer himself as a sacrifice so that men might be made sharers of his kingdom and of his royal power. For everywhere in the Scriptures he promised the kingdom of heaven to the faithful but nowhere the priesthood. It is clear, therefore, that in Christ the royal power is greater and higher than the priestly in proportion as his divinity is greater and higher than his humanity. Hence some hold that among men likewise the royal power is greater and higher than the priestly and the king greater and higher than the priest, as being an imitation and emulation of the better and higher nature or power of Christ. And so it is not contrary to the justice of God, they say, if the sacerdotal dignity is instituted by the royal or subjected to it, for so it was done in Christ; he was made a priest by his royal power and was subjected to the Father in his priestly power while he was equal to him in his royal power.

2 The Reform of the Papacy

*Various reform movements grew up in the church during
the tenth and eleventh centuries. The Roman church began
to take the lead in such activity only after the Emperor
Henry III had carried through a reform of the papacy itself.
In 1046 he deposed three would-be pontiffs and installed
another of his own choosing. The following account is by a
contemporary Roman cleric who was favorable to the emperor.*

FROM *Roman Annals*

IN THE YEAR 1046 from the incarnation of the Lord, in the thirteenth
indiction and in the twelfth year of the reign of Pope Benedict VIII, a great
sedition arose in the city against him. All the people came together and
expelled him from the pontificate. Later in that same year, on the feast of St.
Cecilia the sun was darkened for a space of three hours. . . . Then all the
Romans assembled together and chose for themselves John, Bishop of Sabina, as pope, giving him the name of Sylvester. He held the pontificate for
forty-nine days, then he was expelled and they re-installed Pope Benedict in
his see. Finding the Roman people insufferable, Benedict resigned the
pontificate by a charter in favor of his godfather, John, archpriest of St. John
Lateran, on the first of May. They gave him the name of Gregory, and he
held the pontificate for eleven days short of a year and a month.

When the news of this unheard-of dispute reached Henry, invincible
emperor by the grace of God, he set out for Italy with a great force and an
immense army. When he had reached the city of Sutri he summoned there
the Roman clergy, together with Pope Gregory, and decreed that an extraordinary council be held in the holy church of Sutri. Then, judging canonically
and justly and demonstrating this to the holy and pious bishops by the
canons, he bound with perpetual anathema John, bishop of Sabina, whom

L. Duchesne, ed., *Annales Romani* in *Liber Pontificalis,* II (1892), 331–2. Translated by Brian
Tierney by permission of Editions E. de Boccard, Paris.

they called Sylvester; John, the archpriest, whom they called Gregory; and the above-mentioned Pope Benedict. And so he came to the city of Rome with such a great host that even the city could not accommodate so vast an army.

Henry, pious and benevolent king by the mercy of God, gathered together a multitude of the Roman people along with bishops and abbots and all the Roman clergy in the basilica of St. Peter, prince of the apostles, and held there a holy and glorious council; and he appointed an admirable, holy, and benign pontiff of the holy Roman church called Clement on the vigil of the Nativity of the Lord. On the day of the Nativity of our Lord Jesus Christ the aforesaid king was crowned by his holy and benign pontiff, the city of Rome was filled with joy, and the Roman church was exalted and glorified because at last, by the mercy of God, such a great heresy had been eradicated.

> *In 1049 Henry chose as pope a close kinsman who took the title Leo IX. The new pope initiated a program of sweeping reform directed especially against simony (the buying and selling of spiritual office) and clerical marriage. He not only promulgated reform decrees in Rome but also traveled north of the Alps to publicize and enforce them. The following modern account of a papal council held at Rheims is based on a narrative by a contemporary monk.*

FROM *The Making of the Middle Ages*
BY R. W. SOUTHERN

THE FEAST OF ST. REMIGIUS, 1 October, had been fixed for the ceremony of translation, and the Pope arrived in Rheims on 29 September. The King of France had refused to be present, and he was largely responsible for the poor attendance of bishops. But the vast concourse of people who filled the town formed a striking and instructive contrast to the sparse gathering of notabilities. The 30 September was spent in rest; then, on the appointed day, amid scenes of immense popular enthusiasm and excitement, the bones of St. Remigius were carried round the town. The time had now arrived for the Pope to place them in their new resting place, but instead of

R. W. Southern, *The Making of the Middle Ages* (1953), pp. 125–7. Reprinted by permission of Yale University Press and Hutchinson Publishing Group Ltd., London.

doing so, he had them laid on the high altar of the church in which the Council was to be opened on the following day. The awful presence of the apostle of the Franks appeared from that moment to dominate the meeting. When the Council opened, the Pope—through the mouth of his chancellor, the cardinal deacon Peter, who was in charge of the business—made an unusual demand: before proceeding to the business of the meeting, each bishop and abbot was enjoined to rise and declare whether he had paid any money to obtain his office. The proposal caused considerable consternation. The Archbishop of Rheims asked for a personal interview with the Pope; the Bishops of Langres, Nevers, Coutances and Nantes remained silent. Of the abbots, only a few seem to have made the necessary declaration: the silence of the remainder expressed their embarrassment or guilt. Apparently the case against the abbots was allowed to drop; but during the remaining two days of the Council, in the intervals of the humdrum business of ecclesiastical disputes, the Papal Chancellor relentlessly pressed the bishops who had not dared to make the required declaration. The position of the Archbishop of Rheims, who was the host, was delicate: he was spared to the extent of being ordered to appear at Rome in the following year to make his explanation at the Council to be held in the middle of April. The full weight of the Chancellor's attack fell on the Bishop of Langres, a somewhat learned man, who, we notice, had just written a pamphlet against the heresy of Berengar of Tours. He asked for counsel: two archbishops undertook his defence, but one of them (the archbishop of Besançon) found some difficulty in speaking when his turn came, and the other (the archbishop of Lyons) made a partial admission of guilt on behalf of his client. The matter was adjourned, and came to a climax on the following day. The Bishop of Langres was found to have disappeared in the night. He was excommunicated; and his counsel, the archbishop of Besançon, revealed that he himself had been struck dumb on the previous day when he attempted a defence of his guilty colleague. The assembly felt the influence of the awful presence on the altar, and a wave of excitement ran through the church. The Pope rose with the name of St. Remigius on his lips, and the business was interrupted while they all sang the antiphon *Sancte Remigi*. After these excitements, the case against the other bishops was quickly disposed of. The Bishop of Nevers confessed that his parents had paid a high price for his bishopric, but declared that he was ignorant of this at the time. He laid down his pastoral staff at the Pope's feet, and the Pope restored him to office, giving him (the symbolism is significant) another staff. The Bishop of Coutances then said that his bishopric had been bought for him by his brother without his knowledge; and that when, on discovering the transaction, he had tried to flee, he had been brought back and forcibly invested with the bishopric. He was declared innocent and he lived to be one of the builders of the Anglo-Norman state and one of the most magnificent prelates of his age. The Bishop of Nantes fared worse: he confessed that his father, who had been bishop before him, had obtained for him from the count the reversion of the bishopric, and that he himself had been obliged to pay a large sum to enter into his inheritance. He was deprived of his episcopal ring and staff, and allowed only to retain the status of a priest.

The business of the Council was now rapidly brought to an end. Various excommunications were pronounced against absent or contumacious bishops, decrees were promulgated which were long remembered for their disciplinary vigour, and a number of sentences and prohibitions were directed against laymen. On the day after the dissolution of the Council, the Pope raised the body of St. Remigius from the high altar and bore it on his own shoulders to its new resting place. He had been in Rheims just a week, and during this time, he had left a mark on the affairs of the Church which would not easily be effaced. The Pope had appeared in a more commanding position than at any time in living memory; out of the handful of bishops present at the Council, a quarter had confessed to simony, and had been judged as if they had committed a crime; an archbishop had been summoned to Rome. The promptings of conscience of men like Reginald of Liège were being stiffened by the sterner voice of authority.

Leo IX died in 1054 and Henry III in 1056. The emperor left only an infant son to succeed him. During the long minority that ensued the reformers at Rome began to criticize the whole practice of lay rulers making ecclesiastical appointments, and not only abuses of that practice. The spokesman for the more radical reform party was Cardinal Humbert. His treatise against simony, quoted here, was completed in 1058.

FROM *III Books Against Simony* BY HUMBERT

WHEREAS MEN VENERABLE THROUGHOUT THE WORLD and supreme pontiffs inspired by the Holy Spirit have decreed that the election of the clergy should be confirmed by the judgment of the metropolitan, and the petition of the nobles and people by consent of the prince, now everything is done in such disorder that the first are last and the last first, so that the sacred canons are rejected and the whole Christian religion trampled underfoot. The

Brian Tierney, *The Crisis of Church and State,* © 1964, pp. 40–2. Reprinted by permission of Prentice-Hall, Inc., Englewood Cliffs, N. J.

secular power is first in choosing and confirming; the consent of nobles, people and clergy and then finally the decision of the metropolitan come afterwards whether they are willing or not. Hence, as stated above, men promoted in this fashion are not to be regarded as bishops, for the manner of their appointment is upside down; what ought to be done last is done first and by men who should not be concerned in the matter at all. For how does it pertain to lay persons to distribute ecclesiastical sacraments and episcopal or pastoral grace, that is to say crozier staffs and rings, with which all episcopal consecration is principally effected and by which it functions and is sustained?

. . . Among the other absurd deceptions with which sycophants, like bird-catchers, snare the unwary for the sake of gain, they exalt the worldly power and especially the imperial and royal power beyond all measure to the open and avid ears of princes, while minimizing the dignity of the church. And since everything under the sun has its vicissitudes, sometimes prospering, sometimes declining, they estimate the merit and power of the priestly dignity according to the outward prosperity or decline of the church's cause, sometimes preferring the secular power to the priestly like sun to moon, sometimes setting them together like two suns, sometimes—but this is very rare—by the one title of son subordinating the secular power like a son to a father.

Hence any prince who seeks to attain felicity on earth and to prepare himself for beatitude in the life to come should take care to pay no heed to such persons, for "a Prince that gladly heareth lying words hath all his servants wicked" (Proverbs 29:12). They should not treat the priests of Christ and the things that pertain to them differently than did the great Constantine and his orthodox successors in the empire. . . . Anyone then who wishes to compare the priestly and royal dignities in a useful and blameless fashion may say that, in the existing church, the priesthood is analogous to the soul and the kingship to the body, for they cleave to one another and need one another and each in turn demands services and renders them one to another. It follows from this that, just as the soul excels the body and commands it, so too the priestly dignity excels the royal or, we may say, the heavenly dignity the earthly. Thus, that all things may be in due order and not in disarray the priesthood, like a soul, may advise what is to be done. The kingship in turn, like a head, excels all the members of the body and leads them where they should go; for just as kings should follow churchmen so also layfolk should follow their kings for the good of church and country. And so the people should be taught by one power and ruled by the other, but neither power should heedlessly follow the people.

In 1059, Pope Nicholas II, with the support of the reform group at Rome, promulgated an election decree that de-

*prived the emperor and the Roman aristocracy of any
effective voice in the appointment of future popes.*

Papal Election Decree of 1059

SUPPORTED BY THE AUTHORITY of our predecessors and the other
holy fathers, we decree and order that:

When the pontiff of this universal Roman church dies the cardinal
bishops shall first confer together most diligently concerning the election;
next they shall summon the other cardinal clergy; and then the rest of the
clergy and the people shall approach to give their assent to the new election,
the greatest care being taken lest the evil of venality creep in by any way
whatsoever. The most eminent churchmen shall be the leaders in carrying
out the election of a pope, the others followers. Certainly this order of
election will be found right and lawful if anyone examines the rules and acts
of the various fathers and also calls to mind the judgment of our holy
predecessor Leo. "No reason permits," he says, "that men should be regarded
as bishops who have not been chosen by the clergy or requested by the people
or consecrated by the bishops of the province with the approval of the
metropolitan." But since the apostolic see is superior to all the churches in the
world it can have no metropolitan set over it, and so the cardinal bishops
who raise the chosen pontiff to the summit of the apostolic dignity undoubtedly act in place of a metropolitan. They shall make their choice from the
members of this church if a suitable man is to be found there, but if not they
shall take one from another church, saving the honor and reverence due to
our beloved son Henry who is now king and who, it is hoped, will in future
become emperor with God's grace, according as we have now conceded this
to him and to his successors who shall personally obtain this right from the
apostolic see.

If, however, the perversity of corrupt and evil men so prevails that
a pure, sincere and free election cannot be made in the City, the cardinal
bishops, together with the God-fearing clergy and the Catholic laity, even
though they are few, may have the right and power of electing a pontiff
for the apostolic see in any convenient place.

If, after an election has been made, a time of war or the efforts of any
malignant men shall make it impossible for the person elected to be enthroned in the apostolic see according to custom, it is clear that, nonetheless,
the person elected shall acquire authority to rule the Roman church and to

Brian Tierney, *The Crisis of Church and State,* © 1964, pp. 42–3. Reprinted by permission of
Prentice-Hall, Inc., Englewood Cliffs, N.J.

dispose of all its resources as a true pope, for we know that the blessed Gregory acted thus before his consecration.

> *In the same Roman council Nicholas II for the first time forbade lay investiture. The decree appears rather inconspicuously as number 6 in the following group of canons. There was no serious attempt to enforce the new prohibition at this time.*

Reform Decrees of 1059

1. Firstly it was enacted in the sight of God that the election of the Roman pontiff should be in the power of the cardinal bishops, so that anyone who is enthroned without their previous agreement and canonical election and without the subsequent consent of the other orders of clergy and of the people shall not be held for a pope and an apostle, but rather for an apostate.
2. That when the bishop of Rome or of any city dies no one shall dare to plunder their possessions, but these shall be preserved intact for their successors.
3. That no one shall hear the mass of a priest who, he knows for certain, keeps a concubine or has a woman living with him. . . .
4. And we firmly decree that those of the above-mentioned orders who, in obedience to our predecessors, have remained chaste shall sleep and eat together near the church to which they have been ordained as is fitting for pious clergy and that they shall hold in common whatever revenues come to them from the church, and we urge them especially that they strive to attain the apostolic way of life, which is a life in common.
5. Further, that tenths and first fruits and gifts of living or dead persons be faithfully handed over to the church by lay folk and that they be at the disposal of the bishop. Any who keep them back are cut off from the communion of holy church.
6. That no cleric or priest shall receive a church from laymen in any fashion, whether freely or at a price.
7. That no one shall receive the habit of a monk in the hope or with the promise of becoming an abbot.
8. Nor shall any priest hold two churches at the same time.
9. That no one shall be ordained or promoted to any ecclesiastical office by simoniacal heresy.

Brian Tierney, *The Crisis of Church and State*, © 1964, pp. 43–4. Reprinted by permission of Prentice-Hall, Inc., Englewood Cliffs, N. J.

3 The Program of Pope Gregory

One of the leaders of the reform movement at Rome from the days of Leo IX onward was Hildebrand, archdeacon of the Roman church. In 1073 Hildebrand ascended the papal throne as Gregory VII. Certain documents from the opening years of his reign—before he became involved in major political disputes—illustrate the attitudes he brought to the papacy. The following letter, written in December, 1074, dealt with ecclesiastical reform.

Hildebrand's Letter to Otto of Constance

Gregory . . . to Otto, bishop of Constance, greeting . . .

A REPORT has come to us with regard to Your Fraternity, which I have heard with grief and regret—a report which, if it had been made to us of the lowest member of the Christian community, would undoubtedly have called for a severe disciplinary sentence. While we were zealously striving to wipe out the heresy of Simony and to enforce the chastity of the clergy, inspired by apostolic authority and the authentic opinions of holy fathers, we enjoined upon our colleague, the venerable archbishop of Mainz, whose suffragans are numerous and widely scattered, that he should diligently impress this decree upon his whole clergy, in person and through his assistants, and should see that it was carried out without exception.

To you also, who preside over the numerous clergy and the widespread population of the church of Constance, it has, for the same reason, seemed good to us to send a special letter under our own seal. With this as your authority you can more safely and more boldly carry out our orders and expel from the Lord's holy place the heresy of Simony and the foul plague of carnal contagion. The apostolic authority of St. Paul is here of especial force, where, counting in fornicators and adulterers with other vicious persons, he gives this plain decision: "With such a one, no, not to eat."

Furthermore the whole body of the Catholic Church consists of virgins

E. Emerton, *The Correspondence of Pope Gregory VII* (1932), pp. 52–3. Reprinted by permission of Columbia University Press, New York.

or married persons or those holding themselves in restraint. Whoever, therefore, is outside those three classes is not to be counted among the sons of the
Church or within the bounds of the Christian religion. Wherefore we also, if
we should know for certain that even the lowest layman was involved in
concubinage, would cut him off completely from the body and blood of the
Lord until he should perform due penance. How then shall one be the
distributor or server of the holy sacraments who cannot in any wise be
partaker of them? Further, we are urged to this by the authority of the
blessed Pope Leo [I] who deprived subdeacons of the right to marry, a
decree to which his successors in the Holy Roman Church, especially that
famous doctor Gregory [I], gave such force of law that henceforth the
marriage bond has been absolutely forbidden to the three orders of priests,
levites and subdeacons.

But when we, in our pastoral forethought, sent word to you that these
orders were to be carried out you, not setting your mind on the things that
are above, but on the things that are upon the earth, loosed the reins of lust
within the aforesaid orders so that, as we have heard, those who had taken
concubines [mulierculis] persisted in their crime, while those who had not
yet done so had no fear of your prohibitions. Oh, what insolence! Oh, what
audacity, that a bishop should despise the decrees of the Apostolic See,
should uproot the precepts of holy fathers—nay more, by orders from his
high place and his priestly office should impose upon his subjects things
contrary and repugnant to the Christian faith.

Wherefore we command you to present yourself before us at the approaching synod in the first week of Lent to give answer according to canon
law as well for this disobedience and contempt of the Apostolic See as for all
the other offenses charged against you.

> *Gregory's first prohibition of lay investiture came in Febru-*
> *ary, 1075. The text of this decree has been lost. The text*
> *given below is a re-enactment of the same prohibition made*
> *in 1078.*

Prohibition of Lay Investiture, 1078

INASMUCH AS WE HAVE LEARNED that, contrary to the establishments of the holy fathers, the investiture with churches is, in many places,
performed by lay persons; and that from this cause many disturbances arise

---

E. F. Henderson, *Select Historical Documents of the Middle Ages* (1892), p. 365. Reprinted
by permission of G. Bell & Sons Ltd., London.

in the church by which the Christian religion is trodden under foot: we decree that no one of the clergy shall receive the investiture with a bishopric or abbey or church from the hand of an emperor or king or of any lay person, male or female. But if he shall presume to do so he shall clearly know that such investiture is bereft of apostolic authority, and that he himself shall lie under excommunication until fitting satisfaction shall have been rendered.

The propositions set out below, the so-called Dictatus Papae, *were entered in the pope's official Register in March, 1075. They have been interpreted as chapter headings for a proposed collection of canons.*

Dictatus Papae

1. That the Roman Church was founded by God alone.
2. That the Roman Pontiff alone is rightly to be called universal.
3. That he alone can depose or reinstate bishops.
4. That his legate, even if of lower grade, takes precedence, in a council, of all bishops and may render a sentence of deposition against them.
5. That the Pope may depose the absent.
6. That, among other things, we also ought not to stay in the same house with those excommunicated by him.
7. That for him alone it is lawful to enact new laws according to the needs of the time, to assemble together new congregations, to make an abbey of a canonry; and, on the other hand, to divide a rich bishopric and unite the poor ones.
8. That he alone may use the imperial insignia.
9. That the Pope is the only one whose feet are to be kissed by all princes.
10. That his name alone is to be recited in churches.
11. That his title is unique in the world.
12. That he may depose Emperors.
13. That he may transfer bishops, if necessary, from one See to another.
14. That he has power to ordain a cleric of any church he may wish.
15. That he who has been ordained by him may rule over another church, but not be under the command of others; and that such a one may not receive a higher grade from any bishop.
16. That no synod may be called a general one without his order.

S. Z. Ehler and J. B. Morrall, *Church and State Through the Centuries* (1954), pp. 43–4. Reprinted by permission of Newman Press and Burns & Oates Ltd., London.

17. That no chapter or book may be regarded as canonical without his authority.
18. That no sentence of his may be retracted by any one; and that he, alone of all, can retract it.
19. That he himself may be judged by no one.
20. That no one shall dare to condemn a person who appeals to the Apostolic See.
21. That to this See the more important cases of every church should be submitted.
22. That the Roman Church has never erred, nor ever, by the witness of Scripture, shall err to all eternity.
23. That the Roman Pontiff, if canonically ordained, is undoubtedly sanctified by the merits of St. Peter; of this St. Ennodius, Bishop of Pavia, is witness, many Holy Fathers are agreeable and it is contained in the decrees of Pope Symmachus the Saint.
24. That, by his order and with his permission, subordinate persons may bring accusations.
25. That without convening a synod he can depose and reinstate bishops.
26. That he should not be considered as Catholic who is not in conformity with the Roman Church.
27. That the Pope may absolve subjects of unjust men from their fealty.

4 Gregory VII Versus Henry IV

*At the time of Gregory's accession the young King Henry
IV of Germany was grievously embarrassed by a rebellion
in Saxony. He therefore adopted a most conciliatory tone in
his first letters to the pope.*

Henry IV's Letter to Gregory VII, 1073

TO THE MOST WATCHFUL and best beloved lord, Pope Gregory, by
divine will invested with the apostolic dignity, Henry, by the grace of God
King of the Romans, presents his due and faithful service.

Kingdom and priesthood, if they are to be duly administered in Christ,
need his continual support, and therefore, my beloved lord and father, they
must never be in dissension but must inseparably cleave to each other in
the bonds of Christ. For in this way and no other can the harmony of
Christian unity and the institution of the Church be held in the bond of
perfect love and peace.

But we, who by God's will have now for some time held the kingly
office, have not in all respects shown toward the priesthood such reverence
and honor as was due to it. Not without reason have we borne the sword of
justice entrusted to us by God; but we have not always unsheathed it as we
should have done against the guilty. Now, however, somewhat repentant
and remorseful, we turn to your fatherly indulgence, accusing ourselves and
trusting to you in the Lord that we may be found worthy of absolution by
your apostolic authority.

Alas for me, guilty and unhappy that I am! Partly through the impulses
of my deceitful youth, partly through the seductive counsels of my advisers,
I have sinned against heaven and before you with fraudulent disloyalty and
am no more worthy to be called your son. Not only have I encroached upon
the property of the Church, but I have sold churches themselves to unworthy
persons, men poisoned with the gall of Simony, men who entered not by the

E. Emerton, *The Correspondence of Pope Gregory VII* (1932), pp. 18–9. Reprinted by permission of Columbia University Press, New York.

gate but by other ways, and I have not defended the churches as I ought to have done.

But now, since I cannot regulate the churches alone, without authority from you, I most earnestly beg your advice and help in this and in all my affairs. Your directions shall be scrupulously followed in all respects. And first, in regard to the church of Milan, which has fallen into error through my fault, I beg that it may be restored according to law by your apostolic sentence and that then you will proceed to the regulation of other churches by your authority. I shall not fail you, so God will, and I humbly beseech your fatherly support in all my interests.

You will soon receive letters from me by the hands of most trustworthy messengers and from these you will, please God, learn more fully what remains to be said.

> *In June, 1075, Henry IV defeated the Saxon rebels and soon made it plain that he would never obey the recent papal decree against lay investiture. When he insisted on supporting a royal candidate for the bishopric of Milan against a papal nominee, Gregory wrote rebuking him and threatening excommunication (December, 1075). Henry thereupon summoned a synod of German bishops and, having won their support, denounced Gregory as a usurper and heretic.*

Henry IV's Letter to Gregory VII, 1076

Henry, King not by usurpation, but by the pious ordination of God, to Hildebrand, now not Pope, but false monk:

YOU HAVE DESERVED such a salutation as this because of the confusion you have wrought; for you left untouched no order of the Church which you could make a sharer of confusion instead of honor, of malediction instead of benediction.

For to discuss a few outstanding points among many: Not only have you dared to touch the rectors of the holy Church—the archbishops, the bishops, and the priests, anointed of the Lord as they are—but you have trodden them under foot like slaves who know not what their lord may do. In crushing them you have gained for yourself acclaim from the mouth of

T. E. Mommsen and K. F. Morrison, *Imperial Lives and Letters of the Eleventh Century* (1962), pp. 150–1. Reprinted by permission of Columbia University Press, New York.

the rabble. You have judged that all these know nothing, while you alone know everything. In any case, you have sedulously used this knowledge not for edification, but for destruction, so greatly that we may believe Saint Gregory, whose name you have arrogated to yourself, rightly made this prophesy of you when he said: "From the abundance of his subjects, the mind of the prelate is often exalted, and he thinks that he has more knowledge than anyone else, since he sees that he has more power than anyone else."

And we, indeed, bore with all these abuses, since we were eager to preserve the honor of the Apostolic See. But you construed our humility as fear, and so you were emboldened to rise up even against the royal power itself, granted to us by God. You dared to threaten to take the kingship away from us—as though we had received the kingship from you, as though kingship and empire were in your hand and not in the hand of God.

Our Lord, Jesus Christ, has called us to kingship, but has not called you to the priesthood. For you have risen by these steps: namely, by cunning, which the monastic profession abhors, to money; by money to favor; by favor to the sword. By the sword you have come to the throne of peace, and from the throne of peace you have destroyed the peace. You have armed subjects against their prelates; you who have not been called by God have taught that our bishops who have been called by God are to be spurned; you have usurped for laymen the bishops' ministry over priests, with the result that these laymen depose and condemn the very men whom the laymen themselves received as teachers from the hand of God, through the imposition of the hands of bishops.

You have also touched me, one who, though unworthy, has been anointed to kingship among the anointed. This wrong you have done to me, although as the tradition of the holy Fathers has taught, I am to be judged by God alone and am not to be deposed for any crime unless—may it never happen—I should deviate from the Faith. For the prudence of the holy bishops entrusted the judgment and the deposition even of Julian the Apostate not to themselves, but to God alone. The true pope Saint Peter also exclaims, "Fear God, honor the king." You, however, since you do not fear God, dishonor me, ordained of Him.

Wherefore, when Saint Paul gave no quarter to an angel from heaven if the angel should preach heterodoxy, he did not except you who are now teaching heterodoxy throughout the earth. For he says, "If anyone, either I or an angel from heaven, preach any other gospel unto you than that which we have preached unto you, let him be accursed." Descend, therefore, condemned by this anathema and by the common judgment of all our bishops and of ourself. Relinquish the Apostolic See which you have arrogated. Let another mount the throne of Saint Peter, another who will not cloak violence with religion but who will teach the pure doctrine of Saint Peter.

I, Henry, King by the grace of God, together with all our bishops, say to you: Descend! Descend!

Gregory replied by declaring Henry excommunicated and deposed from his kingship.

Excommunication of Henry IV, 1076

O BLESSED PETER, prince of the Apostles, mercifully incline thine ear, we [*sic*] pray, and hear me, thy servant, whom thou hast cherished from infancy and hast delivered until now from the hand of the wicked who have hated and still hate me for my loyalty to thee. Thou art my witness, as are also my Lady, the Mother of God, and the blessed Paul, thy brother among all the saints, that thy Holy Roman Church forced me against my will to be its ruler. I had no thought of ascending thy throne as a robber, nay, rather would I have chosen to end my life as a pilgrim than to seize upon thy place for earthly glory and by devices of this world. Therefore, by thy favor, not by any works of mine, I believe that it is and has been thy will, that the Christian people especially committed to thee should render obedience to me, thy especially constituted representative. To me is given by thy grace the power of binding and loosing in Heaven and upon earth.

Wherefore, relying upon this commission, and for the honor and defense of thy Church, in the name of Almighty God, Father, Son and Holy Spirit, through thy power and authority, I deprive King Henry, son of the emperor Henry, who has rebelled against thy Church with unheard-of audacity, of the government over the whole kingdom of Germany and Italy, and I release all Christian men from the allegiance which they have sworn or may swear to him, and I forbid anyone to serve him as king. For it is fitting that he who seeks to diminish the glory of thy Church should lose the glory which he seems to have.

And, since he has refused to obey as a Christian should or to return to the God whom he has abandoned by taking part with excommunicated persons, has spurned my warnings which I gave him for his soul's welfare, as thou knowest, and has separated himself from thy Church and tried to rend it asunder, I bind him in the bonds of anathema in thy stead and I bind him thus as commissioned by thee, that the nations may know and be convinced that thou art Peter and that upon thy rock the son of the living God has built his Church and the gates of hell shall not prevail against it.

The pope's condemnation of Henry touched off another rebellion in Germany. Henry was defeated and undertook

E. Emerton, *The Correspondence of Pope Gregory VII* (1932), pp. 90–1. Reprinted by permission of Columbia University Press, New York.

to appear before a Diet of German princes at Augsburg in February, 1077. The pope was to preside over the Diet and the future of the German kingship was to be decided there. To avoid the humiliation of a public trial before his subjects, Henry journeyed over the Alps in December, 1076, met the pope at Canossa, and pleaded as a penitent sinner to be released from the papal sentence of excommunication. Gregory subsequently wrote the following account of the episode to the German princes.

Gregory VII's Letter to the German Princes

WHEREAS, FOR LOVE OF JUSTICE you have made common cause with us and taken the same risks in the warfare of Christian service, we have taken special care to send you this accurate account of the king's penitential humiliation, his absolution and the course of the whole affair from his entrance into Italy to the present time.

According to the arrangement made with the legates sent to us by you we came to Lombardy about twenty days before the date at which some of your leaders were to meet us at the pass and waited for their arrival to enable us to cross over into that region. But when the time had elapsed and we were told that on account of the troublous times—as indeed we well believe—no escort could be sent to us, having no other way of coming to you we were in no little anxiety as to what was our best course to take.

Meanwhile we received certain information that the king was on the way to us. Before he entered Italy he sent us word that he would make satisfaction to God and St. Peter and offered to amend his way of life and to continue obedient to us, provided only that he should obtain from us absolution and the apostolic blessing. For a long time we delayed our reply and held long consultations, reproaching him bitterly through messengers back and forth for his outrageous conduct, until finally, of his own accord and without any show of hostility or defiance, he came with a few followers to the fortress of Canossa where we were staying. There, on three successive days, standing before the castle gate, laying aside all royal insignia, barefooted and in coarse attire, he ceased not with many tears to beseech the apostolic help and comfort until all who were present or who had heard the story were so moved by pity and compassion that they pleaded his cause with

E. Emerton, *The Correspondence of Pope Gregory VII* (1932), pp. 111–2. Reprinted by permission of Columbia University Press, New York.

prayers and tears. All marveled at our unwonted severity, and some even cried out that we were showing, not the seriousness of apostolic authority, but rather the cruelty of a savage tyrant.

At last, overcome by his persistent show of penitence and the urgency of all present, we released him from the bonds of anathema and received him into the grace of Holy Mother Church, accepting from him the guarantees described below, confirmed by the signatures of the abbot of Cluny, of our daughters, the Countess Matilda and the Countess Adelaide, and other princes, bishops and laymen who seemed to be of service to us.

And now that these matters have been arranged, we desire to come over into your country at the first opportunity, that with God's help we may more fully establish all matters pertaining to the peace of the Church and the good order of the land. For we wish you clearly to understand that, as you may see in the written guarantees, the whole negotiation is held in suspense, so that our coming and your unanimous consent are in the highest degree necessary. Strive, therefore, all of you, as you love justice, to hold in good faith the obligations into which you have entered. Remember that we have not bound ourselves to the king in any way except by frank statement—as our custom is —that he may expect our aid for his safety and his honor, whether through justice or through mercy, and without peril to his soul or to our own.

> *Once Henry had made his peace with the pope he found new support in Germany. Many of the princes thought that Gregory had betrayed them by dealing with Henry individually before the proposed Diet had met. The dissident princes elected an anti-king, Rudolf, and civil war broke out once more. After hesitating for three years Gregory agreed to support Rudolf and condemned Henry for a second time in March, 1080.*

Excommunication of Henry IV, 1080

O BLESSED PETER, chief of the Apostles, and thou, Paul, teacher of the Gentiles, deign, I pray, to incline your ears to me and mercifully to hear my prayer. Ye who are disciples and lovers of the truth, aid me to tell the truth to you, freed from all falsehood so hateful to you, that my brethren may be more united with me and may know and understand that through faith in

---

E. Emerton, *The Correspondence of Pope Gregory VII* (1932), pp. 149–52. Reprinted by permission of Columbia University Press, New York.

you, next to God and his mother Mary, ever virgin, I resist the wicked and give aid to those who are loyal to you. For you know that I entered holy orders not of my own pleasure, and that I accompanied the lord Pope Gregory [VI] unwillingly beyond the mountains, but still more unwillingly returned with my master Pope Leo [IX] to your special church, where I have served you as best I could; and then most unwillingly and unworthy as I was, to my great grief and with groans and lamentations I was set upon your throne.

I say this because it is not I that have chosen you, but you that have chosen me and laid upon me the heavy burden of your Church. And because you have commanded me to go up into a high mountain and denounce their crimes to the people of God and their sins to the sons of the Church, those limbs of the Devil have begun to rise up against me and have dared to lay hands upon me even unto blood.

The kings of the earth, and the princes, both secular and clerical, have risen up, courtiers and commons have taken counsel together against the Lord, and against you, his anointed, saying, "Let us burst their chains and throw off their yoke," and they have striven utterly to overwhelm me with death or banishment.

Among these especially Henry, whom they call "king," son of the emperor Henry, has raised his heel against your Church in conspiracy with many bishops, as well ultramontanes as Italians, striving to bring it under his control by overturning me. Your authority withstood his insolence and your power defeated it. In confusion and humiliation he came to me in Lombardy begging for release from his excommunication. And when I had witnessed his humiliation and after he had given many promises to reform his way of life, I restored him to communion only, but did not reinstate him in the royal power from which I had deposed him in a Roman synod. Nor did I order that the allegiance of all who had taken oath to him or should do so in future, from which I had released them all at that same synod, should be renewed. I held this subject in reserve in order that I might do justice as between him and the ultramontane bishops and princes, who in obedience to your Church had stood out against him, and that I might establish peace amongst them, as Henry himself had promised me to do on his oath and by the word of two bishops.

The above-mentioned ultramontane bishops and princes, hearing that he had not kept faith with me, and, as it were, in despair about him, chose Duke Rudolf for their king, without my approval as you will bear witness. Then King Rudolf immediately sent an envoy to me declaring that he had assumed the government of the kingdom under compulsion, but nevertheless was prepared to obey me in every way. And to make this the more acceptable, from that time on he repeatedly sent me the same declaration, adding that he would confirm his promise by sending as hostages his own son and the son of his liegeman Bertaldus [of Zähringen].

Meanwhile Henry was beginning to beg for my help against Rudolf. I replied that I would gladly take action after I had heard both sides in order that I might learn which was the more in accord with what was right. But he, thinking himself strong enough to overcome his opponent, paid no attention to my reply. Later, however, as he saw that he could not do as he had hoped, the two bishops of Verdun and Osnabrück came to Rome on the part of his followers and at a synod requested me in behalf of Henry to do what was right by him. The envoys of Rudolf made the same request. Finally, by divine inspiration as I believe, I decreed at the same synod that a conference should be held beyond the mountains that peace might be restored there, or else that he should be recognized as king whose cause seemed to be the more just. For I, as you, my fathers and my lords, will bear me witness, have never to the present day taken either side except as justice required. And because I reckoned that the wrong side would not be willing to have a conference in which justice was to prevail, I excommunicated and placed under the bonds of anathema all persons, whether of a king or a duke or a bishop or of any vassal, who should try by any device to prevent the holding of a conference. But the aforesaid Henry together with his supporters, not fearing the perils of disobedience—which is the crime of idolatry— incurred excommunication by preventing a conference and bound himself in the bonds of anathema and caused a great multitude of Christians to be delivered to death, churches to be scattered abroad and almost the whole kingdom of the Germans to be desolated.

Wherefore, trusting in the justice and mercy of God and of his most worshipful mother Mary, ever virgin, and relying upon your authority, I place the aforesaid Henry, whom they call "king," and all his supporters under excommunication and bind them with the chains of anathema. And again forbidding him in the name of Almighty God and of yourselves to govern in Germany and Italy, I take from him all royal power and state. I forbid all Christians to obey him as king, and I release all who have made or shall make oath to him as king from the obligation of their oath. May Henry and his supporters never, so long as they may live, be able to win victory in any encounter of arms. But that Rudolf, whom the Germans have chosen for their king in loyalty to you, may rule and protect the kingdom of the Germans, I grant and allow in your name. And relying upon your assurance, I grant also to all his faithful adherents absolution of all their sins and your blessing in this life and the life to come. For as Henry is justly cast down from the royal dignity for his insolence, his disobedience and his deceit, so Rudolf, for his humility, his obedience and his truthfulness is granted the power and the dignity of kingship.

And now, most holy fathers and princes, I pray you to take such action that the whole world may know and understand that if you are able to bind and loose in Heaven, you are able also on earth to grant and to take away from everyone according to his deserts empires, kingdoms, principalities, dukedoms, marquisates, earldoms and the property of all men. You have often taken patriarchates, primacies, archbishoprics and bishoprics away from wicked and unworthy men and have granted them to pious holders. And if you can give judgment in spiritual things, what may we not believe as to your power over secular things? Or, if you can judge the angels who guide all haughty princes, what can you [not] do to their servants? Now let kings and all princes of the earth learn how great is your power, and let them fear to neglect the commands of your Church. And against the aforesaid Henry send forth your judgment so swiftly that all men may know that he falls and is overwhelmed, not by chance but by your power—and would that it were to repentance, that his soul be saved in the day of the Lord!

5 The Aim of Gregory's Pontificate

We are fortunate in having a detailed explanation of Gregory's ideas and intentions written by the pope himself in a letter to Bishop Hermann of Metz (March, 1081).

FROM *Gregory VII's Letter to Hermann of Metz*

YOU ASK US TO FORTIFY YOU against the madness of those who babble with accursed tongues about the authority of the Holy Apostolic See not being able to excommunicate King Henry as one who despises the law of Christ, a destroyer of churches and of the empire, a promoter and partner of heresies, nor to release anyone from his oath of fidelity to him; but it has not seemed necessary to reply to this request, seeing that so many and such convincing proofs are to be found in Holy Scripture. Nor do we believe that those who abuse and contradict the truth to their utter damnation do this as much from ignorance as from wretched and desperate folly. And no wonder! It is ever the way of the wicked to protect their own iniquities by calling upon others like themselves; for they think it of no account to incur the penalty of falsehood.

To cite but a few out of the multitude of proofs: Who does not remember the words of our Lord and Savior Jesus Christ: "Thou art Peter and on this rock I will build my Church, and the gates of hell shall not prevail against it. And I will give thee the keys of the kingdom of heaven and whatsoever thou shalt bind on earth shall be bound in heaven and whatsoever thou shalt loose on earth shall be loosed in heaven." Are kings excepted here? Or are they not of the sheep which the Son of God committed to St. Peter? Who, I ask, thinks himself excluded from this universal grant of the power of binding and loosing to St. Peter unless, perchance, that unhappy man who, being unwilling to bear the yoke of the Lord, subjects

E. Emerton, *The Correspondence of Pope Gregory VII* (1932), pp. 166–75. Reprinted by permission of Columbia University Press, New York.

himself to the burden of the Devil and refuses to be numbered in the flock of Christ? His wretched liberty shall profit him nothing; for if he shakes off from his proud neck the power divinely granted to Peter, so much the heavier shall it be for him in the day of judgment.

*   *   *

To whom, then, the power of opening and closing Heaven is given, shall he not be able to judge the earth? God forbid! Do you remember what the most blessed Apostle Paul says: "Know ye not that we shall judge angels? How much more things that pertain to this life?"

So Pope Gregory declared that kings who dared to disobey the orders of the Apostolic See should forfeit their office. He wrote to a certain senator and abbot in these words:

> If any king, priest, judge or secular person shall disregard this decree of ours and act contrary to it, he shall be deprived of his power and his office and shall learn that he stands condemned at the bar of God for the wrong that he has done. And unless he shall restore what he has wrongfully taken and shall have done fitting penance for his unlawful acts he shall be excluded from the sacred body and blood of our Lord and Savior Jesus Christ and at the last judgment shall receive condign punishment.

Now then, if the blessed Gregory, most gentle of doctors, decreed that kings who should disobey his orders about a hospital for strangers should be not only deposed but excommunicated and condemned in the last judgment, how can anyone blame us for deposing and excommunicating Henry, who not only disregards apostolic judgments, but so far as in him lies tramples upon his mother the Church, basely plunders the whole kingdom and destroys its churches—unless indeed it were one who is a man of his own kind?

As we know also through the teaching of St. Peter in his letter touching the ordination of Clement, where he says: "If any one were friend to those with whom he [Clement] is not on speaking terms, that man is among those who would like to destroy the Church of God and, while he seems to be with us in the body, he is against us in mind and heart, and he is a far worse enemy than those who are without and are openly hostile. For he, under the forms of friendship, acts as an enemy and scatters and lays waste the Church." Consider then, my best beloved, if he passes so severe a judgment upon him who associates himself with those whom the pope opposes on account of their actions, with what severity he condemns the man himself to whom the pope is thus opposed.

But now, to return to our point: Is not a sovereignty invented by men of this world who were ignorant of God subject to that which the providence of

Almighty God established for his own glory and graciously bestowed upon the world? The Son of God we believe to be God and man, sitting at the right hand of the Father as High Priest, head of all priests and ever making intercession for us. He despised the kingdom of this world wherein the sons of this world puff themselves up and offered himself as a sacrifice upon the cross.

Who does not know that kings and princes derive their origin from men ignorant of God who raised themselves above their fellows by pride, plunder, treachery, murder—in short, by every kind of crime—at the instigation of the Devil, the prince of this world, men blind with greed and intolerable in their audacity? If, then, they strive to bend the priests of God to their will, to whom may they more properly be compared than to him who is chief over all the sons of pride? For he, tempting our High Priest, head of all priests, son of the Most High, offering him all the kingdoms of this world, said: "All these will I give thee if thou wilt fall down and worship me."

Does anyone doubt that the priests of Christ are to be considered as fathers and masters of kings and princes and of all believers? Would it not be regarded as pitiable madness if a son should try to rule his father or a pupil his master and to bind with unjust obligations the one through whom he expects to be bound or loosed, not only on earth but also in heaven? Evidently recognizing this the emperor Constantine the Great, lord over all kings and princes throughout almost the entire earth, as St. Gregory relates in his letter to the emperor Mauritius, at the holy synod of Nicaea took his place below all the bishops and did not venture to pass any judgment upon them but, even addressing them as gods, felt that they ought not to be subject to his judgment but that he ought to be bound by their decisions.

Pope Gelasius, urging upon the emperor Anastasius not to feel himself wronged by the truth that was called to his attention said: "There are two powers, O august Emperor, by which the world is governed, the sacred authority of the priesthood and the power of kings. Of these the priestly is by so much the greater as they will have to answer for kings themselves in the day of divine judgment;" and a little further: "Know that you are subject to their judgment, not that they are to be subjected to your will."

In reliance upon such declarations and such authorities, many prelates have excommunicated kings or emperors. If you ask for illustrations: Pope Innocent excommunicated the emperor Arcadius because he consented to the expulsion of St. John Chrysostom from his office. Another Roman pontiff deposed a king of the Franks, not so much on account of his evil deeds as because he was not equal to so great an office, and set in his place Pippin, father of the emperor Charles the Great, releasing all the Franks from the oath of fealty which they had sworn to him. And this is often done by Holy Church when it absolves fighting men from their oaths to bishops who have been deposed by apostolic authority. So St. Ambrose, a holy man but not bishop of the whole Church, excommunicated the emperor Theodosius the Great for a fault which did not seem to other prelates so very grave and excluded him from the Church. He also shows in his writings that the priestly office is as much superior to royal power as gold is more precious than lead. He says: "The honor and dignity of bishops admit of no comparison. If you liken them to the splendor of kings and the diadem of princes, these are as lead compared to the glitter of gold. You see the necks of kings and princes bowed to the knees of priests, and by the kissing of hands they believed that they share the benefit of their prayers." And again: "Know that we have said all this in order to show that there is nothing in this world more excellent than a priest or more lofty than a bishop."

Your Fraternity should remember also that greater power is granted to an exorcist when he is made a spiritual emperor for the casting out of devils, than can be conferred upon any layman for the purpose of earthly dominion. All kings and princes of this earth who live not piously and in their deeds show not a becoming fear of God are ruled by demons and are sunk in miserable slavery. Such men desire to rule, not guided by the love of God, as priests are, for the glory of God and the profit of human souls, but to display their intolerable pride and to satisfy the lusts of their mind. Of these St. Augustine says in the first book of his Christian doctrine: "He who tries to rule over men—who are by nature equal to him—acts with intolerable pride." Now if exorcists have power over demons, as we have said, how much more over those who are subject to demons and are limbs of demons! And if exorcists are superior to these, how much more are priests superior to them!

Furthermore, every Christian king when he approaches his end asks the aid of a priest as a miserable suppliant that he may escape the prison of hell, may pass from darkness into light and may appear at the judgment seat of God freed from the bonds of sin. But who, layman or priest, in his last moments has ever asked the help of any earthly king for the safety of his soul? And what king or emperor has power through his office to snatch any Christian from the might of the Devil by the sacred rite of baptism, to confirm him among the sons of God and to fortify him by the holy chrism? Or—and this is the greatest thing in the Christian religion—who among them is able by his own word to create the body and blood of the Lord? or to whom among them is given the power to bind and loose in Heaven and upon earth? From this it is apparent how greatly superior in power is the priestly dignity.

Or who of them is able to ordain any clergyman in the Holy Church—much less to depose him for any fault? For bishops, while they may ordain other bishops, may in no wise depose them except by authority of the Apostolic See. How, then, can even the most slightly informed person doubt that priests are higher than kings? But if kings are to be judged by priests for their sins, by whom can they more properly be judged than by the Roman pontiff?

In short, all good Christians, whosoever they may be, are more properly to be called kings than are evil princes; for the former, seeking the glory of

God, rule themselves rigorously; but the latter, seeking their own rather than the things that are of God, being enemies to themselves, oppress others tyrannically. The former are the body of the true Christ; the latter, the body of the Devil. The former rule themselves that they may reign forever with the supreme ruler. The power of the latter brings it to pass that they perish in eternal damnation with the prince of darkness who is king over all the sons of pride.

*   *   *

It seems therefore especially useful for emperors and kings, while their hearts are lifted up in the strife for glory, to learn how to humble themselves and to know fear rather than joy. Let them therefore consider carefully how dangerous, even awesome is the office of emperor or king, how very few find salvation therein, and how those who are saved through God's mercy have become far less famous in the Church by divine judgment than many humble persons. From the beginning of the world to the present day we do not find in all authentic records [seven] emperors or kings whose lives were as distinguished for virtue and piety as were those of a countless multitude of men who despised the world—although we believe that many of them were saved by the mercy of God. Not to speak of Apostles and Martyrs, who among emperors and kings was famed for his miracles as were St. Martin, St. Antony and St. Benedict? What emperor or king ever raised the dead, cleansed lepers or opened the eyes of the blind? True, Holy Church praises and honors the emperor Constantine, of pious memory, Theodosius and Honorius, Charles and Louis, as lovers of justice, champions of the Christian faith and protectors of churches, but she does not claim that they were illustrious for the splendor of their wonderful works. Or to how many names of kings or emperors has Holy Church ordered churches or altars to be dedicated or masses to be celebrated?

Let kings and princes fear lest the higher they are raised above their fellows in this life, the deeper they may be plunged in everlasting fire. Wherefore it is written: "The mighty shall suffer mighty torments." They shall render unto God an account for all men subject to their rule. But if it is no small labor for the pious individual to guard his own soul, what a task is laid upon princes in the care of so many thousands of souls! And if Holy Church imposes a heavy penalty upon him who takes a single human life, what shall be done to those who send many thousands to death for the glory of this world? These, although they say with their lips, *mea culpa,* for the slaughter of many, yet in their hearts they rejoice at the increase of their glory and neither repent of what they have done nor regret that they have sent their brothers into the world below. So that, since they do not repent with all their hearts and will not restore what they have gained by human bloodshed, their penitence before God remains without the fruits of a true repentance.

Wherefore they ought greatly to fear, and they should frequently be reminded that, as we have said, since the beginning of the world and throughout the kingdoms of the earth very few kings of saintly life can be found out of an innumerable multitude, whereas in one single chair of successive bishops—the Roman—from the time of the blessed Apostle Peter nearly a hundred are counted among the holiest of men. How can this be, except because the kings and princes of the earth, seduced by empty glory, prefer their own interests to the things of the Spirit, whereas pious pontiffs, despising vainglory, set the things of God above the things of the flesh. The former readily punish offenses against themselves but are not troubled by offenses against God; the latter quickly forgive those who sin against them but do not easily pardon offenders against God. The former, far too much given to worldly affairs, think little of spiritual things; the latter, dwelling eagerly upon heavenly subjects, despise the things of this world.

All Christians, therefore, who desire to reign with Christ are to be warned not to reign through ambition for wordly power. They are to keep in mind the admonition of that most holy pope Gregory in his book on the pastoral office: "Of all these things what is to be followed, what held fast, except that the man strong in virtue shall come to his office under compulsion? Let him who is without virtue not come to it even though he be urged thereto." If, then, men who fear God come under compulsion with fear and trembling to the Apostolic See where those who are properly ordained become stronger through the merits of the blessed Apostle Peter, with what awe and hesitation should men ascend the throne of a king where even good and humble men like Saul and David become worse! What we have said above is thus stated in the decrees of the blessed pope Symmachus—though we have learned it by experience: "He, that is St. Peter, transmitted to his successors an unfailing endowment of merit together with an inheritance of innocence;" and again: "For who can doubt that he is holy who is raised to the height of such an office, in which if he is lacking in virtue acquired by his own merits, that which is handed down from his predecessor is sufficient. For either he [Peter] raises men of distinction to bear this burden or he glorifies them after they are raised up."

Wherefore let those whom Holy Church, of its own will and with deliberate judgment, not for fleeting glory but for the welfare of multitudes, has called to royal or imperial rule—let them be obedient and ever mindful of the blessed Gregory's declaration in that same pastoral treatise: "When a man disdains to be the equal of his fellow men, he becomes like an apostate angel. Thus Saul, after his period of humility, swollen with pride, ran into excess of power. He was raised in humility, but rejected in his pride, as God bore witness, saying: 'Though thou wast little in thine own sight, wast thou not made the head of the tribes of Israel?'" and again: "I marvel how, when he was little to himself he was great before God, but when he seemed great to himself he was little before God." Let them watch and remember what God says in the Gospel: "I seek not my own glory," and, "He who would be first among you, let him be the servant of all." Let them ever place the honor of God above their own; let them embrace justice and maintain it by preserving to everyone his right; let them not enter into the counsels of the ungodly, but cling to those of religion with all their hearts. Let them not seek to make Holy Church their maid-servant or their subject, but recognizing priests, the eyes of God, as their masters and fathers, strive to do them becoming honor.

If we are commanded to honor our fathers and mothers in the flesh, how much more our spiritual parents! If he that curseth his father or his mother shall be put to death, what does he deserve who curses his spiritual father or mother? Let not princes, led astray by carnal affection, set their own sons over that flock for whom Christ shed his blood if a better and more suitable man can be found. By thus loving their own son more than God they bring the greatest evils upon the Church. For it is evident that he who fails to provide to the best of his ability so great and necessary an advantage for our holy mother, the Church, does not love God and his neighbor as befits a Christian man. If this one virtue of charity be wanting, then whatever of good the man may do will lack all saving grace.

But if they do these things in humility, keeping their love for God and their neighbor as they ought, they may count upon the mercy of him who said: "Learn of me, for I am meek and lowly of heart." If they humbly imitate him, they shall pass from their servile and transient reign into the kingdom of eternal liberty.

> *J. A. Wylie maintained that all Gregory's policies aimed at establishing a theocratic system of papal world monarchy, and he saw a political motivation even in the campaign for clerical celibacy. His book was awarded the first prize for an essay on popery in a contest conducted by the Evangelical Alliance in 1852.*

FROM *The Papacy* BY J. A. WYLIE

WE BEHOLD ON THE THRONE of the empire a child, Henry IV; and in the chair of St. Peter, the astute Hildebrand. We find the empire torn by insurrections and tumults, whilst the Papacy is guided by the clear and bold genius of Gregory VII. Savoy had the honour to give birth to this man. He

J. A. Wylie, *The Papacy* (1852), pp. 72–4.

was the son of a carpenter, and comprehended from the first the true destiny of the Papacy, and the height to which its essential principles, vigorously maintained and fearlessly carried out, would exalt the popedom. To emancipate the pontificate from the authority of the empire, and to establish a visible theocracy with the vicar of Christ at its head, became the one grand object of his life. He brought to the execution of his task a profound genius, a firm will, a fearless courage, and a pliant policy,—a quality in which the popes have seldom been deficient. From the moment that he chid Leo IX for accepting the tiara from the hands of the secular power, his spirit had governed Rome. At length, in A.D. 1073, he ascended the pontifical throne in person. "No sooner was this man made Pope," says Du Pin, "but he formed a design of becoming lord, spiritual and temporal, over the whole earth; the supreme judge and determiner of all affairs, both ecclesiastical and civil; the distributer of all manner of graces, of what kind soever; the disposer not only of archbishopricks, bishopricks, and other ecclesiastical benefices, but also of kingdoms, states, and the revenues of particular persons. To bring about this resolution, he made use of the ecclesiastical authority and the spiritual sword." The times were favourable in no ordinary degree. The empire of Germany was enfeebled by the disaffection of the barons; France was ruled by an infant sovereign, without capacity or inclination for affairs of state; England had just been conquered by the Normans; Spain was distracted by the Moors; and Italy was parcelled out amongst a multitude of petty princes. Everywhere faction was rife throughout Europe, and a strong government existed nowhere. The time invited him, and straightway Gregory set about his high attempt. His first care was to assemble a Council, in which he pronounced the marriage of priests unlawful. He next sent his legates throughout the various countries of Europe, to compel bishops and all ecclesiastics to put away their wives. Having thus dissevered the ties which connected the clergy with the world, and given them but one object for which to live, namely, the exaltation of the hierarchy, Gregory rekindled, with all the ardour and vehemence characteristic of the man, the war between the throne and the mitre. The object at which Gregory VII aimed was twofold: 1. To render the election to the pontifical chair independent of the emperors; and, 2. To resume the empire as a fief of the Church, and to establish his dominion over the kings and kingdoms of the earth. His first step towards the accomplishment of these vast designs was, as we have shown, to enact clerical celibacy. His second was to forbid all ecclesiastics to receive investiture at the hands of the secular power. In this decree he laid the foundation of the complete emancipation of the Church from the State; but half a century of wars and bloodshed was required to conduct the first enterprise, that of the investitures, to a successful issue; while a hundred and fifty years more of similar convulsions had to be gone through before the second, that of universal domination, was attained.

Philip Hughes presented the pope as a saintly reformer.

FROM *A History of the Church* BY PHILIP HUGHES

THE PRINCIPLE THAT GIVES UNITY to the whole of Gregory VII's varied activity is his ever present realisation that he is responsible to God for all the souls entrusted to him. Political activity may be a necessary means, but the end in view is always wholly supernatural. The pope must answer to God for the souls of kings no less than for those of priests and peasants; for kings too must keep God's law, or find themselves in hell for all eternity. And to William the Conqueror Gregory VII wrote this explicitly, "If then, on that day of terrible judgement it is I who must represent you before the just judge whom no lies deceive and who is the creator of all creatures, your wisdom will itself understand how I must most attentively watch over your salvation, and how you, in turn, because of your salvation and that you may come to the land of the living, must and ought to obey me without delay." There is nothing new in this: it is but a particular application of the general principle that the shepherd is charged to guide the whole flock which Gelasius I, for example, had stated no less explicitly to the emperor Anastasius six hundred years before St. Gregory VII. Nor, despite the ingenuity of later, anti-papal, historians—was this meant as a thinly-disguised means of bringing about a political system in which the pope should rule all the affairs of the Christian world. Nowhere in the pope's own declarations is there any hint that he hoped for such a position, nor in the multitudinous writings of his supporters, whether publicists or canonists, that argue for the rights he did claim; nor is there any sign that the emperor believed this to be Gregory's aim, or any of the emperor's men. To none of the pope's contemporaries, to none of those who were at the heart of the struggle, did it ever occur, even to allege, that what Gregory VII was aiming at was to be the emperor of a Christian world state.

Henry IV, too, had his problems, and chief among them that of recovering what the crown had lost during his own long minority. Appointments to sees, and the accompanying simony, were at the moment important political expedients. This return to the evil ways of his grandfather had already, in the last years of Alexander II, led to difficulties between Henry and the Holy See; and the candidate to whom the king had sold the see of Constance was, thanks to the pope, denied consecration. Despite the king, a council, presided over by papal legates, was held at Mainz (1071) and the bishop-elect of

From *A History of the Church*, II (1935), 224–8, by Philip Hughes, published in three volumes by Sheed & Ward Inc., New York, and Sheed & Ward Ltd., London.

Constance was compelled to resign. In another dispute, which divided the bishops and abbots of Thuringia—where the allocation of tithes was in question—the king had intervened to prevent an appeal to Rome. It was already more than evident that, in Henry IV, the reform movement faced the most serious opponent who had so far arisen. In Germany itself his determination to dominate the great feudatories could only end in war, and in 1073 a general revolt broke out which came near to sweeping him away altogether. In his despair Henry appealed to the pope, acknowledging his simony and his many usurpations in the matter of ecclesiastical jurisdiction, asking for aid and humbly promising amendment of his life. Gregory VII had already planned his policy with regard to the German king. He was not by nature an intransigent. He would do his best, by kindly warnings, to turn Henry from an opponent into an ally of the reform. Only when he proved obdurate did the pope return to the drastic remedies of Cardinal Humbert and Nicholas II in order to secure the freedom of religion. Already, in September, 1073, he had forbidden the new Bishop of Lucca to receive investiture from the king, and now came the king's submission and appeal.

The pope's reply was to despatch two legates, to reconcile Henry and his subjects and to settle the details of the dispute between king and pope still hanging over from the last pontificate. By May, 1074, the war seemed practically over, and the pope and king were reconciled. The pope resumed his activities on behalf of reform in the great German sees. It was, very largely, to these great bishops, of Cologne, Mainz, Augsburg, and Hamburg, that the ruling of Germany during the minority had fallen. The accession of Gregory VII found them as little subordinate to the pope as they were to the king. It was only with the greatest difficulty that the pope's legates were able to bring together the council he desired, and strong protests came from the German clergy against the new discipline and especially against the newly enforced clerical celibacy. There was not too much hope that, in any conflict between Rome and Henry IV, the churches of Germany would make common cause with the pope.

That conflict was not long in coming. Gregory VII had begun by renewing the decrees against simony and clerical ill-living (Roman Council of March, 1074). By the Lent of 1075 it was evident to him that almost nowhere had the legates despatched to enforce these decrees met with any general support from the bishops. The pope now determined to strike at the two chief causes of this failure on the part of the bishops. The abuse that appointments to sees had everywhere fallen into the hands of the lay lord, Gregory met by a solemn renewal of Nicholas II's decree of 1059, which had never been enforced. No prelate must, henceforth, receive an abbey or a see from any lay lord; no lay lord must, for the future, make such grants. And in the *Dictatus Papae* the pope reminded disobedient bishops that his authority was of divine institution, and that it extended to a power of deposing bishops and, if need be, of the emperor too.

This decree of February, 1075, against lay investiture was not intended, the thing seems certain, as an aggressive move against the princes—still less was it an act which especially envisaged Henry IV; the pope was in no hurry to promulgate the decree to princes generally, and his policy in applying the law varied greatly. In the English kingdom of William the Conqueror, for example, where simony had no place in the royal appointments, and where king and bishops were at one with the pope in the work of reform, Gregory VII never raised the question at all. The new law was, indeed, "a preventive weapon designed to assist the struggle against simony." In a country where simony on the part of the king was systematic, and the king hardened in his resolve to maintain the system, conflict—speedy conflict—was inevitable; and such was the case with Henry IV. And, as the decree was a challenge to Henry IV so too were the blunt declarations of the *Dictatus Papae* a challenge to the feudalised ecclesiastical princes who occupied the sees of Germany. In these twenty-seven terse propositions king and bishops were warned that the pope's laws against simony, clerical ill-living, and the usurpation of rights to appoint were no dead letter, and that none, whatever his rank, would escape the sanctions enacted against those who broke these laws.

> *Gerd Tellenbach also saw Gregory VII as a great pope dedicated to reform, but to a kind of reform that would have involved a reordering of the whole political structure of Christian society. His views are explained by R. F. Bennett in the following reading.*

FROM *Introduction to Tellenbach's Church, State and Christian Society* BY R. F. BENNETT

IT IS NO PART of the purpose of this introduction to recapitulate what Professor Tellenbach has to say. It is sufficient to remark that he distinguishes three main attitudes on the part of the Church: (i) the ascetic, based on withdrawal from the world; (ii) the sacerdotal, based on conversion of the world by the priestly hierarchy; (iii) the monarchic, based on the conversion of the world by the action of a divinely-instituted kingship to which the clergy should be subordinate—here, of course, it comes into

Gerd Tellenbach, *Church, State and Christian Society at the Time of the Investiture Contest* (1940), translated with an Introduction by R. F. Bennett, pp. xi–xvii. Reprinted by permission of Basil Blackwell & Mott Ltd., Oxford.

conflict with the sacerdotal outlook—and not by a clerical hierarchy subject to the bishop of Rome.

The attitude of withdrawal, which was dominant in the early centuries of Christianity, could be reconciled with the conception of monarchical control; devout men, withdrawing from a world which did not interest them because they regarded it as fundamentally evil, were content to leave secular society to be ordered by the kingship. The sacerdotal point of view, which exalted the power of the priest and regarded it as his duty to convert the world and lead it to the Kingdom of God, could not accept the monarchy in this way. There are, then, in reality only two lines of thought: withdrawal, which is reconcilable with the theocratic monarchy, and conversion, which is not, because it must involve the subjection of lay society to the priestly authority. The interaction of these two tendencies in Christianity, writes Professor Tellenbach, has at all times been of vital importance, and they ultimately determined the course of the reform movement in the tenth and eleventh centuries. The chief interest of the pontificate of Gregory VII is the fact that it marked the final rejection by the official Church of the old attitude of mistrust towards the world. To Gregory, this attitude had no meaning; his historic rôle was to enunciate logically and unequivocally the opposite principle, the conversion of the world by the priesthood.

This was the positive side of his task, and for its successful execution there was one indispensable prerequisite: that the world should be ready to accept the claim of Christianity to be the moral basis upon which its affairs should rest. This is an aspect of the age of Canossa which is sometimes too little stressed; both parties approached the quarrel from a high ethical standpoint, neither grounded its actions solely upon considerations of power-politics (this applies with particular force to the argument that, in view of the governmental system set up by Otto I, the emperors needed complete control of Church appointments within their territories lest the government itself should collapse—an argument which is sometimes accorded an importance greater than it deserves), both really felt that they were right in the fullest sense of the word and that their claims were in accordance with the will of God. Many things had contributed towards the attainment of this situation—the first victory of the principle of conversion in St Augustine's *De Civitate Dei,* the theocracy of Charlemagne and the wide extent of the proprietary system, to mention only a few—and even something approaching a dissolution of society, caused by the invasions of Saracens, Norsemen and Magyars in the ninth and tenth centuries, had been unable to prevent its development: the popularity of the reforming movement with all classes of the laity amply demonstrates the truth of this statement. In one way, then, the interest of the Investiture Contest lies in the fact that it deserves to be set beside the missionary journeys of St Paul and Constantine the Great's edict of Milan as one of the few notable steps in the long process by which the Christian religion has sought to lead the world to complete acceptance of its principles and to incline it towards the canons of conduct laid down in the

Gospels. This is a process which Catholic and Protestant have equally at heart, and it is of particular interest at the present time, when it seems to many that the root cause of our ills is the very incompleteness of the process; there is a painful abundance of force in the contention that a new step forward is needed—a step forward by the whole of society, akin to that which not only made possible the work of Gregory VII but also set the tone for the arguments used on both sides throughout the earlier part of the Investiture Contest.

On the negative side, Gregory's task could only be the destruction of the hitherto dominant régime in Church and State; and this involved, as its primary object, the attempt to deprive princely dominion over the Church of the divine and sacramental character in which it had so long appeared. The "right order in the world" could not be established until this object had been secured, since, in Gregory's eyes, the "right order" implied the existence of a "free" Church in a reorganised society. This part of his programme clearly amounted to an attack upon the political institutions of his time, and the question at once arises, "Was Gregory a 'politician'?" The answer can only be "No." Reform in its widest sense was undoubtedly the ideal Gregory set before himself—a reform of the whole of society was the thing which he most desired to see—but reform in the narrower sense was at most a part of his object; he was not concerned solely with the condition of the Church in the sense of an ecclesiastical organisation, and was not opposed only to monarchy if—or because—monarchy prevented the eradication of abuses. The theory that Gregory set out to establish the primacy of Rome because the weakness of the Church had led to its "enslavement" by temporal princes, whose control had in turn resulted in simony and nicolaitism—so that from an attack on simony and clerical incontinence the rest of the Gregorian programme follows logically—is attractively simple, but it quite fails to do justice to Gregory. He was indeed deeply concerned about simony and the marriage of priests, but these things were not the core of the movement to which he has given his name, nor the explanation of the struggle with kings and emperors. If it is true, as we have said, that the real issue was the establishment of the "right order in the world," and if this meant the supremacy of priests over laymen—and the supremacy of the pope in particular, as the chief of all priests—then one conclusion alone can follow: Whether the results of royal control were good (as they were under Henry III), or bad (as they may be admitted to have been under Henry IV), it still remained true that, for Gregory, royal control was in itself an evil. There could be no compromise on this principle, though doubtless there had to be *de facto* compromises in certain cases, like that of William the Conqueror.

This analysis shows how truly Gregory VII deserves to be called "the great Innovator;" his outstanding quality was his ability clearly and directly to assert first principles and to apply them to the practical requirements of the situation in which he found himself. At the same time, the fundamental

importance of Professor Tellenbach's careful distinction between Gregory
and his supposed precursors is revealed: only such a distinction brings to
light the essential novelty of Gregory's position—which is otherwise in
danger of being obscured in the shadows cast by the great reforming
movements which preceded him—and throws his real greatness into bold
relief.

In what sense may we speak of the "novelty" of Gregory's position? The
following pages will make it clear that there was in his programme a
relatively small proportion of new ideas; there were precedents for most of
Gregory's actions, and all arguments to the contrary must fail. Gregory drew
upon tradition, yet made a new use of it. He took the oldest of traditions—
that of the Catholic Church, with the irrefutable claims its sacramental
doctrines gave to the demand of the priesthood that their supremacy should
be recognized—and showed how no true Catholic could resist the entirely
novel construction he placed upon it. While there are strong reasons for
denying that, at the time of the synod of Sutri, for instance, the alliance of
the monarchy with reform was already foredoomed to turn into opposition, a
more wide-ranging view must reveal the truth of the assertion that the
dogmatic structure of the early Church made the emergence of the Gregorian programme a logical necessity. Gregory was the completest and most
ruthless Catholic who had yet held office in the Church, and yet he was a
revolutionary; innovation and an obstinate refusal to abate one jot or tittle of
the law met in him to form a paradoxical and yet entirely consistent whole.

Gregory attained a very considerable measure of success, but his victory
was far from complete. During his pontificate, we have said, the Church
finally abandoned the old attitude of withdrawal and turned to attempt the
conversion of the world; in spite of this, however, the old outlook persisted:
the next century saw a monastic revival on a hitherto unprecedented scale,
and generations of historians have agreed in awarding to St Bernard, its
leading figure, the title of "the ideal monk"—in describing him, that is to
say, as the chief exponent of some of the ideas against which Gregory VII
had fought. So, too, it proved impossible to confine the laity to a purely
passive rôle in Church matters, because more settled and more prosperous
conditions gave many of them leisure to ponder upon spiritual truth, and led
to the conclusion that all men were called to play an equal part in religious
activity. Accordingly, the twelfth and thirteenth centuries saw a wide development of popular religion, which frequently ended in heresy and was often
tainted with anti-sacerdotalism; and this last is, of course, no less than a
denial of the sacramental principles for which Gregory stood and upon
which the subordinate position assigned to the laity was based. Even when
the "conversion" *motif* appeared again with new force in the mendicant
movements of St Francis and St Dominic, it was in the end unable to deal
effectively with the problem of the layman's religion. Finally, despite the
creation of a papal monarchy in the thirteenth and fourteenth centuries, the
"national church" tendency persisted with undiminished force; Divine Right

itself lasted many hundred years more—the long continuance of the practice of touching for the King's Evil shows how difficult it was to eradicate the feeling that the king was more than an ordinary layman—while the reign of Philip the Fair, the Gallican movement and the concordats of the fifteenth century, for instance, show that princely control of the Church had lost little of its theocratic dress, if it was also beginning to clothe itself in a more secular garb and to appeal to expediency and the new conception of the sovereign State.

For a short time, Gregorianism may have conquered both Church and World, but from early in the thirteenth century at latest the old tendencies of episcopalism, nonresistance and royal control raised their heads again. If the lessons taught by the conflict of ideals in the Investiture Contest of the eleventh century are of permanent value to a world which aspires to arrange its affairs according to Christian principles, it is equally clear that contemporary society failed properly to learn them; and this failure in its turn—at least in so far as its unintended effect was to drive the papal monarchy to an ever more intransigent assertion of its authority, and in the end to separate it from the religion of the world which it set out to convert—was in some way responsible for the occurrence of the next great crisis in Christian history, the Reformation.

G. Barraclough emphasized the revolutionary implications of Gregory's policies in the sphere of German politics.

FROM *Origins of Modern Germany*
BY G. BARRACLOUGH

BEHIND ALL THE RESOUNDING APPEALS to principle, therefore, we must take into account the play and cross-currents of political interests. The opponents of Henry were a motley crowd, pursuing divergent interests; and it required all the efforts of the pope and his legates to hold them together. Gregory was not fastidious in his choice of allies. Unlike the earlier reforming popes, from Leo IX to his own immediate predecessor, Alexander II, he was not by birth a member of the episcopal aristocracy, and this was probably one reason why he did not hesitate to enlist the people and stir up popular discontent both in Germany and Italy. His alliance with the Pataria and

G. Barraclough, *Origins of Modern Germany* (1946), pp. 118–20. Reprinted by permission of Basil Blackwell & Mott Ltd., London.

the nascent communes in Lombardy brought him into disrepute; but he showed no hesitation in allying with forces which were seeking to revolutionize the existing order for secular ends. He appeared to throw over principle in favour of expediency when, in order to find a safe refuge at the moment of Henry IV's triumph, he came to terms with the Norman prince, Robert Guiscard, who had been excommunicated for occupying papal territory. His alliance with the German aristocracy was hard to justify save on political grounds; for its leaders were notorious despoilers of the Church, and the civil war unleashed by the excommunication of Henry in 1076 resulted in unparalleled depredation, of which Gregory himself was well aware as early as 1078. By his alliance with the German aristocracy Gregory sacrificed the prospect of lasting reform; for reform, in the eyes of the German princes, was little more than a pretext—as once again in the sixteenth century it was to be a pretext—to enable them to establish control over the Church. It is difficult to escape the conclusion that, for Gregory and his successors, the end justified the means, and that they were more intent on breaking the power of the crown within the Church than on purifying the Church from abuse. In this the Gregorian party was at loggerheads with the moderate party within the Church, the party led by Peter Damiani, which held that the movement against lay investiture was a false step which fatally distracted attention from the main task, the moral regeneration of the Church, and that cooperation with the monarchy was not impossible. For the Gregorians, on the other hand, the political struggle with the German monarchy overshadowed all else; and in this struggle they were willing to ally indiscriminately with princes, Saxons, Normans, communes and Pataria. In this sense the Gregorian movement was a truly revolutionary movement; just as its ultimate object was to overturn the accepted order, so its instruments and methods and alliances and associations were revolutionary in character. For the attack on the Salian monarchy and its principles of government, the papacy mobilized every revolutionary force within the empire: hence the unparalleled fury when the cataclysm was, at last, let loose.

6 The End of the Dispute

The issue of lay investiture was never settled in the life-times of Gregory VII and Henry IV. Pope Calixtus II and King Henry V reached a compromise agreement, known as the "Concordat of Worms," in 1122. The King gave up the actual ceremony of "investiture" with ring and staff but retained considerable influence in the nomination of bishops. Some historians regard this outcome as a victory for Gregorian principles. Others point out that the King "gave up the shadow but retained the substance" of royal power.

Concordat of Worms

PRIVILEGE OF THE POPE

I, BISHOP CALIXTUS, servant of the servants of God, concede to you, beloved son Henry—by the grace of God August Emperor of the Romans—that the election of those bishops and abbots in the German kingdom who belong to the kingdom shall take place in your presence without simony and without any violence; so that if any discord occurs between the parties concerned, you may—with the counsel or judgment of the metropolitan and the co-provincials—give your assent and assistance to the party which appears to have the better case. The candidate elected may receive the "regalia" from you through the sceptre and he shall perform his lawful duties to you for them. But he who is elected in the other parts of the Empire shall, within six months, receive the "regalia" from you through the sceptre and shall perform his lawful duties for them, saving all things which are known as pertaining to the Church. If you complain to me in any of these matters and ask for help, I will furnish you the aid, if such is the duty of my office. I grant true peace to you and to all those who are or have been of your party during this discord.

S. Z. Ehler and J. B. Morrall, *Church and State Through the Centuries* (1954), pp. 48–9. Reprinted by permission of Newman Press and Burns & Oates Ltd., London.

PRIVILEGE OF THE EMPEROR

In the name of Holy and Indivisible Trinity. I, Henry, by the grace of God August Emperor of the Romans, for the love of God and of the Holy Roman Church and of the lord Pope Calixtus and for the healing of my soul, do surrender to God, to the Holy Apostles of God, Peter and Paul, and to the Holy Roman Church all investiture through ring and staff; and do agree that in all churches throughout my kingdom and empire there shall be canonical elections and free consecration. I restore to the same Roman Church all the possessions and temporalities ["regalia"] which have been abstracted until the present day either in the lifetime of my father or in my own and which I hold; and I will faithfully aid in the restoration of those which I do not hold. The possessions also of all other churches and princes and of every one else, either cleric or layman, which had been lost in that war, I will restore, so far as I hold them, according to the counsel of the princes or according to justice; and I will faithfully aid in the restoration of those that I do not hold. And I grant a true peace to the lord Pope Calixtus and to the Holy Roman Church and to all who are or have been on its side. In matters where the Holy Roman Church would seek assistance I will faithfully grant it; and in those where she shall complain to me, I will duly grant justice to her.

The Medieval Mind—

Faith or Reason?

CONTENTS

The twelfth century saw a great revival of culture throughout Western Europe. In many centers of learning men began to study the legacy of the ancient world —Greek philosophy, Roman law, patristic theology— with new eagerness and new insight. Since virtually all medieval thinkers were sincere believing Christians, the problem soon arose of defining the right relationship between rational inquiry and religious faith. This became a central issue of medieval intellectual life; it has remained a major problem for Western man down to the present day.

QUESTIONS FOR STUDY

1 *Peter Abelard has been called an "orthodox skeptic." Do you think the description appropriate?*

2 *How did a medieval university resemble and how did it differ from a modern one?*

3 *Why did the study of Aristotle raise problems for thirteenth-century Christians? What do you think of the "double truth" theory as a solution to these problems?*

4 *Can you discern any significant differences between Roger Bacon and Thomas Aquinas in their attitudes toward human knowledge and revealed truth?*

5 *Were Aquinas's arguments about the family and the state dependent on his theological presuppositions?*

6 *Could Aquinas have replied effectively to Ockham's assertion that, in every proof for the existence of God, "something doubtful or derived from faith is assumed"?*

1 Peter Abelard

*The problem of reason and faith was posed in striking
fashion at the beginning of the twelfth century by the
greatest teacher of the age, Peter Abelard (1079–1142). He
pointed out, in a provocative work called* Sic et Non *(Yes
and No),* that a scholar could not simply accept all the
writings of the old Fathers of the church uncritically because the Fathers often seemed to contradict themselves.*

FROM *Sic et Non* BY PETER ABELARD

AMONG THE MULTITUDINOUS WORDS of the holy Fathers some
sayings seem not only to differ from one another but even to contradict one
another. Hence it is not presumptuous to judge concerning those by whom
the world itself will be judged, as it is written, "They shall judge nations"
(Wisdom 3:8) and, again, "You shall sit and judge" (Luke 22:30). We do
not presume to rebuke as untruthful or to denounce as erroneous those to
whom the Lord said, "He who hears you hears me; he who despises you
despises me" (Luke 10:16). Bearing in mind our foolishness we believe that
our understanding is defective rather than the writing of those to whom the
Truth Himself said, "It is not you who speak but the spirit of your Father
who speaks in you" (Matthew 10:20). Why should it seem surprising if we,
lacking the guidance of the Holy Spirit through whom those things were
written and spoken, the Spirit impressing them on the writers, fail to understand them? Our achievement of full understanding is impeded especially
by unusual modes of expression and by the different significances that can be
attached to one and the same word, as a word is used now in one sense, now
in another. Just as there are many meanings so there are many words. Tully
says that sameness is the mother of satiety in all things, that is to say it gives
rise to fastidious distaste, and so it is appropriate to use a variety of words in
discussing the same thing and not to express everything in common and
vulgar words . . .

We must also take special care that we are not deceived by corruptions
of the text or by false attributions when sayings of the Fathers are quoted

J. P. Migne, ed., *Patrologia Latina*, CLXXVIII (1855), columns 1339–54, translated by
Brian Tierney.

that seem to differ from the truth or to be contrary to it; for many apocryphal writings are set down under names of saints to enhance their authority, and even the texts of divine Scripture are corrupted by the errors of scribes. That most faithful writer and true interpreter, Jerome, accordingly warned us, "Beware of apocryphal writings. . . ." Again, on the title of Psalm 77 which is "An Instruction of Asaph," he commented, "It is written according to Matthew that when the Lord had spoken in parables and they did not understand, he said, 'These things are done that it might be fulfilled which was written by the prophet Isaias, *I will open my mouth in parables.*' The Gospels still have it so. Yet it is not Isaias who says this but Asaph." Again, let us explain simply why in Matthew and John it is written that the Lord was crucified at the third hour but in Mark at the sixth hour. There was a scribal error, and in Mark too the sixth hour was mentioned, but many read the Greek *epismo* as *gamma*. So too there was a scribal error where "Isaias" was set down for "Asaph." We know that many churches were gathered together from among ignorant gentiles. When they read in the Gospel, "That it might be fulfilled which was written by the prophet Asaph," the one who first wrote down the Gospel began to say, "Who is this prophet Asaph?" for he was not known among the people. And what did he do? In seeking to amend an error he made an error. We would say the same of another text in Matthew. "He took," it says, "the thirty pieces of silver, the price of him that was prized, as was written by the prophet Jeremias." But we do not find this in Jeremias at all. Rather it is in Zacharias. You see then that here, as before, there was an error. If in the Gospels themselves some things are corrupted by the ignorance of scribes, we should not be surprised that the same thing has sometimes happened in the writings of later Fathers who are of much less authority . . . .

It is no less important in my opinion to ascertain whether texts quoted from the Fathers may be ones that they themselves have retracted and corrected after they came to a better understanding of the truth as the blessed Augustine did on many occasions; or whether they are giving the opinion of another rather than their own opinion . . . or whether, in inquiring into certain matters, they left them open to question rather than settled them with a definitive solution . . . *that is true*

In order that the way be not blocked and posterity deprived of the healthy labor of treating and debating difficult questions of language and style, a distinction must be drawn between the work of later authors and the supreme canonical authority of the Old and New Testaments. If, in Scripture, anything seems absurd you are not permitted to say, "The author of this book did not hold to the truth"—but rather that the codex is defective or that the interpreter erred or that you do not understand. But if anything seems contrary to truth in the works of later authors, which are contained in innumerable books, the reader or auditor is free to judge, so that he may approve what is pleasing and reject what gives offense, unless the matter is established by certain reason or by canonical authority (of the Scriptures) . . . *Scriptures cant be questioned later works can*

In view of these considerations we have undertaken to collect various sayings of the Fathers that give rise to questioning because of their apparent contradictions as they occur to our memory. This questioning excites young readers to the maximum of effort in inquiring into the truth, and such inquiry sharpens their minds. Assiduous and frequent questioning is indeed the first key to wisdom. Aristotle, that most perspicacious of all philosophers, exhorted the studious to practice it eagerly, saying, "Perhaps it is difficult to express oneself with confidence on such matters if they have not been much discussed. To entertain doubts on particular points will not be unprofitable." For by doubting we come to inquiry; through inquiring we perceive the truth, according to the Truth Himself. "Seek and you shall find," He says, "Knock and it shall be opened to you." In order to teach us by His example He chose to be found when He was about twelve years old sitting in the midst of the doctors and questioning them, presenting the appearance of a disciple by questioning rather than of a master by teaching, although there was in Him the complete and perfect wisdom of God. Where we have quoted texts of Scripture, the greater the authority attributed to Scripture, the more they should stimulate the reader and attract him to the search for truth. Hence I have prefixed to this my book, compiled in one volume from the sayings of the saints, the decree of Pope Gelasius concerning authentic books, from which it may be known that I have cited nothing from apocryphal books. I have also added excerpts from the Retractations of St. Augustine, from which it will be clear that nothing is included which he later retracted and corrected.

[*Abelard then presented 156 questions dealing with such topics as these: "That God is one—and the contrary." "That the Son is without beginning—and the contrary." "That God can do all things—and the contrary." "That God knows all things—and the contrary." "That our first parents were created mortal—and the contrary." "That Adam was saved—and the contrary." "That Peter and Paul and all the apostles were equal—and the contrary." "That Christ alone is the foundation of the church—and the contrary." "That Peter did not deny Christ—and the contrary." "That without baptism of water no one can be saved—and the contrary." "That all are permitted to marry—and the contrary." "That saintly works do not justify man—and the contrary." "That it is permitted to kill men—and the contrary." The first question is given below—B. T.*]

THAT FAITH SHOULD BE BASED ON HUMAN REASON—AND THE CONTRARY

Gregory in Homily XXVI. We know that the works of the Lord would not excite wonder if they were understood by reason; nor is there any merit in faith where human reason offers proof.

Idem to Theodoric and Theudebert, Kings of the Franks. Faith and a good life are chosen by priests; if a good life is lacking so is faith.

Idem in Homily V. At one word of command Peter and Andrew left their nets and followed the Redeemer. They had seen him work no miracles; they had heard nothing from him about eternal retribution; and nevertheless, at one command of the Lord, they forgot what they had seemed to possess . . .

From the First Book of Augustine against Faustus. Faustus: It is a weak profession of faith if one does not believe in Christ without evidence and argument. You yourself are accustomed to say that Christian belief is simple and absolute and should not be inquired into too curiously. Why then are you destroying the simplicity of the faith by buttressing it with judgments and evidences.

From the Life of St. Sylvester, where, disputing with the Jews, he said to the Rabbi Roasus, "Faith is not submitted to human reason, and faith teaches us that this God, whom you confess to be one God, is Father, Son, and Holy Spirit."

Augustine, On the Morals of the Church against the Manicheans. The order of nature is such that, when we state anything, authority precedes reason for a reason might seem weak if, after it has been presented, authority is cited to confirm it . . .

Ambrose. If I am convinced by reason I give up faith . . .

Gregory to Bishop Dominicus. Although these things are so I wish that all heretics be held in check by Catholic priests vigorously and always by reasoning.

Idem in Pastoral Care. The wise of this world and the dull are to be admonished differently. The former are for the most part converted by the arguments of reason, the latter sometimes better by examples. Doubtless it profits the former to be defeated in their arguments; it is sometimes sufficient for the latter to know of the praiseworthy deeds of other men . . .

Hilary, On the Trinity, Book XII. It is fitting for those who preach Christ to the world to refute the irreligious and unsound doctrines of the world through their knowledge of omnipotent wisdom, according as the Apostle says, "Our weapons are not carnal but mighty before God for the destruction of strongholds and the destroying of arguments and of every obstacle raised up against the knowledge of God. . . ." (2 Corinthians 10:4.)

Augustine to Count Valerian, discussing marriage and concupiscence. While you satirize with a most robust faith it is good nevertheless that you also know how to support what we believe by defending it; for the Apostle Peter commanded us to be always ready to give satisfaction to anyone asking us the reason for our faith and hope. . . . We should give an account of our faith and hope to enquirers in a two-fold fashion. We should always explain the just grounds of our faith and hope to questioners, whether they ask honestly or dishonestly, and we should hold fast to the pure profession of our faith and hope even amid the pressures of our adversaries.

Abelard's technique of exposing the contradictions of the Fathers in order to provide an intellectual exercise for his students aroused the indignation of St. Bernard of Clairvaux. Bernard attacked certain specific teachings of Abelard and also his whole approach to sacred learning.

Bernard of Clairvaux's Letter to the Bishops and Cardinals

To the lords and reverend fathers, the Bishops and Cardinals in Curia, from the child of their holiness.

NO ONE HAS ANY DOUBT that it belongs especially to you to remove scandals from the Kingdom of God, to cut back the growing thorns, to calm quarrels. For this is what Moses commanded when he went up the mountain, saying: "Wait here till we come back to you. You have Aaron and Hur with you; to them refer all matters of dispute." I speak of that Moses who came through water, and "not by water only, but by water and blood." And therefore he is greater than Moses because he came through blood. And because by Aaron and Hur the zeal and authority of the Roman Church are signified, I do well to refer to her, not questions about the faith, but wounds to the faith, injuries to Christ, insults and dishonours to the Fathers, the scandals of the present generation and the dangers of those to come. The faith of the simple is being held up to scorn, the secrets of God are being reft open, the most sacred matters are being recklessly discussed, and the Fathers are being derided because they held that such matters are better allowed to rest than solved. Hence it comes about that, contrary to the law of God, the Paschal Lamb is either boiled or eaten raw, with bestial mouth and manners. And what is left over is not burned with fire, but trodden under foot. So mere human ingenuity is taking on itself to solve everything, and leave nothing to faith. It is trying for things above itself, prying into things too strong for it, rushing into divine things, and profaning rather than revealing what is holy. Things closed and sealed, it is not opening but tearing asunder, and what it is not able to force open, that it considers to be of no account and not worthy of belief.

Read, if you please, that book of Peter Abelard which he calls a book of Theology. You have it to hand since, as he boasts, it is read eagerly by many

The Letters of Bernard of Clairvaux (1953), pp. 315–7, translated by Bruno Scott James. Reprinted by permission of Henry Regnery Co., Chicago.

in the Curia. See what sort of things he says there about the Holy Trinity, about the generation of the Son, about the procession of the Holy Spirit, and much else that is very strange indeed to Catholic ears and minds. Read that other book which they call the *Book of Sentences,* and also the one entitled *Know Thyself,* and see how they too run riot with a whole crop of sacrileges and errors. See what he thinks about the soul of Christ, about the person of Christ, about his descent into hell, about the Sacrament of the Altar, about the power of binding and loosing, about original sin, about the sins of human weakness, about the sins of ignorance, about sinful action, and about sinful intention. And if you then consider that I am rightly disturbed, do you also bestir yourselves and, so as not to bestir yourselves in vain, act according to the position you hold, according to the dignity in which you are supreme, according to the power you have received, and let him who has scanned the heavens go down even into hell, and let the works of darkness that have braved the light be shown up by the light, so that while he who sins in public is publicly rebuked, others, who speak evil in their hearts and write it in their books, may restrain themselves from putting darkness for light, and disputing on divine matters at the crossroads. Thus shall the mouth that mutters wickedness be closed.

> *Although Bernard succeeded in obtaining a condemnation of various technical points in Abelard's theological writings, Abelard's "dialectical" method of juxtaposing conflicting authorities was widely adopted by the scholars of the next generation. They took more care than Abelard, however, to show how the apparently contradictory texts could be reconciled with one another. Abelard himself continued to fascinate and attract the students of Paris. He describes in his autobiography how, after the condemnation of his work at the Council of Soissons in 1121, he withdrew to a hermitage and the students of Paris followed him into the wilderness.*

FROM *Historia Calamitatum* BY PETER ABELARD

AND SO I WITHDREW into a solitude in the district of Troyes already known to me. There on a plot which was given to me I built with the

The Story of Abelard's Adversities (1954), 51–3, translated by J. T. Muckle. Reprinted by permission of Pontifical Institute of Mediaeval Studies, Toronto.

approval of the bishop of the diocese an oratory of reeds and thatch and called it the Holy Trinity. Secreted there with a certain cleric, I could sing the verse to the Lord: *Lo, I have gone far off flying away; and I abode in the wilderness.*

When my former students discovered my whereabouts, they began to leave the cities and towns and to flock there to dwell with me in my solitude. Instead of large houses, they built cottages; instead of delicate foods, they lived on wild herbs and coarse bread; instead of soft beds, they used thatch and straw and for tables they heaped up sods so that you would think they were imitating the philosophers of old . . .

*   *   *

Such a life also the sons of the Prophets who followed Eliseus are said to have lived. Jerome also speaks of them as the monks of that time when he writes to Rusticus the monk:

> The sons of the Prophets, the monks of the Old Testament, built huts for themselves by the waters of the Jordan; and forsaking the crowded cities lived on pulse and wild herbs.

Such were our disciples, who building their huts there by the river Arduzon appeared to be hermits rather than students.

The more scholars flocked to me and the harder the life they endured, under my teaching, the greater the glory which my rivals thought accrued to me and the greater the ignominy to them. And when they had done everything they could against me, they were grieved that all things worked together to my good, and as Jerome says:

> In hiding, as I was, far from the cities, the forum, the courts and crowds, as Quintilian says, envy discovered me.

Secretly complaining and bemoaning among themselves, they kept saying: "*Behold the whole world has gone after him,* we have got nowhere persecuting him and gained for him greater renown. We have tried to blot out his name and we have made it better known. Behold, students, who have at hand in the cities everything they need, despise the comforts of city life and flock to a solitude with its poverty, and of their own accord become wretched."

2   The Rise of the Universities

The fame of Abelard's teaching helped to make Paris the leading center of learning north of the Alps. Around 1200 the masters who were teaching there organized themselves into a guild—in Latin, universitas. *C. H. Haskins pointed out that this development marked the beginning of "university" education in Europe.*

FROM *The Renaissance of the Twelfth Century*
BY C. H. HASKINS

BESIDES PRODUCING the earliest universities, the twelfth century also fixed their form of organization for succeeding ages. This was not a revival of some ancient model, for the Graeco-Roman world had no universities in the modern sense of the term. It had higher education, it is true, really superior instruction in law, rhetoric, and philosophy, but this was not organized into faculties and colleges with the mechanism of fixed curricula and academic degrees. Even when the state took on the responsibility of advanced instruction in the state-paid teachers and public law schools of the later Roman empire, it did not establish universities. These arise first in the twelfth century, and the modern university is derived in its fundamental features from them, from Salerno, Bologna, Paris, Montpellier, and Oxford. From these the continuity is direct to our own day, and there was no other source. The university is a mediaeval contribution to civilization, and more specifically a contribution of the twelfth century.

The word university originally meant a corporation or gild in general, and the Middle Ages had many such forms of corporate life. Only gradually did the term become narrowed so as to denote exclusively a learned corporation or society of masters and scholars, *universitas societas magistrorum discipulorumque,* as it is expressed in the earliest and still the best definition

Reprinted by permission of the publishers from Charles Homer Haskins, *The Renaissance of the Twelfth Century,* pp. 369–71, 377–9, 383–4. Cambridge, Mass.: Harvard University Press, Copyright, 1927, by the President and Fellows of Harvard College and, 1955, by Clare Allen Haskins.

of a university. In this general sense there might be several universities in the same town, just as there were several craft gilds, and these separate universities of law or of medicine were each jealous of their corporate life and were slow to coalesce into a single university with its special faculties. Speaking broadly, the nucleus of the new development was in Northern Europe a gild of masters and in the South a gild of students, but in both cases the point of chief importance centres about admission to the gild of masters or professors. Without such admission there could be no license to teach; until then one could be only a student, thereafter one was a master, in rank if not by occupation, and had passed out of the journeyman stage. In order to guard against favoritism and monopoly, such admission was determined by an examination, and ability to pass this examination was the natural test of academic attainment in the several subjects of study. This license to teach (*licentia docendi*) was thus the earliest form of academic degree. Historically, all degrees are in their origin teachers' certificates, as the names doctor and master still show us; a Master of Arts was a qualified teacher of arts, a Doctor of Laws or Medicine was a certified teacher of these subjects. Moreover the candidate regularly gave a specimen lecture, or, as it was said, incepted, and this inception is the origin of the modern commencement, which means commencing to teach. An examination presupposes a body of material upon which the candidate is examined, usually a set of standard textbooks, and this in turn implies systematic teaching and a minimum period of study. Curriculum, examinations, commencement, degrees, are all part of the same system; they are all inherited from the Middle Ages, and in some form they go back to the twelfth century.

*   *   *

At Paris the situation was complicated by the presence of three schools: that of the cathedral of Notre Dame, that of the canons regular of Saint-Victor, of which William of Champeaux at the beginning of this century was the first known master, and that of the collegiate church of Sainte-Geneviève, which passed into the hands of canons regular in 1147. Thus Abaelard began his studies and teaching at Notre Dame, where he seems to have become canon, later listened in the external schools of William of Champeaux at Saint-Victor, but in his maturer years taught on the Mount of Sainte-Geneviève where John of Salisbury heard him in the passage quoted above. The fame of Abaelard as an original and inspiring teacher, with a ready command of the ancient authorities and a quick perception of their inconsistencies, and withal "able to move the minds of serious men to laughter," had much to do with the resort of students to Paris, although Abaelard was for one reason or another absent from Paris for long stretches of time and was followed by large bodies of students to Melun and Corbeil and even into the desert. Still it was in his day that Paris became the great centre of dialectic study, and if his later teaching was associated only with

Sainte-Geneviève and its direct influence suffered from the decline of this school, in a larger sense he contributed powerfully to the habitual resort of students to Paris for advanced study. It is true that our fullest description of his success as a teacher is given by himself, but this receives general confirmation from unimpeachable witnesses like John of Salisbury and Otto of Freising, as well as by more casual evidence. It will be noted in John of Salisbury's account that Abaelard is only one of many masters with whom he studied at Paris, so that already we see signs of the change which Rashdall observes in the next generation, when "Paris became a city of teachers—the first city of teachers the medieval world had known." The masters, like the students, came from many lands. John of Salisbury had been preceded shortly by Otto, future bishop of Freising and uncle of Frederick Barbarossa, and by Adalbert the future archbishop of Mainz; a list of masters *ca.* 1142 mentions not only Bretons like Abaelard and Thierry of Chartres and a Norman like William of Conches, but Englishmen such as Robert of Melun, Adam of the Little Bridge, and the future bishop of Exeter, and an Italian in the person of Peter Lombard. A little later we hear of students from still more remote countries, the nephews of the archbishop of Lund in Sweden and an Hungarian friend of Walter Map who becomes archbishop of Gran.

*   *   *

   While the University of Paris thus originated of itself, it came to depend upon royal and still more upon papal support, and with papal support came papal control. The first specific document of the university's history belongs to the year 1200, the famous charter of Philip Augustus from which the existence of a university is sometimes dated, though such an institution really existed years earlier. There is here no suggestion of a new creation, but merely the recognition of a body of students and teachers which already exists: the *prévôt* and his men had attacked a hospice of German students and killed some of their number, including the bishop-elect of Liége; the king disciplines the *prévôt* severely and provides that students and their chattels shall have justice and be exempt from the jurisdiction of lay courts. The name university is not mentioned, but the assembly of scholars is recognized as the body before which the royal officers shall take oath. In 1208 or 1209 the earliest statutes deal with academic dress and funerals and with "the accustomed order in lectures and disputations," and the Pope recognizes the corporate character of this academic society, or university. Its right to self-government is further extended by the papal legate in 1215 in a document which gives the earliest outline of the course of study in arts. With the great papal privilege of 1231, the result of another town and gown row and a prolonged cessation of lectures, the fundamental documents of the university are complete. Indeed, the chancellor has begun to complain that there is too much organization and too much time consumed with university business:

"in the old days when each master taught for himself and the name of the university was unknown, lectures and disputations were more frequent and there was more zeal for study." Paris has already fallen from the traditions of the good old times!

The first detailed information that we have about the or-ganization of studies at the University of Paris comes from a decree promulgated by a papal legate in 1215.

Rules of the University of Paris

ROBERT, SERVANT OF THE CROSS of Christ by divine pity cardinal priest of the title, St. Stephen in Mons Caelius, legate of the apostolic see, to all the masters and scholars of Paris eternal greeting in the Lord. Let all know that, since we have had a special mandate from the pope to take ef-fective measures to reform the state of the Parisian scholars for the better, wishing with the counsel of good men to provide for the tranquillity of the scholars in the future, we have decreed and ordained in this wise:

No one shall lecture in the arts at Paris before he is twenty-one years of age, and he shall have heard lectures for at least six years before he begins to lecture, and he shall promise to lecture for at least two years, unless a reasonable cause prevents, which he ought to prove publicly or before examiners. He shall not be stained by any infamy, and when he is ready to lecture, he shall be examined according to the form which is contained in the writing of the lord bishop of Paris, where is contained the peace confirmed between the chancellor and scholars by judges delegated by the pope, namely, by the bishop and dean of Troyes and by P. the bishop and J. the chancellor of Paris approved and confirmed. And they shall lecture on the books of Aristotle on dialectic old and new in the schools ordinarily and not *ad cursum*. They shall also lecture on both Priscians ordinarily, or at least on one. They shall not lecture on feast days except on philosophers and rhetoric and the quadrivium and *Barbarismus* and ethics, if it please them, and the fourth book of the *Topics*. They shall not lecture on the books of Aristotle on metaphysics and natural philosophy or on summaries of them or concern-ing the doctrine of master David of Dinant or the heretic Amaury or Mauritius of Spain.

In the *principia* and meetings of the masters and in the responsions or

Lynn Thorndike, *University Records and Life in the Middle Ages* (1944), pp. 27–30. Reprinted by permission of Columbia University Press, New York.

oppositions of the boys and youths there shall be no drinking. They may summon some friends or associates, but only a few. Donations of clothing or other things as has been customary, or more, we urge should be made, especially to the poor. None of the masters lecturing in arts shall have a cope except one round, black and reaching to the ankles, at least while it is new. Use of the pallium is permitted. No one shall wear with the round cope shoes that are ornamented or with elongated pointed toes. If any scholar in arts or theology dies, half of the masters of arts shall attend the funeral at one time, the other half the next time, and no one shall leave until the sepulture is finished, unless he has reasonable cause. If any master in arts or theology dies, all the masters shall keep vigils, each shall read or cause to be read the Psalter, each shall attend the church where is celebrated the watch until midnight or the greater part of the night, unless reasonable cause prevent. On the day when the master is buried, no one shall lecture or dispute.

We fully confirm to them the meadow of St. Germain in that condition in which it was adjudicated to them.

Each master shall have jurisdiction over his scholar. No one shall occupy a classroom or house without asking the consent of the tenant, provided one has a chance to ask it. No one shall receive the licentiate from the chancellor or another for money given or promise made or other condition agreed upon. Also, the masters and scholars can make both between themselves and with other persons obligations and constitutions supported by faith or penalty or oath in these cases: namely, the murder or mutilation of a scholar or atrocious injury done a scholar, if justice should not be forthcoming, arranging the prices of lodgings, costume, burial, lectures and disputations, so, however, that the university be not thereby dissolved or destroyed.

As to the status of the theologians, we decree that no one shall lecture at Paris before his thirty-fifth year and unless he has studied for eight years at least, and has heard the books faithfully and in classrooms, and has attended lectures in theology for five years before he gives lectures himself publicly. And none of these shall lecture before the third hour on days when masters lecture. No one shall be admitted at Paris to formal lectures or to preachings unless he shall be of approved life and science. No one shall be a scholar at Paris who has no definite master.

Moreover, that these decrees may be observed inviolate, we by virtue of our legatine authority have bound by the knot of excommunication all who shall contumaciously presume to go against these our statutes, unless within fifteen days after the offense they have taken care to emend their presumption before the university of masters and scholars or other persons constituted by the university. Done in the year of Grace 1215, the month of August.

Some of the difficulties that plague modern universities made their appearance very early. Student discipline was a problem from the beginning as the following proclamation of 1269 indicates.

Proclamation of the Official of the Episcopal Court of Paris Against Clerks and Scholars Who Go About Paris Armed by Day and Night and Commit Crimes

THE OFFICIAL OF THE COURT of Paris to all the rectors of churches, masters and scholars residing in the city and suburb of Paris, to whom the present letters may come, greeting in the Lord. A frequent and continual complaint has gone the rounds that there are in Paris some clerks and scholars, likewise their servants, trusting in the folly of the same clerks, unmindful of their salvation, not having God before their eyes, who, under pretense of leading the scholastic life, more and more often perpetrate unlawful and criminal acts, relying on their arms: namely, that by day and night they atrociously wound or kill many persons, rape women, oppress virgins, break into inns, also repeatedly committing robberies and many other enormities hateful to God. And since they attempt these and other crimes relying on their arms, we, having in mind the decree of the supreme pontiff in which it is warned that clerks bearing arms will be excommunicated, also having in mind that our predecessors sometimes excommunicated those who went about thus, and in view of the fact that this is so notorious and manifest that it cannot be concealed by any evasion and that their proclamation was not revoked, wishing to meet so great evils and to provide for the peace and tranquillity of students and others who wish to live at peace, at the instance of many good men and by their advice do excommunicate in writing clerks and scholars and their servants who go about Paris by day or night armed, unless by permission of the reverend bishop of Paris or ourself. We also excommunicate in writing those who rape women, break into inns, oppress virgins, likewise all those who have banded together for this purpose. No less do we excommunicate all those who have known anything about the aforesaid, unless within seven days from the time of their information, after the proclamation issued against the aforesaid has come to their notice, they shall have revealed what they know to the said reverend bishop or ourselves and have submitted to fitting emendation. Nevertheless

---

Lynn Thorndike, *University Records and Life in the Middle Ages* (1944), pp. 78–80. Reprinted by permission of Columbia University Press, New York.

we specially reserve to the lord bishop or ourselves the right to absolve clerks excommunicated for the aforesaid reasons.

But inasmuch as some clerks and scholars and their servants have borne arms in Paris, coming there from their parts or returning to their parts, and likewise certain others, knowing that clerks, scholars and their servants have borne arms in Paris, fear that for the said reasons they have incurred the said penalty of excommunication, we do declare herewith that it neither is nor was our intention that those clerks, scholars and their servants should be liable to the said sentence who, coming to Paris for study and bearing arms on the way, on first entering the city bear the same to their lodgings, nor, further, those, wishing to return home or setting out on useful and honest business more than one day's journey from the city of Paris, who have borne such arms going and returning while they were outside the city. We further declare that in the clause in which it is said, "We excommunicate all those who have known anything about the aforesaid," etc., we do not understand that word, *aforesaid,* to refer to all and each of the aforesaid but to the clauses immediately preceding, namely, concerning those who rape women, break into inns, oppress virgins and those who band together for these ends. Moreover, you shall so observe the present mandate that you cannot be charged with or punished for disobedience. Given in the year 1268 A.D., the Friday following Epiphany.

Hazing of freshmen was forbidden in 1340.

Hazing of Freshmen Forbidden

THIS IS THE ORDINANCE made by the deputies of the university as to the punishment of those hazing Freshmen. First, that no one, of whatever faculty he be, shall take any money from a Freshman because of his class or anything else, except from roommates with whom he lives or as a voluntary gift, under penalty of deprivation of any honor now held or to be held from the university, which deprivation from now as from then the said university brings upon any offending thus.

*   *   *

Fourth, the said university bids the said Freshmen, under penalty of deprivation of any honor from the said university, that if anyone does any

Lynn Thorndike, *University Records and Life in the Middle Ages* (1944), pp. 192–3. Reprinted by permission of Columbia University Press, New York.

wrong to them by word or deed on account of their class, they shall straightway secretly reveal this to the proctors and deans of the faculties who in general congregation shall be required to reveal the names of the offenders by their oaths.

Fifth, the said university enjoins all those renting lodgings to students that, as soon as they know that any corporal violence or threats have been made to a Freshman because of his class, they immediately reveal this, as above directed.

Sixth, the said university enjoins all who have taken its oaths that, if they know any person or persons to have inflicted bodily violence or insult, threats and any injury upon Freshmen because of their class, they reveal this by their oaths as quickly as they can, as has been said above.

Professors came in for some criticism too.

On the Vices of the Masters BY ALVARUS PELAGIUS

THE FIRST [*vice—B. T.*] is that, although they be unlearned and insufficiently prepared, they get themselves promoted to be masters by prayers and gifts. . . . And when they are called upon to examine others, they admit inept and ignorant persons to be masters.

Second, moved by envy, they scorn to admit well-prepared subordinates to professorial chairs, and, full of arrogance, they despise others and censure their utterances unreasonably. . . .

Third, they despise simple persons who know how to avoid faults of conduct better than those of words. . . .

Fourth, they teach useless, vain, and sometimes false doctrines, a most dangerous course in doctrine of faith and morals, yet one especially characteristic of doctors of theology. These are fountains without water and clouds driven by whirlwinds and darkening the landscape. . . .

Fifth, they are dumb dogs unable to bark, as Isaiah inveighs against them, 66:10. Seeing the faults of peoples and lords, they keep silent lest they displease them, when they ought to argue at least in secret—which they also sometimes omit to do because they are involved in like vices themselves. . . .

Sixth, they retain in their classes those who have been excommunicated, or do not reprove scholars who are undisciplined and practice turpitudes publicly. For they ought to impress morality along with science.

Lynn Thorndike, *University Records and Life in the Middle Ages* (1944), pp. 171–2. Reprinted by permission of Columbia University Press, New York.

Seventh, although receiving sufficient salaries, they avariciously demand beyond their due or refuse to teach the poor unless paid for it, and want pay whether they teach on feast days or not, or fail to lecture when they should, attending to other matters, or teach less diligently.

Eighth, they try to say what is subtle, not what is useful, so that they may be seen of men and called rabbis, which is especially reprehensible in masters of theology. And in this especially offend, remarks the aforesaid Alvarus, the masters of Paris and those in England at Oxford, secular as well as regular, Dominicans as well as Franciscans, and others, of whom the arrogance of some is inexplicable. In their classes not the prophets, nor the Mosaic law, nor the wisdom of the Father, nor the Gospel of Christ, nor the doctrine of the apostles and holy doctors are heard, but Reboat, the idolatrous philosopher, and his commentator, with other teachers of the liberal arts, so that in classes in theology not holy writ but philosophy is taught. Nay more, now doctors and bachelors do not even read the text of the *Sentences* in class but hurry on to curious questions which have no apparent connection with the text.

Teaching methods were debated; some techniques were approved and others condemned.

Method of Lecturing in the Liberal Arts Prescribed, Paris

IN THE NAME of the Lord, amen. Two methods of lecturing on books in the liberal arts having been tried, the former masters of philosophy uttering their words rapidly so that the mind of the hearer can take them in but the hand cannot keep up with them, the latter speaking slowly until their listeners can catch up with them with the pen; having compared these by diligent examination, the former method is found the better. Wherefore, the consensus of opinion warns us that we imitate it in our lectures. We, therefore, all and each, masters of the faculty of arts, teaching and not teaching, convoked for this specially by the venerable man, master Albert of Bohemia, then rector of the university, at St. Julien le Pauvre, have decreed in this wise, that all lecturers, whether masters or scholars of the same faculty, whenever and wherever they chance to lecture on any text ordinarily

Lynn Thorndike, *University Records and Life in the Middle Ages* (1944), p. 237. Reprinted by permission of Columbia University Press, New York.

or cursorily in the same faculty, or to dispute any question concerning it, or anything else by way of exposition, shall observe the former method of lecturing to the best of their ability, so speaking forsooth as if no one was taking notes before them, in the way that sermons and recommendations are made in the university and which the lectures in other faculties follow. Moreover, transgressors of this statute, if the lecturers are masters or scholars, we now deprive henceforth for a year from lecturing, honors, offices and other advantages of our faculty. Which if anyone violates, for the first relapse we double the penalty, for the second we quadruple it, and so on. Moreover, listeners who oppose the execution of this our statute by clamor, hissing, noise, throwing stones by themselves or by their servants and accomplices, or in any other way, we deprive of and cut off from our society for a year, and for each relapse we increase the penalty double and quadruple as above.

> *A distinguished law professor, Odofredus, explained* c. *1250 his method of expounding the books of the* Corpus Iuris Civilis.

Method of Expounding the Law BY ODOFREDUS

CONCERNING THE METHOD of teaching the following order was kept by ancient and modern doctors and especially by my own master, which method I shall observe: First, I shall give you summaries of each title before I proceed to the text; second, I shall give you as clear and explicit a statement as I can of the purport of each law [included in the title]; third, I shall read the text with a view to correcting it; fourth, I shall briefly repeat the contents of the law; fifth, I shall solve apparent contradictions, adding any general principles of law [to be extracted from the passage], commonly called "'Brocardica,'" and any distinctions or subtle and useful problems (*quaestiones*) arising out of the law with their solutions, as far as the Divine Providence shall enable me. And if any law shall seem deserving, by reason of its celebrity or difficulty, of a repetition, I shall reserve it for an evening repetition, for I shall dispute at least twice a year, once before Christmas and once before Easter, if you like.

I shall always begin the *Old Digest* 'on or about the octave of Michaelmas [6 October] and finish it entirely, by God's help, with everything ordinary and extraordinary, about the middle of August. The *Code* I

Reprinted by permission of the publishers from Charles Homer Haskins, *The Renaissance of the Twelfth Century,* pp. 203–4. Cambridge, Mass.: Harvard University Press, Copyright, 1927, by the President and Fellows of Harvard College and, 1955, by Clare Allen Haskins.

shall always begin about a fortnight after Michaelmas and by God's help complete it, with everything ordinary and extraordinary, about the first of August. Formerly the doctors did not lecture on the extraordinary portions; but with me all students can have profit, even the ignorant and the newcomers, for they will hear the whole book, nor will anything be omitted as was once the common practice here. For the ignorant can profit by the statement of the case and the exposition of the text, the more advanced can become more adept in the subtleties of questions and opposing opinions. And I shall read all the glosses, which was not the practice before my time.

[*Odofredus ended his course of lectures thus—B. T.*]

Now, gentlemen, we have begun and finished and gone through this book, as you know who have been in the class, for which we thank God and His Virgin Mother and all His Saints. It is an ancient custom in this city that when a book is finished mass should be sung to the Holy Ghost, and it is a good custom and hence should be observed. But since it is the practice that doctors on finishing a book should say something of their plans, I will tell you something, but not much. Next year I expect to give ordinary lectures well and lawfully as I always have, but no extraordinary lectures, for students are not good payers, wishing to learn but not to pay, as the saying is: All desire to know but none to pay the price. I have nothing more to say to you, beyond dismissing you with God's blessing and begging you to attend the mass.

> *The problem of dealing with subversive ideas arose soon after the establishment of the university at Paris. The subversive ideas in question were contained in various newly translated treatises of Aristotle on natural science. In 1210 a council of bishops banned these works.*

Banning of Aristotle's Works

NEITHER THE BOOKS OF ARISTOTLE on natural philosophy nor their commentaries are to be read at Paris in public or secret, and this we forbid under penalty of excommunication.

Lynn Thorndike, *University Records and Life in the Middle Ages* (1944), pp. 26–7. Reprinted by permission of Columbia University Press, New York.

In 1231 Pope Gregory IX promulgated a decretal modifying the foregoing condemnation and requiring that the offending books be expurgated.

Gregory IX on Books Offensive to the Catholic Faith

SINCE OTHER SCIENCES ought to render service to the wisdom of holy writ, they are to be in so far embraced by the faithful as they are known to conform to the good pleasure of the Giver, so that anything virulent or otherwise vicious, by which the purity of the Faith might be derogated from, be quite excluded, because a comely woman found in the number of captives is not permitted to be brought into the house unless shorn of superfluous hair and trimmed of sharp nails, and in order that the Hebrews might be enriched from the despoiled Egyptians they were bade to borrow precious gold and silver vessels, not ones of rusty copper or clay.

But since, as we have learned, the books on nature which were prohibited at Paris in provincial council are said to contain both useful and useless matter, lest the useful be vitiated by the useless, we command your discretion, in which we have full faith in the Lord, firmly bidding by apostolic writings under solemn adjuration of divine judgment, that, examining the same books as is convenient subtly and prudently, you entirely exclude what you shall find there erroneous or likely to give scandal or offense to readers, so that, what are suspect being removed, the rest may be studied without delay and without offense. Given at the Lateran, April 23, in the fifth year of our pontificate.

By 1255 all the condemned books—unexpurgated—were listed as required reading for the degree of Master of Arts at Paris.

Courses in Arts, Paris

IN THE YEAR of the Lord 1254. Let all know that we, all and each, masters of arts by our common assent, no one contradicting, because of the

---

Lynn Thorndike, *University Records and Life in the Middle Ages* (1944), p. 40. Reprinted by permission of Columbia University Press, New York.

Lynn Thorndike, *University Records and Life in the Middle Ages* (1944), pp. 64–5. Reprinted by permission of Columbia University Press, New York.

new and incalculable peril which threatens in our faculty—some masters hurrying to finish their lectures sooner than the length and difficulty of the texts permits, for which reason both masters in lecturing and scholars in hearing make less progress—worrying over the ruin of our faculty and wishing to provide for our status, have decreed and ordained for the common utility and the reparation of our university to the honor of God and the church universal that all and single masters of our faculty in the future shall be required to finish the texts which they shall have begun on the feast of St. Remy at the times below noted, not before.

The Old Logic, namely the book of Porphyry, the *Praedicamenta, Periarmeniae, Divisions* and *Topics* of Boethius, except the fourth, on the feast of the Annunciation of the blessed Virgin or the last day for lectures preceding. *Priscian minor* and *major, Topics* and *Elenchi, Prior* and *Posterior Analytics* they must finish in the said or equal time. The *Ethics* through four books in twelve weeks, if they are read with another text; if *per se,* not with another, in half that time. Three short texts, namely *Sex principia, Barbarismus,* Priscian on accent, if read together and nothing else with them, in six weeks. The *Physics* of Aristotle, *Metaphysics,* and *De animalibus* on the feast of St. John the Baptist; *De celo et mundo,* first book of *Meteorology* with the fourth, on Ascension day; *De anima,* if read with the books on nature, on the feast of the Ascension, if with the logical texts, on the feast of the Annunciation of the blessed Virgin; *De generatione* on the feast of the Chair of St. Peter; *De causis* in seven weeks; *De sensu et sensato* in six weeks; *De sompno et vigilia* in five weeks; *De plantis* in five weeks; *De memoria et reminiscentia* in two weeks; *De differentia spiritus et animae* in two weeks; *De morte et vita* in one week. Moreover, if masters begin to read the said books at another time than the feast of St. Remy, they shall allow as much time for lecturing on them as is indicated above. Moreover, each of the said texts, if read by itself, not with another text, can be finished in half the time of lecturing assigned above. It will not be permitted anyone to finish the said texts in less time, but anyone may take more time.

3   *The Impact of Aristotle*

The influence of Aristotle on medieval science is discussed in the following reading.

FROM *A Sketch of Mediaeval Philosophy*
BY D. J. B. HAWKINS

FOR US, NOWADAYS, Aristotle is a philosopher, and still perhaps the greatest name in the history of philosophy, but until three centuries ago he was more even than that; his work covered the whole range of the natural sciences, and he was considered a grave authority there as well. His systematic scientific conceptions have been superseded, although he is still reckoned to have been an accurate observer. For us his philosophical fame alone remains, but we shall not appreciate his significance for the mediaeval thinkers unless we recapture the idea of him as the master of those who know in every field of human speculation. The recovery of Aristotle was for the middle ages the acquisition not only of a philosophical system but of a whole encyclopaedia of scientific knowledge. To the men of that time he appeared almost as a personification of the human reason which they sought to integrate with the divine revelation acknowledged by them in Christian tradition. . . .

At a later period a rigid adherence to the details of Aristotelian physics was an obstacle to the development of modern science; on this account it must all the more be stressed that the introduction of Aristotelianism in the thirteenth century was a powerful reinforcement of the genuine scientific spirit, of the spirit of exact and dispassionate observation of what things are and how they behave. The superficial religious mind tends to disparage created things and thinks that thereby it does honour to their Creator. Some versions of Platonism strengthen this tendency with their view of the world of experience as a mere shadow of the world of essences, which, for Christian Platonism, was the Divine Word. The new Aristotelianism was a reminder that the things of experience had a being and an activity of their own, and deserved to be looked at for their own sake. The Christian Aristotelians were

D. J. B. Hawkins, *A Sketch of Mediaeval Philosophy* (1946), pp. 49, 58–9. Reprinted by permission of Sheed & Ward Ltd., London.

not slow to point out that it did more honour to God to recognize that he had created a world with its own value and interest than to suppose that men were expected to keep their gaze averted from it. In this way a sound religious philosophy was an encouragement to the spirit of humanism and of scientific investigation.

> *The medieval thinker who insisted most trenchantly on the need for observation and experiment in the pursuit of scientific knowledge was Roger Bacon. The following extract is from a work written for Pope Clement IV in 1266.*

FROM *Opus Maius* BY ROGER BACON

NOW THERE ARE four chief obstacles in grasping truth, which hinder every man, however learned, and scarcely allow any one to win a clear title to learning, namely, submission to faulty and unworthy authority, influence of custom, popular prejudice, and concealment of our own ignorance accompanied by an ostentatious display of our knowledge. Every man is entangled in these difficulties, every rank is beset. For people without distinction draw the same conclusion from three arguments, than which none could be worse, namely, for this the authority of our predecessors is adduced, this is the custom, this is the common belief; hence correct. But an opposite conclusion and a far better one should be drawn from the premises, as I shall abundantly show by authority, experience, and reason. Should, however, these three errors be refuted by the convincing force of reason, the fourth is always ready and on every one's lips for the excuse of his own ignorance, and although he has no knowledge worthy of the name, he may yet shamelessly magnify it, so that at least to the wretched satisfaction of his own folly he suppresses and evades the truth. Moreover, from these deadly banes come all the evils of the human race; for the most useful, the greatest, and most beautiful lessons of knowledge, as well as the secrets of all science and art, are unknown. But, still worse, men blinded in the fog of these four errors do not perceive their own ignorance, but with every precaution cloak and defend it so as not to find a remedy; and worst of all, although they are in the densest shadows of error, they think that they are in the full light of truth. For these reasons they reckon that truths most firmly established are at the extreme limits of falsehood, that our greatest blessings are of no moment,

The Opus Maius of Roger Bacon (1928), pp. 4, 584–5, translated by R. B. Burke. Reprinted by permission of University of Pennsylvania Press.

and our chief interests possess neither weight nor value. On the contrary, they proclaim what is most false, praise what is worst, extol what is most vile, blind to every gleam of wisdom and scorning what they can obtain with great ease.

*   *   *

HE THEREFORE WHO WISHES to rejoice without doubt in regard to the truths underlying phenomena must know how to devote himself to experiment. For authors write many statements, and people believe them through reasoning which they formulate without experience. Their reasoning is wholly false. For it is generally believed that the diamond cannot be broken except by goat's blood, and philosophers and theologians misuse this idea. But fracture by means of blood of this kind has never been verified, although the effort has been made; and without that blood it can be broken easily. For I have seen this with my own eyes, and this is necessary, because gems cannot be carved except by fragments of this stone. . . . Moreover, it is generally believed that hot water freezes more quickly than cold water in vessels, and the argument in support of this is advanced that contrary is excited by contrary, just like enemies meeting each other. But it is certain that cold water freezes more quickly for any one who makes the experiment. People attribute this to Aristotle in the second book of the Meteorologics; but he certainly does not make this statement, but he does make one like it, by which they have been deceived, namely, that if cold water and hot water are poured on a cold place, as upon ice, the hot water freezes more quickly, and this is true. But if hot water and cold are placed in two vessels, the cold will freeze more quickly. Therefore all things must be verified by experience.

But experience is of two kinds; one is gained through our external senses, and in this way we gain our experience of those things that are in the heavens by instruments made for this purpose, and of those things here below by means attested by our vision. Things that do not belong in our part of the world we know through other scientists who have had experience of them. As, for example, Aristotle on the authority of Alexander sent two thousand men through different parts of the world to gain experimental knowledge of all things that are on the surface of the earth, as Pliny bears witness in his Natural History. This experience is both human and philosophical, as far as man can act in accordance with the grace given him; but this experience does not suffice him, because it does not give full attestation in regard to things corporeal owing to its difficulty, and does not touch at all on things spiritual. It is necessary, therefore, that the intellect of man should be otherwise aided, and for this reason the holy patriarchs and prophets, who first gave sciences to the world, received illumination within and were not dependent on sense alone. The same is true of many believers since the time of Christ. For the grace of faith illuminates greatly, as also do divine inspirations, not only in things spiritual, but in things corporeal and in the sciences of philosophy; as Ptolemy states in the Centilogium, namely, that there are two roads by which we arrive at the knowledge of facts, one through the experience of philosophy, the other through divine inspiration, which is far the better way, as he says.

> *Roger Bacon evidently saw no conflict between science and religion. Other contemporary thinkers, however, were perplexed by new problems arising out of the fashionable Aristotelian studies. It seemed to them that the great Arab commentator on Aristotle, Averroës (1126-1198), had demonstrated that certain propositions that were incompatible with the Christian faith were none the less philosophically true. The problem of reason and faith thus arose in a new and more difficult form. Etienne Gilson discusses some thirteenth-century reactions to the situation in the following passage.*

FROM *Reason and Revelation in the Middle Ages*
BY ETIENNE GILSON

IN CONSEQUENCE OF THIS, there was the rise of a new spiritual family: the Latin Averroists.

Among the many members of that family, I beg to distinguish a first variety, which I cannot help considering as entitled to our sincere sympathy. For indeed those poor people found themselves in sore straits. On the one side, they were good Christians and sincere believers. To them, it was beyond a doubt that Christian Revelation was, not only the truth, but the ultimate, supreme and absolute truth. This reason in itself was sufficient to make it impossible for them to be Averroists in identically the same way as Averroës himself. On the other side, and this time as philosophers, this group failed to see how any one of Averroës' philosophical doctrines could be refuted. What were they to do in the many instances where their faith and their reason were at odds? For instance, their philosophy proved by necessary reasons that the world is eternal, perpetually moved by a self-thinking thought or mind, ruled from above by an intelligible necessity wholly indifferent to the destinies of individuals as such. In point of fact, the God of the Averroists does not even know that there are individuals, he knows only himself and that which is involved in his own necessity. Thus, knowing the human species, he is in no wise aware of the existence of those fleeting things, the individuals by which the eternal species is represented. Besides, as individuals, men have no intellect of their own; they do not think, they are merely thought into from above by a separate intellect, the same for the whole of mankind. Having no personal intellect, men can have no personal immortality, nor therefore can they hope for future rewards or fear eternal punishments in another life. Yet, at the same time when their reason was binding them to accept those conclusions, as philosophers, their faith was binding them to believe, as Christians, that the world has been freely created in time, by a God whose fatherly providence takes care of even the smallest among His Creatures; and if God so cares for every sparrow, what shall we say of man, who is of more value than many sparrows? Is not each of us endowed with a personal intellect of his own, responsible for each one of his thoughts as well as of his acts, and destined to live an immortal life of blessedness or of misery according to his own individual merits? In short, theology and philosophy were leading these men to conclusions that could neither be denied nor reconciled.

In order to free themselves from those contradictions, some among the Masters of Arts of the Parisian Faculty of Arts chose to declare that, having been appointed to teach philosophy, and nothing else, they would stick to their own job, which was to state the conclusions of philosophy such as necessarily follow from the principles of natural reason. True enough, their conclusions did not always agree with those of theology, but such was philosophy and they could not help it. Besides, it should be kept in mind that these professors would never tell their students, nor even think among themselves, that the conclusions of philosophy were true. They would say only this, that such conclusions were necessary from the point of view of natural reason; but what is human reason as compared with the wisdom and power of an infinite God? For instance, the very notion of a creation in time is a philosophical absurdity, but if we believe in God Almighty, why should not we also believe that, for such a God to create the world in time was not an impossibility? The same thing could be said everywhere. The conclusions of philosophy are at variance with the teaching of Revelation; let us therefore hold them as the *necessary* results of philosophical speculation, but, as Christians, let us believe that what Revelation says on such matters is *true;* thus, no contradiction will ever arise between philosophy and theology, or between Revelation and reason.

The doctrine of this first group of Latin Averroists is commonly called: the doctrine of the twofold truth. Philosophically justified as I think it is, such a designation is not an historically correct one. Not a single one among those men would have ever admitted that two sets of conclusions, the one in philosophy, the other in theology, could be, at one and the same time, both absolutely contradictory and absolutely true. There still are many medieval writings to be discovered, but with due reservation as to what could be found to the contrary in one of them, I can say that such a position was a most unlikely one, and that I have not yet been able to find a single medieval philosopher professing the doctrine of the twofold truth. Their actual position was a much less patently contradictory and a much less unthinkable one. As so many men who cannot reconcile their reason with their faith, and yet want them both, the Averroists were keeping both philosophy and Revelation, with a watertight separation between them. Why should not a man feel sure that Averroës cannot be refuted, and yet believe that the most necessary reasons fall short of the infinite wisdom of an all-powerful God? I would not say that it is a logically safe position, nor a philosophically brilliant one, but the combination of blind fideism in theology with scepticism in philosophy is by no means an uncommon phenomenon in the history of human thought. I seem to hear one of those divided minds saying to himself: here is all that philosophy can say about God, man and human destiny; it is not much; yet that at least is conclusively proven and I cannot make philosophy say anything else. Were we living in a non-Christian world, such conclusions would not be merely necessary, they would also be truth. But God has spoken. We now know that what appears as necessary in the light of a finite reason is not necessarily true. Let us therefore take philosophy for what it is: the knowledge of what man would hold as true, if absolute truth had not been given to him by the divine Revelation. There have been men of that type in the thirteenth-century University of Paris; to the best of my knowledge, there is no reason whatever to suppose that Siger of Brabant and Boethius of Dacia for instance, both of them Averroists in philosophy, were not also perfectly sincere in their religious faith. Such, at least, was the personal conviction of Dante concerning Siger, for had he entertained the least suspicion about the sincerity of Siger's faith, he would not have put him in the fourth heaven of the Sun, together with Albertus Magnus and Thomas Aquinas.

Besides that first group of Latin Averroists, there was another one, whose members were equally convinced that the philosophy of Averroës was the absolute truth, but felt no difficulty in reconciling it with their religious beliefs, because they had none. It is often said, and not without good reasons, that the civilization of the Middle Ages was an essentially religious one. Yet, even in the times of the Cathedrals and of the Crusades, not everybody was a saint; it would not even be correct to suppose that everybody was orthodox, and there are safe indications that confirmed unbelievers could be met on the streets of Paris and of Padua around the end of the thirteenth century. When such men were at the same time philosophers, the deism of Averroës was their natural philosophy. As to Revelation, they would profess, at least in words, absolute respect for its teachings, but none of them would ever miss an opportunity to demonstrate by necessary reasons the very reverse of what they were supposed to believe. Seen from without, the members of this second group were saying identically the same things as the members of the first one, but their tone was different and, cautious as they had to be, they usually found the way to make themselves understood.

One of the best specimens of that variety was undoubtedly the French philosopher John of Jaudun, better known to historians as the associate of Marsiglio di Padoa in his campaign against the temporal power of the Popes. Every time, in his commentaries upon Aristotle, he reached one of those critical points where his philosophy was at variance with the conclusions of Christian theology, John never failed to restate his complete submission to religious orthodoxy, but he usually did it in a rather strange way. In some cases he so obviously enjoys reminding us of all that which he merely believes, and cannot prove, that one wonders what interests him more about those points, that all of them should be believed, or that none of them can be proved. Here is one of those texts: "I believe and I firmly maintain that the substance of the soul is endowed with natural faculties whose activities are independent from all bodily organs. . . . Such faculties belong in a higher order than that of corporeal matter and far exceed its capacities. . . . And although the soul be united with matter, it nevertheless exercises an (intellectual) activity in which corporeal matter takes no part. All those properties of the soul belong to it truly, simply and absolutely, according to our own faith. And also that an immaterial soul can suffer from a material fire, and be reunited with its own body, after death, by order of the same God Who created it. On the other side, I would not undertake to demonstrate all that, but I think that such things should be believed by simple faith, as well as many others that are to be believed without demonstrative reasons, on the authority of Holy Writ and of miracles. Besides, this is why there is some merit in believing, for the theologians teach us, that there is no merit in believing that which reason can demonstrate." Most of the time, however, John of Jaudun would content himself with cracking some joke, which makes it difficult for his readers to take seriously his most formal professions of faith: "I do believe that that is true; but I cannot prove it. Good luck to those who can!" And again: "I say that God can do that, but how, I don't know; God knows." Another time, after proving at great length that the notion of creation is a philosophical impossibility, John naturally adds that we should nevertheless believe it. Of course, says he, no philosopher ever thought of it, "And no wonder, for it is impossible to reach the notion of creation from the consideration of empirical facts; nor is it possible to justify it by arguments borrowed from sensible experience. And this is why the Ancients, who used to draw their knowledge from rational arguments verified by sensible experience, never succeeded in conceiving such a mode of production." And here is the final stroke: "Let it be added, that creation very seldom happens; there has never been but one, and that was a very long time ago." There was a slight touch of Voltaire in John of Jaudun's irony; and yet, his carefully worded jokes represent only what could then be written; as is usually the case, much more could be said.

4 Thomas Aquinas on Faith and Reason

> Thomas Aquinas held that the anti-Christian tenets of Averroistic philosophy could not be definitively proved, while acknowledging that they could not always be disproved either. It is widely held nowadays that he achieved the most impressive medieval synthesis of Christian doctrine and Aristotelian philosophy. An older generation of scholars, however, was inclined to dismiss him as merely obscurantist. The following reading compares him with Roger Bacon.

FROM *The Warfare of Science* BY A. D. WHITE

MORE THAN THREE CENTURIES before Francis Bacon advocated the experimental method, Roger Bacon practised it, and the results as now revealed are wonderful. He wrought with power in philosophy and in all sciences, and his knowledge was sound and exact. By him, more than by any other man of the middle ages, was the world put on the most fruitful paths of science—the paths which have led to the most precious inventions. Among them are clocks, lenses, burning specula, telescopes, which were given by him to the world, directly or indirectly. In his writings are found formulae for extracting phosphorus, manganese, and bismuth. It is even claimed, with much appearance of justice, that he investigated the power of steam. He seems to have very nearly reached also some of the principal doctrines of modern chemistry. But it should be borne in mind that his method of investigation was even greater than these vast results. In the age when metaphysical subtilizing was alone thought to give the title of scholar, he insisted on *real* reasoning and the aid of natural science by mathematics. In an age when

A. D. White, *The Warfare of Science* (1877), pp. 89–90, 79–81.

experimenting was sure to cost a man his reputation, and was likely to cost him his life, he insisted on experiment and braved all its risks. Few greater men have lived.

*   *   *

But the theological ecclesiastical spirit of the thirteenth century gained its greatest victory in the work of the most renowned of all thinkers of his time, St. Thomas Aquinas. In him was the theological spirit of his age incarnate. Although he yielded somewhat, at one period, to love of studies in natural science, it was he who finally made that great treaty or compromise which for ages subjected science entirely to theology. He it was whose thought reared the most enduring barrier against those who, in that age and in succeeding ages, labored to open for science the path by its own legitimate method toward its own noble ends.

Through the earlier systems of philosophy as they were then known, and through the earlier theologic thought, he had gone with great labor and vigor; he had been a pupil of Albert of Bollstadt, and from him had gained inspiration in science. All his mighty powers, thus disciplined and cultured, he brought to bear in making a treaty or truce, giving to theology the supremacy over science. The experimental method had already been practically initiated; Albert of Bollstadt and Roger Bacon had begun their work in accordance with its methods; but St. Thomas Aquinas gave all his thoughts to bringing science again under the sway of the theological bias, metaphysical methods, and ecclesiastical control. He gave to the world a striking example of what his method could be made to produce. In his commentary upon Aristotle's treatise upon "Heaven and Earth" he illustrates all the evils of such a combination of theological reasoning and literal interpretation of the Scriptural with scientific facts as then understood, and it remains to this day a prodigious monument to human genius and human folly. The ecclesiastical power of the time hailed him as a deliverer; it was claimed that striking miracles were vouchsafed, showing that the blessing of Heaven rested upon his labors. Among the legends embodying the Church spirit of that period is that given by the Bollandists and immortalized by a renowned painter. The great philosopher and saint is represented in the habit of his order, with book and pen in hand, kneeling before the image of Christ crucified; and as he kneels the image thus addresses him: "Thomas, thou hast written well concerning me; what price wilt thou receive for thy labor?" To this day the greater ecclesiastical historians of the Roman Church, like the Abbé Rohrbacher, and the minor historians of science, who find it convenient to propitiate the Church, like Pouchet, dilate upon the glories of St. Thomas Aquinas in thus making a treaty of alliance between religious and scientific thought, and laying the foundations for a "sanctified science." But the unprejudiced historian cannot indulge in this enthusiastic view. The results both for the Church and for the progress of science have been most unfortunate. It was a wretched step backward. The first result of this great man's great compromise was to close that new path in science which alone leads to discoveries of value—the experimental method—and to reopen the old path of mixed theology and science, which, as Hallam declares, "after three or four hundred years had not untied a single knot, or added one unequivocal truth to the domain of philosophy"; the path which, as all modern history proves, has ever since led only to delusion and evil.

A more recent account praises Aquinas for correctly distinguishing between the spheres of faith and reason.

FROM *The Evolution of Medieval Thought*
BY DAVID KNOWLES

St Thomas Aquinas has been hailed by common consent in the modern world as the prince of scholastics, not only the *doctor angelicus,* but also, as he was acclaimed soon after his death, the *doctor communis.* To Thomists of pure blood, as to many others besides, he appears as the authentic voice of reason, interpreting and defending tradition, as the greatest medieval representative of the *philosophia perennis,* the way of thinking that is ever ancient and ever new.

The newcomer to Aquinas who is unacquainted with the language and preoccupations of medieval theology, or whose reading in philosophy has lain among the ancients or the moderns, will probably be dismayed or frustrated by the form of his writings. He will find none of the literary charm that the writer of a dialogue or treatise can diffuse; the great doctor goes remorselessly forward through things great and small, following for the most part an invariable sequence of objection, solution and argument; there is no emphasis, no high lighting, no difference between points that seem trivial or otiose and the supreme problems of existence. All is settled by a personal assertion, with little apparent distinction between what is substantial and of common belief, and what is only a possibility or an opinion. It is this apparent lack of discrimination that repels or confuses many readers of to-day, and it must be admitted that some of the admirers and followers of St Thomas have done him a real disservice by their failure to realize them-

Reprinted by permission of the publishers, Helicon Press, Inc., Baltimore, Maryland, and Longmans, Green & Co. Ltd., Harlow, from David Knowles, *The Evolution of Medieval Thought.* Copyright © 1962 by David Knowles. All rights reserved.

selves, and to communicate to others, the fundamental characteristics of the spirit and doctrine of the master. A rigid and unspiritual Thomist can be the worst of guides to St Thomas.

For the greatness is there. The judgment of his contemporaries and posterity has not been false. As we read, with sympathy and a receptive mind, on and on in the two great *Summae,* the pattern unfolds and the cardinal principles of thought recur and are used, like keen knives, to separate the truth from all else. We come to expect, and never fail to find, a justice and lucidity of thought and expression that thrills and stimulates by the impression it creates that a veil has fallen away and that the pure light of reason and reality is streaming into our minds.

Higher Order of Aristotelian

*   *   *

As a follower of Albert who outran his master, he accepted human reason as an adequate and self-sufficient instrument for attaining truth within the realm of man's natural experience, and in so doing gave, not only to abstract thought but to all scientific knowledge, rights of citizenship in a Christian world. He accepted in its main lines the system of Aristotle as a basis for his own interpretation of the visible universe, and this acceptance did not exclude the ethical and political teaching of the Philosopher. By so doing, and without a full realization of all the consequences, St Thomas admitted into the Christian purview all the natural values of human social activity and, by implication, a host of other activities such as art. All these activities were indeed subordinated by him to the supernatural vocation of man, and were raised to a higher power by the Christian's supernatural end of action, but they had their own reality and value, they were not mere shadows or vanities.

Aquinas did not merely adopt and "baptize" or "Christianize" Aristotle. He had, indeed, no hesitation in extending his thought, in filling gaps within it and in interpreting it in accord with Christian teaching. He also took many elements from elsewhere. But he did more than this: and Aristotle, had he been restored to life to read the *Summa contra Gentiles,* would have had difficulty in recognizing the thought as his. For indeed Aquinas stood the system of Aristotle on its head or, to speak more carefully, supplied the lack of higher metaphysics in Aristotle by framing a conception of the deity which was in part drawn from Judeo-Christian revelation and which, when proposed in Thomist terms embodied all that was most valuable in the metaphysic of Platonism. While Aristotle, the empiricist, looked most carefully at the universe of being as it was displayed to the senses and intelligence, and explored in his *Metaphysics* the veins and sinews of substance, he became imprecise when he rose to consider mind and soul, and hesitant when he looked up towards the First Cause of all things. His God is a shadow, an unseen, unknown, uncaring force and reason necessary to give supreme unity to the universe. In the Aristotelian system reality, existential reality, is strongest in the world of everyday experience; the loftier the gaze, the weaker the reality. With Thomism, on the other hand, the infinitely rich, dynamic existential reality is God, the creator and source of all being, goodness and truth, present in all being by power and essence, holding and guiding and regarding every part of creation, while as the one subsistent Being, the uncaused cause, the *ens a se* in whom alone essence and existence are one, He takes the place of the Platonic forms and exemplars as the One of whose Being all created being, its essence perfected by its God-given existence, is a reflection and (according to its mode as creature) a participant. It is only on a lower level that the Aristotelian universe of being is found, but the two visions of reality are fused by Aquinas under the light of the unifying principles, first proposed by the Greeks, of cause, reason and order.

*   *   *

St. Thomas followed his master, Albert, in a resolute separation of the spheres of reason and revelation, the natural and the supernatural. While on the one hand this recognized the autonomy of human reason in its own field, it also limited its competence severely. Pure mysteries, such as the Trinity and the Incarnation, were no longer susceptible of proof, of comprehension, or even of adequate explanation. The human mind was now bounded by its contacts with the external world, according to the axiom *nihil est in intellectu, nisi prius fuerit in sensu.*[1] It was from observation of external reality, not through the soul's direct consciousness of its own or of God's existence, that a proof of the First Cause could be found. It was from contact with external reality, not from a divine illumination or contact with the divine ideas, that a knowledge of truth came. This was in harmony with a key proposition of Aquinas: *quicquid recipitur, secundum modum recipientis recipitur,* which in the field of epistemology became: *cognitum est in cognoscente per modum cognoscentis*[2]—God is known from His works not in Himself—but it might well seem to theologians of the traditional Franciscan school a despiritualization of religious thought. Yet it gave a new dignity to the human reason by lending philosophical support to a conviction common to all men, viz., that our knowledge comes to us directly or indirectly from the universe of being around us, and that neither our senses nor our reason play us false when they function normally. In other words, the activity of the human mind is as much a factor in the dynamics of the universe as are purely material or mechanistic activities. The human reason is a perfectly adequate precision instrument for perceiving all truth in the world of matter and spirit around it, within the limits of its range. Aquinas thus set his face

[1] "The mind can perceive nothing that has not previously been perceived by the senses."
[2] "Whatever is received, is received according to the mode of being of the receiver," as for example, the sound of a clock striking is heard merely as a sound by an animal, but as a time-signal by a man. "What is known is in the mind of the knower according to his mode of being."

both against any kind of "double truth" and against the Platonic conception of the world as a mere shadow and symbol of true reality. The realms of reason and revelation became separate, and the bounds of theology and philosophy, faith and natural knowledge, stood out sharp and clear. There is only one truth, but there are realms of truth to which the unaided human mind cannot attain; there is only one truth, and we can recognize it when we see it; it is therefore not possible for a man to have faith and natural certainty about one and the same proposition, still less can faith and natural certainty be in opposition. Moreover, all being and therefore all truth comes from a single source; there is therefore an order and harmony in all the parts. In the celebrated and characteristic phrase of Aquinas: "Grace does not destroy nature; it perfects her."

> *Some of Aquinas' own comments on reason and faith are set out below. He held that the whole body of theological truth consisted of two parts. Some truths could be attained by natural human reason. Others were strictly "of faith" in that they could be grasped only through divine revelation. The first reading illustrates Aquinas' pattern of argumentation—a final, sophisticated development of Abelard's "dialectical" method.*

FROM *Summa Theologiae* BY THOMAS AQUINAS

WHETHER, BESIDES PHILOSOPHY, ANY FURTHER DOCTRINE IS REQUIRED?

We proceed thus to the First Article:—

Objection 1 It seems that, besides philosophical science, we have no need of any further knowledge. Man should not seek to know what is above reason: *Seek not the things that are too high for thee* (Eccles. iii. 22). But whatever is not above reason is fully treated of in philosophical science. Therefore any other knowledge besides philosophical science is superfluous.

Objection 2 Further, knowledge can only be concerned with being, for nothing can be known, save what is true; and all that is, is true. But

Quoted from *Summa Theologica*, I (1911), 1–3, translated by the Fathers of the English Dominican Province. Reprinted by permission of Benziger Brothers, New York, publishers and copyright owners, and Burns & Oates Ltd., London. The variations in the title arise from disagreement over the correct Latin original—B.T.

everything that is, is treated of in philosophical science—even God Himself; so that there is a part of philosophy called Theology, or the Divine Science, as Aristotle has proved. Therefore, besides philosophical science, there is no need of any further knowledge.

On the contrary, It is said, *All Scripture inspired of God is profitable to teach, to reprove, to correct, to instruct in justice* (2 Tim. iii. 16). Scripture, inspired of God, is no part of philosophical science, which has been built up by human reason. Therefore it is useful that besides philosophical science there should be other knowledge—i.e., inspired of God.

I answer that, It was necessary for man's salvation that there should be a knowledge revealed by God, besides philosophical science built up by human reason. Firstly, indeed, because man is ordained to God, as to an end that surpasses the grasp of his reason; *The eye hath not seen, besides Thee, O God, what things Thou hast prepared for them that wait for Thee* (Isa. lxiv. 4). But the end must first be known by men who are to direct their thoughts and actions to the end. Hence it was necessary for the salvation of man that certain truths which exceed human reason should be made known to him by Divine Revelation. Even as regards those truths about God which human reason could have discovered, it was necessary that man should be taught by a Divine Revelation; because the Truth about God such as reason could discover, would only be known by a few, and that after a long time, and with the admixture of many errors. Whereas man's whole salvation, which is in God, depends upon the knowledge of this Truth. Therefore, in order that the salvation of men might be brought about more fitly and more surely, it was necessary that they should be taught Divine Truths by Divine Revelation. It was therefore necessary that, besides philosophical science built up by reason, there should be a sacred science learnt through Revelation.

The following extracts give the substance of Aquinas' conclusions on various relevant points.

Philosophical Extracts BY THOMAS AQUINAS

A MAN SHOULD REMIND HIMSELF that an object of faith is not scientifically demonstrable lest, presuming to demonstrate what is of faith, he should produce inconclusive reasons and offer occasion for unbelievers to scoff at a faith based on such grounds.

Summa Theologica, ia. xlvi. 2

St. Thomas Aquinas: Philosophical Texts (1951), pp. 29–31, translated by Thomas Gilby. Reprinted by permission of Oxford University Press, London.

There are two methods of argument, demonstrative and persuasive. Demonstrative, cogent, and intellectually convincing argument cannot lay hold of the truths of faith, though it may neutralize destructive criticism that would render faith untenable. Persuasive reasoning drawn from probabilities, however, does not weaken the merit of faith, for it implies no attempt to convert faith into sight by resolving what is believed into evident first principles.

Opusc. xvi, *de Trinitate,* ii. 1, *ad* 5

There is a double canon for the theological truths we profess. Some surpass the ingenuity of the human reason, for instance the Trinity. But others can be attained by the human reason, for instance the existence and unity of God, also similar truths demonstrated in the light of the philosophical reason.

1 *Contra Gentes,* 3

*　　*　　*

Christian theology issues from the light of faith, philosophy from the natural light of reason. Philosophical truths cannot be opposed to the truths of faith, they fall short indeed, yet they also admit common analogies; and some moreover are foreshadowings, for nature is the preface to grace.

Opusc. xvi, Exposition, *de Trinitate,* ii. 3

From bare acquaintance with the commentary of Averroes it is strange how some have presumed to pronounce that his sentiments are shared by all philosophers, the western Christian philosophers excepted. It is an occasion of greater surprise, indeed of indignation, how any professing Christian can talk so irresponsibly about his faith as to contend that these westerners do not accept the doctrine of an unique intelligence because their religious belief happens to be against it.

Here two mischiefs are at work. First, that the repugnance of religious faith to such teachings should be left in doubt. Second, that their irrelevance to the creed should be alleged. Nor is another assertion less rash, namely that God himself could not produce a multitude of intelligences, for that implies a contradiction. More serious is a later statement, "Rationally I infer of necessity that intelligence must be numerically one, but by faith I firmly hold the opposite." This is tantamount to holding that belief can be about things whose contrary can be demonstrated. Since what can be so demonstrated is bound to be a necessary truth and its opposite false and impossible, the upshot would be that faith avows what is false and impossible. This is intolerable to our ears, for not even God could contrive such a situation.

. . . Opusc. vi, *de Unitate Intellectus contra Averroistas*

Although Aquinas held that there were certain mysteries of religion that had to be accepted by faith alone, he was exceptionally optimistic—for his age—about the capacity of reason to discern truth. He did not concern himself to any significant degree with natural science, but he wrote extensively about what we should call the "social sciences." In this sphere he sought to apply rational argumentation to topics that had usually been treated in the past simply as matters of religious doctrine. He argued, for example, for the "naturalness" of permanent marriage between men and women.

FROM *Summa Theologiae* BY THOMAS AQUINAS

WHETHER MATRIMONY IS OF NATURAL LAW?

We proceed thus to the First Article:—

Objection 1. It would seem that matrimony is not natural. Because the natural law is what nature has taught all animals. But in other animals the sexes are united without matrimony. Therefore matrimony is not of natural law.

I answer that, A thing is said to be natural in two ways. First, as resulting of necessity from the principles of nature; thus upward movement is natural to fire. In this way matrimony is not natural, nor are any of those things that come to pass at the intervention or motion of the free-will. Secondly, that is said to be natural to which nature inclines, although it comes to pass through the intervention of the free-will; thus acts of virtue and the virtues themselves are called natural; and in this way matrimony is natural, because natural reason inclines thereto in two ways. First, in relation to the principal end of matrimony, namely the good of the offspring. For nature intends not only the begetting of offspring, but also its education and development until it reach the perfect state of man as man, and that is the state of virtue. Hence, according to the Philosopher (*Ethic.* viii. 11, 12), we derive three things from our parents, namely *existence, nourishment,* and *education.* Now a child cannot be brought up and instructed unless it have certain and definite parents, and this would not be the case unless there were a tie between the man and a definite woman, and it is in this that matrimony

---

Quoted from *Summa Theologica*, XX (1922), 76–8, translated by the Fathers of the English Dominican Province. Reprinted by permission of Benziger Brothers, New York, publishers and copyright owners, and Burns & Oates Ltd., London. The variations in the title arise from disagreement over the correct Latin original—B. T.

consists. Secondly, in relation to the secondary end of matrimony, which is the mutual services which married persons render one another in household matters. For just as natural reason dictates that men should live together, since one is not self-sufficient in all things concerning life, for which reason man is described as being naturally inclined to political society, so too among those works that are necessary for human life some are becoming to men, others to women. Wherefore nature inculcates that society of man and woman which consists in matrimony. These two reasons are given by the Philosopher (*Ethic.* viii., *loc. cit.*).

Reply Objection 1. Man's nature inclines to a thing in two ways. In one way, because that thing is becoming to the generic nature, and this is common to all animals; in another way because it is becoming to the nature of the difference, whereby the human species in so far as it is rational overflows the genus; such is an act of prudence or temperance. And just as the generic nature, though one in all animals, yet is not in all in the same way, so neither does it incline in the same way in all, but in a way befitting each one. Accordingly man's nature inclines to matrimony on the part of the difference, as regards the second reason given above; wherefore the Philosopher (*loc. cit.; Polit.* i.) gives this reason in men over other animals; but as regards the first reason it inclines on the part of the genus; wherefore he says that the begetting of children is common to all animals. Yet nature does not incline thereto in the same way in all animals; since there are animals whose offspring are able to seek food immediately after birth, or are sufficiently fed by their mother; and in these there is no tie between male and female; whereas in those whose offspring needs the support of both parents, although for a short time, there is a certain tie, as may be seen in certain birds. In man, however, since the child needs the parents' care for a long time, there is a very great tie between male and female, to which tie even the generic nature inclines.

Aquinas thought that the state, as well as the family, was a proper subject for rational analysis.

FROM *On Kingship* BY THOMAS AQUINAS

IN ALL THINGS which are ordered towards an end wherein this or that course may be adopted, some directive principle is needed through which the

Thomas Aquinas, *On Kingship* (1949), pp. 3–7, 23–4, translated by G. B. Phelan and I. T. Eschmann. Reprinted by permission of Pontifical Institute of Mediaeval Studies, Toronto.

due end may be reached by the most direct route. A ship, for example, which moves in different directions according to the impulse of the changing winds, would never reach its destination were it not brought to port by the skill of the pilot. Now, man has an end to which his whole life and all his actions are ordered; for man is an intelligent agent, and it is clearly the part of an intelligent agent to act in view of an end. Men also adopt different methods in proceeding towards their proposed end, as the diversity of men's pursuits and actions clearly indicates. Consequently man needs some directive principle to guide him towards his end.

To be sure, the light of reason is placed by nature in every man, to guide him in his acts towards his end. Wherefore, if man were intended to live alone, as many animals do, he would require no other guide to his end. Each man would be a king unto himself, under God, the highest King, inasmuch as he would direct himself in his acts by the light of reason given him from on high. Yet it is natural for man, more than for any other animal, to be a social and political animal, to live in a group.

This is clearly a necessity of man's nature. For all other animals, nature has prepared food, hair as a covering, teeth, horns, claws as means of defence or at least speed in flight, while man alone was made without any natural provisions for these things. Instead of all these, man was endowed with reason, by the use of which he could procure all these things for himself by the work of his hands. Now, one man alone is not able to procure them all for himself, for one man could not sufficiently provide for life, unassisted. It is therefore natural that man should live in the society of many. . . . This point is further and most plainly evidenced by the fact that the use of speech is a prerogative proper to man. . . .

If, then, it is natural for man to live in the society of many, it is necessary that there exist among men some means by which the group may be governed. For where there are many men together and each one is looking after his own interest, the multitude would be broken up and scattered unless there were also an agency to take care of what appertains to the common-weal. In like manner, the body of a man or any other animal would disintegrate unless there were a general ruling force within the body which watches over the common good of all members. With this in mind, Solomon says: "Where there is no governor, the people shall fall" (Proverbs 11:14).

Indeed it is reasonable that this should happen, for what is proper and what is common are not identical. Things differ by what is proper to each: they are united by what they have in common. But diversity of effects is due to diversity of causes. Consequently, there must exist something which impels towards the common good of the many, over and above that which impels towards the particular good of each individual. Wherefore also in all things that are ordained towards one end, one thing is found to rule the rest. Thus in the corporeal universe, by the first body, *i.e.* the celestial body, the other bodies are regulated according to the order of Divine Providence, and all bodies are ruled by a rational creature. So, too, in the individual man, the soul rules the body; and among the parts of the soul, the irascible and the concupiscible parts are ruled by reason. Likewise, among the members of a body, one, such as the heart or the head, is the principal and moves all the others. Therefore in every multitude there must be some governing power.

Therefore, since the rule of one man, which is the best, is to be preferred, and since it may happen that it be changed into a tyranny, which is the worst . . . a scheme should be carefully worked out which would prevent the multitude ruled by a king from falling into the hands of a tyrant.

First, it is necessary that the man who is raised up to be king by those whom it concerns should be of such condition that it is improbable that he should become a tyrant. Wherefore Daniel, commending the providence of God with respect to the institution of the king says: "The Lord hath sought him a man according to his own heart and the Lord hath appointed him to be a prince over his people" (1 Kings 12:4). Then, once the king is established, the government of the kingdom must be so arranged that opportunity to tyrannize is removed. At the same time his power should be so tempered that he cannot easily fall into tyranny.

> *Aquinas' whole method of philosophizing within a framework of assumed religious truth is open to challenge. Some modern philosophers, like Bertrand Russell, have dismissed it as mere "special pleading." Another approach is suggested by F. C. Copleston.*

FROM *Aquinas* BY F. C. COPLESTON

SOME OBECTIONS against medieval philosophy are connected with features which are more or less peculiar to the intellectual life of the Middle Ages. For example, the fact that most of the leading philosophers of the Middle Ages, including Aquinas, were theologians easily gives rise to the conviction that their philosophizing was improperly subordinated to theological beliefs and interests and that their metaphysical arguments were not infrequently instances of what we call "wishful thinking." But on this matter I must content myself with the observation that if we take any given line of argument in favour of some belief or position the relevant question from the philosophical point of view is whether the argument is sound rather than

F. C. Copleston, *Aquinas* (1955), pp. 17–8. Reprinted by permission of Penguin Books Ltd., Harmondsworth.

whether the writer wished to arrive at the conclusion at which he did in fact arrive or whether he already believed in that conclusion on other grounds. For example, it is possible for a man who has believed in God from childhood to ask himself whether there is any rational evidence in favour of this belief. And if he offers what he considers to be rational evidence, it ought to be considered on its merits and not dismissed from the start on the ground that it cannot be anything more than an instance of wishful thinking. Whether or not we come to the conclusion that his arguments were in fact probably examples of wishful thinking, we should not assume that they were simply on the ground that the man already believed in God.

5 Aquinas and the Existence of God

Aquinas was convinced that human reason, unaided by divine revelation, could prove the existence of God. His "proofs" represent a high-water mark of medieval rationalism.

The technical language in the first paragraph of Aquinas' first "proof" may be confusing, but the point Aquinas was seeking to make is not oversubtle. "Motion" throughout the argument means all change in general; "potentiality" means capacity to change. Aquinas was asserting simply that a thing could not change itself into something else without outside intervention. An acorn is thus potentially an oak tree, but it cannot become an actual oak tree without the play upon it of actually existing environmental factors.

Another problem is posed by the sentence, "This cannot go on to infinity." Here the essential nature of the argument is obscured by extreme compression of statement. In other contexts Aquinas admitted that—so far as human reason could tell—the universe might well have existed from all eternity; and he explicitly acknowledged the possibility of their being an infinite series of causes in time. The argument here must be taken to mean that, even if we postulate such an infinite series in time, it is still necessary to assume the existence of a First Mover or First Cause outside the series to account for the series as a whole.

FROM *Summa Theologiae* BY THOMAS AQUINAS

THE EXISTENCE OF GOD can be proved in five ways.

The first and more manifest way is the argument from motion. It is certain and evident to our senses that some things are in motion. Whatever is

Quoted from *Summa Theologica*, I (1911), 24–7, translated by the Fathers of the English in motion is moved by another, for nothing can be in motion except it have a potentiality for that towards which it is being moved; whereas a thing moves inasmuch as it is in act. By "motion" we mean nothing else than the reduction of something from a state of potentiality into a state of actuality. Nothing, however, can be reduced from a state of potentiality into a state of actuality unless by something already in a state of actuality. Thus that which is actually hot as fire, makes wood, which is potentially hot, to be actually hot, and thereby moves and changes it. It is not possible that the same thing should be at once in a state of actuality and potentiality from the same point of view, but only from different points of view. What is actually hot cannot simultaneously be only potentially hot; still, it is simultaneously potentially cold. It is therefore impossible that from the same point of view and in the same way anything should be both moved and mover, or that it should move itself. Therefore, whatever is in motion must be put in motion by another. If that by which it is put in motion be itself put in motion, then this also must needs be put in motion by another, and that by another again. This cannot go on to infinity, because then there would be no first mover, and, consequently, no other mover—seeing that subsequent movers only move inasmuch as they are put in motion by the first mover; as the staff only moves because it is put in motion by the hand. Therefore it is necessary to arrive at a First Mover, put in motion by no other; and this everyone understands to be God.

The second way is from the formality of efficient causation. In the world of sense we find there is an order of efficient causation. There is no case known (neither is it, indeed, possible) in which a thing is found to be the efficient cause of itself; for so it would be prior to itself, which is impossible. In efficient causes it is not possible to go on to infinity, because in all efficient causes following in order, the first is the cause of the intermediate cause, and the intermediate is the cause of the ultimate cause, whether the intermediate cause be several, or one only. To take away the cause is to take away the effect. Therefore, if there be no first cause among efficient causes, there will be no ultimate cause, nor any intermediate. If in efficient causes it is possible to go on to infinity, there will be no first efficient cause, neither will there be an ultimate effect, nor any intermediate efficient causes; all of which is plainly false. Therefore it is necessary to put forward a First Efficient Cause, to which everyone gives the name of God.

The third way is taken from possibility and necessity, and runs thus. We find in nature things that could either exist or not exist, since they are found to be generated, and then to corrupt; and, consequently, they can exist, and then not exist. It is impossible for these always to exist, for that which can one day cease to exist must at some time have not existed. Therefore, if

Dominican Province. Reprinted by permission of Benziger Brothers, New York, publishers and copyright owners, and Burns & Oates Ltd., London. The variations in the title arise from disagreement over the correct Latin original—B.T.

*something
... to will to create*

everything could cease to exist, then at one time there could have been nothing in existence. If this were true, even now there would be nothing in existence, because that which does not exist only begins to exist by something already existing. Therefore, if at one time nothing was in existence, it would have been impossible for anything to have begun to exist; and thus even now nothing would be in existence—which is absurd. Therefore, not all beings are merely possible, but there must exist something the existence of which is necessary. Every necessary thing either has its necessity caused by another, or not. It is impossible to go on to infinity in necessary things which have their necessity caused by another, as has been already proved in regard to efficient causes. Therefore we cannot but postulate the existence of some being having of itself its own necessity, and not receiving it from another, but rather causing in others their necessity. This all men speak of as God.

The fourth way is taken from the gradation to be found in things. Among beings there are some more and some less good, true, noble, and the like. But "more" and "less" are predicated of different things, according as they resemble in their different ways something which is in the degree of "most," as a thing is said to be hotter according as it more nearly resembles that which is hottest; so that there is something which is truest, something best, something noblest, and, consequently, something which is uttermost being; for the truer things are, the more truly they exist. What is most complete in any genus is the cause of all in that genus; as fire, which is the most complete form of heat, is the cause whereby all things are made hot. Therefore there must also be something which is to all beings the cause of their being, goodness, and every other perfection; and this we call God.

The fifth way is taken from the governance of the world; for we see that things which lack intelligence, such as natural bodies, act for some purpose, which fact is evident from their acting always, or nearly always, in the same way, so as to obtain the best result. Hence it is plain that not fortuitously, but designedly, do they achieve their purpose. Whatever lacks intelligence cannot fulfil some purpose, unless it be directed by some being endowed with intelligence and knowledge; as the arrow is shot to its mark by the archer. Therefore some intelligent being exists by whom all natural things are ordained towards a definite purpose; and this being we call God.

Aquinas did not succeed in convincing all of the next generation of philosophers. William of Ockham, the most influential thinker of the fourteenth century, declared that, in all arguments for the existence of God, something doubt-

ful or derived from faith was assumed. The Thomistic "proofs" continue to be argued by modern philosophers. The following discussion views them favorably.

FROM *The Vindication of Religion*
BY A. E. TAYLOR

THE POINT OF THE ARGUMENT about the necessity of an "unmoving source of motion" must not be missed. We shall grasp it better if we remember that "motion" in the vocabulary of Aristotle means change of every kind, so that what is being asserted is that there must be an unchanging cause or source of change. Also, we must not fancy that we have disposed of the argument by saying that there is no scientific presumption that the series of changes which make up the life of Nature may not have been without a beginning and destined to have no end. St. Thomas, whose famous five proofs of the existence of God are all of them variations on the argument from "motion," or, as we might say, the appeal to the principle of causality, was also the philosopher who created a sensation among the Christian thinkers of his day by insisting stiffly that, apart from the revelation given in Scripture, no reasons can be produced for holding that the world had a beginning or need have an end, as indeed Aristotle maintained that it has neither. The dependence meant in the argument has nothing to do with succession in time. What is really meant is that our knowledge of any event in Nature is not complete until we know the full reason for the event. So long as you only know that A is so because B is so, but cannot tell why B is so, your knowledge is incomplete. It only becomes complete when you are in a position to say that ultimately A is so because Z is so, Z being something which is its own *raison d'être,* and therefore such that it would be senseless to ask *why* Z is so. This at once leads to the conclusion that since we always have the right to ask about any event in Nature why that event is so, what are its conditions, the Z which is its own *raison d'être* cannot itself belong to Nature. The point of the reasoning is precisely that it is an argument from the fact that there is a "Nature" to the reality of a "Supernature," and this point is unaffected by the question whether there ever was a beginning of time, or a time when there were no "events."

*   *   *

A. E. Taylor, "The Vindication of Religion" in G. Selwyn, ed., *Essays Catholic and Critical* (1926), pp. 49–55. Reprinted by permission of The Society for Promoting Christian Knowledge, London.

The nerve of the whole reasoning is that every explanation of given facts or events involves bringing in reference to further unexplained facts; a complete explanation of anything, if we could obtain one, would therefore require that we should trace the fact explained back to something which contains its own explanation within itself, a something which is and is what it is in its own right; such a something plainly is not an event or mere fact and therefore not included in "Nature," the complex of all events and facts, but "above" Nature. Any man has a right to say, if he pleases, that he personally does not care to spend his time in exercising this mode of thinking, but would rather occupy himself in discovering fresh facts or fresh and hitherto unsuspected relations between facts. We need not blame him for that; but we are entitled to ask those who are alive to the meaning of the old problem how they propose to deal with it, if they reject the inference from the unfinished and conditioned to the perfect and unconditioned. For my own part I can see only two alternatives.

1. One is to say, as Hume did in his "Dialogues on Natural Religion," that, though every "part" of Nature may be dependent on other parts for its explanation, the *whole* system of facts or events which we call Nature may as a whole be self-explanatory; the "world" itself may be that "necessary being" of which philosophers and divines have spoken. In other words, a complex system in which every member, taken singly, is temporal, may as a complex be eternal; every member may be incomplete, but the whole may be complete; every member mutable, but the whole unchanging. Thus, as many philosophers of yesterday and to-day have said, the "eternal" would just be the temporal fully understood; there would be no contrast between Nature and "supernature," but only between "Nature apprehended as a whole" and Nature as we have to apprehend her fragmentarily. The thought is a pretty one, but I cannot believe that it will stand criticism. The very first question suggested by the sort of formula I have just quoted is whether it is not actually self-contradictory to call Nature a "whole" at all; if it is, there can clearly be no apprehending of Nature as something which she is not. And I think it quite clear that Nature, in the sense of the complex of events, is, in virtue of her very structure, something incomplete and not a true whole. I can explain the point best, perhaps, by an absurdly simplified example. Let us suppose that Nature consists of just four constituents, A, B, C, D. We are supposed to "explain" the behaviour of A by the structure of B, C, and D, and the interaction of B, C, and D with A, and similarly with each of the other three constituents. Obviously enough, with a set of "general laws" of some kind we can "explain" why A behaves as it does, if we know all about its structure and the structures of B, C, and D. But it still remains entirely unexplained why A should be there at all, or why, if it is there, it should have B, C, and D as its neighbours rather than others with a totally different structure of their own. That this is so has to be accepted as a "brute" fact which is not explained nor yet self-explanatory. Thus no amount of knowledge of "natural laws" will explain the present actual state of Nature unless we also assume it

as a brute fact that the distribution of "matter" and "energy" (or whatever else we take as the ultimates of our system of physics) a hundred millions of years ago was such and such. With the same "laws" and a different "initial" distribution the actual state of the world to-day would be very different. "Collocations," to use Mill's terminology, as well as "laws of causation" have to enter into all our scientific explanations. And though it is true that as our knowledge grows, we are continually learning to assign causes for particular "collocations" originally accepted as bare facts, we only succeed in doing so by falling back on other anterior "collocations" which we have equally to take as unexplained bare facts. As M. Meyerson puts it, we only get rid of the "inexplicable" at one point at the price of introducing it again somewhere else. Now any attempt to treat the complex of facts we call Nature as something which will be found to be more nearly self-explanatory the more of them we know, and would become quite self-explanatory if we only knew them all, amounts to an attempt to eliminate "bare fact" altogether, and reduce Nature simply to a complex of "laws." In other words, it is an attempt to manufacture particular existents out of mere universals, and therefore must end in failure. And the actual progress of science bears witness to this. The more we advance to the reduction of the visible face of Nature to "law," the more, not the less, complex and baffling become the mass of characters which we have to attribute as bare unexplained fact to our ultimate constituents. An electron is a much stiffer dose of "brute" fact than one of Newton's hard impenetrable corpuscles.

Thus we may fairly say that to surrender ourselves to the suggestion that Nature, if we only knew enough, would be seen to be a self-explanatory whole is to follow a will-of-the-wisp. The duality of "law" and "fact" cannot be eliminated from natural science, and this means that in the end either Nature is not explicable at all, or, if she is, the explanation has to be sought in something "outside" on which Nature depends.

2. Hence it is not surprising that both among men of science and among philosophers there is just now a strong tendency to give up the attempt to "explain" Nature completely and to fall back on an "ultimate pluralism." This means that we resign ourselves to the admission of the duality of "law" and "fact." We assume that there are a plurality of ultimately different constituents of Nature, each with its own specific character and way of behaving, and our business in explanation is simply to show how to account for the world as we find it by the fewest and simplest laws of interaction between these different constituents. In other words we give up altogether the attempt to "explain Nature"; we are content to "explain" lesser "parts" of Nature in terms of their specific character and their relations to other "parts." This is clearly a completely justified mode of procedure for a man of science who is aiming at the solution of some particular problem such as, *e.g.,* the discovery of the conditions under which a permanent new "species" originates and maintains itself. But it is quite another question whether "ultimate pluralism" can be the last word of a "philosophy of Nature." If you take it so,

it really means that in the end you have no reason to assign why there should be just so many ultimate constituents of "Nature" as you say there are, or why they should have the particular characters you say they have, except that "it happens to be the case." You are acquiescing in unexplained brute fact, not because in the present state of knowledge you do not see your way to do better, but on the plea that there is and can be no explanation. You are putting unintelligible mystery at the very heart of reality.

Perhaps it may be rejoined, "And why should we not acknowledge this, seeing that, whether we like it or not, we must come to this in the end?" Well, at least it may be retorted that to acquiesce in such a "final inexplicability" as final means that you have denied the validity of the very assumption on which all science is built. All through the history of scientific advance it has been taken for granted that we are not to acquiesce in inexplicable brute fact; whenever we come across what, with our present light, has to be accepted as merely fact, we have a right to ask for further explanation, and should be false to the spirit of science if we did not. Thus we inevitably reach the conclusion that either the very principles which inspire and guide scientific inquiry itself are an illusion, or Nature itself must be dependent on some reality which is self-explanatory, and therefore not Nature nor any part of Nature, but, in the strict sense of the words, "supernatural" or "transcendent"—transcendent, that is, in the sense that in it there is overcome that duality of "law" and "fact" which is characteristic of Nature and every part of Nature. It is not "brute" fact, and yet it is not an abstract universal law or complex of such laws, but a really existing self-luminous Being, such that you could see, if you only apprehended its true character, that to have that character and to be are the same thing. This is the way in which Nature, as it seems to me, inevitably points beyond itself as the temporal and mutable to an "other" which is eternal and immutable.

Another modern philosopher presents a more critical analysis.

FROM *The Existence of God* BY W. I. MATSON

LOGICIANS WARN US against a certain mistake in reasoning, which they call the fallacy of composition. This error consists in arguing that since every member of a collection has a certain property, therefore the collection itself (as a whole) must also have the same property. Stock examples: every player on the team has a mother, therefore the team has a mother; every-

Wallace I. Matson, *The Existence of God* (1965), pp. 78–83. Copyright © 1965 by Cornell University. Used by permission of Cornell University Press.

thing heavy falls if not supported, therefore the earth would fall if it were not held up by something. Is not this fallacy committed in arguing: There is a sufficient reason why everything that is, is so and not otherwise; therefore there is a sufficient reason why the universe (i.e., the collection of all things) is so and not otherwise?

> But the WHOLE, you say, wants a cause. I answer, that the uniting of these parts into a whole, like the uniting of several distinct counties into one kingdom, or several distinct members into one body, is performed merely by an arbitrary act of the mind, and has no influence on the nature of things. Did I show you the particular causes of each individual in a collection of twenty particles of matter, I should think it very unreasonable, should you afterwards ask me, what was the cause of the whole twenty. This is sufficiently explained in explaining the cause of the parts.

But one must not lightly charge the great logician Leibniz—to say nothing of the Scholastics—with an elementary blunder. It is not always a matter of rote application of a simple rule to discover whether or not this fallacy has been committed. For instance, it is not committed in the following: Every resident of this community is wealthy; therefore this is a wealthy community. Besides, the argument explicitly states a reason for demanding an explanation of the universe: to wit, that it is not the only possible world. We must go somewhat more deeply into the matter. We must reopen our discussion of the nature of explanation.

The primary purpose of explanation of any sort is the elimination, or at least reduction, of puzzlement and uncertainty with their attendant fears. Let us consider first what kind of puzzlement causal explanation removes, and how.

Think of life as a game we play with nature. Success in this game, as in most others, depends on our being able to anticipate our opponent's next move—on the ability to tell from what is happening now what is likely to happen next. To do this we must discern patterns in the operations of nature, connecting events at one time with other events at other times. These patterns we call causal laws; they state that when, and only when, conditions of the kind C are fulfilled, events of the kind E will occur. A causal explanation is an argument of this form:

$$E\text{-events occur only in C-circumstances (causal law).}$$
$$E_0 \text{ is an E-event that has occurred (final condition).}$$

Therefore conditions C_0 must have obtained (initial condition or inferred cause).

For example:

Only when the water supply is contaminated with the bacillus *Vibrio comma* does a cholera epidemic occur.

A cholera epidemic is now occurring in X.

Therefore the water supply in X is contaminated with *Vibrio comma*.

This last is only an expansion of what is contained in the statement "The citizens of X are suffering from cholera because their water supply is contaminated." Of course there is no warrant for calling it *the* explanation of the epidemic; we may want to know how the water supply got infected; or we may want to know more particulars of the process intervening between the contamination and the outbreak. That is to say, a causal chain of indefinitely many links is involved. But each link is expressible in the same form: causal law, final condition (report of observation, phenomenon to be explained), and inferred cause (initial condition, deduced from the preceding two statements).

Prediction differs in form from explanation only in that the minor premise of the argument states an initial rather than a final condition:

> In C-circumstances, E-events occur.
> Conditions C_0 are realized (initial condition).
> Therefore event E_0 will occur (final condition, prediction).

For example:

> Whenever war breaks out, the birth rate increases.
> X and Y have declared war on each other.
> Therefore the birth rates in X and Y will increase.

Every causal explanation requires two elements: a causal law, which as such mentions no particular occurrence at all; and a statement describing a particular occurrence (final condition, that which is to be explained). From these together we deduce a description of the initial condition (particular cause). But if every event has a cause, then the initial condition is itself the final condition in some other explanation, some other link in the causal chain. Hence causal explanation, by its very nature, always generates an infinite regress.

We have reached this conclusion in focusing our attention on the minor premises of explanatory arguments, the statements of particular conditions. But not only are events explained in terms of preceding events; laws themselves are explained in terms of more general laws. Inhalation of carbon monoxide causes death because the carbon monoxide combines with hemoglobin, rendering it incapable of absorbing oxygen. More formally:

Whenever hemoglobin is rendered incapable of absorbing oxygen, death ⎫ Laws
ensues. ⎬ of
When carbon monoxide is brought into contact with hemoglobin, the ⎪ Wider
hemoglobin is rendered incapable of absorbing oxygen. ⎭ Scope
Therefore when carbon monoxide is inhaled, death ensues (law of narrower scope, which was to be explained).

This procedure does not generate an infinite regress; theoretically, the end of the process comes when a law is enunciated broad enough in its scope to cover all lesser laws as particular instances. This condition is approximated in physics. If the supreme law were discovered, clearly it would be senseless to ask for an explanation of it—at least for an explanation in the sense just described.

We now see how causal explanation "eliminates alternative possibilities," how it shows us that such-and-such must be so and not otherwise. Here is E_0; might it not just as well have been F, or G, or . . . ? But now E_0 is explained: the explanation is to the effect that all C's are followed by E's, and there was C_0, therefore there had to be E_0 and not something else. The "must," then, is the "must" of logical necessity: it is logically impossible (literally inconceivable) for the explanatory premises to be true and the conclusion false. But this necessity is only relative to the premises, which are not in themselves necessary. The particular premise may be itself necessary relative to some other set of premises, but unconditional necessity is never attained. As for the major premise, the statement of a law of nature: might nature not have had some other law? No, because the law is explained, that is, deduced from a more inclusive law; and if that more inclusive law holds, then it is logically impossible for the restricted law not to hold. It logically cannot be the case that both (*a*) all interference with oxidation of hemoglobin results in death, and (*b*) carbon monoxide, when inhaled, interferes with oxidation of hemoglobin but does not cause death. But as in explaining events, so also in explaining laws we do not and cannot arrive at unconditional logical necessity. The most general law that we know is, by the very fact of its being the most general law, unexplained; and even in principle some law must ultimately remain unexplained. And if it is unexplained, it has no kind of necessity, and we may ask, if we like, why it should not have been otherwise. But if we ask this, we ought not to be disappointed that no answer is forthcoming. This is no defect in causal explanation; it is not the case that causal explanation is failing to do something that we might reasonably expect it to do.

All this is to show more particularly why it is that causal explanations can never yield a sufficient reason for the universe at large. To put it in a slightly different way, the universe is the framework within which causal explanations operate. And although these explanations show the linkage of one part of the universe to another, it is quite beyond their scope to link the universe to anything else. To ask for the cause of the universe is to ask a question similar to "When is time?" or "Where is space?"

*   *   *

Causal explanation and the prediction it facilitates alleviate puzzlement and fear. If we know that conditions C lead to disaster, then, when we observe C_0, we can take to the hills; further, when we know that D leads to C, and D is controllable by our efforts, we may eliminate D, if we have time. Intellectual, or idle, curiosity may make us wonder what the causes of D are; and if we have nothing better to do, we may investigate them. There is no limit to the lengths to which we may push the inquiry. We shall never come to a cause necessary in itself, but that does not disturb us, either practically or theoretically—unless we are metaphysicians; in which case the proper remedy for our puzzlement on this score is to get clear about why it is senseless to ask for ultimate causal explanations.

The Parliament of Edward I— Royal Court or Representative Legislature?

CONTENTS

*D*uring the thirteenth century, kings in many lands—
in Spain, Sicily, Hungary, and England, for instance—
called into existence representative assemblies of nobles,
clergy, and townsfolk to assist them in their task of
ruling. This beginning of representative government
was the greatest contribution of the Middle Ages to the
tradition of Western constitutionalism.

Of all the medieval assemblies the English Parliament was the one that outlasted the Middle Ages to provide an example of constitutional government for the

QUESTIONS FOR STUDY

1   On what grounds has Stubbs' interpretation of the nature of Parliament in
1300 been criticized?

2   Do the quotations from Bracton and Grosseteste seem more in accordance
with McIlwain's or with Plucknett's views?

3   How do Sayles and Wilkinson differ in their views?

4   What points of resemblance and difference can you find between Edward I's
summons to a parliament and Innocent III's summons to a general council?

5   What is the significance of the dismissal of the assembly in 1305 for the
general problem of the nature of Parliament at that time?

6   Which of the modern scholars would find most support for his views in The
Flowers of History? In the Rolls of Parliament? In the Writs of Summons?

modern world. Many historians have therefore concerned themselves with the question of how Parliament first came to exist.

The word parliamentum—*of medieval coinage—came into use in the first half of the thirteenth century. It did not at first have a technical sense, referring to a particular institution, but could be used to describe any kind of meeting or "parley." King Edward I of England (1272–1307) initiated a policy of summoning meetings called "parliaments" frequently, as often as three times a year at the beginning of his reign. The great nobles and prelates of England attended these meetings together with the King's judges and other royal officials. Sometimes, but not always, elected representatives of towns and counties were also summoned. By the end of Edward's reign Parliament had become a permanent institution of English government. The problem is to decide what kind of institution it was.*

1 Parliament as a Representative Assembly

> *In 1870 William Stubbs gave a classical formulation to the theory of the origins and nature of Parliament most commonly accepted in the nineteenth century. He saw an original heritage of Teutonic liberty deliberately shaped into enduring institutional forms by the genius of a great king. Stubbs thought of Parliament in 1300 as already a representative legislature—indeed something like the Victorian Parliament.*

FROM *Select Charters* BY WILLIAM STUBBS

THE ENGLISH NATION is of distinctly Teutonic or German origin. The Angles, Jutes, and Saxons, who, according to Bede, furnished the mass of immigrants in the fifth century, were amongst those tribes of Lower Germany which had been the least affected by Roman influences. They entered upon a land whose defenders had forsaken it, and had carried away with them most of the adventitious civilization which they had maintained for four hundred years; whose inhabitants were enervated and demoralized by long dependence, wasted by successive pestilences, worn out by the attacks of half-savage neighbors, and by their own suicidal wars; whose vast forests and unreclaimed marsh lands afforded to the new-comers a comparatively easy conquest, and the means of reproducing at liberty on new ground the institutions under which they had lived at home.

This new race was the main stock of our forefathers: sharing the primeval German pride of purity of extraction; still regarding the family tie as the basis of social organization; migrating in groups of allied and kindred character, and commemorating the tribal identity in the names they gave to their new settlements; honouring the women of their nation, and strictly careful of the distinction between themselves and the tolerated remnant of

William Stubbs, *Select Charters* (1870), pp. 1-2, 34-7, 44-51.

their predecessors. The variations of physical and mental characteristics which in the progress of fourteen hundred years have been developed between the English and North German types, may be amply accounted for by natural and political causes: the natural ones, the air, food, water, and other almost imperceptibly efficient workings of the land on its inhabitants; the political ones, the total difference of history, and mental and moral discipline.

It is unnecessary to suppose that any general intermixture either of Roman or of British blood has affected this national identity. Doubtless there were early intermarriages between the invaders and the natives, and probably in the west of England a large and continuous infusion of Celtic blood. But though it may have been locally or relatively great, it could only be in very small proportion to the whole. The language, the personal and local names, the character of the customs and common law of the English, are persistent during historic times. Every infusion of new blood since the first migration has been Teutonic; the Dane, the Norseman, and even the French-speaking Norman of the Conquest, serve to add intensity to the distinctness of the national identity.

*   *   *

The long struggle of the constitution for existence ends with the reign of Edward I. This great monarch, whose commanding spirit, defining and organizing power, and thorough honesty of character, place him in strong contrast not merely with his father, but with all the rest of our long line of kings, was not likely to surrender without a struggle the position which he had inherited. For more than twenty years he reigned as Henry II had done, showing proper respect for constitutional forms, but exercising the reality of despotic power. He loved his people, and therefore did not oppress them: they knew and loved him, and endured the pressure of taxation, which would not have been imposed if it had not been necessary. He admits them to a share, a large share, in the process of government: he develops and defines the constitution in its mechanical character in a way which Simon de Montfort had never contemplated. The organization of parliament, of convocation, of the courts of law, of provincial jurisdiction, is elaborated and completed until it seems to be as perfect as it is at the present day; and the legislation is so full that the laws of the next three centuries are little more than a necessary expansion of it. But until he is compelled by the action of the barons, he retains the substance of royal power; the right to the purse-strings, the right to talliage the towns and the demesnes of the crown without a grant. Edward I would not have been nearly so great a king as he was if he had not thought this right worth a struggle; nor if, when that struggle was going against him, he had not seen that it was time to yield; nor if, when he had yielded, he had not determined honestly to abide by his concessions. The political party that forced him to the concession was not to be compared with the earlier combinations of the century. Bohun and Bigod had doubtless personal claims at heart, and not political ones: but they took advantage of a state of things which Edward saw could not be resisted. The confirmation of the Charters completes the present survey of political history.

The idea of constitutional government, defined by the measures of Edward I, and summarized in the legal meaning of the word parliament, implies four principles: first, the existence of a central or national assembly, a "commune consilium regni"; second, the representation in that assembly of all classes of the people, regularly summoned; third, the reality of the representation of the whole people, secured either by its presence in the council, or by the free election of the persons who are to represent it, or any portion of it; and fourth, the assembly so summoned and elected must possess definite powers of taxation, legislation, and general political deliberation. We will now trace very briefly the origin, growth, and combination of these.

First. The Commune Concilium had existed from the earliest times, first as the witenagemot, and afterwards as the court of the king's vassals, or in a manner as combining the characters of each. It had in neither stage been representative, in the modern meaning of the word. The witenagemot acted for the nation, but was not delegated or elected by it: the great council of the Norman kings included in theory all tenants in chief of the crown, but had no special provision for these to represent their under-tenants, or for the securing of the rights of any not personally present. The witenagemot possessed and exercised all the powers of a free council; the Norman court or parliament, claiming the character of a witenagemot, if it possessed these rights in theory, did not exercise them. At no period, however, of our early history was the assembling of the national council dispensed with.

Second. The representation of all classes of the people is necessary for the complete organization of a national council, and that complete organization is legally constituted by summons to parliament. In this three principles are involved: the idea of representation, the idea of exhaustive representation, and the definite summons.

The idea of representation was familiar to the English in the minor courts, the hundredmoot and the shiremoot. The reeve and four men represented the township in these assemblies; the twelve assessors of the sheriff represented the judicial opinion, sometimes the collective legal knowledge of the shire. At a later period the inquest by sworn recognitors, in civil suits, in the presentment of criminals, and in the assessment of real and personal property, represented the country, that is the shire or hundred or borough, for whose business they were sworn to answer.

The political constituents of the nation (exclusive of the king), the three estates of the realm, are the clergy, the baronage, and the commons. A perfect national council must include all these: the baronage by personal attendance, the clergy and people by representation. The bishops, although their right to appear personally in the Commune Concilium is older than the introduction of the feudal system on which this division of the estates is based, have, by the definition of lawyers, been made to sink their character of witan in that of barons, amongst whom they may for our present purpose be included. The representation of the estates then implies the union in parliament of (1) the baronage lay and clerical, (2) the lower clergy, and (3) the commons.

*   *   *

The status of the parliament was constituted by the writs of summons, addressed to the barons individually, and to the sheriffs for the representation of the third estate. In the latter case both towns and counties chose their representatives in the shiremoot. Where the particular form of writ was not observed,—and both for military levies of the vassals and for great councils a distinct form was in use,—the assembly, although it might contain every element of a parliament, was not regarded as one. The obscurity of our knowledge on this point, caused by the loss of the ancient writs, occasions the difficulty that exists about the assemblies of the reign of Henry III and of the early years of Edward I, during which many councils were held which contained certainly knights of the shire, and possibly deputies from the towns, but which are called great councils rather than parliaments, for this technical reason—either they contained other ingredients besides the regular ones of parliament; or they did not contain all the ingredients of parliament; or the towns were summoned otherwise than through the sheriffs; or the number of representatives varied; or the selection of the boroughs was irregular; or the purpose specified in the writ was other than parliamentary. These great councils were however a part of the process by which the institution of parliaments ripened. The assemblies of later date, to which the name of great council is given, contained all the elements of a proper parliament, and exercised many of its powers: but they were summoned by a special writ; they contained the judges of the courts and other nominated members of the king's ordinary council; taxes imposed and laws enacted by them were regarded as having no sufficient authority. For judicial purposes they exercised a right which parliament as such had not, and which has descended from them to the House of Lords only.

Third. The combination of the principles of election with that of representation has been illustrated by what precedes. The idea of election was very ancient in the nation, and had been theoretically maintained in both the highest and the lowest regions of the polity: the kings and prelates were supposed to be elected; the magistrates of towns, the judicial officers of the counties and forests, were really so from the beginning of the thirteenth century, if not before. In this, as in every other constitutional point, the freedom claimed and often secured by the clergy served to maintain the recollection or idea of a right. In the reign of Edward I the lawyers represented it as an ancient Teutonic right that the ealdorman, the heretoga, and the sheriff were elected officers. The election of sheriff was claimed for the counties during the parliamentary struggle which produced the Provisions of Oxford, and was secured to the freeholders by the Articuli super

Cartas in 1300; but the privilege was withdrawn early in the next reign. The two principles of election and representation have never been divided in England since the reign of Edward I, although the variety of franchises and disputes on the right of voting for members of parliament are for many centuries bewildering in the extreme. The towns, however close the franchise, have never been, as in France, represented by their magistrates as such.

Fourth. Of the four normal powers of a national assembly, the judicial has never been exercised by the parliament as a parliament. The House of Commons is not, either by itself or in conjunction with the House of Lords, a court of justice: the House of Lords has inherited its jurisdiction from the great council. Another power, the political, or right of general deliberation on all national matters, is too vague in its extent to be capable of being chronologically defined; nor was it really vindicated by the parliament until a much later period than that on which we are now employed. The two most important remain, the legislative and the taxative, the tracing of whose history must complete our present survey. . . .

From the reign of Edward I the forms [*of legislation—B. T.*] are those of statutes and ordinances, differing in some ascertained respects, the former formally accepted in the parliament as laws of perpetual obligation, and enrolled: the latter proceeding from the king and his council rather than from the king and parliament, being more temporary in character, and not enrolled among the statutes. All alike express the counsel and consent with which the king fortifies his own enacting power: but several of the early statutes of Edward are worded as if that enacting power resided in the king and his ordinary council; and it is not clear whether this assumption is based on the doctrine of the scientific jurists who were addicted to the civil law, or on imitation of the practice of the French kings, just then made illustrious by the Establishments of Saint Lewis.

The actual force of the expression "counsel and consent," which is preserved during so long a period and under such various developments of the royal power, can only be estimated approximately, according to the occasion or the needs or the character of the sovereign who acknowledges it. It stands, for at least a century after the Conquest, as the record of a right rather than the expression of a fact. Under Henry II and his descendants, by whom a large share of power was actually vested in the ministers and judges, the facility of consultation was much increased, but it remains an obscure point, whether consent could be withheld as well as bestowed, and whether it was not generally taken for granted. From the reign of Henry III it was probably a reality; and from that of Edward I downwards the form has a typical force, and the variations later introduced into it, a great deal of meaning. After the permanent incorporation of the commons, from 1318 downwards, the form is, *by the assent of the prelates, earls, barons, and the commonalty of the realm.*

*   *   *

The share of the commons in taxation takes precedence of their share in legislation. The power of voting money was more necessary than that of giving counsel. . . . Magna Carta enunciates the principle that the payers shall be called to the common council to vote the aids which had been previously negotiated separately; but the clause was never confirmed by Henry III, nor was it applicable to the talliaging of demesne. It is as the towns begin to increase, and at the same time taxation ceases to be based solely on land and begins to affect personal as well as real property, that the difficulties of the king and the hardships of the estates liable to talliage become important. The steps by which the king was compelled to give up the right of taking talliages without a parliamentary grant, are the same as those which led to the confirmation of the charters. It was finally surrendered in the clause then conceded in addition to the charter, and known as the Act *De Tallagio non concedendo*. And this completed the taxative powers of parliament. The further steps of development, the determination of the different proportions in which the various branches of the three estates voted their supplies, and the final engrossing of the taxing power by the House of Commons, the struggles by which the grants were made to depend on the redress of grievances, and the determination of the disposal of supplies assumed by the parliament, belong to later history.

We have thus brought our sketch of Constitutional History to the point of time at which the nation may be regarded as reaching its full stature. It has not yet learned its strength, nor accustomed itself to economize its power. Its first vagaries are those of a people grown up, but not disciplined. To trace the process by which it learned the full strength of its organism—by which it learned to use its powers and forces with discrimination and effect—to act easily, effectually, and economically,—or, to use another metaphor, to trace the gradual wear of the various parts of the machinery, until all roughnesses were smoothed, and all that was superfluous, entangling, and confusing was got rid of, and the balance of forces adjusted, and action made manageable and intelligible, and the power of adaptation to change of circumstances fully realized,—is the story of later politics, of a process that is still going on, and must go on as the age advances, and men are educated into wider views of government, national unity, and political responsibility. We stop, however, with Edward I, because the machinery is now completed, the people are at full growth. The system is raw and untrained and awkward, but it is complete. The attaining of this point is to be attributed to the defining genius, the political wisdom, and the honesty of Edward I, building on the immemorial foundation of national custom; fitting together all that Henry I had planned, Henry II had organized, and the heroes of the thirteenth century had inspired with fresh life and energy.

2   *Parliament as a Royal Court*

In 1893 F. W. Maitland edited the Memoranda de Parliamento, *an official record of Edward's Parliament of 1305. Maitland's introduction pointed out that, at that Parliament, there was no taxation, and little legislation, that the great bulk of the material recorded consisted of petitions to the King's Council, and that the assembly was still referred to as a "full parliament" even after the nobles, prelates, and commons had been dismissed from it. The essential feature of a parliament, it seemed, was not the meeting of a national representative assembly but rather the sitting of the King's Council as a court.*

FROM *Introduction to Memoranda de Parliamento*
BY F. W. MAITLAND

IT WAS A FULL PARLIAMENT in our sense of that term. The three estates of the realm met the king and his council. . . . This assembly was kept together for just three weeks. On the 21st of March a proclamation was made telling the archbishops, bishops and other prelates, earls, barons, knights, citizens and burgesses in general that they might go home, but must be ready to appear again if the king summoned them. Those bishops, earls, barons, justices and others who were members of the council were to remain behind and so were all those who had still any business to transact. But the "parliament" was not at an end. Many of its doings that are recorded on our roll were done after the estates had been sent home. The king remained at Westminster, surrounded by his councillors, and his parliament was still in session as a "full" and "general" parliament as late as the 5th and 6th of April. . . . The king had summoned the estates in order that he might treat "of certain matters specially touching our realm of England and the estab-

---

F. W. Maitland, ed., *Memoranda de Parliamento* (1893), pp. xxxv–xxxvi, xlviii–xlix, l, liii, lv, lxvi–lxviii, lxxv–lxxvi, lxxxviii.

lishment of our land of Scotland," and no doubt the state of Scotland was one of the main matters which required his attention and the advice of his councillors. . . . What Edward did at this parliament was to call upon the Bishop of Glasgow, the Earl of Carrick, and John Mowbray to say how Scotland should be represented at another parliament to be holden later in the year. They reported that two bishops, two abbots, two earls, two barons, and two men elected by the community of Scotland would be representatives enough. . . . However, at the moment what should interest us most is this, that in our lenten parliament the three Scottish spokesmen did not answer the question that had been put to them until after the assembly of the English estates had been dissolved. Those who were not members of the council had been sent home on the 21st of March; not until the 26th did the Bishop of Glasgow, Robert Bruce, and John Mowbray bring in their report.

Whether Edward had sought advice in this matter from the mass of the clergy, baronage, and commoners, we cannot say. . . .

In the way of legislation this Parliament did little. . . . As to taxation, we have every reason to believe that on the present occasion no tax of any kind was imposed. . . . But by far the greater part of our parliament roll is occupied by entries which concern the audience of petitions. . . .

The petitions of which our roll speaks are neither petitions by parliament nor yet are they petitions addressed to parliament. We see at once that they are very different from those petitions of the commons (*petitions de la commune, petitions des communes*) which will occupy the greater part of almost any parliament roll of Edward III.'s day. But again they are not addressed to "parliament," or to "the lords of parliament," or to either house of parliament. They are addressed either "to the king" or "to the king and his council." In a certain sense they are parliamentary petitions, they are presented in or at a parliament. But at present "parliament" or "a parliament" is not conceived as a body that can be petitioned. A parliament is rather an act than a body of persons. One cannot present a petition to a colloquy, to a debate. It is but slowly that this word is appropriated to colloquies of a particular kind, namely, those which the king has with the estates of his realm, and still more slowly that it is transferred from the colloquy to the body of men whom the king has summoned. As yet any meeting of the king's council that has been solemnly summoned for general business seems to be a parliament. These petitions are not addressed to parliament, nor are they addressed to the assembled estates, nor are they addressed to the earls, barons, and prelates. They are addressed either simply to the king or to the king and his council. The formal title for them which is in use in the chancery is "petitiones de consilio," "council petitions."

When we examine the character of these petitions we soon see that for the more part they were not fit subjects for discussion in a large assembly. They do not ask for anything that could be called legislation; the responses that are given to them are in no sort "private acts of parliament." Generally the boon that is asked for is one which the king without transcending his legal powers might either grant or deny. Sometimes we may say that, if the facts are truly stated by the petitioner, the king is more or less strictly bound by the rules of common honesty to give him some relief:—The king owes him wages, or his lands have been wrongfully seized by the king's officers. At other times what is asked for is pure grace and favour:—The petitioner owes the king money and asks that he may be allowed to pay it by instalments, or that in consideration of his poverty part of his debt may be forgiven, or perhaps the University of Cambridge asks that the king will found a college. . . .

As to what was done by the assembled commoners during the three weeks that they spent at Westminster, we shall hardly get beyond guess-work. All that we learn from our roll is, first, that they joined in a petition with the magnates about the exportation of the wealth of the monasteries, to which petition the king gave his assent, though he did not at once convert it into a statute; and secondly, that they presented two petitions of their own, which were refused. The king, so far as we know, did not ask them for money, nor did he desire their consent to any new law. The doctrine that in these days the representatives of the shires and towns were called to parliament not in order that they might act in concert on behalf of the commons of England, but in order that each might represent before the king in council the grievances and the interests of the particular community, county or borough, that sent him thither, may easily be pressed too far, but we shall probably think that there is no little truth in it, if we ask what the knights and burgesses were doing while the king and his councillors were slowly disposing of this great mass of petitions, many of which were presented by shires and boroughs. . . . Without denying that the germ of a "house" of commons already exists, without denying that its members hold meetings, discuss their common affairs and common grievances, without denying that Edward has encouraged them to do this—at the present moment he has a quarrel with the clergy, at least with the archbishop, and no doubt is glad when the assembled commons protest that there are abuses in the church—without denying all this, we may still believe that the council often gives audience, advice, instructions to particular knights and burgesses. After all we have to fall back upon the words of the writ of summons:—the commoners have been told to come in order that they may do what shall be ordained. . . .

Perhaps more than enough has already been said about these controverted matters; but it seemed necessary to remind readers, who are conversant with the "parliaments" of later days, that about the parliaments of Edward I.'s time there is still much to be discovered, and that should they come to the opinion that a session of the king's council is the core and essence of every *parliamentum,* that the documents usually called "parliamentary petitions" are petitions to the king and his council, that the auditors of petitions are committees of the council, that the rolls of parliament are the records of the business done by the council,—sometimes with, but much more often without, the concurrence of the estates of the realm,—that the highest tribunal in England is not a general assembly of barons and prelates, but the king's council, they will not be departing very far from the path marked out by books that are already classical.

3　Proceedings in Parliament

The following references to Edward's Parliaments are from
The Flowers of History, *a contemporary chronicle com-*
piled by the monks of Westminster.

FROM *The Flowers of History*

A.D. 1275. THE KING COMMANDED all the nobles of his kingdom to
assemble in a parliament at Westminster; in which parliament many statutes
for the benefit of the kingdom were published, and among them one which
bridled the usurious extortions of the Jews.

A.D. 1280. The king, and prelates, and nobles of England, agreed together, and enacted, that the members of the religious orders should not be
enriched by any increase of landed estates, saying, that it was to the detri-
ment of the kingdom and of military service, that the military fees and other
possessions had fallen into the dead hands of the religious orders; not
understanding, perchance, that the army of the Amalekites was overthrown
rather by the prayers of Moses, than by the valour in combat of the children
of Israel.

A.D. 1285. . . . About the same time, the king, having convoked the
principal nobles of his land to meet him at Westminster, promulgated some
statutes, which are called the Second Statutes of Westminster; by some of
which he curtailed the jurisdiction of the ecclesiastical judges. And because
he had previously enacted a law that the members of the religious orders
should not add to their territorial possessions, he now chose to ordain that
they should not diminish what they had. Afterwards, at Winchester, about
the time of the festival of the Nativity of the blessed Mary, he caused some
statutes to be published, for the purpose of checking the truculent fury of
robbers and banditti.

A.D. 1294. Edward, king of England, held his parliament at Westminster,
after the feast of Pentecost, which was attended by John, king of Scotland,
and by all the nobles of England; and at this parliament were recited, in the
hearing of all those then present, the reasons for the commencement and

---

The Flowers of History (1853), pp. 469, 474, 481, 501, 504–5, 513, 561–2, translated by C. D.
Yonge.

continuance of this war, and the reports of the ambassadors; and also the promises which had been made of re-establishing peace in England. At which statement each of the ambassadors of the lord the king showed his hand in all good faith, to the utmost of his power. At last, every one agreed to recover Guienne by force of arms. Then the king of Scotland granted to the king of England, for three years, the revenues of all his estates, which belonged to him by hereditary right, in the kingdom of England, as a subsidy towards the recovery of Guienne, contenting himself with those of Scotland alone. And the other earls and nobles promised him aid from their resources. . . .

On the vigil of Saint Matthew the Apostle, all the clergy and laity having been assembled at Westminster, the king demanded of the whole church, throughout the whole kingdom of England, a moiety of all their possessions, both temporal and spiritual. But when this, which was a measure without a precedent in all ages, was heard of, the pontiffs and prelates were disturbed and alarmed, and groaning in anguish of spirit, not daring to offend or contradict the king, but consenting to the royal demands, they granted him a moiety of all their revenues which came in in one year. Which moiety, however, if they had thought more prudently and properly, and had not omitted to consult the Apostolic See, they would by no means have dared to grant to the king. Therefore, having arranged and appointed certain periods for this payment, they returned to their own homes. And the king lost no time; but as soon as the first instalments, according to the taxation of this previously taxed tithe, had been paid, he ordered the goods of the secular knights to be taxed, and a tenth to be paid to him throughout all England. And he levied a tax for the relief of his necessities on all merchants, and on all citizens dwelling in their walled cities and market towns, to the amount of the sixth penny of all that they possessed. It is also said that Master William de Montfort, dean of St. Paul's, in London, coming safe and sound to the court, in the hope of softening the disposition of the monarch, or, at all events, of lightening such an insupportable yoke of slavery, like a good son of the church, and coming before the king in order to deliver the speech which he had conceived in his mind, and which he had come to utter, became suddenly mute, and losing all the strength of his body, he fell down before the king and expired. But as the king passed over this event with indifferent eyes, and persisted the more vehemently in his demand, it was still uncertain how much every one was to pay to the king.

The consequence was, that different persons told different stories, varying from time to time; and so, after eating sour grapes, at last, when they were assembled in the refectory of the monks at Westminster, a knight, John Havering by name, rose up in the midst of them, and said, "My venerable men, this is the demand of the king—the annual moiety of the revenues of your churches. And if any one objects to this, let him rise up in the middle of this assembly, that his person may be recognised and taken note of, as he is guilty of treason against the king's peace." When they heard this, all the prelates were disturbed, and immediately agreed to the king's demands.

A.D. 1295. On the eve of the feast of Saint Andrew, the clergy, nobles, and laity having been summoned to Westminster, the king again requested that they would grant him a subsidy out of their substance, for the defence of the kingdom. And an eleventh was granted him from those who had paid a tenth the year before; and those who had paid a sixth that year, were now to contribute a seventh. Moreover, the archbishop of Canterbury having been indulged with permission to confer with his suffragans on this subject, with their unanimous consent offered the king a tenth of all ecclesiastical property; which having been offered, but not accepted, the bishops returned a second time to consider of this matter. Therefore, the king seeing their firmness, sent to them a great man, fifty years of age, namely, the chief justice of the king's bench, and his subordinate officers, who said, "O bishop, the king says, I neither accept, nor will I accept your offering, but descend speedily and fulfil his will, granting him at least a fourth part, or a third." But one Elias, the archbishop, did not descend with his clergy from their place; nor did the oxen who were supporting the ark of the covenant turn aside to the right hand or to the left. In the meantime, the king sent another man of fifty years of age, belonging to his chancery, and his subordinate officers, and they too made the same request that those who had been previously sent had made. But by all these measures the body of the clergy was not moved from their resolution, but as they had previously granted a tenth, they now repeated the offer. Therefore, the king seeing that his demand was beyond the ability of the clergy to grant, not wishing to afflict them, on the day after the feast of the Conception of the blessed Mary, he received their offering as if welcome. And the clergy received this as a good omen, and so Israel returned to their tents.

A.D. 1302. . . . The king of England then, being desirous that a good peace should be made in his days, sent ambassadors of high rank to the king of France about Easter, to give him notice by their means of the resolutions to which he had come respecting peace and war. And, having received for answer that such important affairs could not be satisfactorily discussed unless twelve peers were assembled with full powers, which was not practicable at that moment, as the peers were now occupied in various places on account of the unexpected emergencies of the new war, but that they might expect that it could be done in a fortnight. And after this period had elapsed, the mayors of France assembled and answered the English ambassadors that they were not inclined to give a definite answer on the above-mentioned subject, without the presence of the Scottish confederates. Having received this answer, the ambassadors returned to England.

On this, the king held his parliament at Westminster, on the first of July. And when they had had recounted to them the disappointing and evasive delays and procrastinating manoeuvres to which the ambassadors had been exposed, they determined to send the same persons back again, as news of the triumphant victory which the Flemings had gained over the

French, had arrived; and the ambassadors now received for answer that the king of England ought to come in his own person, and that then an agreement about peace might well be come to between the two kings, so that the powerful nobles and superiors of each kingdom might applaud it as advantageous to them, and the middle and lower classes might not be grieved at it. Therefore the king of England held his parliament at Westminster, on the feast of the Translation of Saint Edward the King, where this answer was recited, and gave great offence. But it was decided positively by the council of the whole kingdom that the king should remain in his own dominions, and he was not permitted to leave England at the command or suggestion of the king of France.

> *The great majority of entries in the Rolls of Parliament—the official record of parliamentary proceedings kept by the royal government—consists of petitions like those given here. (A petition could be presented on behalf of an individual, of a group, or of the whole community of the realm.)*

FROM *Rolls of Parliament*

COMMUNITY OF THE REALM, 1301

BILL OF THE PRELATES AND LORDS delivered to the lord King on behalf of the whole community at the Parliament of Lincoln in the year aforesaid:

. . . Thus, if it please our lord the King, the said community is of the opinion that the two Charters of Liberties and of the Forest should henceforth be completely observed in all particulars. [Answer] It expressly pleases the lord King.

And the statutes contrary to the said Charters should be annulled and voided. [Answer] It expressly pleases.

And the power of the justices assigned to keep the Charters in the counties should be defined by the counsel of the prelates, earls, and barons. [Answer] It tacitly pleases.

. . . And the offenses and trespasses committed by the King's ministers contrary to the tenor of the said Charters . . . should henceforth cease. [Answer] It expressly pleases.

B. D. Henning, A. S. Foord, and B. L. Mathias, *Crises in English History* (1949), pp. 54–5. Reprinted by permission of Holt, Rinehart and Winston, Inc.

THE POOR MEN OF ENGLAND, 1305

To the petition of the poor men of the land of England, asking the King to give redress in the matter of the men serving on inquests, juries, and assizes, who are so commonly corrupted by gifts from the rich that no truth can be known from them, etc.; and also asking redress in the matter of the ordinaries [ecclesiastical judicial officers] who, to the prejudice of the Crown, strive to take cognizance of pleas of debt, transgressions, and other matters pertaining to the Crown, etc., and who take fines and payments therefor at their own will, etc.:—

It is answered thus: To the first, let them bring suit against jurors for convicting them by writ of attaint, etc. To the second, let them search diligently through the writs of prohibition in cases in which prohibition plays a part.

COUNTY OF NORFOLK, 1290

The poor and middling men of the county of Norfolk, who are ruined by John of Brilond, prosecutor against them for the merchants of Lübeck, and who had been summoned to plead before the King in another Parliament, petition that the King assign judges to give them justice in the county, because the prosecution is so long drawn out and because they can not bring suit there [in Parliament] on account of their poverty.

[Answer] Let them bring their pleas before G. of Thornton and his fellow justices for the pleas of the crown, because they shall have no other judges.

COUNTY OF HERTFORD, 1290

The men of the county of Hertford beg that they may build a prison in the town of Hertford, from doing which William of Valence [Earl of Pembroke] hinders them, as it is said, to the King's loss and the county's vexation.

[Answer] The King granted it.

COUNTY OF CUMBERLAND, 1305

To the petition of the community of Cumberland, seeking redress for that when the lord King by his writ commanded the sheriff of the county to provide the King's larder against the King's arrival in Scotland in the twenty-second year of his reign, the sheriff on pretext of the order took from the community a certain number of oats, and though he had an appropriation for them in his account, he paid nothing to the community:—

It is answered thus: Let suit be brought at the Exchequer, and if the sheriff has received an appropriation but has not paid, let him be punished by the established penalty and let him pay. But if otherwise let the treasurer ordain what is proper.

BURGESSES OF NEWCASTLE, 1305

To the petition of the burgesses of Newcastle-on-Tyne, seeking redress because of the prior of Tynemouth holds a fair by the King's concession there on the feast of St. Oswin in the autumn, lasting for fifteen days, to the prejudice of said town and the burgesses thereof and to the disinheritance of the King, as they say; because ships loaded with divers wares (which were wont to come to the town of Newcastle, from which the King received the customs and dues and murages) now unload at Tynemouth, and the wares are there exposed for sale, since that place is nearer to the port of Tyne than is the town of Newcastle, which port indeed belongs to the King. Thus to the prior accrue the loading and unloading of wares at the port, and the sales of bread and wine and beer, to the prejudice of the King and the great loss of the merchants themselves. And in the nineteenth year of the reign of the present King in a suit brought before the King by the said burgesses, the prior lost thereof by way of consideration [a certain sum], etc.:—

It is answered thus: Let them have a writ from the Chancery to the effect that the two parties shall come together two weeks after Easter before the King, wherever he may be in England; and that the men of Newcastle and the prior of Tynemouth shall likewise have their charters of privilege with them; and that the men of Newcastle shall meanwhile bring suit to Gilbert of Roubiry that they may have the process and judgment which earlier was made before the King in his Parliament, etc.

MERCHANTS OF ENGLAND, 1290

The merchants of England sought £2000 damages from the Count of Flanders, by virtue of the convention made with the king at Mustrel, which damages they suffered by the seizure and detention in Flanders of their chattels valued at £10,000.

[Answer] The King can do nothing except to ask him [the Count] by a letter (which he granted) to satisfy them and cause them to be indemnified; because it is not recorded that any convention was made or discussed for paying damages, and because the Count can seek his damages from the English in the same way.

RELIGIOUS ORDERS, 1292

Concerning the men of religious orders and others who seek to have their charters confirmed by the lord King and who present petitions for this purpose:—

The King orders that they all go to the Exchequer before the treasurer and barons, and let them make an end of the matter. Let the treasurer do what seems fitting to accomplish this, etc.

HOSPITAL OF ST. KATHERINE, 1290

The brothers and sisters of the hospital of St. Katherine petition that the King grant them the fifty shillings which King Henry, father of the present lord King, gave them annually, which they received for the soul of Sanchia, formerly Queen of Germany, that they might maintain a chapel in the Tower of London where they celebrate [masses] for her soul; and the arrears of the same for ten years back.

[Answer] It is not found at the Exchequer that they received any of the said fifty shillings either in the time of King Henry or in the time of the present King, . . . and nothing is to be done in the matter.

COUNTESS OF CORNWALL, 1298

Touching the lands of the Countess of Cornwall, which were assigned to her for her sustenance by her lord, and from which she claims that she was ejected: it seemed to the council that the *Curia Regis* can not interfere in any arrangement made between the Countess and her husband the Earl.

POOR ALICE, 1302

Alice de la Chapele of the Isle of Guernsey begs the magnanimity, grace, and compassion of our lord the King: for that she has taken thirty-five sheaves of various kinds of grain from the sharecrop of our lord the King, which sheaves were of little value, . . . so she begs in charity and compassion that grace be granted her upon her oath that she took them because of her poverty and to nourish her child.

[Answer] Let her have grace. Let the bailiffs certify the King concerning the cause and manner [of the theft], and if they find it as stated, the King concedes that it be done as is petitioned.

> *The Rolls of Parliament also contain records of occasional statutory decrees. The preamble to the Statute of Westminster (1275) illustrates the manner of enactment at the beginning of Edward's reign.*

Preamble to Statute of Westminster

THESE ARE THE ACTS of king Edward, son of king Henry, made at Westminster at his first general parliament after his coronation, . . . by his

Bertie Wilkinson, *Constitutional History of Medieval England,* III (1958), 312. Reprinted by permission of Barnes & Noble, Inc., and Longmans, Green & Co. Ltd., Harlow.

council, and by the assent of archbishops, bishops, abbots, priors, earls, barons and the commonalty of the land there summoned. Because our lord the king had great zeal and desire to redress the state of the realm in such things as required amendment for the common profit of holy church and of the realm: and because the state of the holy church had been ill kept and the prelates and clergy of the land grieved in many ways, and the people treated otherwise than they ought to be, and the peace less kept than it ought and the laws misused and offenders less punished than they ought to be, by reason whereof the people feared less to offend; the king has ordained and established these underwritten acts, which he intends to be profitable and suitable for all the realm.

> *The Statute of Mortmain* (1279) *aimed to prevent feudal lands passing into the "dead hand" of the church.*

Statute of Mortmain

THE KING TO HIS JUSTICES of the bench, greeting. Whereas it was formerly enacted that men of religion should not enter upon the fiefs of any persons without the consent and licence of the principal lords from whom those fiefs were immediately held; and whereas since then men of religion have nevertheless entered upon the fiefs of others as well as their own—by appropriating them, buying them, and sometimes by receiving them through gifts of other men—whereby the services which are owed from fiefs of this sort, and which were originally established for the defence of the kingdom, are wrongfully withheld and the principal lords [are caused to] lose their escheats: [therefore] we, seeking in this connection to provide a suitable remedy for the good of the kingdom, by the counsel of the prelates, earls, and other faithful men of our kingdom who are members of our council, have enacted, established, and ordained that no man of religion or any other whatsoever shall buy or sell lands or tenements, or under colour of donation, lease, or other title of any sort shall receive them from any one, or presume artfully and craftily to appropriate them in any way whatsoever, whereby land and tenements of this sort may somehow come into mortmain—under pain of forfeiting the same [lands or tenements]. . . . And so we command you to have the aforesaid statute read in your presence and henceforth strictly held and observed.

Sources of English Constitutional History, pp. 169–70, edited and translated by Carl Stephenson and Frederick G. Marcham. Copyright 1937 by Harper & Brothers. Reprinted by permission of Harper & Row, Publishers.

By witness of the king, at Westminster, November 25, in the seventh year of our reign.

The Statute of Winchester (1285) was concerned mainly with police measures.

Statute of Winchester

WHEREAS EVERY DAY robbery, homicide, and arson are committed more frequently than used to be the case, and felonies escape presentment by the oaths of jurors who would see the felonies committed on strangers pass unpunished rather than accuse the offenders, many of whom are persons of the same country . . . : [therefore] our lord the king, in order to abate the power of felons, has established a penalty in such cases; so that henceforth, through fear of the penalty rather than of the oath, no one will be spared and no felony will be concealed. . . .

Accordingly, inquests shall be held when necessary in a vill by him who is lord of the vill, and afterwards in hundreds, franchises, and counties—sometimes in two, three, or four counties, in cases where felonies are committed on the borders of counties—so that the offenders may be brought to justice. And if the country will not answer for criminals in this way, the penalty shall be such that each country—that is to say, the people living in the country—shall be responsible for the robberies committed and the damages [thus incurred]. . . .

And for better assuring the peace, the king has commanded that in great towns which are walled the gates shall be closed from sunset to sunrise; and that no man shall be lodged in the suburbs, or in the outskirts of the town, except in the daytime—nor even in the daytime unless his host will be responsible for him. And the bailiffs of towns each week, or at least every fortnight, shall make investigation concerning men lodged in the suburbs or in the outskirts of the towns; and if they find anybody harbouring or otherwise lodging persons suspected of being in any respect violators of the peace, the bailiffs shall have justice done in the matter. And the king has commanded that henceforth all watches shall be kept according to the ancient custom. . . .

Furthermore, it is commanded that highways from one trading town to another shall be enlarged wherever there are woods, hedges, or ditches; so

Sources of English Constitutional History, pp. 173–4, edited and translated by Carl Stephenson and Frederick G. Marcham. Copyright 1937 by Harper & Brothers. Reprinted by permission of Harper & Row, Publishers.

that there shall be neither ditches, underbrush, nor bushes for two hundred feet on the one side and two hundred feet on the other, where men can hide near the road with evil intent; yet so that this statute shall not apply to oaks or to any great trees, so long as they are cleared underneath. . . .

Moreover, it is commanded that every man shall have in his house arms for keeping the peace according to the ancient assize. . . .

Given at Winchester, October 8, in the thirteenth year of the king's reign.

The Statute of Quia Emptores *eliminated abuses of subinfeudation by providing that, if a vassal alienated his fief, the new tenant was to be regarded as holding directly from the "principal lord" of the fief.*

Statute of Quia Emptores

WHEREAS THE BUYERS of lands and tenements belonging to the fiefs of magnates and other men have in times past frequently entered upon their fiefs to the prejudice of the same [lords], because the freeholders of the said magnates and other men have sold their lands and tenements to such purchasers to be held in fee by themselves and their heirs of the feoffors and not of the principal lords of the fiefs, whereby those same principal lords have often lost the escheats, marriages, and wardships of lands and tenements belonging to their fiefs; and whereas this has seemed very hard and burdensome to those magnates and other lords, being in such cases manifest disinheritance: [therefore] the lord king in his parliament at Westminster [held] after Easter in the eighteenth year of his reign . . . , at the suggestion of the magnates of his realm, has granted, provided, and established that henceforth every freeman shall be permitted to sell his land or tenement, or a part of it, at pleasure; yet so that the feoffee shall hold that land or tenement of the same principal lord [of whom the feoffor held] and by the same services and customs by which the feoffor earlier held. . . .

Sources of English Constitutional History, p. 174, edited and translated by Carl Stephenson and Frederick G. Marcham. Copyright 1937 by Harper & Brothers. Reprinted by permission of Harper & Row, Publishers.

The records of Edward I's reign contain many references to grants of taxes in Parliaments. The following letter was written during the Parliament of 1275.

The Earl of Pembroke's Letter

WILLIAM DE VALENCE, earl of Pembroke, to all faithful in Christ before whom the present writing may come, greeting in the Lord. Whereas the archbishops, bishops, and other prelates of the kingdom of England, as well as the earls and barons, and we and the communities of the said kingdom, at the suggestion and request of the merchants, have for a variety of reasons unanimously granted, for ourselves and our heirs, to the magnificent prince, our dearest lord Edward, by the grace of God illustrious king of England, half a mark for each sack of wool and half a mark for every three hundred wool-fells, which make a sack, and one mark for each last of hides exported from the kingdom of England and the land of Wales, to be henceforth collected in each port of England and Wales, both within liberties and without: . . . [therefore we grant the same for Ireland]. From which the said lord king and his heirs shall collect and keep the half-mark from wool and wool-fells and the mark from lasts of hides, in the manner aforesaid. . . . In testimony whereof we have set our seal to the present writing. Given in the general parliament of the lord king aforesaid, at Westminster, on Sunday, the feast of St. Dunstan the Bishop, in the third year of the reign of the same king.

The Rolls of Parliament record another grant in 1290.

FROM *Rolls of Parliament*

MEMORANDUM THAT in the full parliament of our lord the king held on the morrow of the Holy Trinity . . . Robert bishop of Bath and Wells . . . and the rest of the magnates and *proceres* [*nobles—B. T.*] then present in

Bertie Wilkinson, *Constitutional History of Medieval England,* III (1958), 321. Reprinted by permission of Barnes & Noble, Inc., and Longmans, Green & Co. Ltd., Harlow.

Bertie Wilkinson, *Constitutional History of Medieval England,* III (1958), 320–1. Reprinted by permission of Barnes & Noble, Inc., and Longmans, Green & Co. Ltd., Harlow.

parliament granted to the lord king, for themselves and for the community of the whole realm as far as they were competent, that the lord king should receive and have an aid for the marriage of his eldest daughter. It was to be an aid of the same kind and amount as king Henry his father obtained and received for his daughter, sister of the present king, when she married the king of Scots . . . [at the rate of 40 /—instead of about 2 marks] . . . on condition that this does not constitute a custom or precedent to their prejudice. . . .

In 1297 Edward was compelled to issue the following declaration concerning future taxation.

Confirmation of the Charters

EDWARD, BY THE GRACE OF GOD king of England, lord of Ireland, and duke of Aquitaine, to all who may see or hear these present letters, greeting. Know that, for the honour of God and of Holy Church and for the benefit of our entire kingdom, we have granted for ourselves and for our heirs that the Great Charter of Liberties and the Charter of the Forest, which were drawn up by the common assent of the whole kingdom in the time of King Henry, our father, are to be observed without impairment in all their particulars. . . .

And whereas some people of our kingdom are fearful that the aids and taxes which by their liberality and good will they have heretofore paid to us for the sake of our wars and other needs, shall, despite the nature of the grants, be turned into a servile obligation for them and their heirs because these (payments) may at a future time be found in the rolls, and likewise the prises that in our name have been taken throughout the kingdom by our ministers: (therefore) we have granted, for us and our heirs, that, on account of anything that has been done or that can be found from a roll in some other way, we will not make into a precedent for the future any such aids, taxes, or prises. And for us and our heirs we have also granted to the archbishops, bishops, abbots, priors and other folk of Holy Church, and to the earls and barons of the whole community of the land, that on no account will we henceforth take from our kingdom such aids, taxes and prises, except by the common assent of the whole kingdom and for the common benefit of the same kingdom, saving the ancient aids and prises due and accustomed.

Bertie Wilkinson, *Constitutional History of Medieval England,* I (1958), 226–8. Reprinted by permission of Barnes & Noble, Inc., and Longmans, Green & Co. Ltd., Harlow.

The manner of granting taxes at the end of Edward's reign is described in the following extract from the Rolls of Parliament (1306).

FROM *Rolls of Parliament*

MEMORANDUM THAT, after the lord king had recently ordered that Edward, his first-born son, should be decorated with the belt of knighthood at the feast of Pentecost in the thirty-fourth year of his reign, mandates were issued for the archbishops, bishops, abbots, priors, earls, barons, and other magnates to come before the lord king and his council at Westminster on the morrow of Holy Trinity next following, in order to deliberate and ordain with regard to giving the king an aid for the knighting aforesaid and in order to consent to those matters which should further be ordained in that connection, or for them then and there to send procurators or attorneys with sufficient instructions to carry out the aforesaid matters in their place; also each of the sheriffs of England was commanded to cause two knights from his county to come to the said place at the said time, and from each city of his bailiwick two citizens and from each borough of the same bailiwick two burgesses or one, etc., in order to deliberate, ordain, and consent as aforesaid. [Accordingly] there came in person before the king and his council at Westminster on that day . . . ; also through procurators and attorneys . . . ; and there came likewise two knights from each county of the same kingdom, two citizens from each city, and two burgesses from each borough, elected by the communities of the same counties, cities, and boroughs in the place of the same communities, to deliberate, ordain, and consent as aforesaid. And when all the aforesaid persons had assembled before the aforesaid council of the king, and it had been explained to them by the same council on behalf of the king that by right of the royal crown aid should be given the lord king on the occasion aforesaid, and besides that the lord king had incurred multifarious expenses and many other obligations toward suppressing the rebellion and malice of Robert Bruce, traitor to the same lord king, and of his adherents in the parts of Scotland, who were then presuming to make war against the king in those parts; the same prelates, earls, barons, and other magnates, as well as the knights of the shires, having discussed the matter with deliberation, and considering that aid was owed as aforesaid and that the king had incurred many obligations on account of the aforesaid war, at length unanimously granted to the lord king on behalf of themselves and the

Sources of English Constitutional History, pp. 167–9, edited and translated by Carl Stephenson and Frederick G. Marcham. Copyright 1937 by Harper & Brothers. Reprinted by permission of Harper & Row, Publishers.

whole community of the land a thirtieth of all their movable temporal goods which they should happen to possess on Michaelmas next following, to be taken as a competent aid to the lord king for the knighting of his aforesaid son and also as an aid toward the expenditures that should be made in connection with the aforesaid war. This grant, however, [was made] on condition that it should in no way be held to their own prejudice or to that of their successors or heirs in future times, and that it should never be taken as a precedent in a case of this kind; also that in assessing the aforesaid goods all should be excepted which had been excepted in assessing the fifteenth granted by the community of the kingdom to the lord king in the eighteenth year of his reign for exiling the Jews. Moreover, the citizens and burgesses of the cities and boroughs aforesaid and others of the king's demesnes, being assembled and holding a discussion on the said matters, in consideration of the obligations incurred by the lord king as aforesaid, unanimously granted the lord king for the reasons aforesaid the twentieth of their movable goods, to be taken as aforesaid.

The dismissal of March 21, 1305, to which Maitland referred, was recorded in these words.

Edward I's Dismissal of Parliament

THEN AFTER THE TWENTY-FIRST DAY of March was made a proclamation by the command of the King in these words:

"Archbishops, bishops, and other prelates, earls, barons, knights of the counties, citizens and burgesses and other men of the community, who have come here at the command of our lord the King to his Parliament:

"The King greatly thanks them for their coming and wills that for the present they return to their own lands, so that they be prepared to return quickly and without delay whenever they shall at another time be recalled; except for the bishops, earls and barons, justices, and others who are of the Council of our lord the King, who shall not depart without the special permission of the King. And those who have business to do, let them remain and pursue their business.

"And the knights who have come for the counties and the others who have come for the cities and boroughs, let them appear before Sir John of Kirkby [remembrancer of the Exchequer], and he will have writs issued to them for their expenses to be repaid in their own lands. And the said John of

B. D. Henning. A. S. Foord, and B. L. Mathias, *Crises in England History* (1949), p. 64. Reprinted by permission of Holt, Rinehart and Winston, Inc.

Kirkby, by virtue of the above proclamation, shall deliver to the chancellor the names of the knights who came for the counties and the names of the others who came for the cities and boroughs, and he shall proclaim that all those who desire writs for repayment of their expenses, as aforesaid, shall sue there for their writs."

4 King, Law, and Parliament

Maitland's emphasis on the judicial activity of Parliament was carried still further by C. H. McIlwain, who held that medieval parliaments were not truly legislative bodies at all. He argued that medieval men had no idea of legislation—of deliberate lawmaking—and that Parliament was simply the king's high court.

FROM The High Court of Parliament and Its Supremacy BY C. H. MCILWAIN

LEGISLATION IS DISTINGUISHED from other sources of law mainly by the fact of its "deriving its authority from an external body or person." Of law-making of this kind there was very little in mediaeval England. If we run through the various forms of law from the dooms of Ethelbert or Ine, through the charter of the Normans, the assize of the earlier Angevins, through those great transitional documents such as Magna Charta or the Provisions of Oxford, through the statutes of Edward I, the petitions of the Commons, and finally the bills deriving their authority from their enactment "by the King our Sovereign Lord, with the Assent of the Lords and Commons in Parliament assembled,"—if we pass all these stages in review, it seems that the last stage appears only in times that are almost modern, and also that even after it has appeared, the activity of the legislature is greatly restricted up to comparatively recent times. In mediaeval England legislation in its proper sense was all but unknown. Laws in feudal times are in the main declarations of existing customs; they are, as Professor Jenks says, "not enactments, but records." When on a feudal manor there was doubt as to the existence or character of a custom of the manor, the question was settled by an inquest,—the *enquête par tourbe*. There was no declaration of a new law by the lord or by the suitors; the suitors on oath simply declared what the existing custom of the manor was. Thus, to use Mr. Jenks's phrase, it was characteristic of all feudal law that it was "the law of a court." So in England, as in the rest of feudal Europe, not only the laws of the local feudal units, but the laws of the King as well, were the laws of a *court*. . . .

C. H. McIlwain, *The High Court of Parliament and Its Supremacy* (1910), pp. 42–3, 46–7, 51. Reprinted by permission of Yale University Press.

The idea of "making" law is alien to then existing modes of thought, and when changes occur, as they must, if consciously made, they are usually only the correction of defects in the machinery for administering the ancient customs, or they purport to be the restoration of these customs after a period of wrongful desuetude, or the abolishing of abuses that have contravened the ancient rules; or finally, if the changes cannot be brought conveniently under any of these, they are concealed under a fiction. Changes must inevitably occur in any system, and in a system of law and government which is developing as rapidly as was the case in mediaeval England, such changes must be great and fundamental. But the fact that these developments, great as they were, were so carefully covered up shows the attitude of men's minds towards "legislation." As Sidgwick says: "Law was to an important extent conceived by both governors and governed as a subject of science, capable of being learnt by special study, but not capable of being altered by the mere arbitrary will of government, any more than the principles or conclusions of mathematics." Legislation, in fact, "was not the primary business of Parliament." This is sufficiently evidenced by the small number of statutes that we find on the earlier rolls. . . .

To look at the Assemblies of Edward I, and before Edward I, with the expectation of finding "the Supremacy of a Legislative Assembly in Matters of Legislation," is surely to have a disappointing result. Too many things of that time must be described as "extraordinary," which from their frequency we should more truly call ordinary and normal. "We must read our history backwards as well as forwards," and by so doing the modern idea of legislation will almost disappear, Parliament will grow to seem, in so far as the growth of law is concerned, law-declaring rather than law-making. Edward I "created the most effective law-declaring machine in the Teutonic world of his day," but it cannot be described accurately as a "legislative Assembly."

T. F. T. Plucknett criticized the view of McIlwain as "a paradox brilliantly sustained." He pointed to the variability of medieval custom and maintained that medieval men recognized the possibility of changing it by deliberately innovative judicial decisions and by legislative action.

FROM *The Legislation of Edward I*

BY T. F. T. PLUCKNETT

THE STATUTES OF EDWARD I are by no means a unique phenomenon. Indeed, he might well have said that his age had a vocation for

T. F. T. Plucknett, *The Legislation of Edward I* (1949), pp. 2, 6–8. Reprinted by permission of The Clarendon Press, Oxford.

legislation. The Church naturally took the lead and set the pace. The great collection of Decretals published by Gregory IX in 1234 slightly preceded our own statute of Merton of 1236. A supplementary volume published by Gregory X in 1274 coincides with the opening of Edward I's legislative career, just as the publication of the *Sext* (which superseded Gregory X's volume) by Boniface VIII in 1298 marks its close. Nor was ecclesiastical legislation confined to the court of Rome. Canterbury legislated too. Stephen Langton made a notable effort in 1222, and aggressive sets of constitutions came from Boniface of Savoy in 1261, and from John Pecham on several occasions. The most impressive examples of ecclesiastical legislation in England during the thirteenth century came from the great pan-Anglican councils held by papal legates, particularly those held by Cardinal Otto in 1237 and by Cardinal Ottobon in 1267. The closeness of these dates with the dates of the statutes of Merton and Marlborough is notable, and Ottobon was, in fact, mentioned in the preamble as having been present at the making of the statute of Marlborough. Much the same sort of story comes from Aragon, Castile, Sicily, and to some extent, France. A great wave of legislative activity was sweeping over Europe; professional legal opinion welcomed it, and asked for more. . . .

It has been convenient to use the word "legislation," and we shall continue to do so, in its broadest and most general sense of a conscious and deliberate change in a legal rule, carried out by the competent authority. Such changes could be effected in a variety of ways, and it is necessary to observe that statutes are only one form of legislation. Much legal change was carried out by informal means, and it is well to bear this in mind lest the appearance of "statutes" should seem sudden and catastrophic, and create the impression that our law made a sudden leap into maturity during the reign of Edward I.

We naturally contrast statute law with common law, and legislation with custom, for the common law is indubitably the custom of the realm. Here we must beware of the modern conception of custom as immemorial and immutable. True and living custom was neither the one nor the other, as the middle ages well knew. How old must a usage be before it can be dignified with the name and acquire the legal validity of custom? There was much speculation. Thus the civilian Azo regards ten or twenty years' usage as a "long custom"; thirty years make a "very long," *longissima,* custom; forty years make it "age-old," *longaeva.* Canonists adopted much the same calculus of age, but with a strong preference for forty years as the qualifying age. Both civilians and canonists showed a marked hostility to custom, which accorded ill with their authoritarian principles.

If customs could come into existence so unceremoniously, then one might expect to find that they were, in fact, instruments for legal change rather than the fossilized remains of a remote past which modern legal theory has made them. Confirmation for this view comes from two different quarters. In the first place there is historical material of the sort collected in a very suggestive note by Julius Goebel in his remarkable study of *Felony and*

Misdemeanor. This material seems to show that in the dark ages virtual legislation might spread outwards from the great monasteries. Ancient charters had given them the right to their "customs"; and those customs were not confined to the regulation of the domestic and internal affairs of the community, but overflowed to the surrounding country-side which the monastery owned and governed. An examination of them shows that they contained novelties which we are bound to regard as virtually legislation. As Professor Goebel remarks, with trans-Atlantic tartness, "such a custom may have been a folkway, but it was the way of the folk in power." In the second place, not only did this sort of thing happen, but medieval theorists also knew that it happened. The civilians and canonists of the thirteenth and fourteenth centuries had a proper reverence for the ancient Digest, Code, and Institutes, but that did not prevent them from watching with keen interest the living law around them. Their observations of the contemporary scene convinced them that customs were born, and made, and changed.

*   *   *

It is easy to demonstrate, if demonstration be needed, that the common law of England is just such a custom, alive and vigorous, growing and changing. Both king and people desired amendments from time to time, and achieved them. The theorists were laying it down that custom derived its force from the consent of the prince *or* of the people, and this unresolved disjunctive is full of significance. Some customs may well have been genuine folkways, but we may properly allow a large place (as does Professor Goebel) to the folk in power. In short, we must recognize the possibility that much of the common law may be ultimately of legislative origin. . . .

> *It is interesting to compare the views of McIlwain and Plucknett with some thirteenth-century comments on law and lawmaking. The quotations that follow are from Henry Bracton, a royal judge under King Henry III (1216–1272), who wrote a famous treatise on the laws of England.*

FROM *On the Laws and Customs of England*
BY HENRY BRACTON

I T   W I L L   N O T   B E   A B S U R D to call the laws of England laws even though they are not written for whatever is justly defined and approved by the

T. Twiss, ed., *Henrici de Bracton De Legibus et Consuetudinibus Angliae, Rolls Series,* I (1878), 3, 6–8, 38; III (1880), 92.

counsel and consent of the magnates and the common agreement of the realm, with the authority of the prince or king preceding, that has the force of a law. There are also in England many customs which differ according to the diversity of places. . . .

These English laws and customs . . . since they have been approved by consent of those using them and confirmed by the oath of the king cannot be changed or destroyed without the common consent of all those by whose counsel and consent they were promulgated. They can be improved even without common consent, for what is altered for the better is not destroyed. But if any new and unwonted matters, not previously in use in the kingdom, shall arise then, if similar cases have arisen before, they shall be judged according to the similar case since this is a suitable occasion for proceeding from similar to similar. But if nothing of the kind has arisen before and judgement on such matters proves difficult and obscure then the judgements are to be set aside until the great court so that they may be decided there by the counsel of the court. . . .

The king has no equal in his kingdom for thus he would lose his power of command since an equal has no authority over an equal. Still less does he have a superior . . . The king should be under no man but under God and under the law since law makes the king. . . .

If a prince or king or anyone who has no superior except God (commits an injury) there is no remedy against him by assize; rather there is room only for a petition that he will amend and correct his act. If he does not do so it suffices for his punishment that he await the vengeance of God who says "Vengeance is mine and I will repay"—unless one might say that the community of the realm and his baronage can and should do this in the king's own court.

The following letter was written by Robert Grosseteste, Bishop of Lincoln, to one of the king's judges in 1236.

FROM *Bishop of Lincoln's Letter to a King's Judge*

. . . You INSINUATE that I have tried to change the laws of the realm by the witness of the Old Testament. But you will not find in the course of the letter which I have sent you a claim to do this, if you will read it through without prejudice. I try to persuade you by my letter to attempt to change the laws and customs which are contrary to the divine law and the church's

Bertie Wilkinson, *Constitutional History of Medieval England*, III (1958), 257. Reprinted by permission of Barnes & Noble, Inc., and Longmans, Green & Co. Ltd., Harlow.

decree—to persuade you, and also those with whom lies the power of changing and establishing laws who are won over by your effective persuasion. Nor have I suggested anywhere in the letter I have sent that you alone should be the maker of laws, or that you could do anything you wished at court; nor am I so simple as to believe any suggestion that laws can be made or changed by you or anyone else without the counsel of the ruler and of the magnates.

Fleta, *an anonymous book on English law written c. 1300, gives us the only actual definition of Parliament that has survived from the age of Edward I.*

FROM *Fleta*

THE KING HAS HIS COURT in his council in his parliaments, there being present his prelates, earls, barons, magnates and other skilled men; and there are terminated doubts concerning judgements, and new remedies are devised for new wrongs which have arisen, and justice is done to each one according to his deserts.

Fleta, II (1955), 109, translated by H. G. Richardson and G. O. Sayles. Reprinted by permission of Selden Society, London.

5   Representation Reconsidered

Although McIlwain's extreme formulation of the theory of "fundamental law" has been much criticized, his argument that Parliament was at first essentially a high court concerned with judicial business has found wide acceptance. G. O. Sayles, who has contributed greatly to our understanding of these matters by his editions of medieval records, called Parliament "a court placed above other courts." He summed up his views as follows.

FROM *The Medieval Foundation of England*
BY G. O. SAYLES

IT IS PROBABLE that England will be remembered *sub specie aeternitatis* for that experimentation in the art of government which ultimately produced the English parliament. Yet its history in the formative period of its growth is only now in process of being written. For its outline has been seriously distorted under the democratic and liberal bias of a modern age. The root cause of confusion has lain in the assumption that the history of parliament is identical with the history of popular representation, whereas it is the crux of the problem to understand why these two currents of development, once separate and separable, should have found their way eventually into a single channel. For at first they had little to do with one another: for example, between 1258 and 1300 some seventy parliaments were convoked, and only at nine of them were popular representatives summoned to be present, and we must accept the fact that during the thirteenth and early fourteenth centuries the presence of the commons was not regarded as essential to parliament, whose work was as effectively accomplished without them as with them.

G. O. Sayles, *The Medieval Foundation of England* (1948), pp. 448, 453–6. Reprinted by permission of Methuen & Co. Ltd., London.

What then is a parliament? When medieval men are permitted to supply their own answer, it is plain that all the emphasis is being placed upon the reform of administration and law and the dispensation of justice as the essential work of parliament, and that parliament was valued by the people at large because it provided a means of obtaining relief which for some reason or other could not be obtained elsewhere. The presence of the commons, the granting of taxes, the issue of legislation, are non-essentials: parliament can exist and do its work irrespective of them. If they are found associated with it, that arises from the convenience of the moment and not from any obligation, for they are found associated equally well with other types of assemblies, which made no formal provision for the righting of wrongs and which were not termed parliaments by contemporaries.

✻   ✻   ✻

The abundant records which exist for the reign of Edward I enable us to get a clear and detailed picture of parliament at that time. During the first half of his reign there was obviously a deliberate scheme for holding parliaments at Westminster twice a year, at Easter and at Michaelmas: thus eighteen parliaments were in session between 1275 and 1286. Between 1290 and 1307, when the king's time was greatly occupied with affairs in Scotland, Wales and Gascony, parliament had to meet when convenient opportunities arose, and it assembled on twenty-seven occasions. Since parliament was a court placed above other courts and devised to dispense the highest justice in the land, it was covered by the special peace which attached to all such institutions: the place in which it assembled was sacrosanct and no one must come there possessed of arms; those who attended must not be interfered with either in coming or departing, nor must their property or their household be molested during their absence; those responsible for the conduct of affairs, like councillors and clerks, were immune from the ordinary process of law for wrongdoing so long as parliament remained in session. Indeed, if we seek the origins of the parliamentary privileges of later times, like freedom of speech and freedom from arrest, it is in the peculiar sanctities, accruing to a court of law, that we must look for them.

We can classify the business of parliament under seven heads: (i) the discussion of affairs of state, more especially foreign affairs; (ii) legislation; (iii) taxation or supply; (iv) the audience of petitions; (v) judicial business, such as the determination of causes, criminal and civil; (vi) administrative matters of difficulty; (vii) feudal ceremonial, such as the taking of homage. Not all of these kinds of business were transacted at every parliament, and little of the time of parliament was taken up with politics—with debating state affairs or questions of supply or public grievances. The surviving parliament rolls of Edward I are in overwhelming measure occupied by entries about the hearing of large numbers of private petitions. Indeed, if we took out of these rolls all the passages relating to petitions and pleas and other legal processes, the remaining entries would be found to fill but a small space and to provide relatively little information. The history of parliament is not made up of great monuments of legislation or of dramatic political incidents: these have their place, but they take up little of parliament's time and are given little space upon its records. If the king so willed it, high politics could be, and very often were, transacted elsewhere than in parliament, and no one objected. What concerned the ordinary man was that his personal grievances and requests should receive attention, and to him it was parliament as the dispenser of the highest justice available to him that was most essential. For there was a general understanding that a petition, presented in parliament, should receive an answer before the session came to an end and, though this understanding was not always faithfully observed, a breach of it was resented. As for the subject-matter of parliamentary petitions, it fell into two broad categories: those which prayed for relief which the common law of the land did not for some reason or other afford, and those which solicited special favours not touching law at all, pure matters of grace.

The fact that parliament was an institution open to every man in the land inevitably determined the structure of the parliamentary machine. Parliament was an afforced council—that is to say, a council strengthened both in numbers and ability. But, sitting as a single body, it could not get through the vast amount of trivial business to be transacted, even if it had been proper to assemble so many important people in one place to do so much that was unimportant. So experiment after experiment was made to obtain workmanlike arrangements. The first business of the petitioners was with receivers of petitions, who performed a preliminary weeding-out and rejected such as need not have been brought to parliament. Those they accepted were then passed to a tribunal of auditors or triers, to whom the receivers acted as clerks. The auditors might deal with the matters out of hand: their directions would then be written briefly on the back of the petitions. But if they did not feel competent to give a final decision, the petition went to a yet higher tribunal, a body which was technically the council, though that might mean only a select number of its members. And there, if the subject-matter of the petition in some way affected the king's interests, it was reserved for the attention of persons who could act on the king's behalf and who perhaps received his personal instructions. Already by 1290 the tribunals of receivers and auditors were overburdened with work and had to be divided into panels so that one group of receivers and a corresponding group of auditors could concentrate on the English petitions, another on Irish petitions, and a third on Gascon petitions. In ascending scale, therefore, a petition might pass before four tribunals. The replies given were rarely final. There was no time during a parliamentary session for thorough investigations. But a favourable reply would secure a remedy or accelerate a decision in the appropriate court or government department. But this was not the end of refinements in organization. For, although the creation of special tribunals to deal with petitions relieved the council of much detailed work, although its time was carefully reserved for important matters, even then it was often found necessary to refer various items of council business, including litigation, to specially constituted committees. Only in this way could the work of parliament be dispatched. The occasions on which the full body of councillors met—ministers and magnates—were few and only for very solemn and formal business.

The men who arranged the business of each parliament and who composed its tribunals were mainly men in the service of the king: they were predominantly clerks, trained in the various branches of the king's administration, and justices employed on one of the benches or on eyre, though there were lesser barons and knights among them who were regularly employed by the king in positions of trust. It is rare to find barons, whose relationship to the king was essentially feudal and not ministerial, and whose appearance in parliament hinged upon their responsibility to do suit at the king's court, achieving anything of consequence save in quite unusual circumstances. And there are few signs of any activity on the part of popular representatives on the few occasions when they were summoned to be present. It is true that sometimes the assent of the magnates and the "community" was required to taxation or legislation, or their support was wisely solicited in the prosecution of foreign policy; that homage was rendered or royal marriages discussed or services in war rewarded in parliament: parliament has sprung in part, as we have seen, from a feudal court and may bear the guise of a feudal court from time to time. But the important element of parliament was the official element, and the important aspect of the business of parliament was the dispensation of justice and the expedition of matters of administration. Under Edward I parliament was an institution staffed by men trained in English and even Roman and canon law, men who were in every way professionally competent to cope with the kind of business which took up nearly the whole time of parliament. Their contribution was immeasurably greater than that of any other body of men represented there regularly or intermittently—barons, knights, or burgesses.

It may seem strange that so little has been said so far about the representatives of the shires and towns who figure so prominently in the usual discussions of the rise of parliament. In fact, under Henry III and Edward I their presence was rarely required. Though between 1258 and 1286 nearly fifty parliaments were convoked, the commons were summoned to less than half-a-dozen; between 1290 and 1310 they attended only thirteen out of thirty-four parliaments; between 1311 and 1327 seventeen out of nineteen parliaments; after 1327 they were invariably present at the forty-eight parliaments of Edward III's reign of fifty years. The tendency was evidently towards an increasingly regular attendance of the commons. Still, it is evident that parliaments, at which they were present, had no more authority than those from which they were absent.

*Stubbs himself understood of course that elected repre-
sentatives did not invariably attend the Parliaments of Edward I. He conceived of a baronial parliament that represented the nation imperfectly giving place step by step to a
broader assembly that represented it more nearly perfectly.
Bertie Wilkinson, who has been called a "neo-Stubbsian,"
has argued that this position is defensible if we give due
weight to other classes of source material beside the Rolls of
Parliament.*

FROM *Constitutional History of Medieval England*
BY BERTIE WILKINSON

THE CONSEQUENCES which flow from this fundamental divergence between the "schools" of Maitland and Stubbs extend to almost every problem
of the medieval parliament; from its origin to its composition, from its
relation to the monarch to its evolution into the High Court of the Realm.
One view tends to make parliament the instrument of the ruler; the other
makes it essentially a meeting between the king and the *universitas* [*community—B. T.*], serving the purpose of both. There are many concepts of
parliament which lie between these extremes. Some of these, for example,
reject the notion that parliament was essentially a court, but nevertheless
hold that it was a "conciliar" assembly. Sometimes it may be suspected that
such compromises entail the combination of incompatible elements; and it
seems probable that historians will have to make a choice between the two
main lines of interpretation which cannot be reconciled. According to one,
parliament was a political assembly; according to the other, it was a body
whose essence is to be found in the judicial functions which it exercised in
common with the council, and which expanded in due course into those of
the High Court of the Realm.

Of the sources which throw light on this problem, the most obvious are
the Rolls of Parliament. Unfortunately, they only begin in the reign of
Edward I. At that time, they consist almost exclusively of a record of judicial
proceedings—the unsystematic recordings of the activities of a court. The
haphazard arrangement and fragmentary character of the records appear,
not as something to be explained away, but rather as something to be

Bertie Wilkinson, *Constitutional History of Medieval England*, III (1958), 267–9, 274–6.
Reprinted by permission of Barnes & Noble, Inc., and Longmans, Green & Co. Ltd., Harlow.

expected from a body whose business mostly originated in written petitions to the king. Like the rolls of any court of law, those of parliament were at first merely a "putting together of odds and ends." Unfortunately it has not been possible to translate them below; for if we wished to give a true picture of their nature we should have to illustrate them at length. It must be emphasized, however, that no historian can properly deny their judicial nature: one reason for not translating them at length is that their nature is not in any way in doubt. It is only the conclusions which are to be drawn from them which are a matter of debate.

Despite the character of the early Rolls, it may still be doubted whether the activities they reflect provided the essential reason why parliament was summoned. Of course the different people who attended had different reasons for placing a high value upon it. Those who put forward petitions probably cherished their access to king and council; but petitions to the king could be made at any time, and did not need a session of parliament. Moreover, it seems likely that anybody, whether summoned to parliament or not, could petition the king during a parliamentary assembly. These facts seem to suggest that the judicial work which took place there, derived from petitions, was incidental. The main purpose for which "members" were summoned, and which was peculiar to them, was the weighty business of the realm and of foreign lands, referred to by Edward I in 1280. Finally, and this is of great importance, we know that in the early parliaments much political business was transacted which was never, or very rarely, recorded on the rolls of the parliaments of Edward I. The parliament of Edward I was becoming an institution with an entity and traditions of its own; but it had not developed so far as to have a record of its "corporate" activities, distinct from those of the king and council who acted in the assembly of parliament or who acted, as *Fleta* put it, in the presence of the magnates. It was the king and council in parliament who judged and heard petitions in the age of *Fleta*, not the High Court of Parliament.

Two other major sources of our knowledge of parliament before the death of Edward I are the chronicles, which contain frequent and important references to particular assemblies, and the writs of summons . . . which often indicate briefly the purpose for which individuals or representatives were commanded to attend. The former were no doubt inconsistent and lacking in precision in their references to parliament; and the latter probably tended to become conventional; but together they represent a formidable body of evidence. They tell us what purpose was seen in the actual assemblies by the educated opinion of the age, and also what the king and his ministers proclaimed to be the purpose of the parliamentary assembly. Matthew Paris in particular wrote in great detail and with a sensitive ear for significant formulae, and he has left a fine memorial to some of the great public assemblies which occurred between 1232 and 1258.

The first conclusion suggested by these documents is that the general concern of the early parliaments was with what we may call politics. The second is that the general assemblies which were summoned after 1242 were as much genuine parliaments as those which were later summoned by Edward I. The third, which will, indeed, only become fully apparent at a later stage, is that there was no real break in the early development of the parliamentary assembly. It follows from all this that parliament was already well established, and its problems were already very familiar, long before the end of the thirteenth century. The fourth and final conclusion is that there was a deep distinction between the council and parliament. In particular, the two bodies were summoned for different purposes, or at least in a different relationship to the king.

*   *   *

According to the thesis which he [*Maitland—B. T.*] propounded in 1893, everybody except the members of the council was dismissed from the assembly of 1305; the dismissal took place on 21 March, but nevertheless transactions were recorded after this date as taking place in "full" parliament. The only possible conclusion, Maitland suggested cautiously, from such official testimony was that parliament and council were in essence the same. Those members outside the council who were dismissed in 1305 may have added to the solemnity of the assembly but did not contribute anything that was essential to its full existence. Maitland himself made more reservations in drawing out the consequences of his discovery than has generally been recognized. He actually claimed that he did not depart far, in his conclusions, from accepted views; and it is probably unwise to sweep this assertion aside as meiosis. Nevertheless, the fact remains that his telling juxtaposition of the dismissal of 21 March and subsequent transaction in full assembly, with its far-reaching implications, has hardly ever been subjected to a critical examination; his conclusions were fully supported by Gaillard Lapsley on the only occasion when they were squarely brought into question; and they make it almost impossible to escape from one all-important logical consequence. This is the ultimate identity of parliament and council which has provided a basis for by far the greater part of modern research into the nature of the parliamentary assembly. Maitland's argument still stands athwart all efforts to exploit the good elements in the great Stubbsian tradition. It is true that one penetrating modern analysis of the medieval parliament at work contained the observation that Maitland had come very close to paradox; but even this judgement, weighty though it is, does not dispose of the stubborn fact of evidence which seems to drive historians inexorably only to one end.

Yet this apparently decisive evidence has all along had an element of ambiguity which should at least have served to warn historians against pressing very far any conclusions they derived from it. It is true that everybody was dismissed in 1305 except "the bishops and earls and barons and others who are of the council"; but it has not been (and may never be) placed beyond all doubt who these magnates and others of the council really were. In a crucial passage of this kind it is most dangerous to argue that there is a plain meaning of the words. It is, indeed, a good canon of historical writing to prefer the simplest interpretation of any passage, other things being equal; but the question of simplicity is hardly relevant in this case. It may be said at once that there is no plain meaning of these particular words; nor has an examination of the contemporary usage provided clear guidance as to their interpretation. Far from there being one plain meaning, there are two clear alternatives; either the king retained the council alone (including magnates) or he retained his magnates and his council; and the only guidance which has so far been produced from contemporary sources suggests that the second alternative is very slightly preferable to the former. Certainly we should not characterize a preference for this as a straining of the text. If it is, indeed, the better reading, the case for Maitland's view that the king's council was the core and essence of every *parliamentum,* and that the highest tribunal in England was not a general assembly of barons and prelates, but the king's council, seems to be greatly weakened, if not entirely destroyed.

> *A major problem in treating Parliament simply as a court is to explain why elected commons were ever summoned to it at all. The king had no obvious interest in stimulating floods of petitions from his people. Wilkinson put forward this objection vigorously.*

FROM *Studies in Constitutional History*
BY BERTIE WILKINSON

THE KING NEVER SUMMONED (representatives) especially to hear their petitions . . . it was the business of the subject to approach the monarch for this purpose, not the monarch to summon the subject; and it seems probable that the king was accessible to petitioners outside the meetings of parliament, as well as within. The growing custom of using the meetings of parliament to approach the king for remedies was, indeed, clearly unwelcome to Edward I. "Because the folk who come to the king's parliament are delayed and disturbed to their great grievance and that of the court by the multitude of petitions that are brought before the king, many of which can be considered by the chancellor or by the justices," the king said in 1280, "it is

Bertie Wilkinson, *Studies in Constitutional History* (1937), pp. 21–3. Reprinted by permission of Manchester University Press, Manchester.

provided that all petitions which concern the seal shall come first to the chancellor, and those which concern the exchequer shall come to the exchequer . . ."

Edward I wrote of parliament as essentially a place for the discussion of matters of state, not as a court in the modern sense. "It is the custom of the realm of England," he wrote, "that in all things touching the state of the same realm there should be asked the counsel of all whom the matter concerns." He had caused the question of Peter's Pence to be reserved for deliberation in parliament, he told the Pope in 1275; but though he there ordained many things for the amelioration of the state of the church and the realm, before he was able to conclude the parliament, by reason of the multitude of matters needing reformation, he fell ill and was unable to deal with that matter; he cannot answer now because he is bound by his oath not to do anything touching the crown of the realm, without the counsel of the *proceres* [*nobles—B. T.*]. Judicial matters were, as we have seen, regarded in 1280 as an impediment to such necessary debates. In his summonses to parliament he repeatedly showed that to him, at any rate, the main business of parliament was not judicial, whatever it was to his subjects, who unfortunately are inarticulate on the point: the mere fact that they presented petitions in parliament in no wise proving that they went to parliament primarily for that purpose. There is less tendency now than there was, perhaps, to minimise the importance of that famous tag of Edward's chancery—"quod omnes tangit ab omnibus approbetur, sic et nimis evidenter ut communibus periculis per remedia provisa communiter obvietur" [*"as what touches all should be approved by all, so also, very evidently, common dangers should be met by remedies provided in common"—B. T.*]; and it suggests the same conception of the business of the assembly. In summoning the clergy to the parliament of November 3rd 1296, the king said that in their last assembly at Westminster they had promised a subsidy unless peace should be achieved between England and France; he therefore summoned them to fix the amount of the subsidy. On another occasion parliament was summoned "Propter quedam specialia et ardua negocia nos et statum regni nostri tangencia que noviter emerserunt, et que sine vestra presencia nolumus expediri" [*"On account of certain special and arduous affairs touching us and the state of our realm that we are not willing to handle without your presence"—B. T.*]; in 1308 the king wrote, "Quia diversa negocia nos et statum regni tangencia super quibus vobiscum . . . in parliamento nostro . . . tractare incepimus, propter aliquod impedimentum interveniens quod benedicto Altissimo modo cessat, adhuc remanent pertractanda. . . ." [*"Because various matters touching us and the state of our realm which we had begun to treat . . . in our parliament . . . still remain to be treated on account of an impediment which, through God's blessing, has now ceased to exist. . . ."—B. T.*] Judicial activities were increasing greatly under Edward I; but we cannot say that there is evidence, even in *Fleta*, that the essence of a parliament was considered to be that of a court of law. The political and legislative functions of the assembly still seem to have been considered the essential ones.

> *Wilkinson also urged that the ideas and ideals of medieval men be taken into account by modern historians of Parliament.*

FROM *English Politics and Politicians of the Thirteenth and Fourteenth Centuries*

BY BERTIE WILKINSON

ON TWO FINAL POINTS I would confess myself his [*Stubbs'*—B. T.] disciple and claim support from his wisdom. The first is the importance, in thirteenth- and fourteenth-century politics, of ideas and ideals. I have ventured to go further than Stubbs did in this direction, but the difference is only a matter of degree. I have seen a greater challenge to contemporaries presented by the politics of the period, but assumed the same qualities of human nature in the reply. I would react strongly, as I believe Stubbs did, against the stern and uncompromising realism of a Horace Walpole who believed that "the probability is both kings and nobles wished to encroach on each other; and if any sparks of liberty were struck out, in all likelihood it was contrary to the intention of either the flint or the steel." How far reaction against such "realism" should go is a matter of opinion. Sir Lewis Namier recently reminded us how Graham Wallas wished that his contemporaries would preface their treatises on political science by a definition of their views on human nature, and possibly there is something in this idea for historians as well. We should certainly find deep differences of opinion on this point underlying some of our conflicting interpretations; but perhaps we should also find that we were not as sure about our differences as was the generation of Graham Wallas, and that there is a greater, not a less, disposition to accept the importance of intellectual processes and the compelling force of ideals.

The second point on which there is complete agreement with Stubbs has already been referred to in the quotation given at the outset of this paper. It is the importance to our generation, and in particular to the historians, of the theme of political liberty. The recognition of this importance is indeed common, if I may venture to associate two somewhat dissimilar writers, to

Bertie Wilkinson, "English Politics and Politicians of the Thirteenth and Fourteenth Centuries," *Speculum*, XXX (1955), 48. Reprinted by permission of The Mediaeval Academy of America.

both Mr. Taylor and Bishop Stubbs. Though the theme is as old as history itself, it should have a special appeal to those who have lived through the early years of the twentieth century. We cannot afford by neglecting it to impoverish our subject. It seems undeniable that interest in it has declined, at least as far as the writing of history is concerned, since the heady days when Stubbs talked hearteningly of the cry of liberty being first heard in the North. In this respect, once again, we have probably done an injustice to both the politics and politicians of the thirteenth and fourteenth centuries. There is a case for believing that both were profoundly influenced by the problem of liberty, even if it was then formulated in terms very different from our own. In the sense of an undying hostility to absolute power, the defense of liberty everywhere is, and always has been, the same.

> *Carl Stephenson thought that the presence of commons in Edward's Parliaments was adequately accounted for by the king's need to raise taxes from them.*

FROM *Medieval Institutions* BY CARL STEPHENSON

WHY A KING LIKE EDWARD I should have insisted on these assemblies merely to facilitate the presentation of petitions I cannot understand. But I can understand how the bringing of petitions in parliament would be encouraged by the constant election of burgesses and knights of the shires for other purposes. The principal purpose, I am convinced, was to obtain money —a conclusion that agrees with the known character of the king and the social and economic changes of the age.

The euphemistic language of the royal writs should not mislead us. In 1241 Henry III called at Worcester an assembly of the wealthier Jews from all his boroughs "ad tractandum nobiscum tam de nostra quam sua utilitate" [*to treat with us concerning our advantage and theirs—B. T.*]. But the matter of mutual advantage of which they were to treat was actually a tallage of 20,000 marks. When Edward I notified his good men of various towns that he had commissioned John of Kirkby to explain to them and expedite through them "certain arduous and especial concerns" of his, no one could have been surprised to discover that he was negotiating for a subsidy. And contemporaries were as little mystified when parliamentary representatives were summoned to consider those other "difficult and momentous affairs" to which the writs constantly refer. They knew that they would be fortunate to escape further demands for taxes. . . . On re-examining the

Carl Stephenson, *Medieval Institutions*, pp. 136–8. Copyright 1954 Cornell University. Used by permission of Cornell University Press.

records of his [*Edward's—B. T.*] sixteen parliaments that included deputations of the commons, Miss M. V. Clarke has found only three in which no question of a grant was apparently raised. . . .

Accordingly, if the view here expressed is justified, the core of the English representative system has not been a vague sympathy on the part of self-appointed spokesmen, a primitive custom of deeming dooms in the name of the people, or even the selection of jurors for a sort of national inquest. Rather it has been a matter of sheer political necessity, occasioned on the one hand by the king's lack of money and on the other by the growing strength of the social groups who could supply it. Although the king might use communal delegates in a variety of ways, the compelling motive behind their incorporation as an estate of parliament was economic. Without the recurring need for general taxation, there would, I believe, have been no house of commons.

> *As Stephenson noted, M. V. Clarke called attention to taxation as an immediate motive for Edward's summoning of representatives to Parliament. But she did not regard that as the whole story. In many civilizations, kings have had to collect taxes and dispense justice and "treat" about political matters. Only in the medieval West did they respond to these needs by creating representative assemblies. Miss Clarke could find no adequate precedents in the ancient world for such representative institutions. Furthermore, by the 1930s, theories of innate Teutonic virtue as sufficient explanation for the rise of medieval constitutionalism were becoming highly unfashionable. Miss Clarke herself thought that the councils of the Christian Church provided an indispensable link in the evolution of representative government.*

FROM *Medieval Representation and Consent*
BY M. V. CLARKE

THE IDEA OF REPRESENTATION in the widest sense is probably as old as the first primitive community which was aware of itself as a whole. In

M. V. Clarke, *Medieval Representation and Consent* (1936), pp. 278–80, 294–6. Reprinted by permission of Sir Charles Morris.

its earliest application it appears in close association with religion, as part of the ritual of primitive worship. In more sophisticated societies its value for legal purposes was slowly recognised. Out of uses so different, the religious and the legal, its political importance was at last developed. To understand how this came about we may begin by a summary discussion of its rudimentary forms in primitive society and also its use by the Greeks and Romans. Fuller consideration must be given to its medieval development, both in secular affairs and within the Catholic Church.

The earliest sign of the representative principle may be found when, for a religious purpose, some creature or object is deemed to be the symbol or agent of hidden or unearthly power. In primitive society, as Frazer has shown in *The Golden Bough,* the king or chief stood half-way between his people and the unseen world, typifying or representing both humanity and divinity. His office carried with it responsibility for the weather and the fertility of the soil and in times of drought or other calamity he might even be offered up as a vicarious sacrifice for his subjects. . . . No doubt as civilisation advanced, the personification became less concrete and more symbolic, but from the first the general idea of representation, or substitution of the part for the whole, was constantly present. As the idea itself was familiar, its extension from religious to secular life was bound to occur.

The Greek city state was too compact for the idea of political representation to grow up easily; every citizen was able to attend in person political discussions in the public assembly. In Greek law, however, the representative idea found expression. Vinogradoff has collected a number of examples showing how the city could be represented by a group of prominent citizens. This was done in making treaties and in raising loans for public purposes, but there were no permanent officials or groups who were empowered to act regularly for the city as a whole. Representation was not so much a principle as a temporary administrative convenience. The nearest that the Greeks came to its true political use was probably the Council of Five Hundred in Athens. Its members were chosen by lot out of the whole body of citizens and certain administrative functions were delegated to them. Sometimes political trials, in form resembling the English bill of attainder, were conducted before the Five Hundred, which for a time was vested with full powers of punishment. These powers, however, were afterwards resumed by the people and it was enacted that no Athenian citizen could be sentenced to death, imprisonment, or confiscation without a direct, popular decision. The resumption of power is significant of a failure to recognise or understand the principle of representation.

The great territorial expansion of Rome did not make representation (in the ordinary political sense of the term) an element of the Roman Constitution. There was no such pressure on the Roman governing class as to induce it to replace the popular assemblies and the Senate of the old Roman city-state by a body or bodies of elected representatives from different parts of Roman territory. There were disadvantages for that class in the city-state form of constitution, but there would have been other disadvantages for it in a representative system, besides the initial trouble and difficulty of making such a radical change in the political structure of the community.

The first Christian assembly, convoked for purposes of debate and decision, is described in the Acts of the Apostles, when disputes over the Mosaic law led to a meeting of the Apostles, elders and brethren in Jerusalem. After "much questioning," an unanimous decision was reached and despatched to the churches in Antioch, Syria and Cilicia. This decision may be described as the earliest legislation of the Church. In the first three centuries of the Christian era diocesan and provincial assemblies met fairly often; they seem to have been attended mainly by bishops, who represented their dioceses by reason of their sacred office. They were first described as *concilia* by Tertullian (*fl.* 200); he may have had heathen provincial councils in mind when he wrote "at councils of all the churches high matters are treated in common (*in commune*) and this representation of the whole Christian world is solemnised with great veneration." It can hardly be accidental that the word *concilia* first appears in close association with *representatio*. No elaborate organisation was possible during the centuries of persecution, but the conversion of the Emperor Constantine was soon followed by the summons of the first General Council at Nicea (325). It is unknown whether the idea came from the Emperor or from the Church; the question is of minor importance, as general councils were the logical consequence of the conception of the Church as one and indivisible. The representative character of this first oecumenical Council has never been questioned; over 200 bishops were present, drawn from the whole Christian world. Its chief work was the condemnation of Arius, the insertion of *Homoousios* ("of one substance with the Father") into the creed since called Nicene and the issue of a series of laws, which are the beginning of the canon law of the Church. Thus the Council of Nicea was a representative assembly which exercised both judicial and legislative functions; these powers were maintained in succeeding assemblies.

*   *   *

The first Lateran Council of 1123 was the ninth General Council, and the first to meet since the Council of Constantinople (869). Its sessions mark the beginning of the second great age of councils, falling between 1123 and 1274. Within that period six General Councils were held: the four Lateran Councils of 1123, 1139, 1179 and 1215, and the two Councils of Lyons, 1245 and 1274; they amount to almost a third of the total number (19) held between Nicea (325) and Trent (1548). It is significant that this revival of the General Council should coincide in time with the rise of national legislative assemblies. The three General Councils of the twelfth century were chiefly concerned with particular issues; though important decrees were issued by each, the main attention of members was directed to policy and administration. At the fourth Lateran Council (1215) the emphasis was reversed. It was summoned by Innocent III, when the Papacy was at the height of its power, for the express purpose of reform. In Innocent's own words, it was called "to extirpate vices and implant virtues, to correct excesses and reform manners, to eliminate heresies and strengthen faith, to allay discords and establish peace, to end oppressions and to increase liberty." To fulfil this vast design, the council was summoned in 1213, two and a half years before the time of session, and attendance was enjoined as a solemn obligation. Not only archbishops and bishops, but abbots and priors and all the monarchs of western Christendom were cited to appear. No such gathering had met in Europe since the great councils of the age of the Fathers; 412 archbishops and bishops and over 800 abbots and priors were present, and many others were represented by proctors. The proctor representing an individual was not an innovation, but there were also proctors representing the chapters of cathedral churches. Innocent had commanded each bishop to see that every chapter in his diocese sent the provost, dean or other suitable men to act for the whole body; he gave as a reason for this new departure that business relating to chapters would be brought before the council. It was part of his scheme of reform to compel the chapters to allot one prebend for the support of a schoolmaster and, in commanding the attendance of their representatives, he was acting on the principle already expressed in his canons—*quod omnes tangit, ab omnibus approbetur* [*what touches all should be approved by all—B. T.*].

The Fourth Lateran Council put the representative principle into action on a scale and with a prestige which made it known throughout the whole of western Europe.

The papal bull that summoned the Fourth Lateran Council of 1215 is given here.

Papal Summons to the Fourth Lateran Council, 1215

T o   t h e   a r c h b i s h o p , bishops, abbots and priors of the province of Vienne:

Many kinds of beasts strive to ruin the vineyard of the Lord and their attacks have so prevailed that in no small part of it thorns have grown up in place of vines. Furthermore—we state it with grief—the vines themselves, infected and corrupted in many ways, may bring forth bad fruit. We therefore invoke the witness of Him who is a faithful witness in Heaven that among all the desires of our heart there are two that we principally wish for

J. P. Migne, *Patrologia Latina*, CCXVI (1891), Columns 823–5, translated by Brian Tierney.

in this world, that we may be able to bring about the recovery of the Holy Land and the reform of the universal church. . . . Accordingly, having held diligent and frequent consultations with our brothers and other prudent men, as the responsibility of such a great undertaking demanded, we have finally decided with their counsel that, in order to achieve these things and because they concern the common state of all the faithful, we shall convoke a general council to be celebrated solely for the profit of souls at an opportune time according to the ancient custom of the holy Fathers; in which council, to extirpate vice and implant virtues, to correct excesses and reform morals, to eliminate heresies and strengthen the faith . . . there may be established, to be inviolably observed by prelates and subjects both regular and secular, whatsoever shall be seen by the approval of the council to be expedient for the praise and glory of His name who is the healer and savior of our souls and for the profit and advantage of the Christian people. . . .

Believing then that this healthful intention comes from Him from Whom is every good gift and every perfect gift, we command you all by these apostolic letters to so prepare that in two and a half years from this twelve hundred and thirteenth year from the Incarnation of our Lord you may present yourselves in our sight. . . . Furthermore, O brother archbishops and bishops, you shall charge all chapters of churches, not only cathedral churches but others as well, to send provosts or deans or other suitable men to the council on their behalf, since various matters that especially concern the chapters of churches are to be treated in it. . . . No one shall plead as an excuse difficulties of the journey or obstacles of strife, which for the most part is beginning to cease (a good sign from God). The greater the dangers that threaten the stronger the remedies that should be applied. No one ever sailed through calm waters who always waited for the sea to stop throwing up waves.

[*Similar letters were sent to prelates throughout Europe—B. T.*]

> *By way of comparison, the following writs show how members were summoned to the Parliaments of Edward I.*

Writs of Summons to Parliament

TO AN ARCHBISHOP, 1295

THE KING TO THE VENERABLE FATHER in Christ Robert, by the same grace Archbishop of Canterbury, Primate of all England, greeting. As

B. D. Henning, A. S. Foord, and B. L. Mathias, *Crises in English History* (1949), pp. 54–5. Reprinted by permission of Holt, Rinehart and Winston, Inc.

a most just law, established by the careful providence of sacred princes, exhorts and decrees that what affects all, by all should be approved, so also, very evidently should common danger be met by means provided in common. You know sufficiently well, and it is now as we believe, divulged through all regions of the world, how the King of France fraudulently and craftily deprives us of our land of Gascony by withholding it unjustly from us. Now, however, not satisfied with the before-mentioned fraud and injustice, having gathered together for the conquest of our kingdom a very great fleet, and an abounding multitude of warriors, with which he has made a hostile attack on our kingdom and the inhabitants of the same kingdom, he now proposes to destroy the English language altogether from the earth if his power should correspond to the detestable proposition of the contemplated injustice, which God forbid.

Because, therefore, darts seen beforehand do less injury, and your interest especially, as that of other fellow citizens of the same realm, is concerned in this affair, we command you, strictly enjoining you in the fidelity and love in which you are bound to us, that on the Lord's Day next after the feast of St. Martin [Nov. 11], in the approaching winter, you be present in person at Westminster; citing beforehand the dean and chapter of your church, the archdeacons and all the clergy of your diocese, causing the same dean and archdeacons in their own persons, and the said chapter by one suitable proctor, and the said clergy by two, to be present along with you, having full and sufficient power of themselves from the chapter and clergy, for considering, ordaining, and providing along with us and with the rest of the prelates and principal men and other inhabitants of our kingdom how the dangers and threatened evils of this kind are to be met.

Witness the King at Wangham, the thirtieth day of September.

[Identical summons were sent out to the two archbishops and eighteen bishops, and, with the omission of the last paragraph, to seventy abbots.]

TO AN EARL, 1295

The King to his beloved and faithful relative, Edmund, Earl of Cornwall, greeting. Because we wish to have a consultation and meeting with you and with the rest of the principal men of our kingdom, as to provision for remedies against the dangers which in these days are threatening our whole kingdom; we command you, strictly enjoining you in the fidelity and love in which you are bound to us, that on the Lord's Day next after the feast of St. Martin, in the approaching winter, you be present in person at Westminster, for considering, ordaining, and doing along with us and with the prelates, and the rest of the principal men and other inhabitants of our kingdom, as may be necessary for meeting dangers of this kind.

Witness the King at Canterbury, the first of October.

[Similar summons were sent to seven earls and forty-one barons.]

TO A SHERIFF, 1295

The King to the sheriff of Northamptonshire. Since we intend to have a consultation and meeting with the earls, barons, and other principal men of our kingdom with regard to providing remedies against the dangers which are in these days threatening the same kingdom; and on that account have commanded them to be with us on the Lord's Day next after the feast of St. Martin in the approaching winter, at Westminster, to consider, ordain, and do as may be necessary for the avoidance of these dangers; we strictly require you to cause two knights from the aforesaid county, two citizens from each city in the same county, and two burgesses from each borough, of those who are especially discreet and capable of laboring, to be elected without delay, and to cause them to come to us at the aforesaid time and place.

Moreover, the said knights are to have full and sufficient power for themselves and for the community of the aforesaid county, and the said citizens and burgesses for themselves and the community of the aforesaid cities and boroughs separately, then and there for doing what shall be ordained by the common council in the premises; so that the aforesaid business shall not remain unfinished in any way for defect of this power. And you shall have there the names of the knights, citizens, and burgesses and this writ.

Witness the King at Canterbury on the third day of October.

[Identical summons were sent to every sheriff.]

TO A ROYAL OFFICIAL, 1299

The King, to his faithful and beloved Philip of Willoughby. Chancellor of his Exchequer, greeting.

Since, for the safety of our Crown and the common advantage of the people of our realm, we wish to hold a Parliament at London on the second Sunday of Lent and to have a consultation and meeting with you and the rest of our council upon matters especially touching us and our kingdom; we command you, strictly enjoining you in the fidelity and love in which you are bound to us, that you be personally present at the said time and place to consult with us and the rest of our council and to give your advice. And under no circumstances fail to do this.

Witness the King at Berwick-on-Tweed, the twenty-ninth day of December.

[Similar summons went to thirty-seven others.]

TO A ROYAL JUSTICE, 1300

The King to his beloved and faithful Walter of Gloucester, greetings.

Since, for the common benefit of the people of our realm, we have recently granted that the Charter of the Forest be strictly observed in all its articles, by assigning you and others of our faithful men in every county of the realm in which our forests exist to make a perambulation of these forests:

And so that this perambulation, clearly and carefully made, may be reported to us before any action be taken thereon, and so that our oath, the rights of the English Crown, and our claims and accounts may be kept safe as well as the claims and accounts of all others:

We now for the first time permit you and our other faithful men to report to us what you have done in this matter. . . .

And since . . . we wish to have a consultation and meeting with the prelates, earls, barons, magnates, and other men of the community of the realm concerning both this matter and certain other arduous matters touching us and our realm:

We strictly enjoin and command you to be with us and the prelates and magnates aforesaid at our Parliament [at Lincoln] in the octave of St. Hilary next [Jan. 20, 1301], to discuss these matters with them and give your advice; bringing with you all the perambulations of the forests which we have caused to be made by you and your agents assigned to this purpose in the various counties of our kingdom and all other things pertaining to the perambulations. And under no circumstance fail to do this.

Witness the King at La Rose, the twenty-ninth day of September.

[Similar writs were sent to seventeen others.]

Renaissance Man—
Medieval or Modern?

CONTENTS

QUESTIONS FOR STUDY

1   *What characteristics of the Renaissance have been regarded as distinctively "modern"? Do you agree that these characteristics are in fact typical of the modern world?*

In *its* *simplest* *literal* *meaning* *the* *term* *Renaissance refers to a "rebirth" of classical art and letters in Italy during the fourteenth, fifteenth, and sixteenth centuries. Many works of the ancient world had been known all through the Middle Ages of course, but the Renaissance humanists studied them in a fresh spirit, with a new enthusiasm for the felicities of Latin style and the poetic values of Greek literature. Moreover the revived classical studies inspired—or were inspired by—a changing attitude to nature and to man that expressed itself in a brilliant outburst of art and literature and also in new forms of political experimentation. Many historians have seen in this period a decisive break with the medieval tradition and the beginnings of a distinctively modern civilization. Others have reacted against this interpretation. The argument is still continuing.*

---

2 *How did political conditions in Renaissance Italy encourage the growth of individualism according to Burckhardt? Are his arguments convincing?*

3 *What do Petrarch, Pico della Mirandola, Vasari, Castiglione tell us about Renaissance attitudes toward nature and art?*

4 *Do you think that the qualities Castiglione praises in a Renaissance courtier would fit a man well to serve in the entourage of a modern head of state— as a White House aide, for instance?*

5 *Burckhardt held that the spirit of Italian humanism was "irreligious and pagan." What evidence can you find for and against this view?*

6 *Was the culture of the Renaissance essentially different from that of the Middle Ages? If so, in what ways?*

1   Burckhardt's Renaissance

*The most brilliant of the nineteenth-century works on the
Renaissance was that of Jacob Burckhardt. In his view the
Renaissance saw the beginning of both the modern state
and modern man.*

FROM *The Civilisation of the Renaissance in Italy*
BY JACOB BURCKHARDT

THE STRUGGLE BETWEEN THE POPES and the Hohenstaufen left
Italy in a political condition which differed essentially from that of other
countries of the West. While in France, Spain and England the feudal system was so organized that, at the close of its existence, it was naturally
transformed into a unified monarchy, and while in Germany it helped to
maintain, at least outwardly, the unity of the empire, Italy had shaken it off
almost entirely. The Emperors of the fourteenth century, even in the most
favourable case, were no longer received and respected as feudal lords, but
as possible leaders and supporters of powers already in existence; while the
Papacy, with its creatures and allies, was strong enough to hinder national
unity in the future, not strong enough itself to bring about that unity. Between the two lay a multitude of political units—republics and despots—in
part of long standing, in part of recent origin, whose existence was founded
simply on their power to maintain it. In them for the first time we detect
the modern political spirit of Europe, surrendered freely to its own instincts,
often displaying the worst features of an unbridled egotism, outraging every
right, and killing every germ of a healthier culture. But, wherever this vicious
tendency is overcome or in any way compensated, a new fact appears in
history—the State as the outcome of reflection and calculation, the State as a
work of art. . . .

   The deliberate adaptation of means to ends, of which no prince out of
Italy had at that time a conception, joined to almost absolute power within
the limits of the State, produced among the despots both men and modes of

Jacob Burckhardt *The Civilisation of the Renaissance in Italy* (1921), pp. 4, 8–10, 61–2, 73–4,
83–4, 129–34, 171–2, translated by S. G. C. Middlemore. Reprinted by permission of George
Allen & Unwin Ltd., London.

life of a peculiar character. The chief secret of government in the hands of the prudent ruler lay in leaving the incidence of taxation so far as possible where he found it, or as he had first arranged it. The chief sources of income were: a land tax, based on a valuation; definite taxes on articles of consumption and duties on exported and imported goods; together with the private fortune of the ruling house. The only possible increase was derived from the growth of business and of general prosperity. Loans, such as we find in the free cities, were here unknown; a well-planned confiscation was held a preferable means of raising money, provided only that it left public credit unshaken—an end attained, for example, by the truly Oriental practice of deposing and plundering the director of the finances.

Out of this income the expenses of the little court, of the bodyguard, of the mercenary troops, and of the public buildings were met, as well as of the buffoons and men of talent who belonged to the personal attendants of the prince. The illegitimacy of his rule isolated the tyrant and surrounded him with constant danger; the most honourable alliance which he could form was with intellectual merit, without regard to its origin. The liberality of the northern princes of the thirteenth century was confined to the knights, to the nobility which served and sang. It was otherwise with the Italian despot. With his thirst for fame and his passion for monumental works, it was talent, not birth, which he needed. In the company of the poet and the scholar he felt himself in a new position, almost, indeed, in possession of a new legitimacy.

No prince was more famous in this respect than the ruler of Verona, Can Grande della Scala, who numbered among the illustrious exiles whom he entertained at his court representatives of the whole of Italy. The men of letters were not ungrateful. Petrarch, whose visits at the courts of such men have been so severely censured, sketched an ideal picture of a prince of the fourteenth century. He demands great things from his patron, the lord of Padua, but in a manner which shows that he holds him capable of them. "Thou must not be the master but the father of thy subjects, and must love them as thy children; yea, as members of thy body. Weapons, guards, and soldiers thou mayest employ against the enemy—with thy subjects goodwill is sufficient. By citizens, of course, I mean those who love the existing order; for those who daily desire change are rebels and traitors, and against such a stern justice may take its course."

Here follows, worked out in detail, the purely modern fiction of the omnipotence of the State. The prince is to take everything into his charge, to maintain and restore churches and public buildings, to keep up the municipal police, to drain the marshes, to look after the supply of wine and corn; so to distribute the taxes that the people can recognize their necessity; he is to support the sick and the helpless, and to give his protection and society to distinguished scholars, on whom his fame in after ages will depend.

But whatever might be the brighter sides of the system, and the merits of individual rulers, yet the men of the fourteenth century were not without a more or less distinct consciousness of the brief and uncertain tenure of most of these despotisms. Inasmuch as political institutions like these are naturally secure in proportion to the size of the territory in which they exist, the larger principalities were constantly tempted to swallow up the smaller. Whole hecatombs of petty rulers were sacrificed at this time to the Visconti alone. As a result of this outward danger an inward ferment was in ceaseless activity; and the effect of the situation on the character of the ruler was generally of the most sinister kind. Absolute power, with its temptations to luxury and unbridled selfishness, and the perils to which he was exposed from enemies and conspirators, turned him almost inevitably into a tyrant in the worst sense of the word. . . . The tyrants destroyed the freedom of most of the cities; here and there they were expelled, but not thoroughly, or only for a short time; and they were always restored, since the inward conditions were favourable to them, and the opposing forces were exhausted.

Among the cities which maintained their independence are two of deep significance for the history of the human race: Florence, the city of incessant movement, which has left us a record of the thoughts and aspirations of each and all who, for three centuries, took part in this movement, and Venice, the city of apparent stagnation and of political secrecy. . . .

The most elevated political thought and the most varied forms of human development are found united in the history of Florence, which in this sense deserves the name of the first modern State in the world. Here the whole people are busied with what in the despotic cities is the affair of a single family. That wondrous Florentine spirit, at once keenly critical and artistically creative, was incessantly transforming the social and political condition of the State, and as incessantly describing and judging the change. Florence thus became the home of political doctrines and theories, of experiments and sudden changes, but also, like Venice, the home of statistical science, and alone and above all other States in the world, the home of historical representation in the modern sense of the phrase. The spectacle of ancient Rome and a familiarity with its leading writers were not without influence; Giovanni Villani confesses that he received the first impulse to his great work at the jubilee of the year 1300, and began it immediately on his return home. Yet how many among the 200,000 pilgrims of that year may have been like him in gifts and tendencies and still did not write the history of their native cities! For not all of them could encourage themselves with the thought: "Rome is sinking; my native city is rising, and ready to achieve great things, and therefore I wish to relate its past history, and hope to continue the story to the present time, and as long as my life shall last." And besides the witness to its past, Florence obtained through its historians something further—a greater fame than fell to the lot of any other city of Italy.

*   *   *

In many of their chief merits the Florentines are the pattern and the earliest type of Italians and modern Europeans generally; they are so also in many of their defects. When Dante compares the city which was always mending its constitution with the sick man who is continually changing his posture to escape from pain, he touches with the comparison a permanent feature of the political life of Florence. The great modern fallacy that a constitution can be made, can be manufactured by a combination of existing forces and tendencies, was constantly cropping up in stormy times; even Machiavelli is not wholly free from it. Constitutional artists were never wanting who by an ingenious distribution and division of political power, by indirect elections of the most complicated kind, by the establishment of nominal offices, sought to found a lasting order of things, and to satisfy or to deceive the rich and the poor alike. They naïvely fetch their examples from classical antiquity, and borrow the party names "ottimati," "aristocrazia," as a matter of course. The world since then has become used to these expressions and given them a conventional European sense, whereas all former party names were purely national, and either characterized the cause at issue or sprang from the caprice of accident. But how a name colours or discolours a political cause!

But of all who thought it possible to construct a State, the greatest beyond all comparison was Machiavelli. He treats existing forces as living and active, takes a large and an accurate view of alternative possibilities, and seeks to mislead neither himself nor others. No man could be freer from vanity or ostentation; indeed, he does not write for the public, but either for princes and administrators or for personal friends. The danger for him does not lie in an affectation of genius or in a false order of ideas, but rather in a powerful imagination which he evidently controls with difficulty. The objectivity of his political judgement is sometimes appalling in its sincerity; but it is the sign of a time of no ordinary need and peril, when it was a hard matter to believe in right, or to credit others with just dealing. Virtuous indignation at his expense is thrown away upon us who have seen in what sense political morality is understood by the statesmen of our own century. Machiavelli was at all events able to forget himself in his cause. In truth, although his writings, with the exception of very few words, are altogether destitute of enthusiasm, and although the Florentines themselves treated him at last as a criminal, he was a patriot in the fullest meaning of the word. But free as he was, like most of his contemporaries, in speech and morals, the welfare of the State was yet his first and last thought.

*   *   *

In the character of these States, whether republics or despotisms, lies, not the only, but the chief reason for the early development of the Italian. To this it is due that he was the first-born among the sons of modern Europe.

In the Middle Ages both sides of human consciousness—that which was turned within as that which was turned without—lay dreaming or half awake beneath a common veil. The veil was woven of faith, illusion, and childish prepossession, through which the world and history were seen clad in strange hues. Man was conscious of himself only as a member of a race, people, party, family, or corporation—only through some general category. In Italy this veil first melted into air; an *objective* treatment and consideration of the State and of all the things of this world became possible. The *subjective* side at the same time asserted itself with corresponding emphasis; man became a spiritual *individual,* and recognized himself as such. In the same way the Greek had once distinguished himself from the barbarian, and the Arab had felt himself an individual at a time when other Asiatics knew themselves only as members of a race. It will not be difficult to show that this result was owing above all to the political circumstances of Italy.

In far earlier times we can here and there detect a development of free personality which in Northern Europe either did not occur at all, or could not display itself in the same manner. The band of audacious wrongdoers in the tenth century described to us by Liudprand, some of the contemporaries of Gregory VII (for example, Benzo of Alba), and a few of the opponents of the first Hohenstaufen, show us characters of this kind. But at the close of the thirteenth century Italy began to swarm with individuality; the ban laid upon human personality was dissolved; and a thousand figures meet us each in its own special shape and dress. Dante's great poem would have been impossible in any other country of Europe, if only for the reason that they all still lay under the spell of race. For Italy the august poet, through the wealth of individuality which he set forth, was the most national herald of his time. But this unfolding of the treasures of human nature in literature and art— this many-sided representation and criticism—will be discussed in separate chapters; here we have to deal only with the psychological fact itself. This fact appears in the most decisive and unmistakable form. The Italians of the fourteenth century knew little of false modesty or of hypocrisy in any shape; not one of them was afraid of singularity, of being and seeming unlike his neighbours.

Despotism, as we have already seen, fostered in the highest degree the individuality not only of the tyrant or Condottiere himself, but also of the men whom he protected or used as his tools—the secretary, minister, poet, and companion. These people were forced to know all the inward resources of their own nature, passing or permanent; and their enjoyment of life was enhanced and concentrated by the desire to obtain the greatest satisfaction from a possibly very brief period of power and influence.

But even the subjects whom they ruled over were not free from the same impulse. Leaving out of account those who wasted their lives in secret opposition and conspiracies, we speak of the majority who were content with a strictly private station, like most of the urban population of the Byzantine empire and the Mohammedan States. No doubt it was often hard for the subjects of a Visconti to maintain the dignity of their persons and families, and multitudes must have lost in moral character through the servitude they lived under. But this was not the case with regard to individuality; for

political impotence does not hinder the different tendencies and manifestations of private life from thriving in the fullest vigour and variety. Wealth
and culture, so far as display and rivalry were not forbidden to them, a
municipal freedom which did not cease to be considerable, and a Church
which, unlike that of the Byzantine or of the Mohammedan world, was not
identical with the State—all these conditions undoubtedly favoured the
growth of individual thought, for which the necessary leisure was furnished
by the cessation of party conflicts. The private man, indifferent to politics,
and busied partly with serious pursuits, partly with the interests of a *dilet-*
tante, seems to have been first fully formed in these despotisms of the
fourteenth century. Documentary evidence cannot, of course, be required on
such a point. The novelists, from whom we might expect information,
describe to us oddities in plenty, but only from one point of view and in so
far as the needs of the story demand. Their scene, too, lies chiefly in the
republican cities.

In the latter, circumstances were also, but in another way, favourable to
the growth of individual character. The more frequently the governing party
was changed, the more the individual was led to make the utmost of the
exercise and enjoyment of power. The statesmen and popular leaders, especially in Florentine history, acquired so marked a personal character, that we
can scarcely find, even exceptionally, a parallel to them in contemporary
history, hardly even in Jacob van Artevelde.

The members of the defeated parties, on the other hand, often came into
a position like that of the subjects of the despotic States, with the difference
that the freedom or power already enjoyed, and in some cases the hope of
recovering them, gave a higher energy to their individuality. Among these
men of involuntary leisure we find, for instance, an Agnolo Pandolfini (d.
1446), whose work on domestic economy is the first complete programme of
a developed private life. His estimate of the duties of the individual as
against the dangers and thanklessness of public life is in its way a true
monument of the age.

Banishment, too, has this effect above all, that it either wears the exile
out or develops whatever is greatest in him. "In all our more populous
cities," says Gioviano Pontano, "we see a crowd of people who have left their
homes of their own free will; but a man takes his virtues with him wherever
he goes." And, in fact, they were by no means only men who had been
actually exiled, but thousands left their native place voluntarily, because they
found its political or economical condition intolerable. The Florentine emigrants at Ferrara and the Lucchese in Venice formed whole colonies by
themselves.

The cosmopolitanism which grew up in the most gifted circles is in itself
a high stage of individualism. Dante, as we have already said, finds a new
home in the language and culture of Italy, but goes beyond even this in the
words, "My country is the whole world." And when his recall to Florence
was offered him on unworthy conditions, he wrote back: "Can I not every-

where behold the light of the sun and the stars; everywhere meditate on the noblest truths, without appearing ingloriously and shamefully before the city and the people. Even my bread will not fail me." The artists exult no less defiantly in their freedom from the constraints of fixed residence. "Only he who has learned everything," says Ghiberti, "is nowhere a stranger; robbed of his fortune and without friends, he is yet the citizen of every country, and can fearlessly despise the changes of fortune." In the same strain an exiled humanist writes: "Wherever a learned man fixes his seat, there is home."

An acute and practised eye might be able to trace, step by step, the increase in the number of complete men during the fifteenth century. Whether they had before them as a conscious object the harmonious development of their spiritual and material existence, is hard to say; but several of them attained it, so far as is consistent with the imperfection of all that is earthly. It may be better to renounce the attempt at an estimate of the share which fortune, character, and talent had in the life of Lorenzo il Magnifico. But look at a personality like that of Ariosto, especially as shown in his satires. In what harmony are there expressed the pride of the man and the poet, the irony with which he treats his own enjoyments, the most delicate satire, and the deepest goodwill!

*   *   *

Now that this point in our historical view of Italian civilization has been reached, it is time to speak of the influence of antiquity, the "new birth" of which has been one-sidedly chosen as the name to sum up the whole period. The conditions which have been hitherto described would have sufficed, apart from antiquity, to upturn and to mature the national mind; and most of the intellectual tendencies which yet remain to be noticed would be conceivable without it. But both what has gone before and what we have still to discuss are coloured in a thousand ways by the influence of the ancient world; and though the essence of the phenomena might still have been the same without the classical revival, it is only with and through this revival that they are actually manifested to us. The Renaissance would not have been the process of world-wide significance which it is, if its elements could be so easily separated from one another. We must insist upon it, as one of the chief propositions of this book, that it was not the revival of antiquity alone, but its union with the genius of the Italian people, which achieved the conquest of the western world. The amount of independence which the national spirit maintained in this union varied according to circumstances. In the modern Latin literature of the period, it is very small, while in plastic art, as well as in other spheres, it is remarkably great; and hence the alliance between two distant epochs in the civilization of the same people, because concluded on equal terms, proved justifiable and fruitful. The rest of Europe was free either to repel or else partly or wholly to accept the mighty impulse which came forth from Italy. Where the latter was the case we may as well be spared the complaints over the early decay of mediaeval faith and civilization. Had these been strong enough to hold their ground, they would be alive to this day. If those elegiac natures which long to see them return could pass but one hour in the midst of them, they would gasp to be back in modern air. That in a great historical process of this kind flowers of exquisite beauty may perish, without being made immortal in poetry or tradition, is undoubtedly true; nevertheless, we cannot wish the process undone. The general result of it consists in this—that by the side of the Church which had hitherto held the countries of the West together (though it was unable to do so much longer) there arose a new spiritual influence which, spreading itself abroad from Italy, became the breath of life for all the more instructed minds in Europe.

2   The Cult of the Classics

Petrarch (1304–1374) was the first of the great Italian hu-manists. The following letter illustrates his devotion to Latin literature.

FROM *Petrarch's Letters*

YOUR CICERO has been in my possession four years and more. There is a good reason, though, for so long a delay; namely, the great scarcity of copyists who understand such work. It is a state of affairs that has resulted in an incredible loss to scholarship. Books that by their nature are a little hard to understand are no longer multiplied, and have ceased to be generally intelligible, and so have sunk into utter neglect, and in the end have perished. This age of ours consequently has let fall, bit by bit, some of the richest and sweetest fruits that the tree of knowledge has yielded; has thrown away the results of the vigils and labours of the most illustrious men of genius, things of more value, I am almost tempted to say, than anything else in the whole world. . . .

But I must return to your Cicero. I could not do without it, and the incompetence of the copyists would not let me possess it. What was left for me but to rely upon my own resources, and press these weary fingers and this worn and ragged pen into the service? The plan that I followed was this. I want you to know it, in case you should ever have to grapple with a similar task. Not a single word did I read except as I wrote. But how is that, I hear someone say; did you write without knowing what it was that you were writing? Ah! but from the very first it was enough for me to know that it was a work of Tullius, and an extremely rare one too. And then as soon as I was fairly started I found at every step so much sweetness and charm, and felt so strong a desire to advance, that the only difficulty which I

Epistolae in *Petrarch, the First Modern Scholar and Man of Letters* (1899), pp. 275–8, trans-lated by J. H. Robinson and H. W. Rolfe.

experienced in reading and writing at the same time came from the fact that my pen could not cover the ground so rapidly as I wanted it to, whereas my expectation had been rather that it would outstrip my eyes, and that my ardour for writing would be chilled by the slowness of my reading. So the pen held back the eye, and the eye drove on the pen, and I covered page after page, delighting in my task, and committing many and many a passage to memory as I wrote. For just in proportion as the writing is slower than the reading does the passage make a deep impression and cling to the mind.

And yet I must confess that I did finally reach a point in my copying where I was overcome by weariness; not mental, for how unlikely that would be where Cicero was concerned, but the sort of fatigue that springs from excessive manual labour. I began to feel doubtful about this plan that I was following, and to regret having undertaken a task for which I had not been trained; when suddenly I came across a place where Cicero tells how he himself copied the orations of—someone or other; just who it was I do not know, but certainly no Tullius, for there is but one such man, one such voice, one such mind. These are his words: "You say that you have been in the habit of reading the orations of Cassius in your idle moments. But I," he jestingly adds, with his customary disregard of his adversary's feelings, "have made a practice of *copying* them, so that I might *have* no idle moments." As I read this passage I grew hot with shame, like a modest young soldier who hears the voice of his beloved leader rebuking him. I said to myself, "So Cicero copied orations that another wrote, and you are not ready to copy his? What ardour! what scholarly devotion! what reverence for a man of godlike genius!" These thoughts were a spur to me, and I pushed on, with all my doubts dispelled. If ever from my darkness there shall come a single ray that can enhance the splendour of the reputation which his heavenly eloquence has won for him, it will proceed in no slight measure from the fact that I was so captivated by his ineffable sweetness that I did a thing in itself most irksome with such delight and eagerness that I scarcely knew I was doing it at all.

So then at last your Cicero has the happiness of returning to you, bearing you my thanks. And yet he also stays, very willingly, with me; a dear friend, to whom I give the credit of being almost the only man of letters for whose sake I would go to the length of spending my time, when the difficulties of life are pressing on me so sharply and inexorably and the cares pertaining to my literary labours make the longest life seem far too short, in transcribing compositions not my own. I may have done such things in former days, when I thought myself rich in time, and had not learned how stealthily it slips away: but I now know that this is of all our riches the most uncertain and fleeting; the years are closing in upon me now, and there is no longer any room for deviation from the beaten path. I am forced to practice strict economy; I only hope that I have not begun too late. But Cicero! he assuredly is worthy of a part of even the little that I still have left. Farewell.

Petrarch admired Greek literature too, but he had to read it
in translation, as the next letter indicates. A century later
any scholar of comparable eminence would have been
trained in both Greek and Latin.

FROM *Petrarch's Letters*

YOU ASK ME FINALLY to lend you the copy of Homer that was on sale at Padua, if, as you suppose, I have purchased it; since, you say, I have for a long time possessed another copy; so that our friend Leo may translate it from Greek into Latin for your benefit and for the benefit of our other studious compatriots. I saw this book, but neglected the opportunity of acquiring it, because it seemed inferior to my own. It can easily be had with the aid of the person to whom I owe my friendship with Leo; a letter from that source would be all-powerful in the matter, and I will myself write him.

If by chance the book escape us, which seems to me very unlikely, I will let you have mine. I have been always fond of this particular translation and of Greek literature in general, and if fortune had not frowned upon my beginnings, in the sad death of my excellent master, I should be perhaps today something more than a Greek still at his alphabet. I approve with all my heart and strength your enterprise, for I regret and am indignant that an ancient translation, presumably the work of Cicero, the commencement of which Horace inserted in his *Ars Poetica,* should have been lost to the Latin world, together with many other works. It angers me to see so much solicitude for the bad and so much neglect of the good. . . .

As for me, I wish the work to be done, whether well or ill. I am so famished for literature that just as he who is ravenously hungry is not inclined to quarrel with the cook's art, so I await with lively impatience whatever dishes are to be set before my soul. And in truth, the morsel in which the same Leo, translating into Latin prose the beginning of Homer, has given me a foretaste of the whole work, although it confirms the sentiment of St. Jerome, does not displease me. It possesses, in fact, a secret charm, as certain viands, which have failed to take a moulded shape, although they are lacking in form, nevertheless preserve their taste and odor. May he continue with the aid of Heaven, and may he give us Homer, who has been lost to us!

In asking of me the volume of Plato which I have with me, and which escaped the fire at my trans-Alpine country house, you give me proof of your

---

Epistolae in *A Literary Source Book of the Renaissance* (1900), pp. 13–5, translated by M. Whitcomb.

ardor, and I shall hold this book at your disposal, whenever the time shall come. I wish to aid with all my power such noble enterprises. But beware lest it should be unbecoming to unite in one bundle these two great princes of Greece, lest the weight of these two spirits should overwhelm mortal shoulders. Let your messenger undertake, with God's aid, one of the two, and first him who has written many centuries before the other. Farewell.

> *The mixture of introspection and sensitivity to natural beauty in the following passage has sometimes been taken as reflecting the "medieval" and "modern" elements in Petrarch's personality. The whole passage can be read as an allegory of "the ascent of the soul to God."*

FROM *Petrarch's Letters*

TO-DAY I MADE THE ASCENT of the highest mountain in this region, which is not improperly called Ventosum [*i.e., windy—B. T.*]. My only motive was the wish to see what so great an elevation had to offer. I have had the expedition in mind for many years; for, as you know, I have lived in this region from infancy, having been cast here by that fate which determines the affairs of men. Consequently the mountain, which is visible from a great distance, was ever before my eyes, and I conceived the plan of some time doing what I have at last accomplished to-day. The idea took hold upon me with especial force when, in re-reading Livy's *History of Rome,* yesterday, I happened upon the place where Philip of Macedon, the same who waged war against the Romans, ascended Mount Haemus in Thessaly, from whose summit he was able, it is said, to see two seas, the Adriatic and the Euxine. Whether this be true or false I have not been able to determine, for the mountain is too far away, and writers disagree. Pomponius Mela, the cosmographer—not to mention others who have spoken of this occurrence—admits its truth without hesitation; Titus Livius, on the other hand, considers it false. I, assuredly, should not have left the question long in doubt, had that mountain been as easy to explore as this one. Let us leave this matter to one side, however, and return to my mountain here,—it seems to me that a young man in private life may well be excused for attempting what an aged king could undertake without arousing criticism.

*   *   *

Epistolae in *Petrarch, the First Modern Scholar and Man of Letters* (1899), pp. 307–17, translated by J. H. Robinson and H. W. Rolfe.

At the time fixed we left the house, and by evening reached Malaucène, which lies at the foot of the mountain, to the north. Having rested there a day, we finally made the ascent this morning, with no companions except two servants; and a most difficult task it was. The mountain is a very steep and almost inaccessible mass of stony soil. But, as the poet has well said, "Remorseless toil conquers all." It was a long day, the air fine. We enjoyed the advantages of vigour of mind and strength and agility of body, and everything else essential to those engaged in such an undertaking, and so had no other difficulties to face than those of the region itself. We found an old shepherd in one of the mountain dales, who tried, at great length, to dissuade us from the ascent, saying that some fifty years before he had, in the same ardour of youth, reached the summit, but had gotten for his pains nothing except fatigue and regret, and clothes and body torn by the rocks and briars. No one, so far as he or his companions knew, had ever tried the ascent before or after him. But his counsels increased rather than diminished our desire to proceed, since youth is suspicious of warnings. So the old man, finding that his efforts were in vain, went a little way with us, and pointed out a rough path among the rocks, uttering many admonitions, which he continued to send after us even after we had left him behind. Surrendering to him all such garments or other possessions as might prove burdensome to us, we made ready for the ascent, and started off at a good pace. But, as usually happens, fatigue quickly followed upon our excessive exertion, and we soon came to a halt at the top of a certain cliff. Upon starting on again we went more slowly, and I especially advanced along the rocky way with a more deliberate step. While my brother chose a direct path straight up the ridge, I weakly took an easier one which really descended. When I was called back, and the right road was shown me, I replied that I hoped to find a better way round on the other side, and that I did not mind going farther if the path were only less steep. This was just an excuse for my laziness; and when the others had already reached a considerable height I was still wandering in the valleys.

After being frequently misled in this way, I finally sat down in a valley and transferred my winged thoughts from things corporeal to the immaterial, addressing myself as follows:—"What thou hast repeatedly experienced to-day in the ascent of this mountain, happens to thee, as to many, in the journey toward the blessed life. But this is not so readily perceived by men, since the motions of the body are obvious and external while those of the soul are invisible and hidden. Yes, the life which we call blessed is to be sought for on a high eminence, and strait is the way that leads to it. Many, also, are the hills that lie between, and we must ascend, by a glorious stairway, from strength to strength. At the top is at once the end of our struggles and the goal for which we are bound. All wish to reach this goal, but, as Ovid says, "To wish is little; we must long with the utmost eagerness to gain our end." Thou certainly dost ardently desire, as well as simply wish, unless thou deceivest thyself in this matter, as in so many others. What, then, doth hold thee back? Nothing, assuredly, except that thou wouldst take a path which seems, at first thought, more easy, leading through low and worldly pleasures. But nevertheless in the end, after long wanderings, thou must perforce either climb the steeper path, under the burden of tasks foolishly deferred, to its blessed culmination, or lie down in the valley of thy sins, and (I shudder to think of it!), if the shadow of death overtake thee, spend an eternal night amid constant torments." These thoughts stimulated both body and mind in a wonderful degree for facing the difficulties which yet remained. . . .

One peak of the mountain, the highest of all, the country people call "Sonny," why, I do not know, unless by antiphrasis, as I have sometimes suspected in other instances; for the peak in question would seem to be the father of all the surrounding ones. On its top is a little level place, and here we could at last rest our tired bodies.

Now, my father, since you have followed the thoughts that spurred me on in my ascent, listen to the rest of the story, and devote one hour, I pray you, to reviewing the experiences of my entire day. At first, owing to the unaccustomed quality of the air and the effect of the great sweep of view spread out before me, I stood like one dazed. I beheld the clouds under our feet, and what I had read of Athos and Olympus seemed less incredible as I myself witnessed the same things from a mountain of less fame. I turned my eyes toward Italy, whither my heart most inclined. The Alps, rugged and snow-capped, seemed to rise close by, although they were really at a great distance; the very same Alps through which that fierce enemy of the Roman name once made his way, bursting the rocks, if we may believe the report, by the application of vinegar. I sighed, I must confess, for the skies of Italy, which I beheld rather with my mind than with my eyes.

*   *   *

The sinking sun and the lengthening shadows of the mountain were already warning us that the time was near at hand when we must go. As if suddenly wakened from sleep, I turned about and gazed toward the west. I was unable to discern the summits of the Pyrenees, which form the barrier between France and Spain; not because of any intervening obstacle that I know of but owing simply to the insufficiency of our mortal vision. But I could see with the utmost clearness, off to the right, the mountains of the region about Lyons, and to the left the bay of Marseilles and the waters that lash the shores of Aigues Mortes, altho' all these places were so distant that it would require a journey of several days to reach them. Under our very eyes flowed the Rhone.

While I was thus dividing my thoughts, now turning my attention to some terrestrial object that lay before me, now raising my soul, as I had done my body, to higher planes, it occurred to me to look into my copy of St. Augustine's *Confessions,* a gift that I owe to your love, and that I always have about me, in memory of both the author and the giver. I opened the compact little volume, small indeed in size, but of infinite charm, with the intention of reading whatever came to hand, for I could happen upon nothing that would be otherwise than edifying and devout. Now it chanced that the tenth book presented itself. My brother, waiting to hear something of St. Augustine's from my lips, stood attentively by. I call him, and God too, to witness that where I first fixed my eyes it was written: "And men go about to wonder at the heights of the mountains, and the mighty waves of the sea, and the wide sweep of rivers, and the circuit of the ocean, and the revolution of the stars, but themselves they consider not." I was abashed, and, asking my brother (who was anxious to hear more), not to annoy me, I closed the book, angry with myself that I should still be admiring earthly things who might long ago have learned from even the pagan philosophers that nothing is wonderful but the soul, which, when great itself, finds nothing great outside itself. Then, in truth, I was satisfied that I had seen enough of the mountain; I turned my inward eye upon myself, and from that time not a syllable fell from my lips until we reached the bottom again.

> *Many Renaissance men expressed a sense of affinity with classical civilization and of alienation from medieval culture. This attitude is apparent in the following comments by the sixteenth-century painter and art historian, Giorgio Vasari.*

FROM *Lives of the Most Eminent Painters, Sculptors and Architects* BY GIORGIO VASARI

IT IS WITHOUT DOUBT a fixed opinion, common to almost all writers, that the arts of sculpture and painting were first discovered by the nations of Egypt, although there are some who attribute the first rude attempts in marble, and the first statues and relievi, to the Chaldeans, while they accord the invention of the pencil, and of colouring, to the Greeks. But I am myself convinced, that design, which is the foundation of both these arts, nay, rather the very soul of each, comprising and nourishing within itself all the essential parts of both, existed in its highest perfection from the first moment of creation, when the Most High having formed the great body of the world,

Giorgio Vasari, *Lives of the Most Eminent Painters, Sculptors and Architects* (1855), pp. 9–10, 12–3, 15–6, 20–2, 30–1, translated by Mrs. Jonathan Foster.

and adorned the heavens with their resplendent lights, descended by his spirit, through the limpidity of the air, and penetrating the solid mass of earth, created man; and thus unveiled, with the beauties of creation, the first form of sculpture and of painting. For from this man, as from a true model, were copied by slow degrees (we may not venture to affirm the contrary), statues and sculptures: the difficulties of varied attitude,—the flowing lines of contour—and in the first paintings, whatever these may have been, the softness, harmony, and that concord in discord, whence result light and shade. The first model, therefore, from which the first image of man arose, was a mass of earth; and not without significance, since the Divine Architect of time and nature, Himself all-perfect, designed to instruct us by the imperfection of the material, in the true method of attaining perfection, by repeatedly diminishing and adding to; as the best sculptors and painters are wont to do, for by perpetually taking from or adding to their models they conduct their work, from its first imperfect sketch, to that finish of perfection which they desire to attain. The Creator further adorned his model with the most vivid colours, and these same colours, being afterwards drawn by the painter from the mines of earth, enable him to imitate whatsoever object he may require for his picture. . . .

We find, then, that the art of sculpture was zealously cultivated by the Greeks, among whom many excellent artists appeared; those great masters, the Athenian Phidias, with Praxiteles and Polycletus, were of the number, while Lysippus and Pyrgoteles, worked successfully in intaglio, and Pygmalion produced admirable reliefs in ivory—nay, of him it was affirmed, that his prayers obtained life and soul for the statue of a virgin which he had formed. Painting was in like manner honoured, and those who practised it successfully were rewarded among the ancient Greeks and Romans; this is proved by their according the rights of citizenship, and the most exalted dignities, to such as attained high distinction in these arts, both of which flourished so greatly in Rome, that Fabius bequeathed fame to his posterity by subscribing his name to the pictures so admirably painted by him in the Temple of *Salus,* and calling himself Fabius Pictor. It was forbidden, by public decree, that slaves should exercise this art within the cities, and so much homage was paid by the nations to art and artists, that works of rare merit were sent to Rome and exhibited as something wonderful, among other trophies in the triumphal processions, while artists of extraordinary merit, if slaves, received their freedom, together with honours and rewards from the republics. . . .

I suggested above that the origin of these arts was Nature herself—the first image or model, the most beautiful fabric of the world—and the master, that divine light infused into us by special grace, and which has made us not only superior to all other animals, but has exalted us, if it be permitted so to speak, to the similitude of God Himself. This is my belief, and I think that every man who shall maturely consider the question, will be of my opinion. And if it has been seen in our times—as I hope to demonstrate presently by various examples—that simple children, rudely reared in the woods, have begun to practise the arts of design with no other model than those beautiful pictures and sculptures furnished by Nature, and no other teaching than their own genius—how much more easily may we believe that the first of mankind, in whom nature and intellect were all the more perfect in proportion as they were less removed from their first origin and divine parentage,— that these men, I say, having Nature for their guide, and the unsullied purity of their fresh intelligence for their master, with the beautiful model of the world for an exemplar, should have given birth to these most noble arts, and from a small beginning, ameliorating them by slow degrees, should have conducted them finally to perfection? . . .

But as fortune, when she has raised either persons or things to the summit of her wheel, very frequently casts them to the lowest point, whether in repentance or for her sport, so it chanced that, after these things, the barbarous nations of the world arose, in divers places, in rebellion against the Romans; whence there ensued, in no long time, not only the decline of that great empire, but the utter ruin of the whole and more especially of Rome herself, when all the best artists, sculptors, painters, and architects, were in like manner totally ruined, being submerged and buried, together with the arts themselves, beneath the miserable slaughters and ruins of that much renowned city. . . .

But infinitely more ruinous than all other enemies to the arts above named, was the fervent zeal of the new Christian religion, which, after long and sanguinary combats, had finally overcome and annihilated the ancient creeds of the pagan world, by the frequency of miracles exhibited, and by the earnest sincerity of the means adopted; and ardently devoted, with all diligence, to the extirpation of error, nay, to the removal of even the slightest temptation to heresy, it not only destroyed all the wondrous statues, paintings, sculptures, mosaics, and other ornaments of the false pagan deities, but at the same time extinguished the very memory, in casting down the honours, of numberless excellent ancients, to whom statues and other monuments had been erected, in public places, for their virtues, by the most virtuous times of antiquity. Nay, more than this, to build the churches of the Christian faith, this zeal not only destroyed the most renowned temples of the heathens, but, for the richer ornament of St. Peter's, and in addition to the many spoils previously bestowed on that building, the tomb of Adrian, now called the castle of St. Angelo, was deprived of its marble columns, to employ them for this church, many other buildings being in like manner despoiled, and which we now see wholly devastated. And although the Christian religion did not effect this from hatred to these works of art, but solely for the purpose of abasing and bringing into contempt the gods of the Gentiles, yet the result of this too ardent zeal did not fail to bring such total ruin over the noble arts, that their very form and existence was lost. . . .

In like manner, the best works in painting and sculpture, remaining buried under the ruins of Italy, were concealed during the same period, and continued wholly unknown to the rude men reared amidst the more modern usages of art, and by whom no other sculptures or pictures were produced, than such as were executed by the remnant of old Greek artists. They formed images of earth and stone, or painted monstrous figures, of which they traced the rude outline only in colour. These artists—the best as being the only ones—were conducted into Italy, whither they carried sculpture and painting, as well as mosaic, in such manner as they were themselves acquainted with them: these they taught, in their own coarse and rude style, to the Italians, who practised them, after such fashion, as I have said, and will further relate, down to a certain period. The men of those times, unaccustomed to works of greater perfection than those thus set before their eyes, admired them accordingly, and, barbarous as they were, yet imitated them as the most excellent models. It was only by slow degrees that those who came after, being aided in some places by the subtlety of the air around them, could begin to raise themselves from these depths; when, towards 1250, Heaven, moved to pity by the noble spirits which the Tuscan soil was producing every day, restored them to their primitive condition. It is true that those who lived in the times succeeding the ruin of Rome, had seen remnants of arches, colossi, statues, pillars, storied columns, and other works of art, not wholly destroyed by the fires and other devastations; yet they had not known how to avail themselves of this aid, nor had they derived any benefit from it, until the time specified above. When the minds then awakened, becoming capable of distinguishing the good from the worthless, and abandoning old methods, returned to the imitation of the antique, with all the force of their genius, and all the power of their industry.

3   Renaissance Man Described

*One characteristic of Renaissance humanism was a buoyant
confidence in the dignity and capabilities of human nature
itself. Pico della Mirandola (1463–1494) gave eloquent expression to this sentiment.*

FROM *Oration on the Dignity of Man*
BY PICO DELLA MIRANDOLA

I HAVE READ in the records of the Arabians, reverend fathers, that Abdala
the Saracen, when questioned as to what on this stage of the world, as it
were, could be seen most worthy of wonder, replied: "There is nothing to be
seen more wonderful than man." In agreement with this opinion is the
saying of Hermes Trismegistus: "A great miracle, Asclepius, is man." But
when I weighed the reason for these maxims, the many grounds for the
excellence of human nature reported by many men failed to satisfy me—that
man is the intermediary between creatures, the intimate of the gods, the king
of the lower beings; by the acuteness of his senses, by the discernment of his
reason, and by the light of his intelligence the interpreter of nature; the
interval between fixed eternity and fleeting time, and (as the Persians say)
the bond, nay, rather, the marriage song of the world, on David's testimony
but little lower than the angels. Admittedly great though these reasons be,
they are not the principal grounds, that is, those which may rightfully claim
for themselves the privilege of the highest admiration. For why should we
not admire more the angels themselves and the blessed choirs of heaven? At
last it seems to me I have come to understand why man is the most fortunate
of creatures and consequently worthy of all admiration and what precisely is
that rank which is his lot in the universal chain of Being—a rank to be
envied not only by brutes but even by the stars and by minds beyond this
world. It is a matter past faith and a wondrous one. Why should it not be?

For it is on this very account that man is rightly called and judged a great miracle and a wonderful creature indeed. But hear, Fathers, exactly what this rank is and, as friendly auditors, conformably to your kindness, do me this favor. God the Father, the supreme Architect, had already built this cosmic home we behold, the most sacred temple of His godhead, by the laws of His mysterious wisdom. The region above the heavens He had adorned with Intelligences, the heavenly spheres He had quickened with eternal souls, and the excrementary and filthy parts of the lower world He had filled with a multitude of animals of every kind. But, when the work was finished, the Craftsman kept wishing that there were someone to ponder the plan of so great a work, to love its beauty, and to wonder at its vastness. Therefore, when everything was done (as Moses and Timaeus bear witness), He finally took thought concerning the creation of man. But there was not among His archetypes that from which He could fashion a new offspring, nor was there in His treasure-houses anything which He might bestow on His new son as an inheritance, nor was there in the seats of all the world a place where the latter might sit to contemplate the universe. All was now complete; all things had been assigned to the highest, the middle, and the lowest orders. But in its final creation it was not the part of the Father's power to fail as though exhausted. It was not the part of His wisdom to waver in a needful matter through poverty of counsel. It was not the part of His kindly love that he who was to praise God's divine generosity in regard to others should be compelled to condemn it in regard to himself. At last the best of artisans ordained that that creature to whom He had been able to give nothing proper to himself should have joint possession of whatever had been peculiar to each of the different kinds of being. He therefore took man as a creature of indeterminate nature and, assigning him a place in the middle of the world, addressed him thus: "Neither a fixed abode nor a form that is thine alone nor any function peculiar to thyself have we given thee, Adam, to the end that according to thy longing and according to thy judgment thou mayest have and possess what abode, what form, and what functions thou thyself shalt desire. The nature of all other beings is limited and constrained within the bounds of laws prescribed by Us. Thou, constrained by no limits, in accordance with thine own free will, in whose hand We have placed thee, shalt ordain for thyself the limits of thy nature. We have set thee at the world's center that thou mayest from thence more easily observe whatever is in the world. We have made thee neither of heaven nor of earth, neither mortal nor immortal, so that with freedom of choice and with honor, as though the maker and molder of thyself, thou mayest fashion thyself in whatever shape thou shalt prefer. Thou shalt have the power to degenerate into the lower forms of life, which are brutish. Thou shalt have the power, out of thy soul's judgment, to be reborn into the higher forms, which are divine." O supreme generosity of God the Father, O highest and most marvelous felicity of man! To him it is granted to have whatever he chooses, to be whatever he wills.

Baldassare Castiglione (1478–1529) described the qualities of an ideal Renaissance courtier.

FROM *The Book of the Courtier*

BY BALDASSARE CASTIGLIONE

I WISH, THEN, that this Courtier of ours should be nobly born and of gentle race; because it is far less unseemly for one of ignoble birth to fail in worthy deeds, than for one of noble birth, who, if he strays from the path of his predecessors, stains his family name, and not only fails to achieve but loses what has been achieved already; for noble birth is like a bright lamp that manifests and makes visible good and evil deeds, and kindles and stimulates to virtue both by fear of shame and by hope of praise. . . .

But to come to some details, I am of opinion that the principal and true profession of the Courtier ought to be that of arms; which I would have him follow actively above all else, and be known among others as bold and strong, and loyal to whomsoever he serves. And he will win a reputation for these good qualities by exercising them at all times and in all places, since one may never fail in this without severest censure. And just as among women, their fair fame once sullied never recovers its first lustre, so the reputation of a gentleman who bears arms, if once it be in the least tarnished with cowardice or other disgrace, remains forever infamous before the world and full of ignominy. Therefore the more our Courtier excels in this art, the more he will be worthy of praise; and yet I do not deem essential in him that perfect knowledge of things and those other qualities that befit a commander; since this would be too wide a sea, let us be content, as we have said, with perfect loyalty and unconquered courage, and that he be always seen to possess them. . . .

Not that we would have him look so fierce, or go about blustering, or say that he has taken his cuirass to wife, or threaten with those grim scowls that we have often seen in Berto, because to such men as this, one might justly say that which a brave lady jestingly said in gentle company to one whom I will not name at present; who, being invited by her out of compliment to dance, refused not only that, but to listen to the music, and many other entertainments proposed to him,—saying always that such silly trifles were not his business; so that at last the lady said, "What is your business, then?" He replied with a sour look, "To fight." Then the lady at once said, "Now that you are in no war and out of fighting trim, I should think it were

Baldassare Castiglione, *The Book of the Courtier* (1903), pp. 22, 25–31, 59, 62–3, 65–6, 93–5, translated by Leonard E. Opdycke.

a good thing to have yourself well oiled, and to stow yourself with all your battle harness in a closet until you be needed, lest you grow more rusty than you are;" and so, amid much laughter from the bystanders, she left the discomfited fellow to his silly presumption.

Therefore let the man we are seeking, be very bold, stern, and always among the first, where the enemy are to be seen; and in every other place, gentle, modest, reserved, above all things avoiding ostentation and that impudent self-praise by which men ever excite hatred and disgust in all who hear them. . . .

I say, however, that he, who in praising himself runs into no errour and incurs no annoyance or envy at the hands of those that hear him, is a very discreet man indeed and merits praise from others in addition to that which he bestows upon himself; because it is a very difficult matter. . . .

I would have our Courtier's aspect; not so soft and effeminate as is sought by many, who not only curl their hair and pluck their brows, but gloss their faces with all those arts employed by the most wanton and unchaste women in the world; and in their walk, posture and every act, they seem so limp and languid that their limbs are like to fall apart; and they pronounce their words so mournfully that they appear about to expire upon the spot: and the more they find themselves with men of rank, the more they affect such tricks. Since nature has not made them women, as they seem to wish to appear and be, they should be treated not as good women but as public harlots, and driven not merely from the courts of great lords but from the society of honest men.

Then coming to the bodily frame, I say it is enough if this be neither extremely short nor tall, for both of these conditions excite a certain contemptuous surprise, and men of either sort are gazed upon in much the same way that we gaze on monsters. Yet if we must offend in one of the two extremes, it is preferable to fall a little short of the just measure of height than to exceed it, for besides often being dull of intellect, men thus huge of body are also unfit for every exercise of agility, which thing I should much wish in the Courtier. And so I would have him well built and shapely of limb, and would have him show strength and lightness and suppleness, and know all bodily exercises that befit a man of war: whereof I think the first should be to handle every sort of weapon well on foot and on horse, to understand the advantages of each, and especially to be familiar with those weapons that are ordinarily used among gentlemen; for besides the use of them in war, where such subtlety in contrivance is perhaps not needful, there frequently arise differences between one gentleman and another, which afterwards result in duels often fought with such weapons as happen at the moment to be within reach: thus knowledge of this kind is a very safe thing.

*   *   *

There are also many other exercises, which although not immediately dependent upon arms, yet are closely connected therewith, and greatly foster manly sturdiness; and one of the chief among these seems to me to be the chase, because it bears a certain likeness to war: and truly it is an amusement for great lords and befitting a man at court, and furthermore it is seen to have been much cultivated among the ancients. It is fitting also to know how to swim, to leap, to run, to throw stones, for besides the use that may be made of this in war, a man often has occasion to show what he can do in such matters; whence good esteem is to be won, especially with the multitude, who must be taken into account withal. Another admirable exercise, and one very befitting a man at court, is the game of tennis, in which are well shown the disposition of the body, the quickness and suppleness of every member, and all those qualities that are seen in nearly every other exercise. Nor less highly do I esteem vaulting on horse, which although it be fatiguing and difficult, makes a man very light and dexterous more than any other thing; and besides its utility, if this lightness is accompanied by grace, it is to my thinking a finer show than any of the others.

*   *   *

I think that the conversation which the Courtier ought most to try in every way to make acceptable, is that which he holds with his prince; and although this word "conversation" implies a certain equality that seems impossible between a lord and his inferior, yet we will call it so for the present. Therefore, besides daily showing everyone that he possesses the worth we have already described, I would have the Courtier strive, with all the thoughts and forces of his mind, to love and almost to adore the prince whom he serves, above every other thing, and mould his wishes, habits and all his ways to his prince's liking. . . .

Moreover it is possible without flattery to obey and further the wishes of him we serve, for I am speaking of those wishes that are reasonable and right, or of those that in themselves are neither good nor evil, such as would be a liking for play or a devotion to one kind of exercise above another. And I would have the Courtier bend himself to this even if he be by nature alien to it, so that on seeing him his lord shall always feel that he will have something agreeable to say; which will come about if he has the good judgment to perceive what his prince likes, and the wit and prudence to bend himself thereto, and a deliberate purpose to like that which perhaps he by nature dislikes. . . . He will not be an idle or untruthful tattler, nor a boaster nor pointless flatterer, but modest and reserved, always and especially in public showing that reverence and respect which befit the servant towards the master. . . .

He will very rarely or almost never ask anything of his lord for himself, lest his lord, being reluctant to deny it to him directly, may sometimes grant it with an ill grace, which is much worse. Even in asking for others he will choose his time discreetly and ask proper and reasonable things; and he will so frame his request, by omitting what he knows may displease and by skilfully doing away with difficulties, that his lord shall always grant it, or shall not think him offended by refusal even if it be denied; for when lords have denied a favour to an importunate suitor, they often reflect that he who asked it with such eagerness, must have desired it greatly, and so having failed to obtain it, must feel ill will towards him who denied it; and believing this, they begin to hate the man and can never more look upon him with favour.

> *The autobiography of the artist Benvenuto Cellini provides many vignettes of life in Renaissance Italy.*

FROM *Autobiography* BY BENVENUTO CELLINI

[*Cellini has shown Pope Clement VII a model of a jeweled ornament B. T.*] While we were waiting for the money, the Pope turned once more to gaze at leisure on the dexterous device I had employed for combining the diamond with the figure of God the Father. I had put the diamond exactly in the centre of the piece; and above it God the Father was shown seated, leaning nobly in a sideways attitude, which made a perfect composition, and did not interfere with the stone's effect. Lifting his right hand, he was in the act of giving the benediction. Below the diamond I had placed three children, who, with their arms upraised, were supporting the jewel. One of them, in the middle, was in full relief, the other two in half-relief. All round I set a crowd of cherubs, in divers attitudes, adapted to the other gems. A mantle undulated to the wind around the figure of the Father, from the folds of which cherubs peeped out; and there were other ornaments besides which made a very beautiful effect. The work was executed in white stucco on a black stone. When the money came, the Pope gave it me with his own hand, and begged me in the most winning terms to let him have it finished in his own days, adding that this should be to my advantage.

*   *   *

[*Cellini's brother was murdered at this time—B. T.*]
I went on applying myself with the utmost diligence upon the goldwork for Pope Clement's button. He was very eager to have it, and used to send

The Life of Benvenuto Cellini (1893), pp. 102, 114–9, translated by John Addington Symonds.

for me two or three times a week, in order to inspect it; and his delight in
the work always increased. Often would he rebuke and scold me, as it were,
for the great grief in which my brother's loss had plunged me; and one day,
observing me more downcast and out of trim than was proper, he cried
aloud: "Benvenuto, oh! I did not know that you were mad. Have you only
just learned that there is no remedy against death? One would think that
you were trying to run after him." When I left the presence, I continued
working at the jewel and the dies for the Mint; but I also took to watching
the arquebusier who shot my brother, as though he had been a girl I was in
love with. The man had formerly been in the light cavalry, but afterwards
had joined the arquebusiers as one of the Bargello's corporals; and what
increased my rage was that he had used these boastful words: "If it had not
been for me, who killed that brave young man, the least trifle of delay would
have resulted in his putting us all to flight with great disaster." When I saw
that the fever caused by always seeing him about was depriving me of sleep
and appetite, and was bringing me by degrees to sorry plight, I overcame my
repugnance to so low and not quite praiseworthy an enterprise, and made
my mind up one evening to rid myself of the torment. The fellow lived in a
house near a place called Torre Sanguigua, next door to the lodging of one
of the most fashionable courtesans in Rome, named Signora Antea. It had
just struck twenty-four, and he was standing at the house-door, with his
sword in hand, having risen from supper. With great address I stole up to
him, holding a large Pistojan dagger, and dealt him a back-handed stroke,
with which I meant to cut his head clean off; but as he turned round very
suddenly, the blow fell upon the point of his left shoulder and broke the
bone. He sprang up, dropped his sword, half-stunned with the great pain,
and took to flight. I followed after, and in four steps caught him up, when I
lifted my dagger above his head, which he was holding very low, and hit
him in the back exactly at the junction of the nape-bone and the neck. The
poniard entered this point so deep into the bone, that, though I used all my
strength to pull it out, I was not able. For just at that moment four soldiers
with drawn swords sprang out from Antea's lodging, and obliged me to set
hand to my own sword to defend my life. Leaving the poniard then, I made
off, and fearing I might be recognised, took refuge in the palace of Duke
Alessandro, which was between Piazza Navona and the Rotunda. On my
arrival, I asked to see the Duke; who told me that, if I was alone, I need only
keep quiet and have no further anxiety, but go on working at the jewel
which the Pope had set his heart on, and stay eight days indoors. . . .

More than eight days elapsed, and the Pope did not send for me
according to his custom. Afterwards he summoned me through his chamber-
lain, the Bolognese nobleman I have already mentioned, who let me, in his
own modest manner, understand that his Holiness knew all, but was very
well inclined toward me, and that I had only to mind my work and keep
quiet. When we reached the presence, the Pope cast so menacing a glance
towards me that the mere look of his eyes made me tremble. Afterwards,

upon examining my work, his countenance cleared, and he began to praise me beyond measure, saying that I had done a vast amount in a short time. Then, looking me straight in the face, he added: "Now that you are cured, Benvenuto, take heed how you live." I, who understood his meaning, promised that I would. Immediately upon this, I opened a very fine shop in the Banchi, opposite Raffaello, and there I finished the jewel after the lapse of a few months.

The Pope had sent me all those precious stones, except the diamond, which was pawned to certain Genoese bankers for some pressing need he had of money. The rest were in my custody, together with a model of the diamond. I had five excellent journeymen, and in addition to the great piece, I was engaged on several jobs; so that my shop contained property of much value in jewels, gems, and gold and silver. I kept a shaggy dog, very big and handsome, which Duke Alessandro gave me; the beast was capital as a retriever, since he brought me every sort of birds and game I shot, but he also served most admirably for a watchdog. It happened, as was natural at the age of twenty-nine, that I had taken into my service a girl of great beauty and grace, whom I used as a model in my art, and who was also complaisant of her personal favours to me. Such being the case, I occupied an apartment far away from my workmen's room, as well as from the shop; and this communicated by a little dark passage with the maid's bedroom. I used frequently to pass the night with her; and though I sleep as lightly as ever yet did man upon this earth, yet, after indulgence in sexual pleasure, my slumber is sometimes very deep and heavy.

So it chanced one night: for I must say that a thief, under the pretext of being a goldsmith, had spied on me, and cast his eyes upon the precious stones, and made a plan to steal them. Well, then, this fellow broke into the shop, where he found a quantity of little things in gold and silver. He was engaged in bursting open certain boxes to get at the jewels he had noticed, when my dog jumped upon him, and put him to much trouble to defend himself with his sword.... [*The thief succeeded in escaping—B. T.*]

After sunrise my workmen went into the shop, and saw that it had been broken open and all the boxes smashed. They began to scream at the top of their voices: "Ah, woe is me! Ah, woe is me!" The clamour woke me, and I rushed out in a panic. Appearing thus before them, they cried out: "Alas to us! for we have been robbed by some one, who has broken and borne everything away!" These words wrought so forcibly upon my mind that I dared not go to my big chest and look if it still held the jewels of the Pope. So intense was the anxiety, that I seemed to lose my eyesight, and told them they themselves must unlock the chest, and see how many of the Pope's gems were missing. The fellows were all of them in their shirts; and when, on opening the chest, they saw the precious stones and my work with them, they took heart of joy and shouted: "There is no harm done; your piece and all the stones are here; but the thief has left us naked to the shirt, because last night, by reason of the burning heat, we took our clothes off in the shop and left them here." Recovering my senses, I thanked God, and said: "Go and get yourselves new suits of clothes; I will pay when I hear at leisure how the whole thing happened." What caused me the most pain, and made me lose my senses, and take fright—so contrary to my real nature—was the dread lest peradventure folk should fancy I had trumped a story of the robber up to steal the jewels. . . .

After telling the young men to provide themselves with fresh clothes, I took my piece, together with the gems, setting them as well as I could in their proper places, and went off at once with them to the Pope. Francesco del Nero had already told him something of the trouble in my shop, and had put suspicions in his head. So then, taking the thing rather ill than otherwise, he shot a furious glance upon me, and cried haughtily: "What have you come to do here? What is up?" "Here are all your precious stones, and not one of them is missing." At this the Pope's face cleared, and he said: "So then, you're welcome." I showed him the piece, and while he was inspecting it, I related to him the whole story of the thief and of my agony, and what had been my greatest trouble in the matter. During this speech, he often times turned round to look me sharply in the eyes; and Francesco del Nero being also in the presence, this seemed to make him half sorry that he had not guessed the truth. At last, breaking into laughter at the long tale I was telling, he sent me off with these words: "Go, and take heed to be an honest man, as indeed I know you are."

4 The Renaissance State

*In the transitional period at the end of the Middle Ages,
Marsilius of Padua produced a thoroughly secular theory of
politics. Its distinctive characteristic was that the priesthood
was treated as merely a constituent element of the state,
fully subject to the state's authority.*

FROM *The Defender of the Peace*
BY MARSILIUS OF PADUA

THE STATE, ACCORDING TO ARISTOTLE in the *Politics*, Book I,
Chapter 1, is "the perfect community having the full limit of self-sufficiency,
which came into existence for the sake of living, but exists for the sake of
living well." This phrase of Aristotle—"came into existence for the sake of
living, but exists for the sake of living well"—signifies the perfect final cause
of the state, since those who live a civil life not only live, which beasts or
slaves do too, but live well, having leisure for those liberal functions in which
are exercised the virtues of both the practical and the theoretic soul.

*   *   *

But the living and living well which are appropriate to men fall into two
kinds, of which one is temporal or earthly, while the other is usually called
eternal or heavenly. However, this latter kind of living, the eternal, the
whole body of philosophers were unable to prove by demonstration, nor was
it self-evident, and therefore they did not concern themselves with the means
thereto. But as to the first kind of living and living well or good life, that is,
the earthly, and its necessary means, this the glorious philosophers comprehended almost completely through demonstration. Hence for its attainment
they concluded the necessity of the civil community, without which this
sufficient life cannot be obtained. Thus the foremost of the philosophers,

Marsilius of Padua, *The Defender of the Peace*, II (1956), pp. 12–3, 44–5, 61, 100, 174–5, 253,
258, 264–5, translated by A. Gewirth. Reprinted by permission of Columbia University Press,
New York.

Aristotle, said in his *Politics,* Book I, Chapter 1: "All men are driven toward such an association by a natural impulse." Although sense experience teaches this, we wish to bring out more distinctly that cause of it which we have indicated, as follows: Man is born composed of contrary elements, because of whose contrary actions and passions some of his substance is continually being destroyed; moreover, he is born "bare and unprotected" from excess of the surrounding air and other elements, capable of suffering and of destruction, as has been said in the science of nature. As a consequence, he needed arts of diverse genera and species to avoid the afore-mentioned harms. But since these arts can be exercised only by a large number of men, and can be had only through their association with one another, men had to assemble together in order to attain what was beneficial through these arts and to avoid what was harmful.

But since among men thus assembled there arise disputes and quarrels which, if not regulated by a norm of justice, would cause men to fight and separate and thus finally would bring about the destruction of the state, there had to be established in this association a standard of justice and a guardian or maker thereof. . . .

But it must be remembered that the true knowledge or discovery of the just and the beneficial, and of their opposites, is not law taken in its last and most proper sense, whereby it is the measure of human civil acts, unless there is given a coercive command as to its observance, or it is made by way of such a command, by someone through whose authority its transgressors must and can be punished. Hence, we must now say to whom belongs the authority to make such a command and to punish its transgressors. This, indeed, is to inquire into the legislator or the maker of the law.

Let us say, then, in accordance with the truth and the counsel of Aristotle in the *Politics,* Book III, Chapter 6, that the legislator, or the primary and proper efficient cause of the law, is the people or the whole body of citizens, or the weightier part thereof, through its election or will expressed by words in the general assembly of the citizens, commanding or determining that something be done or omitted with regard to human civil acts, under a temporal pain or punishment. By the "weightier part" I mean to take into consideration the quantity and the quality of the persons in that community over which the law is made. The aforesaid whole body of citizens or the weightier part thereof is the legislator regardless of whether it makes the law directly by itself or entrusts the making of it to some person or persons, who are not and cannot be the legislator in the absolute sense, but only in a relative sense and for a particular time and in accordance with the authority of the primary legislator. . . .

It now remains to show the efficient cause of the ruler, that is, the cause by which there is given to one or more persons the authority of rulership which is established through election. For it is by this authority that a person becomes a ruler in actuality, and not by his knowledge of the laws, his prudence, or moral virtue, although these are qualities of the perfect ruler.

For it happens that many men have these qualities, but nevertheless, lacking this authority, they are not rulers, unless perhaps in proximate potentiality.

Taking up the question, then, let us say, in accordance with the truth and the doctrine of Aristotle in the *Politics,* Book III, Chapter 6, that the efficient power to establish or elect the ruler belongs to the legislator or the whole body of the citizens, just as does the power to make the laws, as we said in Chapter XII. And to the legislator similarly belongs the power to make any correction of the ruler and even to depose him, if this be expedient for the common benefit. . . . [*The holy Canons—B. T.*] clearly demonstrate that the Roman bishop called pope, or any other priest or bishop, or spiritual minister, collectively or individually, as such, has and ought to have no coercive jurisdiction over the property or person of any priest or bishop, or deacon, or group of them, and still less over any secular ruler or government, community, group, or individual, of whatever condition they may be; unless, indeed, such jurisdiction shall have been granted to a priest or bishop or group of them by the human legislator of the province. . . . Since, then, the heretic, the schismatic, or any other infidel is a transgressor of divine law, if he persists in this crime he will be punished by that judge to whom it pertains to correct transgressors of divine law as such, when he will exercise his judicial authority. But this judge is Christ, who will judge the living, the dead, and the dying, but in the future world, not in this one. For he has mercifully allowed sinners to have the opportunity of becoming deserving and penitent up to the very time when they finally pass from this world at death. But the other judge, namely, the pastor, bishop or priest, must teach and exhort man in the present life, must censure and rebuke the sinner and frighten him by a judgment or prediction of future glory or eternal damnation; but he must not coerce, as is plain from the previous chapter.

Now if human law were to prohibit heretics or other infidels from dwelling in the region, and yet such a person were found there, he must be corrected in this world as a transgressor of human law, and the penalty fixed by that law for such transgression must be inflicted on him by the judge who is the guardian of human law by the authority of the legislator, as we demonstrated in Chapter XV of Discourse I. But if human law did not prohibit the heretic or other infidel from dwelling among the faithful in the same province, as heretics and Jews are now permitted to do by human laws even in these times of Christian peoples, rulers, and pontiffs, then I say that no one is allowed to judge or coerce a heretic or other infidel by any penalty in property or in person for the status of the present life. And the general reason for this is as follows: no one is punished in this world for sinning against theoretic or practical disciplines precisely as such, however much he may sin against them, but only for sinning against a command of human law.

*   *   *

But with reference to our main thesis, this must be noted most of all: that even though it may for some reasons seem fitting that certain men should be called the successors of St. Peter, because they are more reverent than the successors of the other apostles, and especially because they occupy the episcopal seat at Rome, yet the sacred Scripture shows no necessary reason why the successors of the other apostles should be regarded as subject to them in any power. And even if the apostles were unequal in authority, yet St. Peter or any other apostle did not, by virtue of the words of the Scripture, have the power to appoint or depose them, with reference either to the priestly dignity which we have called essential, or to their being sent or assigned to a certain place or people, or to the interpretation of the Scripture or of the catholic faith, or to coercive jurisdiction over anyone in this world; any more than, conversely, the other apostles had any such power over St. Peter or some other apostle.

*   *   *

And now I wish to show that after the time of the apostles and of the first fathers who succeeded them in office, and especially now when the communities of believers have become perfected, the immediate efficient cause of the assignment or appointment of a prelate (whether of the major one, called the "bishop," or of the minor ones, called "curate priests," and likewise of the other minor ones) is or ought to be the entire multitude of believers of that place through their election or expressed will, or else the person or persons to whom the aforesaid multitude has given the authority to make such appointments. And I also wish to show that it pertains to the same authority lawfully to remove each of the afore-mentioned officials from such office, and to compel him to exercise it, if it seems expedient.

*   *   *

As for the distribution of temporal things, usually called "ecclesiastic benefices," it must be remembered that these things are set aside for the support of ecclesiastic ministers and other poor persons (which we discussed in Chapters XIV and XV of this discourse) either by the legislator or by some individual person or group. Now if such temporal goods have been thus set aside by the gift and establishment of the legislator, then, I say, the legislator can lawfully, in accordance with divine law, entrust to whomever it wants, and at any time, the authority to distribute these goods, and can, for cause, when it so wishes, revoke such authority from the individual or group to whom it has entrusted it.

*The Florentine diplomat, Niccolò Machiavelli (1469–1527),
startled his contemporaries by writing a book on politics*

that did not aim at instructing rulers in the moral virtues
but rather gave them pragmatic advice on how to win and
hold power.

FROM *The Prince* BY NICCOLÒ MACHIAVELLI

IT NOW REMAINS for us to consider what ought to be the conduct and bearing of a Prince in relation to his subjects and friends. And since I know that many have written on this subject, I fear it may be thought presumptuous in me to write of it also; the more so, because in my treatment of it I depart from the views that others have taken.

But since it is my object to write what shall be useful to whosoever understands it, it seems to me better to follow the real truth of things than an imaginary view of them. For many Republics and Princedoms have been imagined that were never seen or known to exist in reality. And the manner in which we live, and that in which we ought to live, are things so wide asunder, that he who quits the one to betake himself to the other is more likely to destroy than to save himself; since any one who would act up to a perfect standard of goodness in everything, must be ruined among so many who are not good. It is essential, therefore, for a Prince who desires to maintain his position, to have learned how to be other than good, and to use or not to use his goodness as necessity requires.

*   *   *

Beginning, then, with the first of the qualities above noticed, I say that it may be a good thing to be reputed liberal, but, nevertheless, that liberality without the reputation of it is hurtful; because, though it be worthily and rightly used, still if it be not known, you escape not the reproach of its opposite vice. Hence, to have credit for liberality with the world at large, you must neglect no circumstance of sumptuous display; the result being, that a Prince of a liberal disposition will consume his whole substance in things of this sort, and, after all, be obliged, if he would maintain his reputation for liberality, to burden his subjects with extraordinary taxes, and to resort to confiscations and all the other shifts whereby money is raised. But in this way he becomes hateful to his subjects, and growing impoverished is held in little esteem by any. So that in the end, having by his liberality offended many and obliged few, he is worse off than when he began, and is exposed to

Niccolò Machiavelli, *The Prince* (1897), pp. 109–10, 113–5, 118–9, 125–30, translated by N. H. Thompson. Reprinted by permission of The Clarendon Press, Oxford.

all his original dangers. Recognizing this, and endeavouring to retrace his steps, he at once incurs the infamy of miserliness.

A Prince, therefore, since he cannot without injury to himself practise the virtue of liberality so that it may be known, will not, if he be wise, greatly concern himself though he be called miserly. Because in time he will come to be regarded as more and more liberal, when it is seen that through his parsimony his revenues are sufficient; that he is able to defend himself against any who make war on him; that he can engage in enterprises against others without burdening his subjects; and thus exercise liberality towards all from whom he does not take, whose number is infinite, while he is miserly in respect of those only to whom he does not give, whose number is few.

*   *   *

Passing to the other qualities above referred to, I say that every Prince should desire to be accounted merciful and not cruel. Nevertheless, he should be on his guard against the abuse of this quality of mercy. Cesare Borgia was reputed cruel, yet his cruelty restored Romagna, united it, and brought it to order and obedience; so that if we look at things in their true light, it will be seen that he was in reality far more merciful than the people of Florence, who, to avoid the imputation of cruelty, suffered Pistoja to be torn to pieces by factions.

A Prince should therefore disregard the reproach of being thought cruel where it enables him to keep his subjects united and obedient. For he who quells disorder by a very few signal examples will in the end be more merciful than he who from too great leniency permits things to take their course and so to result in rapine and bloodshed; for these hurt the whole State, whereas the severities of the Prince injure individuals only.

*   *   *

A Prince should, therefore, understand how to use well both the man and the beast. And this lesson has been covertly taught by the ancient writers, who relate how Achilles and many others of these old Princes were given over to be brought up and trained by Chiron the Centaur; since the only meaning of their having for instructor one who was half man and half beast is, that it is necessary for a Prince to know how to use both natures, and that the one without the other has no stability.

But since a Prince should know how to use the beast's nature wisely, he ought of beasts to choose both the lion and the fox; for the lion cannot guard himself from the toils, nor the fox from wolves. He must therefore be a fox to discern toils, and a lion to drive off wolves.

To rely wholly on the lion is unwise; and for this reason a prudent Prince neither can nor ought to keep his word when to keep it is hurtful to him and the causes which led him to pledge it are removed. If all men were good, this would not be good advice, but since they are dishonest and do not keep faith with you, you, in return, need not keep faith with them; and no Prince was ever at a loss for plausible reasons to cloak a breach of faith. Of this numberless recent instances could be given, and it might be shown how many solemn treaties and engagements have been rendered inoperative and idle through want of faith in Princes, and that he who has best known to play the fox has had the best success.

It is necessary, indeed, to put a good colour on this nature, and to be skilful in simulating and dissembling. But men are so simple, and governed so absolutely by their present needs, that he who wishes to deceive will never fail in finding willing dupes. One recent example I will not omit. Pope Alexander VI had no care or thought but how to deceive, and always found material to work on. No man ever had a more effective manner of asseverating, or made promises with more solemn protestations, or observed them less. And yet, because he understood this side of human nature, his frauds always succeeded.

It is not essential, then, that a Prince should have all the good qualities which I have enumerated above, but it is most essential that he should seem to have them; I will even venture to affirm that if he has and invariably practises them all, they are hurtful, whereas the appearance of having them is useful. Thus, it is well to seem merciful, faithful, humane, religious, and upright, and also to be so; but the mind should remain so balanced that were it needful not to be so, you should be able and know how to change to the contrary.

And you are to understand that a Prince, and most of all a new Prince, cannot observe all those rules of conduct in respect whereof men are accounted good, being often forced, in order to preserve his Princedom, to act in opposition to good faith, charity, humanity, and religion. He must therefore keep his mind ready to shift as the winds and tides of Fortune turn, and, as I have already said, he ought not to quit good courses if he can help it, but should know how to follow evil courses if he must.

A Prince should therefore be very careful that nothing ever escapes his lips which is not replete with the five qualities above named, so that to see and hear him, one would think him the embodiment of mercy, good faith, integrity, humanity, and religion. And there is no virtue which it is more necessary for him to seem to possess than this last; because men in general judge rather by the eye than by the hand, for every one can see but few can touch. Every one sees what you seem, but few know what you are, and these few dare not oppose themselves to the opinion of the many who have the majesty of the State to back them up.

Moreover, in the actions of all men, and most of all of Princes, where there is no tribunal to which we can appeal, we look to results. Wherefore if a Prince succeeds in establishing and maintaining his authority, the means will always be judged honourable and be approved by every one. For the vulgar are always taken by appearances and by results, and the world is made up of the vulgar, the few only finding room when the many have no longer ground to stand on.

A distinguished modern historian of the Renaissance has evaluated Machiavelli's work as follows.

FROM *Machiavelli and the Renaissance* BY F. CHABOD

THE *leitmotiv* of Machiavelli's posthumous life was his great assertion as a thinker, representing his true and essential contribution to the history of human thought, namely, the clear recognition of the autonomy and the necessity of politics, "which lies outside the realm of what is morally good or evil." Machiavelli thereby rejected the mediaeval concept of "unity" and became one of the pioneers of the modern spirit.

However, in the generations that immediately followed the Florentine Secretary's death such a motif of spiritual enrichment could not be revived, developed and perfected. Amid the vacillation and the uncertainty of thought and feeling which characterizes all periods of transition it remained as a guide-post and no more. . . .

But it did remain; and—albeit almost surreptitiously, without appearing in all its theoretical potency—it also upheld the historical value of the work, and by its clarity made it possible for the European significance of the composition to emerge.

For Machiavelli accepted the political challenge in its entirety; he swept aside every criterion of action not suggested by the concept of *raison d'état*, i.e. by the exact evaluation of the historical moment and the constructive forces which the Prince must employ in order to achieve his aim; and he held that the activities of rulers were limited only by their capacity and energy. Hence, he paved the way for absolute governments, which theoretically were completely untrammelled, both in their home and in their foreign policies.

If this was made possible by the Florentine Secretary's recognition of the autonomy of politics, it depended, conversely, on his own peculiar conception of the State, which he identified with the government, or rather with its personal Head. Accordingly, in *The Prince* all his attention was riveted on the human figure of the man who held the reins of government and so epitomized in his person the whole of public life. Such a conception, determined directly by the historical experience which Machiavelli possessed in

Reprinted by permission of the publishers from Federico Chabod, *Machiavelli and the Renaissance*, pp. 116–8, 121–3, translated by David Moore. Cambridge, Mass.: Harvard University Press, Copyright, 1958, by Federico Chabod; and Bowes & Bowes Ltd., London.

such outstanding measure and presupposing a sustained effort on the part of the central government, was essential to the success and pre-eminence of his doctrine.

This was a turning-point in the history of the Christian world. The minds of political theorists were no longer trammelled by Catholic dogma. The structure of the State was not yet threatened in other directions by any revolt of the individual conscience. An entire moral world, if it was not eclipsed, had at any rate receded into the shadows, nor was any other at once forthcoming to take its place and to inspire a new fervour of religious belief; hence, political thought could express itself without being confused by considerations of a different character. It was an era in which unitarian States were being created amid the ruins of the social and political order of the Middle Ages, an era in which it was necessary to place all the weapons of resistance in the hands of those who had still to combat the forces of feudalism and particularism. It was, in short, an era in which it was essential that the freedom and grandeur of political action and the strength and authority of central government should be clearly affirmed. Only thus was it possible to obliterate once and for all the traces of the past and to offer to the society of the future, in the guise of a precept, the weapons which would preserve the life of the united nation in face of disruptive elements old and new.

*　　　*　　　*

Thus by its unadorned and axiomatic pronouncements Machiavelli's work contributed to keep alive the memory of the greatness which Italy had achieved before the peninsula was obliged to submit to foreign sovereignty. The Seigneurs and the Princes had failed in their purpose; and in the end, overwhelmed by Powers that were wealthier, stronger, and more deeply versed in the arts of war and politics, they had had to yield, either taking to flight or resigning themselves to the idea of leaving the conduct of Italian life to others. Yet in the course of an effort twice repeated within a hundred years they had created something which was not destined to perish, even if it was only completely and successfully developed abroad. The wisdom and administrative ability which had enabled them gradually to establish their power; the clarity and preciseness of political vision which had led them to adopt a vigorous unitarian policy, at any rate within the borders of their domains; their stubborn fight to ensure the absolute supremacy of the sovereign authority and to unite the various elements of the State—all these things established a tradition of civic wisdom and political energy which was destined to survive even when it was left to others to bring about its ultimate triumph.

This was the course on which Western Europe had embarked. It was the unique good fortune of the Italian tradition to be seized upon and epitomized in a few pages by Machiavelli, so that it became a model for Europe.

5   The Revolt of the Medievalists

W. K. Ferguson has described one modern trend in Renaissance historiography as a "revolt of the medievalists." The following extract will serve to illustrate the meaning of the phrase.

FROM *Héloïse and Abélard* BY ETIENNE GILSON

THERE IS NOTHING quite comparable to the passion of the historians of the Renaissance for its individualism, its independence of mind, its rebellion against the principle of authority, unless perchance it is the docility with which those same historians copy one another in dogmatizing about the Middle Ages of which they know so little. We should not attach much importance to this attitude, save that those who speak thus of things they understand so poorly pretend to act in defense of reason and of personal observation. Their charge that all those who hold a different opinion are yielding to prejudice would, indeed, be sad, were it not so comic. Indifference to facts, distrust of direct observation and personal knowledge, the tendency to prune their data to suit their hypotheses, the naïve and dogmatic tendency to charge that those who would refute their position with self-evident facts lack a critical sense—these are the substance of their charge against the Middle Ages. Certainly, the Middle Ages had its fair share of these limitations. But at the same time these same limitations provide a perfect picture of the attitude of these historians of the Renaissance. They themselves possess the weaknesses of which they accuse the Middle Ages.

For Jacob Burckhardt, who only echoes the Preface to Volume VII of Michelet's *History of France,* the Renaissance is characterized by the discovery of the world and by the discovery of man. . . . What he wishes to prove before everything else is that such strong individuals could only have appeared first in the tiny Italian tyrannies of the fourteenth century where men led so intense a personal life that they had to talk about it. And so we read that "Even autobiography (and not merely history) takes here and there in Italy a bold and vigorous flight, and puts before us, together with the most

E. Gilson, *Héloïse and Abélard* (1951), pp. 124–8, translated by L. K. Shook. Reprinted by permission of Henry Regnery Co., Chicago.

varied incidents of external life, striking revelations of the inner man. Among other nations, even in Germany, at the time of the Reformation, it deals only with outward experiences, and leaves us to guess at the spirit within. It seems as though Dante's *La Vita nuova,* with the inexorable truthfulness that runs through it, had shown his people the way." We can, moreover, find a reason for this absence of individuality among medieval folk. Need we speak it? It is to be found in the subjugation and standardization which Christianity forced upon them. "Once mistress, the Church does not tolerate the development of the individual. All must be resigned to becoming simple links in her long chain and to obeying the laws of her institutions."

A man lacking individuality, incapable of analyzing himself, without the taste for describing others in biography or himself in autobiography, such is the man Christianity produces. Let us cite, as an example, St. Augustine! But to confine ourselves to the twelfth century, and without asking from what unique mould we could fashion at the same time a Bernard of Clairvaux and a Pierre Abélard, let us make a simple comparison between the Renaissance of the professors and the facts which become manifest in the correspondence of Héloïse and Abélard.

If all we need for a Renaissance is to find individuals developed to the highest point, does not this pair suffice? To be sure, Abélard and Héloïse are not Italians. They were not born in some tiny Tuscan "tyranny" of the fourteenth century. They satisfy, in brief, none of the conditions which the theory demands except that they were just what they ought not to have been if the theory were true. One insists, however, upon persons capable of "freely describing the moral man," even as the great Italians could do it. Perhaps even here Abélard and Héloïse labored with some success! No one would be so foolish as to compare their correspondence with the *Vita nuova* as literature. But if it is just a matter of stating in which of the two works one finds the moral man more simply and more directly described, the tables are turned. It is the *Vita nuova* that can no longer bear the comparison. Historians still wonder whether Beatrice was a little Florentine or a symbol. But there is nothing symbolic about Héloïse, nor was her love for Abélard but the unfolding of allegorical remarks. This story of flesh and blood, carried along by a passion at once brutal and ardent to its celebrated conclusion, we know from within as, indeed, we know few others. Its heroes observe themselves, analyze themselves as only Christian consciences fallen prey to passions can do it. Nor do they merely analyze themselves, but they talk about themselves as well. What Renaissance autobiographies can be compared with the correspondence of Abélard and Héloïse? Perchance Benvenuto Cellini's? But even Burckhardt recognizes that this does not claim to be "founded on introspection." Moreover, the reader "often detects him bragging or lying." On the contrary, it is absolutely certain that it is their inmost selves about which Abélard and Héloïse instruct us; and if they sometimes lie to themselves, they never lie to us.

Before such disagreement between facts and theory, we might reasonably expect the theory to yield a little. But not a bit of it! . . . No fact, whatever it may be, no facts, however numerous they may be, can ever persuade those who hold this theory that it is false, because it is of its very essence and by definition that the Renaissance is the negation of the Middle Ages.

Gaines Post argued that the origins of the modern state are to be found in the twelfth and thirteenth centuries rather than in the age of the Renaissance.

FROM *Studies in Medieval Legal Thought*
BY GAINES POST

ALMOST FORTY YEARS AGO Charles Homer Haskins applied the word renaissance to the twelfth century. Whether or not it was a renaissance, the twelfth century was in fact a period of great creative activity. The revival of political, economic, and social life, along with the appearance of new learning, new schools, and new literatures and styles of art and architecture, signified the beginnings, in the West, of modern European civilization. In the thirteenth century what had begun in the twelfth arrived at such maturity that it is safe to say that early modern Europe was coming into being.

Among the institutions and fields of knowledge created by medieval men, the university and the State and the legal science that aided in the creation of both were, as much as the rise of an active economy and the organization of towns, important manifestations of the new age. While accepting and respecting tradition and believing in the unchanging higher law of nature that came from God, kings, statesmen, and men of learning confidently applied reason and skill to the work of introducing order into society and societies, into feudal kingdoms, Italian communes, and lesser communities of the clergy and laity. Long before the recovery of Aristotle's *Politics,* the naturalness of living in politically and legally organized communities of corporate guilds, chapters, towns, and States was recognized both in practice and in legal thought. Nature itself sanctioned the use of human reason and art to create new laws for the social and political life on earth —provided always, of course, that the new did not violate the will of God.

Gaines Post, *Studies in Medieval Legal Thought,* pp. 3–4, 248–9, 20–4. Reprinted by permission of the Princeton University Press. Copyright © 1964 by Princeton University Press.

At the very time when merchants, artisans, townsmen, and schoolmen were forming their associations for mutual aid and protection, the study of the Roman and Canon law at Bologna introduced lawyers, jurists, and secular and ecclesiastical authorities to the legal thought of Rome on corporations. When kings were trying to overcome the anarchy of feudalism, the new legal science furnished those principles of public law that helped them convert their realms into States. . . .

The objection is often raised, however, that medieval kingdoms were not States because (1) they accepted the spiritual authority of the pope and the universal Church, (2) king and realm were under God and the law of nature, and (3) the royal government was poorly centralized. As for the first argument, it might be raised against the use of the term "State" for Eire and Spain today. Yet we assume that these two countries are States even though they are essentially Catholic and in some fashion recognize the spiritual authority of the Roman Church. With respect to other ideals of universalism, the United States and Italy, not to mention other nations, are sovereign States while belonging to the United Nations. As for the second argument, on subjection to God and a moral law, it must be replied that the official motto of the United States is "In God We Trust," and Americans take an oath of loyalty to "one nation indivisible under God." Furthermore, the sovereignty of the American people and their State is surely limited in fact by a moral law that belongs to the Judaeo-Christian tradition: it is not likely that the representatives of the people in Congress will ever think of making laws that violate the Ten Commandments, nor that the Supreme Court will approve them. It is therefore not absurd to call medieval kingdoms States despite limitations within which derived from the ideal of law and justice, and despite limitations from without (also within) from the universalism of Christianity and the Church. Papal arbitration of "international" disputes in the thirteenth century interfered with the sovereign right of kings to go to war (always the "just war" in defense of the *patria* and the *status regni*) no more and no less than international organizations do in the twentieth century. And "world opinion" was respected as much or as little.

In reply to the third argument, regarding the amount of centralization, one must ask, what degree of centralization is necessary for a State to exist? If the central government must be absolute in power, then the United States might not qualify, since a great many powers remain in the fifty states within. And did France become a State only with the more thorough centralization that resulted from the Revolution? Logically we might conclude that only a totalitarian State is a true State.

*   *   *

[*During the Middle Ages—B. T.*], in the emergency of a danger that threatened the safety of all, the ruler had a superior right to take such action as would ensure the public welfare or safety, that is, maintain the *status* or state of the realm. This emergency was a case of necessity—usually, as I have had occasion to say above, a just war of defense. Now the case of necessity, Meinecke has shown, was asserted by Machiavelli as a part of his theory of the State: the State is above all; and the prince, to assure the noble end of the State, has the right to use any means to meet the necessity and preserve the State. Necessity is Guicciardini's reason of State. But it had its medieval background—Meinecke finding the earliest statement in the maxim, "necessity knows no law," in the late fourteenth century—in Gerson: Helene Wieruszowski finding it stated, along with public utility, in the time of Frederick II.

Actually it goes back farther—if not to the Greeks, at any rate to Mark 2, 25–26; and above all to the *Corpus Iuris Canonici* and the *Corpus Iuris Civilis*. A pseudo-Isidorian canon in Gratian (*De cons.,* Dist. 1, c. 11) uses the very expression, "quoniam necessitas non habet legem"; decretists and decretalists from the late twelfth century on state the maxim and in their glosses explain its meaning in connection with the equitable interpretation of the law. For example, the necessity of hunger, says one, excuses theft; poverty, says another, knows no law; and the law ends, says a glossator, when necessity begins. Azo in his *Brocardica* discusses the rule and gives many citations *pro* and *con* to *Code* and *Digest*. To *D*. 9, 2, 4, where we find that it is lawful to kill a thief in the night (the correspondence to *Exod*. 22, 2–3, had been noted by St. Augustine and was discussed by the canonists) because "natural reason" permits one to defend oneself against danger, Accursius gives complete approval.

Here, "Necessity knows no law" was a principle of private law. But because of the theory of the just war, that is, the right of the kingdom to defend itself against the aggressor (St. Augustine stated it, as did the scholastic philosophers), the case of necessity became a principle of public laws in the thirteenth century; the equivalent of "just cause," "evident utility," and the common welfare, it was perforce connected with the preservation of the *status regni*. From the twelfth century on, the kings of France and England appealed to necessity as the justification for demanding extraordinary taxes. As we have seen, the Church had already recognized the validity of necessity in the lay taxation of the clergy. No wonder, then, that in the late thirteenth century French lawyers, not only Beaumanoir and Pierre Dubois, but royal councillors like Pierre Flot and William of Nogaret, were asserting that in a case of necessity the defense of the kingdom and all its members was a superior right of the *status regni;* and that if "what touched all must be approved of all," the king had the right to compel all, even the clergy, to consent to measures taken to meet the danger.

At the same time, the situation of "international wars," necessity, public welfare, and the rise of powerful monarchies broke down the corporate hierarchy of communities within the Empire. Each great kingdom, like England or France, by the middle of the thirteenth century was independent of the Empire in theory and practice alike. And at the end of the century each was independent of the Church—and even above the Church, except in purely spiritual matters.

*   *   *

On the foundation of the two laws and of the rise of feudal monarchies, the theory, and some practice, of public law and the State thus arose in the twelfth and thirteenth centuries. Private rights and privileges remained powerful and enjoyed a recrudescence in localism and privileged orders in the fourteenth century and later. At times, in periods of war and civil dissension, they weakened the public authority of kings and threatened the very survival of the State.[1] But the ideas and ideal of the State and public order, of a public and constitutional law, were constantly at hand to remind statesmen of their right to reconstitute the State.

> *Lynn Thorndike criticized Burckhardt's interpretation of the Renaissance from the standpoint of a historian of science.*

FROM *Renaissance or Prenaissance?*
BY LYNN THORNDIKE

MICHELET CALLED THE RENAISSANCE "the discovery of the world and of man," and was followed in this lead by the very influential book of Burckhardt, in which, on what seem too often to be dogmatic or imaginary grounds without sufficient presentation of facts as evidence, the

[1] Naturally I cannot attempt to outline the history of the failures of the public order of the State and of the public authority of the king in the fourteenth and fifteenth centuries. At times, in France for example, king and realm meant little except in the continuity of the ideas and ideal of the public law symbolized by the crown. As late as the eighteenth century, local and individual privileges and local resistance to the commands of the central government made the State weak. On this see in general the excellent book by R. R. Palmer, *The Age of the Democratic Revolution.* To return to the fourteenth century, in France, after the time of Philip IV, particularly in the period of the disasters of the Hundred Years' War and the Black Death, there was far less of a State than in the thirteenth century. *Plena potestas, quod omnes tangit,* and *status regni* apparently no longer manifested the power as well as the theoretical right of the king to obtain more than haphazard and sporadic consent, chiefly in local assemblies, to extraordinary taxes. In England the situation was different, but even there the legal thought I have investigated needs study in relation to the political events. For the situation in France see, besides C. H. Taylor in Strayer and Taylor, *Studies,* Fredric Cheyette, "Procurations by Large-Scale Communities in Fourteenth-Century France," *Speculum,* XXXVII (1962), 18–31.

Lynn Thorndike, "Renaissance or Prenaissance?" *Journal of the History of Ideas,* IV (1943), 69–74.

Renaissance was no longer regarded as primarily a rebirth of classical learning and culture but rather as a prebirth or precursor of present society and of modern civilization—"a period," to quote the *Boston Transcript* (February 27, 1926) concerning Elizabethan England, "that witnessed the birth pangs of most that is worth while in modern civilization and government."

This made a well-calculated appeal to the average reader who is little interested to be told that Erasmus was a great Greek scholar or that Leonardo da Vinci copied from Albert of Saxony, but whose ego is titillated to be told that Leonardo was an individual like himself or that Erasmus's chief claim to fame is that he was the first modern man—the first one like you and me. All this was quite soothing and flattering and did much to compensate for one's inability to read Horace or to quote Euripides.

*   *   *

Was the individual freed and personality enhanced by the Renaissance or Prenaissance? Burckhardt affirmed that with it "man became a spiritual individual and recognized himself as such," whereas "in the middle ages both sides of human consciousness—that which was turned within as that which was turned without—lay dreaming or half awake beneath a common veil." It might be remarked that individualism may be a mark of decline rather than progress. The self-centered sage of the Stoics and Epicureans rang the knell of the Greek city-state. Basil, on the verge of the barbarian invasions, complained that men "for the greater part prefer individual and private life to the union of common life." Carl Neumann held that "true modern individualism has its roots in the strength of the barbarians, in the realism of the barbarians, and in the Christian middle ages." Cunningham believed that the Roman Empire "left little scope for individual aims and tended to check the energy of capitalists and laborers alike," whereas Christianity taught the supreme dignity of man and encouraged the individual and personal responsibility. Moreover, in the thirteenth century there were "fewer barriers to social intercourse than now." According to Schäfer, "So far as public life in the broadest sense, in church and state, city and country, law and society, is concerned, the middle ages are the time of most distinctive individuality and independent personality in volition and action." We may no longer think of the Gothic architects as anonymous, and de Mely discovered hundreds of signatures of miniaturists hidden in the initials and illuminations of medieval manuscripts. No period in the history of philosophy has discussed individuality and its problems more often or more subtly than did the medieval schoolmen. Vittorino da Feltre and other humanist educators may have suited their teaching to the individual pupil; at the medieval university the individual scholar suited himself. The humanists were imitative in their writing, not original. Vitruvius was the Bible of Renaissance architects who came to follow authority far more than their creative Gothic predecessors. For the middle ages loved variety; the Renaissance, uniformity.

Not only has it been demonstrated that the thirteenth and fourteenth centuries were more active and penetrating in natural science than was the quattrocento, but the notion that "appreciation of natural beauty" was "introduced into modern Europe by the Italian Renaissance" must also be abandoned. Burckhardt admitted that medieval literature displayed sympathy with nature, but nevertheless regarded Petrarch's ascent of Mount Ventoux (which is only 6260 feet high) in 1336 as epoch-making. Petrarch represented an old herdsman who had tried in vain to climb it fifty years before as beseeching him to turn back on the ground that he had received only torn clothes and broken bones for his pains and that no one had attempted the ascent since. As a matter of fact, Jean Buridan, the Parisian schoolman, had visited it between 1316 and 1334, had given details as to its altitude, and had waxed enthusiastic as to the Cevennes. So that all Petrarch's account proves is his capacity for story-telling and sentimental ability to make a mountain out of a molehill. Miss Stockmayer, in a book on feeling for nature in Germany in the tenth and eleventh centuries, has noted various ascents and descriptions of mountains from that period. In the closing years of his life archbishop Anno of Cologne climbed his beloved mountain oftener than usual.

As for the feeling for nature in medieval art, let me repeat what I have written elsewhere anent the interest displayed by the students of Albertus Magnus in particular herbs and trees.

This healthy interest in nature and commendable curiosity concerning real things was not confined to Albert's students nor to "rustic intelligences." One has only to examine the sculpture of the great thirteenth-century cathedrals to see that the craftsmen of the towns were close observers of the world of nature, and that every artist was a naturalist too. In the foliage that twines about the capitals of the columns in the French Gothic cathedrals it is easy to recognize, says M. Mâle, a large number of plants: "the plantain, arum, ranunculus, fern, clover, coladine, hepatica, columbine, cress, parsley, strawberry-plant, ivy, snapdragon, the flower of the broom, and the leaf of the oak, a typically French collection of flowers loved from childhood." *Mutatis mutandis,* the same statement could be made concerning the carved vegetation that runs riot in Lincoln cathedral. "The thirteenth-century sculptors sang their *chant de mai*. All the spring delights of the Middle Ages live again in their work—the exhilaration of Palm Sunday, the garlands of flowers, the bouquets fastened on the doors, the strewing of fresh herbs in the chapels, the magical flowers of the feast of Saint John—all the fleeting charm of those old-time springs and summers. The Middle Ages, so often said to have little love for nature, in point of fact gazed at every blade of grass with reverence."

It is not merely love of nature but scientific interest and accuracy that we see revealed in the sculptures of the cathedrals and in the note-books of the thirteenth-century architect, Villard de Honnecourt, with its sketches of insect as well as animal life, of a lobster, two parroquets on a perch, the spirals of a snail's shell, a fly, a dragonfly, and a grasshopper, as well as a bear and a lion from life, and more familiar animals such as the cat and the swan. The sculptors of gargoyles and chimeras were not content to reproduce existing animals but showed their command of animal anatomy by creating strange compound and hybrid monsters—one might almost say, evolving new species—which nevertheless have all the verisimilitude of copies from living forms. It was these breeders in stone, these Burbanks of the pencil, these Darwins with the chisel, who knew nature and had studied botany and zoology in a way superior to the scholar who simply pored over the works of Aristotle and Pliny. No wonder that Albert's students were curious about particular things.

* * *

The concept of the Italian Renaissance or Prenaissance has in my opinion done a great deal of harm in the past and may continue to do harm in the future. It is too suggestive of a sensational, miraculous, extraordinary, magical, human and intellectual development, like unto the phoenix rising from its ashes after five hundred years. It is contrary to the fact that human nature tends to remain much the same in all times. It has led to a chorus of rhapsodists as to freedom, breadth, soaring ideas, horizons, perspectives, out of fetters and swaddling clothes, and so on. It long discouraged the study of centuries of human development that preceded it, and blinded the French *philosophes* and revolutionists to the value of medieval political and economic institutions. It has kept men in general from recognizing that our life and thought is based more nearly and actually on the middle ages than on distant Greece and Rome, from whom our heritage is more indirect, bookish and sentimental, less institutional, social, religious, even less economic and experimental.

But what is the use of questioning the Renaissance? No one has ever proved its existence; no one has really tried to. So often as one phase of it or conception of it is disproved, or is shown to be equally characteristic of the preceding period, its defenders take up a new position and are just as happy, just as enthusiastic, just as complacent as ever.

6 A Suggested Synthesis

W. K. Ferguson has recently defended the older interpretation of the Renaissance as an age of brilliant innovation, while taking note of the criticisms of the medievalists.

FROM *The Reinterpretation of the Renaissance*
BY W. K. FERGUSON

IT SHOULD BE UNDERSTOOD, of course, that recognition of the Renaissance as a period in history does not imply that it was completely different from what preceded and what followed it. Even in a dynamic view of history, periodization may prove a very useful instrument if properly handled. The gradual changes brought about by a continuous historical development may be in large part changes in degree, but when they have progressed far enough they become for all practical purposes changes in kind. To follow a good humanist precedent and argue from the analogy of the human body, the gradual growth of man from childhood to maturity is an unbroken process, yet there is a recognizable difference between the man and the child he has been. Perhaps the analogy, as applied to the Middle Ages and the Renaissance, is unfortunate in that it suggests a value judgment that might be regarded as invidious. However that may be, it is my contention that by about the beginning of the fourteenth century in Italy and somewhat later in the North those elements in society which had set the tone of medieval culture had perceptibly lost their dominant position and thereafter gradually gave way to more recently developed forces. These, while active in the earlier period, had not been the determining factors in the creation of medieval culture but were to be the most influential in shaping the culture of the Renaissance.

That somewhat involved statement brings me to the hazardous question of what were the fundamental differences between medieval and Renaissance civilization, and to the approach to the problem which I have found most generally satisfactory. It is an approach suggested by the work of the

Wallace K. Ferguson, "The Reinterpretation of the Renaissance," W. H. Werkmeister, ed., *Facets of the Renaissance* (1959), pp. 13–7. Reprinted by permission of University of Southern California, Los Angeles.

recent economic historians who have called attention to the dynamic influence of the revival of trade, urban life, and money economy in the midst of the agrarian feudal society of the high Middle Ages. Unfortunately, economic historians have seldom spared much thought for the development of intellectual and aesthetic culture, having been content to leave that to the specialists, while, on the other hand, the historians whose special interests was religion, philosophy, literature, science, or art have all too frequently striven to explain the developments in these fields without correlating them with changes in the economic, social, and political structure of society. In the past few years, however, historians have become increasingly aware of the necessity of including all forms of human activity in any general synthesis, an awareness illustrated by Myron Gilmore's recent volume on *The World of Humanism*. Further, there has been a growing tendency to find the original motive forces of historical development in basic alterations of the economic, political, and social system, which in time exert a limiting and directing influence upon intellectual interests, religious attitudes, and cultural forms. As applied to the Renaissance, this tendency has been evident in the work of several historians, notably, Edward P. Cheyney, Ferdinand Schevill, Eugenio Garin, Hans Baron, and some of the contributors to the *Propyläen Weltgeschichte*.

To state my point as briefly as possible, and therefore more dogmatically than I could wish: let us begin with the axiomatic premise that the two essential elements in medieval civilization were the feudal system and the universal church. The latter represented an older tradition than feudalism, but in its external structure and in many of its ideals and ways of thought it had been forced to adapt itself to the conditions of feudal society. And feudalism in turn was shaped by the necessity of adapting all forms of social and political life to the limitations of an agrarian and relatively moneyless economy. Into this agrarian feudal society the revival of commerce and industry, accompanied by the growth of towns and money economy, introduced a new and alien element. The first effect of this was to stimulate the existing medieval civilization, freeing it from the economic, social, and cultural restrictions that an almost exclusive dependence upon agriculture had imposed upon it, and making possible a rapid development in every branch of social and cultural activity. That the twelfth and thirteenth centuries were marked by the growth of a very vigorous culture no longer needs to be asserted. They witnessed the recovery of much ancient learning, the creation of scholastic philosophy, the rise of vernacular literatures and of Gothic art, perhaps on the whole a greater advance than was achieved in the two following centuries. Nevertheless, it seems to me that, despite new elements and despite rapid development, the civilization of these two centuries remained in form and spirit predominantly feudal and ecclesiastical.

But medieval civilization, founded as it was upon a basis of land tenure and agriculture, could not continue indefinitely to absorb an expanding urban society and money economy without losing its essential character, without gradually changing into something recognizably different. The changes were most obvious in the political sphere, as feudalism gave way before the rise of city states or centralized territorial states under princes who were learning to utilize the power of money. The effect upon the church was almost equally great. Its universal authority was shaken by the growing power of the national states, while its internal organization was transformed by the evolution of a monetary fiscal system which had, for a time, disastrous effects upon its moral character and prestige. Meanwhile, within the cities the growth of capital was bringing significant changes in the whole character of urban economic and social organizations, of which not the least significant was the appearance of a growing class of urban laymen who had the leisure and means to secure a liberal education and to take an active part in every form of intellectual and aesthetic culture.

Taking all these factors together, the result was an essential change in the character of European civilization. The feudal and ecclesiastical elements, though still strong, no longer dominated, and they were themselves more or less transformed by the changing conditions. The culture of the period we call the Renaissance was predominantly and increasingly the product of the cities, created in major part by urban laymen whose social environment, personal habits, and professional interests were different from those of the feudal and clerical aristocracy who had largely dominated the culture of the Middle Ages. These urban laymen, and with them the churchmen who were recruited from their midst as the medieval clergy had been recruited from the landed classes, did not break suddenly or completely with their inherited traditions, but they introduced new materials and re-stated the old in ways that reflected a different manner of life. The Renaissance, it seems to me, was essentially an age of transition, containing much that was still medieval, much that was recognizably modern, and, also, much that, because of the mixture of medieval and modern elements, was peculiar to itself and was responsible for its contradictions and contrasts and its amazing vitality.

This interpretation of the Renaissance leaves many of the old controversial points unanswered, though a partial answer to most of them is implied in it. It may be as well not to attempt to answer all questions with a single formula. There was certainly enough variety in the changing culture of western Europe during both the Middle Ages and the Renaissance to provide historians with material to keep them happily engaged in controversy for some time to come. All that can be claimed for the approach I have suggested is that it seems to offer the broadest basis for periodization, that it points to the most fundamental differences between the civilization of the Renaissance and the Middle Ages, while recognizing the dynamic character of both. At the same time, by suggesting a broad theory of causation in the gradual transformation of the economic and social structure of western Europe, it tends to reduce the controversial questions regarding the primary influence of the classical revival, of the Italian genius, Germanic blood, medieval French culture, or Franciscan mysticism to a secondary, if not irrelevant, status. Finally, such an approach to the problem might make it possible to take what was genuinely illuminating in Burckhardt, without the exaggerations of the classical-rational-Hegelian tradition, and also without the necessity of attacking the Renaissance *per se* in attacking Burckhardtian orthodoxy.

Martin Luther—
Reformer or
Revolutionary?

CONTENTS

QUESTIONS FOR STUDY

1   What was Luther's position on the relation of God to man?

2   To what extent was Luther heretical before the indulgence controversy?

3   What, according to Luther, was the true liberty of a Christian?

4   What role in the making of the Reformation do the various historians cited assign to Luther?

5   Would there have been a Reformation if Martin Luther had never lived?

The Reformation is one of the great events in the history of Europe. The unity of Western Christendom had been strained many times before; now it was broken. Why did this occur in the early sixteenth century? The answers given are many and various, but they all have to begin with Martin Luther—Augustinian monk and devout Christian. The role of the individual in history is difficult to evaluate. With Luther, it becomes almost impossible, for man and circumstances came together at a particular time in so complex a fashion that the contribution of either is difficult, if not impossible, to measure. Yet, one can question Luther's intentions. Was he out to reform the church—or was his position so incompatible with the church doctrine he knew so well that the result necessarily had to be revolutionary? Or, one may ask, did he not even know what he was doing?

1 The Road to Reformation

The English historian, Gordon Rupp, puts Luther and the problems facing him at the very outset of the Reformation in historical perspective.

FROM *The Righteousness of God* BY GORDON RUPP

IT WAS A CRITICAL MOMENT during the Leipzig Disputation (1519) when Martin Luther, out-manoeuvred by his opponent, Dr. Eck, was goaded into declaring that "among the articles of John Huss . . . which were condemned, are many which are truly Christian." The audience was horrified, and perhaps Luther himself was a little shocked. For he had grown to accept the judgment of contemporary opinion against the heretic of a former generation. "I used to abhor the very name of Huss. So zealous was I for the Pope that I would have helped to bring iron and fire to kill Huss, if not in very deed, at least with a consenting mind." In this verdict faith and party loyalty combined, for the Erfurt Augustinians were proud that a member of their own order, John Zachariae, had earned the title "Scourge of Huss" and his tomb bore in effigy the Golden Rose bestowed upon him by a grateful Pope. It was not until Luther himself entered a similar context of Papal condemnation that he turned to examine the writings of Huss, and to criticize this unexamined assumption. Then indeed he could cry to Spalatin, "We are all Hussites, without knowing it . . . even Paul and Augustine!"

Luther did not know that in later centuries, a similar weight of received opinion would lie against himself, and that faith and party loyalty, formidable vested interests of the mind, would come to obscure the truth about himself. To every age there belong mental patterns, involving assumptions about causes and persons, for the most part accepted without reference to the canons of historical criticism, and even the expert in one particular field of historical investigation is bound to take over certain general assumptions when he considers matters beyond his own exact knowledge. Yet it is needful for the soul's health of any culture that there should exist places where these assumptions may be roughly handled. Above all, it would seem

Gordon Rupp, *The Righteousness of God: Luther Studies* (1953), pp. 3–15. Reprinted by permission of Hodder & Stoughton Ltd., London.

that Universities might be centres of vigorous and unremitting self criticism, where there are few closed questions, and where at any time a case may be heard afresh, if it can reasonably be shown that evidence has been ignored, or that new facts have been brought to light.

There are reasons why a good deal of received academic opinion should be unfriendly towards Martin Luther. There is the modern reaction against the judgments of the Victorian Age, not least among those who have shed the Protestantism of their fathers. The virile theological tradition deriving from the Oxford Movement has made great and positive theological contributions to English religion, but from the time of Hurrell Froude onwards, its "blind spot" has been a rigid, narrow and wooden hostility towards the Reformers and their works. Then there is the tradition of the liberal historians with their wistful preference for a Reformation "along Erasmian lines" which, they consider, might have been, but for the violent intervention of Luther and his friends. To the liberal historians and theologians, aloof from theology and dogma, Martin Luther could hardly be a congenial figure. The events of our generation have hardly disposed us to a sympathetic judgment of the course of German history, and made only too plausible the arguments of those who derive all our ills from the Reformation, and not a few from the influence of Martin Luther.

The case for the reconsideration of Luther is that all these judgments, good or ill, rest upon an insufficient consideration of facts. Of the many thousands of Luther's writings, hardly more than a score have been available in English throughout the greater part of four centuries. There has been little awareness of the problems and discoveries of modern Luther study which both in detail and in principle have been of a quality and intricacy high among historical disciplines, second only, it may be, to that of Biblical criticism.

Reconsideration must not prejudge the issue. It must be confessed that so much of the writing about Luther in four centuries has been polemical that it is very difficult not to be on the defensive, or offensive, about him. When Protestants admit faults, and Catholics virtues, in his character, these concessions are bound to be taken from their context and used for polemical purposes. Yet we have the soundest reasons for supposing that an infallible Luther is no part of any Protestant confession. It was a disciple of Melanchthon, Joachim Camerarius, who wrote, "Those who count it a reproach to great and famous people when anything blameworthy is found in them, have too soft a conception of the position of such people. For only God has this privilege, to be without a fault: human nature is not capable of it."

When we have confessed that loyalty and party judgment are inevitably involved, we must face more formidable difficulties. There is first, the vastness of the material to be mastered. . . . A sound historical background: familiarity with secular and ecclesiastical history, and with dogmatic theology, including a more than nodding acquaintance with late scholasticism: a knowledge of Protestant theology in its origin and development. These are essential preliminaries. Then, leaving out of account secondary studies (in half a dozen languages) which run into thousands, there remain the works of Luther himself.

We know that at the Diet of Worms, the Emperor Charles V and the Papal Nuncio, Aleander, were reluctant to believe that the pile of Luther's works heaped before them could have been the work of one man in a few months. Yet that man continued to produce something like a treatise a fortnight over the next twenty-five years. As the great Weimar edition with ninety-four folio volumes draws within sight of completion, we admire a feat of theological engineering, but we remember that such engineering achievements are never finished, always under repair, and that often the beginning is in need of amendment while the work is being finished. So it seems to be with the works of Luther. . . .

If the historian has a mass of material of undoubted authenticity, there is a penumbra which is his titillation and despair. There are many volumes of sermons and lectures by Luther which we possess only in their reported form, and some, like a great part of the Genesis commentary, were published only after Luther's death. The historian is constantly tempted to have his cake, and eat it. But if he rejects the "Sermon on Marriage" (1519) for the sound reason that it is a pirated version very strongly repudiated by Luther, then he has also to admit that Luther did not sponsor the most famous of all sayings attributed to him, the famous "Hier stehe ich: ich kann nicht anders." [*Here I stand: I cannot do otherwise—L. P. W.*]

Above all, there is the nice problem of the Table Talk. One hardly knows whether to be grateful or not for that hospitality of Luther which allowed a motley club of inferior Boswells to frequent his table, and that their garbled remembrances have, in sundry portions and in divers manners, been transmitted to posterity. We know how it irked Frau Luther to play Martha to half a dozen male Marys who made Luther talk while the food got cold. And we know how they intruded into the most domestic privacies, as in that solemn hour when Luther's beloved Magdalena lay dying in her father's arms. But they were all made welcome: the Wittenberg theologians as and when they could come: including, of course, the Melanchthons, though Frau Luther seldom could forget that while she was a Von Bora, Frau Melanchton was the daughter of a small town mayor. There came travelling scholars and distinguished refugees, and the students. And then, from 1530 onwards, the reporters. Cordatus perhaps, seven years the senior of Luther, irascible and ungracious, a teutonic Crawley of Hogglestock: or the melancholy Schlaginhaufen, always in the dumps, but who softened Kate Luther's tongue because, really, he was wonderful with the children. And Mathesius, that enterprising young usher who smuggled some of his pupils to Luther's table until the master of the house decided that this was a little too much, even for Liberty Hall.

It is very tantalizing. Here is richly personal material, offering again and again to fill critical gaps in our knowledge. We are tempted to select what suits us, and to complain when others do the same. Moreover, while the conscious mind may reject testimony, or suspend judgment, the mind is subtly influenced by reading. Not that we need to be too sceptical. Enough of the real Luther has got into even the most dubious collections. But on the whole it is safer to use the Table Talk to confirm rather than to establish, and not to use it as a sufficient source for Luther's exact words or technical vocabulary. Modern research has established a pedigree of the sources, and brought to light some of the original note-books, so that the Weimar edition has a careful compilation in six volumes. But there it all is: letters, sermons, tracts, commentaries, polemic, Table Talk providing material so heterogeneous that select quotation can support the most varied and opposite interpretations.

Luther's method aggravates the difficulty. In a preface to the Book of Exodus Luther has words about Moses, and his apparent inconsistencies, which apply also to himself. "Moses writes as the case demands, so that his book is a picture and illustration of government and life. For this is what happens when things are moving . . . now this work has to be done, and now that . . . and a man must be ready every hour for anything, and do the first thing that comes to hand. The books of Moses are mixed up in just this way." Luther's writing is invariably called forth by a concrete, particular historical occasion: he had neither the leisure nor the talent to produce a systematized text-book, after the manner of the "Loci Communes" of Melanchthon, or the "Institutes" of Calvin. When we consider how for Luther, as for Moses, things were moving (between 1517 and 1546), we need not wonder that historians and theologians have found it hard to reconcile apparent differences, or driven wedges between various sections of his life.

Then there is the difficulty of Luther's personal character. When Frederick the Wise met Erasmus at Cologne in November 1520 and asked for a plain judgment on Luther, he got instead an enigmatic epigram which drove him to complain, "What a wonderful little man that is! You never know where you are with him." That kind of reticence was completely foreign to Luther, about whom even his enemy Duke George had to admit "those people at Wittenberg are at least not mealy-mouthed. They do say what they really mean, frankly and straightforwardly." The result is that for good and ill, what Luther thought came straight out, and his few attempts to be subtle, or to restrain himself, usually ended in tragi-comedy. Like St. Jerome, Luther had a physical excuse, especially in his last years, for his tantrums. But some of his best, as well as his worst, writing was done in the heat of righteous anger. When his blood was up, he would charge into battle, and when he did, his pen was not so much a sword as the spiked club with which Holbein pictures him as the Hercules Germanicus. And when the first impetus had spent itself, sheer pig-headedness might keep him going, while on such occasions he delighted to greet the scared expostulations of his timid friends with something really shocking. For he was a thorough polemic divine, and not Rabelais or Sir Thomas More had more violent and varied ways of calling a spade a spade. His sense of humour was elephantine, large and clumsy, and since it was often misunderstood by his contemporaries, it can be imagined what a mine of potential misconception it bequeathed to owl-like theologians fumbling with what is called "the jocular element in Luther."

There is a good deal in the controversial writings of Luther which repels and disgusts, and polemic has made the most of it. Yet to concentrate the muck in a few pages is to give a completely false impression. Certainly the Luther of the polemical writings is not the whole Luther. We must turn elsewhere to find the surprising reticences, the unexpected mildness, the swift contritions, and the melancholy so closely related to his fun. He had no sympathy with the obscenities of humanist literature.

Finally, there is the whole matter of the Reformation. We read our Luther according to our interpretation of the sixteenth century. "Luther apart from the Reformation would cease to be Luther," wrote Hare. "His work was not something external to him. . . . It was his own very self, that grew out of him, while he grew out of his work. Wherefore they who do not rightly estimate the Reformation cannot rightly understand Luther." But "rightly to understand the Reformation" is a great complexity.

The distinction is capital between the historical Luther—what Luther was, and did, and said: and the Luther myth—what men have believed he said, and did, and was. The historical Luther made an abiding impress on European history, and the story of the Western Church. But what men have believed about Luther throughout four centuries is itself a "factor in modern history." And the Luther of this creative tradition is a different Luther from the figure with whom a modern historian grapples from within an elaborate critical apparatus. The modern historian is confronted with the whole range of Luther's writings, but over most of four centuries very much of this material has been inert, dormant, unknown to more than a tiny band of scholars. Those early Latin commentaries, so precious to modern scholarship, were unheeded for many generations, and their influence on history has been far less than the garbled collection of Aurifaber's Table Talk, with its numerous editions and translations. Nobody can weigh imponderables, but it is possible that "Eyn feste Burg" and the little Catechism have influenced history more profoundly than all the rest of Luther's writings. And we have not only to ask what men read of Luther, but we have to remember what they neglected. We have to ask not only how well they understood him, but where they misunderstood him. Leaving on one side the perennial question whether Melanchthon is the great expositor or perverter of the legacy of Martin Luther, there is much evidence that generations of Court chaplains expounded Luther's doctrine of "Obrigkeit" for the benefit of Protestant Princes and their subjects in a way which disastrously over-simplified Luther's profound and subtle teaching, and with far-reaching practical result. Thus the Luther myth, of legend and of caricature, many-sided, taking form and colour from the changing mental environment, has itself become a creative historical force. No interpretation of Luther can afford to ignore what Lutherans have believed about Martin Luther.

At the close of his great history of dogma, which he conceived to have been brought to an end by Luther, Adolf Harnack wrote, "Catholicism is not the Pope, neither is it the worship of saints, or the Mass, but it is the slavish dependence on tradition, and the false doctrines of sacrament, of repentance and of faith." But in Luther's own estimate of his work, the Pope occupied a more important place, to which the famous epitaph of the Reformer bears witness:

Pestis eram vivus, moriens ero mors tua, papa.
[Living I was thy plague, dying I shall be thy death, O Pope.]

If we are to understand Luther's violence against the papacy we must treat this inscription seriously, and recognize that for the sixteenth century Lutherans, Luther and the Pope are "apocalyptic figures within the action of the history of salvation."

Luther prided himself on the fact that while others had attacked the manners and the morals of particular popes, or the abuses and corruptions of the Curia, he had begun with doctrine. We know that in its essentials Luther's theology existed before the opening of the Church struggle in 1517, and that it was not an improvization devised in the course of that conflict. Nevertheless, it was as the conflict developed out of the Indulgence controversy that he began to question the basis of the Papal power, and turned to the issues raised in a preceding generation by the theologians of the Conciliar movement, the question whether the Papacy were of divine or of human institution. Early in 1519 he could still write "If unfortunately there are such things in Rome as might be improved, there neither is, nor can be, any reason that one should tear oneself away from the Church in schism. Rather, the worse things become, the more a man should help, and cling to her, for by schism and contempt nothing can be mended." In fateful weeks before the Leipzig Disputation, Luther studied church history and the papal decretals. On 13th March 1519 he wrote to his friend Spalatin, "I do not know whether the Pope is Anti-Christ himself, or only his apostle, so grievously is Christ, i.e. Truth, manhandled and crucified by him in these decretals."

The Leipzig Disputation forced Luther to face the implications of his revolt, and made him realize that he could not come so far, without going further in repudiation of papal authority. Then, early in 1520, he read Hutten's edition of Valla's exposure of the "Donation of Constantine," and he wrote in disgust, "I have hardly any doubt left that the Pope is the very Anti-Christ himself, whom the common report expects, so well do all the things he lives, does, speaks, ordains, fit the picture."

In June 1520 he wrote solemn, final words, in a writing of exceptional vehemence. "Farewell, unhappy, hopeless, blasphemous Rome! The wrath of God is come upon thee, as thou deservest. . . . We have cared for Babylon, and she is not healed: let us leave her then, that she may be the habitation of dragons, spectres and witches, and true to her name of Babel, an everlasting confusion, a new pantheon of wickedness."

There are battles of the mind which most men cannot go on fighting again and again. We make up our minds, as we say, and the account is settled. Thereafter we reopen that particular issue only with great reluctance. No doubt this is a weakness of our spirit, though to be able to keep an open mind requires perhaps detachment from the hurly-burly of decision, and is more easily achieved in academic groves than in the battlefield or market-place or temple. Luther's words here perhaps show us the point at which he hardened his mind with terrible finality against the Papacy, as later on he reached a point at which Zwingli and Erasmus were to him as heathen men and publicans. He had become convinced that the Papacy had become the tool of the Devil, that it was blasphemous . . . "possessed and oppressed by Satan, the damned seat of Anti-Christ."

The papacy which Luther attacked was not the Post-Tridentine papacy. On the other hand, he meant something more when he called it "Anti-Christ" than we mean by the adjective "Anti-Christian." Like many great Christians from St. Cyprian to Lord Shaftesbury, Luther believed himself to be living in the last age of the world, on the very edge of time. He believed that the papacy was toppling to its doom, and that this fate was a merited judgment upon a perversion of spiritual power to which there could be no parallel in the temporal realm, and for which only one category would serve, the Biblical category of Anti-Christ.

There are striking words in his "Of Good Works" (1520) which go to the root of this conviction. "There is not such great danger in the temporal power as in the spiritual, when it does wrong. For the temporal power can do no harm, since it has nothing to do with preaching and faith, and the first three commandments. But the spiritual power does harm not only when it does wrong, but also when it neglects its duty and busies itself with other things, even if they were better than the very best works of the temporal power." For Luther the blessed thing for men and institutions is that they should be where God intends them, doing what God has called them to do, and the cursed thing for men and institutions is when they run amok in God's ordered creation, going where God has not sent them, and occupied with other things than their divine vocation.

The papacy had become entangled in diplomatic, juridical, political, financial pressure. Its crime was not that these things were necessarily bad in themselves, but that for their sake the awful supreme, God-given task of the pastoral care and the cure of souls had been neglected and forsaken. Two consequences had followed. In the first place, it had become a tyranny, like any other institution which succumbs before the temptation of power. In that exposition of the Magnificat, which was interrupted by the famous journey to Worms in 1521, Luther had profoundly diagnosed this corrupting effect of power upon institutions. The tract embodies Luther's reflections upon the fate of great Empires in the Bible and in secular history. It is not empire, but the abuse of it which is wrong. "For while the earth remains authority, rule, power . . . must needs remain. But God will not suffer men to abuse them. He puts down one kingdom, and exalts another: increases one people and destroys another: as he did with Assyria, Babylon, Persia, Greece and Rome, though they thought they should sit in their seats forever."

But when empire is abused, then power becomes an incentive to arrogance, and a terrible inflation begins. These institutions or individuals swell and stretch their authority with a curious bubble-like balloon-like quality. Outwardly they seem omnipotent, and those who take them at their face value can be paralysed and brought into bondage to them. But in fact they are hollow shams, corroded from within, so that doom comes upon them, that swift collapse so often the fate of tyrants and empires. "When their bubble is full blown, and everyone supposes them to have won and overcome, and they feel themselves safe and secure, then God pricks the bubble . . . and it is all over . . . therefore their prosperity has its day, disappears like a bubble, and is as if it had never been." It is interesting that Shakespeare turns to the same metaphor when he describes the fall of Wolsey:

> I have ventured,
> Like little wanton boys that swim on bladders,
> This many summers in a sea of glory,
> But far beyond my depth: my high-blown pride
> At length broke under me.

Luther is fond of punning on the double meaning of the Latin word "Bulla," which means bubble, but also the papal bull.

It may well be that Luther's meditation on this quality of tyranny derives from his own experiences, 1517–20. The initial threat of excommunication, and the final promulgation of the papal bull had a deep significance for him. These were the challenge which focussed all his doubts and fears, and evoked his courage at a time when he had no reason to anticipate anything but the dire fate prophesied for him by friends and foes. But, in fact, these papal sanctions led to the revelation of the weakness of the papal authority, a revelation of immense significance, from which all over Christendom (not forgetting the England of Henry VIII) men could draw their own conclusions. It was not that a man could defy the papacy and get away with it. After all, Wyclif had died in his bed, and throughout most of the Middle Ages there were parts of Europe where heresy flourished openly. But there was a new background which echoed and reverberated Luther's defiance, and a concentration of public attention on it which rallied great historical forces.

For centuries the papal sanctions had been as thunder and lightning, and there had been times and places when princes and peoples had cowered before them. Even now the sonorous phrases, the hallowed ritual, did not lack of menacing effect and struck deep into Luther's mind, always hyper-sensitive to words. The extraordinary agitation of his sermon, "On the Power of Excommunication" (1518), an utterance so outspoken that it was perhaps more effectual than the Ninety-five Theses in securing his impeach-ment, reveals the tension in his mind. It is noticeable that in the printed elaboration of this sermon he turns to the "bladder" motif. "They say . . . our Ban must be feared, right or wrong. With this saying they insolently comfort themselves, swell their chests, and puff themselves up like adders, and almost dare to defy heaven, and to threaten the whole world: with this bugaboo they have made a deep and mighty impression, imagining that there is more in these words than there really is. Therefore we would explain them more fully, and prick this bladder which with its three peas makes such a frightful noise." The publication of the Bull in 1520 evoked the same tension, and in his writings against it he affirms, "The Truth is asserting itself and will burst all the bladders of the Papists."

Only gradually did Luther and his friends realize how the world had changed since the days of Huss, that the Diet of Worms would not be as the Council of Constance, though the devout Charles V might be as anxious to dispose of heretics as any Emperor Sigismund. Now the accumulated weight of the past intervened, with paralysing effect. An enormous moral prestige had been frittered away, and the papal authority was revealed as a weak thing in comparison with the deep moving tide of anti-clericalism, national-ism and the fierce energies of a changing society.

But the papacy is for Luther not simply a tyranny, which can be described, as a liberal historian might describe it, in terms of the corrupting influence of power. Its tyranny is of a unique kind, for which there can only be one category, the demonic, Biblical category of Anti-Christ. By its en-tanglement with law and politics, the papacy has brought the souls of men and women into bondage, has confused disastrously the Law and Gospel, has become the antithesis of the Word of God which comes to free and liberate men's souls. Thus he cannot regard the papacy simply as a corrupt institu-tion, as did the mediaeval moralists and the heretics. In Luther's later writings the papacy is included along with the Law, Sin and Death among the tyrants who beset the Christians, and is part of a view of salvation which demands an apocalyptic interpretation of history.

Two sets of Luther's writings are of special virulence: those against the Jews, the apostates of the Old Israel, and those against the Pope, the apostate of the New. Against what he considered the capital sin of blasphemy Luther turned all his invective. It is noticeable that like Ezekiel, he turned to an imagery of physical repulsion. Blasphemy and apostasy are not simply evil: they are filthy things, which must be described in language coarse enough and repulsive enough to nauseate the reader. That is not in any sense to excuse Luther's language, or to justify his reading of the papacy. But those sadly over-simplify who see in these tracts the vapourings of a dirty mind.

Luther's epitaph was premature. He had indeed plagued the papacy. He could say, "While I slept or drank Wittenberg beer with my Philip and my Amsdorf, the Word so greatly weakened the Papacy that never Prince or Emperor inflicted such damage on it." He did not kill the papacy, but in strange partnership with Ignatius Loyola, the Popes of the Counter-Reformation, the Society of Jesus, not to mention the Anabaptists, he had provoked a new historical pattern which made an end, for good and all, of the peculiar perversions of the later Middle Ages. But I think we can understand how it seemed to him that the papacy was doomed and dying, how it seemed to him the engine of Satan, the embodiment of Anti-Christ in what he believed to be the closing act of the human drama.

If the papacy belongs to the dramatic, dualistic, apocalyptic view of history, the rôle of Luther himself belonged to the same setting. . . . It goes back to the moment when Melanchthon broke the news of Luther's death to the students at Wittenberg with "Alas, gone is the horseman and the chariots of Israel."

For this first generation (which included the first sketches of Luther's career by Melanchthon, Bugenhagen, Jonas, Mathesius), Luther is, as for Coelius, "a veritable Elijah and a John the Baptist, whom God has sent before the Great Day." Both Melanchthon and Mathesius drew upon Luther's own interpretation of history, the conception of the "Wundermann," the inspired hero, and the theme of the Word going forth conquering and to conquer. For Melanchthon, Luther stands within a long succession which began with the patriarchs and which includes the great Fathers of the Church, men sent by God, one after another, "just as those who fall in an order of battle, are replaced by others."

We should expect, that as the contemporaries of Luther passed from the scene, there should be a diminishing sense of the personality of the Reformer. The change was accelerated by the fact that the Lutheran Churches were now fighting for their existence, and finding a dogmatic norm in their great Confessional Documents (which included the Catechisms, and the Schmalkaldic Articles of Luther). The result was an emphasis upon those confessional documents and upon the pure doctrine to which they witnessed which led in the seventeenth century to a remarkable neglect of the writings of Luther himself. This was the period of fierce dogmatic strife between disparate elements within the Lutheran tradition, evoking Shakespeare's reference to "spleeny Lutherans," and reaching comedy when Cyriacus Spangenberg interpreted Luther's famous hymn:

> Erhalt uns, Herr, bei deinem Wort,
> Und steur des Papsts und Türken Mord

to mean "all our enemies are to be understood by these two titles (Papists and Turks) . . . Interimists, Adiaphorists, Sacramentarians, Anabaptists, Calvinists, Osiandrists, Schwenckfeldists, Stancarists, Servetianists, Sabbatarians, Davidists, Majorists, Synergists, etc., etc."! . . . Luther's teaching, reflected by the Confessions, became more important than Luther. "He acquired his own stereotyped work, which belonged to him, like the Wheel of St. Catherine, or the Dragon of St. George. . . . He lost his individual proportions and grew into the superhuman and mythical . . . the greatness of his work pushed him into the background."

The polemic of the Counter-Reformation did useful service in preventing the Luther myth from escaping altogether from its connection with history. A century after the beginning of the Reformation Johann Gerard disputed with Becanus and Bellarmine about the "Vocation of Luther" and had to admit the test of accuracy "if Luther's writings can be shown to be lying, erroneous and false, then we shall at once recognize that Luther was no prophet."

2   Luther Before the Controversy Over Indulgences

The Reuchlin case, to which Luther alludes in this letter, is one of considerable complexity involving the place of Hebraic studies in Christian theology. This issue need not concern us here; what is important is Luther's attitude toward both Reuchlin's approach—which he was to imitate when he proposed the Ninety-Five Theses for debate in 1517—and the importance of Scripture.

Martin Luther's Letter to George Spalatin

Wittenberg (January or February, 1514).

PEACE BE WITH YOU, Reverend Spalatin! Brother John Lang has just asked me what I think of the innocent and learned John Reuchlin and his prosecutors at Cologne, and whether he is in danger of heresy. You know that I greatly esteem and like the man, and perchance my judgment will be suspected, because, as I say, I am not free and neutral; nevertheless as you wish it I will give my opinion, namely that in all his writings there appears to me absolutely nothing dangerous.

I much wonder at the men of Cologne ferreting out such an obscure perplexity, worse tangled than the Gordian knot as they say, in a case as plain as day. Reuchlin himself has often protested his innocence, and solemnly asserts he is only proposing questions for debate, not laying down articles of faith, which alone, in my opinion, absolves him, so that had he the dregs of all known heresies in his memorial, I should believe him sound and pure of faith. For if such protests and expressions of opinion are not free from danger, we must needs fear that these inquisitors, who strain at gnats though they swallow camels, should at their own pleasure pronounce the orthodox heretics, no matter how much the accused protested their innocence.

Luther's Correspondence and other Contemporary Letters, I (1913), 28–9, translated and edited by Preserved Smith. Reprinted by permission of Fortress Press.

What shall I say? that they are trying to cast out Beelzebub but not by the finger of God. I often regret and deplore that we Christians have begun to be wise abroad and fools at home. A hundred times worse blasphemies than this exist in the very streets of Jerusalem, and the high places are filled with spiritual idols. We ought to show our excessive zeal in removing these offences which are our real, intestine enemies. Instead of which we abandon all that is really urgent and turn to foreign and external affairs, under the inspiration of the devil who intends that we should neglect our own business without helping that of others.

Pray can anything be imagined more foolish and imprudent than such zeal? Has unhappy Cologne no waste places nor turbulence in her own church, to which she could devote her knowledge, zeal and charity, that she must needs search out such cases as this in remote parts?

But what am I doing? My heart is fuller of these thoughts than my tongue can tell. I have come to the conclusion that the Jews will always curse and blaspheme God and his King Christ, as all the prophets have predicted. He who neither reads nor understands this, as yet knows no theology, in my opinion. And so I presume the men of Cologne cannot understand the Scripture, because it is necessary that such things take place to fulfill prophecy. If they are trying to stop the Jews blaspheming, they are working to prove the Bible and God liars.

But trust God to be true, even if a million men of Cologne sweat to make him false. Conversion of the Jews will be the work of God alone operating from within, and not of man working—or rather playing—from without. If these offences be taken away, worse will follow. For they are thus given over by the wrath of God to reprobation, that they may become incorrigible, as Ecclesiastes says, for every one who is incorrigible is rendered worse rather than better by correction.

Farewell in the Lord; pardon my words, and pray the Lord for my sinning soul.

Your brother,
Martin Luther

Spenlein was a fellow Augustinian brother to whom Luther could reveal his most intimate thoughts on theology and the relation of man to God. The date (April 8, 1516) is significant, a year and a half before Luther posted his Ninety-Five Theses.

Martin Luther's Letter to George Spenlein

Wittenberg, April 8, 1516.

Grace and peace to you from God the Father and the Lord Jesus Christ. Dear Brother George:

NOW I WOULD LIKE to know whether your soul, tired of her own righteousness, would learn to breathe and confide in the righteousness of Christ. For in our age the temptation to presumption besets many, especially those who try to be just and good before all men, not knowing the righteousness of God, which is most bountifully and freely given us in Christ. Thus they long seek to do right by themselves, that they may have courage to stand before God as though fortified with their own virtues and merits, which is impossible. You yourself were of this opinion, or rather error, and so was I, who still fight against the error and have not yet conquered it.

Therefore, my sweet brother, learn Christ and him crucified; learn to pray to him despairing of yourself, saying: Thou, Lord Jesus, art my righteousness, but I am thy sin; thou hast taken on thyself what thou wast not, and hast given to me what I was not. Beware of aspiring to such purity that you will not wish to seem to yourself, or to be, a sinner. For Christ only dwells in sinners. For that reason he descended from heaven, where he dwelt among the righteous, that he might dwell among sinners. Consider that kindness of his, and you will see his sweetest consolation. . . .

If you firmly believe this (and he is accursed who does not believe it) then take up your untaught and erring brothers, patiently uphold them, make their sins yours, and, if you have any goodness, let it be theirs. Thus the apostle teaches: Receive one another even as Christ received you, for the glory of God, and again: Have this mind in you which was also in Christ Jesus, who, when he was in the form of God, humbled himself, &c. Thus do you, if you seem pretty good to yourself, not count it as booty, as though it were yours alone, but humble yourself, forget what you are, and be as one of

Luther's Correspondence and other Contemporary Letters, I (1913), 33–5, translated and edited by Preserved Smith. Reprinted by permission of Fortress Press.

them that you may carry them. . . . Do this, my brother, and the Lord be with you. Farewell in the Lord.

Your brother,
Martin Luther, *Augustinian.*

Luther, as a Professor of theology, had been thoroughly grounded in the Scholastic philosophy of the Middle Ages. Of the three pillars upon which Scholastic theology rested— Scripture, the writings of the Church Fathers, and the philosophy of Aristotle—Scripture had become increasingly de-emphasized by Luther's time. It was to remind men that the central point of the Scriptural message was not the achievement of philosophical distinctions but the salvation of man's soul that Luther composed the Disputation against Scholastic theology in 1517.

Disputation Against Scholastic Theology
BY MARTIN LUTHER

IT IS THEREFORE TRUE that man, being a bad tree, can only will and do evil. [Cf. Matt. 7:17–18].

It is false to state that man's inclination is free to choose between either of two opposites. Indeed, the inclination is not free, but captive. This is said in opposition to common opinion.

It is false to state that the will can by nature conform to correct precept. . . .

As a matter of fact, without the grace of God the will produces an act that is perverse and evil.

It does not, however, follow that the will is by nature evil, that is, essentially evil, as the Manichaeans maintain.

It is nevertheless innately and inevitably evil and corrupt.

*　　*　　*

No act is done according to nature that is not an act of concupiscence against God.

Helmut T. Lehmann and Jaroslav Pelikan, general eds., *Luther's Works,* XXXI (1957), 9–12, edited by Harold J. Grimm. Reprinted by permission of Fortress Press.

Every act of concupiscence against God is evil and a fornication of the spirit.

*   *   *

The best and infallible preparation for grace and the sole means of obtaining grace is the eternal election and predestination of God.

On the part of man, however, nothing precedes grace except ill will and even rebellion against grace.

*   *   *

In brief, man by nature has neither correct precept nor good will.

It is not true that an invincible ignorance excuses one completely (all scholastics notwithstanding);

For ignorance of God and oneself and good works is by nature always invincible.

Nature, moreover, inwardly and necessarily glories and takes pride in every work which is apparently and outwardly good.

There is no moral virtue without either pride or sorrow, that is, without sin.

We are never lords of our actions, but servants. This in opposition to the philosophers.

We do not become righteous by doing righteous deeds but, having been made righteous, we do righteous deeds. This in opposition to the philosophers.

Virtually the entire *Ethics* of Aristotle is the worst enemy of grace. This in opposition to the scholastics.

It is an error to maintain that Aristotle's statement concerning happiness does not contradict Catholic doctrine. This in opposition to the doctrine on morals.

It is an error to say that no man can become a theologian without Aristotle. This in opposition to common opinion.

Indeed, no one can become a theologian unless he becomes one without Aristotle.

To state that a theologian who is not a logician is a monstrous heretic— this is a monstrous and heretical statement. This in opposition to common opinion.

In vain does one fashion a logic of faith, a substitution brought about without regard for limit and measure. This in opposition to the new dialecticians.

No syllogistic form is valid when applied to divine terms. . . .

Nevertheless it does not for that reason follow that the truth of the doctrine of the Trinity contradicts syllogistic forms. . . .

If a syllogistic form of reasoning holds in divine matters, then the doctrine of the Trinity is demonstrable and not the object of faith.

Briefly, the whole Aristotle is to theology as darkness is to light. This in opposition to the scholastics.

3   *Luther and the Break with Rome*

The doctrine of indulgences had a long history before Luther posted his opposition to it on October 31, 1517. It was based on Matthew, xvi:18–19: "Thou art Peter, and Upon this rock I will build my church; and the gates of hell shall not prevail against it. And I will give unto thee the keys of the kingdom of heaven: and whatsoever thou shalt bind on earth shall be bound in heaven: and whatsoever thou shalt loose on earth shall be loosed in heaven."

Thus Christ granted to St. Peter (and to his successors, the popes) the power to remit the penalties for sins. This power was eagerly exploited by the Renaissance popes, who found themselves in almost constant financial difficulties.

Luther's challenge to debate the doctrine of indulgences, however, was not restricted to a narrow issue. It ranged over many fundamental points of church doctrine. Did Luther really believe that such basic things could be reformed? Or, without really facing up to it, must he not have known that he was proposing nothing less than a revolution?

Ninety-Five Theses BY MARTIN LUTHER

OUT OF LOVE AND ZEAL for truth and the desire to bring it to light, the following theses will be publicly discussed at Wittenberg under the chairmanship of the reverend father Martin Luther, Master of Arts and Sacred Theology and regularly appointed Lecturer on these subjects at that place. He requests that those who cannot be present to debate orally with us will do so by letter.

In the Name of Our Lord Jesus Christ. Amen.

Helmut T. Lehmann and Jaroslav Pelikan, general eds., *Luther's Works*, XXXI (1957), 25–9, 33, edited by Harold J. Grimm. Reprinted by permission of Fortress Press.

When our Lord and Master Jesus Christ said, "Repent" [Matt. 4:17], he willed the entire life of believers to be one of repentance.

This word cannot be understood as referring to the sacrament of penance, that is, confession and satisfaction, as administered by the clergy.

Yet it does not mean solely inner repentance; such inner repentance is worthless unless it produces various outward mortifications of the flesh.

The penalty of sin remains as long as the hatred of self, that is, true inner repentance, until our entrance into the kingdom of heaven.

The pope neither desires nor is able to remit any penalties except those imposed by his own authority or that of the canons.

The pope cannot remit any guilt, except by declaring and showing that it has been remitted by God; or, to be sure, by remitting guilt in cases reserved to his judgment. If his right to grant remission in these cases were disregarded, the guilt would certainly remain unforgiven.

*　　*　　*

The dying are freed by death from all penalties, are already dead as far as the canon laws are concerned, and have a right to be released from them.

Imperfect piety or love on the part of the dying person necessarily brings with it great fear; and the smaller the love, the greater the fear.

This fear or horror is sufficient in itself, to say nothing of other things, to constitute the penalty of purgatory, since it is very near the horror of despair.

Hell, purgatory, and heaven seem to differ the same as despair, fear, and assurance of salvation.

*　　*　　*

If remission of all penalties whatsoever could be granted to anyone at all, certainly it would be granted only to the most perfect, that is, to very few.

For this reason most people are necessarily deceived by that indiscriminate and high-sounding promise of release from penalty.

*　　*　　*

The pope does very well when he grants remission to souls in purgatory, not by the power of the keys, which he does not have, but by way of intercession for them.

They preach only human doctrines who say that as soon as the money clinks into the money chest, the soul flies out of purgatory.

It is certain that when money clinks in the money chest, greed and avarice can be increased; but when the church intercedes, the result is in the hands of God alone.

*   *   *

Any truly repentant Christian has a right to full remission of penalty and guilt, even without indulgence letters.

Any true Christian, whether living or dead, participates in all the blessings of Christ and the church; and this is granted him by God, even without indulgence letters.

*   *   *

If, therefore, indulgences were preached according to the spirit and intention of the pope, all these doubts would be readily resolved. Indeed, they would not exist.

Away then with all those prophets who say to the people of Christ, "Peace, peace," and there is no peace! [Jer. 6:14].

Blessed be all those prophets who say to the people of Christ, "Cross, cross," and there is no cross!

Christians should be exhorted to be diligent in following Christ, their head, through penalties, death, and hell;

And thus be confident of entering into heaven through many tribulations rather than through the false security of peace [Acts 14:22].

> *That Luther's position as stated in the Ninety-Five Theses involved more than technical and abstruse questions of theology can be seen in the reaction of the Holy Roman Emperor to Luther's proposed debate.*

Maximilian's Letter to Leo X

Augsburg, August 5, 1518.

MOST BLESSED FATHER and most revered Lord! We have recently heard that a certain Augustinian Friar, Martin Luther by name, has published certain theses on indulgences to be discussed in the scholastic way, and that in these theses he has taught much on this subject and concerning the

Luther's Correspondence and other Contemporary Letters, I (1913), 98, translated and edited by Preserved Smith. Reprinted by permission of Fortress Press.

power of papal excommunication, part of which appears injurious and heretical, as has been noted by the Master of your sacred palace. This has displeased us the more because, as we are informed, the said friar obstinately adheres to his doctrine, and is said to have found several defenders of his errors among the great.

And as suspicious assertions and dangerous dogmas can be judged by no one better, more rightly and more truly than by your Holiness, who alone is able and ought to silence the authors of vain questions, sophisms and wordy quarrels, than which nothing more pestilent can happen to Christianity, for these men consider only how to magnify what they have taught, so your Holiness can maintain the sincere and solid doctrine approved by the consensus of the more learned opinion of the present age and of those who formerly died piously in Christ.

There is an ancient decree of the Pontifical College on the licensing of teachers, in which there is no provision whatever against sophistry, save in case the decretals are called in question, and whether it is right to teach that, the study of which has been disapproved by many and great authors.

Since, therefore, the authority of the Popes is disregarded, and doubtful, or rather erroneous opinions are alone received, it is bound to occur that those little fanciful and blind teachers should be led astray. And it is due to them that not only are many of the more solid doctors of the Church not only neglected, but even corrupted and mutilated.

We do not mention that these authors hatch many more heresies than were ever condemned. We do not mention that both Reuchlin's trial and the present most dangerous dispute about indulgences and papal censures have been brought forth by these pernicious authors. If the authority of your Holiness and of the most reverend fathers does not put an end to such doctrines, soon their authors will not only impose on the unlearned multitude, but will win the favor of princes, to their mutual destruction. If we shut our eyes and leave them the field open and free, it will happen, as they chiefly desire, that the whole world will be forced to look on their follies instead of on the best and most holy doctors.

Of our singular reverence for the Apostolic See, we have signified this to your Holiness, so that simple Christianity may not be injured and scandalized by these rash disputes and captious arguments. Whatever may be righteously decided upon in this our Empire, we will make all our subjects obey for the praise and honor of God Almighty and the salvation of Christians.

The reaction which followed the publication of his Ninety-Five Theses forced Luther to define and defend his position in some detail. This he did in 1520 in the two treatises from which the selections that follow are taken. After their publication, a reconciliation with Rome appeared doubtful.

FROM *Address to the Christian Nobility of the German Nation* BY MARTIN LUTHER

GRACE AND POWER FROM GOD, Most Illustrious Majesty, and most gracious and dear Lords.

It is not out of sheer forwardness or rashness that I, a single, poor man, have undertaken to address your worships. The distress and oppression which weigh down all the Estates of Christendom, especially of Germany, and which move not me alone, but everyone to cry out time and again, and to pray for help, have forced me even now to cry aloud that God may inspire some one with His Spirit to lend this suffering nation a helping hand. Ofttimes the councils have made some pretense at reformation, but their attempts have been cleverly hindered by the guile of certain men and things have gone from bad to worse. I now intend, by the help of God, to throw some light upon the wiles and wickedness of these men, to the end that when they are known, they may not henceforth be so hurtful and so great a hindrance. God has given us a noble youth to be our head and thereby has awakened great hopes of good in many hearts, wherefore it is meet that we should do our part and profitably use this time of grace.

In this whole matter the first and most important thing is that we take earnest heed not to enter on it trusting in great might or in human reason, even though all power in the world were ours; for God cannot and will not suffer a good work to be begun with trust in our own power or reason. Such works He crushes ruthlessly to earth, as it is written in the Thirty-third Psalm, "There is no king saved by the multitude of an host; a mighty man is not delivered by much strength." On this account, I fear, it came to pass of old that the good Emperors Frederick I and II and many other German emperors were shamefully oppressed and trodden under foot by the popes, although all the world feared them. It may be that they relied on their own might more than on God, and therefore they had to fall. In our own times, too, what was it that raised the bloodthirsty Julius II to such heights? Nothing else, I fear, except that France, the Germans and Venice relied upon themselves. The children of Benjamin slew 42,000 Israelites because the latter relied on their own strength.

That it may not so fare with us and our noble young Emperor Charles,

Martin Luther, *Three Treatises* (1947), pp. 10–6, 20–5. Reprinted by permission of Fortress Press.

we must be sure that in this matter we are dealing not with men, but with the princes of hell, who can fill the world with war and bloodshed, but whom war and bloodshed do not overcome. We must go at this work despairing of physical force and humbly trusting God; we must seek God's help with earnest prayer, and fix our minds on nothing else than the misery and distress of suffering Christendom, without regard to the deserts of evil men. Otherwise we may start the game with great prospect of success, but when we get well into it the evil spirits will stir up such confusion that the whole world will swim in blood, and yet nothing will come of it. Let us act wisely, therefore, and in the fear of God. The more force we use, the greater our disaster if we do not act humbly and in God's fear. The popes and the Romans have hitherto been able, by the devil's help, to set kings at odds with one another, and they may well be able to do it again, if we proceed by our own might and cunning, without God's help.

THE THREE WALLS OF THE ROMANISTS

The Romanists, with great adroitness, have built three walls about them, behind which they have hitherto defended themselves in such wise that no one has been able to reform them and this has been the cause of terrible corruption throughout all Christendom.

First, when pressed by the temporal power, they have made decrees and said that the temporal power has no jurisdiction over them, but, on the other hand, that the spiritual is above the temporal power. Second, when the attempt is made to reprove them out of the Scriptures, they raise the objection that the interpretation of the Scriptures belongs to no one except the pope. Third, if threatened with a council, they answer with the fable that no one can call a council but the pope.

In this wise they have slyly stolen from us our three rods, that they may go unpunished, and have ensconced themselves within the safe stronghold of these three walls, that they may practice all the knavery and wickedness which we now see. Even when they have been compelled to hold a council they have weakened its power in advance by previously binding the princes with an oath to let them remain as they are. Moreover, they have given the pope full authority over all the decisions of the council, so that it is all one whether there are many councils or no councils—except that they deceive us with puppet-shows and sham battles. So terribly do they fear for their skin in a really free council! And they have intimidated kings and princes by making them believe it would be an offense against God not to obey them in all these knavish, crafty deceptions.

Now God help us, and give us one of the trumpets with which the walls of Jericho were overthrown, that we may blow down these walls of straw and paper, and may set free the Christian rods for the punishment of sin, bringing to light the craft and deceit of the devil, to the end that through punishment we may reform ourselves, and once more attain God's favor.

Against the *first wall* we will direct our first attack.

It is pure invention that pope, bishops, priests and monks are to be called the "spiritual estate"; princes, lords, artisans and farmers the "temporal estate." That is indeed a fine bit of lying and hypocrisy. Yet no one should be frightened by it and for this reason—viz., that all Christians are truly of the "spiritual estate," and there is among them no difference at all but that of office, as Paul says in I Corinthians 12. We are all one body, yet every member has its own work, whereby it serves every other, all because we have one baptism, one Gospel, one faith, and are all alike Christians; for baptism, Gospel, and faith alone make us "spiritual" and a Christian people.

But that a pope or a bishop anoints, confers tonsures, ordains, consecrates, or prescribes dress unlike that of the laity—this may make hypocrites and graven images, but it never makes a Christian or "spiritual" man. Through baptism all of us are consecrated to the priesthood, as St. Peter says in I Peter 2, "Ye are a royal priesthood, a priestly kingdom," and the book of Revelation says, "Thou hast made us by thy blood to be priests and kings." For if we had no higher consecration than pope or bishop gives, the consecration by pope or bishop would never make a priest, nor might anyone either say mass or preach a sermon or give absolution. Therefore when the bishop consecrates it is the same thing as if he, in the place and stead of the whole congregation, all of whom have like power, were to take one out of their number and charge him to use this power for the others; just as though ten brothers, all king's sons and equal heirs, were to choose one of themselves to rule the inheritance for them all—they would all be kings and equal in power, though one of them would be charged with the duty of ruling.

To make it still clearer. If a little group of pious Christian laymen were taken captive and set down in a wilderness, and had among them no priest consecrated by a bishop, and if there in the wilderness they were to agree in choosing one of themselves, married or unmarried, and were to charge him with the office of baptizing, saying mass, absolving and preaching, such a man would be as truly a priest as though all bishops and popes had consecrated him. That is why in cases of necessity anyone can baptize and give absolution, which would be impossible unless we were all priests. This great grace and power of baptism and of the Christian Estate they have well-nigh destroyed and caused us to forget through the canon law. It was in the manner aforesaid that Christians in olden days chose from their number bishops and priests, who were afterwards confirmed by other bishops, without all the show which now obtains. It was thus that Sts. Augustine, Ambrose, and Cyprian became bishops.

Since, then, the temporal authorities are baptized with the same baptism and have the same faith and Gospel as we, we must grant that they are priests and bishops, and count their office one which has a proper and a useful place in the Christian community. For whoever comes out of the water of baptism can boast that he is already consecrated priest, bishop, and pope, though it is not seemly that everyone should exercise the office. Nay, just because we are all in like manner priests, no one must put himself forward and undertake, without our consent and election, to do what is in the power of all of us. For what is common to all, no one dare take upon himself without the will and the command of the community; and should it happen that one chosen for such an office were deposed for malfeasance, he would then be just what he was before he held office. Therefore a priest in Christendom is nothing else than an office-holder. While he is in office, he has precedence; when deposed, he is a peasant or a townsman like the rest. Beyond all doubt, then, a priest is no longer a priest when he is deposed. But now they have invented *characteres indelebiles,* and prate that a deposed priest is nevertheless something different from a mere layman. They even dream that a priest can never become a layman, or be anything else than a priest. All this is mere talk and man-made law.

From all this it follows that there is really no difference between laymen and priests, princes and bishops, "spirituals" and "temporals," as they call them, except that of office and work, but not of "estate"; for they are all of the same estate—true priests, bishops and popes—though they are not all engaged in the same work, just as all priests and monks have not the same work.

*   *   *

The *second wall* is still more flimsy and worthless. They wish to be the only Masters of the Holy Scriptures even though in all their lives they learn nothing from them. They assume for themselves sole authority, and with insolent juggling of words they would persuade us that the pope, whether he be a bad man or a good man, cannot err in matters of faith, and yet they cannot prove a single letter of it. Hence it comes that so many heretical and unchristian, nay, even unnatural ordinances have a place in the canon law, of which, however, there is no present need to speak. For since they think that the Holy Spirit never leaves them, be they never so unlearned and wicked, they make bold to decree whatever they will. And if it were true, where would be the need or use of the Holy Scriptures? Let us burn them, and be satisfied with the unlearned lords at Rome, who are possessed of the Holy Spirit—although He can possess only pious hearts! Unless I had read it myself, I could not have believed that the devil would make such clumsy pretensions at Rome, and find a following.

But not to fight them with mere words, we will quote the Scriptures. St. Paul says in I Corinthians 14: "If to anyone something better is revealed, though he be sitting and listening to another in God's Word, then the first, who is speaking, shall hold his peace and give place." What would be the use of this commandment, if we were only to believe him who does the talking or who has the highest seat? Christ also says in John 6 that all Christians shall be taught of God. Thus it may well happen that the pope and his followers are wicked men, and no true Christians, not taught of God, not having true understanding. On the other hand, an ordinary man may have true understanding; why then should we not follow him? Has not the pope erred many times? Who would help Christendom when the pope errs, if we were not to believe another, who had the Scriptures on his side, more than the pope?

Therefore it is a wickedly invented fable, and they cannot produce a letter in defense of it, that the interpretation of Scripture or the confirmation of its interpretation belongs to the pope alone. They have themselves usurped this power; and although they allege that this power was given to Peter when the keys were given to him, it is plain enough that the keys were not given to Peter alone, but to the whole community. Moreover, the keys were not ordained for doctrine or government, but only for the binding and loosing of sin, and whatever further power of the key they arrogate to themselves is mere invention. But Christ's word to Peter, "I have prayed for thee that thy faith fail not," cannot be applied to the pope, since the majority of the popes have been without faith, as they must themselves confess. Besides, it is not only for Peter that Christ prayed, but also for all Apostles and Christians, as he says in John 17: "Father, I pray for those whom thou hast given me, and not for these only, but for all who believe on me through their word." Is not this clear enough?

Only think of it yourself! They must confess that there are pious Christians among us, who have the true faith, Spirit, understanding, word, and mind of Christ. Why, then, should we reject their word and understanding and follow the pope, who has neither faith nor Spirit? That would be to deny the whole faith and the Christian Church. Moreover, it is not the pope alone who is always in the right, if the article of the Creed is correct: "I believe one holy Christian Church"; otherwise the prayer must run: "I believe in the pope at Rome," and so reduce the Christian Church to one man—which would be nothing else than a devilish and hellish error.

Besides, if we are all priests, as was said above, and all have one faith, one Gospel, one sacrament, why should we not also have the power to test and judge what is correct or incorrect in matters of faith? What becomes of the words of Paul in I Corinthians 2: "He that is spiritual judgeth all things, yet he himself is judged of no man," and II Corinthians 4: "We have all the same Spirit of faith"? Why, then, should not we perceive what squares with faith and what does not, as well as does an unbelieving pope?

All these and many other texts should make us bold and free, and we should not allow the Spirit of liberty, as Paul calls Him, to be frightened off by the fabrications of the popes, but we ought to go boldly forward to test all that they do or leave undone, according to our interpretation of the Scriptures, which rests on faith, and compel them to follow not their own interpretation, but the one that is better. In the olden days Abraham had to listen to his Sarah, although she was in more complete subjection to him than we are to anyone on earth. Balaam's ass, also, was wiser than the prophet himself. If God then spoke by an ass against a prophet, why should

He not be able even now to speak by a righteous man against the pope? In like manner St. Paul rebukes St. Peter as a man in error. Therefore it behooves every Christian to espouse the cause of the faith, to understand and defend it, and to rebuke all errors.

The *third wall* falls of itself when the first two are down. For when the pope acts contrary to the Scriptures, it is our duty to stand by the Scriptures, to reprove him, and to constrain him, according to the word of Christ in Matthew 18: "If thy brother sin against thee, go and tell it him between thee and him alone; if he hear thee not, then take with thee one or two more; if he hear them not, tell it to the Church; if he hear not the Church, consider him a heathen." Here every member is commanded to care for every other. How much rather should we do this when the member that does evil is a ruling member, and by his evil-doing is the cause of much harm and offense to the rest! But if I am to accuse him before the Church, I must bring the Church together.

They have no basis in Scripture for their contention that it belongs to the pope alone to call a council or confirm its actions; for this is based merely upon their own laws, which are valid only in so far as they are not injurious to Christendom or contrary to the laws of God. When the pope deserves punishment, such laws go out of force, since it is injurious to Christendom not to punish him by means of a council.

Thus we read in Acts 15 that it was not St. Peter who called the Apostolic Council, but the Apostles and elders. If, then, that right had belonged to St. Peter alone, the council would not have been a Christian council, but a heretical *conciliabulum*. Even the Council of Nicaea—the most famous of all—was neither called nor confirmed by the Bishop of Rome, but by the Emperor Constantine, and many other emperors after him did the like, yet these councils were the most Christian of all. But if the pope alone had the right to call councils, then all these councils must have been heretical. Moreover, if I consider the councils which the pope has created, I find that they have done nothing of special importance.

Therefore, when necessity demands, and the pope is an offense to Christendom, the first man who is able should, as a faithful member of the whole body, do what he can to bring about a truly free council. No one can do this so well as the temporal authorities, especially since now they also are fellow-Christians, fellow-priests, "fellow-spirituals," fellow-lords over all things, and whenever it is needful or profitable, they should give free course to the office and work in which God has put them above every man. Would it not be an unnatural thing, if a fire broke out in a city, and everybody were to stand by and let it burn on and on and consume everything that could burn, for the sole reason that nobody had the authority of the burgomaster, or because, perhaps, the fire broke out in the burgomaster's house? In such case is it not the duty of every citizen to arouse and call the rest? How much more should this be done in the spiritual city of Christ, if a fire of offense breaks out, whether in the papal government, or anywhere else? In the same way, if the enemy attacks a city, he who first rouses the others deserves honor and thanks; why then should he not deserve honor who makes known the presence of the enemy from hell, and awakens the Christians, and calls them together?

But all their boasts of an authority which dare not be opposed amount to nothing after all. No one in Christendom has authority to do injury, or to forbid the resisting of injury. There is no authority in the Church save for edification. Therefore, if the pope were to use his authority to prevent the calling of a free council, and thus became a hindrance to the edification of the Church, we should have regard neither for him nor for his authority; and if he were to hurl his bans and thunderbolts, we should despise his conduct as that of a madman, and relying on God, hurl back the ban on him, and coerce him as best we could. For this presumptuous authority of his is nothing; he has no such authority, and he is quickly overthrown by a text of Scripture; for Paul says to the Corinthians, "God has given us authority not for the destruction, but for the edification of Christendom." Who is ready to overlap this text? It is only the power of the devil and of Antichrist which resists the things that serve for the edification of Christendom; it is, therefore, in no wise to be obeyed, but is to be opposed with life and goods and all our strength.

FROM *A Treatise on Christian Liberty*
BY MARTIN LUTHER

MANY HAVE THOUGHT Christian faith to be an easy thing, and not a few have given it a place among the virtues. This they do because they have had no experience of it, and have never tasted what great virtue there is in faith. For it is impossible that anyone should write well of it or well understand what is correctly written of it, unless he has at some time tasted the courage faith gives a man when trials oppress him. But he who has had even a faint taste of it can never write, speak, meditate, or hear enough concerning it. For it is a living fountain springing up into life everlasting, as Christ calls it in John 4. For my part, although I have no wealth of faith to boast of and know how scant my store is, yet I hope that, driven about by great and various temptations, I have attained to a little faith, and that I can speak of it, if not more elegantly, certainly more to the point, than those literalists and all too subtle disputants have hitherto done, who have not even understood what they have written.

That I may make the way easier for the unlearned—for only such do I

Martin Luther, *Three Treatises* (1947), pp. 251–5. Reprinted by permission of Fortress Press.

serve—I set down first these two propositions concerning the liberty and the bondage of the spirit:

A Christian man is a perfectly free lord of all, subject to none.
A Christian man is a perfectly dutiful servant of all, subject to all.

Although these two theses seem to contradict each other, yet, if they should be found to fit together they would serve our purpose beautifully. For they are both Paul's own, who says, in 1 Corinthians 9, "Whereas I was free, I made myself the servant of all," and Romans 8, "Owe no man anything, but to love one another." Now love by its very nature is ready to serve and to be subject to him who is loved. So Christ, although Lord of all, was made of a woman, made under the law, and hence was at the same time free and a servant, at the same time in the form of God and in the form of a servant.

Let us start, however, with something more remote from our subject, but more obvious. Man has a twofold nature, a spiritual and a bodily. According to the spiritual nature, which men call the soul, he is called a spiritual, or inner, or new man; according to the bodily nature, which men call the flesh, he is called a carnal, or outward, or old man, of whom the Apostle writes, in 2 Corinthians 4, "Though our outward man is corrupted, yet the inward man is renewed day by day." Because of this diversity of nature the Scriptures assert contradictory things of the same man, since these two men in the same man contradict each other, since the flesh lusteth against the spirit and the spirit against the flesh (Galatians 5).

First, let us contemplate the inward man, to see how a righteous, free, and truly Christian man, that is, a new, spiritual, inward man, comes into being. It is evident that no external thing, whatsoever it be, has any influence whatever in producing Christian righteousness or liberty, nor in producing unrighteousness or bondage. A simple argument will furnish the proof. What can it profit the soul if the body fare well, be free and active, eat, drink, and do as it pleases? For in these things even the most godless slaves of all the vices fare well. On the other hand, how will ill health or imprisonment or hunger or thirst or any other external misfortune hurt the soul? With these things even the most godly men are afflicted, and those who because of a clear conscience are most free. None of these things touch either the liberty or the bondage of the soul. The soul receives no benefit if the body is adorned with the sacred robes of the priesthood, or dwells in sacred places, or is occupied with sacred duties, or prays, fasts, abstains from certain kinds of food, or does any work whatsoever that can be done by the body, and in the body. The righteousness and the freedom of the soul demand something far different, since the things which have been mentioned could be done by any wicked man, and such works produce nothing but hypocrites. On the other hand, it will not hurt the soul if the body is clothed in secular dress, dwells in unconsecrated places, eats and drinks as others do, does not pray aloud, and neglects to do all the things mentioned above, which hypocrites can do.

Further, to put aside all manner of works, even contemplation, meditation, and all that the soul can do, avail nothing. One thing and one only is necessary for Christian life, righteousness, and liberty. That one thing is the most holy Word of God, the Gospel of Christ, as he says, John 11, "I am the resurrection and the life: he that believeth in me shall not die forever"; and John 8, "If the Son shall make you free, you shall be free indeed"; and Matthew 4, "Not in bread alone doth man live; but in every word that proceedeth from the mouth of God." Let us then consider it certain and conclusively established that the soul can do without all things except the Word of God, and that where this is not there is no help for the soul in anything else whatever. But if it has the Word it is rich and lacks nothing, since this Word is the Word of life, of truth, of light, of peace, of righteousness, of salvation, of joy, of liberty, of wisdom, of power, of grace, of glory, and of every blessing beyond our power to estimate. This is why the prophet in the entire One Hundred and Nineteenth Psalm, and in many other places of Scripture, with so many sighs yearns after the Word of God and applies so many names to it. On the other hand, there is no more terrible plague with which the wrath of God can smite men than a famine of the hearing of His Word, as He says in Amos, just as there is no greater mercy than when He sends forth His Word, as we read in Psalm 107, "He sent His word and healed them, and delivered them from their destructions." Nor was Christ sent into the world for any other ministry but that of the Word, and the whole spiritual estate, apostles, bishops and all the priests, has been called and instituted only for the ministry of the Word.

You ask, "What then is this Word of God, and how shall it be used, since there are so many words of God?" I answer, the Apostle explains that in Romans 1. The Word is the Gospel of God concerning His Son, who was made flesh, suffered, rose from the dead, and was glorified through the Spirit who sanctifies. For to preach Christ means to feed the soul, to make it righteous, to set it free, and to save it, if it believe the preaching. For faith alone is the saving and efficacious use of the Word of God, Romans 10, "If thou confess with thy mouth that Jesus is Lord, and believe with thy heart that God hath raised Him up from the dead, thou shalt be saved"; and again, "The end of the law is Christ, unto righteousness to everyone that believeth"; and, in Romans 1, "The just shall live by his faith." The Word of God cannot be received and cherished by any works whatever, but only by faith. Hence it is clear that, as the soul needs only the Word for its life and righteousness, so it is justified by faith alone and not by any works; for if it could be justified by anything else, it would not need the Word, and therefore it would not need faith. But this faith cannot at all exist in connection with works, that is to say, if you at the same time claim to be justified by works, whatever their character; for that would be to halt between two sides, to worship Baal and to kiss the hand, which, as Job says, is a very great iniquity. Therefore the moment you begin to believe, you learn that all things in you are altogether blameworthy, sinful, and damnable, as Romans 3 says, "For all have sinned and lack the glory of God"; and again, "There is none just, there is none that doeth good, all have turned out of the way: they are become unprofitable together." When you have learned this, you will know that you need Christ, who suffered and rose again for you, that, believing in Him, you may through this faith become a new man, in that all your sins are forgiven, and you are justified by the merits of another, namely, of Christ alone.

Since, therefore, this faith can rule only in the inward man, as Romans 10 says, "With the heart we believe unto righteousness"; and since faith alone justifies, it is clear that the inward man cannot be justified, made free, and be saved by any outward work or dealing whatsoever, and that works, whatever their character, have nothing to do with this inward man. On the other hand, only ungodliness and unbelief of heart, and no outward work, make him guilty and a damnable servant of sin. Wherefore it ought to be the first concern of every Christian to lay aside all trust in works, and more and more to strengthen faith alone, and through faith to grow in the knowledge, not of works, but of Christ Jesus, who suffered and rose for him, as Peter teaches, in the last chapter of his first Epistle; since no other work makes a Christian. Thus when the Jews asked Christ, John 6, what they should do that they might work the works of God, He brushed aside the multitude of works in which He saw that they abounded, and enjoined upon them a single work, saying, "This is the work of God, that you believe in Him whom He hath sent. For Him hath God the Father sealed."

> *Luther's declaration of theological independence was made at Worms in 1521. He had been summoned there to appear before the emperor and appropriate members of the church hierarchy to defend himself against the charge of heresy. The break with Rome now became irrevocable.*

Speech Before Emperor Charles BY MARTIN LUTHER

"MOST SERENE EMPEROR, most illustrious princes, most clement lords, obedient to the time set for me yesterday evening, I appear before you, beseeching you, by the mercy of God, that your most serene majesty and your most illustrious lordships may deign to listen graciously to this my cause—which is, as I hope, a cause of justice and of truth. If through my

Helmut T. Lehmann and Jaroslav Pelikan, general eds., *Luther's Works*, XXXII (1957), 109–12, edited by George W. Forell. Reprinted by permission of Fortress Press.

inexperience I have either not given the proper titles to some, or have offended in some manner against court customs and etiquette, I beseech you to kindly pardon me, as a man accustomed not to courts but to the cells of monks. I can bear no other witness about myself but that I have taught and written up to this time with simplicity of heart, as I had in view only the glory of God and the sound instruction of Christ's faithful.

"Most serene emperor, most illustrious princes, concerning those questions proposed to me yesterday on behalf of your serene majesty, whether I acknowledged as mine the books enumerated and published in my name and whether I wished to persevere in their defense or to retract them, I have given to the first question my full and complete answer, in which I still persist and shall persist forever. These books are mine and they have been published in my name by me, unless in the meantime, either through the craft or the mistaken wisdom of my emulators, something in them has been changed or wrongly cut out. For plainly I cannot acknowledge anything except what is mine alone and what has been written by me alone, to the exclusion of all interpretations of anyone at all.

"In replying to the second question, I ask that your most serene majesty and your lordships may deign to note that my books are not all of the same kind.

"For there are some in which I have discussed religious faith and morals simply and evangelically, so that even my enemies themselves are compelled to admit that these are useful, harmless, and clearly worthy to be read by Christians. Even the bull, although harsh and cruel, admits that some of my books are inoffensive, and yet allows these also to be condemned with a judgment which is utterly monstrous. Thus, if I should begin to disavow them, I ask you, what would I be doing? Would not I, alone of all men, be condemning the very truth upon which friends and enemies equally agree, striving alone against the harmonious confession of all?

"Another group of my books attacks the papacy and the affairs of the papists as those who both by their doctrines and very wicked examples have laid waste the Christian world with evil that affects the spirit and the body. For no one can deny or conceal this fact, when the experience of all and the complaints of everyone witness that through the decrees of the pope and the doctrines of men the consciences of the faithful have been most miserably entangled, tortured, and torn to pieces. Also, property and possessions, especially in this illustrious nation of Germany, have been devoured by an unbelievable tyranny and are being devoured to this time without letup and by unworthy means. [Yet the papists] by their own decrees (as in dist. 9 and 25; ques. 1 and 2) warn that the papal laws and doctrines which are contrary to the gospel or the opinions of the fathers are to be regarded as erroneous and reprehensible. If, therefore, I should have retracted these writings, I should have done nothing other than to have added strength to this [papal] tyranny and I should have opened not only windows but doors to such great godlessness. It would rage farther and more freely than ever it has dared up to this time. Yes, from the proof of such a revocation on my part, their wholly lawless and unrestrained kingdom of wickedness would become still more intolerable for the already wretched people; and their rule would be further strengthened and established, especially if it should be reported that this evil deed had been done by me by virtue of the authority of your most serene majesty and of the whole Roman Empire. Good God! What a cover for wickedness and tyranny I should have then become.

"I have written a third sort of book against some private and (as they say) distinguished individuals—those, namely, who strive to preserve the Roman tyranny and to destroy the godliness taught by me. Against these I confess I have been more violent than my religion or profession demands. But then, I do not set myself up as a saint; neither am I disputing about my life, but about the teaching of Christ. It is not proper for me to retract these works, because by this retraction it would again happen that tyranny and godlessness would, with my patronage, rule and rage among the people of God more violently than ever before.

"However, because I am a man and not God, I am not able to shield my books with any other protection than that which my Lord Jesus Christ himself offered for his teaching. When questioned before Annas about his teaching and struck by a servant, he said: 'If I have spoken wrongly, bear witness to the wrong' [John 18:19-23]. If the Lord himself, who knew that he could not err, did not refuse to hear testimony against his teaching, even from the lowliest servant, how much more ought I, who am the lowest scum and able to do nothing except err, desire and expect that somebody should want to offer testimony against my teaching! Therefore, I ask by the mercy of God, may your most serene majesty, most illustrious lordships, or anyone at all who is able, either high or low, bear witness, expose my errors, overthrowing them by the writings of the prophets and the evangelists. Once I have been taught I shall be quite ready to renounce every error, and I shall be the first to cast my books into the fire.

"From these remarks I think it is clear that I have sufficiently considered and weighed the hazards and dangers, as well as the excitement and dissensions aroused in the world as a result of my teachings, things about which I was gravely and forcefully warned yesterday. To see excitement and dissension arise because of the Word of God is to me clearly the most joyful aspect of all in these matters. For this is the way, the opportunity, and the result of the Word of God, just as He [Christ] said, 'I have not come to bring peace, but a sword. For I have come to set a man against his father, etc.' [Matt. 10:34-35.] Therefore, we ought to think how marvelous and terrible is our God in his counsels, lest by chance what is attempted for settling strife grows rather into an intolerable deluge of evils, if we begin by condemning the Word of God. And concern must be shown lest the reign of this most noble youth, Prince Charles (in whom after God is our great hope), become unhappy and inauspicious. I could illustrate this with abundant examples from Scripture—like Pharaoh, the king of Babylon, and the kings of Israel who, when they endeavored to pacify and strengthen their kingdoms by the wisest counsels, most surely destroyed themselves. For it is He who takes the wise in their own craftiness [Job 5:13] and overturns mountains before they know it [Job 9:5]. Therefore we must fear God. I do not say these things because there is a need of either my teachings or my warnings for such leaders as you, but because I must not withhold the allegiance which I owe my Germany. With these words I commend myself to your most serene majesty and to your lordships, humbly asking that I not be allowed through the agitation of my enemies, without cause, to be made hateful to you. I have finished."

When I had finished, the speaker for the emperor said, as if in reproach, that I had not answered the question, that I ought not call into question those things which had been condemned and defined in councils; therefore what was sought from me was not a horned response, but a simple one, whether or not I wished to retract.

Here I answered:

"Since then your serene majesty and your lordships seek a simple answer, I will give it in this manner, neither horned nor toothed: Unless I am convinced by the testimony of the Scriptures or by clear reason (for I do not trust either in the pope or in councils alone, since it is well known that they have often erred and contradicted themselves), I am bound by the Scriptures I have quoted and my conscience is captive to the Word of God. I cannot and I will not retract anything, since it is neither safe nor right to go against conscience.

"I cannot do otherwise, here I stand, may God help me, Amen."

4   The Problem of Martin Luther

*Erik Erikson of Harvard University is a leader of contem-
porary psychiatric thought. In his book,* Young Man
Luther, *he attempts to account for Luther's actions in terms
of modern depth psychology.*

FROM *Young Man Luther* BY E. H. ERIKSON

I HAVE CALLED THE MAJOR CRISIS of adolescence the *identity
crisis;* it occurs in that period of the life cycle when each youth must forge
for himself some central perspective and direction, some working unity, out
of the effective remnants of his childhood and the hopes of his anticipated
adulthood; he must detect some meaningful resemblance between what he
has come to see in himself and what his sharpened awareness tells him others
judge and expect him to be. This sounds dangerously like common sense;
like all health, however, it is a matter of course only to those who possess it,
and appears as a most complex achievement to those who have tasted its
absence. Only in ill health does one realize the intricacy of the body; and
only in a crisis, individual or historical, does it become obvious what a
sensitive combination of interrelated factors the human personality is—a
combination of capacities created in the distant past and of opportunities
divined in the present; a combination of totally unconscious preconditions
developed in individual growth and of social conditions created and re-
created in the precarious interplay of generations. In some young people, in
some classes, at some periods in history, this crisis will be minimal; in other
people, classes, and periods, the crisis will be clearly marked off as a critical
period, a kind of "second birth," apt to be aggravated either by widespread
neuroticisms or by pervasive ideological unrest. Some young individuals will
succumb to this crisis in all manner of neurotic, psychotic, or delinquent
behavior; others will resolve it through participation in ideological movements passionately concerned with religion or politics, nature or art. Still

Reprinted from *Young Man Luther: A Study in Psychoanalysis and History,* pp. 14–6, 20–1,
206–13, by Erik H. Erikson, by permission of W. W. Norton & Company, Inc., and Faber &
Faber Ltd., London. Copyright © 1958, 1962 by Erik H. Erikson.

others, although suffering and deviating dangerously through what appears to be a prolonged adolescence, eventually come to contribute an original bit to an emerging style of life: the very danger which they have sensed has forced them to mobilize capacities to see and say, to dream and plan, to design and construct, in new ways.

Luther, so it seems, at one time was a rather endangered young man, beset with a syndrome of conflicts whose outline we have learned to recognize, and whose components to analyse. He found a spiritual solution, not without the well-timed help of a therapeutically clever superior in the Augustinian order. His solution roughly bridged a political and psychological vacuum which history had created in a significant portion of Western Christendom. Such coincidence, if further coinciding with the deployment of highly specific personal gifts, makes for historical "greatness." We will follow Luther through the crisis of his youth, and the unfolding of his gifts, to the first manifestation of his originality as a thinker, namely, to the emergence of a new theology, apparently not immediately perceived as a radical innovation either by him or his listeners, in his first Lectures on the Psalms (1513). What happened to him after he had acquired a historical identity is more than another chapter; for even half of the man is too much for one book. The difference between the young and the old Luther is so marked, and the second, the sturdy orator, so exclusive a Luther-image to most readers, that I will speak of "Martin" when I report on Luther's early years, which according to common usage in the Luther literature include his twenties; and of "Luther" where and when he has become the leader of Lutherans, seduced by history into looking back on his past as upon a mythological autobiography.

Kierkegaard's remark has a second part: ". . . of very great import for Christendom." This calls for an investigation of how the individual "case" became an important, an historic "event," and for formulations concerning the spiritual and political identity crisis of Northern Christendom in Luther's time. True, I could have avoided those methodological uncertainties and impurities which will undoubtedly occur by sticking to my accustomed job of writing a case history, and leaving the historical event to those who, in turn, would consider the case a mere accessory to the event. But we clinicians have learned in recent years that we cannot lift a case history out of history, even as we suspect that historians, when they try to separate the logic of the historic event from that of the life histories which intersect in it, leave a number of vital historical problems unattended. So we may have to risk that bit of impurity which is inherent in the hyphen of the psycho-historical as well as of all other hyphenated approaches. They are the compost heap of today's interdisciplinary efforts, which may help to fertilize new fields, and to produce future flowers of new methodological clarity.

*   *   *

We cannot leave history entirely to nonclinical observers and to professional historians who often all too nobly immerse themselves into the very disguises, rationalizations, and idealizations of the historical process from which it should be their business to separate themselves. Only when the relation of historical forces to the basic functions and stages of the mind has been jointly charted and understood can we begin a psychoanalytic critique of society as such without falling back into mystical or moralistic philosophizing.

Freud warned against the possible misuse of his work as an ideology, a *"Weltanschauung";* but as we shall see in Luther's life and work, a man who inspires new ideas has little power to restrict them to the area of his original intentions. And Freud himself did not refrain from interpreting other total approaches to man's condition, such as religion, as consequences of man's inability to shake off the bonds of his prolonged childhood, and thus comparable to collective neuroses. The psychological and historical study of the religious crisis of a young great man renews the opportunity to review this assertion in the light of ego-psychology and of theories of psychosocial development.

*   *   *

In what follows, themes from Luther's first lectures are discussed side by side with psychoanalytic insights. Theological readers will wonder whether Luther saved theology from philosophy only to have it exploited by psychology; while psychoanalysts may suspect me of trying to make space for a Lutheran God in the structure of the psyche. My purposes, however, are more modest: I intend to demonstrate that Luther's redefinition of man's condition—while part and parcel of his theology—has striking configurational parallels with inner dynamic shifts like those which clinicians recognize in the recovery of individuals from psychic distress. In brief, I will try to indicate that Luther, in laying the foundation for a "religiosity for the adult man," displayed the attributes of his own hard-won adulthood; his renaissance of faith portrays a vigorous recovery of his own ego-initiative. To indicate this I will focus on three ideas: the affirmation of voice and word as the instruments of faith; the new recognition of God's "face" in the passion of Christ; and the redefinition of a just life.

After 1505 Luther had made no bones about the pernicious influence which "rancid Aristotelianism" had had on theology. Scholasticism had made him lose faith, he said; through St. Paul he had recovered it. He put the problem in terms of organ modes, by describing scholastic disputations as *dentes* and *linguae:* the teeth are hard and sinister, and form words in anger and fury; the tongue is soft and suavely persuasive. Using these modes, the devil can evoke purely intellectual mirages (*mira potest suggere in intellectu*). But the organ through which the word enters to replenish the heart is the ear (*natura enim verbi est audiri*), for it is in the nature of the word that it should be heard. On the other hand, faith comes from listening, not from looking (*quia est auditu fides, non ex visu*). Therefore, the greatest thing one can say about Christ, and about all Christians, is that they have *aures perfectas et perfossas:* good and open ears. But only what is perceived at the same time as a matter *affectionalis* and *moralis* as well as intellectual can be a matter sacred and divine: one must, therefore, hear before one sees, believe before one understands, be captivated before one captures. *Fides est "locus" animae:* faith is the seat, the organ of the soul. This had certainly been said before; but Luther's emphasis is not on Augustinian "infusion," or on a nominalist "obedience," but, in a truly Renaissance approach, on a self-verification through a God-given inner "apparatus." This *locus,* this apparatus, has its own way of seeking and searching—and it succeeds insofar as it develops its own *passivity.*

Paradoxically, many a young man (and son of a stubborn one) becomes a great man in his own sphere only by learning that deep passivity which permits him to let the data of his competency speak to him. As Freud said in a letter to Fliess, "I must wait until it moves in me so that I can perceive it: *bis es sich in mir ruehrt und ich davon erfahre."* This may sound feminine, and, indeed, Luther bluntly spoke of an attitude of womanly conception— *sicut mulier in conceptu.* Yet it is clear that men call such attitudes and modes feminine only because the strain of paternalism has alienated us from them; for these modes are any organism's birthright, and all our partial as well as our total functioning is based on a metabolism of passivity and activity. Mannish man always wants to pretend that he made himself, or at any rate, that no simple woman bore him, and many puberty rites (consider the rebirth from a kiva in the American Southwest) dramatize a new birth from a spiritual mother of a kind that only men understand.

The theology as well as the psychology of Luther's passivity is that of man in the *state of prayer,* a state in which he fully means what he can say only to God: *Tibi soli peccavi,* I have sinned, not in relation to any person or institution, but in relation only to God, to *my* God.

In two ways, then, rebirth by prayer is passive: it means surrender to God the Father; but it also means to be reborn *ex matrice scripturae nati:* out of the matrix of the scriptures. "Matrix" is as close as such a man's man will come to saying "mater." But he cannot remember and will not acknowledge that long before he had developed those wilful modes which were specifically suppressed and paradoxically aggravated by a challenging father, a mother had taught him to touch the world with his searching mouth and his probing senses. What to a man's man, in the course of his development, seems like a passivity hard to acquire, is only a regained ability to be active with his oldest and most neglected modes. Is it coincidence that Luther, now that he was explicitly teaching passivity, should come to the conclusion that a lecturer should feed his audience as a mother suckles her child? Intrinsic to the kind of passivity we speak of is not only the memory of having been given, but also the identification with the maternal giver: "the glory of a good thing is that it flows out to others." I think that in the Bible Luther at last found a mother whom he could acknowledge: he could attribute to the Bible a generosity to which he could open himself, and which he could pass on to others, at last a mother's son.

Luther did use the words *passiva* and *passivus* when he spoke Latin, and the translation *passive* must be accepted as correct. But in German he often used the word *passivisch,* which is more actively passive, as passific would be. I think that the difference between the old modalities of *passive* and *active* is really that between *erleben* and *handeln,* of being in the state of *experiencing* or of *acting.* Meaningful implications are lost in the flat word *passivity*—among them the total attitude of living receptively and through the senses, of willingly "suffering" the voice of one's intuition and of living a *Passion:* that total passivity in which man regains, through considered self-sacrifice and self-transcendence, his active position in the face of nothingness, and thus is saved. Could this be one of the psychological riddles in the wisdom of the "foolishness of the cross?"

To Luther, the preaching and the praying man, the measure in depth of the perceived presence of the Word was the reaction with a total affect which leaves no doubt that one "means it." It may seem paradoxical to speak of an affect that one could not thus mean; yet it is obvious that rituals, observances, and performances do evoke transitory affects which can be put on for the occasion and afterward hung in the closet with one's Sunday clothes. Man is able to ceremonialize, as he can "automatize" psychologically, the signs and behaviors that are born of the deepest reverence or despair. however, for an affect to have a deep and lasting effect, or, as Luther would say, be *affectionalis* and *moralis,* it must not only be experienced as nearly overwhelming, but it must also in some way be affirmed by the ego as valid, almost as chosen: one means the affect, it signifies something meaningful, it is significant. Such is the relative nature of our ego and of our conscience that when the ego regains its composure after the auditory condemnation of the absolutist voice of conscience we mean what we have learned to believe, and our affects become those of positive conscience: faith, conviction, authority, indignation—all subjective states which are attributes of a strong sense of identity and, incidentally, are indispensable tools for strengthening identity in others. Luther speaks of matters of faith as experiences from which one will profit to the degree to which they were intensive and expressive (*quanto expressius et intensius*). If they are more *frigidus,* however, they are not merely a profit missed, they are a terrible deficit confirmed: for man without intense convictions is a robot with destructive techniques.

It is easy to see that these formulations, once revolutionary, are the commonplaces of today's pulpits. They are the bases of that most inflated of all oratorial currency, credal protestation in church and lecture hall, in political propaganda and in oral advertisement: the protestation, made to order for the occasion, that truth is only that which one means with one's whole being, and lives every moment. We, the heirs of Protestantism, have made convention and pretense out of the very sound of meaning it. What started with the German *Brustton der Ueberzeugung,* the manly chestiness of conviction, took many forms of authoritative appeal, the most recent one being the cute sincerity of our TV announcers. All this only indicates that Luther was a pioneer on one of our eternal inner frontiers, and that his struggle must continue (as any great man's must) exactly at that point where his word is perverted in his own name.

Psychotherapists, professional listeners and talkers in the sphere of affectivity and morality know only too well that man seldom really knows what he really means; he as often lies by telling the truth as he reveals the truth when he tries to lie. This is a psychological statement; and the psychoanalytic method, when it does not pretend to deliver complete honesty, over a period of time reveals approximately what somebody really means. But the center of the problem is simply this: in truly significant matters people, and especially children, have a devastatingly clear if mostly unconscious perception of what other people really mean, and sooner or later royally reward real love or take well-aimed revenge for implicit hate. Families in which each member is separated from the others by asbestos walls of verbal propriety, overt sweetness, cheap frankness, and rectitude tell one another off and talk back to each other with minute and unconscious displays of affect—not to mention physical complaints and bodily ailments—with which they worry, accuse, undermine, and murder one another.

Meaning it, then, is not a matter of credal protestation; verbal explicitness is not a sign of faith. Meaning it, means to be at one with an ideology in the process of rejuvenation; it implies a successful sublimation of one's libidinal strivings; and it manifests itself in a liberated craftsmanship.

When Luther listened to the scriptures he did not do so with an unprejudiced ear. His method of making an unprejudiced approach consisted of listening both ways—to the Word coming from the book and to the echo in himself. "Whatever is in your disposition," he said, "that the word of God will be unto you." Disposition here means the inner configuration of your most meant meanings. He knew that he meant it when he could say it: the spoken Word was the activity appropriate for his kind of passivity. Here "faith and word become one, an invincible whole." *"Der Glawb und das Worth wirth gantz ein Ding und ein unuberwintlich ding."*

Twenty-five times in the Lectures on the Psalms, against once in the Lectures on the Romans, Luther quotes two corresponding passages from Paul's first Epistle to the Corinthians. The first passage:

22. For the Jews require a sign, and the Greeks seek after wisdom;
23. But we preach Christ crucified, unto the Jews a stumblingblock, and unto the Greeks foolishness;
25. Because the foolishness of God is wiser than men; and the weakness of God is stronger than men.

This paradoxical foolishness and weakness of God became a theological absolute for Luther: there is not a word in the Bible, he exclaimed, which is *extra crucem*, which can be understood without reference to the cross; and this is all that shall and can be understood, as Paul had said in the other passage:

1. And I, brethren, when I came to you, came not with excellency of speech or of wisdom, declaring unto you the testimony of God.
2. For I determined not to know any thing among you, save Jesus Christ, and him crucified.
3. And I was with you in weakness, and in fear, and in much trembling.

Thus Luther abandoned any theological quibbling about the cross. He did not share St. Augustine's opinion that when Christ on the cross exclaimed *Deus meus, quare me derelequisti,* He had not been really abandoned, for as God's son and as God's word, He *was* God. Luther could not help feeling that St. Paul came closer to the truth when he assumed an existential paradox rather than a platonic fusion of essences; he insists on Christ's complete sense of abandonment and on his sincere and active premeditation in visiting hell. Luther spoke here in passionate terms very different from those of medieval adoration. He spoke of a man who was unique in all creation, yet lives in each man; and who is dying *in* everyone even as he died *for* everyone. It is clear that Luther rejected all arrangements by which an assortment of saints made it unnecessary for man to embrace the maximum of his own existential suffering. What he had tried, so desperately and for so long, to counteract and overcome he now accepted as his divine gift—the sense of utter abandonment, *sicut jam damnatus,* as if already in hell. The worst temptation, he now says, is not to have any; one can be sure that God is most angry when He does not seem angry at all. Luther warns of all those well-meaning (*bone intentionarii*) religionists who encourage man "to do what he can": to forestall sinning by clever planning; to seek redemption by observing all occasions for rituals, not forgetting to bring cash along to the limit of their means; and to be secure in the feeling that they are as humble and as peaceful as "it is in them to be." Luther, instead, made a virtue out of what his superiors had considered a vice in him (and we, a symptom), namely, the determined search for the rock bottom of his sinfulness: only thus, he says, can man judge himself as God would: *conformis deo est et verax et justus.* One could consider such conformity utter passivity in the face of God's judgment; but note that it really is an active self-observation, which scans the frontier of conscience for the genuine sense of guilt. Instead of accepting some impersonal and mechanical absolution, it insists on dealing with sincere guilt, perceiving as "God's judgment" what in fact is the individual's own truly meant self-judgment.

Is all this an aspect of personal adjustment to be interpreted as a set of unconscious tricks? Martin the son, who on a personal level had suffered deeply because he could not coerce his father into approving his religiosity as genuine, and who had borne with him the words of this father with an unduly prolonged filial obedience, assumes now on a religious level a volitional role toward filial suffering, perhaps making out of his protracted sonhood the victory of his Christlikeness. In his first Mass, facing the altar—the Father in heaven—and at the same time waiting to face his angry earthly father, Martin had "overlooked" a passage concerning Christ's mediatorship. Yet now, in finding Christ in himself, he establishes an inner position which goes beyond that of a neurotic compromise identification. He finds the core of a praying man's identity, and advances Christian ideology by an important step. It is clear that Luther abandoned the appreciation of Christ as a substitute who has died "for"—in the sense of "instead of"—us; he also abandoned the concept of Christ as an ideal figure to be imitated, or abjectly venerated, or ceremonially remembered as an event in the past. Christ now becomes the core of the Christian's identity: *quotidianus Christi adventus,* Christ is today here, in me. The affirmed passivity of suffering becomes the daily Passion and the Passion is the substitution of the primitive sacrifice of others with a most active, most masterly, affirmation of man's nothingness—which, by his own masterly choice, becomes his existential identity.

The men revered by mankind as saviors face and describe in lasting words insights which the ordinary man must avoid with all possible self-deception and exploitation of others. These men prove their point by the magic of their voices which radiate to the farthest corner of their world and out into the millennia. Their passion contains elements of choice, mastery, and victory, and sooner or later earns them the name of King of Kings; their crown of thorns later becomes their successor's tiara. For a little while Luther, this first revolutionary individualist, saved the Saviour from the tiaras and the ceremonies, the hierarchies and the thought-police, and put him back where he arose: in each man's soul.

Is this not the counterpart, on the level of conscience, to Renaissance anthropocentrism? Luther left the heavens to science and restricted himself to what he could know of his own suffering and faith, that is, to what he could mean. He who had sought to dispel the angry cloud that darkened the face of the fathers and of The Father now said that Christ's life *is* God's face: *qui est facies patris.* The Passion is all that man can know of God: his conflicts, duly faced, are all that he can know of himself. The last judgment is the always present self-judgment. Christ did not live and die in order to make man poorer in the fear of his future judgment, but in order to make him abundant today: *nam judicia sunt ipsae passiones Christi quae in nobis abundant.* Look, Luther said at one point in these lectures (IV, 87), how everywhere painters depict Christ's passion as if they agreed with St. Paul that we know nothing but Christ crucified. The artist closest to Luther in spirit was Dürer, who etched his own face into Christ's countenance.

Rupp's discussion of the critical psychological period in Luther's life provides a historical counterweight to Erikson's reading of Luther's psychology.

FROM *The Righteousness of God* BY GORDON RUPP

WE DO NOT KNOW when Luther began to study the Bible, though he must have begun his novitiate by learning portions of scripture which he would recite in the divine offices. It is certain that it became for him an all-important and absorbing study, until his mind was impregnated with the words and themes of the Bible, and he could handle the Biblical material with a facility which was the envy of his enemies, and with a frequent penetration into the exactness of Biblical vocabulary which modern Biblical scholarship has confirmed. But if the Bible was soon to become paramount with him, beyond Augustine and the Fathers, it was initially the meeting-place of all his problems, concentrated in one word. Here is his testimony, in the autobiographical preface which he wrote, at the end of his life (1545), before the Wittenberg edition of his Latin works. After rehearsing his career down to the year 1519, he pauses, and there follows this statement:

"Meanwhile then, in that year (1519), I turned once more to interpret the Psalms, relying on the fact that I was the more expert after I had handled in the schools the letter of St. Paul to the Romans and the Galatians, and that which is to the Hebrews. Certainly I had been seized with a greater ardour to understand Paul in the Epistle to the Romans (captus fueram cognoscendi), but as Virgil says, it was not 'coldness of the blood' which held me up until now, but one word (unicum vocabulum) that is, chapter 1. 'The Justice of God is revealed in it' (Justitia Dei). For I hated this word (vocabulum istud) 'Justitia Dei' which by the use and consent of all doctors I was taught (usu et consuetudine omnium doctorum doctus eram) to understand philosophically of that formal or active justice (as they call it) with which God is just, and punishes unjust sinners.

"For, however irreproachably I lived as a monk, I felt myself in the presence of God (coram Deo) to be a sinner with a most unquiet conscience nor could I trust that I had pleased him with my satisfaction. I did not love, nay, rather I hated this just God who punished sinners and if not with 'open blasphemy' certainly with huge murmuring I was angry with God, saying: 'As though it really were not enough that miserable sinners should be eternally damned with original sin, and have all kinds of calamities laid upon them by the law of the ten commandments, God must go and add

Gordon Rupp, *The Righteousness of God: Luther Studies* (1953), pp. 121–7. Reprinted by permission of Hodder & Stoughton Ltd., London.

sorrow upon sorrow and even through the Gospel itself bring his Justice and his Wrath to bear!' I raged in this way with a fierce and disturbed conscience, and yet I knocked importunately at Paul in this place, thirsting most ardently to know what St. Paul meant.

"At last, God being merciful, as I meditated day and night on the connection of the words, namely, 'the Justice of God is revealed in it, as it is written, "the Just shall live by Faith," ' there I began to understand the Justice of God as that by which the just lives by the gift of God, namely by faith, and this sentence, 'the Justice of God is revealed in the gospel,' to be that passive justice, with which the merciful God justifies us, by faith, as it is written 'The just lives by faith.'

"This straightway made me feel as though reborn, and as though I had entered through open gates into paradise itself. From then on, the whole face of scripture appeared different. I ran through the scriptures then, as memory served, and found the same analogy in other words, as the Work of God (opus) that which God works in us, Power of God (virtus Dei) with which he makes us strong, wisdom of God (sapientia Dei) with which he makes us wise, fortitude of God, salvation of God, glory of God.

"And now, as much as I had hated this word 'Justice of God' before, so much the more sweetly I extolled this word to myself now, so that this place in Paul was to me as a real gate of paradise. Afterwards, I read Augustine, 'On the Spirit and the Letter,' where beyond hope I found that he also similarly interpreted the Justice of God: that with which God endues us, when he justifies us. And although this were said imperfectly, and he does not clearly explain about 'imputation,' yet it pleased that he should teach a Justice of God with which we are justified.

"Armed with these cogitations I began to interpret the Psalms again."

The narrative is in the main straightforward, and most of it can be checked against quotations already cited in these pages. But there are certain problems which must be faced. In the first place, to what period of his career does Luther refer when he speaks of his discovery about "Justitia Dei"? A superficial reading might suggest that he refers to the year (1519), when "armed with these cogitations" he began the second course of lectures on the Psalms. But it can be demonstrated that Luther had developed his teaching on this subject in these terms, at least by the time of his lectures on Romans (1515–16). The notion of a dislocation of the text, that refuge of desperate scholars, put forward by A. V. Müller, has no documentary evidence to support it, and as K. Holl pointed out, would make Luther commit grammatical solecisms. The suggestion that Luther in his old age made a slip of memory and confused his first and second lectures on the Psalms is hardly more convincing. Stracke has made a careful examination of the whole of this autobiographical fragment, and Luther emerges surprisingly well from the test. After thirty years, he is not unnaturally a month or two out here and there, gets a detail misplaced now and again, but when we remember that famous edition of the letters of Erasmus, which had more than half the dates wrong, and some of them years out, we can count this preface yet another disproof of the legend of Luther's anecdotage.

In fact, as Stracke pointed out, Luther's use of the phrase "captus fueram" makes perfectly tenable the interpretation that Luther has gone back in his reflection to an earlier period. Before attempting to identify this date more precisely, we must discuss the authenticity of the statement as a whole.

To impugn this was intended as a crowning demonstration of Denifle's "Luther und Luthertum." Denifle brought forward, in an appendix, a catena of 360 pages, giving the exposition of Rom. 1:17 by sixty doctors of the Western Church, which, he said, demonstrated beyond a doubt "not a single writer from the time of Ambrosiaster to the time of Luther understood this passage (Rom. 1:17) in the sense of the justice of God which punishes, of an angry God. All, on the contrary, have understood it of the God who justifies, the justice obtained by faith." Here, then, is the dilemma. Either Luther was a fool, or he was a liar. Either he was a bragging incompetent, boasting in his senility, or he was adding the last untruth to a long series of lying inventions. For Denifle, the two conclusions were not mutually exclusive.

Denifle included in the demonstration passages from the recently rediscovered lectures of Luther on Romans. This was intended as proof that Luther himself had used the supposed newly discovered meaning at a time anterior to 1515.

That part of his argument falls to the ground if we suppose Luther in fact to have spoken of a period before 1515. We may, therefore, re-sharpen Denifle's usefulness as an advocatus diaboli at this point, and present polemic with an argument here which, as far as we know, has been little noticed. In the Sentences of Peter Lombard, on which Luther lectured in 1509, and in the famous Dist. XVII of Book 1, to which, as we have seen, Luther paid special attention, there is imbedded a quotation from St. Augustine's "Spirit and Letter" which gives the so-called "passive" interpretation of "Justitia Dei":

"The love of God is said to be shed abroad in our hearts, not because he loves us, but because he makes us his lovers: just as the justice of God (Justitia Dei) is that by which we are made just by his gift (justi ejus munere efficimur): and 'salvation of the Lord' by which he saves us: and 'faith of Jesus Christ' that which makes us believers (fideles)."

The words are glossed by the Master of the Sentences, "And this is called the Justice of God, not with which he is just, but because with it he makes us just." At any rate, it seems clear that although in 1509 Luther had not read Augustine's "Spirit and the Letter," he had read an extract concerning this interpretation of the "Justitia Dei" during his study of Peter Lombard.

Denifle's *tour de force* was impressive, and like most polemic of this kind, got a good start of its pursuers. Among many replies the most notable were the essays by Karl Holl and Emmanuel Hirsch.

In the first place, it was pointed out that Luther in speaking of the "use and consent of all doctors" was referring not to Rom. 1:17, but to the "unicum vocabulum" of "Justitia Dei." The distinction is important, for, if granted, it means that the doctors in question were not the exegetes but the systematic theologians, and their views are to be found, not in the commentaries on the Epistles of St. Paul, but in those passages which concerned the conception of divine justice in Commentaries on the Sentences, and the like. Denifle's enormous collection of documents attested a wrong indictment.

Denifle, it is true, could appeal to a passage in Luther's lectures on Genesis, in which he referred to "hunc locum," i.e. Rom: 1:17, as the centre of his difficulties. But these lectures were not published until after Luther's death, and then only in the form in which they were reported. If there is glossing to be done, the 1545 fragment is primary, and Denifle, in his argument, showed some embarrassment at this point. As Holl was not slow to point out, nobody could say how many of Denifle's sixty doctors of the West could have been known, at first- or second-hand, to Luther, or whether he had studied the exegesis concerning Rom. 1:17. Holl proceeded thoroughly to analyse Denifle's authorities and disentangled two main streams of mediaeval exegesis, going back to Ambrosiaster and to Augustine. He showed that Ambrosiaster keeps in mind the problem of the Divine integrity, how the just God can receive sinners, and that while stressing the merciful promises of God, he keeps also the conception of retributive justice. Augustine is less concerned with justice as a divine property than with that bestowed righteousness, the work of grace infused within the human soul, on the ground of which sinners are made just in the presence of God. But Holl pointed out that neither of these expositions, nor all the permutations and combinations of them made thereafter, really met Luther's problem. "That from the time of St. Augustine the Western Church spoke of justifying grace, and that the later schoolmen strengthened this conception by their teaching about an "habitus" is something known to all, and it is quite certain that Luther was not unaware of it." Emmanuel Hirsch dealt with a notable and fundamental omission from Denifle's authorities, namely, the Nominalist doctors whom Luther knew, and whom he had in mind when he said, "I was taught." He showed that Gabriel Biel, though admitting, even stressing the need for grace, and for the divine "Misericordia," normally preferred to reserve "Justitia" for the retributive justice of God which punishes sinners. This interpretation, which Hirsch based on Biel's commentary on the Sentences, seems confirmed by an examination of some scores of sermons by Biel upon the feasts of the Christian year.

Even more important than these arguments is the abundant testimony of Luther's good faith in this matter which is yielded by writings of other years, many of which, since they had never been published, might well have been completely forgotten by Luther. It is quite certain that, whatever the truth about his statement, it was no later invention, made up at the end of his life. Thus, in 1515:

"Wherefore, if I may speak personally, the word 'Justitia' so nauseated me to hear, that I would hardly have been sorry if somebody had made away with me."

In 1531 (published 1538):

"For thus the Holy Fathers who wrote about the Psalms were wont to expound the 'justus deus' as that in which he vindicates and punishes, not as that which justifies. So it happened to me as a young man, and even today I am as though terrified when I hear God called 'the just.'

"Justice, i.e. grace. This word I learned with much sweat. They used to expound justice as the truth of God which punishes the damned, mercy as that which saves believers. A dangerous opinion which arouses a secret hatred of the heart against God, so that it is terrified when he is so much as named. Justice is that which the Father does when he favours us, with which he justifies, or the gift with which he takes away our sin."

There are three passages in the Table Talk which must embody some core of truth. These suggest that Luther met his difficulty, before he came to the Epistle to the Romans, and in the interpretation of Psalm 31:1. "In justitia tua libera me." But the difficulty, "Justitia Dei" understood as retributive justice, is the same.

Two facts seem clear. First, that in his early career Luther found the conception of the "Justitia Dei" a stumbling block. Second, that this rock of offence did become for him the very corner-stone of his theology. The doctrine of Justification by Faith came to hold, in consequence, for him and for subsequent Protestant theology an altogether more important place than in the Catholic and mediaeval framework. In the sixteenth century men like Sir Thomas More and Stephen Gardiner found it hard to understand what all the Protestant fuss was about, and some striking parallels might be cited among modern Anglican scholars. Thus, even if we had not Luther's explicit testimony in the fragment under consideration, it would be necessary to invent something very like it to account for the remarkable and fundamental transformation in his thought. Denifle's demonstration may be held to have failed in so far as he attempted to show that Luther had wittingly perverted mediaeval teaching, and to have failed, too, in the more fundamental charge that Luther had in fact made no theological discoveries at all.

Thus in his narrative Luther explains simply and clearly why Rom. 1:17 was the climax of his difficulties. Luther already knew and believed that God condemned sinners through the Law. Now, in Rom. 1:17, he found that through the Gospel also was revealed the "Justitia Dei," which he took to mean the strict, retributive justice of God.

If the reader, having absorbed the academic roughage of this critical discussion, will turn back to the autobiographical fragment, he will find it tolerably plain. We can understand how, in the presence of a God who weighted everything against the sinner, Luther was filled with that "huge murmuring" which he elsewhere often and eloquently described, but which a man dared hardly admit to himself, so closely did it approximate to "open blasphemy." This inward ferment added to the outward practices of devotion and penitence an element of strain and unreality, and enforced hypocrisy which in turn aggravated the spiritual conflict. This was not merely an academic affair, though we need not shrink from admitting the theological enquiry of a theological professor into such a category. What he learned and taught about the Justice of God became for him a "carnifex theologistria," however, by reason of the unquiet conscience within. It was this fifth column, within the citadel of the soul, which betrayed him. Miegge's judgment is valid: "In the case of Luther, the religious crisis and the theological crisis are not to be separated."

> *Henri Daniel-Rops is a member of the French Academy and has written a number of popular works on the history of the church. The selection that follows gives a view of Luther's evolution toward heresy from a Catholic vantage point.*

FROM *The Protestant Reformation*

BY HENRI DANIEL-ROPS

THE AFFAIR OF THE INDULGENCES

IT WAS 31ST OCTOBER 1517. In the little town of Wittenberg, a part of the Elector of Saxony's possessions, the crush and animation were at their height. Every year the Feast of All Saints attracted countless pious folk, who came to see the precious relics which His Highness the Elector, Frederick the Wise, had collected at great expense, and which were brought out for the occasion from the storerooms of the Schlosskirche. There were plenty of them—several thousand—and they were of the most varied kind: they included not only the complete corpses of various saints, nails from the Passion and rods from the Flagellation, but part of the Child Jesus' swaddling-clothes and some wood from His crib, and even a few drops of His Blessed Mother's milk! Large numbers of most valuable indulgences were attached to the veneration of these distinguished treasures.

That same morning a manifesto, written in scholastic Latin and consisting of ninety-five theses, was found nailed to the door of the castle's chapel.

From the book *The Protestant Reformation,* I, 9, by Henri Daniel-Rops, translated by Audrey Butler. Translation Copyright, ©, 1961 by E. P. Dutton & Co., Inc., and J. M. Dent & Sons Ltd. Reprinted by permission of the publishers.

Its author was an Augustinian monk who was extremely well known in the town, and he declared his intention of defending its contents against any opponent prepared to stand up and argue with him. In fact, the document concerned those very indulgences which honest folk were even then showing such eagerness to obtain by praying before the relics and slipping their guilders into the offertory boxes. The pilgrims assembled outside the church heard the more knowledgeable among them translate its words: "Those preaching in favour of indulgences err when they say such indulgences can deliver man and grant him salvation. The man who gives to the poor performs a better action than the one who buys indulgences." There were three hundred yet more bitter lines in this strain. And the worthy pilgrims wondered what could be the purpose of this monk in thus shaking one of the pillars of the Church.

For this was what indulgences seemed to have become: a pillar of the faith. Palz, Master of Erfurt, actually taught that they were "the modern way of preaching the Gospel." Was there anything intrinsically reprehensible about them? A rereading of the treatise which the learned Johann Pfeffer had devoted to the subject a quarter of a century earlier, in that same town of Wittenberg, or a glance at the sermons of the celebrated Johann Geiler of Kayserberg, makes the real meaning of indulgences clear beyond any shadow of a doubt. What the Church understood by *indulgence* was the total or partial remission of the penalties of sin—to which everyone was liable, either on earth or in Purgatory—after the Sacrament of Penance had afforded him absolution from his fault and remission of eternal punishment. But the state of grace was indispensable for the obtaining of such temporal remission; good works, in the shape of prayers, fasting, pilgrimages, visits to churches and almsgiving, were only an incidental, or, to put it another way, a contributory factor. Where there was no firm resolve or inward glow there was no remission. In strict doctrine an indulgence was certainly not an automatic means of gaining a cheap discharge from penalties that were justly deserved. In 1476 a bull of Sixtus IV had recognized that indulgences could be applied to the souls of the departed, whose sufferings in the next world would be alleviated thereby; and the declaration of this principle had contributed to the success of the jubilee of 1500.

It was not of recent origin. As early as the eleventh century crusaders had reaped the benefits of the plenary indulgence. Since then it had been awarded more generally and bestowed on less heroic occasions. It had had a number of happy results, and countless works of religious or social utility had been financed by the money collected in this way; churches too, hospitals, pawnshops, even dikes and bridges. Thanks to indulgences the Church in France had been materially restored on the morrow of the Hundred Years War. Nor had the spiritual results been insignificant: when proclaimed by special preachers the grant of an indulgence provided a spiritual jolt rather like the "missions" of modern times, and was the means of bringing numerous penitents to the confessional.

But it was not these excellent reasons alone which caused the institution to become so widespread, particularly from the fourteenth century onwards. For close on two centuries years of indulgence had been granted with unrestrained liberality in return for the briefest visit to a church, or the least meritorious of pilgrimages. In a period of twelve months the pious Elector Frederick the Wise laid up no fewer than 127,799 years, sufficient to empty a whole province of Purgatory and ensure himself more than one heaven. It is not difficult to imagine the kind of excesses which found their way into this practice, and they had already been condemned in 1312 by the decretal *Abusionibus*. Simony discovered some splendid material here and it is open to doubt whether preachers of indulgences, with their attendant collectors stationed at the foot of the pulpit, were primarily interested in saving souls or in collecting ducats. All too often the grant of an indulgence was part and parcel of some shady deal, and sometimes the right to collect for it was actually sold at auction. Pope Leo X himself once empowered the Fuggers, a celebrated firm of bankers at Augsburg, to preach an indulgence by way of security for a loan. The climate of the age was only too favourable to this type of proceedings. In 1514, when the Hohenzollern Albert of Brandenberg secured his election as Archbishop of Mainz, the heavy chancellery dues of 14,000 ducats, plus a "voluntary settlement" of a further 10,000 intended to ease the scruples of the Curia, were financed by the Fuggers, who were guaranteed in return one-third of the revenues from the great papal indulgence.

Misconduct such as this was not the only menace to the institution; the doctrine itself was affected by something even worse. Far too many preachers taught that an indulgence possessed a kind of magical quality, and that by spending money to obtain it men were taking out a mortgage on Heaven. One popular jingle ran:

> Sobald das Geld im Kasten klingt
> Die Seele aus dem Fegfeuer springt!

> [*As soon as the money in the collection box rings
> The soul from out of hellfire springs—L. P. W.*]

Moreover Germany was not the only country where such rubbish was taught. In 1482 the Sorbonne had condemned one preacher who recited it from the pulpit; at Besançon, in 1486, a certain Franciscan swore that provided a man wore the habit of his Order, St. Francis would come in person to collect him from Purgatory. Naturally enough there were lively reactions to these specious claims. As early as 1484 a priest named Lallier had publicly rejected the view that the Pope had the power to remit the pains of another world by means of indulgence, and despite objections from the theological faculty, the Bishop of Paris had absolved him. In 1498 the Franciscan Vitrier had been hauled before the Sorbonne for having declared that "money must not be given in order to obtain forgiveness." His disciple Erasmus had lately written: "Any trader, mercenary soldier or judge has but to put down his money, however nefariously acquired, and he imagines that he has purged the whole Lemean Marsh of his life." Views of this sort were taught in the University of Wittenberg, which considered itself the rival of Leipzig and Erfurt; and trenchancy of tone helped to further the renown of that centre, where, during 1516, statements such as the following had been heard: "It is an absurdity to preach that the souls in Purgatory are ransomed by indulgences."

In 1517 the most important indulgence preached in Germany was that which the popes had twice accorded to generous Christians donating money for the new basilica of St. Peter's: Julius II in 1506, in order that building might begin, and Leo X in 1514, to enable it to continue. It was the fruits of this indulgence which had been the object of that extraordinary share-out which we have already noticed on the occasion of the Mainz election. The archbishop had entrusted the task of preaching the indulgence to the Dominicans, and this had provoked a fraternal but somewhat bitter jealousy among the Augustinians.

At the head of these preachers was a certain Brother Tetzel, a burly, voluble fellow, who pleaded his case with extreme enthusiasm. He was a well-intentioned man, whose own moral conduct was perfectly honourable, and he did not deserve the calumnies with which his opponents were to befoul him; but his theology was highly questionable. His method of procedure merely increased the public belief that an indulgence was a mere financial transaction. He visited the whole area dependent on Mainz, and would arrive with a vast retinue, preceded by the bull which was carried on a velvet cushion embroidered with gold. The people would come out in procession to meet him, accompanied by the ringing of bells and waving of banners; and Tetzel would then mount the pulpit, or stand in the town square, offering "passports to cross the sea of wrath and go direct to Paradise." This was indeed a splendid opportunity to make certain of escaping the seven years of suffering—which, as all agreed, any forgiven sin still required in the Beyond—by obtaining the plenary indulgence accorded by a confessor of Tetzel's choice. Besides, here also was an opportunity to snatch some friend or loved one from the fires of Purgatory. Nor was the price extortionate. The penitent must go to confession, visit seven churches, recite five *Paters* and five *Aves,* and place an offering in the indulgence box. The offering demanded was a modest one, scaled to the resources of each individual believer: for the poorest a quarter of a florin was sufficient.

It was against such practices and such teaching that the manifesto nailed to the door of the Schlosskirche protested so strongly. Tetzel had not preached in Wittenberg, which was Saxon territory, but all recognized the target of this attack. It was all very well for the author to maintain discretion by advising his readers to receive "the Apostolic Commissioners with respect"; his theses rejected not only the Dominican's interpretation of the indulgence, but protested against the institution itself. He denounced its financial side. "The indulgences so extolled by preachers have only one merit, that of bringing in money." Or again: "Nowadays the Pope's money-bag is fatter than those of the richest capitalists; why does he not build this basilica with his own resources rather than with the offerings of the poor?" These somewhat clumsy arguments made a deep impression among the common people. He also criticized the theological bases of the institution, suggesting that the indulgence caused men to lose their sense of penitence. "True contrition gladly accepts the penalties and seeks them out; the indulgence remits them and inspires us with aversion for them. When a Christian is truly penitent he has the right to plenary remission, even without an ecclesiastical indulgence. The grace of Jesus Christ remits the penalties of sin, not the Pope. Man can hope to receive this grace by experiencing a hatred of self and of his sin, and not by the accomplishment of a few acts or the sacrifice of a little money." Although, in so far as they contain authentic Catholic doctrine, these theses are acceptable in many respects, they deviate from orthodoxy to the extent that they deny the Pope's power to remit penalties and refer implicitly to a theory of grace according to which man's merits are almost worthless.

What motive had impelled the author of this document to defy the official teaching of the Church? Indignation against traffickers in sacred things? Undoubtedly. Hatred of the Pope and contempt for the simoniacal Roman Curia? No. There was something deeper, more decisive, and it is revealed in the very last sentence of his ninety-five theses. Tetzel was trying to persuade the faithful that salvation was easily effected through works; he was concealing from his hapless listeners that it is necessary "to enter Heaven by way of many tribulations," as the Acts of the Apostles makes quite clear; he was encouraging them to "rest in false security." Here was the crux of the matter. It was against "this appalling error" that the professor of Wittenberg entered the lists; and he entered them with all the violence of a man for whom this theological dispute represented a drama played out in his own life, and whom false security had brought very close indeed to total despair and unbelief. His name was *Martin Luther*.

A BRILLIANT YOUNG MONK

At this date Luther was a tall, lean, bony man with powerful expressive hands. They were never still: they were forever pointing at an enemy or punctuating an argument. Everything about him indicated a passion, unease and a latent violence that was always on the verge of erupting to produce total destruction. The eyes in the rough-hewn face, with its high cheekbones, square chin and lined cheeks, often sparkled with anger or intelligence, but no less frequently they allowed a glimpse of uncontrollable anguish. It is difficult to escape the fascination which this monk in his simple Augustinian robe exerted on everyone who saw him. In 1517 he was thirty-four years old.

What had Luther's life been like up to this time? What events and reasoning had led him to quarrel openly with official conformity and make the gesture which, by setting him in the forefront of world affairs, was to turn him into the living symbol of contradiction? The *Rückblick*, that rapid and superficial glance which he threw back to his youth in 1545, a year before his death, is hardly an adequate answer to these questions; when old people evoke their memories they very often amend both truth and falsehood.

As for the traditional account, still widely believed, it seems best to retain here only the bare outline of the facts and not their substance. The explanation of Martin Luther's attitude must not be sought in his allegedly unhappy childhood and adolescence, nor, as the psychoanalysts would have it, in the crisis of a monk beset by temptations of the flesh, nor even in the scandalized indignation he is supposed to have felt during a brief visit to Rome. It is to be found rather in an inner conflict, something like those experienced by St Paul, St Augustine and Pascal—a conflict through which Luther lived in keen spiritual agony and uncertainty, and from which he unhappily emerged along a path which was no longer that approved by Mother Church.

Martin Luther was born on 10th November 1483, at Eisleben in Saxony, the second of eight children. He was brought up at Mansfeld, where Hans, his father, had settled six months after the boy's birth. His early years were no more and no less happy than that of many sons of ordinary folk. The harsh realities of life brutalized this class of persons, and in a large family there was no time for emotional refinement. Hans was a devout, stern man whose morals were irreproachable but who was easily roused to anger. He was striving with all his might to rise from artisan to foreman, and finally to become a small foundry owner on his own account, and his sole desire was that his entire household should behave with absolute propriety. Hans Luther's hard-working wife, Margaret, *née* Ziegler, was a stolid Franconian. She did not find it difficult to share her husband's ideas and she directed her family with a firm hand which her children occasionally found too heavy.

Martin's parents sent him to school at Mansfeld when he was six years old. There he received the customary education of the age, consisting of the old *trivium* and the catechism, instilled by the pedagogic methods which were then in current use and in which the cane played a large part. When it became apparent that he was an exceptionally gifted boy, his father decided that he should continue his studies with a view to the law. He spent a year in the Cathedral School at Magdeburg, which was excellently conducted by the Brethren of the Common Life, and there he acquired an unhappily all too brief experience of genuine spirituality: it was most probably here that he made his first real contact with the Bible. Then, because his great-uncle was sacristan of St Nicholas's, Luther was drawn back to Eisenach, and there he developed his innate talents for music. Finally, at the age of eighteen, he entered Erfurt University—his father, who was now more comfortably off, was henceforth able to pay him an allowance—where he obtained an outstanding degree and greatly improved his powers of self-expression and reasoning. His teachers, Fathers Usingen and Palz, trained him in their methods, which were those of Ockhamist scholasticism. His fellow students regarded him as an honourable, devout, but merry companion. So far everything about Luther's life had been utterly normal and ordinary. Then, just as he had begun his legal studies, an unforeseen event completely altered his destiny.

On 2nd July 1505, while he was returning alone from Mansfeld to Erfurt, a thunderstorm of unusual violence suddenly broke upon him. The lightning flashed so close that he believed himself lost. In the midst of this danger he invoked St Anne according to custom, and promised: "If you come to my aid I will become a monk." This was perhaps a rash vow, but it was certainly not spontaneous. Various other incidents had preceded this spiritual decision. Legend has embroidered upon them so much that their detail has become obscured, but their meaning is abundantly plain. A serious illness during adolescence, the sudden death of a friend, a sword wound acquired in a student's duel and which had bled for a long time—all these had brought Luther face to face with the one great fact that youth tends to ignore—the fact of death. The episode of the thunderstorm set the seal on this revelation. Luther's impressionable nature and naturally vivid sensibility responded urgently to that mortal fear which the thunderclap had inspired in his soul. He remembered the good Brethren of the Common Life, the Anhalt ruler in the Franciscan habit whom he had known at Magdeburg, the dedicated young Carthusians he often saw at Erfurt. He thought of all the people he knew who seemed to have found peace of heart, and the answer to the most dreadful of all questions beneath the homespun of the monastic robe. This vow of his was undoubtedly forced from his soul by terror, but the terror was not caused by the thunderstorm alone. Neither his family nor his friends could prevent him from remaining faithful to his promise. Fifteen days after the incident on the Erfurt road he set off to knock on the door of the Augustinian monastery there.

In 1517 then, when he nailed his theses on the door of the Schlosskirche in Wittenberg, he was a monk—and a monk of some importance in his Order—and he was moreover a monk who had not the slightest desire to renounce his vows. "I have been a pious monk for twenty years," he was to say; "I have said a Mass every day; I have worn myself out in prayer and fasting." Witnesses have described him as a good monk, "certainly not without sin, but above serious reproach." In 1507 he was ordained priest. Luther mounted the altar steps for the first time with an ardour mingled with fear, as befitted one who was about to hold the living God in his own hands. Theology had made him increasingly fervent; Duns Scotus and St Thomas, Pierre d'Ailly and Gerson, William of Ockham and others in the same tradition, notably Gabriel Biel, had been the object of his voracious reading, together with the Bible, and St Augustine, and all the mystics from St Bernard to Master Eckhart. In 1508, by order of Staupitz, the wise Vicar-General for Germany, who was much interested in this brilliant young man, Luther was transferred to Wittenberg, there to teach philosophy and acquire the title of Bachelor of Arts. He enjoyed a high reputation in his Order.

This was made very clear when, during the winter of 1510–11, he was chosen to go to Rome to submit the dispute between the Augustinians of the strict and conventual observances to the superiors of the Order. Legend has it that what he saw in the Eternal City so upset the young monk that he resolved to undertake the reform of the Church. This is a convenient story, but all the evidence is against it. Luther stayed in Rome for four short weeks, behaving like any other pious pilgrim. He was most anxious to see as many churches as possible, to win the indulgences attached to these visits and to climb the "scala sancta" on his knees; in short, as he himself recalled, he was filled with "holy madness." All he saw of the Papal Court were the usual glimpses that any humble visiting German cleric might expect to obtain. He obviously heard a good deal of gossip, but this did not have much immediate effect upon him. It was not until much later on, when he had been condemned by the Catholic Church, that he sought to justify his own attitude by reviving his memories of Rome. So great was men's ignorance in the capital of Christendom, he recalled, that he had been unable to find a confessor there; in St Sebastian's he had seen seven priests hurry through the Mass within the hour at a single altar; and he himself had witnessed the shameless behaviour of women in church. Perhaps; but he did not pronounce these strictures until twenty-five years after the incidents concerned—very much *a posteriori*.

On his return to Germany Luther was assigned to the Augustinian house in Wittenberg; in the following year, having been made doctor of theology, he was awarded the chair of Holy Scripture at the university. His lectures were outstandingly successful: he spoke on the Psalms and the Pauline Epistles; he was also a celebrated preacher, highly regarded by his congregations. Staupitz, his immediate superior, had a very exalted opinion of him; he made him "district vicar," in other words, provincial, with jurisdiction over eleven of the Order's houses; and he even went so far as to tell Luther: "God speaks through your mouth." Thus Luther's importance and prestige added considerable weight to his stand against the preachers of indulgences on All Saints' Eve 1517.

THE DRAMA OF A SOUL

In order to understand Luther's reasons for acting as he did we must penetrate his soul and reach into those dark and dangerous recesses of the mind wherein each man worthy of the name seeks, amid suffering and contradiction, to give a meaning to his own destiny. Because the light which he himself sheds upon the drama of his youth was given long after the period concerned, a number of critics have treated it all as legend. The aged Luther, they allege, invented the background of a Pascalian debate in order to provide his rebellion with fundamentally lofty and mystical origins. But an impartial study of the documents covering the decisive years—for example, his commentary on the Epistle to the Romans—is sufficient to convince the reader that their author could have adopted certain attitudes at the end of a secret and painful effort to find the answer to the gravest of man's problems. Anyone who refuses to believe that Luther was fundamentally one of those individuals for whom life and belief are serious matters is guilty of traducing historical and psychological truth. He was essentially a protagonist in great spiritual battles. The Augustinian monk who seemed to be making for himself such a brilliant career was inwardly tormented by that peculiarly religious anxiety which it is easier to feel than to define.

Luther had entered the monastery hoping to discover peace of mind, but he had not found it. He was very much a son of his age and of his native land—of Germany, where man's struggle against the powers of darkness was translated into a multitude of terrible or sublime legends; of Christianity at the crossroads, where morbid sermons and dances of death caused the faithful to be haunted with thoughts of their ultimate destiny. He had not been able to get rid of these phantoms merely by donning the monastic robe. "I know a man," he wrote in 1518, "who declares he has experienced such mortal terror that no words can describe it; he who has not suffered the like would never believe him. But it is a fact that if anyone were obliged to endure for long, for half an hour or even the tenth part of an hour, he would perish utterly, and his very bones would be reduced to ashes." Luther was in the grip of terrible anguish, and his friend Melanchthon relates that during the whole of his monastic life he was never able to throw it off. "My heart bled when I said the Canon of the Mass," Luther confesses, in reference to his years as a young priest. These are words that no one can read without emotion.

Whence came this anguish? Certain authors have suggested that it was caused by hereditary neurosis, but there is no real proof of this. It is perfectly clear to anyone reading many of his own confessions that Luther was not so much a sick man as one burdened with the tragic sense of sin in all its intensity. But of what sin? It is futile to pretend to find an answer in the stirrings of his flesh. Some have seen Luther as a monk in the grip of secret lusts, a familiar of the *delectatio morosa,* unable to quell the beast within him and revolting against the discipline of the Church in order to satisfy his craving. Yet if this were a true picture, if he had acted on the strength of such contemptible motives, his influence would scarcely have been so far-reaching, and would scarcely have inflicted so much suffering upon the Church. Besides, Luther himself frequently emphasized that the worst temptations were not carnal: "evil thoughts, hatred of God, blasphemy, despair and unbelief—these are the main temptations." The concupiscence which he had to conquer was not primarily that which draws male to female, but an irresistible craving of both body and soul that urges man to embrace all that is terrestrial and manifest—in a word, human—deflecting him from the invisible and divine.

In the monastery he had hoped to be delivered from these monsters. He was a mystical personality in many ways, and he dreamed of a warm, consoling presence which would shield him from evil and from himself, but he had discovered nothing in the monastic routine to provide such comfort. Was this because he lacked true humility, or because he had not the spirit of prayer? Only God, who has already judged the soul of Martin Luther, can supply an answer. One obstacle, however, certainly prevented him from running like the Prodigal Son to the arms of his Father, for whenever the least flicker of impurity, violence or doubt crossed his mind he believed himself damned. He tried prayer, asceticism, and even daily confession, but none of them could rid him of this ever-present obsession with hell, which continually threatened to overwhelm him. "I did penance," Luther says, "but despair did not leave me."

The obstacle which barred Luther's way to the path of peace and love was his concept of God. He insists that this was the picture shown him in religious life. "We paled at the mere mention of Christ's Name, for He was always depicted as a stern judge who was angry with us." Was it necessary to work oneself to death in prayer, fasting and mortifications from fear of a Master wielding the rod of chastisement, a Divine Executioner? What was the good of it all, since one could not even be sure of melting His wrath? "When will you do enough to obtain God's mercy?" he asked himself in anguish. In that age of misery the message of Christ's love seemed sterile; there remained only the atrocious doctrine of inevitable punishment meted out by an inexorable judge.

It has not been difficult for Catholic critics to show that this doctrine has never been that of Holy Church. In a book of no fewer than 378 pages, Father Denifle has conclusively demonstrated that the "justice of God" mentioned in a famous passage of the Epistle to the Romans (1:17), and which Luther took to be the supreme spiritual reality, was intended to signify something far more than *justitia puniens,* divine wrath punishing the sins of men; the words were used rather of sanctifying grace, of the omnipotent mercy lavished by God on all who believe in Him and submit to His ordinances. Luther's interpretation of the phrase reveals a surprising failure to understand the philosophy of such writers as St Augustine and St Bernard, with whose works he was undoubtedly well acquainted. To explain the spiritual drama of the young Augustinian monk, however, it is sufficient to acknowledge that he himself regarded this erroneous doctrine as valid, and as that which his own professors had taught him.

The fact may have been due to the imperfect theological training offered by the representations of decadent scholasticism who filled all the university chairs. Moreover the teaching then in fashion contained one feature calculated to impel a restless soul along the downward slope. To such a man as Luther, obsessed with the desire to appease his terrible God, and deriving not the slightest comfort from his prayers and mortifications, one system in particular provided a kind of answer: Ockhamist Nominalism, in which, as we have seen, he had been brought up. Luther had discovered from the writings of this school not only that man could overcome sin by will alone, but also that no human action became meritorious unless God acknowledged it and willed it to be so. But if man's will failed it had no means of recovery, for reason was unavailing and grace was not conceived as a supernatural principle raising man's spiritual forces to the level of Divine Justice. Thus nothing was left save a capricious God, granting or withholding His grace and forgiveness for motives that defied all the rules of logic. Before Him stood a defenceless man, inert and passive in relation to the work of salvation. Destiny appeared to be regulated by the cold mechanics of a despot in whose eyes nothing had any merit. Luther strove hard to find confirmation of these theories in certain passages of St Paul and St Augustine, for they corresponded all too well with his fundamental and powerful belief in the futility of all human effort. In several respects he remained an Ockhamist all his life; but he rejected the voluntarism taught by Ockham's disciples, he denied the human liberty which they recognized, and he gave it a ring of predestinationism which was absent from the master's philosophy. None of this did anything to grant him peace of mind.

But a number of more peaceful influences were at work. Luther had read all the mystics, especially the German writers of the late Middle Ages, notably Tauler. Here too he had found elements that tended to deny the importance of external works, to discard free will and to exalt the part played by faith in Christ the Redeemer. Man must lay himself open to God's action, submit to it and do nothing to resist it. This was one of the fundamental ideas of the *Theologica Germanica*. Furthermore Staupitz, anxious to heal this ravaged soul, had gone a long way in the same direction by showing Luther the gentleness of God's love and the need for supreme surrender to Providence. Neither the subtleties of the schools nor ritual practices would give him the divine life to which he aspired, but only the impulse of a believing soul, and the piety which sprang from the most secret recesses of the heart. "True repentance begins with love of justice and of God." Once the young monk felt that part of his burden had been lifted, that he was on the way to a new enlightenment; and it seemed that ideas, arguments and biblical references poured in from all sides to confirm this doctrine "and dance a jig around it."

It was now that there happened the "discovery of mercy," a wholly spiritual event to which Luther's disciples afterwards traced the origins of the Reformation. The date and place of this occurrence are the subject of some dispute. He may have had his first glimpse of it in Rome, while making the pious pilgrimage on his knees up the "Scala sancta." It may, on the other hand, be necessary to advance the date to 1518 or 1519; if so he can have had only a kind of presentiment of his doctrine on the day when he nailed his theses to the chapel door. Its main features, however, are already apparent in the university lectures which he gave between 1514 and 1517. The most probable truth is that the "discovery" took place in his mind by gradual stages, before imposing itself on his soul with such force that all arguments and reservations became as nothing in the blinding clarity of what seemed to him to be incontrovertible evidence.

In the preface to the 1545 edition of his *Works* Luther describes in detail this "sudden illumination of the Holy Spirit." He was pondering once again the terrible seventeenth verse in the first chapter of the Epistle to the Romans when the true meaning—that is to say, the meaning he henceforth considered to be true—was revealed to him. "While I pursued my meditations day and night, examining the import of these words, 'The justice of God is revealed in the Gospel, as it is written, the just live by faith,' I began to understand that the justice of God signifies that justice whereby the just live through the gift of God, namely, through faith. Therefore the meaning of the sentence is as follows: "the Gospel shows us the justice of God, but it is a passive justice, through which, by means of faith, the God of mercy justifies us." To the young monk, tortured by fear and anguish, this was indeed a prodigious discovery! The hangman God, armed with His whip, faded away, yielding place to Him towards whom the soul could turn with perfect trust and confidence. . . .

At this juncture, as always happens where great minds are concerned, all kinds of reflections and arguments crystalized around this one apparently quite straightforward idea. It became the basis of a system. "System". is perhaps the wrong word here; for Luther there was no question of dry doctrine or paper thesis, but of a vital experience, the answer to all his own terrible problems. But he saw the answer so clearly that he was able to express it in the form of categorical principles. Man is a sinner, incapable of making himself just (i.e. righteous) and condemned to impotence by the enemy he bears within himself. Even though he conforms outwardly to the law, he remains in a state of sin. Even though he tries to behave righteously and hopes to acquire merit, he is unable to do so, for at the root of his very being there is a deadly germ. There must therefore be, and indeed there is, a justice exterior to man, which alone will save him. Through the grace of Jesus Christ all the soul's blemishes are, as it were, covered by a cloak of light. Thus the one means and only hope of salvation is to entrust oneself to Christ, as it were to cling to Him. "The faith that justifies is that which seizes Jesus Christ." Compared with this saving reality all man's miserable efforts towards repentance and self-improvement were ridiculous and worthless. "The just live by faith."

It must be admitted that this view was perfectly adapted to set an anguished soul at rest. Where did it deviate from the orthodox? The Church teaches that God is "just" in the simplest sense of the term, that is to say, He distributes His graces to us all in an equitable manner, and not by virtue of a kind of incomprehensible caprice. She teaches that salvation and eternal bliss are earned in the world through positive effort and good works. She affirms the importance of sin, but she refuses to admit that man can do nothing to combat it. She does indeed proclaim the indispensability of the love of God and union with Christ, but she asserts that they demand from man a positive effort to acquire a supernatural resemblance. Faith is but the beginning of justification. It is completed by reception of the sacrament, in the act of contribution or the act of charity. Salvation demands much more than mere belief.

Luther, however, was so intoxicated by his discovery, so exalted by the joy of escaping at last from the vice which had held him in its grip, that he would consider no argument advanced against his theory. "I felt suddenly born anew," he said, "and it seemed that the doors of Paradise itself were flung wide open to me, and I entered in." He was saved! He knew he was a sinner, but Christ had taken upon His shoulders the sins of the whole world. It was distasteful to realize that all the pious exercises and all the theological reasoning to which he had recourse were of no effect, but in the blinding light of the Redemption all human things were nothing but dry dust. The dialectic of sin and grace contained the answer to everything. The exultant professor of Wittenberg announced his discovery at all his lectures even before his own philosophy had been fully defined, before it had been crowned with the maxim (not formulated until after 1518) that in order to be saved all that one needed was the inner certainty of one's own salvation. He set out his thesis at Easter 1517, at the beginning of a series of lectures on the Epistle to the Hebrews. "Man is incapable of obtaining relief from any sin by his own efforts alone. In the sight of God all human virtues are sin." He also directed one of his pupils, Bernhardi, to take "Grace and Free Will" as the subject of his thesis for the doctorate; it was to conform in all respects with the principles of Luther, who later admitted that at this period he felt "divinely possessed."

The preaching of indulgences offered Luther a splendid opportunity to make the truth blindingly clear to everyone. He was disgusted most of all by this computation of so-called merits shamefully acquired, in order to escape the just pains of the after-life. He himself enjoyed true security in that prodigious wager upon Christ which he intended to maintain from now onwards. The false, pitiable thing which these wretched folk believed that they acquired, by kneeling in front of some relics and throwing their money into a box provided by someone like Tetzel, was no true security. As for the authority of the Pope, who guaranteed the value of such practices, the Ockhamist in Luther recalled what the leaders of that school had had to say, their reservations on papal infallibility and indeed on the function of the Papacy in general. He remembered Gabriel Biel's declaration that every Catholic was competent to reform the Church. He had, of course, not the slightest idea that in adopting positions of this kind he was going to set in motion the gravest crisis which Christianity had ever experienced. He was, in his own words, "a blind wretch who set off without knowing where he was going." Spiritual argument did not really interest him. He was fundamentally interested only in making the world hear and understand Heaven's response to his *De Profundis;* but "the voice of Germany, restless and secretly trembling with unrestrained passion," was not slow to answer his cry, and the drama of one soul unleashed a revolution.

> *Gerhard Ritter is one of Germany's leading historians; his interests range from the Reformation to the twentieth century. He views Luther from the position of a modern German and a practicing Lutheran.*

FROM *Luther, His Life and Work* BY GERHARD RITTER

FROM EARLIEST TIMES both the Anglican Church and the Roman Catholic have depicted Luther, not as a "reformer," but as a revolutionary, a destroyer of ancient and hallowed traditions; as a plebeian; as an enemy of all ecclesiastical hierarchy; as a barbarous and immoderate quarrel-seeker. They have accused him, because of his unrestrained accusations against the Old Church, of destroying not only the world dominance of the Roman Papacy but, simultaneously, of shaking the very foundations of that wonderful edifice, a unity of culture in Europe, based upon Christianity. The resultant antipathy was further heightened by the extremely violent polemical treatise written by Luther against Henry VIII, the founder of the English national church.

Anglicans and Roman Catholics have viewed Luther as an extreme revolutionary. Nineteenth-century liberalism in Germany, and also on occasion in France, hailed him as a liberator, freeing the world from the domination of priesthood and dark medieval superstition; but this, too, as first France and later Germany discovered, was a misconception. To the forward-looking liberal, now estranged from Christian dogma, Luther's Reformation was soon to appear simply as a half-measure; it even preached the old dogma and was far removed from that view of the world, secular and freed from religious "prejudices," which the enlightenment of the eighteenth century, as first conceived in England, was to project to the world. Of political freedom of speech, in the sense of liberalism, Luther had not the remotest conception. On the contrary: the greatest reproach which the liberals of Western Europe level against Luther is that, in his sermon "Of the grace of God," he persuaded the Germans to maintain an attitude of pious obedience vis-à-vis the authorities, causing them to become servile lackeys of the princely class and quite devoid of any sense of freedom. It was, indeed, the very memory of Luther which, in the period of nationalism, served to sharpen yet further the contrasts between Germany and Western Europe.

Given these circumstances, does it not seem a hazardous undertaking, to offer to the English-speaking world a biography of Luther, written by a German historian of Lutheran persuasion?

The task would be, perhaps, a hopeless one, had not present-day research on Luther advanced beyond the level it occupied in the nineteenth century and had not the terrible first half of the twentieth brought about considerable change in the spiritual climate of Europe. An attempt has been made in the last chapter of this book to assess Luther's historical significance from the new viewpoint of our own day. It is sufficient here to indicate briefly just why and in what way the picture of Luther today differs from the former image.

In substance, of the writers on Luther before the First World War, by far the majority recognised him only as a campaigner against Rome and the founder of German state churches. Often, and particularly in the case of non-German writers, they were acquainted with only a very limited portion of Luther's writings. During the first decades of this century highly intensive research originated in Germany, and is today keenly pursued in nearly all Protestant countries; this study has been supported in its original premises by new and important manuscript discoveries and has succeeded in penetrating to the innermost structure of Luther's thought.

In spite of the many paradoxes and contradictions contained in his writings, and his own at times inconsistent behaviour, what emerges from this work is the final, magnificent unity of Luther's theology—and this, moreover, a unity rooted in religious experience of quite exceptional depth and power. Luther is a religious prophet: his public acts, his militancy, his efforts as organiser of church life—all stem from this. Only those who view Luther in this light can hope to arrive at any understanding of his essential character.

Such an understanding was only partially attainable in the age of religious liberalism. Today, in a world which has become godless, Europe has had experience of devils so frightful as to render doubtful in her eyes any belief in the steady forward progress of humanity; on the other hand the religious concerns which exercised Luther, the agonising question of the "secret" and invisible aspects of God, have all been brought sharply back into focus. Upon us Germans, at any rate, his spiritual world has dawned anew, and the author of this book has to acknowledge the fact that the basic attitude of his own work, which appeared in its original form shortly after the First World War, was considerably modified by the experience of the Hitler regime and the Second World War. It remains true that Luther reflected to a very high degree the German character and left his own imprint on it, but the fact has become less important. What emerges from our present-day view of him is above all an impression of enormous power of faith and in his dealings with men an astonishing fearlessness, all springing from his true reverence for God.

*   *   *

It is interesting—and yet by no means a matter of pure chance—that it was precisely in the German Mendicant monasteries, those seats of lofty devotion and learned contemplation, that German sensibility and thought came into conflict with the spirit of Roman dogma and first broke through the hard shell of pious obedience to find its own means of expression. From Meister Eckhart, the Dominican, to Luther, the Augustinian Eremite, stretches a series of theologians in whose literary works we believe it is indeed possible to find for the first time certain clearly definable traits of German piety. Nor is their circle by any means limited to the mystics and men of similar temper: in the fifteenth century we find undertones of humanism in these voices, above all with Nicholas of Cusa, about whom now far too little is known, yet who was without doubt the foremost (even if not the most characteristic) figure of his century in Germany. And there were the "silent figures," such as Wessel Gansfort, Johannes Popper of Goch, and other like-minded men. History has passed them all by and many of these men are now partly or wholly buried in obscurity beyond the reach of even academic research. We do not even know the name of the author of the Frankfurt "Theologia Deutsch" which Luther later republished. Only recently has more light been thrown on the writings of Johann of Wesel with their similarities to work of Hus. At first sight the diversity of all these undertakings may seem to far outweigh the one element which they all have in common, and it would certainly be a mistake to see these men as in any sense early reformers—none of them really broke through the magic circle of the medieval, hierarchical world-order. But one can see quite clearly how in these isolated attempts at self-expression a strong spiritual need common to them all struggles to be heard. It is a need to see religion as personal knowledge of God, to gain a deeper spiritual understanding of the religious way of life, and, if not to dispense with the position of the priest as mediator between God and man's soul, at least to let it sink into unimportance by comparison with the one thing which really matters—the immediate experience of God in the heart of the believer. These are external symptoms of a hidden spiritual process, a study of which is more relevant to the history of the German spirit than to the history of Western theology. They begin to show themselves first at the height of the Middle Ages, with the beginnings of German theological speculation, and from the outset they give it—by contrast with Parisian scholasticism—a character which is more edifying than rationalistic. Then, in the later Middle Ages, the growing emphasis on the spiritual life began to upset the harmony between reason and revelation, and between the human and spiritual way of life which had been everywhere dominant in the Western Church in its best days. It was then that the hidden contradiction between the spiritual needs of the devout soul and the seemingly inflexible ordinances of the Church began to assume the character of a spiritual dilemma. It was at this point that religious life in Germany began to be subjected to an extreme tension which already gave signs of its presence in the strange conflict between the increased devotion to the Church and the simultaneously growing criticisms of her internal and external weaknesses. Only in Germany did this conflict become a decisive mark of ecclesiastical development. The Spanish Church drew new vigour through its spiritual roots which stretched back into the thirteenth century, and this produced a new flowering of the old ideals of Roman Catholic piety. On the other hand, in Italy, cultural life began to grow out of the bonds of ecclesiastical tradition as the world of Christian ideas began to lose its completely exclusive hold on the minds of men. It was only in Germany that the growing religious needs of men, that Christian piety in its most intense form, came into conflict with the traditions of the Church because of its own deep spiritual failings. There can be no other explanation: the distinction between the history of the German spirit and the general development of European culture first becomes clear at the point at which the religious needs of the German soul came into conflict with the spirit of the Roman Church; and if the fifteenth century has been called the most German century of our history, this can only be maintained, if indeed it can be, by pointing to the increasing fervour and sincerity with which the Germans of that period tried to make the spiritual treasures of the Christian inheritance their own. Whatever the art and literature of this century may have produced (including the so-called Folk-Books) outside this circle of ideas, in no way bears the unequivocal marks of the true German spirit.

Seen from this standpoint Luther's life-work might well appear as the final crowning point of a development which had started centuries before. He found the decisive word, for which others had searched in vain; he it was who helped their vague lodging to its fulfilment. Indeed without these spiritual antecedents it would be quite impossible to explain the success of the great revolution which attacked the very foundations of the political and spiritual life of the West among a people separated by numerous geographical divisions and noted for its political inertia. Yet it is not possible to speak of a specific development of the reformation idea without completely distorting the course of events. When Luther set in motion the revolution which broke the spell of a tradition which had lasted for more than a thousand years, he was able to do this because he based this revolution in the very depths of his religious consciousness. This decisive element in his action is the element which is completely new, completely unprecedented, completely unexpected. This one startling fact brought the Germans, who till then had been regarded by the other nations more as enjoying, than helping to create,

Western culture, for a few (admittedly short) decades to the forefront of the spiritual development of Europe.

Yet we must be careful, for it is not in this way that we shall find the true meaning of these events. Not as a German, but as a Christian, as a living witness to the reality of God, Martin Luther became the Reformer of the Western Church. There is no real precedent for his work, for his rediscovery of the mystery of primitive Christianity. It can only be understood when we see it relived in the spiritual life of the man himself.

THE EARLY YEARS

It will soon become clear that the central task in any study of the life of Luther is to penetrate to the roots of his personality, into the innermost regions of his spirituality. It may be that biographers of other great spiritual leaders have found it easy to pass from the external to the internal, from the historical evironment to the core of the personality as it gradually develops in response to external influences. Luther's spiritual development has its starting point in the depths of his soul, where no external influence could penetrate. Whoever wishes to understand him must seek him first in his solitude. Of course, the fact that, in contrast to so many other medieval movements which were quickly suppressed, Luther's efforts met with such great external success, was due amongst other things to a most remarkable and unique set of external circumstances which also claim their place in history; but the real secret of his power cannot be found here but in the period of his spiritual development, the foundations of which had been laid long before he stepped out into public life. It can only be found in a spiritual life of such force and depth that nothing comparable to it can be found in the Middle Ages, in spite of all the traces it betrays of its origins in that period. How many had already tried in vain to break the spell of the priestly domination of the medieval church! Some had failed because they could not really break away from the idea of the church as a sacramental institution; others because they gave expression, less to their religious experience than to the rationalistic criticisms of secular thought; a third group (among them forerunners like Wycliffe and Hus) because their opposition was at first inflamed by the external abuses of Church life and was thus from the start tainted with earthly and political demands before they penetrated to the fundamental spiritual issues; but the one thing which all these men had been unable to do was achieved by the monk from Wittenberg with his deeply spiritual and religious firmness of will. It was out of the innermost stirrings of this will that were to come to most far-reaching historical consequences, because it had to draw all its strength from a source which lay beyond the reach of all human and earthly endeavour. The spiritual struggles of this man have become history to an extent which is indeed rare. One is immediately reminded of the great mysterious figures who stand at the very beginning of the history of religion; but they are obscured in the half-light of semi-legendary traditions, while the picture of Martin Luther is already bathed in the full light of historical knowledge.

Now of course it is true that in the life of any man (even if he were as incapable of concealing the thoughts of his heart from others as was Luther) there remain secrets which no book can relate. Even the dedicated study of sources which has for centuries been part of research into Luther's life has not been able to dispel all the shadows which cluster round the figure of the lonely warrior in the monastery cell at Erfurt. Even the criticism of the last few generations had to break through a romantic garland of legend which, not without complicity on the part of the old reformer, whose memories of his early days had grown remarkably dim, had for a long time been twined round the story of his youth. Martin Luther was born on 10th November, 1483, in Eisleben, the son of parents whose circumstances were modest but by no means so far reduced as to have caused him any great suffering. From 1484 he grew up in Mansfeld. There seems to be no need to speak of any particularly severe hardship in his childhood and even less of any disturbance of his nerves and temperament as a result of brutal mishandling by his parents and teachers. But there are indisputably darker undertones in the impressions of these early years. His country parents bore the unbending sober uprightness of people who with tenacious endeavour and sharp business sense had worked themselves up quickly into a position of modest prosperity. This, coupled with the barbaric school discipline of those days, was here brought to bear on a personality in which the powers of genius were slumbering, and which therefore (in spite of his crude and primitive manners) must have been infinitely more susceptible to influence than one would have expected from a glance at his rough village environment. But is it not possible to distinguish positive elements which he inherited from his home environment? One thing above all appears to be determinative; that is his descent from peasant stock, and from the heart of the German country. His heritage is to an extraordinary degree German, and he was never for a moment able to put off the country boy, either outwardly or inwardly. For the rest, there appears to be nothing in what we know of his family home and his forebears which goes beyond the ordinary and everyday. Nor is there anything particularly remarkable in the very ordinary piety of his parents. Thus, to be more precise, the only spiritual inheritance which he brought with him from the miner's house in Mansfeld was an inexhaustible fund of popular wisdom and mother-wit, in speech and thought—but spiced with a strong dose of superstition in which was to be found not a little primitive folk-religion, with its dull fear of invisible, mysterious powers holding sway between heaven and earth. The devil in the mine, the witch in the next-door house, the goblins of all sorts in the woods and fields, against whom one had to invoke all the protective spirits and weather charms: these were the very real trials which even such sober and businesslike people as Hans and Margarete Luther had to put up with. It was only at fourteen, when he went to grammar-school at Magdeburg, that the Church with its mysterious power of attraction seems to have made an impression on the soul of the young boy, particularly in the religious instruction of the Lollards, who had set themselves the task of converting the exponents of wordly scholasticism. When, in 1498 he moved to a new school in Eisenach, his "favourite town," he came into contact with a warmer church life than that to which he was accustomed at home, in the circle of his relations and friends, among them Frau Ursula Cotta, who with her family entourage played a legendary role in the earlier traditions. Yet Luther was hardly a beggar boy whom she took in off the streets, as they would have us believe. Some fortunate recent finds of letters give us a clear picture of the atmosphere of warm friendship, musical company and devotion to the church in which the boy grew up into a youth. Yet in all this, scarcely the outlines even of the man become visible. His biography only really begins in Erfurt, where he entered the university in 1501. But even here the reliable sources for this period, which come from the time of his entry into the monastery, remain extant only in scanty fragments. Little remains but the picture of a hard-working student, sincerely devoted to the Church, held up to others as an example, who quickly assimilated all that the Erfurt philosophers had to impart in his rapid rise through the academic degrees. As well as scholastic learning his interests included the reading of old Roman and Neo-Latin poets, but this hardly entitles one to speak of a circle of "humanist friends." At the same time he was "an alert, gay character," who could play the lute, had many friends, and always carried a sword on his journeys through the countryside. Nothing in this mode of life would indicate that he was destined for any other future than that of the normal German scholar. Nowhere was there any trace of external disturbances which might have thrown the student off his expected course of action. All the same he was a gifted young man for whom his father, who had meanwhile become an alderman in his small town, had great hopes. Since taking his master's degree in philosophy he had been preparing for a lawyer's career, with the aim of a respectable post as counsellor to a prince or town. A suitable match was being considered for him—and then, suddenly, this model son threw over all these plans with the decision to disappear for ever behind monastery walls. The break with his father marked the beginning of the wanderings through the desert which led Martin Luther to the forefront of history. "For I have come to set a man against his father, and a daughter against her mother; and whoever loves father and mother more than me is not worthy of me."

Martin Luther himself was never in doubt that at this point in his life (which otherwise, in spite of great dramatic tensions, bore no sign of any other really remarkable occurrences of this kind) he felt directly the intervention of a higher power. A great deal of doubt surrounds all the reports of his spiritual trials and his fear of sin in that early period, which are supposed to have driven him into the monastery. Nevertheless it does seem that the shadows of deep spiritual unease and of a deep concern with matters of religion were appearing across the picture of the young student with his bright, laughing features. Throughout his life he was subject to a far greater degree than others to stormy changes of mood. Certain events, such as the supposed death of an unknown friend, a narrow escape in an accident in 1503, the raging of the plague in Erfurt in 1505, and others, may have given him cause for deep reflection and spiritual distress, but they hardly offer an explanation for the catastrophe of the summer of 1505, for the entry of the young Master into the monastery of the Augustinian Eremites at Erfurt. Only one thing is certain: the vow to enter the monastery, which he made during a storm in an open field near the village of Stotternheim, was made at a moment when the youth was overcome by terror. "Encircled by the milling forces of the terror and fear of death, I made vows which were wrung and pressed from me." When the lightning struck so close to him that he was thrown to the ground with such force that he "nearly broke his foot," he let forth a cry, which did not come willingly from the heart but was like a cry of terror, and which was decisively to alter the course of his life. Visions, a main characteristic of the Romantic mystics, were always foreign to the temper of the melancholic German; but, at least afterwards, he seems to have thought of this experience as of a voice from heaven. Only much later did he begin to doubt, as did his father, whether it was God or the Devil who had spoken with him then.

For us today the whole occurrence seems to be nothing but the first rumblings of the storm which was to overtake Martin Luther in the monastery.

His "conversion" in the monastery is one of the most disputed points in recent research on Luther. Nevertheless nothing has become clearer than that one cannot in any sense speak of a once-and-for-all conversion. What we see before us is a hard, wearisome struggle step by step over more than ten years in which there are indeed moments of joyful elation, occasioned by moments of sudden insight, but in no sense that flash of enlightenment which in a moment buries an old existence in darkness and opens up a new path clearly in front of one's eyes. "His soul was the battleground of two ages." Even this does not express an entirely accurate view. For this monk with his deep anxiety about the merciful nature of God is not consciously seeking a new answer to old problems. One cannot stress this point too firmly. No echo of the universal opposition to the secularised papal church and its assumption of worldly power can be found in the loneliness of the purely personal struggles in which Luther freed himself from the spiritual world of the Middle Ages and fought for the courage to live on the basis of a new and infinitely deeper understanding of the message of salvation.

The form which these struggles assumed is well enough known, at least in its outward pattern: his crippling feeling of sin; his terror of the wrath of God, which he tried in vain to placate by intense contrition, ascetic penances and an ordered sanctification of his way of life. "If ever a monk got to heaven by monkery, I would have got there too; all my brothers will testify to that. For if it had gone on much longer, I would simply have martyred myself to death with vigils, prayers, reading and other work." This was no exaggeration; during his whole life his body never recovered from the effects of these years. But where did this powerful need for the self-mortification of the earthly man stem from? It is in no sense a purely artificial product of the cloister, just as his fear of sin cannot simply be explained as a "monkish disease." It may indeed be that even before his entry into the monastery Luther had at times felt a burning desire to be reconciled with God through the ascetic life (although in fact we have little specific knowledge of this); and yet he would have been able to find ways and means of having the hurried vow at Stotternheim annulled. What then was the root of all these fears?

People have often tried to produce a psychological or rather medical explanation for his case, and it does suggest itself very readily for a young man of heated temperament. If one reads how Luther portrays the power of original sin, the evil desire which rages like a devouring fire in our veins and destroys all free will, then it is difficult, even if one is without prejudice on the subject, to avoid the impression that it is the sensual passions in a sexual sense which he is describing. But it is unlikely that temptations of this kind played a particularly important part in the life of the young monk. The testimony of all the sources, even when subjected to the most searching inquiry by bitter opponents, speaks against this. It is no mere chance that the vow of celibacy was the last of all the Catholic vows which the reformer renounced. The internal trials which tormented him most of all were set on a much higher plane. They disturbed him as profoundly in old age as in his youth; the only difference was that as he grew older the outward occasion of these trials changed and that above all he had meanwhile achieved an incomparably greater insight into the means of overcoming them. He was never seriously concerned with temptations of a worldly nature, with the struggle of the natural man with the strict monastic vows. All this lies far beneath him, and one can make no more radical misjudgment of him than if one sees his soul as the scene of a battle in which the natural desire for happiness of the earthly man struggled against the ascetic's longing for salvation. It was not that the asceticism of the monastery seemed to him too strict and too impossibly hard to fulfil, but that it seemed totally inadequate in face of the infinite demands of the divine commandment. Nor was it longing for heaven or fear of hell which rent his soul; his own personal well-being fades into total insignificance by comparison with the terrible force with which his spirit was torn by the question of an ethical religion as such.

A more accurate interpretation of his distress of soul may be found not in a "natural" but in a theological explanation, which takes as its starting point the internal tensions of late medieval piety. These sprang from the difficulty of reconciling man's free will in his own actions with the ideas of predestination forged by men like William of Ockham, that is from the internal contradiction between the idea of the retributive justice of God and his irrational and arbitrary election of men. On the one side stood the ability and duty of man in his free will to make himself worthy to receive grace by preparatory works, the ability particularly to produce in himself by means of self-abasement a complete hatred of evil and an infinite love of God; on the other hand the dependence of all moral achievement, of all worth in the eyes of God, on the mysterious co-operation of the grace of God poured into the sacraments, which grace (unaccountably only present in the sacrament through the mediation of a priest) immediately disappears as soon as a mortal sin gains a foothold in a man's heart. Against both these there is God's arbitrary decision either to reject or to accept the works of the man which have been produced in this state of grace; to destine the sinner for eternal salvation or eternal damnation as an act of grace apparently without rhyme or reason. So many propositions, so many doubts and questions, so much cause for inner uncertainty and new fear. In this theology a lively active will meant everything and pious abandonment to God was of no real importance (quite in accordance with the English attitude to the world and life, as one would indeed expect from its ancestry). By its strong emphasis on the responsibility laid on man in his free will and at the same time on the unfettered arbitrariness of God's decisions, it forced the antinomies which are of necessity always to be found slumbering in any high religiosity, right out into the open. One can imagine the effect this must have had on the monk in Erfurt with his intense German sincerity and penetrating insight, as he attempted with trembling conscience to fulfil the moral demands of such a theology and to unravel its secrets with his restless, searching intellect. How could he approach with composure a God on whose grace he could not count with certainty, when his whole life was one long struggle to make himself worthy of this grace? In such circumstances does not justice come to be more a matter for fear than for hope? Did he not indeed have cause for despair as he contemplated a life full of uncertainty and unending yet fruitless striving for righteousness?

*   *   • *

There have been many vain attempts to date the various stages through which Luther struggled to his new position of faith and tore himself free from the scholastic doctrinal system. But what happened here was a piece of pure "revelation" of a deeply spiritual nature; who could ever hope to draw back the veil from processes which by their nature could only partly have been played out in the regions of pure consciousness? Equally, anyone who asks when Luther eventually overcame his spiritual trials will never receive an answer. For Luther never managed to rid himself of them. On the other hand, one must not imagine (as it might well seem from the later accounts of the reformer) that there were years in the monastery which were unrelieved night and despair. Fragmentary records from the early years show that precisely during the period of his much discussed attacks of depression, which at times are reputed to have seriously endangered his physical health (although we have no clear evidence for this), there were also brighter times when he praised the cloister life to others as a "fine, satisfying life." His stormy soul was never without its ups and downs. If we may trust his earliest lecture notes (1509–10) then it seems that as a young theological don he had hardly begun to take even the first steps which would lead him out of the magic circle of the scholastic system. We do however know with some certainty that already individual points of his later theology were fermenting in his mind; but as yet nothing of all this could be stated positively in the lecture room. Only in the years which followed, during the quarrels in the Augustinian orders, the journey to Rome and his second stay at Wittenberg, did the core of his own piety begin to take its place in the centre of his theological thinking, and this in his discovery of a "new conscience," of the duty of the unbounded surrender of the heart to God as the unconditional prerequisite of all true religion; what up till now he had felt rather than known, began now to change his whole thought. At about the time he received his doctorate, he had already forged the basic concepts of his new understanding of justification; they appear more or less clearly in his first great course of lectures on the Psalms (1513 to 1515). But it is deeply characteristic of Luther, the biblicist, that he could never be content until he had made sure that it agreed with all the more important biblical witnesses. Above all, one passage in Paul (Romans 1:17) was for him a source of endless fear and worry, because it proclaimed not the mercy, but the justice, of God as the true content of the Gospel. The solution of this doubt is the only part of his theological development which one might be tempted to call dramatic. One day as he was preparing one of his lectures on the Psalms in the study in the tower of the Black Monastery, he was suddenly overcome by a sense of deep happiness at the discovery of the solution of his worries; for it suddenly became clear to him that Paul in this passage meant not the punitive but the "justifying" justice of God, which gives, pardons and awakes new life—"justitia justificans." He himself always considered this realisation as a turning-point in his spiritual development. Later commentators have even seen it as the "hour of the birth of the Reformation." This, as the lecture notebooks show, is a big exaggeration: in them the new element in his thought grows gradually so that it is impossible anywhere to discern a sudden leap forward or to fix a precise date for the "experience in the tower." Nevertheless, from 1513 onwards, a new stage is reached in his work with the lectures on the Psalms. As Doctor of Theology, he now began to devote himself more and more to the criticisms of the scholastic tradition. It was still a long and wearisome way, but yet every step brought him further out into the open. The decisive turning-point had been reached.

By 1515 we find notes in the margin of the standard theological textbook by G. Biel, which was then used in his school at Erfurt, which dub the latter's scholastic arts with such terms as "utter nonsense" and "enormity of the human mind." One can see clearly in the biblical lectures for that year, on the epistles to the Romans, Galatians and Hebrews, the completion of this truly liberating process of simplification which replaces a mass of theological niceties by a few simple basic concepts. Naturally the lectures retain the scholastic form for a long while; but it is highly interesting to see how this form is imperceptibly filled with a new content. Again and again outmoded elements of thought are reworked to fit in with a completely changed spiritual outlook. Once the antithesis has become really evident, it is no longer possible to think (as many have often tried since then) of synthesising the two elements. The contrast is not so clearly seen in individual theological formulations; indeed in the transitional years it is sometimes difficult to point out the precise difference. But essentially it lies in the strong change of emphasis from the man, from the world, from the Church, to God; in the unexpected and radical way in which he stresses God's exclusive power in his dealings with all living creatures. Clearly Luther's religious sense spoke so strongly on this point that it would hardly brook contradiction from traditional Church doctrine for long. Because his immediate experience was so strongly theocentric, his theology began to develop more and more along these lines. This marked the return to a theological discussion which was pursued with a relentless seriousness of purpose, with a passionate religious force which since the days of Augustine had been gradually losing ground in Scholasticism. If medieval theology's main purpose had been directed towards constructing a well-ordered cosmos with the aid of Greek philosophy, descending by degrees from the divine Trinity to the human creature and his earthly surroundings, in which the Church, the great institution of grace, assumed a decisive position as mediator, then this artistic creation was now gradually to fade away like a castle in the sky before Luther's penetrating gaze. Neither the biblical metaphysic of dogma into which Christianity had been distorted by Greek thought, nor the essentially Roman legalistic concept of the Church, could stand before his exclusive and unconditional interest in the question of the ethical nature of religion. Just as the all-important concept of divine grace had developed from the idea of a spiritual substance into a pure process of the will, so it was with the dogma of the Church and finally with the Church itself—the whole religious tradition was, in the strict sense of the word, now to be spiritualised and stripped of all its magical and miraculous elements. It is not the sacrament, so we read in the lectures on the Epistle to the Hebrews, but faith which justifies. A new, purer, personal belief was to take the place of unthinking devotion to the Church. In this sense Luther's theology may well appear to us as the highest realisation of that tendency which lay deep in the German character, whose first stirrings we have already seen in late medieval piety, of the desire to express the religious way of life in personal terms, to set the direct personal relationship of the individual to God in the place of the mediation of salvation through the priests and the sacraments.

The fulfiller and destroyer of the Middle Ages: in the period of his lectureship we can gradually see Luther assuming this unusual position.

There was nothing new in religious opposition and in criticism of the spiritual roots of the hierarchical system of the Church. But Luther was the first to get to the very heart of the matter by, in a remarkable way, both developing and countering these older tendencies. The earlier critics had for the most part refrained from active opposition, burying themselves in the silence of pious contemplation. If Luther's message was to have a wider audience, then one day he would have to be drawn out of the confines of his monastery and be forced to speak freely in front of the whole country. There on the stage of public life in Germany and elsewhere the wild and unruly cries of the most varied factions had long rung out against Rome and the Romish priests: there was no slogan which provoked the masses to louder cheers than the call to fight against papal usurpation and the lust for power and the hypocrisy of the priests. But all this would die away again so long as the Church held the keys in its hands which were to decide between bliss and damnation. With these it could always in the last resort compel even the most defiant spirits to submit to its will. The criticism remained vague and aimless, clinging to externals, attacking political institutions, here and there trying to achieve more by political means, but all without lasting effect. Did it not seem as if time was just waiting for the man who would unite all who were discontented and ready to fight, the pious and the impious, the "silent figures" and the politicians, and with his spiritual aims give to their zeal the necessary impetus and direct it with deadly aim right at the heart of the Church's key position,—a man who was at once a prophet and a nationalist, a religious thinker and a popular agitator in the grand manner?

*   *   *

THE BREAK WITH ROME (1517-19)

Luther himself stepped on to the scene with the happy and naïve confidence without which no truly great work of man has yet been ventured: that is, in the belief that one need only put the light of truth on its stand for it to light up the whole world of its own accord. In 1518 he was already protesting to Staupitz that he would rather have stayed "in his corner," if it were not that others had dragged him out of it. And it was certainly not the mere desire for a fight which drove him to the forefront. Academic brawls and tourneys never came naturally to him as they did to his opponent Eck. Whoever inquires into his motives must always go much deeper than that. For him the strongest impulse for external action was always the trials of conscience of the pastor. So here, too, right at the beginning. His attention was drawn by penitents in his congregation at Wittenberg to the scandalous trade in "letters of indulgence" (which released the penitent from ecclesiastical punishments on payment of a sum of money as penance) which was being plied with charlatanistic methods by the Dominican monk, John Tetzel, under a papal commission for the sale of a so-called Jubilee indulgence. Behind his sermons lay a most unsavoury transaction of the great princes of the Church. The Curia, impoverished as ever, had demanded large sums of money from Archbishop Albrecht of Mainz and Magdeburg for the privilege of uniting the benefices of two archbishoprics in his person at the same time, which was contrary to canon law. Albrecht had had to incur large debts with the banking house of Fugger in order to raise this sum of money, and to help him pay back the money, the house of Fugger received a certain portion of the indulgence money which Tetzel collected from his penitent audience, and for this reason he was accompanied by agents from the bank on his journeyings. Luther himself had at first no suspicion of these underhand monetary transactions, a full-scale contrivance of cunning Roman courtiers and aristocratic German prelates and skinflints. What brought him to announce a public disputation on the true nature of penance and indulgence was, in the last resort, the clearly unchristian and unscrupulous exploitation of the sacrament of penance by the travelling sellers of indulgences and preachers of repentance. The methods used by a man like Tetzel to stimulate the fast-waning interest of Church people in indulgences were nothing short of mass deception. It was impossible (in Luther's opinion) that this could be the real intention of the Pope and the Church. He only wanted to warn, not to destroy. He was only concerned with the sanctity of the sacrament, to whose practice he wanted to lend a new spirituality. He knew enough of the centuries-long history of indulgences to give crushing grounds for exposing the late medieval forms as crude distortions of their earlier counterparts. However, unlike all earlier critics he was not content merely to appeal to earlier Church laws, but unearthed the deepest roots of the sacrament of penance in the early Christian revelation; this particular question could now be seen in the light of his new religious understanding. In any case why should he worry about the financial difficulties of the Papal Curia and of the Archbishop of Mainz (for whose benefit the latest sale of indulgences had been instigated) or of other great lords! In the same Castle Church on whose door he nailed up the famous ninety-five theses on October 31st, 1517, there were 217,443 holy bones and similar objects on view—the favourite (and highly lucrative) possessions of the pious Elector Frederick; anyone who managed to get through all the rows on his knees, and donated something for the building of the Castle Church, earned himself each time 127,799 years and 116 days indulgence from the fires of Purgatory as Spalatin, Luther's friend at court, reckoned it up in 1520, not without a mischievous grin. In the next few years the ceaseless and costly activity of the agents of the Elector of Saxony brought about a large increase in the number of these "cures." In 1520 they attracted many thousands to Wittenberg for the great exhibition of relics, for which the year before Pope Leo X had granted an increase of indulgences of nearly two million years (one hundred years for every relic) in order to gain the Elector's support in the Imperial Election. So Luther could have inflicted no greater injury on his own ruler than by taking this public stand on indulgences and the idolatry of relics. Yet he was unable to understand considerations of this sort, just as no one outside in the world could understand his deeply spiritual motives. Already right at the beginning of his journey it becomes clear how lonely his way must be. Those who fêted him still thought only of the most superficial implications of his theses: the unmasking of this profiteering, the bold protest against the extortion of the indulgence vendors. He felt it himself; at first this unexpected response worried him more than it encouraged him. The others, however, diligent servants of the existing authorities, saw nothing but the petty ambition or the devilish defiance of the zealot, casting the tables of the money-changers out of the temple.

It was precisely this which roused him and drove him on further; this contemptuous way in which his warning was treated. At that time the theory of indulgences had still to be formulated in a precise dogma; the discussion about it still seemed open. Despite this, the miserable charlatan Tetzel could dare to threaten him straightway with the stake. And then from the beginning the dispute about relics became involved in the shameful bickerings of the monks, in the Dominicans' jealousy of the Augustinians. For a considerable time Luther remained silent, obedient to the warning of his ecclesiastical superiors. Instead of bursting forth in a series of pamphlets, he first established an unassailable scientific position for himself, by working out the thoroughly scholarly "resolutions" (appendices to his ninety-five theses). Even then he waited obediently for his bishop's decision before he published them. But he could never give in over these issues. At the very moment when Rome was trying unobtrusively to quench the fire, to warn him off through his superiors of his Order, he stepped forward once again. His Heidelberg theses on sin and grace, delivered in 1518 to a chapter of the Augustinian congregation as a conscious challenge to the teaching of the Ockhamites, were received by the audience of this professor who had so rapidly risen to fame, as an academic sensation. Moreover the sermons and writings of the summer of 1518 struck a new note which made the world listen in astonishment. All at once men saw what demonic forces of anger, irony, of supercilious humour, of the most arrogant self-assurance, were released in this man as soon as one touched on that most vital, sensitive point: his conscience. In these writings we find a feeling of personal, practical and scientific superiority, anchored directly in the depths of his religious experience. This gave his self-assertiveness its incomparable, masculine ring. "Here I am at Wittenberg, Doctor Martin Luther, Augustinian, and if there is any grand inquisitor who feels like scoffing iron and tearing down rocks, I'm telling him, there'll be safe conduct and an open gate and free lodging for him here." He graciously suggested to Tetzel that he might do better roasting geese at his stake: for he knew more about that than theology. It was already clear that this monk with his faltering conscience and meek heart was called to pour iron into his nation's blood. People had been complaining for long enough. Now it was time for action. "Ho! ho! he'll do it," was the cry like a sigh of relief on the lips of many. How sorrowfully had all the worldly-wise, even at

Wittenberg, shaken their heads at the beginning. "What you say is true, brother, but you will achieve nothing by it. Go to your cell and say 'God have mercy on me.'" Now he bore them all away with him: the majority of his order, against the specific orders of their Roman superiors and in the face of the hatred of all their enemies; the university, particularly the young students, the Saxon court, and many theological circles elsewhere in the land.

Things seemed to be coming rapidly to a head. We will not pursue here the pattern of intrigue set in motion against him in Rome, the different denunciations brought against him, particularly by the Dominicans, the most reliable champions of papal dominion and its trusty police-force. Luther at first heard of it only from rumours. Any of his supporters with political understanding must have wished that he would prove himself to be a loyal moderate son of the Church and would show his orthodoxy in matters of dogma by skilful reticence. Yet the increasing danger only served to raise his confidence; for him it was nothing other than the surest pledge of the "truth, which is contradicted of man," as he wrote in truly exultant tones. He believed he possessed the truth, even if all the centuries of Scholasticism had taught otherwise. It was just at this point that he first really burnt all the bridges behind him, publicly challenging the unconditionally binding power of the ban and frankly opposing the misuse of this for political and financial ends—one of the greatest evils of late medieval Church practice. On August 7th he received the formal summons to Rome. If he obeyed he knew it meant death or life-imprisonment. The following day he was already at work on a polemical treatise which from start to finish, with a sort of mocking respect, tore to shreds the official judgment of the papal palace theologian, Prierias, as a pure contrivance of Italian superficiality. He even reprinted passages from it word for word in order to expose it to the mockery of German theologians. To the horror of the Saxon court this was followed in August by the publication of the sermon on excommunication, whose basic themes had already been spread abroad in a grossly distorted form by his opponents in an attempt to blacken him. "Pray for me," he wrote to Staupitz on September 1st, "lest I should become too jubilant and over-confident in this struggle."

It was precisely this overwhelming conviction of the rightness of his conscience which made it impossible for him to submit to men's judgments without first being allowed the possibility of free discussion, which made it impossible for him to run straight into the clutches of the Roman dragon, which would have devoured him without doubt. Had he obeyed, it would have meant giving himself up and at the same time abandoning his cause. And he clearly never for a moment entertained such an idea. He was still a long way from condemning the Papacy as such; but he was much too firmly convinced of the evil intentions of his Roman judges to waver for a moment. In him they wanted to suppress the pure Word of God. He never considered the idea of pressing forward pathetically to a martyr's death, if the matter did not require it. Just as it never occurred to him to stimulate his "trials" artificially as had so many mystics and pietists (indeed he anticipated them with terror), he equally never pressed forward for the cross which God wished to lay on him. His way was the heroism of suffering rather than of the desire to suffer, which by contrast characterised the ascetic nobility of so many medieval saints.

But how was he to persevere with the power of words alone, now that Rome had spoken? Now all ways were barred to the truth, if secular power would not come to her aid. The German Reformation would have been lost right at the beginning if it had not found political support in the political power of the landed princes. Without hesitation, and yet reluctantly, Luther appealed to the Elector to intervene. It embarrassed him not a little that his cause should now become the affair of the princes and the great lords; how far this pact would one day lead him, he could clearly not have suspected at that time. For the rest he did not refuse outright to come before the judges; he was not minded to creep into a corner, without giving reasons and answers, for this would only have harmed his cause. So it was in accordance with his wishes and proposals that the Elector agreed with Cajetan, the Papal Legate, to hold first an inquiry on German soil. Of the details of the agreement with the Legate, Luther could learn nothing more precise. When at the end of September he set out for Augsburg, he knew little more than that the decisive turning-point of his life was now before him.

It was without doubt the hardest journey of his life; incomparably harder than later the triumphal procession to Worms. In Wittenberg he had hardly had time to worry. Melanchthon had just moved there and Luther had been concerned along with everything else with the reform of the college. Now, however, on the journey he was assailed by uneasy thoughts. Now that the affair was becoming serious, he met with nothing but dark pessimism on all sides. "My dear Doctor, the Italians are learned people in God. I am worried that you will not be able to maintain your cause before them. They will tax you sorely," Staupitz wrote darkly of the cross which had now become inevitable. The brothers in his order from all the houses advised him to turn back. Lonely and depressed, he went on his way, tortured by physical illness and depression. "All the time I was thinking, now you will have to die. I was so frightened by the flesh." Or in a childlike way typical of him: "Oh what a disgrace I shall be to my parents." Moods of Gethsemane. But it was not the fear of the flesh alone which overwhelmed him. We can only suspect what was taking place in the depths of his soul. At the beginning of September he had written to Staupitz hinting at the incomparably more terrible thing which he had to suffer and which compelled him to think of all temporal terror as insignificant. The summons to Rome worried him little, "only that I genuinely want to honour the power of the Church." Now, it seems, the old religious terrors assailed him, more terrifying than ever. But now they clearly sprang from another source. "How often," he wrote later from the Wartburg, "my heart wavered and punished me and reproached me with its strongest argument; are you the only one who's clever? Can you really say that all the others are wrong and have been wrong for such a long time?" Now his thoughts may have begun to run along these lines. Up till now he had always hoped that truth would conquer by virtue of its own pure power if only one could give it space and time to have its effect—it must transform from within the old Church, on which, as a good Catholic, he hung with all his heart. Now for the first time he was faced with the real and immediate danger of a complete break with Rome. His own destiny reared itself up like a terrible monster before him. He arrived at Augsburg in a state of extreme spiritual distress, deep depression and physical exhaustion.

Yet his will remained as firm as iron. "Even in Augsburg, even in the midst of his enemies, Christ reigns. May Christ live and may Martin and every sinner die, as it is written," he wrote on his way in answer to the voices which warned him against his course of action. But as soon as he came into contact with the urbane Italian diplomats who surrounded the papal envoys, he was overcome by a proud sense of his own German nature which he felt to be so far superior. With what contempt he rejected the "typically Italian" suggestion of one of these lords, that he should go through the form of recanting merely to avoid condemnation as a heretic—after all, others had done it before! Indeed two worlds confronted each other here, the politicians par excellence and the man who in the Italian sense was certainly the person the least qualified for politics in the whole of Germany at that time.

Was it possible that there could be a compromise between them, that the already gaping crack in the building of the Church could be patched over? This was, at bottom, the object of the discussions. Cajetan was not the judge Luther took him for. For some weeks now the wind had again been blowing in a different direction. A happy chance in higher politics, the estrangement of the Saxons and the Hapsburgs, had given the Curia cause to hope that they could rapidly overcome the Saxon heresy with the power of the Empire. And so it went quickly ahead with condemnation and warrants for arrest; all this in a great hurry, without giving the accused a hearing or a regular trial. And yet the wind changed again just as quickly. Even before the thunderbolt had arrived in Augsburg from Rome, it had become clear that it would have been best not to have sent it in the first place. The election of a new Emperor was due. All hope of defeating the Spanish candidate the Hapsburg Charles, hated by the Curia because he was the greatest threat to the Papal State and to the House of Medici in Florence, rested on the Saxon vote. It was impossible that they should drive the reluctant, procrastinating, pious Saxon into opposition just at this time—just at the very moment when, to the joy of the Curia, he had refused to sign an agreement which would have committed him in the Imperial Election to casting his vote in favour of the Emperor's grandson, Charles (August 27th). Over and above all this, Cajetan was left in no doubt about the present hostility of the Imperial Diet towards Rome. The tithe which was so urgent for the Crusade against the Turks could not be carried through in any circumstances. Never before had so much dust been raised in the Imperial Diet against Italian arrogance and the deception of the priests whose only purpose was to exploit the Germans. Also, at this time the danger from the Turks was more pressing than ever. If papal diplomacy did not proceed with extreme caution in the matter of indulgences, everything would be lost. Cajetan himself, one of the most honourable figures in the Curia of Leo X and the only theologian in the Renaissance court who was capable of making a judgment of his own accord on the dogmatic aspect of the dispute, recognised perfectly well that Luther's teaching about indulgences was by no means to be condemned out of hand as, in the strict sense, heretical. He had himself only just finished a treatise on indulgences which equally condemned certain abuses in recent practice. And so he had agreed to the wish of the Saxon, even though it meant going against his own instructions, to summon his professor with safe-conduct and without any danger of arrest, to justify himself, in the hope that he might gently persuade him to make the recantation which was so urgently needed. If this did not succeed, then perhaps threats might help. But for the moment there could be no real force behind them.

This was the state of affairs which Martin Luther found in Augsburg, even if he did not see it quite so clearly. No sooner had he arrived than he found himself entangled in the confused net of higher politics. What enormous consequences for world history were to result from the fact that during the development of this crisis, which shook the Western Church, its leaders were more deeply involved than ever in political action which distracted their attention from their universal spiritual task; that precisely at this moment Peter's seat was occupied by a very average man, living only for pleasure, who was basically, and indeed wished for nothing better than to be, an Italian patron and "tyrant" in the style of his Florentine house, with all its calculating subtlety, all the delight in underhand diplomatic techniques, but also all the impoverishment in higher aims, which was now natural in the politics of these small states. What did this bright, corpulent, elegant Medici with his puffy, blasé features, who spent the majority of his days in his hunting lodge at Magliana in diversions which were not always of the most tasteful kind, what did he understand of the religious ideas of this remarkable, pious German, or what at all of the spiritual torments of the rebellious Saxon Mendicant! True the politicians of the Curia with their traditional political instinct needed no theological understanding to sense that the man was a firebrand of the most dangerous kind who must be quickly stamped out. But to be able to appreciate the spiritual depths from which this time the outburst had sprung forth was a task for which they had no scale of values. They knew of no other way of controlling it than by the blind affirmation of papal authority, and yet, because of the political troubles of the day, possessed no means of enforcing its recognition—least of all by a man like Luther! Even in conversation he made an uncanny impression on Cajetan—if later reports are not legendary. From the deep flashing eyes, and the lean, bony features of this face, which still bore clearly the marks of countless sleepless nights and days full of activity and fierce spiritual struggles, there spoke a fiery spirit whose demonic glint would not easily escape even less skilful judges of character. However that may be, the small, slender Eminence— himself a professor under his Cardinal's robes—condescended to give in to Luther's demands, which only the day before had been dismissed as laughable by the Italians—an action which he later tried to have deleted from the reports, as it had been expressly forbidden in his instructions: and he embarked on a theological disputation with the notorious heretic over the most important of his theses. In all seriousness he had hoped to be able to convince the rebel by his Thomistic arguments and to win him by the impression of paternal mildness. Indeed if Luther had been at all susceptible to the pressure of earthly might or to the fear of men, he had scarcely found a better opportunity of beating a retreat and making his peace with the Church, as many had done before him. For now the representative of the Roman see was himself attempting to bring him back on to the right way. The Italian cleverly omitted the fearful demands of his instructions— abjuration and church penance (which at the least would have to be made in strict imprisonment) even if he recanted of his own free will—avoided any discussion of the practice of indulgence and instead posed Luther two essential but purely dogmatic questions for debate. But the stubborn German was unable to realise how much these concessions from the highest quarters really meant. He had only heard in all this the one word: "Recant!" It is dramatically clear from the accounts in his letters with what defiance and self-assurance he met this suggestion: the consciousness of the unconditional superiority—both religious and scientific—of his own hard-won conviction in comparison with the "crass Italian idiocy" of the Thomist, which was to him like "children's jibes": and then his demand following naturally from this, not to be admonished like a lost sheep, but to be recognised as an equally privileged opponent of the might of the Church and to be allowed a thorough discussion of all points at issue on neutral ground. Cajetan soon saw what sort of "beast" he had allowed himself to get involved with; his Italians sniggered at the angry Fratello who dared to spite the Legate to his face. Losing his temper, Cajetan shouted him down. But this completely spoilt everything. Even Luther became violent: "Your Excellency must not think that we Germans do not know our grammar either!" The discussion had been in vain. "Get out!" shouted Cajetan, "and don't let me see you again unless you come to recant!" If this was an attempt to scare him into submission, it was unsuccessful. Luther went and did not return.

The English Civil War—
A Fight for Lawful
Government?

CONTENTS

QUESTIONS FOR STUDY

1   *How did James I and his opponents differ in their ideas about the fundamental laws of England?*

2   *Why did the leaders of Parliament oppose the royal government in 1604–1641?*

3   *In what ways do Macaulay and Wingfield-Stratford agree and in what ways do they differ in their accounts of the "Case of the Five Members"?*

4   *Why did civil war break out in 1642? Which side would you have fought on?*

5   *On the scaffold, Charles I said he was "the matyr of the people." Was he?*

6   *How did Oliver Cromwell defend his actions? Do you find the defense convincing?*

7   *All the legislation signed by Charles before the outbreak of war remained in force after the Restoration. How would this affect future relationships between king and Parliament?*

At a time when nearly all the states of Europe were adopting absolutist forms of government, England embarked on a new experiment in parliamentary constitutionalism.

From the accession of James I onward, the religious and fiscal policies of the royal government came under increasing criticism in Parliament; and, in the reign of Charles I, the leaders of the House of Commons openly challenged the right of the king to function as an effective head of state. A peculiar feature of the ensuing crisis was that, even when the situation had degenerated into a naked struggle for power, all parties in the conflict claimed to be defending lawful government and the ancient rights of Englishmen. Partly for this reason perhaps, the English people succeeded in carrying through a constitutional revolution in the seventeenth century without abandoning any of their medieval institutions of government. King, Parliament, and courts of common law entered into new relationships with one another, and all survived into the modern world.

1 King and Parliament, 1604–1640

The following passage describes some views on government that were widely held in England at the beginning of the seventeenth century.

FROM *The Crisis of the Constitution*
BY MARGARET A. JUDSON

[*The king, as head of state—B. T.*] made the important appointments to the council, the law courts, other departments of government, and to the church. As head of the state he summoned and dismissed parliament at his pleasure. Prerogatives of this sort were seldom mentioned in the law courts and, when they were, never denied. They came to be discussed and eventually questioned and challenged in parliament, but they were not directly attacked there until 1641 and 1642. When at that time some members of parliament worked to take away these particular prerogatives from the king and transfer them to parliament, the civil war soon broke out.

In the years leading up to that war, men agreed also that the king as head of the state was peculiarly competent and solely responsible in certain realms they called government. Here he was most particularly the head of the state, practicing the art of governing, a craft possessed only by kings. Within these realms his authority was accepted as absolute. It must be, they believed, or else he would be unable to carry on his craft as a true artist. These realms of government within which his authority was accepted as absolute included foreign policy, questions of war and peace, the coinage, and the control of industries and supplies necessary for the defense of the realm.

*   *   *

As kings possessed prerogatives, so subjects possessed rights; and those rights, like the king's prerogatives, were part of the law and basic in the

Margaret A. Judson, *The Crisis of the Constitution* (1964), pp. 24–5, 34–5, 44–6. Reprinted by permission of Margaret A. Judson and Octagon Books, Inc.

constitution. Only when the nature and extent of the subjects' rights are understood is it possible to present some aspects of the prerogative and some controversies concerning it which have not been discussed up to this point.

The most important of these rights were property rights. To protect them was the principal concern of the common law. It was also the main concern of great English subjects in the sixteenth and early seventeenth centuries. According to the evidence revealed by the law reports and family papers of this time, men in the upper social classes were adding to their landed holdings. In their acquisition of property, parliament helped them by measures, like the Statute of Uses, which made the transfer of property easier than it had been before. The crown helped them also by its sale of the confiscated monastic lands. The great mistake of the Tudors if they wished to be despots (as Harrington clearly pointed out in his *Oceana* in 1656) was their encouragement of such measures. It was a mistake from the point of view of the king's position, because, at the same time as the king's authority was increasing in the sixteenth century and the concept of the divine right of kings was rising to new exalted heights, the amount of property possessed by influential subjects was also increasing and thereby strengthening the old medieval concept that property was a right belonging to subjects. Among the many reasons why the growing absolutism of the Tudors did not become complete absolutism under the Stuarts is the fact that the medieval concept of the inviolability of a man's property did not disappear or become weaker in the sixteenth or early seventeenth centuries. Tudor and Stuart noblemen, gentry, and merchants who were acquiring property did not forget that although "government belonged to kings, propery belonged to subjects."

*   *   *

Englishmen entered into the constitutional controversies of the seventeenth century with a profound belief in the importance of law. To them law was not primarily a decree enacted by a sovereign legislature to deal with a particular problem of the moment. Law was normally regarded as more than human, as the reflection of eternal principles of justice. When men considered it in relation to their own England, they looked upon it as a binding, cohesive force in their polity without which there would be no commonwealth, no government, no rights, and no justice.

They believed that the law was impartial—serving well both the king and the subject, enabling the king to fulfill his divine mission of governing with justice and protecting the subject in his God-given rights. To the seventeenth-century mind, rule by the king and rule by law were harmonious and not competing concepts. As the king's authority gave sanction to the law, so the law gave strength to the king's rule. To Yelverton, a faithful servant of Queen Elizabeth, "to live without government is hellish and to governe without lawes is brutish." James himself remarked that both king and parliament have a "union of interest" "in the lawes of the Kingdome, without which as the Prerogative cannot subsist, soe without that the Lawe cannot be maynteyned.". . .

It is well known that the parliamentarians based much of their case against the king on the law, but it is sometimes forgotten that the royalists also looked to the law to sanction the great authority they claimed for the monarch. In the long period of controversy between 1603 and 1642, both royalists and parliamentarians turned to the law to justify their actions, and both believed that the law was on their side. Even after the civil war broke out with its appeal to force, both groups strove to prove the legality of their actions, and only a few men admitted that the law had failed them.

James I, as King of Scotland, had propounded a theory of absolute monarchy before he inherited the crown of England. The following extract is from his True Law of Free Monarchies, *published in 1598.*

FROM *True Law of Free Monarchies* BY JAMES I

THE KINGS THEREFORE IN SCOTLAND were before any estates or ranks of men within the same, before any Parliaments were holden or laws made; and by them was the land distributed (which at the first was wholly theirs), states erected and decerned [*decreed—B. T.*], and forms of government devised and established. And it follows of necessity that the Kings were the authors and makers of the laws and not the laws of the Kings. . . . And according to these fundamental laws already alleged, we daily see that in the Parliament (which is nothing else but the head court of the King and his vassals) the laws are but craved by his subjects, and only made by him at their rogation and with their advice. For albeit the King make daily statutes and ordinances, enjoining such pains thereto as he thinks meet, without any advice of Parliament or Estates, yet it lies in the power of no Parliament to make any kind of law or statute without his sceptre be to it for giving it the force of a law. . . . And as ye see it manifest that the King is overlord of the whole land, so is he master over every person that inhabiteth the same, having power over the life and death of every one of them. For although a just prince will not take the life of any of his subjects without a clear law, yet the same laws whereby he taketh them are made by himself or his predecessors, and so the power flows always from himself; as by daily experience we see

J. R. Tanner, *Constitutional Documents of the Reign of James I, 1603–1625* (1930), pp. 9–10. Reprinted by permission of Cambridge University Press.

good and just princes will from time to time make new laws and statutes, adjoining the penalties to the breakers thereof, which before the law was made had been no crime to the subject to have committed. Not that I deny the old definition of a King and of a law which makes the King to be a speaking law and the law a dumb King; for certainly a King that governs not by his law can neither be countable to God for his administration nor have a happy and established reign. For albeit it be true, that I have at length proved, that the King is above the law as both the author and giver of strength thereto, yet a good King will not only delight to rule his subjects by the law, but even will conform himself in his own actions thereunto; always keeping that ground, that the health of the commonwealth be his chief law.

Edward Coke, Chief Justice of the Court of Common Pleas, opposed these views of James I with a doctrine of the supremacy of law. In 1607 he informed James that a king of England could administer justice only through the anciently established courts.

Edward Coke on the Supremacy of Law

THEN THE KING SAID that he thought the law was founded upon reason, and that he and others had reason as well as the Judges. To which it was answered by me, that true it was that God had endowed his Majesty with excellent science and great endowments of nature, but his Majesty was not learned in the laws of his realm of England; and causes which concern the life or inheritance or goods or fortunes of his subjects are not to be decided by natural reason but by the artificial reason and judgment of law, which law is an act which requires long study and experience before that a man can attain to the cognizance of it; and that the law was the golden metwand and measure to try the causes of the subjects, and which protected his Majesty in safety and peace. With which the King was greatly offended, and said that then he should be under the law, which was treason to affirm, as he said; to which I said that Bracton saith, *quod Rex non debet esse sub homine sed sub Deo et lege* [*that the King ought not to be under man but under God and under the law—B. T.*].

J. R. Tanner, *Constitutional Documents of the Reign of James I, 1603–1625* (1930), p. 187. Reprinted by permission of Cambridge University Press.

At the very beginning of James's reign in England (1604), the members of the House of Commons thought it necessary to explain to the new king that he had been "misinformed" about their rights.

The Rights of the House of Commons, 1604

NOW CONCERNING THE ANCIENT RIGHTS of the subjects of this realm, chiefly consisting in the privileges of this House of Parliament, the misinformation openly delivered to your Majesty hath been in three things:

First, That we held not privileges of right, but of grace only, renewed every Parliament by way of donature upon petition, and so to be limited.

Secondly, That we are no Court of Record, nor yet a Court that can command view of records, but that our proceedings here are only to acts and memorials, and that the attendance with the records is courtesy, not duty.

Thirdly and lastly, That the examination of the return of writs for knights and burgesses is without our compass, and due to the Chancery.

*　　　*　　　*

And contrariwise, with all humble and due respect to your Majesty our Sovereign Lord and Head, against those misinformations we most truly avouch,

First, That our privileges and liberties are our right and due inheritance, no less than our very lands and goods.

Secondly, That they cannot be withheld from us, denied, or impaired, but with apparent wrong to the whole state of the realm.

Thirdly, And that our making of request in the entrance of Parliament to enjoy our privilege is an act only of manners. . . .

Fourthly, We avouch also, That our House is a Court of Record, and so ever esteemed.

Fifthly, That there is not the highest standing Court in this land that ought to enter into competency [*competition—B. T.*], either for dignity or authority, with this High Court of Parliament, which with your Majesty's royal assent gives laws to other Courts but from other Courts receives neither laws nor orders.

Sixthly and lastly, We avouch that the House of Commons is the sole

J. R. Tanner, *Constitutional Documents of the Reign of James I, 1603–1625* (1930), pp. 220–6, 230. Reprinted by permission of Cambridge University Press.

proper judge of return of all such writs and of the election of all such members as belong to it. . . .

The rights of the liberties of the Commons of England consisteth chiefly in these three things:

First, That the shires, cities, and boroughs of England, by representation to be present, have free choice of such persons as they shall put in trust to represent them.

Secondly, That the persons chosen, during the time of the Parliament as also of their access and recess, be free from restraint, arrest, and imprisonment.

Thirdly, That in Parliament they may speak freely their consciences without check and controlment, doing the same with due reverence to the Sovereign Court of Parliament, that is, to your Majesty and both the Houses, who all in this case make but one politic body whereof your Highness is the Head . . .

For matter of religion, it will appear by examination of truth and right that your Majesty should be misinformed if any man should deliver that the Kings of England have any absolute power in themselves either to alter Religion (which God defend should be in the power of any mortal man whatsoever), or to make any laws concerning the same otherwise than, as in temporal causes, by consent of Parliament. We have and shall at all times by our oaths acknowledge that your Majesty is Sovereign Lord and Supreme Governor in both. . . .

There remaineth, dread Sovereign, yet one part of our duty at this present which faithfulness of heart, not presumption, doth press. We stand not in place to speak or do things pleasing; our care is and must be to confirm the love and tie the hearts of your subjects the commons most firmly to your Majesty. Herein lieth the means of our well deserving of both. There was never prince entered with greater love, with greater joy and applause of all his people. This love, this joy, let it flourish in their hearts for ever. Let no suspicion have access to their fearful thoughts that their privileges, which they think by your Majesty should be protected, should now by sinister informations or counsel be violated or impaired, or that those which with dutiful respects to your Majesty speak freely for the right and good of their country shall be oppressed or disgraced. Let your Majesty be pleased to receive public information from your Commons in Parliament as to the civil estate and government, for private informations pass often by practice: the voice of the people, in the things of their knowledge, is said to be as the voice of God. And if your Majesty shall vouchsafe, at your best pleasure and leisure, to enter into your gracious consideration of our petition for the ease of these burdens under which your whole people have of long time mourned, hoping for relief by your Majesty, then may you be assured to be possessed of their hearts, and if of their hearts, of all they can do or have.

And so we your Majesty's most humble and loyal subjects, whose ancestors have with great loyalty, readiness, and joyfulness served your famous progenitors, Kings and Queens of this Realm, shall with like loyalty and joy, both we and our posterity, serve your Majesty and your most royal issue for ever, with our lives, lands, and goods, and all other our abilities, and by all means endeavour to procure your Majesty honour, with all plenty, tranquillity, content, joy and felicity.

In 1610 Commons complained about new customs duties (impositions) levied by the king.

Parliament and Taxation, 1610

THE POLICY AND CONSTITUTION of this your kingdom appropriates unto the Kings of this realm, with the assent of the Parliament, as well the sovereign power of making laws as that of taxing or imposing upon the subjects' goods or merchandises, wherein they have justly such a propriety as may not without their consent be altered or changed. This is the cause that the people of this kingdom, as they ever shewed themselves faithful and loving to their Kings and ready to aid them in all their just occasions with voluntary contributions, so have they been ever careful to preserve their own liberties and rights when anything hath been done to prejudice or impeach the same. And therefore when their Princes, occasioned either by their wars or their over-great bounty or by any other necessity, have without consent of Parliament set impositions either within the land or upon commodities either exported or imported by the merchants, they have in open Parliament complained of it in that it was done without their consents, and thereupon never failed to obtain a speedy and full redress, without any claim made by the Kings of any power or prerogative in that point. And though the law of propriety be originally and carefully preserved by the common laws of this realm, which are as ancient as the kingdom itself, yet these famous Kings, for the better contentment and assurance of their loving subjects, agreed that this old fundamental right should be farther declared and established by Act of Parliament, wherein it is provided that no such charges should ever be laid upon the people without their common consent, as may appear by sundry records of former times.

We therefore, your Majesty's most humble Commons assembled in Parliament, following the example of this worthy care of our ancestors and out of a duty to those for whom we serve, finding that your Majesty, without advice or consent of Parliament, hath lately in time of peace set both greater impositions and far more in number than any your noble ancestors did ever in time of war, have with all humility presumed to present this most just and necessary petition unto your Majesty, That all impositions set without the assent of Parliament may be quite abolished and taken away.

J. R. Tanner, *Constitutional Documents of the Reign of James I, 1603–1625* (1930), p. 150. Reprinted by permission of Cambridge University Press.

A "protestation" of 1621 declared that any important matter
of state was a fit subject for debate in Parliament.

Commons Protestation, 1621

THE COMMONS NOW ASSEMBLED in Parliament, being justly occasioned thereunto concerning sundry liberties, franchises, and privileges of Parliament, amongst others here mentioned, do make this Protestation following, That the liberties, franchises, privileges, and jurisdictions of Parliament are the ancient and undoubted birthright and inheritance of the subjects of England; and that the arduous and urgent affairs concerning the King, State, and defence of the realm and of the Church of England, and the maintenance and making of laws, and redress of mischiefs and grievances which daily happen within this realm, are proper subjects and matter of counsel and debate in Parliament; and that in the handling and proceeding of those businesses every member of the House of Parliament hath, and of right ought to have, freedom of speech to propound, treat, reason, and bring to conclusion the same.

The accession of Charles I did not improve matters. Charles
was, by conviction, a high-church Anglican. Moreover, he
had married a papist wife (Henrietta Maria of France) and
was inclined to tolerate Catholicism. The leaders of the
House of Commons were deeply suspicious of his religious
policy, and they hated his chief minister, Buckingham.
Accordingly they withheld grants of taxation. Charles re-
sorted to forced loans, which led to another constitutional
protest. the Petition of Right of 1628.

Petition of Right, 1628

HUMBLY SHOW unto our Sovereign Lord the King, the Lords Spiritual and Temporal, and Commons in Parliament assembled, that whereas it is

J. R. Tanner, *Constitutional Documents of the Reign of James I, 1603–1625* (1930), p. 288–9. Reprinted by permission of Cambridge University Press.

S. R. Gardiner, *The Constitutional Documents of the Puritan Revolution* (2nd ed., 1899), pp. 66–9. Reprinted by permission of The Clarendon Press, Oxford.

declared and enacted by a statute made in the time of the reign of King Edward the First, commonly called *Statutum de Tallagio non concedendo,* that no tallage or aid shall be laid or levied by the King or his heirs in this realm, without the goodwill and assent of the Archbishops, Bishops, Earls, Barons, Knights, Burgesses, and other the freemen of the commonalty of this realm: and by authority of Parliament holden in the five and twentieth year of the reign of King Edward the Third, it is declared and enacted, that from thenceforth no person shall be compelled to make any loans to the King against his will, because such loans were against reason and the franchise of the land; and by other laws of this realm it is provided, that none should be charged by any charge or imposition, called a Benevolence, or by such like charge, by which the statutes before-mentioned, and other the good laws and statutes of this realm, your subjects have inherited this freedom, that they should not be compelled to contribute to any tax, tallage, aid, or other like charge, not set by common consent in Parliament.

Yet nevertheless, of late divers commissions directed to sundry Commissioners in several counties with instructions have issued, by means whereof your people have been in divers places assembled, and required to lend certain sums of money unto your Majesty, and many of them upon their refusal so to do, have had an oath administered unto them, not warrantable by the laws or statutes of this realm, and have been constrained to become bound to make appearance and give attendance before your Privy Council, and in other places, and others of them have been therefore imprisoned, confined, and sundry other ways molested and disquieted. . . .

And where also by the statute called, "The Great Charter of the Liberties of England," it is declared and enacted, that no freeman may be taken or imprisoned or be disseised of his freeholds or liberties, or his free customs, or be outlawed or exiled; or in any manner destroyed, but by the lawful judgment of his peers, or by the law of the land.

They do therefore humbly pray your Most Excellent Majesty, that no man hereafter be compelled to make or yield any gift, loan, benevolence, tax, or such like charge, without common consent by Act of Parliament; and that none be called to make answer, or take such oath, or to give attendance, or be confined, or otherwise molested or disquieted concerning the same, or for refusal thereof; and that no freeman, in any such manner as is before-mentioned, be imprisoned or detained. . . .

Charles accepted the Petition of Right. But a new dispute broke out at once over a tax called "tonnage and poundage," not specifically mentioned in the Petition. Charles protested that he had never intended to deprive himself of this source of revenue.

FROM *Charles I's Speech at the Prorogation of Parliament, 1628*

NOW SINCE I AM TRULY INFORMED, that a second Remonstrance is preparing for me to take away the profit of my Tonnage and Poundage, one of the chiefest maintenances of my Crown, by alleging I have given away my right thereto by my answer to your Petition.

This is so prejudicial unto me, that I am forced to end this Session some few hours before I meant, being not willing to receive any more Remonstrances, to which I must give a harsh answer. And since I see that even the House of Commons begins already to make false constructions of what I granted in your Petition, lest it be worse interpreted in the country, I will now make a declaration concerning the true intent thereof.

The profession of both Houses in the time of hammering this Petition, was no ways to trench upon my Prerogative, saying they had neither intention or power to hurt it. Therefore it must needs be conceived that I have granted no new, but only confirmed the ancient liberties of my subjects; yet to show the clearness of my intentions, that I neither repent, nor mean to recede from anything I have promised you, I do here declare myself, that those things which have been done, whereby many have had some cause to expect the liberties of the subjects to be trenched upon—which indeed was the first and true ground of the Petition—shall not hereafter be drawn into example for your prejudice, and from time to time; in the word of a king, ye shall not have the like cause to complain; but as for Tonnage and Poundage, it is a thing I cannot want, and was never intended by you to ask, nor meant by me—I am sure—to grant.

To conclude, I command you all that are here to take notice of what I have spoken at this time, to be the true intent and meaning of what I granted you in your Petition; but especially, you my Lords the Judges, for to you only under me belongs the interpretation of laws, for none of the Houses of Parliament, either joint or separate (what new doctrine soever may be

S. R. Gardiner, *The Constitutional Documents of the Puritan Revolution* (2nd ed., 1899), pp. 73–4. Reprinted by permission of The Clarendon Press, Oxford.

raised) have any power either to make or declare a law without my consent.

> *The Parliament of 1629 continued to attack the fiscal and religious policies of Charles' government. It ended in the unprecedented scene described next.*

FROM *A True Relation of . . . Proceedings in Parliament*

THIS DAY, being the last day of the Assembly, as soon as prayers were ended the Speaker went into the Chair, and delivered the Kings command for the adjournment of the House until Tuesday sevennight following.

The House returned him answer, that it was not the office of the Speaker to deliver any such command unto them, but for the adjournment of the House it did properly belong unto themselves; and after they had settled some things they thought fit and convenient to be spoken of they would satisfy the King.

The Speaker told them that he had an express command from the King as soon as he had delivered his message to rise; and upon that he left the Chair, but was by force drawn to it again by Mr. Denzil Holles, son to the Earl of Clare, Mr. Valentine, and others. And Mr. Holles, notwithstanding the endeavour of Sir Thomas Edmondes, Sir Humphrey May, and other Privy Councellors to free the Speaker from the Chair, swore, Gods wounds, he should sit still until they pleased to rise. . . .

Sir John Eliot. God knows I now speak with all duty to the King. It is true the misfortunes we suffer are many, we know what discoveries have been made; how Arminianism creeps in and undermines us, and how Popery comes in upon us; they mask not in strange disguises, but expose themselves to the view of the world. In search whereof we have fixed our eyes not simply on the actors (the Jesuits and priests), but on their masters, they that are in authority, hence it comes we suffer. The fear of them makes these interruptions. You have seen prelates that are their abettors. That great Bishop of Winchester, we know what he hath done to favour them; this fear extends to some others that contract a fear of being discovered, and they draw from hence this jealousy. This is the Lord Treasurer, in whose person all evil is contracted. I find him acting and building on those grounds laid by

Wallace Notestein and Frances H. Relf, eds., *Commons Debates for 1629* (1921), pp. 101–6.

his Master, the late great Duke of Buckingham, and his spirit is moving for these interruptions. And from this fear they break Parliaments lest Parliaments should break them. I find him the head of all that great party the Papists, and all Jesuits and priests derive from him their shelter and protection.

In this great question of Tonnage and Poundage, the instruments moved at his command and pleasure; he dismays our merchants, and invites strangers to come in to drive our trade, and to serve their own ends.

The Remonstrance was put to the question, but the Speaker refused to do it; and said he was otherwise commanded from the King.

Whereupon Mr. Selden spake as followeth:

"You, Mr. Speaker, say you dare not put the question which we command you; if you will not put it we must sit still, and thus we shall never be able to do any thing; they that come after you may say they have the Kings command not to do it. We sit here by commandment of the King, under the great Seal of England; and for you, you are by his Majesty (sitting in his royal chair before both Houses) appointed our Speaker, and yet now you refuse to do us the office and service of a Speaker."

Then they required Mr. Holles to read certain Articles as the Protestations of the House, which were jointly, as they were read, allowed with a loud *Yea* by the House. The effect of which Articles are as followeth:

First, Whosoever shall bring in innovation in Religion, or by favour or countenance, seek to extend or introduce Popery or Arminianism or other opinions disagreeing from the true and orthodox Church, shall be reputed a capital enemy to this Kingdom and Commonwealth.

Secondly, Whosoever shall counsel or advise the taking and levying of the Subsidies of Tonnage and Poundage, not being granted by Parliament, or shall be an actor or instrument therein, shall be likewise reputed an innovator in the government, and a capital enemy to this Kingdom and Commonwealth.

Thirdly, If any merchant or person whatsoever shall voluntarily yield or pay the said subsidies of Tonnage and Poundage, not being granted by Parliament, he shall likewise be reputed a betrayer of the liberties of England and an enemy to the same.

These being read and allowed of, the House rose up after they had sitten down two hours.

The King hearing that the House continued to sit (notwithstanding his command for the adjourning thereof) sent a messenger for the serjeant with the mace, which being taken from the table there can be no further proceeding; but the serjeant was by the House stayed, and the key of the door taken from him, and given to a gentleman of the House to keep.

After this the King sent Maxwell [*the usher—B. T.*] with the black rod for the dissolution of Parliament, but being informed that neither he nor his message would be received by the House, the King grew into much rage and passion, and sent for the Captain of the Pensioners and Guard to force the door, but the rising of the House prevented the bloodshed that might have been spilt.

Notwithstanding the Parliament was but as yet adjourned until that day sevennight, being the tenth of March, yet were the principal gentlemen attached by pursuivants, some the next morning; and on Wednesday by order from the Council-board sent to sundry prisons.

> *After this incident, Charles ruled for eleven years without Parliament. He obtained revenue by reviving ancient rights of the crown that had fallen into disuse. When such procedures were challenged in the courts, the judges upheld their legality. The following extracts deal with the "Case of Ship Money" (1637).*

Case of Ship Money, 1637

AN ENQUIRY OF CHARLES TO THE JUDGES

WHEN THE GOOD AND SAFETY of the kingdom in general is concerned, and the whole kingdom in danger, whether may not the King, by writ under the Great Seal of England, command all the subjects of our kingdom at their charge to provide and furnish such a number of ships, with men, victuals, and munition, and for such time as we shall think fit for the defence and safeguard of the kingdom from such danger and peril, and by law compel the doing thereof, in case of refusal or refractoriness; and whether in such a case is not the King the sole judge both of the danger, and when and how the same is to be prevented and avoided?

REPLY OF THE JUDGES

May it please your Most Excellent Majesty:

We have, according to your Majesty's command, every man by himself, and all of us together, taken into serious consideration the case and question signed by your Majesty, and inclosed in your royal letter; and we are of opinion, that when the good and safety of the kingdom in general is concerned, and the kingdom in danger, your Majesty may, by writ under the Great Seal of England, command all your subjects of this your kingdom, at their charge to provide and furnish such a number of ships, with men,

S. R. Gardiner, *The Constitutional Documents of the Puritan Revolution* (2nd ed., 1899), pp. 108–14. Reprinted by permission of The Clarendon Press, Oxford.

victuals, and munition, and for such time as your Majesty shall think fit for the defence and safeguard of this kingdom from such danger and peril: and that by law your Majesty may compel the doing thereof in case of refusal, or refractoriness: and we are also of opinion, that in such case your Majesty is the sole judge both of the danger, and when and how the same is to be prevented and avoided.

SPEECH OF OLIVER ST. JOHN AGAINST
SHIP MONEY

My Lords, not to burn daylight longer, it must needs be granted that in this business of defence the *suprema potestas* [*supreme power—B. T.*] is inherent in His Majesty, as part of his crown and kingly dignity.

So that as the care and provision of the law of England extends in the first place to foreign defence, and secondly lays the burden upon all, and for ought I have to say against it, it maketh the quantity of each man's estate the rule whereby this burden is to be equally apportioned upon each person; so likewise hath it in the third place made His Majesty the sole judge of dangers from foreigners, and when and how the same are to be prevented, and to come nearer, hath given him power by writ under the Great Seal of England, to command the inhabitants of each county to provide shipping for the defence of the kingdom, and may by law compel the doing thereof.

So that, my Lords, as I still conceive the question will not be *de persona,* in whom the *suprema potestas* of giving the authorities or powers to the sheriff, which are mentioned in this writ, doth lie, for that it is in the King; but the question is only *de modo,* by what medium or method this supreme power, which is in His Majesty, doth infuse and let out itself into this particular. . . .

And as without the assistance of his Judges, who are his settled counsel at law, His Majesty applies not the law and justice in many cases unto his subjects . . . neither can he out of Parliament alter the old laws, nor make new, or make any naturalizations or legitimations, nor do some other things; and yet is the Parliament His Majesty's Court too, as well as other his Courts of Justice.

That amongst the *ardua Regni negotia,* for which Parliaments are called, this of the defence is not only one of them, but even the chief, is cleared by this, that of all the rest none is named particularly in the summons, but only this; for all the summons to Parliament show the cause of the calling of them to be *pro quibusdam arduis negotiis nos et defensionem Regni nostri Angliae et Ecclesiae Anglicanae concernentibus* [*for certain arduous affairs concerning us and the defence of our realm of England and of the English church—B. T.*].

My Lords, the Parliament, as it is best qualified and fitted to make this supply for some of each rank, and that through all the parts of the kingdom being there met, His Majesty having declared the danger, they best knowing the estates of all men within the realm, are fittest, by comparing the danger and men's estates together, to proportion the aid accordingly.

And secondly, as they are fittest for the preservation of that fundamental propriety which the subject hath in his lands and goods, because each subject's vote is included in whatsoever is there done; so that it cannot be done otherwise, I shall endeavour to prove to your Lordships both by reason and authority.

My first reason is this, that the Parliament by the law is appointed as the ordinary means for supply upon extraordinary occasions, when the ordinary supplies will not do it. . . .

My second reason is taken from the actions of former Kings in this of the defence.

The aids demanded by them, and granted in Parliament, even for this purpose of the defence, and that in times of imminent danger, are so frequent, that I will spare the citing of any of them; it is rare in a subject, and more in a prince, to ask and take that of gift, which he may and ought to have of right, and that without so much as a *salvo,* or declaration of his right.

2   The Limitation of Royal Power, 1640–1641

In 1640 Charles was compelled by a rebellion in Scotland to summon Parliament again. It promptly passed a series of acts curtailing royal power for the future. The first act decreed that Parliament was to meet at least every three years.

Triennial Act

AN ACT FOR THE PREVENTING OF INCONVENIENCES HAPPENING BY THE LONG INTERMISSION OF PARLIAMENTS

I. WHEREAS by the laws and statutes of this realm the Parliament ought to be holden at least once every year for the redress of grievances, but the appointment of the time and place for the holding thereof hath always belonged, as it ought, to His Majesty and his royal progenitors; and whereas it is by experience found that the not holding of Parliaments accordingly hath produced sundry and great mischiefs and inconveniences to the King's Majesty, the Church and Commonwealth; for the prevention of the like mischiefs and inconveniences in time to come.

II. Be it enacted by the King's Most Excellent Majesty, with the consent of the Lords spiritual and temporal, and the Commons in this present Parliament assembled, that the said laws and statutes be from henceforth duly kept and observed; and your Majesty's loyal and obedient subjects, in this present Parliament now assembled, do humbly pray that it be enacted; and be it enacted accordingly, by the authority of this present Parliament, that in case there be not a Parliament summoned by writ under the Great Seal of England, and assembled and held before the 10th of September,

S. R. Gardiner, *The Constitutional Documents of the Puritan Revolution* (2nd ed., 1899), pp. 144–5. Reprinted by permission of The Clarendon Press, Oxford.

which shall be in the third year next after the last day of the last meeting and sitting in this present Parliament, the beginning of the first year to be accounted from the said last day of the last meeting and sitting in Parliament; and so from time to time, and in all times hereafter, if there shall not be a Parliament assembled and held before the 10th day of September, which shall be in the third year next after the last day of the last meeting and sitting in Parliament before the time assembled and held; the beginning of the first year to be accounted from the said last day of the last meeting and sitting in Parliament; that then in every such case as aforesaid, the Parliament shall assemble and be held in the usual place at Westminster. [*The Act required the Lord Chancellor to issue writs for a new Parliament whether the king commanded it or not—B. T.*]

> *The Earl of Strafford was declared guilty of high treason by act of attainder and executed. As his real offense was that he had been an exceptionally loyal and effective servant of the king, the chief prosecutor, John Pym, found it necessary to propound a new theory of treason as an offense against fundamental law.*

Attainder of Strafford

M Y   L O R D S , many days have been spent, in maintenance of the impeachment of the earl of Strafford, by the House of Commons, whereby he stands charged with high treason; and your lordships have heard his defence with patience and with as much favour as justice would allow. We have passed through our evidence, and the result of all this is, that it remains clearly proved, that the earl of Strafford hath endeavoured by his words, actions, and counsels, to subvert the fundamental laws of England and Ireland, and to introduce an arbitrary and tyrannical government. . . .

The law is that which puts a difference betwixt good and evil, betwixt just and unjust; if you take away the law, all things will fall into a confusion, every man will become a law to himself, which in the depraved condition of human nature, must needs produce many great enormities. Lust will become a law, and envy will become a law, covetousness and ambition will become laws; and what dictates, what decisions such laws will produce, may easily be discovered in the late government of Ireland. . . .

S. Reed Brett, *John Pym* (1940), pp. 171–2. Reprinted by permission of John Murray, London.

The law is the boundary, the measure, betwixt the King's prerogative and the people's liberty; whilst these move in their own orbs, they are a support and a security to one another; the prerogative a cover and defence to the liberty of the people, and the people by their liberty are enabled to be a foundation to the prerogative; but if these bounds be so removed, that they enter into contestation and conflict, one of these mischiefs must ensue: if the prerogative of the King overwhelm the liberty of the people, it will be turned to tyranny; if liberty undermine the prerogative, it will grow into anarchy.

Parliament also decreed that it could not be dissolved without its own consent.

Act Against Dissolving the Long Parliament Without Its Own Consent

AN ACT TO PREVENT INCONVENIENCES WHICH MAY HAPPEN BY THE UNTIMELY ADJOURNING, PROROGUING, OR DISSOLVING THIS PRESENT PARLIAMENT

WHEREAS GREAT SUMS of money must of necessity be speedily advanced and provided for the relief of His Majesty's army and people in the northern parts of this realm, and for preventing the imminent danger it is in, and for supply of other His Majesty's present and urgent occasions, which cannot be so timely effected as is requisite without credit for raising the said monies; which credit cannot be obtained until such obstacles be first removed as are occasioned by fears, jealousies and apprehensions of divers His Majesty's loyal subjects, that this present Parliament may be adjourned, prorogued, or dissolved, before justice shall be duly executed upon delinquents, public grievances redressed, a firm peace between the two nations of England and Scotland concluded, and before sufficient provision be made for the repayment of the said monies so to be raised; all which the Commons in this present Parliament assembled, having duly considered, do therefore most humbly beseech your Majesty that it may be declared and enacted.

And be it declared and enacted by the King, our Sovereign Lord, with the assent of the Lords and Commons in this present Parliament assembled, and by the authority of the same, that this present Parliament now assembled

S. R. Gardiner, *The Constitutional Documents of the Puritan Revolution* (2nd ed., 1899), pp. 158–9. Reprinted by permission of The Clarendon Press, Oxford.

shall not be dissolved unless it be by Act of Parliament to be passed for that purpose.

Act Abolishing Star Chamber

AN ACT FOR THE REGULATING OF THE PRIVY COUNCIL AND FOR TAKING AWAY THE COURT COMMONLY CALLED THE STAR CHAMBER

I. WHEREAS by the Great Charter many times confirmed in Parliament, it is enacted that no freeman shall be taken or imprisoned, or disseized of his freehold or liberties or free customs, or be outlawed or exiled or otherwise destroyed, and that the King will not pass upon him or condemn him but by lawful judgment of his Peers or by the law of the land; and by another statute made in the fifth year of the reign of King Edward the Third, it is enacted that no man shall be attached by any accusation nor forejudged of life or limb, nor his lands, tenements, goods nor chattels seized into the King's hands against the form of the Great Charter and the law of the land . . . ; and forasmuch as all matters examinable or determinable before the Court commonly called the Star Chamber, may have their proper remedy and redress, and their due punishment and correction by the common law of the land, and in the ordinary course of justice elsewhere, and forasmuch as the reasons and motives inducing the erection and continuance of that Court do now cease, and the proceedings, censures and decrees of that Court have by experience been found to be an intolerable burden to the subjects, and the means to introduce an arbitrary power and government: and forasmuch as the Council Table hath of late times assumed unto itself a power to intermeddle in civil causes and matters only of private interest between party and party, and have adventured to determine of the estates and liberties of the subject contrary to the law of the land and the rights and privileges of the subject, by which great and manifold mischiefs and inconveniences have arisen and happened, and much uncertainty by means of such proceedings hath been conceived concerning men's rights and estates: for settling whereof and preventing the like in time to come, be it ordained and enacted by the authority of this present Parliament, that the said Court commonly called the Star Chamber, and all jurisdiction, power and authority belonging unto or exercised in the same Court, or by any of the Judges, Officers or Ministers thereof be, from the first day of August in the year of

S. R. Gardiner, *The Constitutional Documents of the Puritan Revolution* (2nd ed., 1899), pp. 179–82. Reprinted by permission of The Clarendon Press, Oxford.

our Lord God one thousand six hundred forty and one, clearly and absolutely dissolved, taken away, and determined.

> *The collection of ship money was declared illegal. Other acts of Parliament abolished all the other nonparliamentary procedures that Charles had used to raise taxes during the preceding ten years. It is important to note that all these acts of 1641 were signed by the king and so became valid statutes.*

Act Abolishing Ship Money

WHEREAS DIVERS WRITS of late time issued under the great seal of England, commonly called ship writs, for the charging of the ports, towns, cities, boroughs, and counties of this realm respectively to provide and furnish certain ships for his majesty's service; and whereas, upon the execution of the same writs . . . , process hath been thence made against sundry persons pretended to be charged by way of contribution for the making up of certain sums assessed for the providing of the said ships, and in especial . . . against John Hampden, esquire . . . ; and whereas some other actions and process depend . . . against other persons for the like kind of charge grounded upon the said writs commonly called ship writs, all which writs and proceedings as aforesaid were utterly against the law of the land: be it therefore declared and enacted by the king's most excellent majesty and the lords and the commons in this present parliament assembled, and by the authority of the same, that the said charge imposed upon the subject for the providing and furnishing of ships commonly called ship money . . . , and the said writs . . . and the said judgment given against the said John Hampden, were and are contrary to and against the laws and statutes of this realm, the right of property, the liberty of the subjects, former resolutions in parliament, and the Petition of Right made in the third year of the reign of his majesty that now is.

And it is further declared and enacted . . . that all . . . particulars prayed or desired in the said Petition of Right shall from henceforth be put in execution accordingly, and shall be firmly and strictly holden and ob-

Sources of English Constitutional History, p. 482, edited and translated by Carl Stephenson and Frederick G. Marcham. Copyright 1937 by Harper & Brothers. Reprinted by permission of Harper & Row, Publishers.

served as in the same petition they are prayed and expressed; and that all . . . the records . . . of all . . . the judgment, enrolments . . . , and proceedings as aforesaid, and all . . . the proceedings whatsoever, upon or by pretext . . . of any of the said writs commonly called ship writs . . . , shall be deemed . . . to be utterly void.

3   The Outbreak of War

Toward the end of 1641 a division between the more moderate and the more radical members of the House of Commons became apparent in debates over the "Grand Remonstrance." This document was a diffuse statement of all the grievances of the preceding twenty years. The petition accompanying the Remonstrance, given below, sets out its main points.

Petition Accompanying the Grand Remonstrance

MOST GRACIOUS SOVEREIGN,

Your Majesty's most humble and faithful subjects the Commons in this present Parliament assembled, do with much thankfulness and joy acknowledge the great mercy and favour of God, in giving your Majesty a safe and peaceable return out of Scotland into your kingdom of England, where the pressing dangers and distempers of the State have caused us with much earnestness to desire the comfort of your gracious presence, and likewise the unity and justice of your royal authority, to give more life and power to the dutiful and loyal counsels and endeavours of your Parliament, for the prevention of that eminent ruin and destruction wherein your kingdoms of England and Scotland are threatened. The duty which we owe to your Majesty and our country, cannot but make us very sensible and apprehensive, that the multiplicity, sharpness and malignity of those evils under which we have now many years suffered, are fomented and cherished by a corrupt and ill-affected party, who amongst other their mischievous devices for the alteration of religion and government, have sought by many false scandals and imputations, cunningly insinuated and dispersed amongst the people, to blemish and disgrace our proceedings in this Parliament. . . .

*   *   *

S. R. Gardiner, *The Constitutional Documents of the Puritan Revolution* (2nd ed., 1899), pp. 202–5. Reprinted by permission of The Clarendon Press, Oxford.

And because we have reason to believe that those malignant parties, whose proceedings evidently appear to be mainly for the advantage and increase of Popery, is composed, set up, and acted by the subtile practice of the Jesuits and other engineers and factors for Rome, and to the great danger of this kingdom, and most grievous affliction of your loyal subjects, have so far prevailed as to corrupt divers of your Bishops and others in prime places of the Church, and also to bring divers of these instruments to be of your Privy Council, and other employments of trust and nearness about your Majesty, the Prince, and the rest of your royal children.

And by this means have had such an operation in your counsel and the most important affairs and proceedings of your government, that a most dangerous division and chargeable preparation for war betwixt your kingdoms of England and Scotland, the increase of jealousies betwixt your Majesty and your most obedient subjects, the violent distraction and interruption of this Parliament, the insurrection of the Papists in your kingdom of Ireland, and bloody massacre of your people, have been not only endeavoured and attempted, but in a great measure compassed and effected.

*   *   *

We, your most humble and obedient subjects, do with all faithfulness and humility beseech your Majesty:

1. That you will be graciously pleased to concur with the humble desires of your people in a parliamentary way, for the preserving the peace and safety of the kingdom from the malicious designs of the Popish party:

For depriving the Bishops of their votes in Parliament, and abridging their immoderate power usurped over the Clergy, and other your good subjects, which they have perniciously abused to the hazard of religion, and great prejudice and oppression to the laws of the kingdom, and just liberty of your people:

For the taking away such oppressions in religion, Church government and discipline, as have been brought in and fomented by them:

For uniting all such your loyal subjects together as join in the same fundamental truths against the Papists, by removing some oppressions and unnecessary ceremonies by which divers weak consciences have been scrupled, and seem to be divided from the rest, and for the due execution of those good laws which have been made for securing the liberty of your subjects.

2. That your Majesty will likewise be pleased to remove from your council all such as persist to favour and promote any of those pressures and corruptions wherewith your people have been grieved, and that for the future your Majesty will vouchsafe to employ such persons in your great and public affairs, and to take such to be near you in places of trust, as your Parliament may have cause to confide in; that in your princely goodness to your people you will reject and refuse all mediation and solicitation to the contrary, how powerful and near soever.

> *The last part of the preceding petition was, in effect, a*
> *demand by Parliament to take control of the king's govern-*
> *ment. Charles refused to assent to it and, in January 1642,*
> *tried to arrest its leading sponsors.*

Case of the Five Members

AND AS HIS MAJESTY CAME through Westminster Hall, the Commanders, etc., that attended him made a lane on both sides the Hall (through which his Majesty passed and came up the stairs to the House of Commons) and stood before the guard of Pensioners and Halbedeers (who also attended the king's person) and, the door of the House of Commons being thrown open, his Majesty entered the House, and as he passed up towards the Chair he cast his eye on the right hand near the Bar of the House, where Mr. Pym used to sit; but his Majesty not seeing him there (knowing him well) went up to the Chair, and said, "By your leave, Mr. Speaker, I must borrow your chair a little." Whereupon the Speaker came out of the Chair and his Majesty stepped up into it; after he had stood in the Chair a while, casting his eye upon the members as they stood up uncovered, but could not discern any of the five members to be there, nor indeed were they easy to be discerned (had they been there) among so many bare faces all standing up together. Then his Majesty made this speech.

"Gentlemen, I am sorry for this occasion of coming unto you. Yesterday I sent a Serjeant at Arms upon a very important occasion, to apprehend some that by my command were accused of high treason; whereunto I did expect obedience and not a message. And I must declare unto you here that, albeit no king that ever was in England shall be more careful of your privileges, to maintain them to the uttermost of his power, than I shall be; yet you must know that in cases of treason no person hath a privilege. And therefore I am come to know if any of these persons that were accused are here. For I must tell you, Gentlemen that so long as these persons that I have accused (for no light crime, but for treason) are here, I cannot expect that this House will be in the right way that I do heartily wish it. Therefore I am come to tell you that I must have them wheresoever I find them. Well, since I see all the birds are flown, I do expect from you that you shall send them unto me as soon as they return hither. But I assure you, on the word of a king, I never did intend any force, but shall proceed against them in a legal and fair way, for I never did intend any other.

"And now, since I cannot do what I came for, I think this no unfit

---

John Rushworth, *Historical Collections*, IV (1721), 477–8.

occasion to repeat what I have said formerly, that whatsoever I have done in favor and to the good of my subjects, I do mean to maintain it.

"I will trouble you no more, but tell you I do expect as soon as they come to the House you will send them to me; otherwise I must take my own course to find them."

When the king was looking about the House, the Speaker standing below by the Chair, his Majesty asked him whether any of these persons were in the House. Whether he saw any of them? And where they were? To which the Speaker, falling on his knee, thus answered, "May it please your Majesty, I have neither eyes to see, nor tongue to speak in this place but as the House is pleased to direct me, whose servant I am here; and humbly beg your Majesty's pardon, that I cannot give any other answer than this to what your Majesty is pleased to demand of me."

The king, having concluded his speech, went out of the House again, which was in great disorder, and many members cried out aloud, so as he might hear them, "Privilege! Privilege!" and forthwith adjourned till the next day at one of the clock.

> *After this abortive attempt Charles withdrew from London. The decisive breach came when the houses of Parliament, without royal consent, raised an army on their own authority. (An army was urgently needed to suppress a rebellion in Ireland.)*

Militia Ordinance

AN ORDINANCE OF THE LORDS AND COMMONS IN PARLIAMENT, FOR THE SAFETY AND DEFENCE OF THE KINGDOM OF ENGLAND AND DOMINION OF WALES

WHEREAS THERE HATH BEEN of late a most dangerous and desperate design upon the House of Commons, which we have just cause to believe to be an effect of the bloody counsels of Papists and other ill-affected persons, who have already raised a rebellion in the kingdom of Ireland; and by reason of many discoveries we cannot but fear they will proceed not only to stir up the like rebellion and insurrections in this kingdom of England, but also to back them with forces from abroad.

S. R. Gardiner, *The Constitutional Documents of the Puritan Revolution* (2nd ed., 1899), pp. 245–6. Reprinted by permission of The Clarendon Press, Oxford.

For the safety therefore of His Majesty's person, the Parliament and kingdom in this time of imminent danger.

It is ordained by the Lords and Commons now in Parliament assembled, that Henry Earl of Holland shall be Lieutenant of the County of Berks, Oliver Earl of Bolingbroke shall be Lieutenant of the County of Bedford, &c.

*   *   *

And shall severally and respectively have power to assemble and call together all and singular His Majesty's subjects, within the said several and respective counties and places, as well within liberties as without, that are meet and fit for the wars, and them to train and exercise and put in readiness, and them after their abilities and faculties well and sufficiently from time to time to cause to be arrayed and weaponed, and to take the muster of them in places most fit for that purpose.

> *The king, in reply, insisted on his ancient right to command the armed forces of the realm.*

Charles I's Proclamation Condemning the Militia Ordinance

WHEREAS, BY THE STATUTE made in the seventh year of King Edward the First, the Prelates, Earls, Barons and Commonalty of the realm affirmed in Parliament, that to the King it belongeth, and his part it is by his royal seigniory straightly to defend wearing of armour and all other force against the peace, at all times when it shall please him, and to punish them which do the contrary according to the laws and usages of the realm; and hereunto all subjects are bound to aid the King as their sovereign lord, at all seasons when need shall be; and whereas we understand that, expressly contrary to the said statute and other good laws of this our kingdom, under colour and pretence of an Ordinance of Parliament, without our consent, or any commission or warrant from us, the trained bands and militia of this kingdom have been lately, and are intended to be put in arms, and drawn into companies in a warlike manner, whereby the peace and quiet of our subjects is, or may be, disturbed; we being desirous, by all gracious and fair admoni-

---

S. R. Gardiner, *The Constitutional Documents of the Puritan Revolution* (2nd ed., 1899), pp. 248–9. Reprinted by permission of The Clarendon Press, Oxford.

tions, to prevent that some malignant persons in this our kingdom do not by degrees seduce our good subjects from their due obedience to us and the laws of this our kingdom . . . do therefore, by this our Proclamation, expressly charge and command all our sheriffs, and all colonels, lieutenant-colonels, sergeant-majors, captains, officers and soldiers, belonging to the trained bands of this our kingdom, and likewise all high and petty constables, and other our officers and subjects whatsoever, upon their allegiance, and as they tender the peace of this our kingdom, not to muster, levy, raise or march, or to summon or warn, upon any warrant, order or ordinance from one or both of our Houses of Parliament.

4 A Whig Interpretation of the Civil War

FROM *The History of England* BY T. B. MACAULAY

AND NOW [1624—*B. T.*] began that hazardous game on which were staked the destinies of the English people. It was played on the side of the House of Commons with keenness, but with admirable dexterity, coolness, and perseverance. Great statesmen who looked far behind them and far before them were at the head of that assembly. They were resolved to place the King in such a situation that he must either conduct the administration in conformity with the wishes of his Parliament, or make outrageous attacks on the most sacred principles of the constitution. They accordingly doled out supplies to him very sparingly. He found that he must govern either in harmony with the House of Commons, or in defiance of all law. His choice was soon made. He dissolved his first Parliament, and levied taxes by his own authority. He convoked a second Parliament, and found it more intractable than the first. He again resorted to the expedient of dissolution, raised fresh taxes without any show of legal right, and threw the chiefs of the opposition into prison. At the same time a new grievance, which the peculiar feelings and habits of the English nation made insupportably painful, and which seemed to all discerning men to be of fearful augury, excited general discontent and alarm. Companies of soldiers were billeted on the people; and martial law was, in some places, substituted for the ancient jurisprudence of the realm.

The King called a third Parliament, and soon perceived that the opposition was stronger and fiercer than ever. He now determined on a change of tactics. Instead of opposing an inflexible resistance to the demands of the Commons, he, after much altercation and many evasions, agreed to a compromise which, if he had faithfully adhered to it, would have averted a long series of calamities. The Parliament granted an ample supply. The King ratified, in the most solemn manner, that celebrated law, which is known by the name of the Petition of Right, and which is the second Great Charter of the liberties of England. By ratifying that law he bound himself never again

Thomas Babington Macaulay, *The History of England*, I (9th ed., 1853), 83–8, 96–111.

to raise money without the consent of the Houses, never again to imprison any person, except in due course of law, and never again to subject his people to the jurisdiction of courts martial.

The day on which the royal sanction was, after many delays, solemnly given to this great act, was a day of joy and hope. The Commons, who crowded the bar of the House of Lords, broke forth into loud acclamations as soon as the clerk had pronounced the ancient form of words by which our princes have, during many ages, signified their assent to the wishes of the Estates of the realm. Those acclamations were reechoed by the voice of the capital and of the nation; but within three weeks it became manifest that Charles had no intention of observing the compact into which he had entered. The supply given by the representatives of the nation was collected. The promise by which that supply had been obtained was broken. A violent contest followed. The Parliament was dissolved with every mark of royal displeasure. Some of the most distinguished members were imprisoned; and one of them, Sir John Eliot, after years of suffering, died in confinement.

Charles, however, could not venture to raise, by his own authority, taxes sufficient for carrying on war. He accordingly hastened to make peace with his neighbours, and thenceforth gave his whole mind to British politics.

Now commenced a new era. Many English Kings had occasionally committed unconstitutional acts: but none had ever systematically attempted to make himself a despot, and to reduce the Parliament to a nullity. Such was the end which Charles distinctly proposed to himself. From March 1629 to April 1640, the Houses were not convoked. Never in our history had there been an interval of eleven years between Parliament and Parliament. Only once had there been an interval of even half that length. This fact alone is sufficient to refute those who represent Charles as having merely trodden in the footsteps of the Plantagenets and Tudors.

It is proved, by the testimony of the King's most strenuous supporters, that, during this part of his reign, the provisions of the Petition of Right were violated by him, not occasionally, but constantly, and on system; that a large part of the revenue was raised without any legal authority; and that persons obnoxious to the government languished for years in prison, without being ever called upon to plead before any tribunal.

For these things history must hold the King himself chiefly responsible. From the time of his third Parliament he was his own prime minister. Several persons, however, whose temper and talents were suited to his purposes, were at the head of different departments of the administration.

Thomas Wentworth, successively created Lord Wentworth and Earl of Strafford, a man of great abilities, eloquence, and courage, but of a cruel and imperious nature, was the counsellor most trusted in political and military affairs. . . . His object was to do in England all, and more than all, that Richelieu was doing in France; to make Charles a monarch as absolute as any on the Continent; to put the estates and the personal liberty of the whole people at the disposal of the crown; to deprive the courts of law of all independent authority, even in ordinary questions of civil right between man and man; and to punish with merciless rigour all who murmured at the acts of the government, or who applied, even in the most decent and regular manner, to any tribunal for relief against those acts.

This was his end; and he distinctly saw in what manner alone this end could be attained. There was, in truth, about all his notions a clearness, coherence, and precision which, if he had not been pursuing an object pernicious to his country and to his kind, would have justly entitled him to high admiration. He saw that there was one instrument, and only one, by which his vast and daring projects could be carried into execution. That instrument was a standing army. To the forming of such an army, therefore, he directed all the energy of his strong mind. In Ireland, where he was viceroy, he actually succeeded in establishing a military despotism, not only over the aboriginal population, but also over the English colonists, and was able to boast that, in that island, the King was as absolute as any prince in the whole world could be.

The ecclesiastical administration was, in the meantime, principally directed by William Laud, Archbishop of Canterbury. Of all the prelates of the Anglican Church, Laud had departed farthest from the principles of the Reformation, and had drawn nearest to Rome. . . . Under his direction every corner of the realm was subjected to a constant and minute inspection. Every little congregation of separatists was tracked out and broken up. Even the devotions of private families could not escape the vigilance of his spies. Such fear did his rigour inspire that the deadly hatred of the Church, which festered in innumerable bosoms, was generally disguised under an outward show of conformity. On the very eve of troubles, fatal to himself and to his order, the Bishops of several extensive dioceses were able to report to him that not a single dissenter was to be found within their jurisdiction.

*   *   *

In November 1640 met that renowned Parliament which, in spite of many errors and disasters, is justly entitled to the reverence and gratitude of all who, in any part of the world, enjoy the blessings of constitutional government.

During the year which followed, no very important division of opinion appeared in the Houses. The civil and ecclesiastical administration had, through a period of near twelve years, been so oppressive and so unconstitutional that even those classes of which the inclinations are generally on the side of order and authority were eager to promote popular reforms, and to bring the instruments of tyranny to justice. It was enacted that no interval of more than three years should ever elapse between Parliament and Parliament, and that, if writs under the Great Seal were not issued at the proper time, the returning officers should, without such writs, call the constituent bodies together for the choice of representatives. The Star Chamber, the

High Commission, the Council of York were swept away. Men who, after suffering cruel mutilations, had been confined in remote dungeons, regained their liberty. On the chief ministers of the crown the vengeance of the nation was unsparingly wreaked. The Lord Keeper, the Primate, the Lord Lieutenant were impeached. Finch saved himself by flight. Laud was flung into the Tower. Strafford was impeached, and at length put to death by act of attainder. On the same day on which this act passed, the King gave his assent to a law by which he bound himself not to adjourn, prorogue, or dissolve the existing Parliament without its own consent.

*   *   *

At a later period the Royalists found it convenient to antedate the separation between themselves and their opponents, and to attribute the Act which restrained the King from dissolving or proroguing the Parliament, the Triennial Act, the impeachment of the ministers, and the attainder of Strafford, to the faction which afterwards made war on the King. But no artifice could be more disingenuous. Every one of those strong measures was actively promoted by the men who were afterwards foremost among the Cavaliers. No republican spoke of the long misgovernment of Charles more severely than Colepepper. The most remarkable speech in favour of the Triennial Bill was made by Digby. The impeachment of the Lord Keeper was moved by Falkland. The demand that the Lord Lieutenant should be kept close prisoner was made at the bar of the Lords by Hyde. Not till the law attainting Strafford was proposed did the signs of serious disunion become visible. Even against that law, a law which nothing but extreme necessity could justify, only about sixty members of the House of Commons voted. It is certain that Hyde was not in the minority, and that Falkland not only voted with the majority, but spoke strongly for the bill. Even the few who entertained a scruple about inflicting death by a retrospective enactment thought it necessary to express the utmost abhorrence of Strafford's character and administration.

But under this apparent concord a great schism was latent; and when, in October 1641, the Parliament reassembled after a short recess, two hostile parties, essentially the same with those which, under different names, have ever since contended, and are still contending, for the direction of public affairs, appeared confronting each other. During some years they were designated as Cavaliers and Roundheads. They were subsequently called Tories and Whigs; nor does it seem that these appellations are likely soon to become obsolete.

*   *   *

Neither party wanted strong arguments for the measures which it was disposed to take. The reasonings of the most enlightened Royalists may be summed up thus:—"It is true that great abuses have existed; but they have been redressed. It is true that precious rights have been invaded; but they have been vindicated and surrounded with new securities. The sittings of the Estates of the realm have been, in defiance of all precedent and of the spirit of the constitution, intermitted during eleven years; but it has now been provided that henceforth three years shall never elapse without a Parliament. The Star Chamber, the High Commission, the Council of York, oppressed and plundered us; but those hateful courts have now ceased to exist. . . . Henceforth it will be our wisdom to look with jealousy on schemes of innovation, and to guard from encroachment all the prerogatives with which the law has, for the public good, armed the sovereign."

Such were the views of those men of whom the excellent Falkland may be regarded as the leader. It was contended on the other side with not less force, by men of not less ability and virtue, that the safety which the liberties of the English people enjoyed was rather apparent than real, and that the arbitrary projects of the court would be resumed as soon as the vigilance of the Commons was relaxed. True it was,—such was the reasoning of Pym, of Hollis, and of Hampden,—that many good laws had been passed: but, if good laws had been sufficient to restrain the King, his subjects would have had little reason ever to complain of his administration. The recent statutes were surely not of more authority than the Great Charter or the Petition of Right. Yet neither the Great Charter, hallowed by the veneration of four centuries, nor the Petition of Right, sanctioned, after mature reflection, and for valuable consideration, by Charles himself, had been found effectual for the protection of the people. If once the check of fear were withdrawn, if once the spirit of opposition were suffered to slumber, all the securities for English freedom resolved themselves into a single one, the royal word; and it had been proved by a long and severe experience that the royal word could not be trusted.

The two parties were still regarding each other with cautious hostility, and had not yet measured their strength, when news arrived which inflamed the passions and confirmed the opinions of both. The great chieftains of Ulster, who, at the time of the accession of James, had, after a long struggle, submitted to the royal authority, had not long brooked the humiliation of dependence. They had conspired against the English government, and had been attainted of treason. Their immense domains had been forfeited to the crown, and had soon been peopled by thousands of English and Scotch emigrants. The new settlers were, in civilisation and intelligence, far superior to the native population, and sometimes abused their superiority. The animosity produced by difference of race was increased by difference of religion. Under the iron rule of Wentworth, scarcely a murmur was heard: but, when that strong pressure was withdrawn, when Scotland had set the example of successful resistance, when England was distracted by internal quarrels, the smothered rage of the Irish broke forth into acts of fearful violence. . . . To raise a great army had always been the King's first object. A great army must now be raised. It was to be feared that, unless some new securities were devised, the forces levied for the reduction of Ireland would be employed against the liberties of England. Nor was this all. A horrible suspicion, unjust indeed, but not altogether unnatural, had arisen in many minds. The Queen was an avowed Roman Catholic: the King was not regarded by the Puritans, whom he had mercilessly persecuted, as a sincere Protestant; and so notorious was his duplicity, that there was no treachery of which his subjects might not, with some show of reason, believe him capable. It was soon whispered that the rebellion of the Roman Catholics of Ulster was part of a vast work of darkness which had been planned at Whitehall.

After some weeks of prelude, the first great parliamentary conflict between the parties which have ever since contended, and are still contending, for the government of the nation, took place on the twenty-second of November 1641. It was moved by the opposition, that the House of Commons should present to the King a remonstrance, enumerating the faults of his administration from the time of his accession, and expressing the distrust with which his policy was still regarded by his people. That assembly, which a few months before had been unanimous in calling for the reform of abuses, was now divided into two fierce and eager factions of nearly equal strength. After a hot debate of many hours, the remonstrance was carried by only eleven votes.

The result of this struggle was highly favourable to the conservative party. It could not be doubted that only some great indiscretion could prevent them from shortly obtaining the predominance in the Lower House. The Upper House was already their own. Nothing was wanting to insure their success, but that the King should, in all his conduct, show respect for the laws and scrupulous good faith towards his subjects.

His first measures promised well. He had, it seemed, at last discovered that an entire change of system was necessary, and had wisely made up his mind to what could no longer be avoided. He declared his determination to govern in harmony with the Commons, and, for that end, to call to his councils men in whose talents and character the Commons might place confidence. Nor was the selection ill made. Falkland, Hyde, and Colepepper, all three distinguished by the part which they had taken in reforming abuses and in punishing evil ministers, were invited to become the confidential advisers of the crown, and were solemnly assured by Charles that he would take no step in any way affecting the Lower House of Parliament without their privity.

Had he kept this promise, it cannot be doubted that the reaction which was already in progress would very soon have become quite as strong as the most respectable Royalists would have desired. Already the violent members of the opposition had begun to despair of the fortunes of their party, to tremble for their own safety, and to talk of selling their estates and emigrating to America. That the fair prospects which had begun to open before the King were suddenly overcast, that his life was darkened by adversity, and at length shortened by violence, is to be attributed to his own faithlessness and contempt of law.

The truth seems to be that he detested both the parties into which the House of Commons was divided: nor is this strange; for in both those parties the love of liberty and the love of order were mingled, though in different proportions. The advisers whom necessity had compelled him to call round him were by no means men after his own heart. They had joined in condemning his tyranny, in abridging his power, and in punishing his instruments. They were now indeed prepared to defend by strictly legal means his strictly legal prerogatives; but they would have recoiled with horror from the thought of reviving Wentworth's projects of Thorough. They were, therefore, in the King's opinion, traitors, who differed only in the degree of their seditious malignity from Pym and Hampden.

He accordingly, a few days after he had promised the chiefs of the constitutional Royalists that no step of importance should be taken without their knowledge, formed a resolution the most momentous of his whole life, carefully concealed that resolution from them, and executed it in a manner which overwhelmed them with shame and dismay. He sent the Attorney General to impeach Pym, Hollis, Hampden, and other members of the House of Commons of high treason at the bar of the House of Lords. Not content with this flagrant violation of the Great Charter and of the uninterrupted practice of centuries, he went in person, accompanied by armed men, to seize the leaders of the opposition within the walls of Parliament.

The attempt failed. The accused members had left the House a short time before Charles entered it. A sudden and violent revulsion of feeling, both in the Parliament and in the country, followed. The most favourable view that has ever been taken of the King's conduct on this occasion by his most partial advocates is that he had weakly suffered himself to be hurried into a gross indiscretion by the evil counsels of his wife and of his courtiers. But the general voice loudly charged him with far deeper guilt. At the very moment at which his subjects, after a long estrangement produced by his maladministration, were returning to him with feelings of confidence and affection, he had aimed a deadly blow at all their dearest rights, at the privileges of Parliament, at the very principle of trial by jury. . . . Had Charles remained much longer in his stormy capital, it is probable that the Commons would have found a plea for making him, under outward forms of respect, a state prisoner.

He quitted London, never to return till the day of a terrible and memorable reckoning had arrived. A negotiation began which occupied many months. Accusations and recriminations passed backward and forward between the contending parties. All accommodation had become impossible. The sure punishment which waits on habitual perfidy had at length overtaken the King.

*   *   *

The change which the Houses proposed to make in our institutions, though it seems exorbitant, when distinctly set forth and digested into articles of capitulation, really amounts to little more than the change which, in the next generation, was effected by the Revolution [*of 1688—B. T.*]. It is true that, at the Revolution, the sovereign was not deprived by law of the power of naming his ministers: but it is equally true that, since the Revolution, no ministry has been able to remain in office six months in opposition to the sense of the House of Commons. It is true that the sovereign still possesses the power of creating peers, and the more important power of the sword: but it is equally true that in the exercise of these powers the sovereign has, ever since the Revolution, been guided by advisers who possess the confidence of the representatives of the nation. In fact, the leaders of the Roundhead party in 1642, and the statesmen who, about half a century later, effected the Revolution, had exactly the same object in view. That object was to terminate the contest between the crown and the Parliament, by giving to the Parliament a supreme control over the executive administration. The statesmen of the Revolution effected this indirectly by changing the dynasty. The Roundheads of 1642, being unable to change the dynasty, were compelled to take a direct course towards their end.

5 *Monarchy, Oligarchy, Democracy, or Dictatorship?*

The parliamentary regime can reasonably be called an oligarchy in that it represented men of property (the masses of the common people had no vote). The idea of instituting a democratic system was put forward in the course of a debate held among the army leaders in 1647 concerning the future form of government. The views expressed by Colonel Rainborow in the following exchange, however, proved totally unacceptable to the monarchists, the parliamentary leaders, and the generals. There was never any serious possibility of their being put into practice.

FROM *The Army Debates*

COL. RAINBOROW. . . . Really I thinke that the poorest hee that is in England hath a life to live as the greatest hee; and therefore truly, Sir, I thinke itt's cleare, that every man that is to live under a Governement ought first by his owne consent to putt himself under that Governement; and I doe thinke that the poorest man in England is nott att all bound in a stricte sence to that Governement that hee hath not had a voice to putt himself under; and I am confident that when I have heard the reasons against itt, somethinge will bee said to answer those reasons, insoemuch that I should doubt whether he was an Englishman or noe that should doubt of these thinges.

COMMISSARY IRETON. Give mee leave to tell you, that if you make this the rule I thinke you must flie for refuge to an absolute naturall Right, and you must deny all Civill Right; and I am sure itt will come to that in the consequence. . . . For my parte I thinke itt is noe right att all. I thinke that noe person hath a right to an interest or share in the disposing or determin-

C. H. Firth, ed., *The Clarke Papers* (1891), pp. 301–9. Reprinted by permission of The Royal Historical Society.

ing of the affaires of the Kingedome, and in chusing those that shall determine what lawes wee shall bee rul'd by heere, noe person hath a right to this,
that hath nott a permanent fixed interest in this Kingedome; and those
persons together are properly the Represented of this Kingedome, and conse-
quentlie are to make uppe the Representors of this Kingedome, who taken
together doe comprehend whatsoever is of reall or permanent interest in the
Kingedome. And I am sure I cannott tell what otherwise any man can say
why a forraigner coming in amongst us—or as many as will coming in
amongst us, or by force or otherwise setling themselves heere, or att least by
our permission having a being heere—why they should nott as well lay
claime to itt as any other. Wee talke of birthright. Truly [by] birthright
there is thus much claime. Men may justly have by birthright, by their very
being borne in England, that wee should nott seclude them out of England,
that wee should nott refuse to give them aire, and place, and ground, and the
freedome of the high wayes and other things, to live amongst us; nott [to]
any man that is borne heere, though by his birth there come nothing att all to
him that is parte of the permanent interest of this Kingedome. That I thinke
is due to a man by birth. Butt that by a man's being borne heere hee shall
have a share in that power that shall dispose of the lands heere, and of all
thinges heere, I doe nott thinke itt a sufficient ground. I am sure if wee looke
uppon that which is the utmost within man's view of what was originally the
constitution of this Kingedome, [if wee] looke uppon that which is most
radicall and fundamentall, and which if you take away there is noe man hath
any land, any goods, [or] any civill interest, that is this: that those that chuse
the Representors for the making of Lawes by which this State and Kingedome are to bee govern'd, are the persons who taken together doe comprehend the locall interest of this Kingedome; that is, the persons in whome all
land lies, and those in Corporations in whome all trading lies. This is the
most fundamentall Constitution of this Kingedome, which if you doe nott
allow you allow none att all. . . .

COL. RAINBOROW. Truly, Sir, I am of the same opinion I was; and am
resolved to keepe itt till I know reason why I should nott. . . . I doe heare
nothing att all that can convince mee, why any man that is borne in England
ought nott to have his voice in Election of Burgesses. Itt is said, that if a man
have nott a permanent interest, hee can have noe claime, and wee must bee
noe freer then the lawes will lett us to bee, and that there is noe Chronicle
will lett us bee freer then that wee enjoy. Something was said to this
yesterday. I doe thinke that the maine cause why Almighty God gave men
reason, itt was, that they should make use of that reason, and that they
should improve itt for that end and purpose that God gave itt them. And
truly, I thinke that halfe a loafe is better then none if a man bee an hungry,
yett I thinke there is nothing that God hath given a man that any else can
take from him. Therefore I say, that either itt must bee the law of God or the
law of man that must prohibite the meanest man in the Kingedome to have

this benefitt as well as the greatest. I doe nott finde any thinge in the law of God, that a Lord shall chuse 20 Burgesses, and a Gentleman butt two, or a poore man shall chuse none. I finde noe such thinge in the law of nature, nor in the law of nations. . . . And truly I have thought somethinge [else], in what a miserable distressed condition would many a man that hath fought for the Parliament in this quarrell bee? I will bee bound to say, that many a man whose zeale and affection to God and this Kingedome hath carried him forth in this cause hath soe spent his estate that in the way the State, the Army are going hee shall nott hold uppe his head; and when his estate is lost, and nott worth 40s. a yeare, a man shall nott have any interest; and there are many other wayes by which estates men have doe fall to decay, if that bee the rule which God in his providence does use. A man when hee hath an estate hath an interest in making lawes, when hee hath none, hee hath noe power in itt. Soe that a man cannott loose that which hee hath for the maintenance of his family, butt hee must loose that which God and nature hath given him. Therefore I doe [think] and am still of the same opinion; that every man born in England cannot, ought nott, neither by the law of God nor the law of nature, to bee exempted from the choice of those who are to make lawes, for him to live under, and for him, for ought I know, to loose his life under.

*   *   *

COMMISSARY GEN. IRETON. . . . All the maine thinge that I speake for is because I would have an eye to propertie. I hope wee doe nott come to contend for victorie, butt lett every man consider with himself that hee doe nott goe that way to take away all propertie. For heere is the case of the most fundamentall parte of the Constitution of the Kingedome, which if you take away, you take away all by that. Heere are men of this and this qualitie are determined to bee the Electors of men to the Parliament, and they are all those who have any permanent interest in the Kingedome, and who taken together doe comprehend the whole interest of the Kingedome. . . . Now I wish wee may all consider of what right you will challenge, that all the people should have right to Elections. Is itt by the right of nature? If you will hold forth that as your ground, then I thinke you must deny all property too, and this is my reason. For thus: by that same right of nature, whatever itt bee that you pretend, by which you can say, "one man hath an equall right with another to the chusing of him that shall governe him"—by the same right of nature, hee hath an equal right in any goods hee sees: meate, drinke, cloathes, to take and use them for his sustenance. Hee hath a freedome to the land, [to take] the ground, to exercise itt, till itt; he hath the [same] freedome to any thinge that any one doth account himself to have any propriety in. Why now I say then, if you, against this most fundamentall parte of [the] civill Constitution (which I have now declar'd), will pleade the law of nature, that a man should, paramount [to] this, and contrary to this, have a power of chusing those men that shall determine what shall bee law in this state, though he himself have noe permanent interest in the State, [but] whatever interest hee hath hee may carry about with him. If this be allowed, [because by the right of nature], wee are free, wee are equall, one man must have as much voice as another, then shew mee what steppe or difference [there is], why by the same right of necessity to sustaine nature [I may not claim property as well]?

COL. RAINBOROW. . . . For my parte, as I thinke, you forgott somethinge that was in my speech, and you doe nott only your selves believe that [we] are inclining to anarchy, butt you would make all men believe that. And Sir, to say because a man pleades, that every man hath a voice [by the right of nature], that therefore itt destroyes [by] the same [argument all property]—that there's a propertie the law of God sayes itt; else why [hath] God made that law, "Thou shalt nott steale?" If I have noe interest in the Kingedome I must suffer by all their lawes bee they right or wronge. I am a poore man, therefore I must bee prest. . . . Therefore I thinke that to that itt is fully answered. God hath sett downe that thinge as to propriety with this law of his, "Thou shalt not steale." For my parte I am against any such thought, and as for yourselves I wish you would nott make the world believe that wee are for anarchy.

> *By the autumn of 1648 the parliamentary armies had defeated both the Cavaliers and the Scots—with whom Charles had formed an alliance in 1647. But at this point a quarrel broke out between the leaders of Parliament and the generals. Parliament wanted to continue negotiating with the king; the army was determined to kill him. Parliament wanted to impose a rigid Presbyterian discipline on the English church; the army sought toleration for the various extremist Protestant sects included in its ranks. Oliver Cromwell justified a take-over of power by the army in the following letter (November 25, 1648).*

Oliver Cromwell's Letter to Colonel Hammond

DEAR ROBIN, thou and I were never worthy to be door-keepers in this service. If thou wilt seek, seek to know the mind of God in all that chain of Providence, whereby God brought thee thither, and that person to thee; how,

Thomas Carlyle, *The Letters and Speeches of Oliver Cromwell,* I (1904), 394–7, edited by S. C. Lomas. Reprinted by permission of Methuen & Co. Ltd., London.

before and since, God has ordered him, and affairs concerning him: and then tell me, whether there be not some glorious and high meaning in all this, above what thou hast yet attained? And, laying aside thy fleshly reason, seek of the Lord to teach thee what that is; and He will do it. . . .

You say: "God hath appointed authorities among the nations, to which active or passive obedience is to be yielded. This resides in England in the Parliament. Therefore active or passive [*obedience should be yielded to Parliament*" —B. T.].

Authorities and powers are the ordinance of God. This or that species is of human institution, and limited, some with larger, others with stricter bands, each one according to its constitution. "But" I do not therefore think the authorities may do anything, and yet such obedience "be" due, but all agree there are cases in which it is lawful to resist. If so, your ground fails, and so likewise the inference. Indeed, dear Robin, not to multiply words, the query is, Whether ours be such a case? This ingenuously is the true question.

To this I shall say nothing, though I could say very much; but only desire thee to see what thou findest in thy own heart as to two or three plain considerations. First, whether *Salus Populi* be a sound position? [*Cromwell referred to the maxim, "The safety of the people is the supreme law."—B. T.*] Secondly, whether in the way in hand, really and before the Lord, before whom conscience must stand, this be provided for, or the whole fruit of the war like to be frustrated, and all most like to turn to what it was, and worse? And this, contrary to engagements, declarations, implicit covenants with those who ventured their lives upon those covenants and engagements, without whom perhaps, in equity, relaxation ought not to be? Thirdly, Whether this Army be not a lawful power, called by God to oppose and fight against the King upon some stated grounds; and being in power to such ends, may not oppose one name of authority, for those ends, as well as another, the outward authority that called them, not by their power making the quarrel lawful, but it being so in itself? If so it may be acting will be justified *in foro humano.*—But truly these kinds of reasonings may be but fleshly, either with or against: only it is good to try what truth may be in them. And the Lord teach us.

My dear friend, let us look into providences; surely they mean somewhat. They hang so together; have been so constant, so clear and unclouded. Malice, swoln malice against God's people, now called Saints, to root out their name; and yet they, "these poor Saints," by providence, having arms, and therein blessed with defence and more. . . .

What think you of Providence disposing the hearts of so many of God's people this way, especially in this poor Army, wherein the great God has vouchsafed to appear. I know not one officer among us but is on the increasing hand. And let me say it is here in the North, after much patience, we trust the same Lord who hath framed our minds in our actings, is with us in this also. And this contrary to a natural tendency, and to those comforts our hearts could wish to enjoy with others. And the difficulties probably to be encountered with, and the enemies, not few, even all that is glorious in this world, with appearance of united names, titles and authorities, and yet not terrified, only desiring to fear our great God, that we do nothing against His will. Truly this is our condition.

And to conclude. We in this Northern Army were in a waiting posture, desiring to see what the Lord would lead us to.

> *On December 6, 1648, a Colonel Pride "purged" Parliament of all the members opposed to the army's policies. The surviving remnant then enacted the following decree.*

Declaration of the Supremacy of Parliament

(RESOLVED) That the commons of England, in parliament assembled, do declare that the people are, under God, the original of all just power. And do also declare, that the commons of England, in parliament assembled, being chosen by and representing the people have the supreme power in this nation. And do also declare, that whatsoever is enacted, or declared for law, by the commons in parliament assembled, hath the force of a law; and all the people of this nation are concluded thereby, although the consent of king, or house of peers, be not had thereunto.

> *This decree was followed by an act creating a high court of justice to try the king. The act was passed by the Commons but not by the Lords.*

Act Erecting a High Court of Justice for the King's Trial

WHEREAS IT IS NOTORIOUS that Charles Stuart, the now King of England, not content with the many encroachments which his predecessors had made upon the people in their rights and freedom, hath had a wicked design totally to subvert the ancient and fundamental laws and liberties of this nation, and in their place to introduce an arbitrary and tyrannical govern-

---

W. Cobbett, *Parliamentary History of England*, III (1808), column 1257.

S. R. Gardiner, *The Constitutional Documents of the Puritan Revolution* (2nd ed., 1899), pp. 357–8. Reprinted by permission of The Clarendon Press, Oxford.

ment, and that besides all other evil ways and means to bring his design to pass, he hath prosecuted it with fire and sword, levied and maintained a civil war in the land, against the Parliament and kingdom; whereby this country hath been miserably wasted, the public treasure exhausted, trade decayed, thousands of people murdered, and infinite other mischiefs committed; for all which high and treasonable offences the said Charles Stuart might long since have justly been brought to exemplary and condign punishment: whereas also the Parliament, well hoping that the restraint and imprisonment of his person, after it had pleased God to deliver him into their hands, would have quieted the distempers of the kingdom, did forbear to proceed judicially against him, but found, by sad experience, that such their remissness served only to encourage him and his accomplices in the continuance of their evil practices, and in raising new commotions, rebellions and invasions: for prevention therefore of the like or greater inconveniences, and to the end no Chief Officer or Magistrate whatsoever may hereafter presume, traitorously and maliciously, to imagine or contrive the enslaving or destroying of the English nation, and to expect impunity for so doing; be it enacted and ordained by the [Lords] and Commons in Parliament assembled, and it is hereby enacted and ordained by the authority thereof, that the Earls of Kent, Nottingham, Pembroke, Denbigh and Mulgrave, the Lord Grey of Wark, Lord Chief Justice Rolle of the King's Bench, Lord Chief Justice St. John of the Common Pleas, and Lord Chief Baron Wylde, the Lord Fairfax, Lieutenant-General Cromwell, &c. [in all about 150], shall be and are hereby appointed and required to be Commissioners and Judges for the hearing, trying and judging of the said Charles Stuart.

> *Charles was not permitted to speak at his trial. He said at that time: "I am not suffered to speak. Expect what justice other people will have." On the scaffold he gave a last defense of his reign.*

Charles I's Defense of His Reign

I THINK IT IS MY DUTY, to God first, and to my country, for to clear myself both as an honest man, a good king, and a good Christian.

I shall begin first with my innocence. In truth I think it not very needful for me to insist long upon this, for all the world knows that I never did begin a war with the two Houses of Parliament; and I call God to witness, to whom I must shortly make an account, that I never did intend to incroach

England's Black Tribunal (5th ed., 1720), pp. 43–6.

upon their privileges. They began upon me. It was the Militia they began upon. They confessed that the Militia was mine but they thought it fit to have it from me. . . . So that the guilt of these enormous crimes that are laid against me, I hope in God that God will clear me of it. I will not (I am in charity) God forbid that I should lay it upon the two Houses of Parliament. There is no necessity of either. I hope that they are free of this guilt, for I do believe that ill instruments between them and me have been the chief cause of all this bloodshed. . . . I will only say this, that an unjust sentence that I suffered to take effect [*i.e., the execution of Strafford—B. T.*] is punished now by an unjust sentence upon me. That is, so far as I have said, to show you that I am an innocent man.

Now for to show you that I am a good Christian. I hope there is a good man that will bear me witness that I have forgiven all the world, and even those in particular that have been the chief causes of my death. Who they are God knows. I do not desire to know. I pray God forgive them. But this is not all. My charity must go further. I wish that they may repent, for indeed they have committed a great sin in that particular. I pray God, with St. Stephen, that this be not laid to their charge; nay, not only so, but that they may take the right way to the peace of the kingdom, for my charity commands me, not only to forgive particular men, but my charity commands me to endeavor to the last gasp the peace of the kingdom. . . .

[As] for the people—truly I desire their liberty and freedom as much as anybody whosoever. But I must tell you that their liberty and freedom consists in having of government those laws by which their lives and goods may be most their own. It is not for having share in government. That is nothing pertaining to them. A subject and a sovereign are clean different things, and therefore, until they do that—I mean that you do put the people in that liberty as I say—certainly they will never enjoy themselves.

Sirs, it was for this that now I am come here. If I would have given way to an arbitrary way, for to have all laws changed according to the power of the sword, I needed not to have come here. And therefore I tell you (and I pray God it be not laid to your charge) that I am the matyr of the people.

Act Declaring England To Be a Commonwealth, 1649

BE IT DECLARED and enacted by this present Parliament, and by the authority of the same, that the people of England, and of all the dominions and territories thereunto belonging, are and shall be, and are hereby consti-

---

S. R. Gardiner, *The Constitutional Documents of the Puritan Revolution* (2nd ed., 1899), p. 388. Reprinted by permission of The Clarendon Press, Oxford.

tuted, made, established, and confirmed, to be a Commonwealth and Free State, and shall from henceforth be governed as a Commonwealth and Free State by the supreme authority of this nation, the representatives of the people in Parliament, and by such as they shall appoint and constitute as officers and ministers under them for the good of the people, and that without any King or House of Lords.

> *Cromwell finally dismissed the surviving "rump" of Parliament in 1653 in the following fashion.*

Oliver Cromwell's Dismissal of the Rump Parliament

CALLING TO MAJOR-GENERAL HARRISON, who was on the other side of the House, to come to him, he told him, that he judged the Parliament ripe for a dissolution, and this to be the time of doing it. The Major-General answered, as he since told me; "Sir, the work is very great and dangerous, therefore I desire you seriously to consider of it before you engage in it." "You say well," replied the General, and thereupon sat still for about a quarter of an hour; and then the question for passing the Bill being to be put, he said again to Major-General Harrison, "this is the time I must do it;" and suddenly standing up, made a speech, wherein he loaded the Parliament with the vilest reproaches, charging them not to have a heart to do any thing for the publick good, to have espoused the corrupt interest of Presbytery and the lawyers, who were the supporters of tyranny and oppression, accusing them of an intention to perpetuate themselves in power, had they not been forced to the passing of this Act, which he affirmed they designed never to observe, and thereupon told them, that the Lord had done with them, and had chosen other instruments for the carrying on his work that were more worthy. This he spoke with so much passion and discomposure of mind, as if he had been distracted. Sir Peter Wentworth stood up to answer him, and said, that this was the first time that ever he had heard such unbecoming language given to the Parliament, and that it was the more horrid in that it came from their servant, and their servant whom they had so highly trusted and obliged: but as he was going on, the General stept into the midst of the House, where continuing his distracted language, he said, "Come, come, I will put an end to your prating;" then walking up and down the House like a mad-man, and kicking the ground with his feet, he cried out, "You are no Parliament, I say you are no Parliament; I will put an end to your sitting; call them in, call

C. H. Firth, ed., *The Memoirs of Edmund Ludlow*, I (1894), 352–4. Reprinted by permission of The Clarendon Press, Oxford.

them in:" whereupon the serjeant attending the Parliament opened the doors, and Lieutenant-Colonel Worsley with two files of musqueteers entered the House; which Sir Henry Vane observing from his place, said aloud, "This is not honest, yea it is against morality and common honesty." Then Cromwell fell a railing at him, crying out with a loud voice, "O Sir Henry Vane, Sir Henry Vane, the Lord deliver me from Sir Henry Vane." Then looking upon one of the members, he said, "There sits a drunkard;" and giving much reviling language to others, he commanded the mace to be taken away, saying, "What shall we do with this bauble? here, take it away." Having brought all into this disorder, Major-General Harrison went to the Speaker as he sat in the chair, and told him, that seeing things were reduced to this pass, it would not be convenient for him to remain there. The Speaker answered, that he would not come down unless he were forced. "Sir," said Harrison, "I will lend you my hand;" and thereupon putting his hand within his, the Speaker came down. Then Cromwell applied himself to the members of the House, who were in number between 80 and 100, and said to them, "It's you that have forced me to this, for I have sought the Lord night and day, that he would rather slay me than put me upon the doing of this work."

> *Six years of army rule made most Englishmen long for a restoration of monarchy. Charles II smoothed the way for his return to the throne by issuing the following declaration.*

Declaration of Breda

WE DO MAKE IT our daily suit to the Divine Providence, that He will, in compassion to us and our subjects, after so long misery and sufferings, remit and put us into a quiet and peaceful possession of that our right, with as little blood and damage to our people as is possible; nor do we desire more to enjoy what is ours, than that all our subjects may enjoy what by law is theirs, by a full and entire administration of justice throughout the land, and by extending our mercy where it is wanted and deserved.

And to the end that the fear of punishment may not engage any, conscious to themselves of what is past, to a perseverance in guilt for the future, by opposing the quiet and happiness of their country, in the restora-

S. R. Gardiner, *The Constitutional Documents of the Puritan Revolution* (2nd ed., 1899), pp. 465–6. Reprinted by permission of The Clarendon Press, Oxford.

tion of King, Peers and people to their just, ancient and fundamental rights, we do, by these presents, declare, that we do grant a free and general pardon, which we are ready, upon demand, to pass under our Great Seal of England, to all our subjects, of what degree or quality soever, who, within forty days after the publishing hereof, shall lay hold upon this our grace and favour, and shall, by any public act, declare their doing so, and that they return to the loyalty and obedience of good subjects; excepting only such persons as shall hereafter be excepted by Parliament, those only to be excepted. . . .

And because the passion and uncharitableness of the times have produced several opinions in religion, by which men are engaged in parties and animosities against each other (which, when they shall hereafter unite in a freedom of conversation, will be composed or better understood), we do declare a liberty to tender consciences, and that no man shall be disquieted or called in question for differences of opinion in matter of religion, which do not disturb the peace of the kingdom; and that we shall be ready to consent to such an Act of Parliament, as, upon mature deliberation, shall be offered to us, for the full granting that indulgence.

And because, in the continued distractions of so many years, and so many and great revolutions, many grants and purchases of estates have been made to and by many officers, soldiers and others, who are now possessed of the same, and who may be liable to actions at law upon several titles, we are likewise willing that all such differences, and all things relating to such grants, sales and purchases, shall be determined in Parliament, which can best provide for the just satisfaction of all men who are concerned.

And we do further declare, that we will be ready to consent to any Act or Acts of Parliament to the purposes aforesaid, and for the full satisfaction of all arrears due to the officers and soldiers of the army under the command of General Monk; and that they shall be received into our service upon as good pay and conditions as they now enjoy.

6   The Case for the King

FROM *Charles King of England 1600–1637*
BY ESMÉ WINGFIELD-STRATFORD

IT WAS NOW [*1629—B. T.*] just upon four years since King Charles had come to the throne, years of continued difficulty and frustration, that had brought him to a pass unprecedented in the history of English monarchy. For now one tremendous fact stared him in the face: Parliamentary government had broken down; had become, for the time being, impossible, from the standpoint of a monarch who aspired to govern as well as to reign.

That riot in the House had been enough to prove that under such leadership as Eliot's, there were no lengths to which the Commons could not be driven along the path to revolution. Not content with openly defying the King's authority, they were capable of inciting his subjects in general to set in at naught—nay more, of actually intimidating them into doing so. They were determined to take all before giving him anything; to destroy everyone on whom he leaned, or on whose loyalty he could count, in Church or State; to strip him of the barest minimum of necessary revenue; and to leave him as abject a puppet as Richard II had been in the days of the Merciless Parliament, or Henry III when he was the crowned captive of Simon de Montfort.

It is therefore misleading to talk as if, after that memorable scene which closed the career of his third Parliament, Charles had formed some novel and sinister design of governing without Parliament. Humanly speaking, he had no choice in the matter. He had to do so if he was to govern at all and the only question was—how to do it?

*   *   *

It is odd that even so prejudiced an historian as John Richard Green should have chosen to describe this period in a section of his famous *Short History* entitled *The Tyranny*. The idea of setting up a despotism on the Continental model had never entered Charles's mind. It was Parliament and not he that had been trying to upset the balance of the Constitution. There

Esmé Wingfield-Stratford, *Charles King of England 1600–1637* (1949), pp 241, 245–6, 318–22. Reprinted by permission of The Bodley Head Ltd., London, and Christy & Moore Ltd., London.

was nothing in the law or practice of that Constitution to compel him to summon Parliament before he needed its help. If he could carry on without it—so much the better for the Taxpayer!

Meanwhile the law, stiffened up as it had recently been against the Crown, remained supreme, and the King had not the power, even if he had the will, to set it at defiance. For unlike the real tyrants overseas, he had practically no armed force to back him. The handful of royal guards would not have been equal to defending his royal person against a really determined mob. Thus the King was compelled to govern with at least the passive acquiescence of a people, who certainly would not have endured any flagrant assertion of arbitrary power.

*   *   *

All that it is essential to know about the affair of ship-money, and Hampden's part in it, can be briefly set down.

Let us remember that the object of King Charles's government was to tide over a situation in which it was only too plain that to summon a Parliament would be to open the flood gates of revolution. The policy of which Wentworth and Laud were to become the two leading exponents, was to observe the strictest bounds of constitutional propriety, narrowed as these were by the Petition of Right; to scrape along on the peace-time income of the Crown without resort to taxation; to withdraw from any attempt to interfere in the politics of the Continent; and to devote all the energy and resources available to building up such a Utopia of ordered prosperity as would in time cause the revolutionary fires to die from lack of fuel, and enable the normal course of Parliamentary government to be resumed in an atmosphere of loyal co-operation between King, Church, Parliament, and people.

Now Hampden, who was an enormously wealthy multiple estate owner, was among those who were determined at all costs to upset this programme.

Sooner or later the Thorough plan, if it were allowed to go through smoothly, would revolutionize the situation the wrong way. You could not go on indefinitely playing propaganda against prosperity. Sooner or later the people would discover that they were well off, and that life under King Charles, without war, without taxes, and without want, was the sort of life that the common Englishman would like to prolong indefinitely. And even the 160,000 or so who constituted the entire electorate, might come round sufficiently to this point of view to return a majority willing to carry on with the existing Constitution.

But that time had not come yet, and the King's position was one of the utmost precariousness. For one thing, the necessity of realizing the last farthing of an income that largely consisted of petty and antiquated calls on the resources of the wealthy, made the government extremely unpopular with just that class which alone could have been said, in any intelligible sense

of the word, to be represented in Parliament. And again, the King's isolation-
ist and pacifist foreign policy, though in the long run it might come to be
reckoned as the most priceless boon ever conferred by any English Sovereign
on his people and their posterity, was not of the sort to appeal to a public
opinion inflamed with ideologist propaganda, and demanding a firm line
and decisive intervention on behalf of God's, and the Prince Palatine's cause,
without counting the cost. And there was a third factor of weakness, in the
personnel of the government itself. The King and his ministers were weakest
just where Pym and his friends were strongest, in the now indispensable art
of propaganda. They could confer benefits much more easily than advertise
them. Neither King Charles, with his tongue-tied dignity, nor Wentworth,
with his thunder-charged brow and explosive temper, nor the little, bustling,
rather old-maidish Archbishop Laud, could be described as competent adver-
tisers of their own goods. No doubt, in course of time, the goods might be
trusted to advertise themselves; but he who waits for that time, as any slick
salesman will tell you, will be in danger of missing his market.

To bring down the King, then, it was necessary to act with the least
possible delay, in order to catch him at a disadvantage that would grow
steadily less the longer time he had for his policy to develop. The best thing
of all would be for him to get involved in war—but to count on this would
be wishful thinking. But what if he could be compelled, with his resources
already strained to breaking point, to foot some extra item of expenditure
that his income would not cover? That—in his extremely delicate position of
the moment—would be just enough to do the trick.

It was only to be expected that Charles's difficulties with the navy should
have presented themselves, to the conspirators, as a golden opportunity for
upsetting that precarious equilibrium between income and expenditure, that
alone enabled him, from year to year, to stave off the revolution that they
were engineering. That they were in the least affected by urgency of the need
for ships, or sympathetic with His Majesty's efforts to meet it, there is no
reason to believe. If he wanted to police the seas, let him come to Parliament
with his crown in his hand, and hear what conditions Parliament was going
to exact for his privilege of performing the most elementary duty to his
subjects. Verily he should not come out thence till he had parted with its
uttermost jewel! That he should find means, legal or otherwise, of escaping
from this dilemma, was sheer tyranny; it was not to be borne!

All that was needed was for some champion to come forward and bring
this new grievance into the light of fullest publicity, by challenging the
legality of ship-money in the courts.

*   *   *

Hampden was selected, possibly because he was known to be excellently
versed in the law; and he chose to resist an assessment of twenty shillings on
one of his many estates. As money was no object to him, he was able to brief

the most eloquent counsel at the Bar, including one of his own group, Oliver St John, who, though of a saturnine and jaundiced disposition, rose magnificently to the occasion. And Hampden displayed his strategic insight in fighting the case, not on the obvious legal ground of the difference between maritime and inland districts, but on the King's right to make the levy at all, except with Parliamentary sanction. In view of the fact that the judges had already certified, by an overwhelming majority, the legality of ship-money, he could hardly have hoped to win. But he could obtain such nation-wide publicity for the opposition propaganda as had not been possible since the doors at Westminster had been locked.

He succeeded probably beyond his expectations. The case came on early in November, 1637, and was argued by counsel till within a week of Christmas. So well had St John, and his colleague, Holborn, done their work, that even the Barons of the Exchequer were sufficiently impressed with the importance of the issue at stake to insist on referring its decision to the entire body of judges. It was not until the following June that all their opinions were collected, and this time the majority for the Crown was no longer 10 to 2, but a bare 7 to 5. Hampden had had a rare piece of luck, in the fact that two of their Lordships had decided the matter for him on technical grounds that had nothing to do with the main contention. The fact that legal technicalities could be strained in this way against the Crown, at least shows how fair, according to their lights, the judges endeavoured to be. To put it mildly, this is not the sort of thing one expects during a tyranny. . . .

Charles had thus got the decision he wanted, and got it fairly enough. But it was one of those victories whose fruits are reaped by the vanquished. The King's zeal for the navy was likely to prove his undoing. Ship-money might be legal, but it had now been advertised throughout the length and breadth of the country as another grievance of grievances.

It was the most fatal time such a thing could have happened. For now clouds of war and rebellion had begun to darken the Northern sky, and the King would have need of all his prestige, and all the loyalty of his subjects, if he were not to be swept off his feet by the plainly impending storm.

FROM *King Charles and King Pym 1637–1643*
BY ESMÉ WINGFIELD-STRATFORD

WHEN THE BELLS of the London steeples were heard ringing in the year 1642, the same thought must surely have come to the mind of every hearer.

Esmé Wingfield-Stratford, *King Charles and King Pym 1637–1643* (1949), pp. 260–70. Reprinted by permission of The Bodley Head Ltd., London, and Christy & Moore Ltd., London.

Long before the end of the year England would again, as in that unforgotten time of troubles when White Rose had contended with Red, be a house divided against itself—a self-created shambles. It was the horror of all others that had been most deeply seared into the English soul. Even Pym, in his lodgings at Westminster, must have regarded the prospect with apprehension. Nature had not made him a man of war, nor even a man of blood; he would no doubt have far preferred to arrive at his goal in what he himself would have described as a Parliamentary way. But having once set his face towards it, neither remorse nor scruple would turn him aside. Though the steeples themselves should be silenced, he at least would see this year out with his head on.

Meanwhile in Whitehall, with its improvised guard house and its informal garrison, King Charles must have been listening to the same sounds with an even keener anxiety, in proportion as he lacked his rival's unimaginative toughness of fibre. To him, with his almost feminine horror of violence, the prospect of civil war must have been more bitter than that of death itself, of which he was never to show the least fear. But in these last months he had come to realize that for him too the die was cast. Nothing of all that he had conceded, nothing that he ever could concede short of the trust that he held for his people, could satisfy these few who were banded together to make their will law for the rest of the community.

And yet it would seem that in the dawn of their New Year, he could not abandon all hope of finding some honourable means of averting this unthinkable catastrophe—a solution by reason and conciliation and not by the sword. That such thoughts must have been passing through his mind is clear from the fact that he chose that very day for making one last desperate effort to give his enemies all that they demanded of him short of the actual overthrow of the Constitution. For the last time he offered to govern the realm through a ministry of their own choice and composition—a Pym ministry.

Of the form in which this offer was made, we are even more in the dark than we are about the two previous occasions, but that it *was* made seems beyond all reasonable doubt, and it is equally certain that Pym turned it down out of hand. We can well believe that his suspicious mind scented a trap in the invitation to take up an office from which his Sovereign retained the right to dismiss him at will. And in any case, it seems certain that he and his friends were now determined to go through to the last item with their programme of revolution, which envisaged a perpetual government in control of a perpetual Parliament. And Pym, conscious of the trump card that he had been keeping all this time up his sleeve and was now ready to produce, can have been in no mood for compromise. Why—we can imagine him putting it to himself—walk into the King's trap, when the jaws of his own trap were ready to close on the King?

Did the King realize what Pym was about to spring on him? And did Pym divine that he realized it? In the light of subsequent events the overwhelming probability would seem to be that they did, both of them. [*The following day Charles appointed three leaders of the moderate party in Parliament to his government.—B. T.*]

*   *   *

This prompt action of the King was none the less calculated to infuriate the revolutionaries, from its having been the result of their own refusal to take office. Instead of the surrender to which they had meant to drive him, he had gone quietly ahead and challenged them, by implication, to do their worst. And he must have known them well enough, by now, to realize that the challenge would be accepted.

Some days must needs elapse before the two new ministers, who were quite without administrative experience, would be ready to take over their departments, and by that time the whole face of the situation was destined to be transformed. For on Monday, the third day of the year, the Attorney General, Sir Edward Herbert, appeared before the Lords, to present, in the King's name, articles of impeachment for treason against Pym, Hampden, and three others of the extremist stalwarts in the Commons, Haslerigg, Denzil Holles, and Strode, as well as one of the Peers, Lord Kimbolton. . . .

It was an amazing and, to those not in the secret, must have seemed an unaccountable move. It is certain that the King's new advisers had had no part in it, and they can hardly have failed to regard it with consternation, since they must have realized to what an extent it was calculated to frustrate all their efforts, and to give the game, in which their Constitutional party had built up for itself a position of winning advantage, into the hands of Pym and his extremists. But the fact that none of the trio, not even Falkland, did what might have seemed the obvious thing, and retired from the service of a master who had to all appearance let them down so hopelessly, suggests that they may have had a more discerning insight into his motives than that of the conventional version in which he figures as a crowned villain plotting to establish his absolute power by eliminating the noblest champions of his peoples' liberties. The truth was not so crudely melodramatic.

Not improbably the person who was least surprised at the news, was Pym himself, who must have felt all the satisfaction of a chess player who has forced his opponent to make a fatal move. Paradoxical as it may seem to characterize him as the prime mover in getting himself arraigned by the highest legal authority in the land on the most heinous charge known to the law, we have only to regard the matter from what must have been his standpoint, to realize that this offered him his only way of escape from otherwise practically certain ruin. He had committed himself to destroying the King, and the King had entrenched himself in a constitutional position from which, so long as he sat quiet, there appeared to be no means of dislodging him, before the not distant date when the forces gathering to his support had rendered him strong enough to turn the tables on his assailants.

It had come to this. The only person who could defeat the King now was the King himself. Once let him quit his secure defensive to launch out with some premature counter-stroke, and the revolutionary forces in the field, with public opinion rallied to their support, would have him at a fatal disadvantage. It is true that the King had hitherto not shown the faintest disposition to oblige his enemies in this way, and that with Hyde at his elbow, he would be even less likely to do so now. But what if his hand could be forced? What if means could be found of compelling him at the last moment to throw patience to the winds, and to rush, with suicidal precipitation, into the trap prepared for him?

Anyone who had followed Pym's strategy up to this point would have seen that such a design was its necessary culmination. For it had been his invariable principle to repeat every once successful manoeuvre as nearly as possible to pattern when the next opportunity occurred. The former great royal surrender he had forced by bringing all his pressure to bear on the King's most vulnerable point, which was constituted by his love for the Queen. In the even more difficult and delicate operation he had now to perform, Pym could not fail to exploit the same weakness. He would force the King to move, by a threat to the Queen. He would confront his opponent with the choice between attacking him, and sacrificing her. Or what was equally to the purpose, bluff him into thinking so.

*   *   *

For months he had waged a war of nerves against her, and through her, against her husband. He had played cat and mouse with her. Every time she had tried to escape, even for a respite, out of his invisible clutches, she had been drawn back with just sufficient firmness. Her feelings had been played upon with that gentle skill which modern progress has prescribed for its technique of the Third Degree. Her love for her children, her sympathy for her persecuted co-religionists, her sensitiveness to calumny—never for one moment had she been allowed the least respite from a menace that was all the more nerve-racking from the fact of its always lurking just out of sight behind the forms of fulsomeness and loyalty. Meanwhile opinion in the country was being exacerbated against her in every conceivable way—the ordinary man was being conditioned to associate her with Army plots, Popish plots, and now with the monstrous libel of having been accessory, before the fact, to all the horrors of the Irish rebellion.

*   *   *

On the last day of the year, a Friday, it had been proposed that a committee of the Commons should sit over the week-end behind closed doors in the city Guild Hall, to deliberate over the safety of the Kingdom. What lay behind this may be gathered from the coded report of the Venetian Ambassador:

"These persons, supplied with arms, proceeded publicly to the destined place, giving every one the impression that there was a plot againt the liberty of Parliament. By this device they redeemed their credit generally and won back the affection of ignorant people. Shut up there in long secret discussions, they persuaded themselves that the King's action [in appointing a guard for the palace] and his resentment were due to the advice of the Queen. Accordingly they decided to accuse her in Parliament of conspiring against the public liberty, and of secret intelligence of the rebellion in Ireland. When their Majesties learned this they decided to put aside all dissimulation, and denounce to the Lower House as guilty of high treason five members of the Lower Chamber and one of the Upper, of the most powerful and factious individuals."

Even if we did not know, specifically, that the committee was open to any member who liked to attend, it is incredible that intelligence of its dire intent can have failed to get through to the King almost at once. Nor can we doubt that this was just what Mr Pym wanted, since such a master in the arts of concealment would never have chosen this theatrical way of wrapping up his bombshell unless he had meant to advertise it. And that such warning was conveyed to the King, probably on Friday night, may be inferred from his desperate last minute attempt to come to terms with Pym on the Saturday, and the energy with which he acted on the two following days.

For the thing that of all others he must have feared was now upon him, and to his troubled conscience it may well have seemed the Nemesis of Strafford. For it had been his love for the Queen, and assuredly no fear for either his life or his Crown, that had induced him to make that fatal compromise with his honour. And his mind may have travelled back to that other failure of his from which it had all started; when at his urgent request, Strafford had come up to London to confront the then all-powerful Parliamentary leaders with the proofs of their own treason; and how he, Charles, had by his failure to appreciate the urgency of the situation, succeeded in delaying his minister's stroke for just the few hours required to enable Pym to get in with his framed up impeachment, and thus keep out of court and publicity the evidence of the real treason that would have branded its perpetrators with a stigma as ineffaceable as that of Guy Fawkes.

And now the same hand that had struck down his friend was lifted to strike down his wife. Behind those doors at the Guild Hall another charge of treason was being framed up. Parliament was resuming its sittings on Monday, and Pym was not the man to let the grass grow under his feet. At any moment he might be expected to rise in his place to read out the list of charges, drawn up with all his proved skill in denigration; and then the Sergeant at Arms, followed by the trained bands, would arrive at the palace, to conduct her through the insults of the mob away from him and her children, to eat her heart out in some gloomy chamber of the Tower until she

left it to mingle her dust with that of two other Queens of England beneath
the floor of St Peter's Chapel.

On the previous occasion it had been through no disloyalty that he had
failed Strafford. He had not realized—and who has to this day!—what sort
of an opponent, in Pym, he had had to deal with. But if he were to fail again
in the same circumstances and through a similar hesitation to grasp the
nettle—what excuse could he plead? This time there should be not a second's
delay in getting the true charge brought home to the real traitors. So he must
have thought; and so Mr Pym must have known, and counted on his
thinking.

But *were* the circumstances the same? Are they ever, in life? There was
one difference that the King may have failed to notice. Last time, Pym had
taken very good care that his victim should not have the least warning of
what was in store for him till the moment of his arrest. This time he
positively went out of his way to warn him in advance—all the more by that
ostentatious make-believe of secrecy. Pym was not likely to act in this way
without some sufficient motive.

If Charles had been playing political chess with the same cold calculation
as his opponent, it might have occurred to him that just because the threat to
the Queen was being made with such ostentation, it was his game to ignore
it. But this was more a matter of the heart than of the head with him. And
that, I think, accounts for the fact that he went ahead without pausing to
take the advice of his new counsellors, who, just because of their loyalty,
would have taken a more detached view than his own. Perhaps he may have
divined, in his innermost soul, the sort of advice he would have received
from Hyde:

"Have no fear, Sir. Pym is desperate, and you can safely dare him to do
his worst. It is to the last degree unlikely that he will go to the length of
moving an impeachment against Her Majesty. That he could get a majority
for it in the Commons is at least doubtful; that he could ever get the Lords to
condemn her is unthinkable. Pym is no fool. Even if he could get her as far
as the Tower, he knows that she would be safer in the care of Sir John Byron
than she would at Whitehall. And the spectacle of its Queen in distress
would rally nine tenths of the nation, in its present mood, to your support.
Be advised, Sir! Hold your hand for a very little longer and all will be well.
But give Pym the opportunity he is seeking, to transfer the issue to one of
Parliamentary privilege, and you give him the one chance he has left of
turnng the tide against you."

That would, I believe, have been not only a just appreciation, but one
that Charles, if he had felt himself free to do so, would have been the first to
endorse. A masterly restraint had been the keynote of his policy during all
these months, and now that he was just about to harvest its fruits, why
should he wish to jettison it unless it was that policy had to give way to
honour? Rather than run the slightest risk of harm to the Queen, he was
ready to forgo any advantage to himself. And the bitter repentance, that

haunted him to the scaffold, for his surrender of Strafford, had planted in him a resolve, from which he never wavered, that his loyalty even to the humblest of his followers—and how much more to the wife he adored—should be unconditional, and unswayed by prudential considerations.

And if this had not been enough to spur him to action, there was the indignation that he must have felt against these men who were striking down right and left his ministers, judges, and bishops, and were now preparing to strike down his Consort, on charges of treason so impudently unsubstantiated that an impeachment had come to signify, in effect, a proscription for loyalty. Whereas they themselves . . .

But let us examine the charges one by one on which he had directed Sir Edward Herbert to proceed against them.

1. *That they have traitorously endeavoured to subvert the fundamental laws and government of this Kingdom; and deprive the King of his regal power; and place his subjects under an arbitrary and tyrannical power.*

A more modestly worded, or historically correct, description of the aims unswervingly held by Pym and his associates, from the days of the Providence Island Company and their Broughton Castle caballing to those of the plot against the Queen, it would be hard, even now, to frame.

2. *That they have endeavoured, by many foul aspersions upon His Majesty, and his government, to alienate the affections of his people and to make His Majesty odious to them.*

Not only endeavoured, but largely succeeded, owing to Pym's consummate mastery of the arts of propaganda.

3. *That they have endeavoured to draw His Majesty's late army to disobedience to His Majesty's command and to side with them in their traitorous design.*

To what other purpose had been their endeavours to place it under the command of their own stooges, to prevent it taking the least step to oppose the invasion or interfere with the occupation of English soil, their relentless proscription of all officers suspected of disloyalty to their faction, and now their open conspiracy to wrest the control of it out of the King's hands altogether and lodge it in their own?

4. *That they have traitorously invaded, and encouraged a foreign power to invade His Majesty's Kingdom of England.*

Their most ardent supporters have not denied the substantial truth of this.

5. *That they have traitorously endeavoured to subvert the very rights and being of Parliament.*

What milder description could be applied to their Perpetual Parliament Act and the means whereby it had been jockeyed through Parliament and forced on the Crown?

6. *That . . . they have endeavoured . . . by force and terror to compel the Parliament to join with them in their traitorous designs, and to that end have actually raised and countenanced tumults against King and Parliament.*

Notoriously and consistently, and Pym had recently gone out of his way openly to applaud and justify such tumults.

7. *That they have traitorously conspired to levy and actually have levied, war against the King.*

By foreign invasion, by terror of the mob, and now—though it had not yet got beyond the stage of conspiracy—by civil war.

I have set down the terms of this brief indictment in order to show that every item of it is as indisputable a statement of historical fact as that England was conquered in 1066, or that Queen Anne died in 1714. Nor are they, in point of fact, any more disputed, the invariable line of justification being that even if these things were done, provided they were done by men like John Hampden against a King like Charles Stuart, they *must* be justified, and that to count them as treason is one of those things that are not done. But even so, it seems a little hard on the King to blame him for being too biased to have anticipated this convenient standpoint.

The Absolutism of Louis XIV—
The End of Anarchy
or the Beginning of
Tyranny?

CONTENTS

QUESTIONS FOR STUDY

1   In what ways does Bossuet's king differ from the medieval king?

2   How does Bossuet define absolutism?

3   How successful did Louis XIV think his absolute rule had been?

4   How well did absolutism work?

5   What did absolutism in France accomplish?

6   In your opinion, was absolutism as practiced by Louis XIV a good thing for France?

The seventeenth century witnessed the acceleration of political change throughout Europe. In France, the temporary peace created by Henri IV and continued by Richelieu was constantly threatened by religious passions and the nobility. When Louis XIV assumed the full royal power at the age of 21 in 1661, he was determined to create a state obedient solely to him. He was to be the absolute ruler of France. If this were to be accomplished, two things had to be done; the old medieval theory of kingship had to be supplanted by one that granted absolute power to the king, and the king had to carry this theory into practice by means of the royal administration. Only in this way could the disorders bordering on anarchy, which had wracked France for a century, be removed. Only when the king ordered and the realm obeyed instantly would the full potential of France be realized. The problem was to achieve such obedience in the face of local traditions, laws, and customs, not to mention the recalcitrance of the aristocracy. Or, to put it another way—how effective, absolute, and beneficial to France was the absolutism of Louis XIV?

1 The France of Louis XIV— A Brief Perspective

FROM *A History of the Modern World*
BY R. R. PALMER

THE DEVELOPMENT OF ABSOLUTISM IN FRANCE

THIS ASCENDANCY OF FRENCH CULTURE went along with a regime in which political liberties were at a discount. It was an embellishment to the absolute monarchy of Louis XIV. France had a tradition of political freedom in the feudal sense. It had the same kind of background of feudal liberties as did the other countries of Europe. It had an Estates-General, which had not met since 1615 but was not legally abolished. In some regions Provincial Estates, still meeting frequently, retained a measure of self-government and of power over taxation. There were about a dozen bodies known as parliaments, which, unlike the English Parliament, had developed as courts of law, each being the supreme court for a certain area of the country. The parliaments upheld certain "fundamental laws" which they said the king could not overstep, and they often refused to enforce royal edicts which they declared to be unconstitutional. We have already observed how France, beneath the surface, was almost as composite as Germany. French towns had won charters of acknowledged rights, and many of the great provinces enjoyed liberties written into old agreements with the Crown. These local liberties were the main reason for a good deal of institutional complication. There were some three hundred "customs" or regional systems of law; it was observed that a traveller sometimes changed laws more often than he changed horses. Internal tariffs ran along the old provincial borders. Tolls were levied by manorial lords. The king's taxes fell less heavily on some regions than on others. Neither coinage nor weights and measures were uniform throughout the country. France was a bundle of territories held together by allegiance to the king.

This older kind of freedom discredited itself in France at the very time when by triumphing in Germany it pulled the Holy Roman Empire to

Reprinted by permission of the publisher from *A History of the Modern World*, pp. 156–63, by R. R. Palmer. Copyright, 1950, 1956, 1964, by Alfred A. Knopf, Inc.

pieces, and when in England it successfully made the transition to a more modern form of political liberty, embodied in the Parliamentary though aristocratic state. In France the old medieval, feudal or local type of liberty became associated with disorder. It has already been related how after the disorders of the sixteenth-century religious wars people had turned with relief to the monarchy and how Henry IV and then Richelieu had begun to make the monarchy strong. The troubles of the Fronde provided additional incentive for absolutism in France.

The Fronde broke out immediately after the Peace of Westphalia, while Louis XIV was still a child, and was directed against Cardinal Mazarin, who was governing in his name. It was an abortive revolution, led by the same elements, the parliaments and the nobility, which were to precipitate the great French Revolution in 1789. The parliaments, especially the Parliament of Paris, insisted in 1648 on their right to pronounce certain edicts unconstitutional. Barricades were thrown up and street fighting broke out in Paris. The nobility rebelled, as often in the past. Leadership was assumed by certain prominent noblemen who, roughly like the great Whigs of England, had enough wealth and influence to believe that, if the king's power were kept down, they might govern the country themselves. The nobility demanded a calling of the Estates-General, expecting to dominate over the bourgeoisie and the clergy in that body. Armed bands of soldiers, unemployed since the Peace of Westphalia and led by nobles, roamed about the country terrorizing the peasants. If the nobles had their way, it was probable that the manorial system would fall on the peasants more heavily, as in Eastern Europe, where triumphant lords were at this very time exacting increased labor services from the peasants. Finally the rebellious nobles called in Spanish troops, though France was at war with Spain. By this time the bourgeoisie, represented in the parliaments, had withdrawn support from the rebellious nobles. The agitation subsided in total failure, because bourgeoisie and aristocracy could not work together, because the nobles outraged the loyalty of many Frenchmen by joining with a power with which France was at war, and because the *frondeurs,* especially after the parliaments deserted them, had no systematic or constructive program, aiming only at the overthrow of the unpopular Cardinal Mazarin, and at obtaining offices and favors for themselves.

After the Fronde, as after the religious wars, the bourgeoisie and peasantry of France, to protect themselves against the claims of the aristocracy, were in a mood to welcome the exercise of strong power by the kings. And in the young Louis XIV they had a man more than willing to grasp all the power he could get. Louis, on Mazarin's death in 1661, announced that he would govern the country himself. He was the third king of the Bourbon line. It was the Bourbon tradition, established by Henry IV and by Richelieu, to draw the teeth from the feudal aristocrats, and this tradition Louis XIV followed. He was not a man of any transcendent abilities, though he had the capacity, often found among successful executives, of learning a good deal from conversation with experts. His education was not very good, having been made purposely easy; but he had the ability to see and stick to definite lines of policy, and he was extremely methodical and industrious in his daily habits, scrupulously loading himself with administrative business throughout his reign. He was extremely fond of himself and his position of kingship, with an insatiable appetite for admiration and flattery; he loved magnificent display and elaborate etiquette, though to some extent he simply adopted them as instruments of policy rather than as a personal whim.

With the reign of Louis XIV the "state" in its modern form took a long step forward. The state in the abstract has always seemed theoretical to the English-speaking world. Let us say, for simplicity, that the state represents a fusion of justice and power. A sovereign state possesses, within its territory, a monopoly over the administration of justice and the use of force. Private persons neither pass legal judgments on others, nor control private armies of their own. For private and unauthorized persons to do so, in an orderly state, constitutes rebellion. This was in contrast to the older feudal practice, by which feudal lords maintained manorial courts and led their own followers into battle. Against these feudal practices Louis XIV energetically worked, though not with complete success, claiming to possess in his own person, as sovereign ruler, a monopoly over the law-making processes and the armed forces of the kingdom. This is the deeper meaning of his reputed boast, *L'état, c'est moi*—"the state is myself." In the France of the seventeenth century, divided by classes and by regions, there was in fact no means of consolidating the powers of state except in a single man.

The state, however, while representing law and order within its borders, has generally stood in a lawless and disorderly relation to other states, since no higher monopoly of law and force has existed. Louis XIV, personifying the French state, had no particular regard for the claims of other states or rulers. He was constantly either at war or preparing for war with his neighbors. The modern state, indeed, was created by the needs of peace at home and war abroad. Machinery of government, as devised by Louis XIV and others, was a means of giving order and security within the territory of the state, and of raising, supporting and controlling armies for use against other states.

The idea that law and force within a country should be monopolized by the lawful king was the essence of the seventeenth century doctrine of absolutism. Its principal theorist in the time of Louis XIV was Bishop Bossuet. Bossuet advanced the old Christian teaching that all power comes from God, and that all who hold power are responsible to God for the way they use it. He held that kings were God's representatives in the political affairs of earth. Royal power, according to Bossuet, was absolute but not arbitrary: not arbitrary because it must be reasonable and just, like the will of God which it reflected; absolute in that it was free from dictation by parliaments, estates or other subordinate elements within the country. Law, therefore, was the will of the sovereign king, so long as it conformed to the higher law which was the will of God. This doctrine, affirming the divine right of kings, was popularly held in France at the time, and was taught in the churches. It was fortified by the principles of Roman law, which also held that laws could be made and unmade, modified and amended, by act of the sovereign power. In addition, the authority of Louis XIV rested on purely practical considerations. Experience showed absolutism to be the corrective to anarchy, and the king was widely believed to represent the interests of the country better than anyone else. . . .

Possibly the most fundamental step taken by Louis XIV was to assure himself of control of the army. Armed forces had formerly been almost a private enterprise. Specialists in fighting, leading their own troops, worked for governments more or less as they chose, either in return for money or to pursue political aims of their own. This was especially common in Central Europe, but even in France great noblemen had strong private influence over the troops, and in times of disorder nobles led armed retainers about the country. Colonels were virtually on their own. Provided with a general commission and with funds by some government, they recruited, trained and equipped their own regiments, and likewise fed and supplied them, often by preying upon bourgeois and peasants in the vicinity. In these circumstances it was often difficult to say on whose side soldiers were fighting. It was hard for governments to set armies into motion, and usually hard to make them stop fighting, for commanders fought for their own interests and on their own momentum. War was not a "continuation of policy"; it was not an act of the state; it easily degenerated, as in the Thirty Years' War, into a kind of aimless and perpetual violence.

Louis XIV made war an activity of state. He saw to it that all armed persons in France fought only for him. This produced peace and order in France, while strengthening the fighting power of France against other states. Under the older conditions there was also little integration among different units and arms of the army. Infantry regiments and troops of horse went largely their own way, and the artillery was supplied by civilian technicians under contract. Louis XIV created a stronger unity of control, put the artillery organically into the army, systematized the military ranks and grades, and clarified the chain of command, placing himself at the top. The government supervised recruiting, required colonels to prove that they were maintaining the proper number of soldiers, and assumed most of the responsibility for equipping, provisioning, clothing and housing the troops. Higher officers, thus becoming dependent on the government, could be subjected to discipline. The soldiers were put into uniforms, taught to march in step, and housed in barracks; thus they too became more susceptible to discipline and control. Armed forces became less of a terror to their own people, and a more effective weapon in the hands of the government. They were employed usually against other governments, but if necessary to suppress rebellion at home. Louis XIV also increased the French army in size, raising it from about 100,000 to about 400,000. These changes, both in size and in degree of government control, were made possible by the growth of a large civilian administration. The heads of this administration under Louis XIV were civilians. They were in effect the first ministers of war, and their assistants, officials, inspectors, and clerks constituted the first organized war ministry.

Louis XIV was not only a vain man, but made it a political principle to overawe the country with his own grandeur. He built himself a whole new city at the old village of Versailles about ten miles from Paris. Where the Escorial had the atmosphere of a monastery, Versailles was a monument to worldly splendor. Tremendous in size alone, fitted out with polished mirrors, gleaming chandeliers, and magnificent tapestries, opening on to a formal park with fountains and shaded walks, the palace of Versailles was the marvel of Europe and the envy of lesser kings. It was virtually a public building, much of it used for government offices, and with nobles, churchmen, notable bourgeois, and servants milling about on the king's affairs. The more exclusive honors of the château were reserved for the higher aristocrats. The king surrounded his daily routine of rising, eating, and going to bed (known as the *lever, dîner,* and *coucher*) with an infinite series of ceremonial acts, so minute and so formalized that there were, for example, six different entries of persons at the *lever,* and a certain gentleman at a specified moment held the right sleeve of the king's nightshirt as he took it off. The most exalted persons thought themselves the greater for thus waiting on so august a being. In this way, and by more material favors, many great lords were induced to live habitually at court. Here, under the royal eye, they might engage in palace intrigue, but were kept away from real political mischief. Versailles completed the political and moral ruin of the French aristocracy as a class. The king himself was one of the few who could proceed through such rounds of elaborate living and still be able to attend regularly to public affairs. Neither the nobles whom he kept about him, nor his own successors Louis XV and Louis XVI, were able to carry the burden.

For positions in the government, as distinguished from his personal entourage, Louis XIV preferred to use men of the bourgeois class, who were dependent on him for salaries and careers, and who unlike noblemen could aspire to no independent political influence of their own. He never called the Estates-General, which in any case no one except some of the nobility wanted. Some of the Provincial Estates, because of local and aristocratic pressures, he allowed to remain functioning. He temporarily destroyed the independence of the parliaments, commanding them to accept his orders, as Henry IV had commanded them to accept the Edict of Nantes. He stifled the old liberties of the towns, turning their civic offices into empty and purchasable honors, and likewise regulating the operation of the gilds. He developed a strong system of administrative coordination, centering in a number of councils of state, which he attended in person, and in "intendants" who represented these councils throughout the country. Councillors of state and intendants were generally of bourgeois origin. Each intendant, within his district, embodied all aspects of the royal government, supervising the flow of taxes and recruiting of soldiers, keeping an eye on the local nobility, dealing with towns and gilds, controlling the more or less heriditary officeholders, stamping out bandits, smugglers and wolves, policing the market places, relieving famine, watching the local law courts and often deciding cases himself. In this way a firm and uniform administration was superimposed upon the heterogeneous mass of the old France. In contrast to England, all local questions were handled by agents of the central government, usually honest and often efficient, but essentially bureaucrats constantly instructed by, and referring back to, their superiors at Versailles.

To support the reorganized and enlarged army, the panoply of Versailles, and the growing civil administration the king needed a good deal of money. Finance was always the weak spot in the French monarchy. Methods of collecting taxes were costly and inefficient. Direct taxes passed through the hands of many intermediate officials; indirect taxes were collected by private concessionnaires called tax-farmers, who made a substantial profit. The state always received far less than what the taxpayers actually paid. But the main weakness arose from an old bargain between the French crown and nobility; the king might raise taxes without consent if only he refrained from taxing the nobles. Only the "unprivileged" classes paid direct taxes, and these came almost to mean the peasants only, since many bourgeois in one way or another obtained exemptions. The system was outrageously unjust in throwing the tax burden on the poor and helpless. It was ruinous to the government, since the government could never raise enough money, however hard it taxed the poor, being unable to tap the real source of ready wealth, namely the wealthier people. It was ruinous also to the French nobility, who in paying no direct taxes lost their hold over the government, lacked incentive to interest themselves in public affairs, and were unable to assume leadership of the bulk of the population. Louis XIV was willing enough to tax the nobles, but was unwilling to fall under their control, and only toward the close of his reign, under extreme stress of war, was he able, for the first time in French history, to impose direct taxes on the aristocratic elements of the population. This was a great step toward equality before the law and toward sound public finance, but so many concessions and exemptions were won by nobles and bourgeois that the reform lost much of its value.

Like his predecessors, Louis resorted to all manner of expedients to increase his revenues. He raised the tax-rates, always with disappointing results. He devalued the currency. He sold patents of nobility to ambitious bourgeois. He sold government offices, judgeships, and commissions in the army and navy. For both financial and political reasons the king used his sovereign authority to annul the town charters, then sell back reduced rights at a price; this produced a little income but demoralized local government and civic spirit. The need for money, arising from the fundamental inability to tax the wealthy, which in turn reflected the weakness of absolutism, of a government which would not or could not share its rule with the propertied classes, corrupted much of the public life and political aptitude of the French people.

Louis XIV wished, if only for his own purposes, to make France economically powerful. His great minister Colbert worked for twenty years to do so. Colbert went beyond Richelieu in the application of mercantilism, aiming to make France a self-sufficing economic unit and to increase the wealth from which taxes were drawn. He managed to abolish local tariffs in a large part of Central France, where he set up a tariff-union oddly entitled the Five Great Farms (since the remaining tolls were collected by tax-farmers); and although vested interests and provincial liberties remained too strong for him to do away with all internal tariffs, the area of the Five Great Farms was in itself one of the largest free-trade areas in Europe, being about the size of England. For the convenience of business men Colbert promulgated a Commercial Code, replacing much of the local customary law, and long a model of business practice and business regulation. He improved communications by building roads and canals, of which the most famous was one joining the Bay of Biscay with the Mediterranean. Working through the gilds, he required the handicraft manufacturers to produce goods of specified kind and quality, believing that foreigners, if assured of quality by the government, would purchase French products more freely. He gave subsidies, tax exemptions, and other privileges to expand the manufacture of silks, tapestries, glassware, and woollens. He helped to found colonies, built up the navy, and established the French East India Company. Export of some goods, notably foodstuffs, was forbidden, for the government wished to keep the populace quiet by holding down the price of bread. Export of other goods, mainly manufactures, was encouraged, partly as a means of bringing money into the country, where it could be funneled into the royal treasury. The growth of the army, and the fact that under Louis XIV the government clothed and equipped the soldiers, and hence placed unprecedentedly large orders for uniforms, overcoats, weapons, and ammunition, greatly stimulated the employment of weavers, tailors and gunsmiths, and advanced the commercial capitalism by which such labors were organized. In general, trade and manufacture developed in France under more direct government guidance than in England. They long gave the English an extremely brisk competition. Not until the age of iron and coal did France begin economically to lag.

2 The Theory of Absolutism

Jacques Bénigne Bossuet (1627–1704) was a bishop, popular preacher, and tutor to the Dauphin under Louis XIV. His political writings provided the most eloquent justification of the Divine Right of Kings.

FROM *Politics Drawn from the Very Words of Holy Scripture* BY J. B. BOSSUET

To His Lordship the Dauphin.

GOD IS THE KING OF KINGS: it is his place to instruct them and to regulate them as his ministers. Hence listen well, Your Lordship, to the lessons that he gives to them in his Scripture, and learn from him the rules and the examples on which they should base their conduct.

BOOK I

In order to form nations and unite peoples, it was necessary to establish a government.

PROPOSITION I

It is not enough that men live in the same country or speak the same language, because becoming unsociable by the violence of their passions, and incompatible by their different humors, they cannot act as one unless they submit themselves altogether to a single government which rules over all.

Without that, even Abraham and Lot could not get along together and were forced to separate. . . .

If Abraham and Lot, two just men who were moreover closely related, could not get along with one another because of their servants, what kind of disorder must be expected among those who are bad! . . .

Justice has no other support than authority and the subordination of powers.

J. B. Bossuet, *Politique tirée des propres paroles de l'Écriture Sainte,* I (1870), 299, 305, 306, 308, 313, 322, 325, 326, 333, 335, translated by L. Pearce Williams (citations from the Bible are taken directly from the King James Version).

It is this order which restrains license. When everyone does what he wishes and has only his own desires to regulate him, everything ends up in confusion.

*   *   *

PROPOSITION 3
It is only by the authority of the government that union is established amongst men.

The effect of this legitimate commandment is marked by these words often repeated in Scripture: to the command of Saul and of legitimate power, "all Israel obeyed as one man. They were forty thousand men, and all this multitude was as one." This is what is meant by the unity of a people, when each man renouncing his own will takes it and joins it to that of the prince and the magistrate. Otherwise there is no union; the people wander as vagabonds like a dispersed flock. . . .

*   *   *

PROPOSITION 5
By means of government each individual becomes stronger.

The reason is that each is helped. All the forces of the nation concur in one and the sovereign magistrate has the right to reunite them. . . .

Thus the sovereign magistrate has in his hand all the forces of the nation which submits itself to obedience to him. . . .

Thus, an individual is not troubled by oppression and violence because he has an invincible defender in the person of the prince and is stronger by far than all those who attempt to oppress him.

The sovereign magistrate's own interest is to preserve by force all the individuals of a nation because if any other force than his own prevails among the people his authority and his life is in peril. . . .

PROPOSITON 6
The law is sacred and inviolable.

In order to understand perfectly the nature of the law it is necessary to note that all those who have spoken well on it have regarded it in its origin as a pact and a solemn treaty by which men agree together under the authority of princes to that which is necessary to form their society.

This is not to say that the authority of the laws depends on the consent and acquiescence of the people; but only that the prince who, moreover by his very station has no other interest than that of the public good, is helped by the sagest heads in the nation and leans upon the experience of centuries gone by.

BOOK II

A monarchy is the most common, the oldest, and the most natural form of government.

The people of Israel themselves formed a monarchy as being the universally received government. "Make us a king to judge us like all the nations."

If God was annoyed it was because up to then he had governed this people by himself and that he had been their true king. This is why he said to Samuel: "They have not rejected thee but they have rejected me, that I should not reign over them."

For the rest, this government was so clearly the most natural, that it is to be found at the beginning in all peoples.

We have seen it in sacred history: but here a short look at profane histories will show us that even those who lived in republics had begun first of all under kings.

Rome started that way and finally came back to it as to its natural state.

It was only later and little by little that the Greek cities formed their republics. The old opinion of Greece was that expressed by Homer in this famous sentence in the *Iliad*: "Many princes is not a good thing: let there be only one prince and one king."

At the present time there is no republic which was not at one time subject to a monarch. The Swiss were the subjects of the princes of the house of Austria. The United Provinces have only just escaped the domination of Spain and that of the house of Burgundy. The free cities of Germany have their individual lords other than the emperor who was the common head of the entire Germanic body. The cities of Italy which turned themselves into republics at the time of the emperor Rudolf bought their liberty from him. Venice even, which so boasts of having been a republic since its founding, was yet subject to the emperors, under the reign of Charlemagne and even long after: since then she has become a popular state from which she has now only recently become the state which we see.

Everybody thus begins with a monarchy and almost everybody has retained it as being the most natural state.

We have also seen that it has its foundation and its model in the rule of the father, that is to say in nature itself.

All men are born subjects: and paternal authority which accustoms them to obey, accustoms them at the same time to have only one chief.

Monarchical government is the best.

If it is the most natural, it is consequently the most durable and from that it follows also the strongest.

It is also the most opposed to divisiveness, which is the worst evil of states, and the most certain cause of their ruin. . . . "Every kingdom divided against itself is brought to desolation; and every city or house divided against itself shall not stand."

We have seen that Our Lord in this sentence has followed the natural progress of government and seems to have wished to show to realms and to cities the same means of uniting themselves that nature has established in families.

Thus, it is natural that when families wish to unite to form a body of State, they will almost automatically coalesce into the government that is proper to them.

When states are formed there is the impulse to union and there is never more union than under a single leader. Also there is never greater strength because everything works in harmony. . . .

BOOK III

Where we begin to explain the nature and properties of royal authority.

ARTICLE I

There are four characters or qualities essential to royal authority:
First, royal authority is sacred; second, it is paternal; third, it is absolute; fourth, it is ruled by reason. . . .

ARTICLE II

Royal authority is sacred.

PROPOSITION I

God established kings as his ministers and rules peoples by them.

We have already seen that all power comes from God. "The prince," St. Paul adds, "is the minister of God to thee for good. But if thou do that which is evil, be afraid; for he beareth not the sword in vain; for he is the minister of God, a revenger to execute wrath upon him that doeth evil."

Thus princes act as ministers of God, and as his lieutenants on earth. It is by them that he exercises his rule. . . .

Thus we have seen that the royal throne is not the throne of a man, but the throne of God himself. . . .

He thus governs all peoples and gives to them all their kings; even though he governs Israel in a more particular and more explicit way. . . .

PROPOSITON 2

The person of kings is sacred.

It thus appears that the person of kings is sacred and that to make an attempt on their lives is a sacrilege.

God has had them anointed by his prophets with a sacred unction as he has his pontiffs and his altars anointed.

But without the external application of this unction, they are sacred by their office, as being the representatives of the divine majesty, deputized by his providence to the execution of his designs. . . .

The title of Christ is given to kings; and they are everywhere called christs, or the anointed of the lord.

ARTICLE 3

Royal authority is paternal and its proper character is goodness.

After what has been said, this truth has no need of proof.

We have seen that kings take the place of God, who is the true father of the human species. We have also seen that the first idea of power which exists among men is that of the paternal power; and that kings are modeled on fathers.

Everybody is also in accord, that the obedience which is owed to the public power can be found in the ten commandments only in the precept which obliges him to honor his parents.

Thus it follows from this that the name of king is a name for father and that goodness is the most natural character of kings. . . .

PROPOSITION 3

The prince must provide for the needs of the people.

It is a royal right to provide for the needs of the people. He who undertakes it at the expense of the prince undertakes royalty: this is why it has been established. The obligation to care for the people is the foundation of all the rights that sovereigns have over their subjects.

This is why, in time of great need, the people have the right to have recourse to its prince. . . .

BOOK IV

ARTICLE I

The royal authority is absolute.

In order to make this term odious and insupportable, many wish to confuse absolute government and arbitrary government. But there is nothing more distinct than these two as we shall see when we speak of justice.

PROPOSITION I

The prince owes no account to anyone on what he orders.

"I counsel thee to keep the king's commandments, and that in regard to the oath of God. Be not hasty to go out of his sight, stand not in an evil thing; for he doeth whatsoever pleaseth him. Where the word of a king is, there is power: and who may say unto him what doest thou? Who so keepeth the commandment shall feel no evil thing."

Without this absolute authority, he cannot do good nor can he repress evil: it is necessary that his power be such that no one can hope to escape him; and finally the only defense of individuals against the public power ought to be their innocence. . . .

The prince is by his office the father of his people; he is placed by his grandeur above all petty interests; even more: all his grandeur and his natural interests are that the people shall be conserved, for once the people fail him he is no longer prince. There is thus nothing better than to give all the power of the state to him who has the greatest interest in the conservation and greatness of the state itself.

*   *   *

PROPOSITION 4
Kings are not by this above the laws.
"Thou shalt in any wise set him king over thee . . . but he shall not multiply horses to himself. . . . Neither shall he multiply wives to himself that his heart turn not away: neither shall he greatly multiply to himself silver and gold. And it shall be, when he sitteth upon the throne of his kingdom, that he shall write him a copy of this law in a book out of that which is before the priest the Levite: and it shall be with him and he shall read therein all the days of his life: that he may learn to fear the Lord his god, to keep all the words of this law and these statutes to do them: that his heart be not lifted up above his brethren and that he turn not aside from the commandment to the right hand, or to the left: to the end that he may prolong his days in his kingdom, he, and his children."
It should be noticed that this law does not include only religion, but the law of the realm as well to which the prince was subject as much as any other, or even more than others by the justness of his will.
It is this that princes find difficult to understand. . . .
Kings therefore are subject like any others to the equity of the laws both because they must be just and because they owe to the people the example of protecting justice; but they are not subject to the penalties of the laws: or, as theology puts it, they are subject to the laws, not in terms of its coactive power but in terms of its directive power.

Louis XIV was in the habit of keeping a journal in which he noted the course of his reign. He was also concerned to pass on to his heirs the lessons he had learned over the years. The selection that follows reveals his thoughts from

the age of twenty-one—when he first assumed full control of
the State—to the end of his reign, when he took stock of
what he had accomplished.

FROM *Louis XIV's Letters to His Heirs*

M A N Y   R E A S O N S, all very important, my son, have decided me, at some labour to myself, but one which I regard as forming one of my greatest concerns, to leave you these Memoirs of my reign and of my principal actions. I have never considered that kings, feeling in themselves, as they do, all paternal affection, are dispensed from the obligation common to fathers of instructing their children by example and by precept. On the contrary, it has seemed to me that in the high rank in which we are placed, you and I, a public duty is added to private, and that in the midst of all the respect which is given us, all the abundance and brilliancy with which we are surrounded—which are nothing more than the reward accorded by Heaven itself in return for the care of the peoples and States confided to our charge—this solicitude would not be very lofty if it did not extend beyond ourselves by making us communicate all our enlightenment to the one who is to reign after us.

I have even hoped that in this purpose I might be able to be more helpful to you, and consequently to my subjects, than any one else in the world; for there cannot be men who have reigned of more talents and greater experience than I, nor who have reigned in France; and I do not fear to tell you that the higher the position the greater are the number of things which cannot be viewed or understood save by one who is occupying that position.

I have considered, too, what I have so often experienced myself—the throng who will press round you, each for his own ends, the trouble you will have in finding disinterested advice, and the entire confidence you will be able to feel in that of a father who has no other interest but your own, no ardent wish but for your greatness.

*   *   *

I have given, therefore, some consideration to the condition of Kings—hard and rigorous in this respect—who owe, as it were, a public account of their actions to the whole world and to all succeeding centuries, and who,

Louis XIV, *Letters to His Heirs,* Jean Longnon, *A King's Lessons in Statecraft: Louis XIV* (1925), pp. 39–45, 47–53, 58, 66–70, 129–31, 149–51, 177–8, translated by Herbert Wilson. Reprinted by permission of Albert & Charles Boni, Inc., and Routledge & Kegan Paul Ltd., London.

nevertheless, are unable to do so to all and sundry at the time without injury to their greatest interests, and without divulging the secret reasons of their conduct. And, not doubting that the somewhat important and considerable affairs in which I have taken part, both within and without my kingdom, will one day exercise diversely the genius and passions of writers, I should not be sorry for you to possess in these Memoirs the means of setting history aright if it should err or not rightly interpret, through not having faithfully reported or well divined my plans and their motives. I will explain them to you without disguise, even where my good intentions have not been happily conceived, being persuaded that only a small mind and one usually at fault could expect never to make a mistake, and that those who have sufficient merit to succeed the more often, discover some magnanimity in recognising their faults.

*   *   *

I made a beginning by casting my eyes over all the different parties in the State, not indifferently, but with the glance of experience, sensibly touched at seeing nothing which did not invite and urge me to take it in hand, but carefully watching what the occasion and the state of affairs would permit. Everywhere was disorder. My Court as a whole was still very far removed from the sentiments in which I trust you will find it. Men of quality and officials, accustomed to continual intrigue with a minister who showed no aversion to it, and to whom it had been necessary, arrogated to themselves an imaginary right to everything that suited them. There was no governor of a city who was not difficult to govern; no request was preferred without some complaint of the past, or some hint of discontent for the future, which I was allowed to expect and to fear. The favours demanded, and extorted, rather than awaited, by this one and that, and always considerable, no longer were binding on any one, and were only regarded as useful in order to maltreat thenceforth those to whom they wished me to refuse them.

The finances, which give movement and action to the great organisation of the monarchy, were entirely exhausted, so much so that we could hardly find the ways and means. Much of the most necessary and most privileged expenses of my house and of my own privy purse were in arrears beyond all that was fitting, or maintained only on credit, to be a further subsequent burden. At the same time a prodigality showed itself among public men, masking on the one hand their malversations by every kind of artifice, and revealing them on the other in insolent and daring luxury, as though they feared I might take no notice of them.

The Church, apart from its usual troubles, after lengthy disputes on matters of the schools, a knowledge of which they allowed was unnecessary to salvation for any one, with points of disagreement augmenting day by day through the heat and obstinacy of their minds, and ceaselessly involving fresh human interests, was finally threatened with open schism by men who were all the more dangerous because they were capable of being very serviceable and greatly deserving, had they themselves been less opinionated. It was not a question only of a few private and obscure professors, but of Bishops established in their Sees and able to draw away the multitude after them, men of high repute, and of piety worthy of being held in reverence had it been accompanied by submission to the sentiments of the Church, by gentleness, moderation, and charity. Cardinal de Retz, Archbishop of Paris, whom for well-known reasons of State I could not permit to remain in the kingdom, encouraged all this rising sect from inclination or interest, and was held in favour by them.

The least of the ills affecting the order of Nobility was the fact of its being shared by an infinite number of usurpers possessing no right to it, or one acquired by money without any claim from service rendered. The tyranny exercised by the nobles over their vassals and neighbours in some of my provinces could no longer be suffered or suppressed save by making severe and rigorous examples. The rage for duelling—somewhat modified by the exact observance of the latest regulations, over which I was always inflexible—was only noticeable in a now well advanced recovery from so inveterate an ill, so that there was no reason to despair of the remedy.

The administration of Justice itself, whose duty it is to reform others, appeared to me the most difficult to reform. An infinity of things contributed to this state of affairs: the appointments filled haphazard or by money rather than by selection and merit; scant experience and less knowledge on the part of some of the judges; the regulations referring to age and service almost everywhere eluded; chicanery firmly established through many centuries, and fertile in inventing means of evading the most salutary laws. And what especially conduced to this was the fact that these insatiable gentry loved litigation and fostered it as their own peculiar property, applying themselves only to prolong and to add to it. Even my Council, instead of supervising the other jurisdictions, too often only introduced disorder by issuing a strange number of contrary regulations, all in my name and as though by my command, which rendered the confusion far more disgraceful.

All this collection of evils, their consequences and effects, fell principally upon the people, who, in addition, were loaded with impositions, some crushed down by poverty, others suffering want from their own laziness since the peace, and needing above all to be alleviated and occupied.

Amid so many difficulties, some of which appeared to be insurmountable, three considerations gave me courage. The first was that in these matters it is not in the power of Kings—inasmuch as they are men and have to deal with men—to reach all the perfection they set before themselves, which is too far removed from our feebleness; but that this impossibility of attainment is a poor reason for not doing all we can, and this difficulty for not always making progress. This, moreover, is not without its uses, nor without glory. The second was that in all just and legitimate enterprises, time, the fact of doing them even, and the aid of Heaven, open out as a rule a thousand channels, and discover a thousand facilities which we had not looked for. And the last was one which of itself seemed to me to hold out visibly that help, by disposing everything to the same end with which it inspired me.

In fact, all was calm everywhere. There was no movement, nor fear or seeming of any movement in my kingdom which might interrupt or oppose my designs. Peace was established with my neighbours, and to all seeming for as long as I myself wished it, owing to the conditions of affairs then prevailing.

It would assuredly have been to make a bad use of conditions of such perfect tranquillity, such as might only be met with very rarely in several centuries, not to turn them to the only account capable of making me appreciate them, at a time when my youth and the pleasure of being at the head of my armies would have caused me to wish to have more matters to deal with abroad. But inasmuch as my chief hope in these reforms was based on my will, their foundation at the outstart rested on making absolute my will by conduct which should impose submission and respect: by rendering scrupulous justice to all to whom I owed it; but in the bestowing of favours, giving them freely and without constraint to whomsoever I would, and when it should please me, provided that my subsequent action should let others know that while giving reasons to no one for my conduct I ruled myself none the less by reason, and that in my view the remembrance of services rendered, the favouring and promoting of merit—in a word, doing the right thing— should not only be the greatest concern but the greatest pleasure of a prince.

Two things without doubt were absolutely necessary: very hard work on my part, and a wise choice of persons capable of seconding it.

As for work, it may be, my son, that you will begin to read these Memoirs at an age when one is far more in the habit of dreading than loving it, only too happy to have escaped subjection to tutors and to have your hours regulated no longer, nor lengthy and prescribed study laid down for you.

On this heading I will not warn you solely that it is none the less toil *by which* one reigns, and *for which* one reigns, and that the conditions of royalty, which may seem to you sometimes hard and vexatious in so lofty a position, would appear pleasant and easy if there was any doubt of your reaching it.

There is something more, my son, and I hope that your own experience will never teach it to you: nothing could be more laborious to you than a great amount of idleness if you were to have the misfortune to fall into it through beginning by being disgusted with public affairs, then with pleasure, then with idleness itself, seeking everywhere fruitlessly for what can never be found, that is to say, the sweetness of repose and leisure without having the preceding fatigue and occupation.

I laid a rule on myself to work regularly twice every day, and for two or three hours each time with different persons, without counting the hours which I passed privately and alone, nor the time which I was able to give on particular occasions to any special affairs that might arise. There was no moment when I did not permit people to talk to me about them, provided that they were urgent; with the exception of foreign ministers who sometimes find too favourable moments in the familiarity allowed to them, either to obtain or to discover something, and whom one should not hear without being previously prepared.

I cannot tell you what fruit I gathered immediately I had taken this resolution. I felt myself, as it were, uplifted in thought and courage; I found myself quite another man, and with joy reproached myself for having been too long unaware of it. This first timidity, which a little self-judgment always produces and which at the beginning gave me pain, especially on occasions when I had to speak in public, disappeared in less than no time. The only thing I felt then was that I was King, and born to be one. I experienced next a delicious feeling, hard to express, and which you will not know yourself except by tasting it as I have done. For you must not imagine, my son, that the affairs of State are like some obscure and thorny path of learning which may possibly have already wearied you, wherein the mind strives to raise itself with effort above its purview, more often to arrive at no conclusion, and whose utility or apparent utility is repugnant to us as much as its difficulty. The function of Kings consists principally in allowing good sense to act, which always acts naturally and without effort. What we apply ourselves to is sometimes less difficult than what we do only for our amusement. Its usefulness always follows. A King, however skilful and enlightened be his ministers, cannot put his own hand to the work without its effect being seen. Success, which is agreeable in everything, even in the smallest matters, gratifies us in these as well as in the greatest, and there is no satisfaction to equal that of noting every day some progress in glorious and lofty enterprises, and in the happiness of the people which has been planned and thought out by oneself. All that is most necessary to this work is at the same time agreeable; for, in a word, my son, it is to have one's eyes open to the whole earth; to learn each hour the news concerning every province and every nation, the secrets of every court, the mood and the weaknesses of each Prince and of every foreign minister; to be well-informed on an infinite number of matters about which we are supposed to know nothing; to elicit from our subjects what they hide from us with the greatest care; to discover the most remote opinions of our own courtiers and the most hidden interests of those who come to us with quite contrary professions. I do not know of any other pleasure we would not renounce for that, even if curiosity alone gave us the opportunity.

I have dwelt on this important subject longer than I had intended, and far more for your sake than for my own; for while I am disclosing to you these methods and these alleviations attending the greatest cares of royalty I am not unaware that I am likewise depreciating almost the sole merit which I can hope for in the eyes of the world. But in this matter, my son, your honour is dearer to me than my own; and if it should happen that God call you to govern before you have yet taken to this spirit of application and to public affairs of which I am speaking, the least deference you can pay to the advice of a father, to whom I make bold to say you owe much in every kind of way, is to begin to do and to continue to do for some time, even under constraint and dislike, for love of me who beg it of you, what you will do all your life from love of yourself, if once you have made a beginning.

I gave orders to the four Secretaries of State no longer to sign anything whatsoever without speaking to me; likewise to the Controller, and that he should authorise nothing as regards finance without its being registered in a book which must remain with me, and being noted down in a very abridged abstract form in which at any moment, and at a glance, I could see the state of the funds, and past and future expenditure.

The Chancellor received a like order, that is to say, to sign nothing with the seal except by my command, with the exception only of letters of justice, so called because it would be an injustice to refuse them, a procedure required more as a matter of form than of principle; and I allowed to remain the administering and remissions of cases manifestly pardonable, although I have since changed my opinion on this subject, as I will tell you in its proper place. I let it be understood that whatever the nature of the matter might be, direct application must be made to me when it was not a question that depended only on my favour; and to all my subjects without distinction I gave liberty to present their case to me at all hours, either verbally or by petitions.

At first petitions came in very great numbers, which nevertheless did not discourage me. The disorder in which my affairs had been placed was productive of many; the novelty and expectation, whether vain or unjust, attracted not less. A large number were presented connected with law-suits, which I could not and ought not to take out of the ordinary tribunals in order to have them adjudicated before me. But even in these things, apparently so unprofitable, I found great usefulness. By this means I informed myself in detail as to the state of my people; they saw that I was mindful of them, and nothing won their heart so much. Oppression on the part of the ordinary tribunals might be represented to me in such a way as to make me feel it desirable to gain further information in order to take special measures when they were required. One or two examples of this kind prevented a thousand similar ills; the complaints, even when they were false and unjust, hindered my officers from giving a hearing to those which were more genuine and reasonable.

Regarding the persons whose duty it was to second my labours, I resolved at all costs to have no prime minister; and if you will believe me, my son, and all your successors after you, the name shall be banished for ever from France, for there is nothing more undignified than to see all the administration on one side, and on the other, the mere title of King.

To effect this, it was necessary to divide my confidence and the execution of my orders without giving it entirely to one single person, applying these different people to different spheres according to their diverse talents, which is perhaps the first and greatest gift that Princes can possess.

I also made a resolution on a further matter. With a view the better to unite in myself alone all the authority of a master, although there must be in all affairs a certain amount of detail to which our occupations and also our dignity do not permit us to descend as a rule, I conceived the plan, after I should have made choice of my ministers, of entering sometimes into matters with each one of them, and when they least expected it, in order that they might understand that I could do the same upon other subjects and at any moment. Besides, a knowledge of some small detail acquired only occasionally, and for amusement rather than as a regular rule, is instructive little by little and without fatigue, on a thousand things which are not without their use in general resolutions, and which we ought to know and do ourselves were it possible that a single man could know and do everything.

* * *

Time has shown what to believe, and I have now been pursuing for ten years fairly consistently, as it seems to me, the same course, without relaxing my application; kept well informed of everything; listening to the least of my subjects; at any hour knowing the number and quality of my troops, and the state of my fortified towns; unremitting in issuing my orders for all their requirements; dealing at once with foreign ministers; receiving and reading dispatches; doing myself a portion of the replies and giving to my secretaries the substance of the others; regulating the State receipts and expenditure; requiring those whom I placed in important posts to account directly to me; keeping my affairs to myself as much as any one before me had ever done; distributing my favours as I myself chose; and retaining, if I mistake not, those who served me in a modest position which was far removed from the elevation and power of prime ministers, although loading them with benefits for themselves and their belongings.

The observation by others of all these things doubtless gave rise to some opinion of me in the world; and this opinion has in no small measure contributed to the success of what I have since undertaken, inasmuch as nothing could have produced such great results in so short a time as the reputation of the Prince.

* * *

After having thus fully informed myself in private discussions with them I entered more boldly into practical action. There was nothing that appeared more pressing to me than to alleviate the condition of my people, to which the poverty of the provinces and the compassion I felt for them strongly urged me. The state of my finances, as I have shown you, seemed to oppose this, and in any case counselled delay; but we must always be in haste to do well. The reforms I took in hand, though beneficial to the public, were bound to be irksome to a large number of private people. It was appropriate to make a beginning with something that could only be agreeable, and besides, there was no other way of maintaining any longer even the name of peace without its being followed by some sort of sop of this kind as a promise of greater hopes for the future. I therefore put aside any other considerations and, as a pledge of further alleviation, I first remitted three millions of the taxes for the following year which had already been prescribed and were awaiting collection.

At the same time, but with the intention of having them better observed than heretofore, I renewed the regulations against wearing gold and silver on clothes, and a thousand other foreign superfluities which were a kind of charge and contribution, outwardly voluntary but really obligatory, which my subjects, especially those most qualified and the persons at my Court, paid daily to neighbouring nations, or, to be more correct, to luxury and vanity.

For a thousand reasons, and also to pave the way for the reform of the administration of justice so greatly needed, it was necessary to diminish the authority of the chief jurisdictions which, under the pretext that their judgments were without appeal, and, as we say, sovereign and of final resort, regarded themselves as separate and independent sovereignties. I let it be known that I would no longer tolerate their assumptions. The *Cour des Aides* in Paris having been the first to exceed its duties and in some degree its jurisdiction, I exiled a few of its most offending officers, believing that if this remedy were thoroughly employed at the outset, it would relieve me of the necessity of its frequent application afterwards; and my action has been successful.

Immediately afterwards I gave them to understand my intentions still better in a solemn decree by my Supreme Council. For it is quite true that these jurisdictions have no cause to regulate each other in their different capacities, which are defined by laws and edicts. In former times these sufficed to make them live in peace with each other, or in the event of certain differences arising between them, especially in matters regarding private individuals, these were so rare and so little difficult of adjustment, that the Kings themselves decided them with a word, more often than not during a walk, on the report of the Magistrates, who then consisted of a very small number, until, owing to the growth in the kingdom of these matters and still more of chicanery, this duty was entrusted principally to the Chancellor of France and to the Administrative Council of which I have spoken already to you. Now these officials of necessity should be fully authorised to regulate the competence of the other jurisdictions (and also all other matters of which from time to time we deem it suitable for reasons of public utility or of our own proper service, to give them cognisance exceptionally) by taking it over from them inasmuch as they derive their power only from us. Notwithstanding, owing to this spirit of self-sufficiency and the disorder of the times, they only yielded in so far as seemed good to them, and outstepped their powers daily and in all manner of cases in spite of their proper limitations, often enough going so far as to say that they recognised the King's will in no other form than that contained in the Ordinances and the authorised Edicts.

By this decree I forbade them all in general to give any judgments contrary to those of my Council under any pretext whatsoever, whether in their own jurisdiction or in their private capacity, and I commanded them, when one or the other felt they had suffered hurt to make their complaint to me and have recourse to my authority, inasmuch as I had only entrusted to them to exercise justice towards my subjects and not to create their own justice of themselves, which thing constitutes a part of sovereignty so closely united to the Crown and so much the prerogative of the King alone that it cannot be communicated to any other.

In the same year, but a little later, for I shall not observe too closely the order of dates, in a certain matter connected with the finances of all the record offices in general, and one which they had never dared carry through in connection with those of the Parliament in Paris, because the property belonged to the officers of that body and sometimes to the chambers as a whole, I made it be seen that these officers must submit to the common law, and that there was nothing to prevent my absolving them from it when it pleased me to give this reward for their services.

About the same time, I did a thing which seemed even too bold, so greatly had the gentlemen of the law profited by it up till then, and so full were their minds of the importance they had acquired in the recent troubles through the abuse of their power. From three quarters I reduced to two all the fresh mortgages which were charged upon my revenue, which had been effected at a very extortionate rate during the war, and which were eating up the best of my farms of which the officials of the corporations had acquired the greater part. And this made them regard it as a fine thing to treat them as harshly as possible in their most vital interests. But at bottom this action of mine was perfectly just, for two quarters was still a great deal in return for what they had advanced. The reform was necessary. My affairs were not in such a state that I had nothing to fear from their resentment. It was more to the purpose to show them that I feared nothing they could do and that the times were changed. And those who from different interests had wished that these corporations might win the day learnt on the contrary from their submission what was due to me.

*   *   *

I also made a change in my household at that time, in which all the nobility of the realm had an interest. This had to do with my chief stables in which I increased the number of pages by more than half, and took pains both that the selection was made with more care and that they were better instructed than they had been up till then.

I was aware that what had prevented people of quality from aspiring to these kinds of positions was either the ease with which all conditions of folk had been recommended and admitted to them, or the scant opportunity afforded to them as a rule of approaching my person, or the neglect to perfect them in their duties which had insensibly arisen. To remedy all this I determined to take care to appoint all the pages myself, to make them share with those of my private stables all the domestic services which the latter rendered me, and to choose the best instructors in my realm to train them.

As regards the public, the results I hoped to obtain were to provide an excellent education for a large number of gentlemen, and for my own private benefit to have always a supply of people coming from this school more capable, and better disposed than the general run of my subjects, to enter my service.

I had yet another object for my personal attention which concerned principally people of substance, but the effect of which was afterwards spread over my kingdom generally. I knew what immense sums were spent by private individuals and were perpetually being withdrawn from the State by the trade in lace of foreign manufacture. I saw that the French were wanting neither in industry nor in the material for undertaking this work themselves, and I had no doubt that if they did this on the spot they could provide it far more cheaply than what they imported from such a distance. From these considerations I determined to establish works here, the effect of which would be that the great would moderate their expenditure, the people would derive the entire benefit of what the rich spent, and the large sums leaving the State would insensibly produce additional abundance and wealth by being retained in it, and beyond this would provide occupation for many of my subjects who up till then had been forced either to become slack through want of work or to go in search of it among our neighbours.

However, inasmuch as the most laudable plans are never carried out without opposition, I foresaw well that the lace merchants would oppose this with all their power, because I had no doubt that they found it paid them better to sell their wares which came from a distance, whereof the proper value could not be known, than those which were manufactured here within sight of everybody.

But I was determined to cut short by my authority all the trickery they might use, and so I gave them sufficient time to sell the foreign lace which they had before my edict was published, and when this time had expired I caused all that they still had to be seized as having come in since my prohibition, while, on the other hand, I caused shops filled with new manufactures to be opened, at which I obliged private individuals to make their purchases.

The example of this in a short while set up the manufacture of many other things in my State, such as sheets, glass, mirrors, silk stockings, and similar wares.

I took special plans to find out how to augment and assure to my subjects their maritime trade by making the ports I possessed safer, and seeking places to construct new ones. But while doing this I took in hand another enterprise of no lesser utility, which was to link by a canal the Ocean with the Mediterranean, in such wise that it would be no longer necessary to go round Spain to pass from one sea to the other. It was a great and difficult undertaking. But it was infinitely advantageous to my realm, which thus became the centre, and as it were the arbiter of the trade of the whole of Europe. And it was no less glorious for me who in the accomplishing of this object raised myself above the greatest men of past centuries who had undertaken it without result.

$$* \qquad * \qquad *$$

I have never failed, when an occasion has presented itself, to impress upon you the great respect we should have for religion, and the deference we should show to its ministers in matters specially connected with their mission, that is to say, with the celebration of the Sacred Mysteries and the preaching of the doctrine of the Gospels. But because people connected with the Church are liable to presume a little too much on the advantages attaching to their profession, and are willing sometimes to make use of them in order to whittle down their most rightful duties, I feel obliged to explain to you certain points on this question which may be of importance.

The first is that Kings are absolute *seigneurs,* and from their nature have full and free disposal of all property both secular and ecclesiastical, to use it as wise dispensers, that is to say, in accordance with the requirements of their State.

The second is that those mysterious names, the Franchises and Liberties of the Church, with which perhaps people will endeavour to dazzle you, have equal reference to all the faithful whether they be laymen or tonsured, who are all equally sons of this common Mother; but that they exempt neither the one nor the other from subjection to Sovereigns, to whom the Gospel itself precisely enjoins that they should submit themselves.

The third is that all that people say in regard to any particular destination of the property of the Church, and to the intention of founders, is a mere scruple without foundation, because it is certain that, inasmuch as the founders of benefices when transmitting their succession were not able to free them either from the quit-rental or the other dues which they paid to particular *seigneurs,* so for a far stronger reason they could not release them from the first due of all which is payable to the Prince as *Seigneur* over all, for the general welfare of the whole realm.

The fourth is that if up till now permission has been given to ecclesiastics to deliberate in their assemblies on the amount which it is their duty to provide, they should not attribute this custom to any special privilege, because the same liberty is still left to the people of several provinces as a former mark of the probity existing in the first centuries, when justice was sufficient to animate each individual to do what he should according to his ability and, notwithstanding, this never prevented either laymen or ecclesiastics when they refused to fulfil their obligations of their own free will, from being compelled to do so.

And the fifth and last is that if there are dwellers in our Empire more bound than others to be of service to us as regards their property as a whole, these should be the beneficiaries who only hold all they have at our option. The claims attaching to them have been established as long as those of their benefices, and we have titles to them which have been preserved from the first period of the monarchy. Even Popes who have striven to despoil us of this right have made it more clear and more incontestable by the precise retractation of their ambitious pretensions which they have been obliged to make.

But we might say that in this matter there is no need of either titles or examples, because natural equity alone is sufficient to illustrate this point. Would it be just that the Nobility should give its services and its blood in the defence of the realm and so often consume its resources in the maintenance of the offices with which it is charged, and that the people (with so little substance and so many mouths to fill) should bear in addition the sole weight of all the expenses of the State, while ecclesiastics, exempt by their profession from the dangers of war, from the profusion of luxury and the burden of families, should enjoy in abundance all the advantages of the general public without ever contributing anything to its necessities?

*   *   *

I have sustained this war with the high hand and pride which becomes this realm; through the valour of my Nobility and the zeal of my subjects I have been successful in the undertakings I have accomplished for the good of the State; I have given my whole concern and application to reach a successful issue; I have also put in motion the measures I thought necessary in fulfilling my duties, and in making known the love and tenderness I have for my people, by procuring by my labours a peace which will bring them rest for the remainder of my reign so that I need have no other care than for their welfare. After having extended the boundaries of this Empire, and protected my frontiers with the important strongholds I have taken, I have given ear to the proposals of peace which have been made to me, and I have exceeded perhaps on this occasion the limits of prudence in order to accomplish so great a work. I may say that I stepped out of my own character and did extreme violence to myself in order promptly to secure repose for my subjects at the expense of my reputation, or at least of my own particular satisfaction, and perhaps of my renown, which I willingly risked for the advantage of those who have enabled me to acquire it. I felt that I owed them this mark of gratitude. But seeing at this hour that my most vehement enemies have only wished to play with me and that they have employed all the artifices they could to deceive me as well as their allies by forcing them to contribute to the immense expenditure which their disordered ambition demanded, I do not see any other course to take than that of considering how to protect ourselves securely, making them understand that a France thoroughly united is stronger than all the powers they have got together at so great pains, by force and artifice, to overwhelm her. Up to now I have made use of the extraordinary measures which on similar occasions I have put into practice in order to provide sums proportionate to the expenditure indispensable to uphold the glory and safety of the State. Now that all sources are *quasi*-exhausted I come to you at this juncture to ask your counsel and your assistance, whence a safe issue will arise. Our enemies will learn from the efforts we shall put forth together that we are not in the condition they would have people believe, and by means of the help which I am asking of you and which I believe to be indispensable, we shall be able to force them to make a peace which shall be honourable to ourselves, lasting for our tranquillity, and agreeable to all the Princes of Europe. This is what I shall look to up to the moment of its conclusion, even in the greatest stress of the war, as well as to the welfare and happiness of my people which have always been, and will continue to be to the last moment of my life, my greatest and most serious concern.

3　Absolutism in Practice

The Duke of Saint-Simon (1675–1755) came from one of the oldest noble families in France. He was, in many ways, typical of the feudal nobility that Louis XIV was concerned to tame and bring under the authority of the monarchy. His Memoirs *describe court life and give considerable insight into the ways in which Louis XIV tried to control the aristocracy. His reports on politics in the provinces were clearly influenced by his own position at court.*

FROM *The Memoirs of the Duke of Saint-Simon*

LOUIS XIV WAS MADE for a brilliant Court. In the midst of other men, his figure, his courage, his grace, his beauty, his grand mien, even the tone of his voice and the majestic and natural charm of all his person, distinguished him till his death as the King Bee, and showed that if he had only been born a simple private gentleman, he would equally have excelled in fêtes, pleasures, and gallantry, and would have had the greatest success in love. The intrigues and adventures which early in life he had been engaged in—when the Comtesse de Soissons lodged at the Tuileries as superintendent of the Queen's household, and was the centre figure of the Court group—had exercised an unfortunate influence upon him: he received those impressions with which he could never after successfully struggle. From this time, intellect, education, nobility of sentiment, and high principle in others, became objects of suspicion to him, and soon of hatred. The more he advanced in years the more this sentiment was confirmed in him. He wished to reign by himself. His jealousy on this point unceasingly, became weakness. He reigned, indeed, in little things; the great he could never reach: even in the former, too, he was often governed. The superior ability of his early ministers and his early generals soon wearied him. He liked nobody to be in any way superior to him. Thus he chose his ministers, not for their knowl-

The Memoirs of the Duke of Saint-Simon on the Reign of Louis XIV and the Regency, I (1857), 315–9; II (1857), 3–6, 64–6, 95–8, 214–9, 354–7; III (1857), 225–8, 232–3, translated by Bayle St. John.

edge, but for their ignorance; not for their capacity, but for their want of it. He liked to form them, as he said; liked to teach them even the most trifling things. It was the same with his generals. He took credit to himself for instructing them; wished it to be thought that from his cabinet he commanded and directed all his armies. Naturally fond of trifles, he unceasingly occupied himself with the most petty details of his troops, his household, his mansions; would even instruct his cooks, who received, like novices, lessons they had known by heart for years. This vanity, this unmeasured and unreasonable love of admiration, was his ruin. His ministers, his generals, his mistresses, his courtiers, soon perceived his weakness. They praised him with emulation and spoiled him. Praises, or to say truth, flattery, pleased him to such an extent, that the coarsest was well received, the vilest even better relished. It was the sole means by which you could approach him. Those whom he liked owed his affection for them to their untiring flatteries. This is what gave his ministers so much authority, and the opportunities they had for adulating him, of attributing everything to him, and of pretending to learn everything from him. Suppleness, meanness, an admiring, dependent, cringing manner—above all, an air of nothingness—were the sole means of pleasing him.

This poison spread. It spread, too, to an incredible extent, in a prince who, although of intellect beneath mediocrity, was not utterly without sense, and who had had some experience. Without voice or musical knowledge, he used to sing, in private, the passages of the opera prologues that were fullest of his praises! He was drowned in vanity; and so deeply, that at his public suppers—all the Court present, musicians also—he would hum these self-same praises between his teeth, when the music they were set to was played!

And yet, it must be admitted, he might have done better. Though his intellect, as I have said, was beneath mediocrity, it was capable of being formed. He loved glory, was fond of order and regularity; was by disposition prudent, moderate, discreet, master of his movements and his tongue. Will it be believed? He was also by disposition good and just! God had sufficiently gifted him to enable him to be a good King; perhaps even *a tolerably great King!* All the evil came to him from elsewhere. His early education was so neglected that nobody dared approach his apartment. He has often been heard to speak of those times with bitterness, and even to relate that, one evening he was found in the basin of the Palais Royale garden fountain, into which he had fallen! He was scarcely taught how to read or write, and remained so ignorant, that the most familiar historical and other facts were utterly unknown to him! He fell, accordingly, and sometimes even in public, into the grossest absurdities.

It was his vanity, his desire for glory, that led him, soon after the death of the King of Spain, to make that event the pretext for war; in spite of the renunciations so recently made, so carefully stipulated, in the marriage contract. He marched into Flanders; his conquests there were rapid; the passage of the Rhine was admirable; the triple alliance of England, Sweden, and Holland only animated him. In the midst of winter he took Franche-Comté, by restoring which at the peace of Aix-la-Chapelle, he preserved his conquests in Flanders. All was flourishing then in the state. Riches everywhere. Colbert had placed the finances, the navy, commerce, manufactures, letters even, upon the highest point; and this age, like that of Augustus, produced in abundance illustrious men of all kinds,—even those illustrious only in pleasures.

*   *   *

Thus, we see this monarch grand, rich, conquering, the arbiter of Europe; feared and admired as long as the ministers and captains existed who really deserved the name. When they were no more, the machine kept moving some time by impulsion, and from their influence. But soon afterwards we saw beneath the surface; faults and errors were multiplied, and decay came on with giant strides; without, however, opening the eyes of that despotic master, so anxious to do everything and direct everything himself, and who seemed to indemnify himself for disdain abroad by increasing fear and trembling at home.

*   *   *

A short time after the death of Mademoiselle de l'Enclos, a terrible adventure happened to Courtenvaux, eldest son of M. de Louvois. Courtenvaux was commander of the Cent-Suisse, fond of obscure debauches; with a ridiculous voice, miserly, quarrelsome, though modest and respectful; and in fine a very stupid fellow. The King, more eager to know all that was passing than most people believed, although they gave him credit for not a little curiosity in this respect, had authorised Bontems to engage a number of Swiss in addition to those posted at the doors, and in the parks and gardens. These attendants had orders to stroll morning, noon, and night, along the corridors, the passages, the staircases, even into the private places, and, when it was fine, in the court-yards and gardens; and in secret to watch people, to follow them, to notice where they went, to notice who was there, to listen to all the conversation they could hear, and to make reports of their discoveries. This was assiduously done at Versailles, at Marly, at Trianon, at Fontainebleau, and in all the places where the King was. These new attendants vexed Courtenvaux considerably, for over such new-comers he had no sort of authority. This season, at Fontainebleau, a room, which had formerly been occupied by a party of the Cent-Suisses and of the body-guard, was given up entirely to the new corps. The room was in a public passage of communication indispensable to all in the château, and in consequence, excellently well adapted for watching those who passed through it. Courtenvaux more than ever vexed by this new arrangement, regarded it as a fresh encroachment upon his authority, and flew into a violent rage with the new-comers, and railed at them in good set terms. They allowed him to fume as he would; they had their orders, and were too wise to be disturbed by his rage. The King, who heard of all this, sent at once for Courtenvaux. As soon as he appeared in the cabinet, the King called to him from the other end of the room, without giving him time to approach, and in a rage so terrible, and for him so novel, that not only Courtenvaux, but Princes, Princesses, and everybody in the chamber, trembled. Menaces that his post should be taken away from him, terms the most severe and the most unusual, rained upon Courtenvaux, who, fainting with fright, and ready to sink under the ground, had neither the time nor the means to prefer a word. The reprimand finished by the King saying, "Get out." He had scarcely the strength to obey.

The cause of this strange scene was that Courtenvaux, by the fuss he had made, had drawn the attention of the whole Court to the change effected by the King, and that, when once seen, its object was clear to all eyes. The King, who hid his spy system with the greatest care, had counted upon this change passing unperceived, and was beside himself with anger when he found it made apparent to everybody by Courtenvaux's noise. He never regained the King's favour during the rest of his life; and but for his family he would certainly have been driven away, and his office taken from him.

*   *   *

The death of the Abbé de Vatteville occurred at the commencement of this year, and made some noise, on account of the prodigies of the Abbé's life. This Vatteville was the younger son of a Franche Comté family; early in life he joined the Order of the Chartreux monks, and was ordained priest. He had much intellect, but was of an impetuous spirit, and soon began to chafe under the yoke of a religious life. He determined, therefore, to set himself free from it, and procured some secular habits, pistols, and a horse. Just as he was about to escape over the walls of the monastery by means of a ladder, the prior entered his cell. Vatteville made no to-do, but at once drew a pistol, shot the prior dead, and effected his escape.

Two or three days afterwards, travelling over the country and avoiding as much as possible the frequented places, he arrived at a wretched road-side inn, and asked what there was in the house. The landlord replied—"A leg of mutton and a capon." "Good!" replied our unfrocked monk; "put them down to roast."

The landlord replied that they were too much for a single person, and that he had nothing else for the whole house. The monk upon this flew in a passion, and declared that the least the landlord could do was to give him what he would pay for; and that he had sufficient appetite to eat both leg of mutton and capon. They were accordingly put down to the fire, the landlord not daring to say another word. While they were cooking, a traveller on horseback arrived at the inn, and learning that they were for one person, was much astonished. He offered to pay his share to be allowed to dine off them with the stranger who had ordered this dinner; but the landlord told him he was afraid the gentleman would not consent to the arrangement. Thereupon the traveller went up stairs and civilly asked Vatteville if he might dine with him on paying half of the expense. Vatteville would not consent, and a dispute soon arose between the two; to be brief, the monk served this traveller as he had served the prior, killed him with a pistol shot. After this he went down stairs tranquilly, and in the midst of the fright of the landlord and of the whole house, had the leg of mutton and capon served up to him, picked both to the very bone, paid his score, remounted his horse, and went his way.

Not knowing what course to take, he went to Turkey, and in order to succeed there, had himself circumcised, put on the turban, and entered into the militia. His blasphemy advanced him, his talents and his colour distinguished him; he became *Bacha,* and the confidential man in the Morea, where the Turks were making war against the Venetians. He determined to make use of this position in order to advance his own interests, and entering into communication with the generalissimo of the Republic, promised to betray into his hands several secret places belonging to the Turks, but on certain conditions. These were, absolution from the Pope for all crimes of his life, his murders and his apostasy included; security against the Chartreux and against being placed in any other Order; full restitution of his civil rights, and liberty to exercise his profession of priest with the right of possessing all benefices of every kind. The Venetians thought the bargain too good to be refused, and the Pope, in the interest of the Church, accorded all the demands of the Bacha. When Vatteville was quite assured that his conditions would be complied with, he took his measures so well that he executed perfectly all he had undertaken. Immediately after he threw himself into the Venetian army, and passed into Italy. He was well received at Rome by the Pope, and returned to his family in Franche Comté, and amused himself by braving the Chartreux.

At the first conquest of the Franche Comté, he intrigued so well with the Queen-mother and the ministry, that he was promised the Archbishopric of Besançon; but the Pope cried out against this on account of his murders, circumcision, and apostasy. The King sided with the Pope, and Vatteville was obliged to be contented with the abbey of Baume, another good abbey in Picardy, and divers other advantages.

Except when he came to the Court, where he was always received with great distinction, he remained at his abbey of Baume, living there like a grand seigneur, keeping a fine pack of hounds, a good table, entertaining jovial company, keeping mistresses very freely; tyrannising over his tenants and his neighbours in the most absolute manner. The intendants gave way to him, and by express orders of the Court allowed him to act much as he pleased, even with the taxes, which he regulated at his will, and in his conduct was oftentimes very violent. With these manners and this bearing, which caused him to be both feared and respected, he would often amuse himself by going to see the Chartreux, in order to plume himself on having quitted their frock. He played much at *hombre,* and frequently gained *codille* (a term of the game), so that the name of the Abbé Codille was given to him. He lived in this manner, always with the same licence and in the same consideration, until nearly ninety years of age.

*   *   *

Such was our military history of the year 1706—a history of losses and dishonour. It may be imagined in what condition was the exchequer with so many demands upon its treasures. For the last two or three years the King had been obliged, on account of the expenses of the war, and the losses we had sustained, to cut down the presents that he made at the commencement of the year. Thirty-five thousand louis in gold was the sum he ordinarily spent in this manner. This year, 1707, he diminished it by ten thousand louis. It was upon Madame de Montespan that the blow fell. Since she had quitted the Court the King gave her twelve thousand louis of gold each year. This year he sent word to her that he could only give her eight. Madame de Montespan testified not the least surprise. She replied, that she was only sorry for the poor, to whom indeed she gave with profusion. A short time after the King had made this reduction,—that is, on the 8th of January,—Madame La Duchesse de Bourgogne gave birth to a son. The joy was great, but the King prohibited all those expenses which had been made at the birth of the first-born of Madame de Bourgogne, and which had amounted to a large sum. The want of money indeed made itself felt so much at this time, that the King was obliged to seek for resources as a private person might have done. A mining speculator, named Rodes, having pretended that he had discovered many veins of gold in the Pyrenees, assistance was given him in order that he might bring these treasures to light. He declared that with eighteen hundred workmen he would furnish a million (francs' worth of gold) each week. Fifty-two millions a-year would have been a fine increase of revenue. However, after waiting some little time, no gold was forthcoming, and the money that had been spent to assist this enterprise was found to be pure loss.

The difficulty of finding money to carry on the affairs of the nation continued to grow so irksome that Chamillart, who had both the finance and the war departments under his control, was unable to stand against the increased trouble and vexation which this state of things brought him. More than once he had represented that this double work was too much for him. But the King had in former times expressed so much annoyance from the troubles that arose between the finance and war departments, that he would not separate them, after having once joined them together. At last, Chamillart could bear up against his heavy load no longer. The vapours seized him: he had attacks of giddiness in the head; his digestion was obstructed; he grew thin as a lath. He wrote again to the King, begging to be released from his duties, and frankly stated that, in the state he was, if some relief was not afforded him, everything would go wrong and perish. He always left a large margin to his letters, and upon this the King generally wrote his reply. Chamillart showed me this letter when it came back to him, and I saw upon it with great surprise, in the handwriting of the King, this short note: "Well! let us perish together."

The necessity for money had now become so great, that all sorts of means were adopted to obtain it. Amongst other things, a tax was established upon baptisms and marriages. This tax was extremely onerous and odious. The result of it was a strange confusion. Poor people, and many of humble means, baptised their children themselves, without carrying them to the church, and were married at home by reciprocal consent and before witnesses, when they could find no priest who would marry them without formality. In consequence of this there were no longer any baptismal extracts; no longer any certainty as to baptisms or births; and the children of the marriages solemnised in the way I have stated above were illegitimate in the eyes of the law. Researches and rigours in respect to abuses so prejudicial were redoubled therefore; that is to say, they were redoubled for the purpose of collecting the tax.

From public cries and murmurs the people in some places passed to sedition. Matters went so far at Cahors, that two battalions which were there had great difficulty in holding the town against the armed peasants; and troops intended for Spain were obliged to be sent there. It was found necessary to suspend the operation of the tax, but it was with great trouble that the movement of Quercy was put down, and the peasants, who had armed and collected together, induced to retire into their villages. In Perigord they rose, pillaged the bureaux, and rendered themselves masters of a little town and some castles, and forced some gentlemen to put themselves at their head. They declared publicly that they would pay the old taxes to King, curate, and lord, but that they would pay no more, or hear a word of any other taxes or vexation. In the end it was found necessary to drop this tax upon baptism and marriages, to the great regret of the tax-gatherers, who, by all manner of vexations and rogueries, had enriched themselves cruelly.

It was one thing to claim that the royal will was absolute; it was another thing to enforce it throughout France. To do this, Louis XIV and his great minister, Jean Baptiste Colbert (1619–1683), set out to create a bureaucracy that would extend into the farthest reaches of the realm. Through this bureaucracy, information would flow to Versailles and orders could be carried out in the localities. The effectiveness of absolutism was determined by the efficiency of both operations.

FROM *Memoirs of Nicolas-Joseph Foucault*

Colbert to the Commissioners in the Field, April 28, 1679

YOU KNOW THAT I HAVE WRITTEN you by order of the king every year before this in order to stimulate you to make your visit to all the elections [an administrative unit] of the generality of . . . with great care and also in order to let you know what you should occupy yourself with principally in this visit. Since this is a way of procuring the easing of the people's lot, almost equal to that which the king has given them by the great decrease that he has made in the taxes, His Majesty has ordered me to tell you that he wishes that this year you will make a more complete visit of all the elections and parishes of the above generality that you have not yet made, and that you should start this immediately and without any hesitation; and to this effect I will give you, in a few words, the principal points that you should examine.

The first and the most important is the imposition of the *tailles* [*a property tax from which the nobility and clergy were exempt—L. P. W.*], on which, although I am persuaded that the application that you already have shown prevents many abuses, nevertheless, since it is certain that, either in the drawing up of the tax rolls, or in the levying and collection of the *tailles,* or in the actual reception that the receivers make of the collectors, or in the pressures that one exercises and the expenses that the taxable people are forced to pay, there is still a good deal of disorder of which you are not aware since those who are guilty and who profit from it take care to hide it from you—this being the case the king wants you to enter into detail on all these points, in order that there is nothing on which you are not exactly informed and to which you will not be able to apply whatever remedies may be necessary.

His Majesty also wishes that you should examine the state of commerce and manufactures in the same generality, together with the food supply and the number of domestic animals, and that you should consider these three points as the fertile sources from which the people draw their money, not only for their own subsistence, but also for paying all their taxes; so that His Majesty desires that you should look into with care the means not only of maintaining them but even of augmenting them and of re-establishing

Mémoires de Nicolas-Joseph Foucault (1850), pp. 417 ff., translated by L. Pearce Williams.

commerce and manufactures which have disappeared because of not having received any help. . . .

You know well enough the intentions of the king regarding the garrisoning of troops. . . . This is why I shall rest content merely to add that His Majesty has been informed that in the greater number of cities and places where the inhabitants have furnished the housing of troops for the last ten or twelve years, the mayors and aldermen have kept and distributed amongst themselves the money which was given to them by the general receivers of finances for the reimbursement of the said inhabitants; and since there is no theft more obvious than this, and none which merits more to be punished, since the people are in the hands of their magistrates and since this theft can consequently begin again every day, His Majesty wishes that in the visit that you are going to make, you will examine carefully if the inhabitants of the cities and places of your generality which have furnished housing for troops make the same complaints against the mayors and aldermen, and in case you find someone who has been in charge for five or six years and who has applied for his own profit a large enough sum, let me know about it so that I can render an account to His Majesty and he will be able to send you orders so that you can give an exemplary punishment of this crime. . . .

*   *   *

FROM *Administrative Correspondence Under the Reign of Louis XIV*

The Bishop of Marseilles to Colbert, Lambesc, November 20, 1668

NO MATTER WITH WHAT CARE I tried, I was unable to get the deputies to this assembly to go beyond the sum of 400,000 [*French pounds—L. P. W.*] without certain conditions. The main ones are compensation for the expense that the troops have caused this year, the revocation of the edict on soap, and the revocation of the edict on genealogical experts.

They defend themselves in terms of the sum of money by pointing to the exhaustion of money in the province which is, in truth, very great, and which proceeds from the taxes on the businessmen, from the inquest on false nobility, which has drawn out enormous amounts of money by rather extraordinary avenues, the considerable expenses which have fallen on the communities with the arrangement of the [*royal—L. P. W.*] domain, from which apparently the money does not come back into the treasury, and the

G. B. Depping, ed., *Correspondance administrative sous le règne de Louis XIV*, I (1850), 381–2, 384–5, 389, 390, 398, 399, translated by L. Pearce Williams.

circulation of counterfeit five-sous pieces which has used up a great deal of good money and which will destroy commerce if there is not a true remedy forthcoming. In truth, if the province was only assessed for what the king wishes to draw from it and which he demands as his free gift there would be no trouble in arranging that and in persuading the deputies.

The province by law has a right to compensation [*for garrisoning—L. P. W.*], and this year it has cost almost one hundred thousand livres, and since the king, no doubt, will not wish to subtract this amount from his gift this will mean it will cost the province five hundred thousand pounds and there is some justice to the position that the province should be assured of this compensation for the future in order to dismiss the apprehension under which these people labor that in giving to H. M. a considerable gift they will at the same time be asked, in the province, to pay for the lodging of troops or any other expense that may be demanded.

As for the affair of the soap, it is certain that not everything is being done to carry out the ordinance of H. M. as the price of soap has gone up. Since the old manufactories no longer work and since new ones are being established in neighboring provinces, there is the fear that this manufacture, which is one of the largest in the realm and which gives so much profit in this province, will be destroyed in the end if something is not done about it. You will do, Monsieur, what you will consider just.

As for the edict on the genealogical experts, if this is carried out it will mean the establishment of more than 800 officers at the same time that the King is working so well to abolish those who are useless and a burden on the people; moreover, paying them will force the disbursement of immense sums.

I also feel it necessary, Monsieur, to inform you that the nobility of this province, having the desire to sell their wheat at an excessive price, would like to restrain the public liberty (the right to import wheat by sea) on a foodstuff so necessary to life. They have worked, by all kinds of means, to force this assembly to join with them; but the deputies know the famine that would affect all the poor people of the province, and on this affair I have no doubt that they will oppose themselves to this unjust proposition, which is so harmful to the public. . . . Since the assembly has been meeting for almost three months without accomplishing much, and as it cannot disband until the return of the courier that has been sent to you, you would be doing a great favor to send him back soon, and you will find complete acquiescence to all that H. M. may order.

Colbert to President d'Oppède, Saint-Germain, March 6, 1671

I have given an account to the King of the request that you have made to the assembly of the communities of Provence, in conformity to the orders of H. M. He orders me to tell you that it is necessary to terminate this affair promptly considering how long it has been going on. . . .

I have already received several complaints that the aldermen of the city of Marseilles are not carrying out the execution of the edicts for the liberation (of the port) and particularly for the payment of the 20 per cent, and the confiscation of merchandise which would enter without paying. . . .

March 13 . . . I will not even answer the offer that the province has made of giving 200,000 pounds as the free gift, since you know that the King wishes the amount that is mentioned in your instructions and is waiting for you to get it done.

Colbert to the Count de Grignan, Saint-Germain, March 20, 1671

I have reported to the King what you have been pleased to write me on the offer that the assembly of the communities of Provence have made for his free gift and the difficulty that you are encountering in raising it to the sum that H. M. desires; but he has told me at the same time to let you know that he will not rest content with less than what he has asked for and thus has no doubt that you will employ all the means that you consider necessary to oblige the said assembly to give him this satisfaction.

Colbert to the Count de Grignan, Saint-Germain, October 16, 1671

I can assure you that H. M. wanted 500,000 pounds from the province last year, as this, and it was only the pleading of your letters and those of Monsieur d'Oppède, that led H. M. to reduce it to 450,000 pounds for particular reasons that I cannot remember at present; but this year H. M. wants 500,000 pounds. . . .

Colbert to President d'Oppède, Saint-Germain, October 23, 1671

The King was somewhat surprised to hear that the deputies of the communities have returned to their homes under the pretext of holidays and that after a negotiation of three weeks you have only obtained from them the sum of 300,000 pounds. I ought to tell you that I really fear that the King may take the resolution to dismiss this assembly without taking anything from it since H. M. is not accustomed, by the conduct of other estates, to all these long negotiations for such a modest sum as that which he demands from Provence. . . .

Colbert to the Count de Grignan, Paris, December 25, 1671

I have reported to the King on the bad conduct of the assembly of the communities of Provence and, since H. M. is not disposed to suffer it any longer, he has given the necessary orders to dismiss it and at the same time has sent *lettres de cachet* intended to exile the ten deputies who caused the most trouble to Grandville, Cherbourg, Saint-Malo, Morlaix, and Concarneau. The said letters and orders will be sent to you by the first ordinary post, and I do not think it necessary to recommend that you be punctual and exact in executing them, knowing with how much warmth and zeal you act in everything that concerns the service of the King.

Colbert to the Bishop of Marseilles, Versailles, December 31st, 1671

The King accepts the four hundred and fifty thousand pounds that the assembly of the communities of Provence offered for the free gift, but H. M. is so indignant at the conduct of the deputies in making their deliberation that he has sent orders to exile 10 of the worst troublemakers to the provinces of Normandy and Brittany, which orders have been addressed to Monsieur the Count de Grignan. Provence should easily know how disadvantageous it has been to it to have chosen deputies so little attached to its true interest, but I do not know if these complaints may not be useless since it looks as though H. M. will not permit another such assembly of the communities in Provence.

4 The Evaluation of the Reign

Abolutism depended upon the efficiency of the bureaucracy created to make it effective. This machinery of government is the subject studied by James E. King, who sees its development as the result of the new science of the seventeenth century. Just as the new science emphasized facts over theories, so the government of Louis XIV was an attempt to apply reason to actual situations. To do so, channels of information and chains of command had to be created.

FROM *Science and Rationalism in the Government of Louis XIV* BY JAMES E. KING

SUCH WAS THE CENTRAL GOVERNMENT of France in the period 1661 to 1683. It is necessary to remind oneself that most of its actual work was performed in committees, subcommittees of the councils, and in the bureaus functioning under the various ministers and secretaries of state. In the provinces the will of this organization was exercised, in the main, through four distinct structures: that of justice, finances, the military, and the church. The last of these we can omit from our considerations as it has no direct bearing on our story.

The justice of the King was carried to the kingdom by the "sovereign" parlements. These were, for all but extraordinary cases, the supreme courts of the realm. To them came appeals from all the lower courts, as the *présidiaux, bailliages,* or *sénéchaussées,* in their particular jurisdictions. The chief of these parlements in prestige and real authority was that at Paris. This might be called the king's parlement. Other parlements were situated at Toulouse, Rouen, Grenoble, Bordeaux, Dijon, Aix, Rennes, Pau, Metz, and Besançon, and several sovereign courts functioned elsewhere. The natural head, excluding the king, of all these courts was the chancellor of France, and it was

James E. King, *Science and Rationalism in the Government of Louis XIV, 1661–1683* (1950), pp. 124–30; 136–7. Reprinted by permission of The Johns Hopkins Press.

through his department that appointments to them were made. The *conseil du Roi,* as represented in any of its four divisions, might override the decisions or opinions of the parlements.

The financial administration of the kingdom, and this must be extended to include economic as well as tax administration, was carried on, primarily, by the intendants with their subordinates. In our period, France was divided into twenty-six large tax districts, for administrative purposes, called generalities. There were headed by twenty-five intendants. The generalities, in turn, were subdivided into smaller districts called elections and the elections into parishes. A regular hierarchy of officials, within these areas, supervised the levying and collection of taxes, judged cases involving taxation, performed accounting, kept tax rolls, and allocated sums for local costs of government. Under the intendants operated a separate group of officials, with undefined powers, who supervised or interfered in these functions.

The so-called military government of the king was exercised by royal governors in thirty-seven governments. These men were ordinarily the peers of the realm or princes of the blood. Many of the ancient prerogatives of these gentlemen, as governors, had been drained off by the agents of the secretary of state for war and the intendants, but their prestige was still very considerable and if the governor was a man of capacity, cooperated with the intendants, was friendly to and trusted by the king and ministers, he could still wield considerable influence. Below the governor were usually four or five lieutenant-generals and, beneath them, governors of local places, cities or royal chateaux. Lieutenant-generals and these local governors were often almost independent of the provincial governor and were also usually chosen from the higher nobility. The primary duties of the governors were to maintain order and obedience to the crown in the provinces and to give armed support, if necessary, to the executions and functions of the other administrations.

The administrative prerogatives of the intendant as supervisor of the royal services of justice, police, and finances in the provinces had been rather clearly defined by the time that Colbert assumed his full role in the government. During the personal reign of Louis XIV, these powers were even more definitely organized and solidified and the monarchy assumed the form which it was to retain almost to the end of the *ancien régime.* At the center of this monarchy was the officer called the *contrôleur général,* and, intimately allied to his functions and carrying his authority throughout the realm were the intendants of the provinces. This close relationship, or interdependence, was largely the creation of Colbert. The expression of it was the development of the practice of regular correspondence between the intendants and the *contrôleur général.* From the very beginning of his administration, Colbert maintained a prodigious correspondence with his subordinates and, particularly, with the intendants. The reciprocal necessity of submitting reports, surveys and memoirs to the *contrôleur général* became a regular duty of these officials. This was the most striking innovation of the minister in the government. As Usher writes in his *History of the grain trade in France,* "The development of the informing function of the intendants was thus one of the most direct results of the personal influence of Colbert. Nor was any function of the new administration more important or more literally unique."

Under the regime of Colbert and Louis XIV, the intendant assumed the part of delegate administrator in the most obscure sections that the royal power penetrated. . . . A literal reading of the instructions and circular letters sent to the intendants or *commissaires départis* into the generalities and *pays d'élections* from 1663 through 1683 would probably leave the researcher at a loss to imagine any possible field of government which was not committed to their inspection. But every inspection required the return of a report or written survey to the King, the secretaries of state, or the *contrôleur général,* and it was on such reports that *ordonnances* were formed, policies decreed, and projects drawn up by the ministry for presentation to the councils and the King.

It was the desire of the King, according to his Minister, that the intendants should come to know "perfectly all abuses" in the area of their responsibility, and to know them appears to have been considered as equal to remedying them. The insistence on thorough penetration into the most obscure corners of provincial affairs was the theme dominating instructions. The King recognized the physical limitations of his own personal desire to learn of the details of his realm "piece by piece," details which he would acquire himself if it were possible; therefore, trusted emissaries must perform the vicarious functions of a protean crown.

*   *   *

The intendants were, then, the legal eyes of the Monarchy. Colbert wrote his intendants and ordered them carefully, and personally, to investigate the levying of all taxes in all the elections of their generality "in a way that nothing escapes you." He spurred them on to greater thoroughness by representing these requests as being relayed from "His Majesty" who urged them to make "a serious reflection on all that which happens in the area of the Generality in which you serve . . . that you enter into the detail of the conduct of all those who are employed thereto." He acknowledged the difficulty of knowing all the various matters to "the depth," but this difficulty only emphasized the need of more continuous application to the task, in order that he might give to "His Majesty all your advice on all that which can apply in the future to the end which he sets for himself."

*   *   *

The multifarious functions of the intendants and the essentially informative character of these functions are progressively evident in early correspondence of Colbert with them. Usher asserts that technical and statistical information was less frequently required of the intendant than a statement of the general impression of conditions in his generality; however, as time passed the Minister became ever more exacting in his demands and increasingly discriminating in the segregation of fact from rumor. His persistency in insisting on adequate and valid information had the end result of developing an administrative standard of expectation and compliance which accounts for the fullness of the reports of the intendants after Colbert's death. The requirement of continuous reporting, the necessity for presenting, to the ministry, digested summary statements of the most diverse facts in his generality, placed the intendant, perforce, as another writer has observed, in the midst of numbers. By the very nature of his functions, he became a statistical agent of the central government.

The general pattern of government by inquiry was precisely laid down in the *Instruction pour les maîtres des requêtes, commissaires départis dans les provinces* of September 1663. This circular letter significantly and, in a sense, officially underlined the henceforth consistent policy of Colbert and Louis XIV in regard to the duties of the intendants. It initiated a vast inquest into the state of the realm with the intendants as the royal investigators; an inquest which was never completed in the life of its originator. The correspondence of Colbert reveals that most of the information requested at this time was still being sought by him twenty years later. Twenty years after that the Duke of Beauvillier made almost the same inquiries when forming his famous memoirs for the instruction of Louis XIV's grandson, the Duke of Burgundy. However imperfectly the designs of the inquest might be carried out, the instruction of 1663 was an unqualified endorsement by Louis XIV and his Minister of the ideal of administration based on the accumulation of political and social statistics.

*   *   *

Among the memoirs resulting from the inquest of 1663 those of Charles Colbert de Croissy, a brother of the Minister, are singled out by Clement as of superior quality, displaying, besides a diversity of information, an unusual frankness. His reports on Poitou, Touraine, Anjou, Alsace and the three bishoprics of Metz, Toul and Verdun were notably detailed and revealed the sad plight of their peoples. Other such memoirs have been discovered on Brittany, Rouen, Champagne, Burgundy, Bourges, Berry, and Moulins dating from the early years of Colbert's administration.

The utility of a summary account of the personal qualities of the members of the parlements, and other superior courts, probably seemed particularly pointed to Louis XIV and Colbert, both of whom always kept the lessons of the Fronde carefully nurtured in their memories. We have seen the attention given to this detail in the third section of the memoir. All the intendants of the provinces were requested to submit careful notes on the morals, capacities, influence, property, connections, and functions of the personnel of these courts. The resulting reports were in many cases partial and in most cases must have appeared inadequate. But this might be expected at a time when the intendants were but beginning to assume the new role assigned to them by an exacting Minister. At any rate, the *"Notes sécrètes"* sent to Colbert in response to this request form an extensive and entertaining part of the administrative correspondence edited by Depping.

M. Lamoignon of the Parlement of Paris was a pompous person with an "affectation of great probity and of a great integrity hiding a great ambition." M. Bailleul had a "gentle and easy disposition, acquiring through his civility many friends in the Palais [of the Parlement] and at the court." One de Nesmond "married to the sister of Mr the first president, is governed by her." M. Menardeau-Sampré was "very capable, firm, obstinate . . . governed by a damlle of the rue Saint-Martin." As for M. Fayet, he was "less than nothing." In the *Chambre des Enquestes,* M. Faure was "stupid, ignorant, brutal, fearing extraordinarily M. Hervé; he is a man of letters, but loves extraordinarily his own interests." But this was a report on all the major courts of the kingdom; in the Parlement of Brittany, the sieur De Brequingy had good intention "but he is weak and of a very mediocre mind." Jacquelot, sieur de la Motte was "without capacity, and addicted to debauches with women and wine," but M. Montigny had "many of all kinds of good qualities and no bad ones." The reporter on the councillors of the *cours des Aydes* at Rouen contented himself almost entirely with variations on the two words: *"probité"* and *"capacité."* If his subject was very commendable he had both *"probité"* and *"capacité."*

However deficient some of the first reports of the intendants might be, it would appear that, with practice, the technique could be too well mastered. In July 1676, Colbert wrote in perplexity to M. Le Blanc at Rouen, "I have received the account of the provender which has been consumed in your generality during the winter quarter; but you fail to explain for what reason you send it to me, and I cannot supply it."

François-Marie Arouet (1694–1778), who took the name of Voltaire, was one of the most prominent and prolific writers of the Enlightenment in France. The Age of Louis XIV was, to him, the golden age of French culture, and he attributed much of this excellence to the regime of absolutism instituted by the Sun King.

FROM *The Age of Louis XIV* BY VOLTAIRE

WE OWE IT TO PUBLIC MEN who have benefited their age to look at the point from which they started in order better to appreciate the changes they have brought about in their country. Posterity owes them an eternal debt of gratitude for the examples they have given, even when their achievements have been surpassed, and this well-deserved glory is their only reward. It was certainly the love of this sort of glory that inspired Louis XIV when, as soon as he began to govern for himself, he set out to reform his kingdom, embellish his court and perfect the arts.

Not only did he impose upon himself the duty of working regularly with each one of his ministers, but any man of repute could obtain a private audience with him, and every citizen was free to present him with petitions and projects. The petitions were received, first of all, by a master of requests, who noted his comments in the margin and sent them on to the offices of the ministers. The projects were examined in Council when they deserved it and their authors were more than once admitted to discuss their proposals with the ministers in the King's presence. In this way, despite Louis's absolute power, the nation could still communicate with the monarch.

Louis XIV trained and accustomed himself to work, and this work was all the more difficult because it was new to him and because he could easily be distracted by the lures of pleasure. The first dispatches he sent to his ambassadors he wrote himself, and he later often minuted the most important letters in his own hand. None were written in his name without his having them read to him.

After the fall of Fouquet, Colbert had scarcely re-established order in the finances when the King canceled all the arrears due on taxes from 1647 to 1656 and, above all, three millions of the taille. Five hundred thousand crowns' worth of onerous duties were abolished. So the Abbé de Choisi seems to be either very misinformed or very unjust when he says that the receipts were not decreased. It is clear that they were decreased by these remissions, though they were later increased again as a result of better administration.

The efforts of the First President of Bellièvre, helped by the generosity of the Duchess of Aiguillon and several other citizens, had already established the general hospital in Paris. The King enlarged it and had others built in all the principal towns of the kingdom.

The highways, which up till then had been impassable, were no longer neglected and gradually became what they are today under Louis XV—the admiration of all foreigners. Whatever direction one goes from Paris, one can now travel for nearly two hundred miles, except for a few places, on well-surfaced roads lined with trees. The roads built by the ancient Romans were more lasting, but not as spacious or as beautiful.

Colbert directed his genius principally toward commerce, which was still largely undeveloped and whose basic principles were still unknown. The English, and still more the Dutch, carried almost all French trade in their ships. The Dutch in particular loaded their ships with our goods in our ports and distributed them throughout Europe. In 1662 the King began to exempt his subjects from a duty called the freight tax, which all foreign vessels had to pay, and he gave French merchants every facility for transporting their goods themselves more cheaply. It was then that our maritime trade began to develop. The council of commerce, which still exists today, was established, and the King presided over it every fortnight.

The ports of Dunkirk and Marseilles were declared free, and very soon this advantage attracted the trade of the Levant to Marseilles and that of the North to Dunkirk.

*　　　*　　　*

The West India company was encouraged no less than the others; the King supplied a tenth of all its funds. He gave thirty francs a ton on exports and forty on imports. All those who had ships built in French ports received five francs for each ton their vessel could carry.

*　　　*　　　*

Paris in those days was very far from being what it is now. There was neither lighting, police protection nor cleanliness. Provision had to be made for the continual cleaning of the streets and for lighting them every night with five thousand lamps; the whole town had to be paved; two new gates had to be built and the old ones restored; a permanent guard, both mounted and on foot, was needed for the security of citizens. All this the King took upon himself, allotting the funds for these necessary expenses. In 1667 he appointed a magistrate whose sole duty was to supervise the police. Most of the large cities of Europe only initiated these examples many years later; none has equaled them. There is no city paved like Paris, and even Rome has no street lighting.

Everything was beginning to improve so noticeably that the second holder of the office of lieutenant of police in Paris acquired a reputation which placed him among the distinguished men of his age; and indeed he was a man of great ability. He was afterward in the Ministry and he would have made a fine general. The post of lieutenant of police was below his birth and merit, and yet it gained him a much greater reputation than did the uneasy and transient ministerial office which he obtained toward the end of his life.

It is worth noting here that M. d'Argenson was not the only member of the old nobility to hold the office of magistrate. Far from it; France is almost the only country in which the old nobility has often worn magisterial robes. Almost all other states, from motives which are a remnant of Gothic barbarity, fail to realize that there is greatness in this profession.

From 1661 onward, the King was continually occupied in building the Louvre, Saint-Germain and Versailles. Private individuals, following his example, built hundreds of superb, spacious buildings in Paris. Their number increased to such an extent that there sprang up around the Palais-Royal and Saint-Sulpice two new towns vastly superior to the old one. This same time saw the invention of that splendid convenience, the coach, ornamented with mirrors and suspended on springs; thus a citizen of Paris could travel about this great city in far greater luxury than that in which the ancient Romans rode in triumph to the Capitol. This custom, which began in Paris, soon spread to the rest of Europe and has become so common that it is no longer a luxury.

Louis XIV had a taste for architecture, gardens and sculpture, and his taste was characterized by a liking for grandeur and impressiveness. In 1664, Controller General Colbert assumed the office of director of buildings (which is really the Ministry of the Arts), and no sooner had he done so than he set about furthering his master's schemes. The first task was to complete the Louvre. François Mansart, one of the greatest architects France has ever had, was chosen to construct the vast buildings that were planned. He was unwilling to undertake this commission unless he had freedom to reconstruct any parts of the edifice which seemed to him defective when he had completed them, and this mistrust of himself, which might have involved too great an expenditure, led to his exclusion. The chevalier Bernini was then sent for from Rome, a man whose name was famous by virtue of the colonnade surrounding St. Peter's Square, the equestrian statue of Constantine and the Navonna fountain. Carriages were provided for his journey. He was brought to Paris like a man who came to honor France. Apart from five louis a day during the eight months he stayed, he also received a present of fifty thousand crowns, together with a pension of two thousand, and one of five hundred for his son. Louis XIV's generosity to Bernini was even greater than that of Francis I to Raphael. By way of acknowledgment, Bernini later made, in Rome, the equestrian statue of the King which is now to be seen at Versailles. But when he arrived in Paris with so much circumstance, he was amazed to see the plan of the façade of the Louvre which faces Saint-Germain l'Auxerrois, and which soon after, when executed, became one of the most august monuments of architecture in the world. Claude Perrault had made this plan, and it was put into execution by Louis Levau and Dorbay. Perrault invented the machines by which were transported the stones, fifty-two feet long, that formed the pediment of this majestic edifice. Sometimes people go a long way to find what they already have at home. No palace in Rome has an entrance comparable to that of the Louvre, for which we are indebted to the Perrault whom Boileau dared to ridicule. Travelers admit that the famous Italian villas are inferior to the château of Maisons, which was built at such a small cost by François Mansart. Bernini was magnificently rewarded and did not deserve his rewards; he merely furnished plans which were never put into execution.

While building the Louvre, the completion of which is so greatly to be desired, while creating a town at Versailles near the Château which has cost so many millions, while building the Trianon and Marly and embellishing many other edifices, the King also built the Observatory, which was begun in 1666, at the same time as he founded the Academy of Sciences. But his most glorious monument, by its usefulness and its greatness as much as by the difficulties of its construction, was the canal which joins the two seas and which finds an outlet at the port of Sète, built especially for the purpose. All this work was begun in 1664 and continued without interruption until 1681. The foundation of the Invalides, with its chapel, the finest in Paris, and the establishment of Saint-Cyr, the last of many works built by the King—these by themselves would suffice to make his memory revered. Four thousand soldiers and a large number of officers find consolation in their old age and relief for their wounds and wants in the first of these great institutions; two hundred and fifty daughters of noblemen receive an education worthy of them in the other; together they are like so many voices praising Louis XIV. The establishment of Saint-Cyr will be surpassed by the one which Louis XV has just created for the education of five hundred noblemen; but so far from causing Saint-Cyr to be forgotten, it serves to remind one of it; the art of doing good has been brought to perfection.

At the same time, Louis XIV wanted to achieve something even greater and more generally useful, though more difficult; he wanted to reform the laws. For this task he employed the Chancellor Seguier, Lamoignon, Talon, Bignon, and above all, the councilor of state, Pussort. Sometimes he attended their meetings himself. The year 1667 was marked both by his first laws and by his first conquests. The civil ordinance appeared first and was followed by the code for the rivers and forests, and then by statutes concerning all the industries, by a criminal code, one for commerce and one for the marine. These followed one another in an almost annual succession. New laws were even established in favor of the Negroes of our colonies, a race of men who had hitherto not enjoyed the common rights of humanity.

One cannot expect a sovereign to possess a profound knowledge of jurisprudence, but the King was well informed about the principal laws; he was imbued with their spirit and knew how to enforce or mitigate them as the occasion demanded. He often judged his subjects' cases, not only in the Council of the Secretaries of State, but also in the so-called Council of Parties. There are two celebrated judgments of his in which he decided against his own interest.

In the first, in 1680, the issue was one between himself and some private citizens of Paris who had built on his land. He decided that they should keep the houses, together with the land which belonged to him and which he ceded to them.

The other case concerned a Persian called Roupli, whose goods had been seized by his revenue commissioners in 1687. His decision was that all should be returned to him, and the King added a present of three thousand crowns. Roupli returned to his country full of admiration and gratitude. When we later met Mehemet Rizabeg, the Persian ambassador to Paris, we found that he had known about this incident for a long time, for it had become famous.

*   *   *

He was the legislator of his armies as well as of his people as a whole. It is surprising that, before his time, there was no uniform dress among the troops. It was he who, in the first year of his administration, ordered that each regiment should be distinguished by the color of its dress or by different badges; this regulation was soon adopted by all other nations. It was he who instituted brigadiers and who put the household troops on their present footing. He turned Cardinal Mazzarin's guards into a company of musketeers and fixed the number of men in the companies at five hundred; moreover, he gave them the uniform which they still wear today.

Under him there were no longer constables, and after the death of the Duke of Epernon, no more colonel generals of infantry; they had become too powerful, and he quite rightly wanted to be sole master. Marshal Grammont, who was only colonel of horse of the French Guards under the Duke of Epernon and who took his orders from this colonel general, now took them only from the King, and was the first to be given the title of Colonel of the Guards. The King himself installed his colonels at the head of their regiments, giving them with his own hand a gilt gorget with a pike, and afterward, when the use of pikes was abolished, a spontoon, or kind of half-pike. In the King's Regiment, which he created himself, he instituted grenadiers, on the scale of four to a company in the first place; then he formed a company of grenadiers in each regiment of infantry. He gave two to the French Guards. Nowadays there is one for each battalion throughout the whole infantry. He greatly enlarged the Corps of Dragoons, and gave them a colonel general. The establishment of studs for breeding horses, in 1667, must not be forgotten, for they had been completely abandoned beforehand and they were of great value in providing mounts for the cavalry, an important resource which has since been too much neglected.

It was he who instituted the use of the bayonet affixed to the end of the musket. Before his time, it was used occasionally, but only a few companies fought with this weapon. There was no uniform practice and no drill; everything was left to the general's discretion. Pikes were then thought of as the most redoubtable weapon. The first regiment to have bayonets and to be trained to use them was that of the Fusiliers, established in 1671.

The manner in which artillery is used today is due entirely to him. He founded artillery schools, first at Douai, then at Metz and Strasbourg; and the Regiment of Artillery was finally staffed with officers who were almost all capable of successfully conducting a siege. All the magazines in the kingdom were well stocked, and they were supplied annually with eight hundred thousand pounds of powder. He created a regiment of bombardiers and one of hussars; before this only his enemies had had hussars.

In 1688 he established thirty regiments of militia, which were provided and equipped by the communes. These militia trained for war but without abandoning the cultivation of their fields.

Companies of cadets were maintained in the majority of frontier towns; there they learned mathematics, drawing and all the drills, and carried out the duties of soldiers. This institution lasted for ten years, but the government finally tired of trying to discipline these difficult young people. The Corps of Engineers, on the other hand, which the King created and to which he gave its present regulations, is an institution which will last forever. During his reign the art of fortifying strongholds was brought to perfection by Marshal Vauban and his pupils, who surpassed Count Pagan. He built or repaired a hundred and fifty fortresses.

To maintain military discipline, the King created inspectors general and later directors, who reported on the state of the troops; from their reports it could be seen whether the war commissioners had carried out their duties.

He instituted the Order of Saint-Louis, an honorable distinction which was often more sought after than wealth. The Hôtel des Invalides put the seal on his efforts to merit loyal service.

It was owing to measures such as these that he had, by 1672, a hundred and eighty thousand regular troops, and that, increasing his forces as the number and strength of his enemies increased, he finished with four hundred and fifty thousand men under arms, including the troops of the navy.

Before his time such powerful armies were unknown. His enemies could scarcely muster comparable forces, and to do so they had to be united. He showed what France, on her own, was capable of, and he always had either great successes or great resources to fall back on.

*   *   *

This short account is enough to illustrate the changes which Louis XIV brought about in the state; and that they were useful changes is shown by the fact that they still exist. His ministers vied with each other in furthering his plans. They were responsible for all the details and for the actual execution, but the over-all plan was his. Of one thing one can be certain: the magistrates would not have reformed the laws; order would not have been restored in the finances; discipline would not have been introduced into the armies and into the general policing of the kingdom; there would have been no fleets; the arts would not have been encouraged; and all this would not have been achieved in such an organized and determined fashion at one single time (though under different ministers) if there had not been at the head of affairs a master who conceived in general terms all these great aims, and had the will power to accomplish them.

He never separated his own glory from the well-being of France, and he never looked on his kingdom in the same light as a lord looks on the lands from which he extracts all he can in order to live a life of luxury. Every king who loves glory loves the public welfare; Colbert and Louvois were no longer there when, in 1698, he ordered each intendant to produce a detailed description of his province for the instruction of the Duke of Burgundy. In this way it was possible to have an exact account of his kingdom and an accurate census of his peoples. This was a most useful achievement, although not every intendant had the capacity or the attention to detail of M. de Lamoignon de Bâville. If the King's intentions had been carried out as thoroughly in every other province as they were by this magistrate in his census of Languedoc, this collection of reports would have been one of the finest monuments of the age. Several others were well done; but a general plan was lacking, insofar as the intendants did not all receive the same instructions. What would have been most desirable was for each intendant to give, in columns, an account of the number of inhabitants of each district— nobles, citizens, farm workers, artisans and workmen—together with live-stock of all kinds, lands of various degrees of fertility, the whole of the regular and secular clergy, their revenues, those of the towns and those of the communes.

In most of the reports returned, these aims are confused; some subjects are dealt with superficially and inaccurately, and it is often quite difficult to find the information one is looking for and which should be immediately available to a minister wanting to discover, at a glance, the forces, needs and resources of the community. The plan was an excellent one, and it would be most useful if someday it is executed in a uniform manner.

This, then, in general terms, is what Louis XIV did or tried to do to make his country more flourishing. It seems to me hardly possible to consider all this work and all these efforts without a feeling of gratitude and without being filled with the concern for the welfare of the people which inspired them. Consider what the country was like at the time of the *Fronde* and what it is like today. Louis XIV did more for his people than twenty of his predecessors put together; and even then he did not do everything he might have done. The war which ended with the Peace of Rijswijk began the ruin of the flourishing commerce established by his minister Colbert, and the War of Spanish Succession completed it.

He spent immense sums on the aqueducts and works of Maintenon and on conveying water to Versailles, and both these projects were abandoned and thereby rendered useless. If he had spent this money, or a fifth part of what it cost to force nature at Versailles, on embellishing his capital, Paris today would be, throughout its whole extent, as beautiful as is the area around the Tuileries and the Pont-Royal, and would have become the most magnificent city in the universe.

It is a great achievement to have reformed the laws, but legal chicanery could not be abolished by legislation. The government tried to make justice uniform, and it has become so in criminal matters and in those of commerce and procedure; it could become so in the laws regulating the fortunes of individual citizens. It is most inconvenient that the same tribunal often has to give judgment on the basis of a hundred different customs. Certain land rights, which are either equivocal, onerous or harmful to society, still exist like remnants of a feudal government which no longer survives; they are the rubbish from a ruined Gothic building.

We are not claiming that the different orders in the state should all be subjected to the same laws. It will be realized that the customs of the nobility, the clergy, the magistracy and the peasantry must be different. But there is no doubt that it is desirable that each order should have its own law, which should be uniform throughout the kingdom, and that what is just or true in Champagne should not be considered false or unjust in Normandy. In every branch of administration, uniformity is a virtue; but the difficulties of achieving it have deterred people from the attempt.

Louis XIV could much more easily have done without the dangerous assistance of tax-farmers, to whom he was forced to have recourse because he almost always anticipated on his revenues, as will be seen in the chapter on finances.

If he had not believed that his will was sufficient to make a million men change their religion, France would not have lost so many citizens. Yet despite these upsets and losses, the country is still one of the most prosperous in the world, because all the good which Louis did remains and the evil which it was difficult to avoid doing in those stormy times has been repaired. In the final analysis it is posterity which judges kings and of whose judgment they must always be mindful; and when it comes to weigh up the virtues and weaknesses of Louis XIV, posterity will admit that, although he received too much praise during his lifetime, he deserves the praise of all future ages and was worthy of the statue which was erected to him at Montpellier, with a Latin inscription the sense of which is "To Louis the Great after his death." Don Ustariz, a statesman who has written on the finances and commerce of Spain, calls Louis XIV "an astounding man."

All these changes in government and in all the orders of society, which we have just examined, necessarily produced a vast change in our manners. The spirit of faction, intemperance and rebellion which had possessed the citizens of France ever since the time of Francis II gave place to a desire to excel in serving the King. The lords of large estates no longer remained quartered at home; the governors of provinces no longer had important posts to bestow; and as a result, the sovereign's favors were the only ones people strove to deserve; in this way, the state acquired a sort of geometrical unity, with each line leading to the center.

> *Charles Guignebert was, for many years, Professor of History at the University of Paris. Educated under the Third Republic, he saw the Age of Louis XIV with somewhat different eyes from Voltaire's.*

FROM *A Short History of the French People*
BY CHARLES GUIGNEBERT

THE DESPOTISM OF LOUIS XIV

IT WAS A GREAT MISFORTUNE for France and the monarchy that every means of resisting royal absolutism and every desire to do so should have disappeared towards 1661. The evolution of royalty, which might have proceeded in closer and closer adaptation to the needs of the country, was cut short and crystallised into a practical *deification of the king*. And since, in fact, *the uncontrolled authority* of the prince cannot possibly do all that is needed, it gives less than it takes away, and any government which it provides has inevitably many shortcomings; further, by supplanting every other principle on which public action can be based, *it rapidly vitiates its own administration and transforms it into a mere exploitation of the subjects for the benefit of the monarch.*

The character and the political theories of Louis XIV largely contributed to this disastrous result; but this character assumed its visible shape under the influence of a definite environment. These theories did not spring spontaneously to birth in the spirit of the young king; they are the result of impressions made on him by his surroundings. When Bossuet, preaching before him in the Lent of 1662, said, *"Il se remue pour votre Majesté quelque chose d'illustre et de grand et qui passe la destinée des rois vos*

Charles Guignebert, *A Short History of the French People* (1930), pp. 86–105, translated by F. G. Richmond.

prédécesseurs" (*There broods over your Majesty something illustrious and great, foreshadowing a destiny above that of the kings your predecessors*), he expressed a prevalent opinion. It was with the complicity of his own subjects that Louis XIV developed his despotic egotism. Neither they nor he understood from the start the danger they were running.

At the death of Mazarin the king was twenty-two, and was commonly considered the handsomest man in his kingdom. It was said at court that only the poet Racine could compare with him. In other words, he fulfilled the ideal of royal beauty, formed by his contemporaries. Though he was but of moderate stature, he had a perfect nobility and majesty of deportment, so natural as never to seem in the least affected. Easy and gracious, with the most courteous manners in the world, he exercised an extraordinary attraction when he cared to trouble himself so far. Saint-Simon, who had no affection for him, nevertheless praises his fine manners and his perfect politeness. His subjects had a genuine admiration for him. *"The respect aroused by his presence, no matter where or when,"* writes Saint-Simon, *"imposed silence and almost terror on all."* Even in old age and depression he never lost his grand air.

His mind without being *"below mediocrity,"* as the redoubtable memorialist alleges, was ordinary and above all *passive,* but *"capable of forming itself,"* being well able both to attend and to reflect. It was, in other respects, ill-served by a most inadequate education, conducted without order or method during the Fronde, which Mazarin made no effort to remedy effectively, in so far as essentially political knowledge was concerned, until the last years of his life. Louis XIV in compensation for these insufficiencies had indeed the precious gift of *knowing how to be silent, and how to listen,* and another, even rarer among absolute monarchs: he could tolerate ability in those about him and turn it to his own use and profit.

His character was headstrong and his temper in all probability violent, but he could keep it under control; a perfect self-mastery seemed to him essential to his dignity, and Saint-Simon assures us that he did not lose his self-control *"more than ten times in the whole of his life";* that is to say, he did not allow himself to be visibly angered more than ten times. He was endowed with a certain instinct for right, justice and equity which he did not always follow, but never completely lost. His politeness, too, tempered and controlled his keen susceptibilities, but it unfortunately fostered a tendency to dissimulation, a fault to which he was by nature only too prone, and this dissimulation was accompanied by a tendency to be vindictive which led him at times to ill-feeling and ill-dealing. His *pride* was unbounded, such that *"but for the fear of the devil which God never took from him, however disturbed he might be, he would have caused himself to be worshipped."* His pride never pardoned an offense, and to offend him was easy.

It is possible that his good will, his diligence, certain qualities of prudence and moderation, his basic benevolence, if not real generosity—an assortment, in fact, of inconspicuous but by no means negligible virtues—might, after some years of experience of life, if each reinforced the other, have made him a type of much that a king should be, had not all been ruined by flattery. Unfortunately Louis XIV was the prey *"of flattery so egregious as to deify him in the very heart of Christianity."* During his whole life he drank deep of this deadly poison. It gave him extreme pleasure and cost him his sense of reality. Thus he came to believe himself of a different kind and of a different clay from other men, to find it both natural and necessary that all men and everything should be sacrificed to him. His egotism developed into a kind of unconscious ferocity and his *Ego,* his *"Moi,"* became a monstrosity. The interested and ingenious servility of courtiers, the crowd of adulators constantly pressing about him, were more responsible than himself for this disastrous distortion of his judgment.

He was extremely devout, or at least he became so when his early youthful fires had waned. He believed himself in all respects a good Christian. In reality he neither professed nor comprehended any but a religion of outward show, compounded of habit, ceremony, superstition and *"fear of the devil."* It was impotent either to make him moral or repress his inordinate sensuality. His private life was a scandal up to the threshold of middle age and he paraded his irregularities before the world with a sedate absence of all shame, apparently in the belief that he was privileged by Heaven and need not concern himself with the code that must rule the rest of the world. Not only did he live openly in adultery, but he had the assurance to give his bastards the rank of princes of the blood. It is probable that the eminent preachers whose office it was, every Lent, to remind him of the Christian virtues and of repentance for sin, sometimes found themselves in an embarrassing position. The warnings and the stern rebukes, to which he had to listen from some among them, fell on deaf ears till he had grown old, or at least was aging after 1681.

He owed the dignity of the latter part of his life, in all probability, to Madame de Maintenon. It was she who brought him and the queen again together in 1681, and after the death of the latter, in 1683, she was secretly married to the king, probably in January, 1684. Thenceforward he was a faithful husband and grew steadily more absorbed in religious devotion. On his death-bed he asked pardon from the bystanders for the scandals occasioned by his transgressions.

His political theories, which he took the trouble to embody by his own hand in writing for the instruction of his son, were in keeping with the education which had persuaded him that for him there was no law but his own will, and no control but that of God. One of his childish copybook headings, which has been preserved, is in these words, *"Homage is due to kings, they do everything that pleases them."* His youth was spent in hearing this reiterated by all about him, and the Fronde itself helped to convince him that all hung attendant on the king's will.

That kings were *"instituted by God,"* held their sceptre from Him

alone, need render no account of their acts but to Him alone, was the
complete conviction of his contemporaries as of himself and the few bold
spirits, who still recalled the political doctrines of the jurists of the Renaissance and their chimeras concerning *Organised Monarchy*—that is to say,
monarchy controlled and limited—were careful after the end of the troubles
to raise no voice in France. The work of Bossuet *Politique tirée des propres
paroles de l'Ecriture sainte,* has been commonly considered as the classical
presentation of the doctrine of the divine right of kings. Its chief merit was
the exposition of this doctrine in precise propositions and in a style of great
magnificence. Fundamentally it added nothing essential to what had been
said again and again for forty or fifty years by every political theorist of
royalty. Is it not curious to hear on the lips of Parliamentarians formulas
which no servility could surpass, taken as a matter of course as the expression
of received opinion?—the king is *"a visible divinity"* or *"a divine image of
the divinity. . . , an august law-giver, who with one hand has access to the
laws in the breast of God himself, and with the other communicates the
gathered treasure through us to his people."*

Louis XIV was thus naturally led to believe himself of a *"station above
that of other men."* He saw himself as *"standing in the place of God"* and as
"sharing in his knowledge as well as in his authority." He persuaded himself
that for a man of his rank to be under *"the necessity of receiving the law
from his people"* was the *"greatest calamity"* into which he could fall, that
every man who was his *"born subject"* must *"blindly obey,"* and that
"however bad" a prince might be, revolt against him was *"always infinitely
criminal,"* because a prince could be judged only by God. These convictions
were held by him to be clearly established both by direct evidence and by the
sovereign strength of revelation.

However, he did not, for a moment, imagine that divine favour had
raised him to the throne merely to indulge himself with a life of ease and
material satisfaction. He believed thoroughly that the *interest of the State
must come first* and that his own duty was clear: he must never *"reproach
himself in any important matter with having done less than his best."* It was
borne in upon him that the *"trade"* he practised was one which exacted
abnegation and forgetfulness of self. *"The trade of king,"* he wrote, *"is great,
noble and delightful when the workman can feel that he has acquitted
himself worthily in all his undertakings, but it does not exempt him from
pain, fatigue and anxiety."* Above all, it exacts continual labour: *"it is by this
he reigns, for this he reigns, and it were ingratitude and insolence towards
God, injustice and tyranny towards men to desire the one without the other."*

Louis XIV was indeed a life-long labourer; that is to say, he devoted
several hours a day to audiences with his ministers and councils, he made
decisions, he really believed that he himself transacted all the chief business
of the State, though in this he was not free from illusions; neither in
quantity nor in quality was his work all that he believed it to be. Nevertheless he did his best according to the measure of his ability and was persuaded
that he was the inspirer of his ministers.

There is certainly some grandeur in this conception which shows the sovereign, rising superior to human frailty, to all individual interests and to his own inclinations, bending his mind and will to the sole service of his State. Unfortunately Louis XIV thought that *"when one has the State in view one works for oneself"* and he held that *the nation* had no embodiment in France, save as it might express itself solely *"in the person of the king."* Thus *it was easy for him to confuse the State with his person, and the public service with worship of himself.*

A strange phenomenon indeed is the feeling displayed at this time towards the monarch, professed as it is by men in whom a genuine revival of faith has engendered an energetic Catholicism and amounting as it does to a kind of *idolatry.* Louis XIV had merely to make a gesture to inaugurate a cult. Did not, in 1686, the Marshal of La Feuillade go so far as to have lighted lanterns placed at night about the prince's statue on the Place des Victoires at Paris? Other acts of like servility are met with; we feel that more than one of those courtiers to whom the king's countenance was *"felicity complete,"* as La Bruyère puts it, tended to accept as truth the ejaculation of Bossuet, *"O kings, ye are gods"!* And this devotional sentiment and this religious respect undoubtedly are a better explanation than the universal lassitude which followed the Fronde, of the abasement of character and the abdication of all will in face of the king.

*   *   *

Louis XIV always claimed to govern by himself; the examples of his father dominated by Richelieu, and of his mother led by Mazarin, the memories of his youth, which were certainly not unmixed so far as his associations and personal relations with the late cardinal were concerned, had taught him a salutary lesson. He was determined that another should never be *"king in function"* while he was but King in name. Thus he decided to do without a prime minister and entrusted the preparation and the execution of business only to *commis* (clerks). Nor did he ever make of any man a favourite, or at any rate he allowed no one with whom he formed a friendship to exercise any influence whatever in State affairs any more than he allowed his mistresses to do so.

Saint-Simon alleges that in reality he was led by his ministers, even the least able among them, and that he was master only in his own imagination. There is undoubtedly some truth in this view, but it should not be unreservedly accepted. The Fronde had taught him suspicion of men; he knew that they might deceive him and he was always on his guard. Those of his *commis* who really influenced him successfully were those who, as students of human nature, had the address to persuade him that the ideas and the resolutions which he owed to their suggestion were originated by himself. Le Tellier, father of Louvois, relates that of twenty agenda submitted by himself to a Council meeting there was always one which the king returned for examination after refusing the proposed solution, but it was impossible to know beforehand which one it would be. Louis XIV said *No* to show that he was master and in a position to do so, not because he had come to any opinion of his own upon the case in question. As he could not possibly know or examine everything for himself, it may be considered as certain that his ministers sometimes duped him, that they wielded more power than he wished, but this was only achieved surreptitiously and by running a risk from the authority which hung over them, always ready to strike. The perfidious and tenacious rancour which the king displayed towards Fouquet, his superintendent of finance, after his disgrace and arrest, helps us to realise to what lengths he could go when he felt certain that he had been deceived.

He was not a man to think of great innovations in matters of government or even to realise that they might be necessary. On the other hand, he showed himself capable of approving improvements, more or less considerable, on the tradition which he received from the hands of Mazarin, provided that they seemed likely to advance his power or add lustre to his name.

During his reign the organisation of central government on the lines laid down by Francis I was completed. His ministers were six: *the Chancellor,* for justice; *the Controller-General of Finance*—the title of *superintendent* was thus altered, as being unacceptable to the king—*the four Secretaries of State:* of the *King's Household,* of *Foreign Affairs,* of *War* and of the *Navy.* But it must not be assumed that the apparent precision of their titles implied a clear and invariable ascription of duties among these four last functionaries. The limits of their respective jurisdictions are always giving rise to doubt, dispute and transpositions between them. The confusion is still further increased by the fact that each retains the general administration of one of the four sections into which the kingdom is still divided; each minster has a numerous staff, assigned to different *bureaux*. In these, current business is considered and carried on by the officials who form their staff, and are soon to become an important factor in the State. *The reign of the bureaucracy is beginning*.

The traditional practice of the French monarchy was to surround itself with competent advisers. These came to form what were practically government Councils. Under Louis XIV the tendency to specialisation, already frequently mentioned, has reached a definite result; we see four regular and largely specialised *Councils* now at work. The *Council* "par excellence," called also the *High Council,* examines all great questions of policy and government, as does our Council of Ministers today. Its numbers do not exceed four or five persons, including the king. They are entitled *Ministers of State*. The *Council of Despatches* has cognisance of all business affecting the interior administrative life of the kingdom. It conducts, with the four Secretaries of State as intermediaries, correspondence with the intendants. It consists of not more than a dozen or so members and is presided over by the king: it includes the dauphin, the Ministers of State, the Chancellor, the Controller-General of Finance and the Secretaries of State. The *Council of Finance* dealt with the assessment and distribution of direct taxes, conducted negotiations with the financiers and examined all that the financial administration thought fit to submit to it. The king sat as its president twice a week.

The *Privy Council* or *Council of Parties* was essentially, like our present Council of State, a *superior* court; that is to say all the administrative difficulties, conflicts as to jurisdiction, besides a number of purely judicial affairs that the king consigned to it, came within its province which was both extremely vague and extensive. It consisted of thirty members assisted by eighty-eight *Masters of Requests,* who examined and reported upon cases. These masters paid high prices for their posts, since their work prepared them for that of higher administration and the king chose his provincial *Intendants* from among them. The Privy Council was presided over by the Chancellor, the king rarely attending, though its business was conducted in his name as though he himself were present.

This organisation of the central government of Louis XIV is undoubtedly still far from perfection. It still fails in the distinct differentiation between functions which we know to be necessary to the smooth working of a political machine. It is nevertheless a great advance on its predecessor though it runs on similar lines. The *Duke of Beauvilliers,* who was head of the Council of Finance and afterwards Minister of State, was almost the only exception to the rule that no authentic noble had part or portion in this central government; no prince of the blood except the dauphin had even the right to membership of any of the four Councils. This despotism meant, as Saint-Simon said, *"the reign of the long robe"* in all things. The titles of nobility borne by many among these confidential men or ministers of the king should not mislead us as to their origin; they are bourgeois or they come from the ranks of the *officers* of the robe. Ennoblement was the reward for their services.

The provincial government likewise becomes better defined; the provinces are now fixed areas, each has its governor, a noble and a swordsman, well paid and much looked up to, but in reality now no more than a figurehead, indeed so much so that except on special ceremonial occasions the majority of these great personages dispense with residence in their "government." The real authority is in the hands of the *Intendant.* As the experiment attempted by Richelieu proved successful, it was continued by Mazarin and completed by Louis XIV. In his reign the kingdom was divided into financial districts, known as *Généralités* or *Intendances,* of which there were thirty-one in 1700. Their limits did not coincide with those of the provinces in which they were established.

The *Intendant,* his appointment being decided by the Council of the Parties, was chosen by the king, under whose control he remained. He started his career in an intendantship of small importance and his advancement depended on his zeal and success in the *"execution of the orders of his Majesty."* His powers may be described as extending over the whole provincial administration and his work as comprising all duties such as now fall to the heads of the various services in a modern department. Taxes, police, public works, commerce, industry, religious matters, recruiting, supervision and control of the courts of justice and of the administrators of all ranks, the judgment of many contentious or even criminal cases and the selection of those chosen for submission to the king; his work and his authority both covered an immense field.

Louis XIV would naturally wish to abolish such *Provincial States* as still survived, many of which did, in fact, disappear during his reign, for instance, those of Auvergne, Normandy, Quercy and others. If he left some as they were (Brittany, Flanders, Artois, Burgundy, Provence, Languedoc) this would be because they gave him no trouble and because he had probably no intention of abolishing wholesale all the institutions of the past still extant in the provinces. He allowed various anomalies in local administrative usage to continue, and left uncorrected defects of organisation, highly detrimental to those who came under them. They could be justified by established custom and the king seems to have been little concerned with them, being, as he always was, supremely preoccupied with securing two things from his people: *passive obedience and money.*

The government is one which settles all questions in secret. It is absolutely uncontrolled. The *nobility* are no longer a separate body, and politically they count for nothing; to the prince they are *"mere people,"* says Saint-Simon. The *Assembly of the clergy,* held at regular intervals, deals only with its own affairs, except that it is attempting to secure the abolition of the Edict of Nantes. All ecclesiastical appointments are in the hands of the king. The *States-General* are now altogether out of the field. Their name alone was sufficient to set Louis XIV beside himself. There was now not even an Assembly of Notables. The *Parliament,* deprived of all right of remonstrance, could now do no more than register the edicts of the king without comment. As to the *subjects,* they had merely to take their orders. Discussion is considered as revolt and as a kind of sacrilege. It will be only towards the end of the reign that *opposition,* born from the misery of the country and from the failures of the king, will venture to find a home in men's minds and occasionally an outward expression. Not even a genius could have succeeded in realising the immeasurable pretensions of this appalling despotism; and Louis XIV was no genius.

The administration of the kingdom is entirely directed for the service and benefit of the king, against which no consideration whatever can prevail. The care, which it outwardly devotes to the public interest, is no more than a way of promoting the king's. If the subjects are well off and contented they will be able to pay better and more. Although men of all ranks are merely "people" before the king, equally subjected to his will, in practice the administration takes account of the *social inequalities* that the founders of the French monarchy had never attempted to abolish, which were so unfortunately confirmed by the States-General of 1614 and which were now maintained by Louis XIV. It seems probable that no idea that they were unjust or detrimental to the State ever entered his head; all prescription was in their favour. His absolutism, in fact, heavy as it was upon all men, was particularly severe upon the *small folk,* on whose shoulders it laid the greater portion of public expenditure.

In principle, they are the sole bearers of the direct impost (*la taille,* a tax on real property), besides most of those which are indirect, the chief of which are *aids,* diverse taxes upon merchandise of prime necessity and common consumption and *gabelle,* a tax upon salt. These imposts are raised in a way which makes them particularly difficult to bear. The State farms them out to private companies which can appeal to public force for support; they greatly abuse the power thus given them to bring pressure upon the defenceless tax-payers. In those times it was no honour to a man to say that he was in the *Farms* or *Parties;* this last word designating the tenders made to the State by financiers in relation to the adjudication of taxes. From this deplorable system the peasants were the sufferers in chief.

After the death of Colbert (1683), who had done his best to restrain the insane extravagance of the king, the impoverishment of the country proceeded apace, assisted by the exigencies of an expensive foreign policy. The returns from the ordinary taxes then diminished as the need of the royal treasury for money grew greater. The government had recourse to various expedients, not altogether honourable, which furthermore were far from fulfilling expectation. The verses of Boileau are well known (*Satire* III).

> *D'où vous vient aujourd'hui cet air sombre et sévère,*
> *Et ce visage enfin plus pâle qu'un rentier*
> *A l'aspect d'un édit qui supprime un quartier?*

> Why do you look so sombre and severe today,
> With a face indeed paler than a rentier's
> At the appearance of an edict which abrogates a quarter?

A *quartier* of the *rentes* covers a *trimestre,* period of three months; to abrogate it was a method of raising a special tax on the creditors of the State. The creation of useless and sometimes ridiculous posts is an indirect method of establishing new taxes, as the newly created officials will not fail to reimburse themselves from the pockets of the public; thus we find controllers appointed for faggots, fresh butter, oysters and the like, without mentioning *conseillers semestres* (semestrial councillors) who, sitting in their courts for six months only, enable the State to double the number of those functionaries.

The fiscal necessities became so great that even a restriction in the number of the *privileged* had to be accepted. The poll-tax, established in 1695, was to be paid by all Frenchmen without distinction in proportion to their income; only the poorest were exempted. As a matter of fact the privileged, by diverse expedients, for instance, by paying a composition by which they escaped on good terms—as was done by the Assembly of the

Clergy—or by obtaining the appointment of special receivers, materially decreased their obligations. This was similarly the case with another tax upon income, the *tenth,* superimposed in 1710, upon all contributions and upon all subjects.

The government was not unaware of the defects in its fiscal system and could easily realise the disastrous results to which they must lead, but it seems to have been only concerned to fill the treasury by no matter what means, and to have considered inevitable, if not natural, evils for which it had neither leisure nor will to devise adequate remedies. Those which were suggested to it from without, for instance by *Vauban* beginning in 1695 and by *Boisguillebert* starting from 1699, left it indifferent or brought more or less disagreeable consequences upon the heads of their authors.

Justice remained in the hands of the old local jurisdictions, over which were the *Présidiaux,* which went back to Henry II (over them again were the *Parliaments,* then about twelve in number) but its orderly working is disturbed by the privileges of the clergy, who have their own tribunals, and of the nobles, who still often enjoy the abusive right to be judged only by the Parliament of Paris; above all, it is impaired by the *right of evocation* retained by the king. He, being theoretically supreme judge and the fountain-head of all justice, is able, when he thinks fit, to transfer any case from its regular judges and bring it before the *Council of Parties.* These exceptions and privileges are detrimental to the proper working of one of the essential functions of the State.

The diversity of laws and customs had similar effects. It is impossible to find a way through their inextricable confusion. A methodical synopsis would have been indispensable. Colbert thought of having one made and of drafting a kind of civil code, but his plans came to nothing.

The criminal procedure remains barbarous and the penalties are harsh in the extreme. When the king wants oarsmen for his galleys, conviction for any petty crime is enough to send a man to the benches. Generally speaking, the law takes no thought for the moral improvement of delinquents; its one aim is to induce terror by extreme severity. Here as elsewhere the government follows its most immediate interest, regardless of equity, of the needs of its subjects, or of the progress of manners, which are much milder than those of the Middle Ages though its spirit still survives in the practice of torture.

The administration of Louis XIV is in close correspondence with the principles and intentions of the government for which it acts. Rigorous, exacting, and generally exact, it confounds the service of the king with the good of the State, and for the good of the State it deliberately sacrifices individual interests, even those which most call for respect. It is, in fact, an instrument of despotism and not in the least an organism established and set to work for the good of the nation.

> *In a general work on the sixteenth and seventeenth centuries,*
> *the modern French historian, Roland Mousnier, Professor at*

the University of Strasbourg, defined the dimensions of
Louis XIV's absolutism and its effect.

FROM *The XVIth and XVIIth Centuries*
BY ROLAND MOUSNIER

THE ABSOLUTE MONARCHY

ABSOLUTISM WAS THE WISH of the crowds who saw their salvation
in the concentration of powers in the hands of one man—the incarnation of
the realm, the living symbol of order and of the desired unity. Everyone
wished to see in the king the image of God: "You are God on earth. . . ."
To this conception was added, with many, the old humanist dream: the king
ought to be a hero, lover of glory as in antiquity, protector of Letters like
Augustus, protector of the Church like Constantine, a legislator like Justinian, but with a "predilection for arms," because "the role of conqueror is
esteemed to be the most noble and the highest of titles," by all contemporaries.

As lieutenant of God, the king is sovereign. "The sovereign Prince
makes the law, consequently he is absolved of the law." He acts according to
his own good pleasure. Thus it results that kings "naturally have the full and
free disposition of all properties, secular as well as ecclesiastic, to make wise
use of like good stewards, that is to say according to the needs of their states."
Public good is above the right of property. Thus it follows that the Church is
subject to the sovereign and owes him rental on its possessions which have
been given to it "for the general welfare of the entire realm. . . ." (The
comparison with the sun arose by itself, and Louis XIV, Nec Pluribus Impar
[None His Equal] did no more than insist on an old monarchical symbol.)

But, as an image of God, the king ought to be a providence on earth. He
should make justice reign "precious trust that God has put in the hand of
kings as a participation in his wisdom and his power." He ought to bring to
perfection each of the professions of which society is constituted, because
"each of them has its functions, which the others may do without only with
great difficulty. . . . This is why, far from disdaining any of these conditions, or of raising one at the expense of others, we should take care to bring
them all, if it can be done, to the perfection of which they are capable,"
[realizing] the ideal of a society where social work is directed and the

Roland Mousnier, *Les XVIè et XVIIè Siècles. Les progrès de la civilisation européenne et le
déclin de l'Orient (1492–1715)*, Tome IV, *Histoire Générale des Civilisations* (1954), pp. 229–
36. Translated by L. Pearce Williams by permission of Presses Universitaires de France, Paris.

professions form a hierarchy according to the needs of man. Finally, the king should be the protector of the weak, he ought "to give to the people who are subject to us the same marks of paternal goodness that we receive from God every day," to have "nothing more at heart than to guarantee the most feeble from the oppression of the most powerful and to find some ease for the neediest in their misery."

The king mistrusted his ministers and his secretaries of state. He reverted to a division of labor, and tried to divide up the affairs which were interconnected in such a way that no specialist would be able to block his will. He opposed his officials to one another, provoked them, divided them, stimulated their mutual jealousies, saw in the opposition of Colbert and of Le Tellier a guarantee of his power.

. . . The problem for the king is not only to make his subjects obey, but also to subject to his will his own officers who had become independent thanks to the venality of office, and to exercise the fullness of the legislative judiciary police or administrative powers.

For this purpose the king used *lettres de cachet* by which he made known his will directly to individuals or to bodies. By *lettres de cachet,* the king arrested, emprisoned, exiled; at the request of families, he punished the bad conduct of a son or of a spouse; he weakened resistance, arbitrarily punished seditions and plots with the enemy. When the king himself had spoken, there was nothing else to do but to bow before his authority, the legal source of justice.

More and more, the king utilized commissioners named by him and removeable at his will. The Counselors of State of the administrative councils were only commissioners. . . .

The king used the intendants of the army and the intendants of justice, police, and finance. They were above all inspectors, charged with the surveillance of the officers and subjects of the king, and were required to give an account to the council. The council could then either deal with the question itself by a decree or give the necessary powers to the intendant to decide, judge, or regulate the problem by means of an ordinance. The intendant could thus meet with the council of the governor and give his advice; he could preside over courts of justice, reform justice by means of ordinances, make sure that the officers carried out their functions and suspend them if they did not, listen to the complaints of the king's subjects and make sure justice was given them by the judges. The intendant presided over the assemblies of the cities, . . . elections, checked the debts of communities, and oversaw the carrying out of orders and regulations. . . . The intendant supervised the raising of taxes, presided over the bureau of the finances, and guaranteed the observance of ordinances and regulations. Only in two cases did he have a general and discretionary power and a sovereign judgment: malpractices and falsification of accounts by financial officers, and illicit assemblies, seditions, riots, and raising of armed men.

The intendant was a very supple instrument. In time of war or of internal crisis, the council could extend his powers indefinitely, to the point that the intendant could perform all the functions of the officers and leave them only their hollow title. At these times, with their assistants the intendants formed an administration of commissioners in competition with the administration of the regular officers. But the royal government, Richelieu, and Colbert considered such times as exceptional and as an unhappy necessity. In time of peace, the king strove to keep the intendant, who always wanted to extend his powers, in his role of inspector. He forbade him to substitute himself for the royal officers—he was instructed only to supervise them, and, if they were not working well, to let the council know and to wait for the necessary powers to remedy the situation.

The king used a political police. It was run by the intendants, by spies and agents to be found everywhere—at Paris by the governor of the Bastille, the chief criminal officer, and, since 1667, the lieutenant general of police, La Reynie. One misinterpretation and, duke or lackey, one was in the Bastille. On such feeble suspicions, the intendants or the council constructed accusations of *lèse majesté,* judgment was given on mere suspicion because Richelieu, Louis XIII, and Louis XIV all believed that when conspiracy was concerned it was almost impossible to have mathematical proofs, and one should not wait for the event itself by which everything would be lost. More often than for mere trials, the king had recourse to preventive imprisonment of indefinite length by means of the *lettres de cachet.* . . .

In all important offices, like that of ministers, secretaries of state, controller general, and so on, Louis XIV desired only "devoted servants" who joined to their public functions domestic services and, like Colbert, carried the notes from the monarch to his favorites or received the adulterine children of the king at the childbirth of the royal mistresses. He used the sentiments of vassalage but he wished to be the sole object of them. He wished to achieve absolutism by tying all Frenchmen directly to the king by means of a personal connection, just as vassals were tied to their suzerain. He wished to be the unique and universal suzerain or at least the universal patron. . . . All ties of sentiment and of interest converged on the king, who thus incarnated the wishes and the hopes of all his subjects, and in this way, not less than by the personal exercise of power, concentrated the state in himself; achieved in himself the unity of the State and thus prepared his subject, by means of very old sentiments, to pass to the concept of the abstract State. Through the intermediary of medieval survivals, Louis XIV prepared the foundations of the modern State.

The king prepared them by opposing class to class and by making the bourgeois rise in a social scale. His ministers, his counselors, and his intendants were drawn more and more in the course of the century from among the bourgeois officers. These were his men, "rising from pure and perfect commonness," but "exalted above all grandeur." The king ennobled the Le Tellier and the Colbert families, made marquises of them, lords were known by the name of their estates, Louvois, Barbezieux, Croissy, Torcy. He created dynasties of ministers, bourgeois family groups and dynasties whose strength he used in face of the dynasties and noble family groups. . . .

The gentlemen grumbled. They despised these "bourgeois." "It was the reign of the vile bourgeoisie," complained Saint-Simon. They suffered by the leveling accomplished by a state which broke all resistance. The prisons were filled with eminent prisoners: the Count of Cramaing, the Marshal of Bassompierre, Barabas—one of the favorites of Louis XIII. The kings also sought, however, to procure honors and a means of existence for the nobility. The place of governor was reserved for them, and they filled most of grades in the army. To their younger sons went the greater part of the ecclesiastical functions; they [the Kings] used them in their service inculcating in them the spirit of subordination and little by little turning them into functionaries. Louis XIV succeeded in organizing the court. Around him he grouped, at Saint Germaine, at Fontainebleau, at Versailles, all who counted among the nobility. He ruined them by alternating between the onerous life of military camps and the ostentatious life of the Court. He had no hesitation in waging war to find them employment and the opportunity for glory and reputation. He rendered them servile by pensions, dowries, and properties of the church. . . . He even provided a psychological alibi to this nobility. In a series of marvelous fairy-like festivals, the king appeared costumed as a god from Olympus, the courtiers appearing as secondary divinities or as heroes. Thus they could transpose their false dream of power and grandeur to this copy of the life of the immortals, raised above common humanity and, if it had to obey, at least obeyed the "Lord Jupiter," the king-god. Etiquette habituated them to see in the king a superhuman being. Men uncovered themselves before the king's bed, women curtsied to it as in church before the high altar. The princes of the blood disputed the honor of handing him the sleeve of his shirt at his rising. A whole ceremonial filled with reverences was present at his rising in the morning, at his retiring, at his meals, and for his whole life. . . .

Thus the king, by dividing governmental functions between two classes but reserving the most important to the lower one—the bourgeoisie—and by systematically raising this one and opposing the other—the strongest— brought the class struggle to an equilibrium which assured his personal power and—both in the government and in the state—unity, order, and hierarchy. But also, perhaps forced by crises and war, and without wishing to change the social structure of the realm, the king leveled and equalized more and more in the service due to the state. When Louis XIV had achieved total submission and limitless obedience his power became autocratic and revolutionary.

A Note on the Type

This book is set in Granjon, a type named in compliment to Robert Granjon, type-cutter and printer—Antwerp, Lyons, Rome, Paris—active from 1523 to 1590. The boldest and most original designer of his time, he was one of the first to practice the trade of type-founder apart from that of printer.

This type face was designed by George W. Jones, who based his drawings on a type used by Claude Garamond (1510–1561) in his beautiful French books, and more closely resembles Garamond's own than do any of the various modern types that bear his name.

This book was designed by Betty Anderson. It was composed, printed, and bound by Kingsport Press, Inc., Kingsport, Tennessee.